Symbol, Service, and Song

Symbol, Service, and Song

The Levites of 1 Chronicles 10–29 in Rhetorical, Historical, and Theological Perspectives

J. Nathan Clayton

FOREWORD BY
James K. Bruckner

◥PICKWICK *Publications* • Eugene, Oregon

SYMBOL, SERVICE, AND SONG
The Levites of 1 Chronicles 10–29 in Rhetorical, Historical, and Theological Perspectives

Copyright © 2021 J. Nathan Clayton. All rights reserved. Except for brief quotations in critical publications or reviews, no part of this book may be reproduced in any manner without prior written permission from the publisher. Write: Permissions, Wipf and Stock Publishers, 199 W. 8th Ave., Suite 3, Eugene, OR 97401.

Pickwick Publications
An Imprint of Wipf and Stock Publishers
199 W. 8th Ave., Suite 3
Eugene, OR 97401

www.wipfandstock.com

PAPERBACK ISBN: 978-1-5326-8677-1
HARDCOVER ISBN: 978-1-5326-8678-8
EBOOK ISBN: 978-1-5326-8679-5

Cataloguing-in-Publication data:

Names: Clayton, J. Nathan, author. | Bruckner, James K., foreword.

Title: Symbol, service, and song : the Levites of 1 Chronicles 10–29 in rhetorical, historical, and theological perspectives / by J. Nathan Clayton ; foreword by James K. Bruckner.

Description: Eugene, OR: Pickwick Publications, 2021 | Includes bibliographical references and index.

Identifiers: ISBN 978-1-5326-8677-1 (paperback) | ISBN 978-1-5326-8678-8 (hardcover) | ISBN 978-1-5326-8679-5 (ebook)

Subjects: LCSH: Levites | Priests, Jewish—Biblical teaching | Bible—Chronicles—Criticism, interpretation, etc. | Public Worship—Biblical teaching. | Worship in the Bible.

Classification: BS1345 C53 2021 (print) | BS1199.P7 (ebook)

11/05/21

To Maureen Janet Clayton

Contents

List of Tables | viii
Foreword by James K. Bruckner | ix
Acknowledgements | xiii
Abbreviations | xv

1　The Levites of 1 Chronicles 10–29: Contextual OT Data and Scholarly Approaches | 1

2　Exegetical Methodologies: Rhetorical Criticism, Historiography, and Biblical Theology | 39

3　The Rhetorical Aspect in 1 Chronicles 15:1—16:3: The Levites and the Symbol of God's Presence | 90

4　The Historical Aspect in 1 Chronicles 23: On the Plausibility of David's Establishment of an Expanded Levitical Duty in the Early First Millennium | 140

5　A Biblical-Theological Reflection on Levitical Song: Proclamation about God in 1 Chronicles 16 and Promise from God in Psalm 73 | 205

6　Conclusion: Summary, Contributions, and Further Research | 261

Appendix: A Rhetorical-Critical Outline of 1 Chronicles 15:1—16:3 | 275
Bibliography | 285
Index of Ancient Sources | 343

Tables

Table 1: The Structure of Scobie's BT | 88
Table 2: Sacred Song and BT | 89
Table 3: The Placement of the APN within the DKN1 | 105
Table 4: Relationship between 1 Sam 6 and 1 Chr 15 | 111
Table 5: Structure of Unit A (1 Chr 15:1–3) | 113
Table 6: Structure of Unit B (1 Chr 15:4–15) | 117
Table 7: Structure of Unit C (1 Chr 15:16–24) | 127
Table 8: Structure of Unit B' (1 Chr 15:25–29) | 130
Table 9: Structure of Unit A' (1 Chr 16:1–3) | 133
Table 10: Overall Structure of the APN1 (1 Chr 15:1—16:3) | 134
Table 11: Throntveit's Structure for 1 Chr 16:8–36 | 220
Table 12: Throntveit's Structure for 1 Chr 16:35–36 | 228
Table 13: Chiastic Outline of 1 Chr 16:25–26 | 234

Foreword

OF ALL THE TYPES of literature to read and interpret, "the Bible is most difficult," as Mortimer Adler reminds us in his classic *How to Read a Book*.[1] Scholarly interpretation of a difficult canonical book like Chronicles requires competency in languages, text criticism, form criticism, historiography, redaction criticism, rhetorical criticism, cultural anthropology, religious practice, deconstruction, and theological traditions. Fortunately, Dr. Clayton has mastered this combination of crafts for Chronicles in *Symbol, Service, Song*.

His monograph does what every excellent canonical reading of Scripture ought to do. It brings all the best historical and literary tools to bear to produce a theologically constructive illumination of the biblical text. This combination of historical-critical, literary, and theological interpretation represents a "type of wisdom" amid various post-modern approaches to Scripture.[2] Expertly handling a discerning range of interpretive tools, Dr. Clayton reveals the enduring value of Chronicles. Incisively applying a range of methodologies to the data found in key texts, he opens the second temple world of Chronicles for the present day. The result is truly multidimensional and deeply canonical.

---

1. Adler, Mortimer J. and Van Doren, Charles, "How to Read Canonical Books" in *How to Read a Book: The Classic Guide to Intelligent Reading* (New York: Simon & Schuster, 1972), 293–94.

2. Dennis R. Edwards quotes this Stephen Fowl phrase in a recent essay. Edwards' description of the tension between modern and post-modern approaches to the Bible is instructive for sorting the current landscape of biblical interpretation. See Dennis R. Edwards, "Hermeneutics and Exegesis," in Scot McKnight, ed., *The State of New Testament Studies: A Survey of Recent Research* (Grand Rapids: Baker, 2019), 63–82; Stephen Fowl, "Theological Interpretation of the Bible," in Michael J. Gorman, ed., *Scripture and Its Interpretations: A Global, Ecumenical Introduction to the Bible* (Grand Rapids: Baker, 2017), 211.

Such an interpretation is all the more welcome in view of the traditional marginalization of Chronicles in western scholarship. Its stigmatization as an unwelcome late-comer to the canon has led to a widespread judgment that it is "less than" Kings in assessments of quality and value in the canon. The previous problem in the judgment against Chronicles has been the longstanding presuppositions of former critics, leaning toward the earlier versions of events. When a reader and an ancient text meet, however, conflict is rarely the fault of the text.

Clayton's approach is made possible by a relatively recent shift in biblical studies. For many years, the narrow philosophical interests of historical-critical methods solely dominated the interpretation of biblical texts. Scholarly interpretation of the biblical text as Scripture now goes beyond a focus on the grammar and history of the literature behind the biblical text. Canonical interpretation, which embraces a wide spectrum of critical tools in service of the Scripture as a living Word, is a hopeful result of western biblical scholarship. The possibilities for the keenest minds in scholarship are now much more interesting and fruitful.

In the fall of 1999, at the Society of Biblical Literature meeting in Boston, Rolf Rendtorff (Heidelberg University) and Walter Brueggemann (CST, Emory University) joined the call of Brevard Childs (Yale), who had sounded the trumpet of crisis in biblical scholarship much earlier in 1970. He pointed to how fragmented the Bible had become in the hands of historical-critical scholars. He called on scholars to begin to deal with the biblical text as a whole canon.[3]

The public nature of the event in 1999, and the weighty repudiation of the historical-critical method by Rendtorff and Brueggemann dramatically altered the landscape of Old Testament scholarship. A return to the final redaction of the received biblical text had begun.

At an even earlier SBL gathering, James Barr (Oxford) had argued that history itself is a human construct that ignores the text itself. History and its critical tools cannot subsume biblical categories of God's action and revelation.[4] Dr. Clayton follows Barr, Childs, and a handful of canonical interpreters of Chronicles (Gary Knoppers, Richard Pratt, Mark Boda) who demonstrate a new appreciation of the value of Chronicles *as* Scripture. Dr. Clayton reinforces the value of canonical interpretation for understanding Chronicles. He brings the strength of the biblical canon to bear on interpreting the role of the Levites' service at the temple.

---

3. Brevard S. Childs, *Biblical Theology in Crisis* (Philadelphia: Westminster, 1970).
4. Presidential Inaugural Address, Society of Biblical Literature, 1962.

This form of canonical interpretation does what narrower methodologies cannot do on their own. Modern criticisms strive to be scientific, but only to understand specific historical or literary elements of the text. These premises have reduced Chronicles to a derivative text, deemed lesser simply because it is a much later re-written version of an earlier history. Scientific approaches are not particularly interested in the biblical text as a Word of God for a specific time and place, e.g., the value of Chronicles in the history of the second temple period. A self-limiting "scientific" interest in the genius behind the composition of the text provides some preliminary information for understanding a book like Chronicles but cannot unearth its full value.

The best interpretation of an ancient text is to read the received text as it functioned in its original sociological context, i.e., how it functioned *as Scripture* in the Second Temple period. Why was it accepted as Scripture? What were and are its salient attributes for the people who self-identify as the people of God? What does it tell us about God? Other methodologies do not ask this question or pursue it. Canonical interpretation intentionally uses historical and literary methodologies in service of the prior theological question. In this sense, it shares the post-modern focus on generating meaning from a distinct hermeneutical perspective.

Dr. Clayton's thesis is that the Levitical passages of the Davidic narratives in First Chronicles have much to teach us about the leadership of ordered ministry in times of crisis and transition. Their leadership is threefold: facilitating the songs of the people; expanding their elements of service in times of the community's leadership crisis; and mediating God's presence in their symbolic ministries. The doubled historical-cultural situations of the first and second temple periods provide the necessary depth-perspective for understanding this Levitical leadership in each historical-cultural crisis context. This focus on three-fold leadership paints an enduring and relevant picture of Levitical "service, symbol, and song."

Each of Dr. Clayton's chapters on Chronicles fifteen, sixteen, and twenty-three stands on their own as distinct and useful explications and elucidations of the central role of worship leadership in the first and second temple periods. Using three distinct methodological tools, he mines the veins of data for its best materials. In his work on chapter fifteen, he emphasizes the establishment of Levitical music ministry which serves to encourage a renewed identity in the post-exilic community (using the tools of rhetorical criticism). In his work on chapter twenty-three, he employs a maximalist understanding of priestly practices in the historiography of the ancient Near East (Sumerian, Akkadian, Canaanite, and Egyptian) to establish a common cognitive milieu for comparison to the Davidic descriptions of Levitical service. In his work on First Chronicles sixteen, he exegetes the theological nature of Levitical song and its function of creating exuberant, care-full, and joyful hope for the post-exilic community.[5] Finally, Dr. Clayton combines these three in an integrated conclusion that is a bonified constructive treatment of Chronicles as a living Word of God. Ultimately, Dr. Clayton advances scholarship on this marginalized and maligned book. He also demonstrates the value of an eclectic, multi-dimensional canonical approach to interpreting Scripture.

James K. Bruckner
North Park Theological Seminary

---

5. The fifty-eight page bibliography is worth its weight for any serious student of Chronicles or the temple priestly tradition.

Acknowledgements

I would like to briefly acknowledge four sets of people who have been particularly instrumental in bringing this study of Levitical worship function in 1 Chronicles to publication.

First, this work began life some years ago as my PhD dissertation at Trinity Evangelical Divinity School in Deerfield, IL. Three professors were especially significant to me during my time as a doctoral student at TEDS: Richard Averbeck, Willem VanGemeren, and Lawson Younger. Each one of these gentlemen modeled for me what it means to be a gracious and Christ-centered teacher and scholar. I am grateful for their teaching, advice, and support.

Secondly, I am thankful for the opportunity given to me by Wipf and Stock Publishers. Two editors in particular have encouraged me in my work along the way: earlier on, Chris Spinks, and more recently, Robin Parry. I am thankful for their editorial advice and support.

Thirdly, over the past few years, I have had the joy of serving full-time on the faculty of North Park Theological Seminary in Chicago, IL. I have grown in ministry while serving with all of the faculty and staff. I would especially like to acknowledge my OT and NT colleagues at the seminary, who have all been thoughtful in their support: Max Lee, Dennis Edwards, Stephen Chester (now serving at Wycliffe College in Canada), and Jim Bruckner. I have also benefited from conversations with my Bible-teaching North Park friend Jonathan Teram. It is a joy to serve with, and learn from, these servant-leaders. I would also like to acknowledge Joseph DeNeui's careful proofreading of the manuscript and his work in compiling the index of ancient sources.

Finally, I am most grateful to God for my family. My father John and my mother Sandra have always encouraged in me a love of God and of his Word. My four children, Elizabeth, Adam, Mary and Benjamin, are a continuing blessing for my wife and me. In the end, this work, and my Christian ministry in general, would not be possible at a human level without the constant partnership, encouragement and support from my wife Maureen. I love her dearly and this study is dedicated to her.

Loué soit Dieu!

Lake Forest, IL, USA
July 2021

Abbreviations

AB	Anchor Bible
ABD	*The Anchor Bible Dictionary*. 6 vols. Edited by David Noel Freedman. New York: Doubleday, 1992.
AnBib	*Analecta Biblica*
BAR	Biblical Archaeology Review
BBR	*Bulletin for Biblical Research*
BDB	Francis Brown, S. R. Driver, and Charles A. Briggs. *Hebrew and English Lexicon of the Old Testament*. Oxford: Clarendon, 1907.
BEATAJ	Beiträge zur Erforschung des Alten Testaments und des antiken Judentums
Bib	*Biblica*
BibInt	*Biblical Interpretation*
BN	*Biblische Notizen*
BSOT	Jonathan S. Greer et al., eds. *Behind the Scenes of the Old Testament: Cultural, Social, and Historical Contexts*. Grand Rapids: Baker, 2018.
BWA(N)T	Beiträge zur Wissenschaft vom Alten (und Neuen) Testament
BZAW	Beihefte zur Zeitschrift für die alttestamenliche Wissenschaft
CANE	Jack M. Sasson, ed. *Civilizations of the Ancient Near East*. 4 vols. New York: Scribners 1995. [Reprinted in 2 vols. Peabody: Hendrickson, 2006].

CAT		Commentaire de l'Ancien Testament
CahRB		Cahiers de la Revue Biblique
ChrA		M. Patrick Graham and Steven L. McKenzie, eds. *The Chronicler as Author: Studies in Text and Texture.* JSOTSup 263. Sheffield: Sheffield Academic, 1999.
CaH		M. Patrick Graham et al., eds. *The Chronicler as Historian.* JSOTSup 238. Sheffield: Sheffield Academic, 1997.
CaT		M. Patrick Graham et al., eds. *The Chronicler as Theologian: Essays in Honor of Ralph W. Klein.* JSOTSup 371. New York: T&T Clark, 2003.
CBQ		*Catholic Biblical Quarterly*
CLGB		Leland Ryken and Tremper Longman III, eds. *A Complete Literary Guide to the* Bible. Grand Rapids: Zondervan, 1993.
COS		William W. Hallo and K. Lawson Younger Jr., eds. *The Context of Scripture.* 4 vols. Leiden: Brill, 2003–2018.
CTJ		*Calvin Theological Journal*
CTM		*Concordia Theological Monthly*
CtheC		Paul S. Evans and Tyler F. Williams, eds. *Chronicling the Chronicler: The Book of Chronicles and Early Second Temple Historiography.* Winona Lake: Eisenbrauns, 2013.
CVO		A. Lemaire and M. Sæbø, eds. *Congress Volume: Oslo, 1998.* VTSup 80. Leiden: Brill, 2000.
DCH		Harry Ritter. *Dictionary of Concepts in History.* Reference Sources for the Social Sciences and Humanities 3. New York: Greenwood, 1986.
DCM		Francis Joannès, ed. *Dictionnaire de la Civilisation Mésopotamienne.* Paris: Lafont, 2001.
DOTP		T. Desmond Alexander and David W. Baker. *Dictionary of the Old Testament: Pentateuch,* Downers Grove: InterVarsity, 2003.
DOTHB		David W. Baker and H. G. M. Williamson, eds. *Dictionary of the Old Testament: Historical Books.* Downers Grove: InterVarsity, 2005.

DTIB	Kevin J. Vanhoozer, ed. *Dictionary for Theological Interpretation of the Bible,* Grand Rapids: Baker, 2005.
EncJud	Cecil Roth, ed. *Encyclopedia Judaica.* 16 vols. New York: MacMillan, 1972.
EDT	Walter A. Elwell, ed. *Evangelical Dictionary of Theology.* Grand Rapids: Baker, 2001.
FAOTS	David W. Baker and Bill T. Arnold, eds. *The Face of Old Testament Studies: A Survey of Contemporary Approaches.* Grand Rapids: Baker, 1999.
FAT	Forschungen zum Alten Testament
FOTL	Forms of Old Testament Literature
FTH	A. R. Millard et al., eds. *Faith, Tradition, and History: Old Testament Historiography in Its Near Eastern Context.* Winona Lake: Eisenbrauns, 1994.
GtS	David M. Howard Jr. and Michael A. Grisanti, eds. *Giving the Sense: Understanding and Using Old Testament Historical Texts.* Grand Rapids: Kregel, 2003.
GKC	W. Gesenius et al. *Gesenius' Hebrew Grammar as Edited and Enlarged by the Late E. Kautzsch.* Reprint. Oxford: Clarendon, 1990 (1885).
HALOT-SE	Ludwig Köhler and Walter Baumgartner, eds. *The Hebrew and Aramaic Lexicon of the Old Testament: Study Edition.* 2 vols. Translated by M. E. J. Richardson. Leiden: Brill, 2001.
HSMS	Harvard Semitic Monograph Series
ISBR	Geoffrey W. Bromiley, ed. *The International Standard Bible Encyclopedia, Revised.* 4 vols. Grand Rapids: Eerdmans, 1986.
LBHOTS	Library of Hebrew Bible/Old Testament Studies
Int	*Interpretation*
IDB	G. A. Buttrick, ed. *The Interpreter's Dictionary of the Bible.* 4 vols. New York: Abingdon, 1962.
JANES	*Journal of the Ancient Near Eastern Society*
JAOS	*Journal of the American Oriental Society*
JBL	*Journal of Biblical Literature*

JETS	*Journal of the Evangelical Society*
Joüon	Paul Joüon and T. Muraoka. *A Grammar of Biblical Hebrew*. Subsida Biblica 27. Rome: Gregorian & Biblical, 2018.
JSOT	*Journal for the Study of the Old Testament*
JSNTSup	Journal for the Study of the New Testament: Supplement Series
JSOTSup	Journal for the Study of the Old Testament: Supplement Series
LHBOTS	Library of Hebrew Bible/Old Testament Studies
NAC	New American Commentary
NDBT	T. Desmond Alexander and Brian S. Rosner, eds. *New Dictionary of Biblical Theology*. Downers Grove: InterVarsity, 2000.
NIB	Leander E. Keck, ed. The *New Interpreter's Bible*. 10 vols. Nashville: Abingdon, 1999.
NICOT	New International Commentary on the Old Testament
NIDOTTE	Villem VanGemeren, ed. *New International Dictionary of Old Testament Theology and Exegesis*. 5 vols. Grand Rapids: Zondervan, 1997.
NIVAC	New International Version Application Commentary
OBT	Overtures to Biblical Theology
OTE	*Old Testament Essays*
OTL	Old Testament Library
OTTFF	Ben C. Ollenburger, ed. *Old Testament Theology: Flowering and Future*. Sources for Biblical and Theological Study 1. Winona Lake: Eisenbrauns, 2004.
RB	*Revue Biblique*
SB	*Studia Biblica*
SBLDS	Society of Biblical Literature Dissertation Series
ShaTal	M. Fishbane and E. Tov, eds. *"Sha'arei Talmon" Studies in the Bible, Qumran, and the Ancient Near East Presented to Shemaryahu Talmon*. Winona Lake: Eisenbrauns, 1992.
SJLA	Studies in Judaism in Late Antiquity

SPreIs	John Day, ed. *In Search of Pre-Exilic Israel: Proceedings of the Oxford Old Testament Seminar*. JSOTSup 406. New York: T&T Clark, 2004.
SNTSMS	Society for New Testament Studies: Monograph Series
SP	Sacra Pagina
SSN	Studia Semitica Neerlandica
VTSup	Supplements to Vetus Testamentum
TDOT	*Theological Dictionary of the Old Testament*. 14 vols. Edited by G. Johannes Botterweck and Helmer Ringgren. Translated by Geoffrey W. Bromiley et al. Grand Rapids: Eerdmans, 1974–2004.
TOTC	Tyndale Old Testament Commentaries
Transeu	*Transeuphratène*
TynBul	*Tyndale Bulletin*
VT	*Vetus Testamentum*
VTSup	Supplements to Vetus Testamentum
WTJ	Westminster Theological Journal
WOT	Bill T. Arnold, and Brent A. Strawn, eds. *The World Around the Old Testament: The People and Places of the Ancient Near East*. Grand Rapids: Baker, 2016.
WBC	Word Biblical Commentary
ZAW	*Zeitschrift für alttestamentliche Wissenschaft*

1

The Levites of 1 Chronicles 10–29

Contextual OT Data and
Scholarly Approaches

WITHIN ONE STREAM OF ongoing research, scholars have argued that the books of 1–2 Chronicles are carefully composed and display abundant literary techniques, historical outlooks, and theological accents that provide judicious contrast and complementarity to the parallel history of Samuel-Kings.[1] These views, indeed, give greater emphasis to the purposeful shape and goals of the Chronicler's history.[2] This broad perspective has also pro-

---

1. In fact, in the context of the 1970s, Childs, *Introduction to the Old Testament*, 643–44, noted that "scholars remain in considerable disagreement as to the purpose of the Chronicler's writing his history. Much of the disagreement stems from a critical assumption that the author has cloaked his real intentions behind some tendentious handling of his sources.... However, if one takes the statements of the author of Chronicles at face value, *his purpose in writing seems entirely straightforward. The author was attempting to interpret to the restored community in Jerusalem the history of Israel as an eternal covenant between God and David which demanded an obedient response to the divine law*" (emphasis added). Childs, *Introduction to the Old Testament*, 647–55, goes on to suggest ways in which the Chronicler may be viewed as a *coherent* exegete of Scripture. For some recent authors who build on this call to more fully engage the specific purposes of the Chronicler, see for example: Boda, *1–2 Chronicles*, 3–19; Leithart, *1 & 2 Chronicles*, 1–7; Japhet, "The Writings," 115–26; Kleinig, "Recent Research," 43–76; Knoppers, *I Chronicles 1–9*, 72–89. For instance, in reflecting on how the Chronicler presents king Jehoshapat's reforms, Hess, *The Old Testament*, 338, highlights the way God's *past* saving actions are brought forth as a source of encouragement for a *postexilic* audience: "[t]he God who created and redeemed Israel from its enemy at the exodus from Egypt is the same God to whom Jehoshaphat can pray and from whom he can receive the same sort of victory from overwhelming number of enemies. This is the same God to whom the present [postexilic] community can pray at the temple in Jerusalem, the same God who can act again to preserve and protect from their enemies."

2. For some principal views and arguments in this area, note for example Kalimi,

duced studies that engage with the distinct biblical-theological perspectives found in the Chronicler's work.³

Kalimi, for instance, after interacting with certain approaches that strongly criticize the historical reliability of the book of Chronicles, concludes that "the major literary nature of Chronicles, the book as a whole, is historiography (rather than 'historical fiction' or 'fantasy literature'), though it is indeed a 'sacred' but not 'secular' historiography."⁴ Selman, in turn, has argued that "the Old Testament as a whole plays a central role in Chronicles . . . [as] the Chronicler's overall aim was to offer an interpretation of the Bible as he knew it."⁵ Other authors note that literary competence is needed in interpreting Samuel-Kings and Chronicles and in ascertaining the distinct contributions to the biblical canon made by both sets of histories. They write, indeed:

> The two renditions of Israel's monarchical period, the one in Samuel-Kings and the other in Chronicles, are anything but identical, though they cover much the same ground. *A wooden reading of one or both could easily give the impression that they are mutually contradictory, but a wooden reading would be*

An Ancient Israelite Historian, 1–82; Kalimi, "Die Abfassungskeit der Chronik," 223–33; Kalimi, *The Reshaping*, 1–17; Japhet, *I and II Chronicles*, 1–49. In this vein, Merrill, *A Commentary*, 52–53, writes, "[t]he Chronicler's message somehow had to redress [the] despair [of his postexilic audience] while at the same time tracing the history of the nation from the time of the patriarchs to his present time to demonstrate how God's covenant people time and time again had rebelled against his gracious covenant with them. . . . In doing so, a certain 'rewriting' or at least 'revisionism' of the DH and other earlier historical writings was essential in order to view that history from the standpoint of the Chronicler's *Sitz im Leben*. Such a method need not and did not question the historical reliability of either the Chronicler or his revised sources."

3. For a constructive perspective on the Chronicler's theological methods and perspectives, see for instance Mosis, *Untersuchungen zur Theologie*, 45–125; Japhet, *The Ideology*, 111–91; Murray, "Retribution and Revival," 77–99; Pratt, *1 and 2 Chronicles*, 14–54. And note as well the recent study by Ahn, *The Persuasive Portrayal*, 1–32. Kalimi has produced a full study of the reception history of Chronicles—especially in biblical and Jewish-Hellenistic sources. In this analysis, Kalimi argues that the Chronicler reveals himself to be an effective writer, closer in tone to intertestamental Jewish writers (than the earlier writer of Samuel-Kings). Kalimi, *Das Chronikbuch und Seine Chronik*, 177–78, indeed concludes, in part, that "[i]hr Verfasser war ein äußerst kreativer Historiker mit einer soliden literarischen, historiographischen und theologischen Kompetenz. Die theologischen Linien und Gedanken sind viel näher zu jenen späteren normativen jüdischen Werke und Gedanken als jene in Samuel-Könige." For a study of the broader reception history of David's temple preparations in 1 Chr 22–29, note French, *Chronicles through the Centuries*, 82–101.

4. Kalimi, *An Ancient Israelite Historian*, 82. And see further Selman, "Chronicler's History," 157–61; Weinberg, *Der Chronist*, 121–47; Riley, *King and Cultus*, 15–36.

5. Selman, *1 Chronicles*, 26, emphasis added, and also see 20–26 as a whole.

entirely inappropriate. Recognition of the distinct purposes and audiences of the two histories goes a long way towards accounting for many of the differences between the two.[6]

Furthermore, researchers have also noted that a distinct focus for the Chronicler may be found in the emphasis laid on worship and the central role played by the priests and Levites therein. In a recent essay, for instance, Boda has essentially argued that—when it comes to the theme of the temple and worship—we find both a *present* purpose and a *future* expectation embedded in the Chronicler's theology, that is, "[t]he Chronicler cannot be restricted to the priestly *or* the eschatological, to the status quo *or* the charismatic. Rather, firmly planted in the present, he looks for and longs for a future when God's people will fully realize the core values of God's kingdom."[7] As a further example, we may also note Street's study, which focuses squarely on the Ark Narrative of 1 Chr 15–16. One of his major conclusions highlights the interwoven relationship between worship in both preexilic Israel—*historically*—and postexilic Israel—*rhetorically*. As Street writes:

> The theology of the ark narrative comes directly out of its attention to proper worship. Thus, the roles of the priests and Levites are essential because they are maintaining the cultic objects and come into close contact with these sacred objects that have been set apart for the worship of Yahweh. . . . The Chronicler's readers would have seen the connection between Mosaic traditions and the Davidic institutions as a continuation of legitimate worship. It is this worship that the Chronicler is arguing for in his own day. Worship in the Second Temple is just as legitimate as the worship that took place in David's and Moses' day. . . . In the Chronicler's day, maintaining a proper covenant relationship with Yahweh can only be achieved through the cult and the proper sacrificial worship in the temple.[8]

---

6. Provan et al., *A Biblical History of Israel*, 263, (emphasis added); see pp. 261–66 for the larger argument on this main point.

7. Boda, "Gazing Through the Cloud of Incense," 245, (emphasis added).

8. Street, *The Significance of the Ark Narrative*, 138–39. In his recent study of monotheism in Chronicles, Lynch, *Monotheism and Institutions*, 261, presents a very similar conclusion, as he writes, "the fundamental conclusion of this study is that, for Chronicles, the oneness and supremacy of Yhwh find congruent expression in the temple, the temple's priesthood, and in the rule of the temple's royal patron. For a postexilic audience lacking visible markers of national greatness that flow from divine favor, Chronicles weaves a sacred tapestry in which the temple and its supporting institutions mediate and participate in Yhwh's preeminence as it was known and experienced in Israel's glorious past."

With rootedness in these types of approaches to the Chronicler's history, the principal aim of our study is to articulate a *multidimensional* reading of select passages that are focused on the ministry of the Levites in the Davidic narratives of 1 Chr 10–29. The Jerusalem temple and its personnel represent, indeed, a major emphasis in Chronicles. This is evident throughout the corpus and, in a foundational way, in David's reign, where the role of the Levites (הלוים) is particularly accentuated in two broad sets of passages.[9]

First, the Levites are central to the ark narrative of 1 Chr 15–16.[10] Second, they play an important role in the narrative unit focused on David's preparations for the Solomonic temple in 1 Chr 22–29. This unit includes the establishment of Levitical musical function for the eventual temple worship services (especially in 1 Chr 25).[11] Our analysis will present a methodical

---

9. As Kalimi, *An Ancient Israelite Historian*, 12, remarks further, "[i]t is no exaggeration to conclude that in Chronicles little happens without some connection to Jerusalem." See further Japhet, *The Ideology*, 199–266; Selman, "Jerusalem in Chronicles," 43–56; Dennerlein, *Die Bedeutung*, 85–120; Kuntzmann, "David, constructeur du temple?" 139–56. Even as Endres, *First and Second Chronicles*, 6, comments, "[t]he Chronicler's idiosyncrasies show a great interest in how Israel (i.e, Judah in postexilic times) should pray and worship, and ultimately what religious practices can help the divided sectors of Israel come together in unity."

10. The narratives of 1 Chr 15 and 16 are partly drawn from, and contrasted to, the ark narrative in 2 Sam 6. On the synoptic issues, note Lemke, "The Synoptic Problem," 349–63; Brunet, "Le Chroniste et ses sources," 481–508. More recently, see Rezetko, *Source and Revision*, especially 5–42. And on the text-critical matters more broadly, see Throntveit, *When Kings Speak*, 77–107; Knoppers, *I Chronicles 1–9*, 52–71, 118–34; Japhet, *I and II Chronicles*, 14–22. Note also Endres et al., *Chronicles and Its Synoptic Parallels*, 49–152, for an English-based synoptic presentation of the Davidic narratives. For a detailed text-critical study of the synoptic texts between 1–2 Samuel and 1–2 Chronicles, see the recent study by Schenker, *Une Bible archétype*. He essentially concludes that based on common scribal mistakes in parallel passages, a common "archetypal" textual antecedent must have existed—he writes indeed, "[ceci] implique un manuscript achétype commun antérieur à la composition des Chroniques ... Avant l'éclosion de nombreuses formes textuelles aux derniers siècles avant J.-C., il y avait un texte reçu, reconnu comme archétype, et transmis avec soin à travers ces mêmes siècles." Schenker, *Une Bible archétype*, 173. For a recent and detailed rhetorical study of the Ark Narrative as a whole, see Street, *The Significance of the Ark Narrative*, especially 45–112.

11. On the literary and theological significance of Levitical song, note especially Kleinig, *The LORD's Song*, 13–27, 182–91; Leithart, *From Silence to Song*, 11–18, 101–32; Leithart, *1 & 2 Chronicles*, 1–8, 71–96; Ko, *The Levite Singers in Chronicles*, especially 151–82, 183–213; Boda, *1-2 Chronicles*, 185–202. For a discussion of the prophetic aspects of Levitical function, as it is set up by David in 1 Chr 25, note Knoppers, "To Him You Must Listen," 188–91, who concludes (p. 191) on the relationship between David and the "prophetic" Levites, "[i]n the Chronistic writing, the references to Asaph, Heman, and Jeduthun justify a long-standing tradition of cultic prophecy by associating the appointment of these critical figures with the formative arrangements

analysis of select passages within these two broader sets of narrative units. As a starting point, the topic of Levitical service will be introduced in this first chapter as follows: (1) the broad background will be set up by looking generally at the Levites in OT texts and major scholarly theories, (2) a more specific background will be established with key texts and theories about the Levites in Chronicles itself, and (3) a guiding thesis related to an exegetical approach for these Levitical texts in 1 Chr 10–29 will finally be proposed.

The Levites in OT Texts and Theories: The Broad Background

In this introductory section, we will proceed by (1) noting the foundational OT texts related to the ministry of the Levites, (2) highlighting the principal aspects of historical-critical theories related to the Levites in ancient Israelite religious history, and (3) commenting on some of the canonical-based theories concerning the service and ministry of the Levites in the OT.

Foundations: The Levites in OT Texts

In this section, key OT texts will be summarized, with an attempt at maintaining a distinction between the basic biblical *data* in the MT and scholarly *theories* related to that data.[12] Awareness of these passages should enhance the closer study envisaged for the specific texts in 1 Chronicles.

First, a brief survey of Pentateuchal texts may be effectively organized around the Sinai revelation.[13] The first set of data is genealogical and concerns those passages leading up to the Sinai texts, which begin with Exod 19. The priests and the Levites of later passages all trace their lineage to Levi. The account of Isaac (Gen 25:19–35) includes a section detailing the birth of Jacob's first eleven sons (Gen 29:31—30:24). The Isaac cycle also comprises the birth of Jacob's twelfth son, Benjamin (Gen 35:16–18), and

---

of the united monarchy. . . . Yahwistic prophecy in Chronicles is a rich and diverse phenomenon."

12. This follows Averbeck's call to distinguish between textual data and scholarly theory in biblical scholarship. See his "Ancient Near Eastern Mythography," 328.

13. Some have argued that when looking at Genesis through Joshua as a literary unit, the texts encompassing the Sinai treaty form a literary center (Exod 19–40, the book of Leviticus, and Num 1:1—10:10; i.e., between the geographical/temporal notices of Exod 19:1 and Num 10:10). See for example Dorsey, *The Literary Structure*, 97–102; Steiner, "Literary Structure," 544–66. On the cohesive function of the Sinai narratives in the Pentateuch more broadly, see Sailhammer, *The Meaning of the Pentateuch*, 44–56; Alexander, *From Paradise to Promise Land*, 64–81.

a summary of Jacob's twelve sons as a whole (Gen 35:23–26). Leah claims (Gen 29:34) that, with the birth of her third son, Jacob would now become *attached* to her (יִלָּוֶה), hence the name *Levi* (לֵוִי).[14] Furthermore, the genealogy in Gen 46:8–27 includes Levi's three sons (Gen 46:11): Gershon, Kohath, and Merari (גרשן קהת ומררי), the founders of three important Levitical clans for the tabernacle and temple ministry. In Gen 34, Simeon and Levi overreact to the rape of their sister Dinah by Shechem—to become a threat to Jacob's line (Gen 34:30–31). They incur a curse from Jacob who, in Gen 49:7, promises dispersion in the land because of their rash violence. As Matthews remarks of Jacob's utterance at this juncture, "[h]is vivid language heightens the imagery of ruthless violence."[15]

In Exodus, the chapters preceding the Sinai unit reinforce and develop this initial genealogical data. (1) Levi is included in the notice of Jacob's eleven sons, who sojourn to Egypt and join Joseph (Exod 1:1–7). (2) Moses' parents belong to the house of Levi in Exod 2:1—connecting Moses to that line. (3) After Moses' initial calling from the LORD, a family record of Jacob's sons occurs in Exod 6:14–25.[16] Levi's three sons are listed, along with additional lines (Gershon: Libni, Shimei; Kohath: Amram, Izhar, Hebron; Merari: Uzziel, Mahli, Mushi), which are all significant in the Chronicler's perspective.

The second major set of Pentateuchal texts relates to the Sinai experience itself, as recorded in sections of Exodus, Leviticus, and the early chapters of Numbers. After the proclamation and ratification of the covenant at Sinai (Exod 19–24), at least two issues stand out in Exodus. (1) The special function of Aaron and his sons is underscored. As Yahweh gives Moses the pattern of the tabernacle complex (Exod 25–27), his brother Aaron and his sons (also Levites, a key expression: אהרן ובניו) are given the role of serving Yahweh as priests (כהן) in Exod 28–30, which is a section focused on the

---

14. In *HALOT-SE*, 522, this niphal imperfect form of יִלָּוֶה is glossed as "to join oneself to." Note the implication, then, of Deut 10:9. The precise etymology of לוה or לוי, however, is rather obscure. See Jensen, "לוי," 772–78; Kellerman, "לְוִיִּם לֵוִי," 486–90.

15. Matthews, *Genesis 11:27–50:26*, 889.

16. In historical-critical views, this genealogy is seen as an insertion in the narrative, which would "suggest that a priestly redactor, and not the original Priestly writer, has carefully inserted the genealogy within the narrative," according to Childs, *The Book of Exodus*, 111. In this light, note that Stuart, *Exodus*, 175, argues with regards to this genealogy, "[i]n the style of ancient Near Eastern writing and according to the concerns of ancient Near Eastern culture, a genealogy here [in chapter 6] is neither out of place nor stylistically intrusive but welcome and perfectly placed. . . . Most ancient narratives had no concern for preservation of suspense per se, but neither did it hurt to place a review and retrospective, which is what 6:13–27 functions as in Exodus." See further Twersky, "Genesis 49," 317–33.

institution of this priestly ministry.¹⁷ (2) The Levites' refusal to participate in the sin of the golden calf in Exod 32 is viewed positively: they rally to Moses and are recognized with a special ordination.¹⁸

In Leviticus, (1) the distinction between Aaron's line and the rest of the Levitical clans is assumed, as the priestly sacrificial duties at the altar are assigned to "Aaron and his sons" (Lev 8:2, in context of the institution of the priesthood in Lev 8–10). (2) An awareness of the special status of the Levitical clans within the tribes of Israel is also apparent in the discussion of the Levitical cities in Lev 25:32–34—within the larger literary complex of the Holiness Code in chapters 17–27.¹⁹

In Numbers, the status of the Levites is noted in the general context of the wilderness camp preparations (chs. 1 and 2). The census in Num 1:1–46 provides the tribal lists of men of twenty years or more able to serve in a military function, except the tribe of Levi. Indeed, in Num 1:47–54, the Levites are not listed according to the "tribe of their fathers" (v. 47, והלוים למטה אבתם), but are set apart to *carry, take care of, take down*, and *set up* the tabernacle, and to *put to death* any intruder—activities encompassing their service of *keeping guard*.²⁰ The passage in Num 1:47–54 can be understood as a summary of Levitical service, while the later texts in Numbers *expand* on this basic statement. The Levitical clans are physically located around the tent (i.e., following their distinct clans) in the encampment and during the procession (Num 2:17)—in both contexts in a graded manner.²¹

Second, Num 3 and 4 provide further detail. In chapter 3: (1) the contrast between the duty of "Aaron and his sons" and the rest of the Levites is given in vv. 1–13. (2) The purpose of this census (of counting every firstborn male) is given in vv. 14–20. (3) The three clans provide structure to the

---

17. For a short synthesis of priestly theology, see for instance Dozeman, "The Priestly Vocation," 117–28.

18. For some, strands of Exodus 32 are taken as propaganda for various rival Levitical clans—such as Cody, *A History*, 146–55. However, note the contrasted positions on this issue in Durham, *Exodus*, 427–28 and Jensen "לוי," 773, for example.

19. See further Milgrom, *Leviticus 23–27*, 2201–4; Hartley, *Leviticus*, 103–8, 414–48; Jepsen, "Mose und die Leviten," 318–23. On the literary and theological coherence of Leviticus as a whole, note Averbeck, "Leviticus," 907–23.

20. These terms represent the core activities of the Levites in the wilderness: נשׂא שרת ירד קום מות שמר. See further Spencer, "The Tasks of the Levites," 267–71; Milgrom, *The Encroacher*, 82–90.

21. Some historical-critical scholars approach Numbers as the product of a long process of growth where the J, E (and the redacted JE), and P sources make up the MT's final text. Thus, many view Num 1:1—10:10 as the legendary organization of the sanctuary campaign. On this, see Knierim and Coats, *Numbers*, 4–26. For a (contrasted) canonical perspective, see Wenham, *Numbers*, 13–34.

description of duties in vv. 21–39 (parallel to the clans of Exod 6:16–19). The Gershonites are responsible for the tent and curtains. The Kohathites oversee the holiest tabernacle vessels. The Merarites care for the structural items of the tabernacle. (4) In vv. 40–51, the Levites' function of standing in the place of the firstborn Israelites is also affirmed.

The second major census in Num 4 ascertains the number of Levites actually able to perform their required service (4:1–3: all Levites from thirty to fifty years old are now counted). Under Aaronide supervision, the role of the Kohathites is central, with the expanded detail of their care for the tabernacle's holy articles (4:1–17)—followed by the Gershonites' (4:21–28) and the Merarites' (4:29–33) respective responsibilities. The final tally of "working" Levites is given at the conclusion of this chapter (4:34–49).[22]

Third, in Num 8:5–26, the special status of the Levites is again highlighted, as Moses is commanded to take the Levites and perform a ceremonial cleansing to prepare them for their wilderness duties at the tent of meeting. A key section of this text occurs in Num 8:12–26. The Levites are to be presented as a wave offering before Aaron and his sons, since they stand in the place of the firstborn of the Israelites. In turn, having laid their hands on the heads of the sacrificial bulls (v. 12), the Levites become a gift to Aaron and his sons for the work of the tabernacle. Based on this special ritual status, they are thus able to make atonement for all Israelites (v. 19).[23]

The final section of Pentateuchal biblical data on the Levites concerns those passages related to the wilderness journey and, especially, the final preparations at the threshold of entry into the land—that is, in the later sections of Numbers and Deuteronomy.[24] Four passages stand out in Numbers: (1) In Num 16, in contrast to Exod 32, the Levite Korah (of the Kohathite clan) organizes a rebellion against Moses, which leads to judgment in death for Korah's family and the other clans involved, as well as a deadly plague in the camp. Only the ministry of Aaron quells this divine judgment (Num 16:46–50).

(2) In Num 18, (a) "fellow Levites" are called to assist Aaron and his sons in ministry "before the tent of meeting" (vv. 1–7), and (b) the offerings from the people are noted as a source of support (vv. 8–24). In turn,

---

22. On the Levitical clans, see further Jensen, *Graded Holiness*, 130–35; Douglas, "Levite," 89.

23. As Cole, *Numbers*, 152, remarks in this regard, "[c]learly the Levites' role in the tabernacle service was multifaceted.... The Levites became the substitute redemption price for all Israelite firstborn because of their demonstrated faithfulness to Yahweh during the golden calf incident."

24. See further Sherwood, *Leviticus*, 97–140, 99–240; Lee, *Punishment and Forgiveness*, 1–45.

in vv. 25-32, the Levites are called to return a tenth of their offerings as a tithe to the LORD—a portion that is to be given to Aaron the priest (לאהרן הכהן). (3) The second census of Num 26 occurs while the people are in Moab, to the east of the land, across the Jordan. The notice for the tribe of Levi includes the three major clans, some of the same sub-clans found in Exod 6 (Libni, Hebron, Mahli, Mushi), and additional detail on the sub-clan of Korah (Num 26:5-59, of the Kohathite clan through Amram). (4) Building on Lev 25:32-34, Num 35:1-4 establishes detail for the provision of Levitical cities and pasturelands.

Moreover, four sets of texts in Deuteronomy should also be pointed out.[25] (1) In Moses' first address (Deut 4:44—11:32), Deut 10:6-9 stands as a narrative interlude recalling Eleazar's succession as the primary Aaronide priest (after the death of his father, Aaron), and the establishment of the Levites' duty in (a) carrying the ark, (b) standing before the LORD to minister, and (c) pronouncing blessings in the name of the LORD.

(2) In the section reiterating the laws of worship and conduct for Israel (Deut 12-26), a number of texts provide information on the responsibilities envisaged for the Levites in the land: (a) particular duties planned for the Levites are described: they will live throughout the territory and, also, participate in the central cult (12:11-12; 18:6-7) and the feast of Weeks (16:11-12). (b) The Levites' dependence on the LORD is also emphasized: they are to receive offerings of firstfruits and tithes as support (14:27; 26:12-15). (c) Broader language referring to the priests and the Levites is used: on the one hand, the basic term "Levite" continues to refer to the non-Aaronite clans (as with הלוי in Deut 12:12), while on the other hand, the term "Levite" also carries a broader connotation with its association to "priest," as in the expression "the priests, who are Levites" (הכהנים הלוים; 17:9, 18; 18:1; 24:8; 27:8). Furthermore, the expression "the priests, the sons of Levi" is also used twice in Deuteronomy (הכהנם בני לוי; 21:5; 31:9).[26] With fewer rigors than the more formal priestly texts, these expressions still appear to recognize the special function of the Aaronite priests, while also connecting them to the larger sacerdotal tribe of Levi.[27]

---

25. For a succinct discussion of Deuteronomy (and key bibliography) see McConville, "Deuteronomy," 82-93, and, in methodological contrast, note for instance Dahmen, *Leviten und Priester*, 388-407.

26. Note Duke, "The Portion of the Levite," 193-201, who counters the prevailing thesis, rooted in Wellhausen's work, of the sharp distinctions between D and P in the Deut 18 passage.

27. Wright argues that some have drawn too sharp a difference in the Levitical and priestly terminology of the priestly and Deuteronomic texts. See Wright, "The Levites in Deuteronomy," 325-30 and the response by Emerton, "Priests and Levites," 129-38. Note as well Abba, "Priests and Levites in Deuteronomy," 257-67.

(3) In Moses' third address (Deut 27–30), the Levites are instructed to loudly recite the curses to the people, once in the land (for disobedience to basic laws; cf. 27:14, [15–26]). (4) In the context of the passages dealing with the conclusion to Moses' ministry (Deut 31–34), two texts related to the tribe of Levi should be noted. (a) In Deut 31:24, the Levites receive the book of the Law from Moses and are to place it to the side of the ark as a witness against the people. (b) In Moses' final address to the tribes in chapter 33, the tribe of Levi also receives its blessing in 33:8–11, which details its role of keeping the Law and *teaching* it, and of being involved in the cult and worship leadership.[28] In this sense, we remember the fundamental call for the tribe of Levi in Lev 10:11, "to *teach* [ולהורת] the Israelites all the decrees the LORD has given them through Moses."

Beyond the Pentateuch, we may observe some key issues in the books of Joshua, Judges, and Samuel-Kings. In Joshua, the data connects logically with Deuteronomy. (1) The duty of the Levitical priests in carrying the ark is emphasized (הכהנים הלוים; 3:3; 8:33). (2) The fact that the Levites do not receive land inheritance is also noted (Josh 13:14, 32; 14:2; 18:7). (3) Further, the Levitical leaders request that Eleazar fulfill the Pentateuchal promise of receiving Levitical cities (Josh 21:2; cf. Lev 25:32–34; Num 35:1–4).

Following this initial establishment in the land, the presentation of the Levites in Judges fits within this book's overall negative assessment of the people's faithfulness to the LORD in the pre-monarchic period (cf. Judg 21:25). In Judg 17–18, Micah makes a young Levite his own priest, who then allows for idolatry both with Micah and his neighbors, and also some Danites. Judg 18:3–31 makes note of the sin of another Levite (Jonathan, a Gershonite), whose sons continue his tradition of idolatry in the tribe of Dan. In Judg 19 and 20, yet another Levite takes a concubine and acts rashly with her (Judg 19:25–30). Later, the Levites are connected with the ark (1 Sam 6:15; 2 Sam 15:24–29; 1 Kgs 8:4) and Rehoboham, who appoints non-Levites as priests (1 Kgs 12:29).[29]

In contrast to the biblical corpus of Joshua through 1 Kings, the Levites are more significantly portrayed in the postexilic books of Ezra-Nehemiah.[30]

---

28. On Moses in Chronicles, note Dörrfuss, *Mose in den Chronikbüchern*, 119–71. Cole, *Numbers*, 439, argues that in Deut 33:8–11, the responsibilities of the Levites are essentially twofold: "teaching Torah and offering incense and burning offerings." He remarks further that it is interesting to note how the second responsibility (related to worship function, even as it expands) is fairly clear in the subsequent history of Israel and that the *Torah-teaching* function is also present, but "especially in post-Old Testament times when teaching of Torah became the very center of Judaism." See Cole, *Numbers*, 439–40.

29. On this issue, note the classic study by Noth, "The Background," 68–85.

30. On the basic compositional issues related to Ezra-Nehemiah, see Williamson,

In Ezra, (1) they are included in the list of returnees in Ezra 2 (vv. 40-42), including the temple servants in vv. 43-58, following the returning priests (vv. 36-39). (2) The Levites also help rebuild and dedicate the temple in song "according to the directions of David king of Israel" (Ezra 2:10). The divisions of priests and Levites are set up in chapter 6 and the Levitical role at Passover is emphasized (Ezra 6:19-22). (3) Ezra, a Levite, also returns to the land intent on teaching the Law (Ezra 7:10). (4) In 8:15-20, he further ensures that Levites are part of the returnees to provide "ministers for the house of our God," (v. 17). (5) Levites, finally, participate in the sin of intermarriage and in its ceremonial confession (Ezra 9:1-2; 10:1-4, 23-24).

In Nehemiah, (1) the role of the Levites at the rebuilding of the Jerusalem wall is noted (Neh 3:17; 12:27-47). (2) Genealogical data for Levites, who are a part of the community of the return, is also included (Neh 7:43-60; 11:10-24; 12:1-26). (3) The specific role of Ezra and other Levites in teaching the Law is shown (Neh 8:1-12), which leads to a renewal of the feast of Booths (Neh 8:13-18), and to confession of sin (Neh 9:1-5, 6-38). (4) A Levitical covenant renewal ceremony also follows (Neh 9:39—10:27; 10:28-39). (5) Finally, Nehemiah promotes reforms with: (a) the restoration of Levitical temple service (Neh 13:4-10); (b) the renewal of tithing (Neh 13:10-14); (c) the role of the Levites in the Sabbath (Neh 13:22); and (d) the establishment of cultic rotations (Neh 13:30).

In the poetic and prophetic books, basic biblical data related to the Levites (or the tribe of Levi generally) is especially found in Ezekiel, and within the Levitical psalms of the Psalter.[31] In Ezekiel, the key text is chapter 44, set within the broader context of Ezekiel's vision of a restored Jerusalem temple in chapters 40-48 where, in the twentieth year of Ezekiel's exile, God leads him back to Israel through supernatural visions (Ezek 40:1-4). In chapter 44, part of Ezekiel's vision includes the duties of the Levites and priests.[32] The LORD challenges Ezekiel by calling for the purity of the temple (vv. 6-9). Levites are accused of having strayed from God. Accordingly, they cannot serve as priests, but are put in charge of temple duties (vv. 10-14). Only Zadokite priests (in line with the priest faithful to David

---

Ezra, Nehemiah, 525; Min, *The Levitical Authorship*, 6-31, 142-46; VanderKam, "Ezra-Nehemiah," 55-75; Eskenazi, "The Missions of Ezra and Nehemiah," 509-29.

31. For other texts, note Ps 135:19-21; Isa 66:14-21; Jer 33:17-18; Zech 12:1-14; Mal 2:1-9; 3:1-7. And see further Grabbe, "A Priest Without Honor," 79-97.

32. On Ezek 44:4-31, Blekinsopp agrees with critical scholars who view this text as the fruit of later editorializing—thus affirming the centrality of priestly Zadokites and the demotion of non-Zadokites as Levites. See Blenkinsopp, *Ezekiel*, 219. Block, *The Book of Ezekiel*, 626-37, however, argues for a "re-commissioning" rather than a "demotion." Conclusions similar to Block's are also defended in: McConville, "Priests and Levites in Ezekiel," 1-35, and Duke, "Punishment or Restoration," 61-81.

and Solomon, cf. 1 Kgs 1:28–53) will be allowed to carry out the sacrificial duties and must then behave appropriately as Aaronides (vv. 15–28). For the restored temple, the *Zadokite priestly* Levites are the only Levites to be involved with temple sacrifice—Aaronide priests and Levites thus remain distinct (cf. Ezek 40:44–46; 43:18–21; 45:1–5; 48:9–14).

Also, in the canonical form of the Psalter, a number of psalms are attributed to Levitical origins.[33] The psalm titles connect these texts to several Levitical groups that are also described in the narrative historical contexts of Chronicles. The content of these Levitical psalms is often focused on the sovereignty and beneficence of the LORD in Jerusalem/Zion and, also, on the theological significance of the temple complex. For instance, Levitical Korahite Ps 48 opens with a call to praise that distinctly relates God's worthiness with his presence in Zion (MT Ps 48:2–3): גדול יהוה ומהלל מאד בעיר אלהינו הר־קדשו יפה נוף משוש כל־הארץ הר־ציון ירכתי צפון קרית מלך רב.

Or, Asaphite Ps 50 opens with a commentary on the relationship between God and Zion in the context of the LORD's control over creation (MT Ps 50:1–2): אל אלהים יהוה דבר ויקרא־ארץ ממזרח־שמש עד־מבאו מציון מכלל־יפי אלהים הופיע. Further, the Levitical psalms both affirm the blessing of being in God's presence in the temple such as MT Ps 73:16–17a, ואחשבה לדעת זאת עמל היא בעיני עד־אבוא אל־מקדשי־אל, and the mourning related to the destruction of the temple complex, such as in MT Ps 74:2–3, זכר עדתך קנית קדם גאלת שבט נחלתך הר־ציון זה שכנת בו הרימה פעמיך למשאות נצח כל הרע אויב בקדש.

The Levitical psalms are organized around two major groups.[34] (1) A first group of texts is related to the sons of Korah (Pss 42; 44–49; 84–85; 87–88; [89]).[35] In the MT, each of these psalms contains a title related to the Korahite Levitical temple guild.[36]

---

33. For a recent and helpful introduction to the function of the Levitical psalms in the composition of the Psalter, see Gillingham, "The Levites," 201–13, and note the further discussion in chapter five of this work.

34. For a recent summary of the discussion surrounding the titles/superscriptions in the Psalms, see deClaissé-Walford et al., *The Book of Psalms*, 9–12. And note as well, Slomovic, "Toward an Understanding," 350–80.

35. For the data on Korah in Chronicles, see 1 Chr 1:35; 6:7, 22; 9:19.

36. All MT references: Ps 42:1 למנצח משכיל לבני־קרח; Ps 44:1 למנצח לבני־קרח משכיל; Ps 45:1 למנצח על־ששנים לבני־קרח משכיל שיר ידידת; Ps 46:1 למנצח לבני־קרח על־עלמות שיר; Ps 47:1 למנצח לבני־קרח מזמור; Ps 48:1 שיר מזמור לבני־קרח; Ps 49:1 למנצח לבני־קרח מזמור; Ps 84:1 למנצח על־הגתית לבני־קרח מזמור; Ps 85:1 למנצח לבני־קרח מזמור; Ps 87:1 לבני־קרח מזמור שיר; Ps 88:1 שיר מזמור לבני קרח למנצח על מחלת לענות משכיל להימן האזרחי; [Ps 89:1 משכיל לאיתן האזרחי].

The title of Ps 89 does not bear the name of Korah directly. However, this psalm should also be seen as at least generally Levitical since: (1) Ethan, in Ps 89, is part of the same Ezrahite Levitical sub-clan as Heman in the title of Ps 88, who is also connected to

(2) Another group of texts is connected to the Asaphite Levitical tradition (Pss 50; 73–83). In the Psalter, twelve psalms are specifically related to Asaph, who in Chronicles is presented as a key Levitical music leader in Jerusalem under David (see 1 Chr 16:4–7).[37]

While the compositional and historical issues related to the meaning of the Levitical (and other) psalm titles are complex, at a minimum we may state with Wilson at this juncture that these Levitical sections within the Psalter "probably represent the remains of collections of songs written by [the Asaphite and Korahite] guilds of temple singers."[38]

The Levites in the Old Testament: Historical-Critical Theories

In the context of OT historical-criticism, the cornerstone scholarly approach to the biblical data on the Levites briefly summarized above is that of Wellhausen and his source-critical documentary hypothesis (which, in turn, follows earlier theories by Graf and De Wette).[39] Wellhausen's key claim was that the priestly and legal system cannot be rooted in the early historical period of Moses, but is a representation of the late postexilic Jewish era.[40] In fact, as Boda has pointed out, "unquestionably the fragment from Julius Wellhausen's *Prolegomena* most frequently cited by researchers"[41] is the following quote:

---

the Korahite Levitical line, and (2) Ethan is regularly connected to the Levitical singing guilds in Chronicles (cf. 1 Chr 2:6; 6:33; 15:17, 19; 25:1–5; 2 Chr 5:12; 35:15). It is an important psalm that concludes Book III of the Psalter with a reflection on the transformation in the perception of the Davidic covenant (compare 89:1–37 vs. 89:38–52).

37. Ps 50:1 מזמור לאסף; Ps 73:1 מזמור לאסף; Ps 74:1 משכיל לאסף; Ps 75:1 למנצח אל־תשחת מזמור לאסף שיר; Ps 76:1 למנצח בנגינת מזמור לאסף שיר; Ps 77:1 למנצח על־ידיתון למנצח אל־ששנים עדות לאסף מזמור; Ps 78:1 משכיל לאסף; Ps 79:1 מזמור לאסף; Ps 80:1 שיר מזמור לאסף; Ps 81:1 לאסף מזמור; Ps 82:1 מזמור לאסף; Ps 83:1 למנצח על־הגתית לאסף. For the basic data on Asaph in Chronicles, see 1 Chr 6:24; 9:15; 15:17, 19; 16:5, 7, 37; 25:1–2, 6, 9; 26:1; 2 Chr 5:12; 20:14; 29:13, 30; 35:15.

38. Wilson, *Psalms*, 20. Some of the data related to these Levitical psalms will be investigated in more detail in the second major section of chapter five of this study.

39. See especially "Priester und Leviten," in Wellhausen, *Prolegomena zur Geschichte*, 121–54. And note further Rehm, "Priests and Levites," 297–98. Broadly, see the studies and bibliographies provided in Klingbeil, "Historical Criticism," 401–20. See as well the helpful discussion in Harrison, *Introduction to the Old Testament*, 33–61.

40. So writes Rendtorff, "The Paradigm Is Changing," 35.

41. Boda, "Gazing Through the Cloud of Incense," 215, and note also, 215–16, for a list of scholars since the 1950s who have been at odds when it comes to understanding the Chronicler's presentation of David (and the Levites) and the Chronicler's eschatological theology.

> See what Chronicles has made out of David! The founder of the kingdom has become the founder of the temple and the public worship, the king and hero at the head of his companions in arms has become the singer and master of ceremonies at the head of a swarm of priests and Levites; his clear-cut figure has become a feeble holy picture, seen through a cloud of incense.[42]

For Wellhausen, then, the contrasts in the Levitical data demonstrate how separate literary sources have been combined in the final form of the text. Underlying this final form, however, is a much different historical reality for the Levites. The earliest literary traditions of the Jawhist and the Elohist (J, E) portray the Levites as secular tribesmen (Genesis) operating in a free environment of multiple shrines and eventually taking on priestly duties (Judges). In this theoretical reading, the book of Judges does not bear witness to the remains of an earlier cult, but to the natural *beginnings* of civil authority.[43] Consequently, during the monarchy, priests are able to ally closely with the growing power of the king. While these priests gain in prominence, other Levites continue to operate elsewhere. With Josiah's reforms (following De Wette on D), the centrality of the Jerusalem priests is affirmed; still, "provincial" Levites can participate at the central shrine (Deut 18).

In Wellhausen's reading, Ezekiel 44 represents the linchpin between the earlier views of J, E, and D and the latest views of P. Ezekiel anticipates the priestly division between "Levites" and "priests" (the sons of Aaron), since, for him, chapter 44 *introduces* the systematic separation of holy and profane. Hence, in this view, the Priestly Code was not yet in existence during Ezekiel's exilic period. The Levites had acted as priests of their own right; however, during the exile, they are punished for ministering at the outer shrines and *degraded* to the status of servants at the central shrine (a role earlier taken on by heathen slaves). *Zadokite* Levites—those who faithfully ministered in Jerusalem—alone remain as priests (a quasi-subversive move).[44] Accordingly, the priestly distinction between Aaronide priests and inferior Levitical

---

42. Wellhausen, *Prolegomena*, 182. The original German, in Wellhausen, *Prolegomena zur Geschichte*, 181–82, reads, "[w]as hat die Chronik aus David gemacht! Der Gründer des Reichs ist zum Gründer des Tempels und des Gottesdienstes geworden, der König und Held an der Spitze eines Schwarmes von Priestern und Leviten, seine so scharf gezeichnete Figur zu einem matten Heiligenbilde, umnebelt von einer Wolke von Weihrauch."

43. "Sondern die ersten naturwüchsigen Anfänge staatlicher Autorität, die sich weiter und weiter entwickelnd schließlich zum Königtum geführt haben." See Wellhausen, *Prolegomena zur Geschichte*, 128.

44. "Mit anderen Worten hängt Ezekiel bloss der Logik der Tatsachen einen moralischen Mantel um." See Wellhausen, *Prolegomena zur Geschichte*, 124.

"hieroduli" becomes a reality *after* Ezekiel in the postexilic period.[45] P (i.e., Leviticus, strands of Exodus and Numbers, and supplements in Chronicles) presents a complicated system that is projected back onto "Mosaic" times. Dissonance, then, exists between P and earlier strands like Judges.

A number of scholars have followed Wellhausen's broad trajectory in assuming the late date of P and the view, hence, of the *degradation* of the Levites' functions. For example, Vogelstein has examined the effects of Ezekiel's "demotion" of the non-Zadokite Levites in Ezra-Nehemiah and Chronicles.[46] Baudissin separates the evidence of P, J, D, Ezekiel, the postexilic books of Chronicles and Ezra-Nehemiah, and the Samuel-Kings corpus in examining the OT priesthood. For him, Chronicles establishes a distinction between the attending Levites and the priests, thus conforming to the authoritative and late status of P.[47] Van Hoonacker similarly argues that source-critical differences existed between the priests and the Levites.[48] In a related approach, De Vaux has proposed three developmental stages: (1) earliest non-Levitical priests (Judges); (2) monarchical Levitical priests (Deut 18); (3) Priests and Levites ("idealized" in Ezekiel, "realized" in Numbers). In this sense, the cultic heritage of the secular tribe of Levi was the fruit of priestly redaction.[49]

For Cody, as a further example, the book of Judges also reflects the earliest priestly activities of *secular* Levites—sojourners who operated as priests for economic reasons. Deuteronomy, while in part representing older laws, takes its final shape, then, under Josiah and presents a closer relationship between the central priests and other Levites, unlike earlier times in the monarchy. The biblical text of Ezekiel moves *toward* the distinction

---

45. In line with Wellhausen, note the comment by Van Hoonacker, "Les prêtres et les lévites," 183, "c'est que la peine infligée aux prêtres infidèles consiste formellement dans leur dégradation au rang de portiers, de desservants de 'la maison,' de ministres au service du temple." And on Van Hoonacker, see further Post, "Levi," 101-2.

46. See Vogelstein, *Der Kampf*, 5-14. Note further, Biberfeld, *Der Übergang*, 1-8; Berry, "Priests and Levites," 227-38.

47. Baudissin, *Die Geschichte*, 28-35, 151-58.

48. Van Hoonacker, *Sacerdoce lévitique*, 117. For similar views, note Wiener, "Priests and Levites," 2446-52; Harper, *The Work*, 13-61, 208-17; Lefèvre, "Lévitique (Organisation)," 389-98; James, *The Nature*, 68-100, 282-84.

49. de Vaux, *Les institutions*, 214-30. He notes that most of the data (except the most "ancient" texts of Judges): (1) "reports" priestly prerogatives for the Levites, and (2) assumes the centrality of Jerusalem. However, in his words, these are "deux prérogatives qui ne furent acquises qu'au terme de toute une historique." See de Vaux, *Les institutions*, 217. And similarly, see Fohrer, *History*, 151-222, 307-91; Vanhoye, *Old Testament Priests*, 19-38.

between priest and Levite, which is fully realized in the priestly strands of the Pentateuch and in the Chronicler's work.[50]

Following earlier work by Gunneweg, Sabourin further highlights the *ancient* nature of cultic clergy throughout the ANE—unlike Wellhausen. Still, he largely follows Wellhausen on the priest vs. Levite issue, by attempting to elucidate historical ambiguities found in differing literary strands. For him, Judges presents *secular* Levites taking on priestly duties. Deuteronomy displays the closer relationship between Levites and priests that was evident in the *later monarchy*. Ezekiel *first* notes the division between priest and Levite, which is, for him, characteristic of P, Chronicles, and Ezra-Nehemiah.[51]

More recent historical-critical studies on the religious leadership of ancient Israel assume, in the main, the majority position of this broad-based Wellhausian trajectory, while differing in reconstructive details.[52] Nurmela, for instance, assumes that Zadok was from the south and Abiathar was from the north and, hence, argues: (1) Ezekiel 44 is the best *starting point* for the emergence of the "second-class priesthood" (the Levites), as this passage contains the least amount of redaction by rival factions; (2) assuming the northern origin of Deuteronomy, the Levites would largely be former northern royal priests who fled south and emerged as lower class priests to the Jerusalem Zadokites, following Jeroboam's revolt; (3) Zadok would then be "a historical person" contemporary to David and Solomon, "whereas Aaron definitely belongs to the prehistorical period in Israel's life," the (imaginary) fruit of priestly revision.[53]

Haran, in contrast, has argued for the priority of P over D (contra Wellhausen).[54] In his view, the distinction between priests and Levites is not an *innovation* introduced by Ezekiel but actually originates in the early monarchy. Consequently, Haran counters the prevailing notion of the late development of a *hierarchical* priestly and Levitical clergy. In this approach to the biblical data, an ancient priestly line can be traced back

---

50. See Cody, *Ezekiel*, 256–63; *A History*, 29–38, 151–56, 82–92; Strauss, *Untersuchungen*, 13–65.

51. Sabourin, *Priesthood*, 102–16. Similarly, see Schulz, *Leviten*, 15–85.

52. See especially Blenkinsopp, *Sage, Priest, Prophet*, 66–114; Grabbe, *Priests, Prophets*, 41–65; Millar, *Priesthood*; 85–104; Miller, *The Religion*, 162–73; Nelson, *Raising Up*, 1–16; Collins, "Israel," 181–88. Polk, "The Levites," 3–22, suggests certain Levites only gained priestly privileges as a reward from David.

53. Nurmela, *The Levites*, 177–81. See also White, "The Elohistic," 149–60. For further critical study of the Israelite religion during the united monarchy, see Albertz, *A History of Israelite Religion*, 105–242. For recent critical study of the history of the Levites in OT texts, see Samuel, *Von Priestern*, 1–15, for his introduction.

54. Haran, *Temples and Temple-Service*, 7. Similarly, see Abba, "Priests and Levites," 876–91; Milgrom, *Studies in Cultic Theology*, 1–66.

to the tribe of Levi through Moses. In fact, for him, the evidence suggests that the postexilic period could *not* sustain a complex cult, while an earlier preexilic monarchy could.[55]

The Levites in the Old Testament: Canonical-Based Theories

Haran's earlier view of P leads us naturally to discussing more canonically rooted views, which locate "P" within a pre-monarchic, cohesive, and essentially Mosaic literary tradition. These views take the final, canonical form of the MT as the starting point. Interestingly, in a few earlier studies, scholars even suggested typological relationships between the Mosaic ministry of the Levites and the ministry leadership of God's people in the NT church. Ritchie, for instance, argued for links between the duties of the Levitical clans and later functions, since the service of the Levites can be seen as rooted historically in God's dealings with Moses. He proposed a typological relationship between the responsibilities of the Merarites, Gershonites, and Kohathites and certain NT church leaders.[56] Further, Kurtz assumed both the reliability of the texts and the validity of the early gradation of priest and Levite.[57] In a similar vein, Keil defended the early division of priest and Levite in the wilderness and its adaptation in Canaan.[58] In his study, Legendre argued that the Pentateuch cohesively presents the Levites as active under Moses' leadership and engaged in major cultic duties.[59]

More recent canonically-based studies reveal further discussion of the Levites and, also, interaction with historical-critical issues more directly. For instance, Childs first acknowledged the presence of multiple theories related to the historical development of the priests and the Levites. He remarked further that the study of the *canonical* form, despite possible historical uncertainties, should prove more fruitful and, in the end, represents the intended focus of the sacred texts.[60] Duke largely agrees with Childs and also contends for an early view of the distinction between

---

55. Haran, *Temples and Temple-Service*, 84–111. And note as well, Haran, "Priests and Priesthood," 1070–86.

56. Ritchie, *The LORD's Work*, 24–31. Ritchie was a Reformed Scottish writer from the late nineteenth to early twentieth centuries.

57. See Kurtz, *Sacrificial Worship*, 34–35, 340–41. In the same vein, note Curtiss, *The Levitical Priests*, 9–21, 100–20.

58. Keil, *The Pentateuch*, 651–77, 729–32, 905–11, 930–35, 1010–12.

59. Lengendre, "Lévi," 209.

60. Childs, *Biblical Theology*, 140–43, 59–62; Childs, *Old Testament Theology*, 145–55.

the Aaronide priests and the Levites, rooted historically in Moses' ministry and communicated *theologically*.[61]

In the following discussion, the views of three representative scholars (Garrett, Klingbeil, and Pratt) will be highlighted as examples of more recent approaches to a broader OT understanding of the Levites, based on the final form of the MT. For Garrett, the Pentateuchal texts related to the Levites raise two questions: (1) When do the Levites *receive* their sacerdotal duties? (2) What is the *relationship* between the Levites and the Aaronide priests? In response to (1), he argues that in Exod 32, at Sinai, Aaron and the Levites are *already* recognized as the priestly tribe as a whole. This text serves, then, to *confirm* their function, but not radically alter their status. On (2), Garrett contends that Deuteronomy (and even Judges) shows that the Levite is not merely a *servant*, even if Leviticus and Numbers established distinct roles for the priests and the Levites.[62]

In fact, four aspects structure Garrett's proposal for a broad canonical solution. (1) The Levites were not originally secular tribesmen in Canaan (per the historical-critical perspective, in the main), but at the Exodus, they had a recognized priestly status (cf. Exod 32). (2) Texts like Ezek 44 do not *require* the existence of propaganda among rivals for the priesthood—since even in passages like Num 16–18, Levites and priests *agree* on the specific duties of the non-Aaronide Levites. (3a) During the *wilderness* period, the Aaronides officiated at the one sanctuary and the rest of the Levites served as support staff, while (3b), Deuteronomy *anticipated* entry into Canaan when the tabernacle would no longer be mobile, nor require the large practical support of the various Levitical clans. This would have allowed the Levites to move throughout the land and freely lead in the worship of Yahweh at other legitimate altars—the reality portrayed during the period of the judges and the early monarchy. At this time, the Levites would have taught the Torah throughout the land, which was also part of their ministry function. (4) 1 Kgs 12:31 bears witness to a growing *syncretism* with Canaanite religious traditions, with the emergence of non-Levitical shrines. This eventually prompted Josiah's centralizing reforms and led to finally closing down any outlying sanctuary. After the exile, the Jerusalem temple with its Aaronide priesthood was kept as the only legitimate shrine, but, as Garrett notes, "the Levites were *not demoted* in the process."[63]

---

61. Duke, "Priests, Priesthood," 646–55.

62. See Garrett, "Levi, Levites," 519–22. And similarly, note McCready, "Priest and Levites," 965–70.

63. Garrett, "Levi, Levites," 522 (emphasis added).

Furthermore, Klingbeil develops the following argument with regards to the OT historical books, more specifically.[64] (1) Relating literary testimony with historical reality is a significant endeavor—as the historical credibility of a preexilic clergy is plausible, although historical reliability is only *one* aspect of the passages since they are principally *theological* texts. (2) The picture of the priests and Levites is "complex and multifaceted," but it generally agrees with the Pentateuch. Part of this complexity lies in the different literary *genres* of the texts in which the data occurs. (3) Adaptation and contextualization to later historical realities are also evident, notably with the Levites' ministry at the Solomonic temple. The variation in Levitical age restrictions is probably due to the lesser number of Levites during the postexilic period. (4) The destruction of the temple has a profound impact on Israel, evident in the historical and theological "processing" visible in the Chronicler's work, but also in Joshua–2 Kings. (5) In the end, then, based on a reading of the canonical data, both priests and Levites should be seen as "personal attendants to Yahweh in his house," within a precise system of gradated holiness.[65]

Finally, Pratt has offered an overall canonical perspective built around the following six key historical periods.[66] (1) *Patriarchal*: Levi is one of the twelve patriarchs, with three sons: Gershon, Kohath and Merari (cf. Gen 46:11; 1 Chr 6). (2) *Mosaic*: Kohath and his son Amram are Levi's most prominent descendants; Moses, Aaron, and Miriam come from this line (1 Chr 6:3). Aaron and his sons are consecrated as priests, in *contrast* to all other Levites (Exod 28–29). Of Aaron's four sons, Nadab and Abihu die with no descendants (Exod 6:23; Num 3:2). The sons of Eleazar and Ithamar, then, maintain the priestly line. Also, Phineas' zeal for God (Num 25:10–13) allows Eleazar's line to continue as the high priestly one.

(3) *Davidic*: David sets up two high priests in Jerusalem to account for *both* remaining lines of Eleazar and Ithamar (the surviving two sons of Aaron): Abiathar is a descendant of Ithamar (1 Chr 15:11; 24:6) and Zadok is a descendant of Eleazar (1 Chr 6:4, 12); both share in the high priestly office (1 Chr 18:16; 2 Sam 20:25).[67] (4) *Solomonic*: however, Abiathar sides with

---

64. Klingbeil, "Priests and Levites," 811–19, and similarly, Jensen, "לוי," 772–78.

65. Jensen, "לוי," 818. Following Jensen, *Graded Holiness*, 133. See further Jensen, "Priest and Levites," 1066–67; Leithart, "Attendants of Yahweh's House," 3–24; Crossley, "The Levite as a Royal Servant," 80–182.

66. See Pratt, *1 and 2 Chronicles*, 55–57.

67. With the priestly genealogy of 1 Chr 6, Boda, *1–2 Chronicles*, 74, reminds us of the need to observe the Chronicler's overall concerns with both priestly and non-priestly Levitical clans—he writes: "[t]o focus on Zadok would be to miss the fact that the Chronicler is open to the involvement of not only non-priestly Levitical clans with the priests (see 6:48), but also of the other priestly clan descended from Aaron through Ithamar."

Adonijah against Solomon for David's throne (1 Kgs 1:7) and is removed (1 Kgs 2:26–27, 35), in fulfillment of divine prophecy (1 Sam 2:27–36). Consequently, Zadok and his descendants are established as the high priests, up to the exile (1 Chr 29:2; 1 Kgs 2:35; 4:1–4). (5) *Exilic*: yet, as a large number of Zadokite priests are deported after the fall of Judah, non-Zadokite Levites take up duties in Jerusalem during the exile. The exilic Ezekiel (a *Zadokite* priest) prophesies that upon the return of the exiles, the Zadokite line would once again assume its priestly leadership duty at the second temple of Jerusalem (the Zadokites are Aaronides, through Eleazar). The other clans would return to their subordinate duty, under the priestly leadership of the Zadokites/Aaronides (Ezek 40:46; 43:19; 44:1–15).

(6) *Postexilic*: The Zadokite high priest Joshua (or Jeshua/ישוע in 1 Chr 24:11; 2 Chr 31:15) returns with the Davidic Zerrubbabel to lead in Jerusalem. The postexilic prophet Zechariah presents Joshua and Zerrubabel as closely linked in the early restoration (Zechariah 3–4). Ezekiel and Zechariah's focus on the preeminence of the Zadokites indicates that certain Levitical clans were apparently *unwilling* to acquiesce to this leadership. The Chronicler, then, stresses both the *central* Zadokite line and the *other* lines—as both were crucial for the renewal of worship in the restoration period after the return from the exile.[68]

The Levites in OT Texts and Theories: The Background in Chronicles

In this second major section of our introductory chapter, we will transition to the book of Chronicles itself and cover the following four areas: (1) key texts on the Levites throughout Chronicles proper; (2) related historical-critical theories, (3) some newer literary-critical theories, and finally, (4) canonical-based theories on the Levites in Chronicles.

The Levites in Chronicles: Key Texts Summarized

The textual data concerning the Levites in Chronicles will first be summarized as a further foundation for our broader study. A basic canonical stance will also be adopted, as the function of the Levites in the four major sections of Chronicles is briefly summed up.

First, it is widely recognized that the extended and stylized genealogy of the tribe of Levi in chapter 6 stands at the chiastic center of the

---

68. Pratt, *1 and 2 Chronicles*, 57.

genealogical prologue of 1 Chr 1–9. The Levitical genealogy of 1 Chr 6 is itself commonly divided into five major sections.[69] (1) A mixed genealogy introduces the line of Aaron in vv. 1–15 (MT 5:27-41). A segmented genealogy in vv. 1–3 traces the generations of Levi and his three sons (v. 1), the sons of Kohath (v. 2), and the sons of Amram and Aaron (v. 3). A linear genealogy in vv. 4–15 then traces the descending line of Eleazar, one of Aaron's sons, to Jehozadak, the exiled high priest. (2) In vv. 16–30 (MT 6:1–15), the basic threefold clan structure is again recorded in v. 16, with development of the Levitical lines in vv. 17–19. In vv. 20–30, lines within the Levitical clans are highlighted, including Gershom (vv. 20–22), Kohath (vv. 22–24), Elkanah (vv. 25–27, a Kohathite), Samuel (v. 28, a Hemanite Kohathite, cf. v. 33), and Merari (vv. 29–30).

(3) In vv. 31–48, the Levitical singers are introduced, with their "service of song" in the house of the LORD (על־ידי־שיר בית יהוה; MT 6:16–17). Significantly, each singer is traced back to *Aaron*: Heman's line through Kohath (vv. 33–39); Asaph's line through Gershom (vv. 39–43); and Ethan's line through Merari (vv. 44–47). (4) A disjunctive clause sets apart the passage on the ministry of Aaron and his sons (ואהרן ובניו מקטירים MT 6:34) and, in vv. 49–53, introduces the duties of the Aaronide priests (cf. v. 49, of making offerings [מקטירים] and making atonement [ולכפר] for Israel) and, also, briefly traces a descending Aaronide line through Eleazar (vv. 50–53). (5) Finally, based on Joshua 21, chapter 6 concludes with a statement regarding the Levitical settlements, by following the clan structure: Kohathites (vv. 54–70); Gershomites (vv. 71–76), and Merarites (vv. 77–81).[70]

---

69. For analysis of the genealogies in Chronicles, see Johnson, *The Purpose*, 37–76; Wilson, *Genealogy and History*, 137–98. On their unity, see especially Oeming, *Das wahre Israel*, 188–218; Knoppers, *I Chronicles 1–9*, 246–65; Levin, "Who Was the Chronicler's Audience?" 229–45; Braun, "1 Chronicles 1–9," 92–105. Note as well the following more recent essays and the further literature cited there: Schweitzer, "The Genealogies of 1 Chronicles 1–9," 9–27; Bodner, "Reading the Lists," 29–41. On a succinct chiastic overview of the literary structure of the genealogies in 1 Chr 1–9, see Dorsey, *The Literary Structure*, 145–46. For the introduction to a feminist reading of the Chronicler's genealogies, see Löwisch, *Trauma Begets Genealogy*, 1–19. Löwisch notes that "this book integrates research on the genealogies of the Hebrew Bible into a broader discourse on genealogies, memory performance and gender, both academic and artistic. It opens new perspectives for an understanding of why genealogies are a key genre in the Hebrew Bible and how they function." See Löwisch, *Trauma Begets Genealogy*, 17.

70. A long process of textual growth has often been proposed for this chapter, yet, as one author notes, "the highly systematic structure of [chapter 6:1–48] clearly indicates that it is not a haphazard composition." See Japhet, *I and II Chronicles*, 145 (and see 145–49 as a whole). For a defense of the early preexilic reliability of the Levitical settlements (in line with Albright), note Hauer, "David and the Levites," 33–54; Hill, "Levitical Cities," 906–7.

Further, 1 Chr 9 provides lists of returnees from the Babylonian exile (and thus takes the genealogy from Adam in ch. 1 to the postexilic period in ch. 9), including priests (vv. 10-13), Levites (vv. 14-16), Levitical "gatekeepers" (השערים, vv. 17-32), and the Levites assigned to Jerusalem (vv. 33-34).[71] Three issues come to the fore in this text: (a) the gate-keeping duty at the preexilic temple is described as an *expansion* of the much earlier tabernacle duties; (b) the supervisory duty of an Aaronide priest is noted (v. 21); (c) David's role (and Samuel's) in the Levitical "office of trust" (באמונתם) is also emphasized. Overall, we may observe that the Chronicler's concern for the legitimacy of the Levitical guilds is present in the genealogies (most notably from a literary, structural perspective, since the Levitical genealogies occur at the center) and this sets up important concerns for the rest of the narrative. As House has noted of the theological implications of this initial genealogical section of the Chronicler's work:

> Through the use of genealogy as a telescoping device, the author has demonstrated agreement with the canon's conviction that the LORD is Creator, sustainer, covenant maker, judge, giver of land and restorer of the chosen people. Above all, the LORD must rule human history for all these ideas to be correct. No other god is considered part of the rule. No other god is identified as a living identity.[72]

In the context of David's reign (1 Chr 10-29), the Levites provide early military and liturgical support (1 Chr 12:26-28; 13:1-4). However, their duties take center stage with the proper transfer of the ark to Jerusalem and the ensuing celebration in 1 Chr 15-16: (1) David first ensures the set-up of priestly and Levitical supervision for the ark's transfer (1 Chr 15:1-16).[73] (2) Once the ark is set up to be properly carried, David appoints Levitical groups (led by Heman, Asaph, and Ethan [הימן אסף ואיתן], v. 19) to direct in the ministry of music (1 Chr 15:16-29).[74] (3) As the ark

---

71. 1 Chr 9:2-17 is parallel to Neh 11:3-19. On their relationship, see Williamson, *1 and 2 Chronicles*, 87-92; McKenzie, *1-2 Chronicles*, 108-15. And more generally, note Dirksen, "1 Chronicles 9, 26-33," 91-96.

72. House, *Old Testament Theology*, 527.

73. Note Welten, "Lade-Tempel-Jerusalem," 168-83. For a detailed textual analysis of the ark narratives in 1 Chronicles (and comparison to the Samuel sources), see Rezetko, *Source and Revision*, 286-300, for his conclusions.

74. As the German reformer Lucas Osiander (1534-1604) notes of David's responsibility for the musical aspect of Levitical ministry at this juncture: "David chose some Levites to be in charge of certain musical instruments, which became the origin of pleasantly played sacred music . . . Thus musical instruments belong to holiness as a gift of God for rendering praise and glory to God." See Cooper and Lohrman, *1-2 Samuel*, 519.

is placed in a tent in Jerusalem, David appoints Levites, under Asaph, to minister before it (1 Chr 16:1–7).

(4) A psalm of praise follows in 1 Chr 16:8–36 (based on canonical Pss 105, 96, and 106), after David's appointment of the Asaphites for thanksgiving and worship (v. 7 להדות ליהוה ביד־אסף ואחיו). (5) This section concludes with the transitional liturgical situation of twin worship sites (1 Chr 16:37–43): (a) David appoints Asaphites to continue ministry at the ark in Jerusalem (vv. 37–38), and (b) he also appoints Zadokites to remain with the tabernacle at Gibeon. Heman and Jeduthun give support by "giving thanks to the LORD" (v. 41 להדות ליהוה) and with "the song of God" (v. 42 שיר האלהים) at the tabernacle.[75]

David's extensive preparations for the Solomonic temple provide the second major set of data related to the Levites in 1 Chronicles (1 Chr 22:2—29:26). (1) 1 Chr 22:2—23:2 sets up the *need* for the preparations established by David in 1 Chr 23:3—27:34 (and finalized in 1 Chr 28–29). David, indeed, organizes building materials (1 Chr 22:2–5), and charges Solomon and Israel's leaders to build the temple (vv. 6–19). Once Solomon is made king, David then assembles "all the *leaders of Israel* and the *priests* and the *Levites*" (1 Chr 23:2 כל־שרי ישראל והכהנים והלוים), the three sets of leaders covered in chapters 23 to 27.

(2) David's vision for the Levitical ministry is first delineated in 1 Chr 23:4–32: (a) David sets up the divisions of Levites (who are thirty or older) in vv. 3–5 and outlines four areas of responsibility: (i) the "work in the house of the LORD" (v. 4a על מלאכת בית יהוה); (ii) "officers and judges" (v. 4b שטרים ושפטים); (iii) "gatekeepers" (v. 5a שערים); and (iv) to "offer praises" to Yahweh (v. 5b מהללים ליהוה). (b) The genealogical division follows in vv. 6–23 with the clans of Gershon, Kohath, and Merari (including the special function of Aaron within the Kohathites, vv. 13–14). (c) A summary statement of Levitical duty is included in vv. 24–32 (those of twenty years and older, a critical issue in comparison to 1 Chr 23:3). The Levites are no longer required to carry the tabernacle (vv. 24–27) and, hence, are to focus on assisting the priests (i.e., care of temple facilities [v. 28], ii. care of sacred food items [v. 29], and iii. regular liturgical duty of song [of "standing, thanking, praising" in vv. 30–32: לעמד בבקר בבקר להדות ולהלל]).

(3) The Aaronide ministry is given detail in 1 Chr 24:1–31, which includes the organization of the priestly lines (vv. 1–6) under Zadok (through Eleazar) and Ahimelech (through Ithamar) and the priestly service rotations (vv. 7–31). (4) 1 Chr 25:1—26:32 emphasizes three subsets of Levitical

---

75. With others, De Vries, *1 and 2 Chronicles*, 48–52, argues that sections of 1 Chr 16:2–43 bear the marks of editorializing from rival Levitical groups. In contrast to this view, note for instance Hill, *1 and 2 Chronicles*, 236–40.

duties envisioned by David: (i) the musicians (ch. 25), (ii) the gatekeepers (1 Chr 26:1-12), (iii) and other Levitical functions (1 Chr 26:20-32).

(5) In his second charge (1 Chr 28:11-21), David gives Solomon the plan of the temple, received from God—included in that plan (v. 11, 12 תבנית) are the divisions of the priests and Levites (v. 13 מחלקות הכהנים והלוים).[76] With respect to the preparations for the temple service, continuation with Moses and innovations by David are thus seen as consistent for the Chronicler.[77]

For Solomon's reign (2 Chr 1-9), the following texts stand out. (1) In 2 Chr 5:2-14, Solomon oversees the transportation of the ark to its proper place in the completed temple complex. Three elements may be noted here in relation to the Levites. (a) Only the Levites carry the ark *to* the temple, along with the tent of meeting and other sacred vessels (vv. 3-6). (b) However, only the Aaronide priests, properly consecrated, carry the ark *into* the temple and set it to rest in the Most Holy Place (v. 7). (c) Finally, the Levitical musical leaders (Asaph, Heman, and Jeduthun) lead in sacred song of worship as the glory of Yahweh fills the temple (vv. 11-14).[78]

(2) The priests and Levites also play a significant role at the dedication of the temple in 2 Chr 7:1-8. The Levites lead in musical ministry, "with instruments of music to the LORD," (v. 6a בכלי־שיר יהוה) according to David's instructions. The priests stand opposite the Levites and sound the trumpets (v. 6b והכהנים מחצצרים נגדם, cf. Num 10:1-10). (3) In 2 Chr 8:14-15, Solomon establishes the regular divisions of priests and Levites for the temple ministry.

Hence, in the Solomonic narratives, the contrasts in duties between the Aaronide priests and other Levites is maintained. David's expansions of the Levitical ministry to include music of praise are also seen as a proper development. Finally, the priests' former duty of blowing the trumpets is maintained—now in the context of the temple ministry.

Furthermore, five sets of texts concerning the Levites may be briefly highlighted, for the large literary complex covering the divided monarchy (2 Chr 10-36, which is mostly focused on the southern kingdom). (1) The

---

76. Wright argues on the basis of literary criticism that 1 Chr 23-27 should not be seen as a later insertion to the original text of Chronicles (contra most historical-critical points of view). See Wright, "The Origin and Function," 248-57.

77. For a careful discussion of the "aggadic exegesis" present in the Chronicler's uses of the Pentateuchal cultic *traditum* (especially in relationship to David's desire to build the temple), see Fishbane, *Biblical Interpretation*, 392-402.

78. On the presentation of Solomon in 2 Chr 1-9 (particularly the uses of historical sources) and arguments supporting the compositional integrity of the Levitical passages in this section, see Dillard, *2 Chronicles*, 1-7, 39-43.

narratives dealing with the conflicts between Rehoboam and Jeroboam (2 Chr 10–12) include, (a) a passage detailing the flight of certain faithful northern priests and Levites to Jerusalem (2 Chr 11:13–17). Two facets of this passage are significant for our purposes: (i) The priests and Levites leave the northern kingdom as Jeroboam forbids them to serve as "priests of the LORD" (v. 14 מכהן ליהוה); (ii) only those priests and Levites "who had set their hearts to *seek* the LORD God of Israel" (v. 16 הנתנים את־לבבם לבקש את־יהוה אלהי ישראל, cf. 2 Chr 11:11–18) faithfully travel to Jerusalem and strengthen Rehoboam's early reign.[79]

(b) Two items stand out in Abijah's speech against Jeroboam in 2 Chr 13: (i) Jeroboam is condemned, in part, for *not* having maintained the LORD's standards for the priests and Levites (by having set up his own priests, worship spaces, and idols; cf. 2 Chr 13:8–9); (ii) Abijah, in contrast, claims divine blessing for *having* faithfully followed the LORD with regards to the duties of the priests and Levites (cf. 2 Chr 13:10–12; the sacrificial service of the priests, "the sons of Aaron" [v. 10b בני אהרן], the Levites, who are at "their service" [v. 10b הלוים במלאכת], and in combat, the priests "with their battle trumpets" [v. 12 הצצרות התרועה]).[80]

(2) The account of Jehoshaphat's reign (2 Chr 17–20), which is altogether viewed positively by the Chronicler (2 Chr 17:6), includes some significant biblical data related to the service of the Levites. (a) At the outset of his reign, Jehoshaphat sends his officials with priests and Levites to teach the book of the Law throughout Judah (2 Chr 17:7–9). For the Chronicler, this teaching mission is instrumental in garnering respect from Judah's neighbors and in reinforcing Jehoshaphat's kingdom (2 Chr 17:10–19). (b) Jehoshaphat also sets up Levites as judges in Jerusalem, under the supervision of the chief priest Amariah (2 Chr 19:8–11). This service entails "giving judgment for the LORD" and "deciding disputed cases" (v. 8 למשפט יהוה ולריב), in line with the earlier duty set out in 1 Chr 26:29–32. The demeanor required of the Levites ("fear of the LORD," "faithfulness," and "your whole heart" [v. 9 ביראת יהוה באמונה ובלבב שלם]) is characteristic of the Chronicler's positive evaluation of faithfulness to the LORD.[81] (c) When Jehoshaphat faces

---

79. Boda, *1–2 Chronicles*, 294, highlights the significance of the priests and Levites in this context (and the connections to David and Solomon as models), when he writes, "[n]ot surprisingly, the Chronicler highlights the faithfulness of the sacred personnel, who have played a significant role in the narrative to this point, as well as to the impact that such faithfulness could have on the people as a whole. The standard of faithfulness continues to be David and Solomon, an allusion to the portrait of these kings in 1 Chronicles 10–2 Chronicles 9."

80. Note the related essay by Halpern, "Levitic Participation," 31–42.

81. On interpretive issues related to the reign of Jehoshaphat, see for example Strübind, *Tradition als Interpretation*, 9–98.

a coalition of Moabites and Ammonites in battle (2 Chr 20), it is upon an Asaphite Levite—Jahaziel—that the Spirit of the LORD descends (v. 13-14). Jahaziel delivers the prophetic message of victory to Jehoshaphat and Judah (vv. 15-17). A number of Kohathite and Korahite Levites then lead in worship in celebration of this delivery (vv. 18-19).

(3) In the context of Joash's reign (2 Chr 23-24), (a) the priest Jehoiada reclaims the Judahite throne from Athaliah for Joash, with the help of Levites, and also restores the divisions of priests and Levites at the temple (2 Chr 23:2-11). (b) He further abolishes pagan worship and posts Levitical watchmen and gatekeepers at the temple (2 Chr 23:16-21). (c) Moreover, Joash forcefully enlists the Levites to gather taxes in Judah to repair the temple (2 Chr 24:1-19).

(4) Hezekiah's reign in Judah includes an extensive focus on the ministry of the priests and the Levites (2 Chr 29-32). Chapter 29 preserves a detailed account of Hezekiah's cleansing of the temple and his restoration of temple worship (with the correctly established ministry of the priests and Levites).[82] Chapter 30 then presents an extended narrative of Hezekiah's Passover celebration, including the proper participation of the Levites (2 Chr 30:13-17).[83] In chapter 31, Hezekiah destroys pagan shrines throughout Judah (v. 1) and re-establishes the priests and Levites at the temple.

(5) Before the downfall and exile of Judah, Josiah's reign (2 Chr 34-36) also includes attention to the ministry of the priests and Levites. (a) The Levites are properly involved in temple repair, which leads to the re-discovery of the book of the Law (2 Chr 34:8-20). (b) As with Hezekiah, in 2 Chr 35, Josiah leads in the celebration of a Passover service correctly involving priests and Levites (vv. 2-6).[84]

Therefore, the faithfulness of a Judean king in preserving the ministry of the priests and Levites represents a central aspect of the historiographic method and theological processing of 2 Chr 10-36. The Levites are also active in a variety of contexts in this large narrative unit: attending the priests in worship and in battle contexts, serving as gatekeepers, as

---

82. For a study of both Hezekiah's and Josiah's reforms, see Bae, *Vereinte Suche*, 1-14, 162-200.

83. For a study focusing on priestly and Levitical sacrificial events in 2 Chronicles, see McEntire, *The Function of Sacrifice*, 21-49.

84. Some have highlighted the presence of Deuteronomistic themes (including terminological issues between "priests and Levites" and "Levitical priests") in these Passover celebration texts of Hezekiah's reign. See for instance Thompson, *1, 2 Chronicles*, 350-56.

watchmen, as treasurers, as judges in Jerusalem, and as teachers of the Law throughout Judea.[85]

On the basis of the preceding basic biblical data, our discussion will now proceed to highlighting some of the main themes in the scholarly understanding of the Levitical texts in the Davidic narratives of 1 Chr 10–29. This may be synthesized around three main approaches: historical-critical theories, newer literary-critical views and more canonically-rooted perspectives.

The Levites in 1 Chr 10–29: The Historical-Critical Heritage

As alluded to earlier in this chapter, De Wette was concerned with the source-critical analysis of the Pentateuch and, especially, the dating of the priestly materials. In this way, he may be understood as instigating the historical-critical approach to Chronicles in earnest. De Wette was not interested in Chronicles *per se*, but with his focus on the dating of Pentateuchal sources, he was led to define the historical perspective of Chronicles as ideological and reflective of postexilic Jewish reality.[86] Matthias, for instance, argued this point in his study: De Wette clearly posited that the Chronicler's text was a *late* creation.[87]

Notably, De Wette's view was championed by Wellhausen, among others, who then influenced an entire generation of subsequent scholars with his negative assessment of the historical reliability of Chronicles.[88] For Wellhausen, as pointed to above as well, the author of the book of Chronicles was writing in the midst of a fully developed Judaism (*after* the Persian domination) and the Levitical texts in 1 Chr 15–16 and 24–27 should, then, be seen as *intrusions* that distort 2 Samuel's original perspective on the Davidic monarchy.[89]

85. See for example Gertner, "The Masorah," 244–48, who has emphasized the teaching function of the Levites. And note as well Sklba, *The Teaching Function*, 62–88.

86. See De Wette, *Lehrbuch*. He writes, "[b]esides the orthography and language [and other factors], the mythological and Levitical spirit of the book, as well as its place in the canon, is evidence in favor of its late origin." See De Wette, *A Critical and Historical Introduction*, 1:265. See the overall discussions of this early period of modern Chronicles research in: Japhet, "The Historical Reliability of Chronicles," 83–107; Williamson, "Introduction," 12; Rogerson, *W. M. L. de Wette*, 87–129, 125–60, 266–70. And on pre-critical exegesis, note for example, Saltman, "Introduction," 11–60.

87. See Mathias, "Die Geschichte der Chronikforschung," especially 14, 17.

88. Wellhausen, *Prolegomena zur Geschichte*, 175–235.

89. Wellhausen, *Prolegomena zur Geschichte*, 181, views the temple preparation narratives in 1 Chr 22–29 as "invention," as he writes "[d]er ganze Abschnitt 1. Chron. 22–29 ist *ein abschreckendes Beispiel des statistschen Phantasie der Juden*" (emphasis

Developing from Wellhausen, another branch of this broader historical-critical approach has offered a more nuanced outlook on the book of Chronicles. While the Levitical texts in 1 Chr 15–16 and 23–27 were still generally viewed as the result of late propaganda, the remaining sections of the Davidic narratives (i.e., those closer to the Samuel source) were investigated with greater theological interest.[90]

In this approach, the work of two scholars stands out in particular. First, Von Rad, following Gunkel's form-critical approach, argued that much of the sermons of Chronicles followed a pre-established "Levitical sermon" form. He also produced a lengthy study of the "picture of history" in Chronicles—giving credence to the Chronicler's *literary* goals, even if these texts were deemed *historically* untrustworthy, in the end.[91] Second, Noth maintained that chapters 23–27 of 1 Chronicles represent late additions and, hence, contribute very little to the overall argument of the Davidic narratives.[92] Other critics adopted similar methods in dealing with the Levitical texts in 1 Chronicles.[93] Rothstein and Hänel, for instance, viewed the ark narrative of 1 Chr 15–16 as highly composite.[94]

On the Levites, more specifically, a number of critical approaches have adopted (to varying degrees) the reconstruction proposed by Gese, who argued that the textual data related to the Levites in Ezra-Nehemiah and Chronicles is reflective of a three-stage *postexilic* development of temple servants.[95] Stage I: at the start of the postexilic period, these temple singers were merely known as "sons of Asaph," not Levites. Stage II: during Nehemiah's time, two groups of temple singers were then known: "sons of Asaph," and "sons of Jeduthun" (Neh 11:3–19; 1 Chr 9:1–18). Stage IIIa: these temple servants further developed into three groups of Levitical singers: Asaph, Heman, and Jeduthun (1 Chr 16:4–7; 2 Chr 5:12). Stage IIIb: the *final* developmental stage occurred with the replacement of Jeduthun by Ethan and the prominence of the Hemanite singers. Gese concludes that stage IIIa is reflective of the Chronicler's postexilic period, while stage

---

added). On Wellhausen's period more generally, see further, Graham, *The Utilization*, 243–49; Peltonen, *History Debated*, 521.

90. Peltonen, *History Debated*, 481–525, argues that this period evinces a renewed attention to the historical and theological dimensions of Chronicles.

91. See von Rad, *Das Geschichtsbild*, 25–37 and his "The Levitical Sermon in 1 and 2 Chronicles." Von Rad seems ambivalent regarding the value of the Chronicler's historical method. See Von Rad, *Theology of the Old Testament, Volume I*, 350.

92. Noth, *The Chronicler's History*, 29–50.

93. See for instance Hanson, "1 Chronicles 15–16," 69–78.

94. Rothstein and Hänel, *Das erste Buch der Chronik*, 7–8.

95. See Gese, "Zur Geschichte des Kultsänger," 223–34.

IIIb is *post*-Chronistic. Some writers have argued that Gese's stage IIIb is also reflective of the Chronicler's time.[96] Knoppers, in contrast, has offered a sharp rebuttal of Gese's influential theory by pointing out that it fundamentally "assumes what it needs to prove."[97] Essentially, Knoppers notes that (1) the textual evidence is more complex than claimed in this theoretical reconstruction, and that (2) the Chronicler can be understood as actually defending the singers, musicians, and gatekeepers as *full-fledged* Levites, based on their preexilic historical moorings in David's Levitical organization and elsewhere.[98]

In the same general vein as Gese, Min has argued (contra Knoppers, then) that in Chronicles, two opposing views are maintained—found in two literary layers. The first layer (Chron.-L) is favorable to the Levites and "promotes them to the status of priests;" the second layer (Chron.-P) is thoroughly priestly and views the Levites merely as minor clergy, as in Ezekiel and the Priestly Code. Thus, in this perspective, "Chronicles preserves these two opposing descriptions of the Levites."[99]

We may also make note of Kim's recent study of the Levites and temple administration in Chronicles. This work is rooted in much of the scholarship discussed in this section, and, in the end, Kim concludes that "the Chronicler's incorporation of all of the non-priestly personnel into the Levites *does not cohere with the realities of his day*" and that, basically, the picture in Chronicles is what the Chronicler *wished for* as a historical reality in his postexilic setting. It is merely an "idealistic temple administration," thus, not rooted in the Davidic period.[100] Similarly, in another recent study, Janzen has proposed that the Chronicler was governed in the postexilic period by his desire to respond to various "pro-Davidic" and "anti-Davidic" political rivalries. In this view, in order to support the Davidides as the preferred local leaders in the context of the postexilic Persian domination, the Chronicler does

---

96. Laato, "The Levitical Genealogies," 77–99; Williamson, "The Origins," 251–68; Williamson, *1 and 2 Chronicles*, 119–22.

97. Knoppers, *I Chronicles 10–29*, 657.

98. Knoppers, *I Chronicles 10–29*, 657 (and 657–59 as a whole). Ko also reminds us that several other recent commentators remain fairly skeptical of Gese's proposed reconstruction. He writes, "these criticisms [from more recent scholars] somewhat undermine Gese's reconstruction. The relationship between the redactional history of Chronicles and the actual diachronic development of the musical guilds seems far more complex and sophisticated than Gese suspected." Ko, *The Levite Singers*, 17.

99. Min, *The Levitical Authorship*, 65–70.

100. Kim, *The Temple Administration*, 191, 192 (emphasis added).

not elide past Davidic failures in regard to the cult, but *creates* a history that demonstrates how God punishes kings who fail in this regard, sending a message to eligible Davidides and a message of reassurance to the assembly that future client rulers would honor temple norms ... The Chronicler also *portrays* the Levites under a monarchy with higher status than they have in the Priestly Writing and with important roles in civil administration. The Chronicler does not wish to alienate the Aaronide priesthood, and so does not attempt to diminish their authority, but he or she is also aware that the Aaronides stand the most to lose from a restoration, and so aims merely not to arouse their opposition while gaining strong Levitical support.[101]

These types of historical-critical approaches to the Levites in Chronicles, hence, affirm the composite and ideological nature of these sections of the Davidic narratives in 1 Chr 10–29. Postexilic Levitical ideology is largely understood to be in tension with priestly concerns of the Second Temple period. Historical reconstructions and compositional theories usually dominate in these discussions, while the exploration of the canonical and theological dimensions of the Levitical theme in Chronicles are less emphasized.[102]

The Levites in 1 Chr 10–29: The Newer Literary-Critical Perspective

In contrast, in his analysis of Chronicles scholarship that has moved away from purely historical-critical methods, Kleinig has suggested that "the discussion of historicity has been replaced by the analysis of Chronicles as a piece of literature," instigated by a threefold shift from historical criticism to literary analysis, from redactional analysis to canonical analysis, and from thematic analysis to theological synthesis.[103] In this more recent history of the study of Chronicles, two scholars have been notably instrumental in effecting this shift—a foundation for which is a concern to approach Chronicles on its own terms.

First, Japhet has certainly approached 1–2 Chronicles in this way, and she generally contends that the Chronicler's biblical text needs to be

101. See Janzen, *Chronicles*, 227, emphasis added, and see 226–28 for Janzen's full concluding statement.

102. For surveys of the various compositional theories related to Chronicles, see Knoppers, *I Chronicles 1–9*, 73–96; Klein, "Chronicles, Book of 1–2," 992–99. Note as well the earlier, influential study by Welch, *The Work of the Chronicler*, 149–60.

103. Kleinig, "Recent Research," 68. And note further the related methodological discussion in the following chapter of this book.

interpreted as a separate work from Ezra-Nehemiah. And second, Williamson has furthered these types of arguments, beginning with his study of the conception of Israel in Chronicles, and in his later works as well.[104] While Chronicles and Ezra-Nehemiah are obviously related (the edict of Cyrus of 2 Chr 36 is repeated in Ezra 1, for instance), their theological concerns and their language differ in some ways. Furthermore, according to Williamson, these key themes are treated differently in Ezra-Nehemiah and Chronicles: mixed marriages, Israel's early history, the northern kingdom, retribution of sin, and the manner of writing, more generally.[105]

Both Japhet and Williamson have produced commentaries and have generally made a case for the *literary* coherence and unity of the *majority* of the text of Chronicles. They have also allowed varying conceptions of human ideology to stand as the guiding force behind the production of certain texts—especially the Levitical ones.[106] For example, in discussing the composition of 1 Chr 25 (David's new assignment of the Levites as temple singers), Japhet argues that while this text represents an artificial literary creation on the Chronicler's part, it is still cohesive on its own *literary* terms, as it is motivated historically by postexilic priestly and Levitical ideological concerns.[107]

As a result, a number of scholars have investigated Chronicles from a variety of literary, theological and/or ideological perspectives. The majority of these writers argue that the Levitical texts of 1 Chr 10–29 contribute to the *literary* unity of these Davidic narratives, while still being examples (in various terms) of later postexilic *ideology*—with only slim possibilities of evincing substantive roots in the traditions of Israel's preexilic history.[108] Several of these scholars have also focused their attention more precisely

---

104. Japhet, "The Supposed," 330–98; Williamson, *Israel*, 5–86. The long-held pre-critical and early critical assumption was that Ezra was responsible for both Chronicles and Ezra-Nehemiah. Zunz, however, argued that both books were indeed written by the same author, but from a much later period than Ezra—the scholarly "Chronicler" was then born. Basically, Zunz's view held the field until Japhet and Williamson's strong challenges to *common* authorship. See Zunz, *Die Gottesdienstlichen*, 13–36. Some have, in turn, challenged Japhet's linguistic arguments, as in Talshir, "A Reinvestigation," 165–94. On this issue, see more broadly Knoppers, *I Chronicles 1–9*, 101–17.

105. See Williamson, *Israel*, 60–69. Similarly, note Klein, *1 Chronicles*, 6–12.

106. Japhet, *I and II Chronicles*, 3–8; Williamson, *1 and 2 Chronicles*, 17–23.

107. Japhet, *I and II Chronicles*, 438.

108. This is the fundamental view of these representative studies; the chapter "Les lévites-chantres, prophètes cultuels," in Tournay, *Voir et entendre*, 17–48; Johnstone, *1 and 2 Chronicles*, 1:174–97, 244–73; Allen, "The First and Second Books of Chronicles," 299–659; Hanspach, *Inspirierte Interpreten*, 1–38; Tuell, *First and Second Chronicles*, 61–63, 94–106; Cardellini, *I Leviti*, 37–44.

on the literary *function* of the Levitical texts in the Davidic narratives of Chronicles.[109] For example, in his monograph, Cudworth finds that the Chronicler definitely "stresses the importance of temple faithfulness by illustrating its great benefit and consequences in war narratives throughout Israel's monarchic past." At the same time, in his conclusions, Cudworth restricts the Chronicler's emphasis on David as the founder of an expanded Levitical temple service mainly to "literary intentions."[110]

Similarly, Abadie has analyzed the Chronicler's presentation of king David. In his reading, David is a *constructed* figure who has been wrenched from the vicissitudes of formal history to be fully idealized as a cultic leader and as a spiritual example for later generations.[111] Other writers further downplay any historical connection to David's monarchy in this context; the Chronicler essentially remains a *creator* of postexilic literature.[112]

As a final example of this approach, we may point to the recent monograph by Ko, who explores the "stabilizing" role of the Levites in postexilic Judah. From the outset, Ko acknowledges the thorny issue of the historicity of the Levite singers for the *first* temple in the history of Chronicles research. He writes:

> Scholarship since Wellhausen has wrestled with the problem of historicity. It would be tempting to see references to singers as either reflecting the author's late projection or presenting a trustworthy account of the pre-exilic temple cult, that is, as either a complete ideological imagination or a complete historical reality. Some scholars have proposed the concept of "historical probability" which provides a reality-imagination spectrum for judging whether Levite singers are historically probable or not. While this concept softens the extreme polarization, I wonder whether the problem of historicity is a worthwhile pursuit, because the history of Israelite religion still contains unbridgeable gaps that cannot be filled up easily with evidence that is available to us. . . . A claim of what is historically probable, or not, is difficult to establish, and thus I do not consider it to be productive.[113]

---

109. See Braun, *1 Chronicles*, 180–94, 228–64, for instance, or Wright, "The Origin and Function," 83–147; Abadie, "La figure de David," 156–86; Willi, "Leviten," 75–98. Note as well Klein, *1 Chronicles*, 345–51.

110. See Cudworth, *War in Chronicles*, 183–86.

111. See the concluding comment by Abadie, "La figure de David," 186.

112. Van Seters attributes the Chronicler's Davidic narratives to "creative imagination." See Van Seters, "Creative Imitation," 395–409; and similarly, Jarick, *1 Chronicles*, 5–6.

113. Ko, *The Levite Singers*, 13.

On the one hand, we appreciate that Ko is engaging with the texts in Chronicles focused on the Levitical singers *as a part* of the Chronicler's purpose. This author also engages with the context of the ANE, although he remains mainly focused on *later* first millennium parallels—not on any possible *earlier* contextual parallels. As such, on the other hand, it seems that Ko (as with other authors) is, in the end, unwilling to view the texts in Chronicles as possible evidence for *first* temple musical guilds, while accepting other, later (biblical and, especially, non-biblical) texts as evidence for *postexilic* realities.[114] As we seek to argue in chapter four, the "gaps" in the religious, cultic history of preexilic Israel do not appear to be completely insurmountable, and in fact it seems possible to, indeed, pursue its historical "plausibility."

The Levites in 1 Chr 10–29: The Canonical-Based Contributions

A final wing of Chronicles scholarship approaches these Levitical texts from the point of view of their received canonical form. These writers argue that the passages are *rooted* in preexilic historical traditions, that they are *shaped* rhetorically in light of the postexilic situation, and, hence, that they *function* as theologically-focused biblical historical narratives. It is granted in these approaches that the topic of Levitical service (especially in 1 Chr 10–29) is a complex one. The complexity involves (1) engaging with the possibility of written (and/or oral) sources existing throughout the life of Israel that preserved the tradition regarding David's institution of expanded Levitical service, and (2) the concomitant reality that, in the postexilic period, the role of the priest and Levite took on a more significant role in the life of Judah, since the prophetic voice was essentially silenced for that period and since a physical royal leadership was non-existent for the majority of this period. That is, on the one hand, the Chronicler claims that David was responsible for the establishment of expanded Levitical duty (to include song and music); on the other hand, this preexilic tradition very likely served as an important impetus towards the establishment, and proper maintenance, of temple worship life in Jerusalem at various times during the postexilic period. As Street, for instance, has concluded on the key interplay between *preexilic* Davidic worship and the *postexilic* situation of the Jewish community in the Chronicler's work:

---

114. See the chapter, "Scholar-Singers in Mesopotamia," in Ko, *The Levite Singers*, 29–61. In the end, Ko sees some "historical value" in the Chronicler's work, especially in the context of his time and place. See his section "The Chronicler's Historical Truth-Claims" in Ko, *The Levite Singers*, 109–12.

> The ark narrative [of 1 Chr 15–16] reveals that proper worship is at the heart of Chronicler's purpose. This worship was instituted by David. The Chronicler came to the same history as that found in the books of Samuel and Kings. However, his selectivity and emphases are clearly different. These differences suggest that he wanted that nation of Israel to understand who they were as the people of God. . . . The Levites' contribution to the worship system is a major emphasis throughout the Chronicler's work. The ordering of the Levites by David allows the Levites to enable the people to take part in the worship services. While ritual forms are fixed, the attitude of the worshiper is what is most important. The Levites are charged with the responsibility of leading the public in this attitude of worship. Thus, the Chronicler's hope for the nation is bound in worship.[115]

Overall, then, the influence of (1) the postexilic need and desire for proper (second) temple-worship and (2) of preexilic traditions related to David's formal expansion of non-Aaronide Levitical duties (at the first temple) represent the two poles effecting one's definition and understanding of this theme in Chronicles. Where expanded Levitical functions fit between these poles represents, in a sense, the crux of the complexity.

Nonetheless, in these canonically-rooted approaches, the Chronicler's use of both synoptic and non-synoptic sources is understood as a sign of effective ancient history-writing during the postexilic era—since it is argued that a variety of literary sources have been used to produce a unique and coherent theological perspective on Israel's history. This perspective stretches from the creation of Adam to the postexilic hope of Cyrus' edict, and, hence, to the notice of the return to the land.[116] Also, following Japhet and Williamson, in part, the author of Chronicles is most often understood in these approaches as being different than the author of Ezra/Nehemiah, while the postexilic compositional date of both histories is usually understood as closely related.[117]

---

115. Street, *The Significance*, 139.

116. For a helpful listing of sources in Chronicles see Hill, *1 and 2 Chronicles*, 43–45; Howard, *An Introduction*, 238–49.

117. Howard, *An Introduction*, 235, 284, for example, cautiously argues that: (1) the composition of Chronicles need not be dated later than 400 BC, (2) the final composition of Ezra/Nehemiah can be safely dated to about the same period. Knoppers, *1 Chronicles 1–9*, 116–17, on the other hand "allows a range of dates [for the composition of Chronicles], from the late fifth century through the mid-third century," and is inclined toward a date in the late fourth or early third century. It is indirect comparison with Greek genealogists that especially leads Knoppers to his later dating. See Knoppers, "Greek Historiography and the Chronicler's History," 647–50, and chapter two of this work for some further discussion of the date and composition of Chronicles.

Childs, for example, argued that the Chronicler's treatment of sources demonstrates that he is an apt exegete of authoritative Scripture, through his use of harmonization, supplementation, typology, and a distinct theology of "cause-and-effect retribution." That is, *theological* motives for the inclusion of the Levitical texts in the Davidic narratives are emphasized, rather than postexilic ideological ones rooted in theories of compositional layering.[118]

Also, Knoppers contends that with the Levitical texts in 1 Chr 15–16 and 23–27, the Chronicler need not be seen as creating a *new* traditum. Chapters 23–27 demonstrate that the Chronicler is in fact emphasizing the *interdependence* of priestly and Levitical clans, based on preexilic traditions.[119] Selman has similarly argued that the representation of Levitical ministry makes most sense *with* a preexilic connection to David (and Solomon).[120] For him, *complex* Levitical duties most likely did *not* exist in the Chronicler's period of composition—they are very likely rooted in the preexilic past to encourage a postexilic audience towards the proper renewal of a Davidic-type worship.[121]

Dorsey, in turn, defines Chronicles as "encouraging stories from Israel's history," and notes that in 1 Chr 23–27, "the author underscores the importance of the temple, the priests, and Levites by structuring the entire unit so that it begins, ends, and centers on this theme."[122] Hill points out the association Chronicles makes to the earlier biblical covenants, thereby establishing *hope* for the postexilic generations and affirming the Levitical priesthood in that later period.[123] Pratt argues that the Chronicler is promoting the Zadokite line to its proper place of Aaronide leadership in postexilic Judah, while also confirming the contributions of the other Levitical clans. The Chronicler thus connects back to very specific genealogical lines within the tribe of Levi.[124]

Furthermore, Boda, in his commentary, notes how Chronicles has often been "ignored and maligned in biblical studies because of its

---

118. Childs, *Introduction to the Old Testament*, 647–54.

119. On arguments for the interdependence of priests and Levites, see Knoppers, *I Chronicles 10–29*, 825–26; "Hierodules, Priests, or Janitors?" 49–72; Leithart, "Attendants of Yahweh's House," 3–24; Fishbane, *Biblical Interpretation*, 381; Endres, "Joyful Worship," 155–88.

120. Selman, *1 Chronicles*, 56–59.

121. Representative of this view are Michaeli, *Les livres des Chroniques*, 115–38; Harrison, *Introduction to the Old Testament*, 1152–73; McConville, *I and II Chronicles*, 76–93; Jones, *1 and 2 Chronicles*, 32–47; Rabinowitz, *Commentary*, 62–83, 186–212.

122. Dorsey, *The Literary Structure*, 147.

123. Hill, *1 and 2 Chronicles*, 43.

124. Pratt, *1 and 2 Chronicles*, 57. Note also Pratt, "Royal Prayer," 355–63.

perceived lack of historical worth."[125] Boda goes on to counter this view by noting that a careful understanding of the setting and purpose of the Chronicler is helpful in seeing the worth of this biblical text. For instance, "[t]he Chronicler has . . . shaped his historical presentation in a certain way to highlight historiographical principles that were key to his worldview and theology and helpful to his readers, who lived in a unique period of history."[126] One of the historiographical principles that Boda highlights is the Chronicler's "legitimizing the present by the past."[127] That is, Boda's position stands as a significant example of a scholar who engages with the final form of the MT of Chronicles. For example, he doesn't see the many genealogies and lists in 1 Chronicles, which include extensive material related to David's expansion of Levitical music and worship duty, as *extraneous* to the Chronicler's historical, literary, and, ultimately, theological purposes. As such, and in contrast to much of the historical-critical perspectives on these text in 1 Chronicles, Boda argues:

> This [historiographic technique of legitimizing the present with the past] can be seen in [the Chronicler's] fixation with genealogies and lists throughout his account, especially in 1 Chronicles (1 Chr 1–9, 11–12, 23–27). These lists offer legitimacy to the people as a whole, reminding them of God's election of Israel from time immemorial, but also to the families who served in the [first] Temple and its services. Such legitimacy is very important in the wake of the stain of the Exile and new circumstances of foreign hegemony.[128]

Similarly, Leithart, in his Chronicles commentary, views David's establishment of the Levitical musical guilds, in preparation for the Solomonic temple, as a major development in salvation history, especially as it is rooted in David's time, in the early first millennium. In fact, Leithart argues for

---

125. Boda, *1–2 Chronicles*, 4.
126. Boda, *1–2 Chronicles*, 4–5.
127. Boda, *1–2 Chronicles*, 17.
128. Boda, *1–2 Chronicles*, 17. Boda views David's establishment of the Levites as newly appointed temple worship musicians and singers in 1 Chr 25, which includes an aspect of prophecy (thus confirmed *royally* by David), as a significant *first temple* historical development that is evident throughout later Judean history. Boda, *1–2 Chronicles*, 195, writes, "[b]oth the link to the royal house [of David] and the link to prophecy strengthen the claim of superior status for the Levitical singers among the Levitical orders. . . . First Chronicles 25 is thus a first in a series of texts in Chronicles that will contribute to the tracing of a prophetic function for the Levites. . . . In 2 Chronicles [for example ch. 20] the Levite Jahaziel would function as prophet on the battlefield, and Levitical singers would sing praise as prophetic utterance to secure victory (2 Chr 20:19)."

both priestly and royal dimensions to this Levitical music and song. On this priestly aspect, he writes of the key text in 1 Chr 25, that it

> encapsulates the Chronicler's theology of music. By placing Levitical singers in the center of the genealogies [in 1 Chr 1-9] that begin with Adam, he indicates that music encapsulates the vocation of human beings. In 1 Chr. 25 he indicates that human beings are made to be singers because we are to be priests, kings, and prophets. Levites are the primary singers, and their song is a form of priestly ministry. In Leviticus, priests turn animal flesh to smoke that ascends as soothing aroma to the Lord. In Chronicles, priests offer their own life breath as a pleasing sound to Yahweh. Chronicles marks an advance in this history of sacrifice: instead of offering animals, Levites offers themselves as living sacrifices.[129]

Finally, we may point to Ahn's study, as a recent example of research contributing to this canonically-based wing of Chronicles study. In his work, Ahn explores the rhetorical strategy that the Chronicler employs in the MT's Davidic narratives (1 Chr 10-29) and Solomonic narratives (2 Chr 1-9). Specifically, Ahn focuses on the speeches and prayers of David and Solomon in these settings. The postexilic rhetorical situation of the Chronicler is examined in detail, but this is not done at the expense of assuming the historical aspects of the Davidic and Solomonic are merely literary or ideologically-driven creations. In the end, Ahn concludes that "the [Chronicler's] portrayal of David and Solomon through the speeches and prayers in the David-Solomon narrative is designed to reformulate the identity of the Yehudite community in the Persian period as a worshipping community based in the Jerusalem temple."[130]

---

129. Leithart, *1 & 2 Chronicles*, 82.

130. Ahn, *The Persuasive Portrayal*, 273. Constructively, Ahn, *The Persuasive Portrayal*, 1-2, makes plain his commitment to both the trustworthy historical underpinnings of David and Solomon (in all of their facets) and the way in which the Chronicler shapes these preexilic traditions to address the postexilic situation of his original audience—indeed, Ahn notes at the outset of his work that "[m]any scholars have claimed that the Chronicler portrays David and Solomon as idealized kings in the narrative of the temple building. However, if they were idealized in Chronicles, why does the Chronicler include David's census and his initial failure to bring the ark to Jerusalem? It seems that the Chronicler's purpose in portraying David and Solomon does not simply lie in idealizing the reign of David and Solomon in order to glorify YHWH. . . . [T]he Chronicler's persuasive portrayal of David and Solomon serves to reconstruct the community identity through the Jerusalem temple, revealing the continuity of the covenantal relationship between YHWH and Israel in the Persian period."

The Levites in 1 Chr 10–29: A Multidimensional Approach

The preceding selective discussion helps illustrate how the field of research concerned with the Levitical texts of 1 Chr 10–29 remains a fertile one. Although a wide variety of methods have been applied to the study of these passages, their function within, and their contribution to, their primary canonical contexts remain an ongoing subject of scholarly conversations. On the one hand, a number of critical theories related to Levitical developments in history (and in the composition of Chronicles) have often guided the discussion with greater force than the canonical narratives themselves (such as with Gese or Nurmela). On the other hand, the situation of the Levites in Chronicles is more often seen as a reflection of the postexilic context of the author (such as with Japhet or Braun), despite the text's association of this theme with the redemptive historical stage of David's United Monarchy.

Accordingly, the Levitical passages of the Davidic narratives in 1 Chronicles continue to offer the potential for opening wider exegetical and theological vistas. Towards these ends, our study will build on canonically-based views of the Levites in the OT and in Chronicles (such as found in the work of Knoppers, Pratt and Boda). In fact, the operating thesis of our study is that 1 Chronicles chapters 15, 16, and 23—key texts concerning the function of the Levites—contribute significantly to the rhetorical argumentation, the historiographic method, and the biblical-theological significance of the canonical books of Chronicles generally, and of the Davidic narratives of 1 Chr 10–29 specifically, as they emphasize the central role played by proper Levitical worship leadership at the time of David *and* during the challenging situation of the Chronicler's postexilic audience.

To flesh out this multidimensional approach, a three-pronged methodology will be adopted. From a literary point of view, the notion that the Levites are closely associated with the *symbol* of God's presence will be explored (chapter three). From a historical perspective, the roles of the Levites in expanding the *service* to God and his people will be examined (chapter four). And from a biblical-theological perspective, the means by which the Levites facilitate the *song* of God's people will also be studied (chapter five). First, however, the basic methodological approaches needed to flesh out this proposed reading of the Levites in 1 Chronicles will be articulated in chapter two.

2

Exegetical Methodologies

Rhetorical Criticism, Historiography
and Biblical Theology

As SHOULD BE EVIDENT from the previous chapter, approaching the biblical texts related to the Levites can prove to be an engaging exegetical enterprise—at least from a methodological point of view. In Chronicles, scholars typically use one type of interpretive methodology (either diachronic or synchronic) when analyzing passages dealing with the genealogies or the cultic functions of the Levites. As one of its main contributions, the present study will engage aspects of the Levitical theme in 1 Chronicles by means of three complimentary exegetical methods. Approaches adopted in applying the methods of rhetorical criticism, historiography, and biblical theology will, hence, be more clearly defined in this chapter. The choice of control passages will also be noted. First, each method will be discussed in very broad terms and, second, each specific exegetical approach proposed will be clarified.[1]

The Literary Aspect: A Rhetorical-Critical Approach to 1 Chr 15:1–16:3

As previously noted, the Davidic narratives of 1 Chr 10–29 are typically divided into two broad sections: (1) the start and consolidation of David's rule (10:1—22:1) and (2) David's oversight of the temple preparations (22:2—29:30). The Levites figure prominently in these narratives, beginning with

---

1. Note the arguments provided for employing multiple methods in Averbeck, "Factors in Reading," 115–37; Long, "Historiography," 174–75.

1 Chr 15:1—16:3, the celebratory movement of the ark into Jerusalem. The following observations will establish the basic methodological parameters for a rhetorical study of the 1 Chr 15:1—16:3 pericope.

Literary Studies and the Old Testament

Understanding rhetorical criticism calls for at least a basic perspective on literary approaches to Scripture in general. Until more recent decades, much of OT biblical scholarship was dominated by historical-critical methods, at least since the nineteenth century generally. In spite of this, a consistent stream of literary approaches may also be discerned. Lowth, Jebb, Boys, or Bullinger (and others) represent an earlier, smaller counterpoint to the prevailing exegetical methods employed by scholars throughout the nineteenth and twentieth centuries—as the former focused primarily on literary style and structure.[2]

However, one prominent OT scholar has argued that by the end of the twentieth century, synchronic methods actually overtook historical ones.[3] Interdisciplinary issues such as philosophy's emphasis on linguistic analysis, historiography's methodological revamping, and the study of the Bible by literary scholars, have all combined with issues in biblical studies proper to enable this shift. Older methods of biblical analysis (such as source, form, and tradition criticisms) have been seen as atomistic by a number of recent writers—since, when applying these methods, theories about historical detail and background are often seen as more significant than literary unity and inherent textual meaning.[4] Clines and Exum have defined this "new" literary criticism as follows:

> It is not a historical discipline, but a strictly literary one, foregrounding the textuality of the biblical literature. Even when it occupies itself with historical dimensions of the texts—its primary concern is the text as an object, a product, not as a window upon historical actuality.[5]

---

2. For a detailed discussion of these scholars' contributions, see Meynet, *L'analyse rhétorique*, 25–174; Dorsey, *The Literary Structure*, 18–19. Some of the most significant original works are Lowth, *Lectures*, and Bullinger, *Figures of Speech*.

3. Rendtorff, "The Paradigm," 51.

4. See further Longman, "Literary Approaches," 97–102.

5. Clines and Exum, "The New Literary Criticism," 11, and 11–25 as a whole.

In the context of these discussions, some have interacted with the work of Abrams—an earlier and prominent literary critic.[6] For Abrams, four elements characterize attempts at explaining and evaluating "literary art." They are: the *work* (the actual literary product), the *artist* (the one creating this product), the *universe* (the referential world surrounding work and artist), and the *audience* ("the listeners, spectators, or readers to whom the work is addressed").[7] Abrams further argued that four basic theories could frame theoretical attempts at explicating the nature of this work. Three of these theories focus on the work in relation to another entity—while one simply focuses on the work in and of itself. *Mimetic* theories explain aesthetic appreciation by means of seeing art as "essentially an imitation of aspects of the universe." With *pragmatic* theories, literary works of art have a "purpose—to achieve certain effects in an audience." In *expressive* theories, literature represents the "imaginative process which modifies and synthesizes the images, thoughts, and feelings of the poet," thus relating the meaning of the work to the artist. *Objective* theories, finally, explain art "in isolation from all these external points of reference." The work itself is the sole means of evaluation.[8]

In a clarifying manner, Barton has adapted Abrams' scheme towards an understanding of biblical criticisms with these categories: historical events or theological ideas (universe), text (work), author(s) (artist), and reader (audience).[9] Source criticism focuses either on the theological truth or the author, while form and tradition criticisms shift towards the author as a group or a "clever compiler." More recent forms of literary-based biblical criticisms have moved to focus on the final form of the text.[10] Such criticisms, focusing on the *text*, represent a marked contrast to the pre-textual concerns of the historical-critical methods—where the literary products are often shrouded by compositional or redactional theories. Synchronic approaches to Scripture, hence, support the *literary* nature of the Bible and underscore the unity of texts without dissecting them further.[11]

---

6. Abrams, *The Mirror and the Lamp* (published in 1953). See the discussion of Abrams' work in Trible, *Rhetorical Criticism*, 5-13; Kessler, "An Introduction," 4-16. Note also the assessment by Lipking, "The Genie in the Lamp," 128-48.

7. Abrams, *The Mirror and the Lamp*, 6.

8. Abrams, *The Mirror and the Lamp*, 8, 14-16, 19-23, 27.

9. See Barton, *Reading the Old Testament*, especially 237-46.

10. Barton, *Reading the Old Testament*, 240. On text and reader-centered developments, see further McKenzie and Haynes, *To Each Its Own Meaning*, 142-82, 230-306. Note also the critique of some of these approaches in Thiselton, *New Horizons*, 80-141, 313-78; Longman, "Literary Approaches," 102-13.

11. See House, "The Rise and Current Status," 3; Leland Ryken, "Literary Criticism," 457.

As a consequence, with these synchronic approaches, Abrams' "work" is understood as the primary material for study and appreciated as a coherent piece of communicative literature. Several characteristics of this "new" literary criticism of the Hebrew Bible have been advanced (the German term *Literarkritik* referring to traditional source criticism).[12] At least one of those applies to the stance adopted here: a basic orientation to *texts*.[13] Thus, a rhetorical approach to 1 Chr 15:1—16:3 is, at its foundation, a literary study. It is concerned with the synchronic unity of the narrative and its contribution to the larger argument developed in 1 Chr 10–29 and will, then, also focus on select intertextual dimensions (especially within 1 Chr 10:1—22:1). Nielsen, for instance, has observed how intertextuality assumes that "no text comes into being or can be read as an isolated unit. It is always part of a network of texts." She also proposes three phases for an intertextual reading: (1) concentrating on the "author's intentions" via the text proper, (2) focusing on the editorial layers, and (3) allowing the reader's tradition to single out the relevant intertexts.[14] Certainly, a biblical text is fruitfully read in context of others.[15]

Rhetorical Criticism and the Old Testament

From the perspective of literary studies, rhetorical criticism, more specifically, has deep roots and has flowered into a number of specific applications.[16] Formal beginnings can be traced to the classical Greek period, with

---

12. Exum and Clines, "The New Literary Criticism," 13. For seminal discussions of the literary study of the OT, note especially Sternberg, *The Poetics of Biblical Narrative*, 1–57; Bar-Efrat, *Narrative Art in the Bible*, 9–46; Alter, *The Art of Biblical Narrative*, 3–46; Alter, *The Art of Biblical Poetry*, 3–26.

13. As Jeanrond, "Text, Textuality," 782, has noted, "the aim of biblical interpretation is not to decipher particular sentences, though this task is a necessary part of the overall exercise, but understanding the meaning of larger communicative units: texts ... In whatever extension a biblical text is read or heard, it is received as a *text*" (emphasis original). See further Jeanrond, *Text and Interpretation*, especially, for this issue, 1–4, 94–128.

14. Nielsen, "Intertextuality and the Hebrew Bible," 18–19. Note as well Fishbane, "Types of Biblical Intertextuality," 39–44.

15. A concept vividly argued for, in the OT/Hebrew Bible context, by Fishbane, *Biblical Interpretation*; note his key statements in 23–43 (on scribal comments), 91–106 (on legal exegesis), 281–91 (on aggadic exegesis), 443–46 (on mantological exegesis).

16. It is notoriously difficult to define this discipline very narrowly, as seen for example in Bizell and Herzberg, "General Introduction," 1. See further King, "The State of Rhetorical Criticism," 365–68; Condit, "Contemporary Rhetorical Criticism," 369–72.

emphases on stylistics and persuasion (mostly in speech).[17] Early Christian fathers further employed and adapted classical categories to their emerging theological discourse.[18] Additionally, an element of rhetorical sensitivity may be distinguished in a number of works dealing with literary and compositional strategies through subsequent periods (in the West at least, in both Christian and non-Christian works).[19] More recently, rhetorical criticism has been developed as a component of literary studies. With the works of theorists such as Perelman, Burke, Richards, and Weaver, the concept of rhetorical criticism has, in fact, been renewed as a fruitful means for studying all spoken and written communication.[20] This "new rhetoric," however, moves further than the classical emphasis on speech, since it is also concerned with discourse theory and epistemology, linguistics, and the interrelationship of the concept of persuasion with sociology.[21]

Moreover, rhetorical criticism has been variously applied to the study of Scripture. For the NT, Kennedy has been influential in using classical Greek categories—notably towards the study of the Pauline corpus.[22] Muilenburg, in turn, is rather universally credited with the formal introduction of "rhetorical criticism" to OT scholarship, even as it has developed in various directions since his initial work.[23] He indeed helped shift

---

17. The principal Greek authors are Gorgias, Plato, Isocrates, Aristotle, Cicero, Quintilian, and the anonymous author of *Rhetorica ad Herennium* (sometimes attributed to Cicero). This final work, dated to about 86 BC, is the first to expound the four classical divisions of rhetoric: *invention, arrangement, style, and memory*. See further Kessler, "A Methodological Setting," 23; Fiore, "Rhetoric and Rhetorical Criticism," 710–11. As examples of these primary sources, see Cicero, *On Oratory*, 5–81; Aristotle, *The "Art" of Rhetoric*, 2–167. Note as well Enos, "Classical Rhetoric and Rhetorical Criticism," 361–65.

18. This is true, for example, in Augustine, *On Christian Doctrine*, ix–xxii.

19. For the historical framework, note Bizell and Herzberg "General Introduction," 13–15, and the fuller discussion of these historical categories in Barilli, *Rhetoric*. The latter work deals with each successive period. See also Tull, "Rhetorical Criticism," 156–64.

20. Perelman, for example, laments the fact that while *classical* rhetoric did emphasize the persuasive aspect of rhetoric, *later* (in this case French) authors, focused merely on *stylistics*. See Perelman, *L'empire rhétorique*, 10. Note also, Perelman and Olbrechts-Tyteca, *Traité de l'argumentation*.

21. See Tull, "Rhetorical Criticism," 157. Further, note Connors et al., "The Revival of Rhetoric in America," 1–15; Olbricht, "The Flowering of Rhetorical Criticism in America," 94–99.

22. See for instance Kennedy, *Classical Rhetoric*, 137–82. Note further, Classen, *Rhetorical Criticism*, 1–98, and as examples of NT application, Edart, *L'Épître aux Phillipiens*; Long, *Ancient Rhetoric*.

23. For a helpful discussion of the relationship of OT rhetorical criticism to the traditional historical-critical methods, see Hauser, "Notes on History and Method," 4–9.

the prevailing exegetical emphasis from historical events or ideas behind the text to the text itself—so that texts "must no longer serve simply as avenues back into history."[24]

Muilenburg appreciated certain aspects of form criticism; he also criticized this method's tendency to "generalize because it is concerned with what is common to all the representatives of a genre, and therefore applies an external measure to the individual pericopes."[25] Muilenburg, thus, encouraged appreciation of the given "incarnation" of a passage, as "it is the creative synthesis of the particular formulation of the pericope with the content that makes it the distinctive composition that is it."[26] After all, the authors of the Hebrew Bible *were* guided by competent literary sensitivities, he argued.

What is central, then, is the search for "Hebrew literary composition," "structural patterns," and the literary devices used to *achieve* such patterns. A key aspect is the focus on the "texture and fabric of the writer's thought" to discover the meaning of a unit. Hence, the basic steps for Muilenburg are logical: (1) divide a passage into units, (2) analyze the movement and flow of the various units (particularly via poetic devices and world play), and (3) synthesize the data to elucidate the intention of the text's author.[27]

Anderson and Kessler, for instance, represent later scholars who embraced Muilenburg's call to synchronically focus on the style and drama of a given OT text.[28] Similarly, Kikawada argued that a *rhetorical* biblical critic should move back to the original intent of a unit by starting with its basic literary data, then studying its structure, titling its component parts, and, on those bases, pursuing its deeper meaning.[29]

Other scholars, however, have pointedly argued that rhetorical criticism should also focus on aspects of *persuasion*. For some, the "Muilenburg School"—and the socio-rhetorical method of Robbins—have been victims of a rhetorical theory reduced merely to literary *style*, without

---

24. House, "The Rise and Current Status," 8.

25. Muilenberg, "Form Criticism and Beyond," 5. For the key essay by Gunkel, see the critical translation by Siedlecki, "The Literature of Ancient Israel," 26–83. For bibliography of Muilenburg's publications, see Hicks, "A Bibliography," 233–42; Ball, "Additions," 285–87.

26. Muilenburg, "Form Criticism and Beyond," 5.

27. Muilenburg, "Form Criticism and Beyond," 7–10. Note also the discussion of Muilenburg's proposals in Trible, *Rhetorical Criticism*, 25–32; Warner, "Introduction: Rhetorical Criticism," 1–25.

28. See Anderson, "Introduction: The New Frontier," ix–xvii; Kessler, "A Methodological Setting," 22–36; Greenwood, "Rhetorical Criticism," 418–26.

29. See Kikawada, "Some Proposals," 67–69.

enough concern for the *effect* of the literary art on the ancient or current audience. To these ends, Wuellner, for example, has promoted Kennedy's stages of rhetorical criticism to pursue the persuasive element of NT texts: define the rhetorical unit, identify its rhetorical situation, arrangement, style, and finally, view the whole synchronically.[30] Similarly, Howard has made an appeal for the application of a rhetorical criticism that is not only sensitive to literary artistry, but also, that is intent on elucidating the *persuasive* aspects of a given OT text.[31]

All in all, the broader discipline of rhetorical criticism has developed in a variety of directions.[32] In biblical studies, however, either "the art of *composition*," following Muilenburg, or the "art of *persuasion*," following classical categories, have tended to dominate.[33] Furthermore, some argue that these classical categories are being "overly" applied in OT/biblical rhetorical studies.[34] It is indeed important, as Hallo has pointed out, to remember that literary shaping *and* communicative persuasion can be detected in some of the earliest Sumerian and Akkadian texts, as well as other early settings of the ANE—which are obviously *prior* to the Greek period (and its classical rhetorical categories).[35] At the same time, a number of "anachronistic" methods are regularly applied in the study of biblical texts (such as semiotics or linguistics).[36]

30. Wuellner, "Where Is Rhetorical Criticism," 455–58, based on Kennedy, *New Testament Interpretation*, 33–38. For Robbins' view, note Robbins, "The Present and Future," 24–52. For a study incorporating elements from both Muilenburg and Robbins, see Hens-Piazza, *Of Methods*.

31. Howard, "Rhetorical Criticism," 99–104. For some rhetorical studies outside of Chronicles variously emphasizing elements of persuasion, see, for instance, "Rhetoric as the Art of Persuasion," in Gitay, *Prophecy and Persuasion*, 34–49; Gitay, "Rhetorical Criticism," 13–24; Marbury, "The Separatist Rhetoric"; Kelly, *Hosea 2*, 2–46; Cook, "Prayers that Form Us," 451–67. Note as well Stulac, "Charting New Paths," 390–412. Also note the rhetorical-critical essays on various OT texts gathered in Lundbom, *Biblical Rhetoric*.

32. See Amador, "Where Could Rhetorical Criticism," 195–222. Further, see Olbricht, "Classical Rhetorical Criticism," 109–24; Compier, *What Is Rhetorical Theology?* 1–48.

33. Per Möller, "Rhetorical Criticism," 689.

34. See for instance, Meynet, *L'analyse rhétorique*, 175–318, whose method accentuates the inherent nature of *biblical* rhetorical composition, without recourse to classical categories. More broadly, note also Meynet, *Initiation à la rhétorique biblique*.

35. See Hallo, "The Birth of Rhetoric," 25–46. See also Lipson, "Ancient Egyptian Rhetoric," 79–88.

36. Möller, for instance, tempers this oft-cited criticism (of the anachronistic use of later Greek rhetorical categories for the study of earlier OT texts). He notes that other "anachronistic" tools are regularly used in the study of ancient documents, such a modern linguistics. See Möller, "Rhetorical Criticism," 690. Similarly, note Duke, "A Rhetorical Approach," 106.

Applying Rhetorical Criticism to 1 Chr 15:1–16:3

Four guiding principles and five steps of application will now be laid out—as an outline framing a rhetorical study of 1 Chr 15:1—16:3, one that will explore the Levites' role in sustaining the symbol of God's *presence* at the ark.[37] First, this rhetorical analysis will be taken up on the basis of an affirmative hermeneutic. The focus will be on the message inherent to the MT "as we have it."[38] The relationship between the Chronicler as the biblical author, his primary audience of postexilic Judah generally, and the textual means of communication between the two will help guide the discussion. In fact, Patrick and Scult have noted that a hermeneutic of "suspicion" merely seeks to elucidate the so-called human ideologies underlying a rhetorical situation. This severely limits a full appreciation of the biblical and theological rhetorical environment—as they note:

> A humanistic hermeneutics of affirmation does not claim to guarantee the power of a text's rhetoric is an indication of its truth, only of its possible truth. . . . *[T]he possible becomes actual through the testimony of the Spirit engendering faith and obedience. Divine inspiration has a very definite role in the rhetorical transaction after all.*[39]

In a sense, this hermeneutical rhetorical approach complements the epistemological stance of critical realism, where the communicative and truthful force of Scripture—in all of its literary genres—is not seen as impossibly distant, but viewed as *adequately* attainable through the filtered means of human intellectual perception.[40] Coupled with the "interpretive virtues," it is

---

37. Chiasm is often recognized as a literary rhetorical tool in biblical texts. See Berger, "Chiasm and Meaning," 1–28, for a recent study of chiastic patterns in the whole of 1 Chronicles. Berger, "Chiasm and Meaning," 1, notes in fact, "in recent decades it has been become increasingly clear that late biblical writers made extensive use of chiasm. In the case of Chronicles, numerous proposed chiastic patterns have substantial support, including some that govern notable large expanses of text." For a detailed literary exegetical analysis of the full ark narrative (1 Chr 15–16) and its broader function in 1–2 Chronicles, see Street, *The Significance*, 45–112.

38. Following the observation of Kennedy, who writes, "rhetorical criticism takes the text as we have it . . . and looks at it from the point of view of the author's or editor's intent, the unified results, and how it would be perceived by an audience of near contemporaries." See Kennedy, *New Testament Interpretation*, 4, and as cited in Duke, "A Rhetorical Approach," 107.

39. Patrick and Scult, "Rhetoric and Ideology," 83, emphasis added. And see further Patrick and Scult, *Rhetoric and Biblical Interpretation*, 45–46.

40. For a helpful discussion, see "Knowledge: Problems and Varieties," in Wright, *New Testament*, 31–46. See further, Thiselton, *New Horizons*, 1–75; the chapter "Critical Realism: Engaging with a Stratified Reality," in McGrath, *The Science of God*, 139–52.

thus arguably possible for the human reader and knower to attain a critically-realist view of this pericope—even of its rhetorical power.[41]

Secondly, and consequently, the rhetorical exegesis will proceed assuming: (1) a generally postexilic and pre-Hellenistic date of composition, and (2) the benefit of a consistent focus on the synchronic unity of the text. Regarding the date of composition, it is difficult to state a very precise period beyond a range of about three hundred years—a date between the late fifth century BC and the mid third century BC is plausible: at the *earliest*, several generations removed from the return, still under Persian domination, and at the *latest*, before more direct Hellenistic influences. First, Chronicles must have been written after the rise of Persian Empire, since it ends with the decree of Cyrus in 2 Chr 36:22—23 (539/538 BC). Second, scholars usually point to two later works that presuppose aspects of the canonical books of Chronicles: Ben Sira's "Praise to the Fathers" appears to assume the Chronicler's depiction of David; the Jewish historian Eupolemus probably made use of Chronicles in Greek translation.[42] As Ben Sira is usually dated to around 190–175 BC and Eupolemus to around 150 BC, "one may conclude that the original Hebrew Chronicles had to be ready by the beginning of the second century BCE at the latest."[43]

Alternatively, based on other allusions to Chronicles in apocryphal texts, in pseudepigraphical works, and in certain Dead Sea scrolls—and coupled with the evidence from the LXX—Knoppers concludes that the latest possible date would reasonably be the mid-third century BC. Since Chronicles is used and alluded to in these various works in the first and second centuries BC, and since Chronicles is translated into Greek in the LXX and cited in Greek with Eupolemos, one has to allow both for MT Chronicles to become established and LXX Chronicles to be translated into Greek and, then, to be cited by a Jewish-Hellenistic author.[44] Knoppers, then, opts for a range between the late fifth century (earliest) and the mid-third century (latest), and tentatively suggests a date of composition in the late fourth or early third century.[45] Although some scholars have argued for a date of composition early in the Persian period (late sixth century to early fifth century), and others have argued for a date late into the third or even second centuries, a number of recent scholars support the view that

---

41. See Vanhoozer, *Is There a Meaning?* 376–77.

42. Note *Sir* 47:8–10. Further, Knoppers remarks that Eupolemus' "quotation of certain texts dealing with David and Solomon is preserved in Eusebius (*Praep. ev.* 9.30.1–34.18)." See Knoppers, *I Chronicles 1–9*, 106n131.

43. As noted by Peltonen, "A Jigsaw Without a Model?" 223.

44. See Knoppers, *I Chronicles 1–9*, 111.

45. Knoppers, *I Chronicles 1–9*, 116; see 101–17 as a whole.

Chronicles was probably composed sometime in the fourth century BC, "be it before or shortly after the fall of the Persian Empire to Alexander the Great in 333 BCE."[46] Indeed, a very early Persian date requires complex literary-critical theories (ones that especially see the Levitical texts as later additions to the core of the Chronicler's work); the fact that no obvious Hellenistic influences (literary or cultural) exists in Chronicles mitigates against a date after the fall of the Persian Empire.[47]

Furthermore, despite certain text-critical challenges, the genealogy in 1 Chr 3:17-24 is helpful in suggesting a date in the early 400s or the late 300s. The genealogy lists the sons of Jehoiachin exiled in 597 BC. The MT, indeed, extends for at least two generations beyond Jeconiah (Jehoiachin) and Zerubbabel, and if one assumes twenty to thirty years per generation, Chronicles could not have been written any sooner that the early fifth century. No internal evidence compels one to affix any later date, so it seems plausible for Chronicles to have been written no later than the early 400s or the very late 300s.[48] Thus, the Chronicler wrote at a time when Israel was reduced to the status of the outlying province of "Yehud" in the context of the larger Persian domination.[49]

46. Following Peltonen, *A Jigsaw*, 226-27. Some of these scholars include: Williamson, *1 and 2 Chronicles*, 15-17; Japhet, *I and II*, 23-28; Selman, *1 Chronicles*, 69-71; Kalimi, "Könnte die aramäische," 79-81; Riley, *King and Cultus*, 24-26.

47. Knoppers, *I Chronicles 1-9*, 228. The early dating views, indeed, entail a number of redactional theories—see, for example, Cross, "A Reconstruction," 4-18; Newsome, "Towards a New Understanding," 201-17; Braun, *1 Chronicles*, xxviii-xxix; Throntveit, *When Kings Speak*, 97-107. For views defending the third or second centuries as compositional dates, see for instance, Welten, *Geschichte*, 199-200; Steins, "Zur Datierung der Chronik," 84-92.

48. Here following, in part, Howard, *An Introduction*, 235. The LXX appears to count several more generations after Zerubbabel. Note Peltonen, *A Jigsaw*, 229. For a thorough study of this genealogy, see Knoppers, *I Chronicles 1-9*, 317-36. Other texts informing the discussion of the date of Chronicles are: 1 Chr 29:7 (with an anachronistic use of the Persian daric, first minted during the reign of Darius I [522-486 BC]; the possibly anachronistic association of Tadmor and Hamath in 2 Chr 8:3-4 (which, perhaps, reflects the Persian system of provincial administration); the apparent use of Zech 4:10 in 2 Chr 16:9; and two passages apparently borrowed from Ezra-Nehemiah: 1 Chr 9:2-17 (the list of the inhabitants of Jerusalem at the return) and 2 Chr 36:22-23 (the edict of Cyrus). See further as well, "The Date of the Book of Chronicles," in Kalimi, *An Ancient Israelite Historian*, 41-66.

49. Five Persian emperors ruled throughout this approximate period (fifth to fourth centuries BC): Artaxerxes II (405/4-359), Artaxerxes III (359-338), Artaxerxes IV (Arses, 338-336), Darius III (336-331), and finally, Artaxerxes V (331). See further Allen, *The Persian Empire*, 86-109, 132-59; Briant, *From Cyrus to Alexander*, 1-30, 422-71, 693-768, 817-76. Weinberg, for example, has argued that the Jews were a minority in "Yehud" in the early postexilic period and only later gained prominence. On this theory, earlier postexilic leaders like Sheshbazzar and Zerubbabel would have

In his recent commentary, for example, Boda surveys the same basic evidence (as noted above) related to the dating of Chronicles, and arrives at a similar conclusion, as he writes:

> These various pieces of evidence suggest that the *earliest* date for the writing of Chronicles is 425 B.C. Regarding the *latest* possible date for the book's composition, there is strong evidence of the use of Chronicles in several books in the Second Temple period (Daniel, 1 Maccabees, Sirach, and various of the DSS). This, together with the fact that Chronicles is part of the Greek translation of the Old Testament (LXX) ... [suggests] that the Chronicler was at work somewhere between 425 and 250 B.C., writing to a community of Jews who needed to return to Jerusalem to the reconstructed temple and to participate in its worship as they awaited the full realization of the restoration of the kingdom of David.[50]

In his study of the broader David-Solomon narratives in 1 Chronicles, Ahn has also carefully investigated the full-fledged "rhetorical situation" of the Chronicler. His main conclusion in this regard is worth noting here, as a concise statement regarding the situation that the Chronicler faced *rhetorically*, as the human author of this biblical corpus:

> The [Chronicler's] rhetorical situation concerns the problems that the Yehudite community faced under Persian rule. These problems are reflected in the [Chronicler's] exigence, audience and constraints. The Judahites in Persian Yehud wished they were still God's people, although their identity as God's people seems to have gone away after exile. Thus, the [Chronicler], responding to

---

had Persian support and control of the smaller Jewish community, but not of the larger province. See further Weinberg, *The Citizen-Temple Community*. However, several have noted that the relationship between Persia and the whole province was broader and that the postexilic Jewish community experienced the same relationship to Persia as others in the larger province. See Provan et al., *A Biblical History*, 396–97 (and 379–409 for an overview of the general historical background for the postexilic period); Williamson, "Exile and After," 251–52. For further study on the interrelationship of the Judean province and the Persian kingdom, see Fried, *The Priest*, 17, 156–233; Carter, *The Emergence of Yehud*, 31–74, 249–324; Williamson, *Studies in Persian*, 3–63, 199–211; Sacchi, *The History*, 160–213; Schiffman, *Texts and Traditions*, 70–95, 106–16.

50. Boda, *1-2 Chronicles*, 8 (emphasis added). Similarly, Konkel, *1 & 2 Chronicles*, 27–28, argues for the *terminus a quo* around 400–350 BC and the *terminus ad quem* as "probably before the first half of the fourth century BCE." Merrill, *A Commentary*, 22–23, argues for the *terminus a quo* for ca. 530 BC and the *terminus ad quem* "as late as the early fourth century BC, well into the era sometimes described as the Second Temple."

this situation, presents the early history of Israel, and he expects fitting responses from his audience, the Yehudite community.⁵¹

Furthermore, as noted in the first chapter of this study, when it comes to texts dealing with the Levites in Chronicles, a number of compositional suggestions (mainly related to theories of warring priestly and Levitical parties in the postexilic period) have the propensity to dictate the discussions. A rhetorical analysis, however, provides the benefit of exploring the nexus between this text viewed as a *unified* narrative and the message present in the *structure* of that narrative. In fact, 1 Chr 15:1—16:3 is part of a larger *historical* narrative, which as one author has argued, can be generally defined as a "representational [depiction] of the world composed for the purpose of conveying meaning to the intended audience."⁵² Consequently, the component parts of this narrative, which are often broken apart, will be investigated in reference to their potential in sustaining a more unified and meaningful message.

Thirdly, thus, the basic notion that literary structure and textual meaning are closely related will be followed. An affirmative hermeneutic of critical realism coupled with a synchronic approach to the text of 1 Chr 15-16 enable the exploration of meaning as it is conveyed in the specific structure of this passage. As one author has argued, literary "structure has rhetorical and expressive value, it is one of the factors governing the effect of the work on the reader and in addition it serves to express or accentuate meaning."⁵³ Dorsey notes, similarly, that in Hebrew texts, meaning is conveyed through structure in three basic manners: (1) the overall configuration of the composition, (2) structural repetition, and (3) positions of prominence.⁵⁴ Our rhetorical analysis of 1 Chr 15:16—16:3 will consider these various elements.

Finally, whether they have been closer to the Muilenburg approach or whether they have moved to stress persuasive rhetoric or ideology, the majority of OT rhetorical-critical studies have often been applied to poetry. However, one scholar in particular, Duke, has done work in applying the method of rhetorical criticism to the narrative texts of Chronicles (and

---

51. Ahn, *The Persuasive Portrayal*, 63.

52. Duke, "The Strategic Use," 129. In this manner, Vanhoozer, *Is There a Meaning*, 462, argues for a "chastened" way forward—out of interpretive skepticism (similarly to Wright above).

53. See Bar-Efrat, "Some Observations," 172 (and as cited in Dorsey, *The Literary Structure*, 36); Bar-Efrat, *Narrative Art in the Bible*, 93-140. And see further Welch, "Introduction," 9-16; Radday, "Chiasmus in Hebrew Biblical Narrative," 50-117. On chiasmus in Chronicles, see especially Kalimi, *The Reshaping*, 215-74; Berger, "Chiasm and Meaning," 1-28.

54. See Dorsey, *The Literary Structure*, 36, and the ensuing discussion, 37-41.

to its other genres).⁵⁵ The proposed study of 1 Chr 15:1—16:3 will seek to build on several rhetorical insights offered by Duke. At this juncture, three should be introduced. First, Duke has argued that the rhetorical purposes of historical narratives in the OT are at least threefold: (1) to preserve Israel's traditions and shape its identity; (2) to respond to the needs of the intended audience; and (3) to argue for a particular worldview, so that this literary genre became a way of "teaching theology."⁵⁶

Second, Duke has noted that an overall rhetorical argument frames the whole work of Chronicles. He posits that 1 Chr 1–9 represents the introduction by establishing the main parameters of the whole work. With 1 Chr 10 through 2 Chr 9, the Chronicler fashions the narratives to present the basic paradigm of "seeking Yahweh." In 2 Chr 10–36, the Chronicler, then, *illustrates* the paradigm (negatively or positively) through the reigns of the southern Davidic kings.⁵⁷ A number of writers have observed this phenomenon generally; Duke, however, has provided much rhetorical detail in support. Thus, third, in the Davidic narratives, Duke's development of the "seeking Yahweh" argument is particularly significant for a study of the proposed text. He maintains that one of the main "purposes of Chr. was to move his audience to seek Yahweh through the proper forms of the Jerusalem cult."⁵⁸ David, hence, represents the embodiment of this "seeking" argument. Each of these aspects will come into play with the focused rhetorical study proposed for chapter three of this study.

Consequently, the following four steps will structure our study proper. First, a translation will be provided—one that covers the main text-critical issues in the passage. The study will also briefly establish the text as a definable rhetorical unit in the Chronicler's developing argument. Second, the "internal" rhetorical aspect will be explored by defining the

55. Note the following representative studies: Duke, "Chronicles," 161–80; Duke, "The Ethical Appeal," 33–51; Duke, "A Rhetorical Approach," 100–35; Duke, "The Strategic Use," 1–77. For a recent exploration of the nature of narrative in the context of rhetorical criticism, engaging with Sternberg's *The Poetics of Biblical Narrative*, see Bonneau, "Socio-Rhetorical," 43–52. Interestingly, Bonneau, "Socio-Rhetorical," 49, notes that "in narrative, there are *two concurrent dramas going on*, the drama of that which is represented (in the story) and the drama of that which is representing (in the telling/reading). They are concurrent, both occurring, and mutually influencing each other, in their interplay through time" (emphasis added). Note as well the recent rhetorical study of Ahn, *The Persuasive Portrayal*, 82–272, who focuses on the prayers and speeches (so, poetry) of David and Solomon, as they are *embedded* in the narrative structure of 1 Chr 10–2 Chr 9 as a whole.

56. Duke, "A Rhetorical Approach," 111–12.

57. This basic argument is presented in Duke, *The Persuasive Appeal*, 54–74. In part, he is following Schaefer, "The Significance of Seeking God," 119–224.

58. Duke, "A Rhetorical Approach," 129.

components of the unit and by arguing for literary strategies employed in bringing these parts together. The relationship to the synoptic text in 1 Samuel will also be noted. In considering the triad of author, text, and reader, this section of the study will focus primarily on author and text. Third, the "external" rhetorical aspect will be examined by looking at the relationship between the specifics of the strategy employed in this unit and the broader structure and argument of the Davidic narratives of 1 Chronicles (1 Chr 10:1—22:1 principally). Our rhetorical study will conclude with a brief synthesis of the investigation.

The Historical Aspect: Historiography and 1 Chr 23:24–32

The second major step will involve a study of the historical aspects of 1 Chr 23:24–32, specifically. In the context of 1 Chr 23–29, this is a passage that formally describes the modification of Levitical service during David's reign. As a general backdrop, some major approaches to historiography will be first noted briefly in this section. A few definitions are pertinent, however, from the outset. *History* may be defined as the "inquiry into the nature of the human past, with the aim of preparing an authentic account of one or more of its facets." *Historiography* represents the writing of history, or more technically, the study of the developments and methods in history-writing. *Historicity* concerns the relationship between an event in time and the witness to that event. A *philosophy of history* entails reflection on the nature of history from speculative, analytical, or pragmatic angles.[59]

Philosophy of History in the Academy: A Broad Background

Modern historiography took root in fourteenth century Renaissance Italy and blossomed thereafter, in the West at least. Some of the major philosophies of history in the nineteenth and twentieth centuries will be highlighted here

---

[59] On these definitions, see further Ritter, "History," 193–94. An older, and still oft-discussed (in biblical studies at least) definition of history is that of Huizinga's, who argued that "history is the intellectual form in which a civilization renders account to itself of its past." See Huizinga, "A Definition," 9. Ritter, "History," 198, argues that Huizinga's definition is "ecumenical," and accordingly, very broad. See also the discussion in Younger, *Ancient Conquest Accounts*, 26–31. More generally on the interrelationship of the concepts of history and historiography, note Kempshall, *Rhetorical and the Writing*, 34–120.

briefly—towards establishing the contours of a theoretical context helpful in ascertaining some recent developments in OT history-writing.[60]

Positivism, idealism, historicism, and Marxism were central to nineteenth century (and earlier twentieth century) historical thinking. Positivism was quintessentially modernistic in its epistemology, since it assumed that the methods of natural science could be transferred to the writing of history. Based initially on the social philosophy of Comte, positivism opposed the supernatural, idealized the natural sciences, and affirmed that *phenomena* alone should provide the basis for historical exploration. Especially popular outside Germany, positivism's emphasis on empirical research thrived during this period. Its principle of searching for overarching rules governing human behavior was, however, eventually abandoned as naïve and limiting. In the twentieth century academy, "positivist" evolved into a pejorative term describing those historians who continued with the methods of natural science in historical enquiry.[61]

Idealism stood as a clear counterpoint to positivism and was more prominent in the German academy. On the basis of Platonic epistemology and Kant's transcendental idealism (in which *phenomena* is contrasted to *noumena*), Hegel developed a theory of *historical* idealism.[62] He indeed elaborated an absolute idealism by identifying reality with human self-consciousness—the Absolute Spirit (*not* a Kantian transcendental ideal).[63] Reason, here, is the goal of history. "Unreflected Consciousness" represents the first stage of world history (infant eastern thought); the second is the union of "Morality" with the subjective "Will" (adolescent Greek thought); the third is the realm of "Abstract Universality" (the adult Roman state with its dominance of the social ideal); the final state is found in the ultimate blending of "Reason and Spirit" (church and state: in the mature German state). Hegelian idealism, thus, is not rooted in the natural sciences, but it is related to a theory of the *development* of human institutions: from limited consciousness (thesis), through contradictions (antithesis), to the ideal of a higher rationality

---

60. On aspects of OT historiography before the nineteenth century, note Hayes, "The History of the Study," 33–53.

61. See Ritter, "Positivism," 327–30. Further, note Steinmetz, "Positivism," 1–58; Karsenti, *Politique de l'esprit*, 211–16.

62. See Kant, *Critique of Pure Reason*, 1–62; Kant, *Kritik*, 31–48. Note further, Ameriks, "The Critique of Metaphysics," 269–302; Simpson, *German Aesthetic*, 1–26; Rockmore, *Kant and Idealism*, 121–200 (for his critique).

63. For a recent exploration of the relationship between Aristotle's idealism and that of Hegel's, note Sauder, "L'Ενεργεια selon Hegel," 213–22. More generally note as well, Grosos, "Lire Hegel," 655–72; Pagès, "De Hegel à Herder," 631–60.

(synthesis). Consequently, this conception of human history is intrinsically non-metaphysical and also anti-supernatural.[64]

"Historicism" is more difficult to define, but it relates to understanding the course of human events "historically," that is, to tracing the origins and developments of a particular facet of a human society. In the nineteenth century, it was steeped in realism and also influenced by idealism. Ranke's famous dictum, "*wie es eigentlich gewesen*," ("as it actually occurred") encapsulated an early notion of this approach, where the past was sought in approximation to reality. Ranke, however, was not pursuing a recreation of the historical past *per se*; rather, he was searching for its "essential" nature.[65] Other important theorists of historicism were Croce, Troeltsch, and Meinecke—whose works variously dealt with relativism and the historicist recreation of the past. In 1913, Troeltsch argued that historicism constituted "one of the outstanding elements" of the nineteenth century's spiritual state (*Seelenverfassung*) and defined this philosophy of history as "the completely relativistic rediscovery of any arbitrary past formations with the burdening and tiring impression of general historical knowledge and skeptical non-productivity for the present."[66] For Scholtz, Meinecke's view of historicism was one of many in the nineteenth century—one that "inhaled Nietzsche's criticism of the historicizing nineteenth century."[67] Historicism is now usually understood as a very limiting method, especially as it is charged with forcing data into preset, meta-historical frameworks.[68] Fischer, for example,

64. See Ritter, "Idealism," 207–12; Hegel, *The Philosophy of History*, 9, 105–10; Iggers, *The German Conception of History*, 38–41, 140–49.

65. On Ranke, see further, Gilbert, "Historiography," 393–97; Fitzsimons, "Ranke," 533–55; Braw, "Vision as Revision," 45–60.

66. See the discussion in Scholtz, "The Notion of Historicism," 149–50. More broadly, note Martli, "Reflections," 479–504.

67. Scholtz, "The Notion of Historicism," 150. Scholtz argues that already in the nineteenth century, five different meanings of historicism could be discerned: (1) as "the universal historical view of the human world, including reason" (with Novalis and Schlegel by 1800); (2) as a philosophy "which presumes to understand the order and rationality of all history in its course, ... the metaphysics of history" (with Braniss, or with Zimmerman in reference to Hegel's views); (3) as a "glorifying retrospect of the past and an adherence to the old values," while criticizing all things new (as with Feuerbach, or with Haym's criticism of Hegel); (4) as a "restriction of historical research to the collection and securing of facts along the guidelines of philological or historical methods" (as with positivism or objectivism); (5) as "the relativity of all value and orientation systems which makes them mere transitory phenomena in the incalculable flow of history" (as with historical relativism). See further Scholtz, "The Notion," 151–64.

68. See further Ritter, "Historicism, Historism," 183–88; Iggers, *The German Conception*, 63–89; Iggers, "Introduction," in Ranke, *The Theory*, xix–xx. Scholt, "The Notion," 149, recalls the distinction in German: *Historismus* can be used very broadly to "characterize, to criticize, and to name [various historicist] programmes," *Historizismus*,

has critiqued historicism's reductionistic emphasis on purely historical categories, which has led to ethical relativism in certain cases.[69]

Marxism, finally, represents the fourth major speculative philosophy of history in Western thought in the nineteenth century and draws on both idealism and positivism.[70] Its philosophical framers, Marx and Engels, rejected the absolute idealism of Hegel and drastically transformed his historical dialectic. For Marx, dialectical tension does not lead to "Reason," but reveals man's *alienation* from his essential humanity. The historical ideal is not pure rationality, but occurs at the humanistic level of a classless society: when the tension between the economic social "basis" (the forces of production) and the "superstructure" of ownership is resolved. Marxism, then, is essentially a materialistic, atheistic and economic view of history.[71] As Weil has noted of this philosophy of history, "there are two kinds of atheism, one of which is a purification of the concept of God."[72]

Further, at least three broad developments in the philosophy of history for the twentieth century may be noted. First, a movement of critical or "analytical" philosophers of history emerged. Early in the twentieth century, some scholars tried to counter rising attacks against the notion of history as a meaningful process. Spengler and Toynbee, for example, argued by means of scientific cyclical theories that history does evince purposeful development. Spengler focused on the "morphology" of the cultures of world history—which formed a human universe in which "there is a wondrous music of the spheres which *wills to be heard* and which a few of our deepest spirits will hear."[73] Toynbee, based on careful empirical research, engaged in a comparative study of the growth of civilizations, and, also, in a historical analysis of the "progress" of "higher" religions—including the relationship of Christianity to other world religions.[74] Also, a number of scholars focused on the epistemological basis for history-writing. This development can be defined

---

on the other hand, "always has a pejorative sense and is a term of criticism." For its American use, note Lee and Beck, "The Meaning of 'Historicism,'" 56–77.

69. Fischer, *Historians' Fallacies*, 156. See also Popper, *The Poverty of Historicism*, 160–61.

70. See further Jameson, "Marxism and Historicism," 41–73; Habib, "Marxist Historiography," 3–13.

71. Note Ritter, "Historical Materialism," 177–83. For introduction and fundamental texts, see Marx and Engels, *Basic Writings*, ix–xxi, 47–68, 133–67. See also, for instance, Cohen, "Functional Explanation," 391–402.

72. Simone Weil is quoted in Preston, *Religion*, 49; and see 50–76 as a whole.

73. Spengler, *The Decline of the West*, 160, emphasis original; see also 1–50, 53–84, 359–436.

74. See Toynbee and Somervell, *A Study of History*, 1:12–34, 2:268–301; Toynbee, *An Historian's Approach*, 1–142. Note also Toynbee, *Christianity Among*, 1–8.

as "neo-idealist," as with Collingwood's work that emphasized centrality of *thought*, since the "historian's method consists in 'rethinking' the ideas and intentions of people in the past."[75] These types of developments continue to raise methodological issues for historiography.

Secondly, the "new history" of the French *Annales* school has exerted significant influence on the conception and process of history-writing—even of "what constitutes and who makes history."[76] Through the work of several French writers (notably Febvre, Bloch, Braudel, le Goff, Nora, le Roy Ladurie, and Foucault), this method has sought to reverse the more traditional idealist or neo-idealist paradigms by focusing on: *local* issues, the analysis of underlying structures, the study of history "from below" (from the perspective of "ordinary" people), the use of more than the "official" sources, and the subjectivity of the historian and the cultural relativism of the historiographic process.[77]

Finally, White introduced the key concept of *rhetorical strategy* employed by historians in their writing. White studied some of the major historical writers of the nineteenth century and demonstrated the significance of imaginative elements brought into their written recreation of the past. A historian has a dominant style seen in the major "trope" of his text. White argued, then, that historical narratives followed one of four principal plots: comedy, tragedy (dominant), satire, or romance. For example, he contended that Ranke's history-writing was plotted as comedy, while Tocqueville's was written as tragedy.[78] In fact, White has further argued that narrative represents a "meta-code," a universal and transcultural means of communication about reality. As he has written, "historiography is an especially good ground on which to consider the nature of narration and narrativity, because it is here that our desire for the imaginary, the possible, must connect with the imperatives of the real, the actual."[79] It could, perhaps, be argued

---

75. Ritter, "Idealism," 210; Collingwood, *The Idea of History*, 1–13, 205–334. Other scholars important in this regard are Croce and Oakeshott (earlier in the century) and Dray, White, and Danto (later in the period). See Ritter, "Idealism," 209–12.

76. Iggers, *Historiography*, 51. For an overview of the *Annales* school, see Hagsor, "Total History," 1–13; Hunt, "French History," 209–24.

77. Note the comment by Ricœur, *Temps et Récit*, 140. See further (for concise synthesis and critique), Burke, "Overture: The New History," 1–23; Younger, "Early Israel," 191–92; Dosse, *New History in France*, especially 1–6, 42–76, 107–36, 215–24. Note also Ankersmit, "Historiography and Postmodernism," 137–53; Lorenz, "Comparative Historiography," 25–39; Noblesse-Rocher, "Die Rezeption des Werkes," 273–82.

78. Note also White, *Metahistory*, 45–80, 163–90, 230–64. For further discussion of postmodern historiography (including a critique of White), see Kofoed, *Text and History*, 5–32. And see more broadly, Tucker, "The Future," 37–56.

79. See "Narrativity," in White, *The Content of the Form*, 4, based on the notion

that the structural triad adopted in this work (symbol, service, and song) characterizes our "imaginative" attempt at framing the literary, historical, and theological elements of this study. This, however, does not seem to necessitate, mainly on epistemological grounds, that the content of this work, as framed, be regarded as fictitious. In the end, however, for White, written histories are both about events *and* "the possible sets of relationships that those events can be demonstrated to figure."[80]

The preceding discussion briefly points to some of the variety in approaches to conceptions of history-writing—many of which have focused on the scientific and analytical task of historical research. White has, however, also promoted the *narrative* aspect of thinking about historiography—by arguing that historical meaning is very much dependent on historiographic *expression*, thus, not only on the events and sources under consideration.[81] The challenge of deciphering historical meaning in the theological texts of the Bible remains a key issue for OT studies as well.

Some Recent Developments in Old Testament Historiography

Developments in the larger field of historiography, noted above, have had some (occasionally direct) impact on historical thinking in biblical studies and, perhaps, have periodically contributed to awkwardly forcing modern methods onto ancient texts. For example, Hegelian historical idealism stands as an underpinning for Wellhausen's skeptical view of the evolution of priests and Levites in Israel's history.[82] Or, later in the twentieth century, historical relativism introduced in the works of certain neo-idealists might be detected in the Alt/Noth school of historians—whose view of the Bible as a source for history was framed by their history-of-tradition method. Further, a more

---

of narrative in Barthes, *Image, Music, Text*, 79 (and note 79–124 as a whole). See also "The Historical Text as Literary Artifact," in White, *Tropics of Discourse*, 81–100. White, *Tropics of Discourse*, 82, argues that historical narrative is, in fact, *verbal fiction*: "in general, there has been a reluctance to consider historical narratives as what they most manifestly are: verbal fictions, the contents of which are as much *invented* as *found* and the forms of which have more in common with their counterparts in literature than they have with those in the sciences" (emphasis original). And see further Kansteiner, "Hayden White's Critique," 379–403.

80. White, "The Historical Text," 94.

81. On this, see further Dray, "Narrative vs. Analysis in History," in *Historiography*, 340–59.

82. So argue, for instance, Harrison, *Introduction to the Old Testament*, 21 (and see 3–32 as a whole); Kitchen, *On the Reliability*, 486–92.

positivistic view of the use of the Bible and archeology in a history of Israel may be found in the Albright/Wright/Bright school.[83]

However, as Evans remarks, the late twentieth century's "linguistic turn," effected by postmodernist thought has challenged the notion of writing history to its very core. Instead of earlier views of historical explanation (which emphasized *causality*), Evans contends that:

> The linguistic turn has given us *discourses*. History is widely argued to be only one discourse among many. The notion of scientific history, based on the rigorous investigation of primary sources, has been widely attacked. . . . *The question is not so much "What is History?" as "Is It Possible to Do History at All?"*[84]

These observations prompt Evans to vigorously defend the historian's ability to adequately study, write about, and learn from the past. His views provide helpful perspective on contemporary developments in OT historiography.[85] Using Hallo's categories, Yamauchi, among others, has indeed noted the existence of two main methodological poles in the broader spectrum of more recent study of OT history: "minimalism" and "maximalism."[86]

On the one hand, minimalists evince a low view of the biblical text as a source for reconstructing history—since many of these writers have embraced what Evans defines as the postmodern/linguistic turn in historiography.[87] This approach is inherently materialistic and anti-supernatural. A majority of minimalist scholars view numerous OT texts as very late and ideological—thus, as intrinsically non-historical. As Long notes of this method, "it is argued not only that the premonarchical traditions from Abraham to the judges are essentially *fictional* but also that the accounts of monarchical times are likewise *inventions* of Persian- and Hellenistic-period

---

83. Note Ollenburger, "Review Essay," 529.

84. Evans, *In Defense of History*, 3 (emphasis added). On postmodern philosophies of history more broadly, see Strauss, "Between Postmodernism," 1–10; Telfer, "The Turbulent Fortunes," 7–19; Oiry, "L'histoire comme récit," 329–61.

85. Note Evans' conclusion in his *In Defense of History*, 192–220.

86. Yamauchi, "The Current State," 1–36; in reference to Hallo, "Biblical History," 1–18. See as well Zvi-Brettler, *The Creation of History*, 1–19. And see further Gericke, "When Historical Minimalism," 412–27; Mykytiuk, "Strengthening Biblical Historicity," 114–55. Note as an example the study by Earl, "'Minimalism' and Old Testament," 207–28; and see Garfinkel, "The Birth and Death," 46–78.

87. On this point (of full-fledge adoption of postmodern theory), note the critique, for example, of Whitelam's 1987 *The Emergence of Early Israel* (and see further below) in Kitchen, *On the Reliability*, 462–63.

novelists."[88] Or, as Howard comments further, "most 'minimalists' insist that archeological evidence *alone* should be used in [reconstructing biblical history], because written texts—especially the Bible—are later, tendentious, and ideologically biased."[89] Some of the original framers of this approach were Thompson, Van Seters, and Gottwald.[90] Minimalist views on Israel's history have been further elaborated by scholars such as Lemche, Ahlström, Coote, Whitelam, Davies, and Garbini, among others.[91] Smith, for example, has argued that certain OT historical texts are late creations of Israel. In his view, the monotheism of the Pentateuch and other OT books would only be a late development projected back onto a polytheistic past—based on the memory-making of later Israel. We encounter a more extreme skepticism with Davies, who argues that the "historical Israel" presented in the Bible did not exist, and with Whitelam, who contends "ancient Israel" is a creation of modern scholars whose political views favor modern-day Israel, not the current Palestinian cause.[92]

88. Long, "Introduction," 1, emphasis added.

89. Howard, "History as History," 45, emphasis added.

90. The literature related to the minimalist/maximalist debate is vast and beyond the full scope of this work. For a critique of the historical revisionism of the minimalist camp and related bibliography, see Howard, "History as History," 25-53. Note also Collins, *The Bible After Babel*, 27-53. For key points of argument by Thompson, Gottwald, and Van Seters, note Gottwald, *The Tribes of Yahweh*, 3-24, 376-86; Thompson, *Early History*, 1-26, 77-126, 401-23; Thompson, *The Historicity*, 1-9, 315-30; Van Seters, *Abraham in History*, 1-4, 7-12, 123-53, 309-12; Van Seters, *In Search of History*, 1-7, 209-48, 354-62. For example, Thompson, *The Historicity*, 315, 330, concludes that the patriarchal narratives are *not* historical, but a late version of Israel's *experience* of their perceived relationship with God. Note, however, the careful critique of this type of position in Wiseman, "Abraham Reassessed," 141-60. See also Millard, "Methods of Studying," 35-52; Klingbeil, "Historical Criticism," 401-20; Arnold, "Pentateuchal Criticism," 622-31.

91. Note the methodological statements in Ahlström, *Ancient Palestine*, 19-55, 812-906; Coote, *Early Israel*, 1-8, 69-74, 141-68; Coote and Ord, *Is the Bible True?* 121-33; Coote and Whitelam, *The Emergence*, 11-26, 167-77; Davies, *In Search of 'Ancient Israel'*, 11-20, 57-71, 149-55; Davies, *Scribes and Schools*, 4-36, 169-83; Garbini, *Myth and History*, 1-20, 170-78; Lemche, *Ancient Israel*, 29-74, 197-258; Lemche, *The Israelites*, 1-34, 163-67; Whitelam, *The Invention of Israel*, 1-36. Lemche, *The Israelites*, 24, 165, for instance, writes that the OT should not have been seen as a source for the history of ancient Israel, as this is especially a creation of modern scholars—since "literary Israel" is merely a creation from the Greek period. For a direct response to this claim, see Kitchen, *On the Reliability*, 461-62. Note further, more generally, Whitelam, *Rhythms of Time*; Davies, *Guide for the Perplexed*.

92. See Smith, *The Memoirs of God*, especially 1-6, 124-58, 162-65; Davies, *In Search of 'Ancient Israel,'* 1-20; Whitelam, *The Invention of Israel*, 223-37. For a critique, note Provan, "The End of (Israel's) History?" 283-300.

On the other hand, a number of maximalist scholars have operated on less skeptical grounds—similar, in viewpoint, to Evans' "defense of history." These writers have also responded (sometimes forcefully) to the revisionism inherent in most minimalist approaches. Some have countered the epistemological underpinnings of the minimalist position.[93] Others have specifically challenged the minimalists' archeological methodology.[94] Still others have critically demonstrated how known extra-biblical data (textual and artifactual) correlate well with the biblical data—from later through earlier biblical periods.[95] And some authors have defended the ability, through careful interpretation, to grasp aspects of historical truth from theologically shaped narratives.[96]

In the context of maximalist OT scholarship, we present here, in agreement, one of the key methodological conclusions given by Provan, Long, and Longman, in the second edition (2015) of their volume on the history of Israel. They write:

> Given the renewed acceptance of narrative histories among historians in general, we argued that biblical scholars are unjustified in dismissing biblical narratives as "essentially useless for the historian's purposes" and the Bible as nothing more than "a holy book that tells stories." We noted, though, that if biblical narratives are to be used in historical reconstruction, they must be properly read. . . . [W]e emphasized the central role played by historians themselves *depicting* history; it is

---

93. As examples, note Provan, "In the Stable with the Dwarves," 280-320; Provan et al., *A Biblical History of Israel*, 1-134; Nicholson, "Current 'Revisionism,'" 1-22; Younger, *Ancient Conquest Accounts*, 25-60; Hallo, "The Limits of Skepticism," 187-99, who concludes, "[t]he history so reconstructed [with careful attention to source material]—be it political or literary, linguistic or socio-economic, religious or Biblical—will then be true to its textual documentation. However limited that documentation may be, *the only limits imposed on it are to set reasonable limits to our own skepticism.*" See Hallo, "The Limits of Skepticism," 199, emphasis added.

94. In particular, see Dever, *What Did the Biblical Writers Know*, 1-52, 245-94; Dever, *Who Were the Early Israelites*, 1-6, 153-66, 223-41. Note that Dever defends the historical reality of the biblical Israel, though he does so from the position of secular humanism (see Dever, *What Did the Biblical Writers Know*, ix-xi). Note as well Dever, *Beyond the Texts*, and the review essay by Hess, "An Archaeological Synthesis of Israel's History," 261-76.

95. See chiefly the conclusions in Kitchen, *On the Reliability*, 449-500. Note also key statements in Hoffmeier, *Israel in Egypt*, 25-51, 223-27; Hoffmeier, *Ancient Israel in Sinai*, 3-26, 23-34, 149-76, 235-50.

96. See for instance Osborne, "Historical Narrative and Truth in the Bible," 673-88; Koefed, *Text and History*, 190-248; Raney, *History as Narrative*, 7-38, 192-206; Long, *The Art of Biblical History*, 58-119; "Old Testament History," 86-102; Merrill, "Old Testament History," 68-85.

historians who must first catch a vision of the past and then devise ways of presenting their vision so as to persuade others that their reconstructions fairly represent some aspect of past reality. . . . We stressed the importance—even (or especially) for historians—of reading biblical texts with as high a degree of literary competence as possible.[97]

Furthermore, for the purposes of looking at the Levites in 1 Chronicles *historically*, two major points stand out in essays by Yamauchi and Long (who write from "maximalist" perspectives). First, Yamauchi argues that in revisionist methods, a large number of biblical texts are rejected as sources of history because their composition is *later* than the events they claim to describe. However, as he notes, "the date of a text's composition is not necessarily a warrant *against* the possibility that it preserves accurate memories, if it was able to use earlier sources."[98] That is, the absence of clear source references for a particular text should not automatically signify they were created later on the basis of a particular ideology. Such *a priori* rejection of primary literary evidence, for lack of internal or external corroboration, is arguably an unwarranted suspicion forced on the text by a post-Enlightenment rationalism (or a postmodern epistemological skepticism, for that matter).[99]

Second, Long shows that recent OT historiography on the minimalist side is guided by: (1) an acutely rationalist application of the three historical-critical principles of criticism (overly skeptical), analogy (limited to a *formal* definition), and correlation (limited to *present* human experience);[100] (2) a heavily *nomothetic* application of social scientific methods (i.e., concerned with structural/general laws of social change—in line with the "new history") that trumps the *ideographic* concerns of theological biblical texts (i.e., related to significant events, nations, and individuals), which are then rejected as historical sources; (3) an application of literary criticism to historical texts that has elucidated their rhetorical shape (as with White's methods), but that has also created a reductionism to "pure literary art," causing actual historical questions to be faded out. These approaches are not helpful in gaining broader insight into the texts themselves, Long argues. A

---

97. Provan et al., *A Biblical History of Israel*, 133 (emphasis original).
98. Yamauchi, "The Current State," 26–27 (emphasis added).
99. See further, House, "God's Design and Postmodernism," 29–54.
100. Long, "Historiography," 152–56. Long notes that Troeltsch, writing in the early twentieth century, is credited with presenting these three canons of the historical-critical method. It is thus interesting to note how Ritter, "Historicism," 184, argues that Troeltsch also introduced the modern concept of relativism to a historical-critical approach to historiography.

"maximalist" *biblical* historian needs to adapt these methods to ensure they align with a necessarily theistic worldview.[101]

Hence, such a theistic approach to historical texts may make use of the methods of historical criticism, social science, and literary criticism in these ways: (1) criticism should entail a thoughtful appraisal of the evidence, analogy should not solely be based on present human experience (the *past* may also serve as a key to the present), and correlation should be defined *personally* not *formally* (allowing, then, for divine intervention); (2) social scientific insights should serve to provide appropriate *background* evidence, without trumping the primary literary evidence; (3) a reductionistic literary criticism is not necessary, as genuine literary sensitivity will do justice to the various types of truth claims embedded in texts.[102]

It is our opinion that Long's methodological proposals are worth embracing, as we proceed with a more historically-focused exegetical analysis of the Levites in 1 Chronicles.

Applying a Historiographic Method to the Study of 1 Chr 23:24-32

As such, the purpose of examining the historical aspect of the Levites in Chronicles is to reflect on their role in expanding the *service* to God and his people at a key juncture in Israel's history. Chapter four will engage this issue with a focused study of 1 Chr 23:24-32.

First of all, it should be remembered that Chronicles, as a work of biblical historiography, can be seen as *complementing* the synoptic history of Samuel-Kings—not as simply plagiarizing or suppressing texts from Samuel-Kings.[103]

---

101. Long, "Historiography," 156-65. For a helpful introduction on the history-writing process from essentially maximalist perspectives, see further the chapter "History and Historiography," in Matthews, *Studying the Ancient Israelites*, 159-96. Matthews strikes a balance in his proposed method, as he writes, "[i]t is the task of the historian of ancient Israel to gather all available information—including the biblical text... piece it together in a variety of ways, and posit an interpretation based on clearly defined research methodologies that do justice to the data while keeping in mind the potential for shaping of the material both in antiquity and today." See Matthews, *Studying the Ancient Israelites*, 196.

102. Long, "Historiography," 168-74. On the appropriateness of theism within historiography, Long is interacting with Abraham, *Divine Revelation*, 158, who argues, "there is nothing unhistorical in relying on theology." See also Abraham, *Divine Revelation*, 116-40, where Abraham concludes, "[b]elief in divine intervention and belief in the resurrection are in principle admissible." For further discussion, see Long, *The Art of Biblical History*, 120-68.

103. Childs, for example, contended that it is a basic error in interpretation to suggest that the Chronicler's method of source-selection is suppressive—for two reasons: (1) he regularly assumes his readers have knowledge of earlier traditions (if not, often,

As some have recently argued, the Deuteronomistic history of Samuel-Kings addresses precisely the *exilic* concerns of the LORD's people: the reasons for the exile and ensuing doubts about Yahweh's continued faithfulness to his earlier covenantal promises.[104] Clearly, in the covenant context of blessing and curse, the LORD was *not* unfaithful to his promise of blessing *and* curse. Chronicles, however, is responding to different issues than those addressed in Samuel-Kings: life *after* the experience of the curse of the exile—as the book addresses those exiles who have returned, or who are returning, to the Promised Land.[105] The questions are, hence, different and relate to Yahweh's continued interest in his people and to the *continuation* of his covenant promises—"[thus t]he Chronicler's chief purpose in writing his history appears to be to exhort and encourage the returnees."[106] As Provan et al. have noted of the distinct historiographic purposes of the Chronicler:

> The books of Chronicles focus on a different set of questions [than Samuel-Kings]. Their addressees were not exilees still in captivity but exilees who had returned or were returning to the promised land from which they had been taken. The questions animating the Chronicler's addressees must have been of the following sort: "Is God still interested in us? Are the covenants still in force?" To such questions, the Chronicler answers with a resounding yes. The Chronicler's chief purpose in writing his history appears to be to exhort and encourage the returnees.[107]

Consequently, it would make sense for the Chronicler's synoptic account: (1) to leave out certain materials which would have been widely known to his hearers (such as David's adultery or Solomon's apostasy) and not in line with his desire for encouragement[108] and (2) to include other material that (a) "underscored the more universal significance of Israel's

---

his account cannot be properly understood), and (2) even if a story is omitted, it is frequently and explicitly referred to through careful use of sources. See Childs, *Introduction*, 646–47.

104. See Provan et al., *A Biblical History*, 261–66. Note also the somewhat contrasted conclusions in Brettler, *The Creation of History*, 46–47.

105. See further Edelman, "The Deuteronomist's David," 67–83; Edelman, "Chronicles as a Model for Biblical History," in Brettler, *The Creation of History*, 20–47.

106. Brettler, *The Creation of History*, 196.

107. Provan et al., *A Biblical History*, 262. For a detailed study of the covenant theme in this "reenvisioned" perspective of the Chronicler, see especially Boda, "Reeinvisioning the Relationship," 391–406, and the further literature cited there.

108. And note that even with the Chronicler, David is the not the fully "idealized" character that some scholars argue for. Some of the sins of David *do* play a part in the Chronicler's rhetorical purposes, such as David's sin at the census in 1 Chr 21.

experiences," (b) emphasized the personal nature of the LORD's covenant with David (in a time when the physical throne of David was empty), (c) "stressed the importance of the Temple as the focus of God's presence among his people (when the temple was [being] rebuilt)," and (d) "highlighted the significance for 'all Israel' of the return from exile."[109]

1 Chr 23, furthermore, is part of the "additions" of the Chronicler's presentation of David's kingdom.[110] This chapter is unmistakably related to a desire to stress the temple and God's presence, since it carefully delineates Levitical duties for the temple service. Verses 24–32 of this chapter will serve as the control text for this phase of the study. A number of other texts are obviously pertinent to a historical discussion of Levites in the Davidic narratives of 1 Chronicles, but within the scope of our analysis, this will be our focused control passage.

Moreover, as it is set within the second major section of 1 Chr 10–29, 1 Chr 22:2—29:30 displays two major concerns from David's perspective: the transferal of the kingdom to his son Solomon and the oversight of the preparations for building the Solomonic temple. More specifically, in chapter 22, David initiates the temple-building preparations (vv. 2–5) and delivers the first charge to Solomon: to oversee the building of the house of the LORD, as, unlike David, Solomon is a man of rest (v. 9: איש מנוחה). David also enlists the help of Israelite leaders to support Solomon in his task (vv. 17–19).[111] Chapters 23–26 are thus concerned with the establishment of the "sacred" duties of priests and Levites in relationship to (upcoming) temple duties, while chapter 27 is dedicated to listing the "secular" duties of military and tribal leaders. Chapter 28 and 29 conclude this main section (and the Davidic narratives as a whole) with further charges and prayers from David.[112]

---

109. Following Brettler, *The Creation of History*, 196–97. For a discussion of the history of modern discussion related to source-use in Chronicles, see Peltonen, "Function, Explanation," 18–69, especially 21–41.

110. This text is in keeping with the "re-focusing" of David in 1 Chronicles that emphasizes his role in instigating proper worship, so that, as one author aptly notes, "the historian recasts a vision of David's role to present him as the priest of praise, a founder and leader of a pattern the Chronicler believes will bring peace and wholeness to a community that is wrestling with new circumstances and shifting political boundaries." See Hoglund, "The Priest of Praise," 190.

111. Selman, for instance, agrees that chapter 22 appears to have "no obvious source in earlier biblical literature." However, he further argues that three separate strands of earlier OT traditions are "readily identifiable": (1) the Davidic covenant promise of 2 Samuel 7 (in vv. 7–10); (2) Moses' appointment of Joshua (Deuteronomy 31; Joshua 1)—serving as the model for the transition between David and Solomon; (3) general association with 1 Kings' presentation of Solomon. See Selman, *1 Chronicles*, 211–12.

112. See further Braun, "The Significance of 1 Chronicles 22, 28, 29," especially 10–99, 200–224.

The Levites, as mentioned earlier, come into focus in chapter 23 with an overview of their responsibilities (vv. 1-6), the traditional threefold list of their genealogical divisions (vv. 7-23), and finally, a more specific description of their duties as established by David (vv. 24-32). One of the key interpretive issues with this whole section concerns the compositional relationship of 23:3—27:34 (all the lists of duties) with the outer frame found in 22:2—23:1 and 28:1—29:26 (various charges, prayers, and narrative comments). Specifically, some commentators have considered the central lists of duties (chs. 23-28) as *additions* to the original text composed by the Chronicler (chs. 22, 28-29)—as certain tensions are perceived within the section itself and in relationship to other parts of Chronicles.[113] Conversely, as McKenzie notes, a number of other recent scholars are of the opinion "that if the Chronicler's compositional techniques are properly understood there is no need to see this section as secondary."[114] Still, as noted previously, writers who argue for compositional *unity* in this section also often contend that its *content* is mostly reflective of postexilic history.[115]

These matters arise very concisely when looking at 2 Chr 23:24-32. On the one hand, as McKenzie remarks further, "the duties of the Levites laid out in verses 25-32 are explicitly described as the result of a change in *historical circumstances* [during the Davidic monarchy]."[116] On the other hand, in certain approaches, ideological tensions are perceived within this text: between the claim that David modified the duties of the Levites

---

113. So, *first*, historical critics have often considered chapters 22 and 28-29 as original to the Chronicler and as his *own* creation. Such, for example, was the view supported by Curtiss and Madsen, who wrote, "[t]his chapter [22] is a free composition by the Chronicler, full of general and exaggerated statements, with a number of short quotations from earlier canonical books woven together," in their *A Critical and Exegetical*, 255. *Secondly*, chapters 23-27, in these views, are regarded as *secondary* to this free composition by the Chronicler. Note the concise discussion in Japhet, *I and II Chronicles*, 406-11. See Rudolph, *Chronikbücher*, 152-59; Noth, *The Chronicler's History*, 31-35—who argued that chapters 22-29 display "a rank growth of literary accretions" (p. 31). In contrast, a number of recent scholars argue for a compositionally cohesive understanding of this unit as a whole. See for example Boda, *1-2 Chronicles*, 179-223; Leithart, *1 & 2 Chronicles*, 71-96; Konkel, *1 & 2 Chronicles*, 220-55; or Merrill, *A Commentary*, 263-315.

114. McKenzie, *1-2 Chronicles*, 179. Such is the opinion of Japhet, *I and II Chronicles*, 409-10; and of Williamson, *1 and 2 Chronicles*, 157-59.

115. Note the related discussion in Wright, "The Legacy of David," 229-42; Wright, "The Origin and Function," 248-57. Wright defends the literary integrity of chapters 23-27 within the larger frame of chapters 22 and 28-29. However, he is more skeptical of the historical relationship of these passages to the Davidic monarchy, as he notes of 1 Chr 23-27, "this passage can tell us nothing concerning preexilic Israel or even early postexilic Judah." See Wright, "The Origin and Function," 252.

116. McKenzie, *1-2 Chronicles*, 180, emphasis added.

during the united monarchy and the "ideologies" of later literary strands (such as the sharp division between priest and Levite in "P," or the view of divine rest in "D").[117]

Therefore, this pericope presents significant data for a study of the historical dimensions of the Levites in the context of the Chronicler's historiography. In pursuing this type of investigation, the interrelationship of the literary, theological, and historical impulses of Scripture needs to be acknowledged.[118] Thus, a theistic and critically-realist approach to the text asks that the careful intermingling of historical reality and theological meaning be affirmed. In fact, it is rather unfortunate that historical criticisms have often been applied from the foundation of a modernist atheism—which is, arguably, fundamentally at odds with the communicative intent of Scriptural texts.[119] As noted earlier, Long has suggested that bringing criticism in line with a theistic approach should bear more interpretive fruit with a historiographic analysis. This is also in keeping with Moritz's argument—as he has written:

> For too long historical criticism has been dominated by atheistic ideological paradigms and movements. *What is needed is a critical realist cognitional theory that starts with an all-powerful loving God whose prime characteristic is his continued interest in creation as evidenced in his biblical self-disclosure.*[120]

And as Millard has noted further, "Israel's history cannot be fully comprehended without knowledge of her faith, nor can her faith be understood without a realistic portrayal of her history."[121] That is, the *historical* impulse

---

117. Note, for instance, the careful discussion in Knoppers, *I Chronicles 10–29*, 817–26.

118. Following the suggestions of Long, "Old Testament History," 95–96. And as Sternberg has commented, "[t]o gather up the threads, biblical narrative emerges as a complex, because multifunctional, discourse. Functionally speaking, it is regulated by a set of three principles: ideological, historiographic, and aesthetic. How they cooperate is a tricky question." See Sternberg, *The Poetics of Biblical Narrative*, 43, and 1–47 as a whole.

119. Philosophically, Abraham has argued that it is *permissible* to proceed as a thoughtful Christian scholar with a belief in divine intervention. See his *Divine Revelation*, 187–89.

120. Moritz, "Critical Realism," 149 (emphasis added). On a theoretical basis, see further Groff, *Critical Realism*, especially "Introduction," 1–24, and "Conclusion," 135–42. Groff, *Critical Realism*, 139, argues that the epistemological stance of critical realism enables the "knower" (1) to counter the challenges of relativism and anti-realism and (2) to ground the ontological roots of post-positivism. Note as well, Collier, "Critical Realism," 327–44; Finn, "What is Critical Realism," 19–28.

121. Millard, "Story, History," 64, and 60–64 as a whole.

embedded in an OT text should naturally bring forth a concomitant focus on its *theological* inclination. Even as Goldingay has noted concisely (and with a sense of balance regarding the relationship between historical enquiry and theological reflection), "the basic historicity of the events related in the Old Testament is important to the validity of its theology, and this is one reason why the study of Israelite history deserves investigation . . . (I do not know how much historicity is enough, but I know God does, and has looked after the matter.) [However], the study of Israelite history is an ancillary and supportive discipline like the study of philosophy."[122]

Furthermore, Fischer has noted that any proper historical analysis ought to begin with a carefully structured question. He suggests that six positive axioms should be followed to avoid common fallacies when framing a historical question: (1) it must be *operational*: resolvable on empirical terms (i.e., pertinent evidence [principally literary] should exist); (2) it must be *open-ended*, though focused: by being a genuinely interrogative statement, but also, by allowing to focus the inquiry through a potentially massive amount of relevant information; (3) it must be a *flexible* question—in the sense that it should acknowledge that certainty in the matter is probably not attainable, but *plausibility* might be: thus, it ought to be open to being "adjusted and amended, revised and ramified"; (3) it should also be adequately *explicit* and *precise*: for the purposes of this study, then, perhaps focused on a main issue raised from a specific biblical text; (4) finally, a good historical question can be *tested*: it should lay out a hypothesis that can be verified by means of relevant evidence.[123] On these bases, the following question will guide this section of the study: *is it plausible that the Chronicler's claim for the Davidic modification and expansion of Levitical duties in 1 Chr 23:24–32—which include musical duties—is based on reliable and preexilic traditions that preserved the witness of this early monarchic development?* Three lines of evidence and one set of key implications will be proposed in defense of an *affirmative* answer to this historical question.

First, the Chronicler's claim is plausible because the canonical form of the MT sustains such a reading. This entails that the argument will begin with a careful examination of the claims of the primary source of evidence—the pericope of 1 Chr 23:24–32—in context of chapter 23 as a whole, and of chapters 22 through 29, more generally. Consideration will be given to arguments of composition and literary structure in elucidating the historical dimension in this passage. Again, the presence of literary and rhetorical shaping should not necessitate the loss of historical reliability. As Millard has noted of the

---

122. Goldingay, "Old Testament Theology and the Canon," 7–8.
123. See Fischer, *Historians' Fallacies*, 38–39.

history-writer in the ANE, his "store of language, experience and imagination can all contribute to enriching the narrative *without smothering the reality of the events he describes or detracting from it.*"[124]

Second, the Chronicler's claim is plausible because contextual evidence from the Levant demonstrates the presence of a rich musical culture in various cultural and cultic contexts, *even before the time of David*. That is, this section of the argument will focus precisely on one aspect of David's development of the Levitical ministry: its musical, cultic function. One section of the pericope under investigation alludes to this ministry of praise (1 Chr 23:30–31, especially verse 30, which states the Levites were "to stand every morning, thanking and praising the LORD, and likewise at evening" [ולעמד בבקר בבקר להדות להלל וכן לערב]) and a subsequent text, in 1 Chr 25:1 (and the chapter as a whole) plainly emphasizes the musical aspect of the Levites' new temple duties, by also mentioning specific musical instruments (this verse states that David and service leaders set apart sons of Asaph, Heman, and Jeduthun for the service, "who prophesied with lyres, with harps, and with cymbals" [הנבאים בכנרות בנבלים ובמצלתים]). The musical and liturgical culture of the area of Syria-Palestine is quite rich from the Stone Age forward. However, for the purposes of this discussion, some of the basic evidence from the late Bronze Ages I (1550–1400) and II (1400–1200) and into Iron Age I will be highlighted.[125] From a maximalist perspective, David's reign is dated from approximately 1010 to 970, which places it within Iron Age IA (1000–900).[126] Following Long's discussion noted above, this evidence should provide appropriate *background* information sustaining the *plausibility* of the specific claim of musical expansion in the religious service of the Levites in 1 Chr 23:30 (and 1 Chr 25:1)—that is, the claim that David was at the origin of this musical expansion (in the early Iron Age).[127] In fact, Klingbeil has noted that when comparing Israelite religious practices (present in "P" and claimed to be late) with other such practices of the ANE, "[w]hat is clear ... is that important ritual elements found in

---

124. Millard, "Story, History," 49, emphasis added.

125. Following the standard archaeological periods as laid out, for instance, in Volkmar, *An Introduction*, 74–77 (and note there the slight dating variations for the archaeological periods among major scholarly traditions on p. 76). The discussions on the musical culture of late Bronze and early Iron ages will be based especially on Braun, *Music in Ancient Israel*, 67–188.

126. See Kitchen, *On the Reliability*, 82–83.

127. On the benefit of contextual analysis, see Hallo, "Biblical History," 3; Hallo, "Introduction," xxiii–xxviii.

the so-called Priestly source *cannot* be marked as 'late' in the context of the history of Israelite religion."[128]

Finally, and consequently, the Chronicler's claim is plausible because it makes good sense of key theological implications related to the significance of the Davidic monarchy and the establishment of the Solomonic temple. If the Chronicler is seeking to encourage his postexilic audience on the basis of God's *past* (preexilic) covenantal faithfulness, how do the claims in this pericope function *theologically*? Answers to these types of questions will represent a final set of implications sustaining a historical argument seeking to elucidate the *plausibility* of the preexilic roots of this section of 1 Chr 23.

The Biblical-Theological Aspect: Sacred Levitical Song in 1 Chr 16 and 25

The third methodological approach proposed for our investigation is that of biblical and OT theology (BT/OTT). Sections of 1 Chr 16:4-43 and 25:1-8 will serve as control texts for investigating certain theological dimensions evident in the ministry of Levitical *song*. First, in this section of the study, some of the central issues in the history and practice of BT and OTT will be briefly noted. Second, some of the theological issues specific to Chronicles and a method for approaching this theme will be presented.

For Vanhoozer, BT has been limited by two major challenges: the rationalistic separation of exegesis and theology, and the more recent pluralistic affirmation of ideological or "advocacy" approaches. The aim of a theological interpretation, however, ought to be the "criticism" of the reader by giving priority to God, who is the main subject of the text. Hence, reading theologically is to read biblical texts "as they wish to be read, and as they should be read in order to do them justice."[129]

Köhler, for example, once argued that the existence of God is an absolute given in the OT.[130] This type of focus, hence, calls for a reading concerned with God's revelation and engaged with some key aspects of the fields of BT and OTT. In our case, the discussion may proceed based on Scobie's initial definition of BT, which states, "[BT] ought to mean something

---

128. Klingbeil, "Historical Criticism," 413, emphasis added.

129. See Vanhoozer, "What Is Theological Interpretation," 20-21. See further for instance, Adam, *Reading Scripture*; Seitz, *Word Without End*, 3-112; Cummins, "The Theological Interpretation," 179-96; and more generally, note Fowl et al., *Reading Scripture*.

130. He wrote, "[d]aß Gott da ist, dieser Satz ist die große Gabe des Alten Testaments an die Menscheit." Köhler, *Theologie*, 1.

like the ordered study of what the Bible has to say about God and his relation to the world and to humankind."[131]

Biblical Theology in Old Testament Studies: Some Principle Issues

The field of OTT represents a broad discipline—historically and currently—as it is also an integral part of the field of BT.[132] Here, some of the major turn-

---

131. Scobie, *The Ways*, 4. For a recent and brief overview of OTT, note "Taking the Pulse of Old Testament Theology," in Boda, *The Heartbeat*, 1–8. After alluding to the interplay of diachronic, synchronic and, more recently, ideological approaches to OTT, Boda raises the key ongoing questions for this discipline when he asks, "Is there a way ahead? Can we speak any longer of a theology that lies at the core of the OT? Are our claims of theology merely perspectival projections, or can we identify something in these ancient texts that witnesses to some form of unity in the biblical corpus?" (p. 6). Boda represents a recent example of an OT scholar who, while recognizing some of the limits of own "situatedness," is nonetheless willing to pursue a constructive theological reflection. His method is a "selective intertextual-canonical approach that identifies core expressions of God that appear throughout the OT canon" (p. 7). The core divine expressions are "narrative" found in God's "historical action" (pp. 9–26), "character" found in God's "active character" (pp. 27–52) and "relational" aspects found in God's "relational identity" (pp. 53–76).

A helpful study of the broader field of BT may be found in Mead, *Biblical Theology*. Mead proceeds on the following definition of BT: "Biblical theology seeks to identify and understand the Bible's theological message, that is, what the Bible says about God and God's relation to all creation, especially to humankind." See Mead, *Biblical Theology*, 2.

For a further analysis of the field of biblical theology, note Klink & Lockett, *Understanding Biblical Theology*. This book "offers a fivefold taxonomy of how biblical theology is currently defined and practiced in an effort to offer substance and clarity concerning the elusive idea of biblical theology" (p. 25). Klink and Lockett define their spectrum of BT as (1) "historical description," with James Barr as the representative scholar (pp. 29–58); (2) "history of redemption," with D. A. Carson as the representative scholar (pp. 59–92); (3) "worldview-story," with N. T. Wright as the representative scholar (pp. 93–124); (4) "canonical approach," with Brevard Childs as the representative scholar (pp. 125–46); and (5) "theological construction," with Francis Watson as the representative scholar (pp. 157–82).

In the end, Klink and Lockett conclude, in part, that "[t]he longer that biblical theologies and biblical theologians speak past one another, the more quickly the term 'biblical theology' will become a nose of wax, so pliant it loses any sense of its own boundaries or form. *While we have offered proof that biblical theology is pliant, at least according to the five types we described, such descriptions also serve as proof that biblical theology does have its own boundaries and innate form. The academy needs to work hard to retrieve the substance of biblical theology, even if debate is allowed to remain in regard to the exact nature and outworking of that substance.*" Klink and Lockett, *Understanding Biblical Theology*, 185 (emphasis added).

132. For some studies of the history of OTT, note Brueggemann, *Theology*, 1–60; Hasel, *Old Testament Theology*, especially 10–27; Prussner and Hayes, *Old Testament*

ing points and key aspects of method can only be briefly highlighted.[133] The formal birth of a "BT" represents the first turning point. Indeed, OTT owes much to Gabler's call for a "discrete" study of the biblical text: one that was not, from the outset, guided by dogmatic presuppositions. The appropriate starting point for discussing BT and OTT, however, remains debated. In the sense of searching for an "inner unity" of Scripture, a biblical-theological impulse can certainly be detected with a number of pre-critical scholars.[134]

Nevertheless, the emergence of the modern field of BT is typically traced to Gabler's 1787 lecture, as a signpost anyhow, since he argued for the separation of a BT from dogmatic or systematic theology (ST).[135] To arrive at the "religion of the Bible," Gabler posited that one must exegetically decipher "sacred ideas," organize them by historical periods, differentiate between the historical-laden and the "truly sacred" ideas, and finally, evaluate any resulting universal notions. This was essentially rationalistic and historical: "true" biblical theology (objective historical data) was distinct,

---

Theology, especially chapters 2 (35–72), 3 (73–142), and 4 (143–218); and Lemke, "Theology (OT)," 448–73. For surveys of the field of BT, see Mead, *Biblical Theology*, 13–59; Reventlow, "Theology (Biblical), History of," 483–505; Rosner, "Biblical Theology," 3–11; Scobie, *The Ways*, 3–45, "History of Biblical Theology," 11–20; Childs, *Biblical Theology*, 1–94; Schuele, "Theology as Witness," 256–67. Note as well: Davidson, "The Legacy," 3–25; Merrill, "Archaeology and OT Theology," 667–78; Gericke, "Rethinking," 86–112; Krüger, "Recent Developments," 5–13; Schmidt, "Die Frage," 168–78; Hamilton, "The Problem of History," 197–211; Goldingay, "Old Testament Theology," 1–26; Seitz, "Canon, Narrative," 27–34; Strawn, "What Would (or Should)," 129–66. From a Jewish perspective, note Kalimi, "Models for Jewish Bible Theologies," 107–33; Rom-Shiloni, "Hebrew Bible Theology," 165–84. Note also Sweeney, "A Jewish Biblical Theology," 397–410.

133. For a succinct overview of developments in OTT up to the early twenty-first century, see Snyman, "Recent Developments," 1–8. For example, two recent German volumes of OTT still show (Snyman, "Recent Developments," 1) that "[t]here is a general agreement that Old Testament theology is about God." Fischer, *Theologien*, 13 (and as cited by Snyman, "Recent Developments," 1), writes, "[i]n der ganzen Bibel gibt es kein umfassenderes und bedeutenderes Thema als ihr Reden von Gott. Das gilt bereits für das Alte Testament, in dem Name Gottes, Jhwh, über 68 mal und Formen ‚Gott' weitere tausend Male genannt werden." And Jeremias, *Theologie*, 1 (and also as cited by Snyman, "Recent Developments," 1), equally notes "[e]ine Theologie des Alten Testaments (AT) zielt darauf ... die zentrale Gottesaussagen des Alten Testaments zu erheben." While the subject of OTT finds some agreement among scholars, the "how" to present OTT remains an ongoing debate. Note further Brueggemann, "Futures," 32–49; Brueggemann, "Theology of the Old Testament," 28–38.

134. So argues, for instance, Bartholomew, "Biblical Theology," 84. For developments prior to Gabler, note further, Rosner, "History of Biblical Theology," 11–20; Scobie, *The Ways*, 9–14; Childs, *Biblical Theology*, 30–52.

135. On further matters of definition between BT and ST, note Carson, "Systematic Theology," 83–104.

here, from "pure" biblical theology (focused dogmatic data).[136] Gabler thus sought to "free biblical study from the chains of church tradition and especially from the categories of dogmatic theology," which quickly led to the separation of OTT from NTT.[137] Scobie, for example, notes that Gabler was limited in his view of God and Scripture, though he still presented a way forward by insisting that BT must not *remain* descriptive.[138]

Throughout the nineteenth century, two main reactions to Gabler were evident: either an embrace of his rationalistic principles or, eventually, a more conservative reply, where OTT was conceived on the basis of inner theological coherence and of ultimate unity with the NT. Bauer was the first to write a complete work of OTT in 1796 and he followed Gabler with a critical search for "universally" true theological ideas.[139] Kaiser and de Wette were similar in their approaches, while Vatke further applied Hegel's historical dialectic.[140] Hengstenberg, however, represents an early conservative response to Gabler, since he emphasized biblical themes that carried through both testaments.[141] Also, with this latter type of response, the course of biblical history and the theological ideas of the OT remained closely linked; this was especially true with von Hoffman.[142] Still, many of these more conservative writers continued with certain aspects of Hegelianism; however, unlike Gabler, Bauer, and their followers, they also remained committed to the following elements: the divine inspiration of the Bible, the validity of the historical element in the OT, the congruence of the biblical text with the supernatural, and the synthesis of history and theology.[143]

---

136. See further Gabler et al., "J. P. Gabler," 133–58; Knierim, *The Task*, 495–556; Prussner and Hayes, *Old Testament Theology*, 2–5; Lemke, "Theology (OT)," 450; Reventlow, "Theology (Biblical)," 485.

137. So notes Vanhoozer, "Exegesis and Hermeneutics," 53.

138. Scobie, *The Ways*, 16.

139. Bauer, *Theologie*, 1–18 for the introduction (and the key statement on the relationship between God and man on p. 1; the work is divided following the main categories of "Theologie" [9–210] and "Anthropologie" [211–430]).

140. See Kaiser, *Die biblische Theologie*; De Wette, *Lehrbuch*; Vatke, *Die biblische Theolgie*, 2–13, 711–19. Vatke clearly argues that "biblische Theologie" ought to be a historical field of knowledge distinct from the teachings of the church and from dogmatics. Vatke, *Die biblische Theolgie*, 10.

141. See Hengstenberg, *Christologie*, 1–124, for example, for his study of messianic prophecy in the Pentateuch, and note also his *Geschichte*; and similarly, see Oehler, *Prolegomena*, 2–12 (p. 2 gives the definition of OTT as a "historical/genetic presentation of the Scriptural teachings of the OT contained in a religion of revelation"), note further his *Theologie des Alten Testaments*.

142. See especially von Hofmann, *Weissagung*, 1–12, 33–40, 153–99.

143. In line with Hayes and Prussner, *Old Testament*, 110–42.

This aspect of the field's history points to a key methodological issue. Should the focus be primarily on the text itself, or on the text as a witness to an *event* in history?[144] Wright, for example, later elaborated his OTT with a view towards the redemptive acts of God in *history*.[145] However, Perdue has argued that in many (more recent) examples of OT theologies, the situation of a particular community vis-à-vis the biblical text has taken on greater prominence than the relationship of the biblical witness to previous history.[146]

Further, the dominance of the "history-of-religions" school characterizes the *second* major turning point for OTT—one that took its cues initially from Wellhausen's work. Just as his *Prolegomena* had a dominating effect on the critical discussion of the priests and Levites (see chapter one of this study), so his critical views of the development of Israel's history (also proposed in his *Prolegomena*) came to govern much of the academic approach to OTT—at least for this period. In essence, Wellhausen argued that Israelite religion was initially rooted in Canaanite nature religion, evolved into an ethical monotheism prompted by the Israelite prophetic ministry, and further mutated into a more centralized monotheistic religion.[147] Finally, it arrived at the complex religious system led by the priests and Levites. For Wellhausen, each of these stages must be deciphered from the various sources underlying OT texts, theoretically.[148]

This understanding of the OT and its religion dominated, at least in academic circles, well into the early twentieth century (within the mode of historicism, as described above in this chapter). OTT was no longer conceived in terms of biblical-theological (or universal) classes, but in terms of historical categories.[149] OTT would, hence, be profoundly influenced by two fundamental aspects of Wellhausen's work: (1) the late date of the Pentateuchal priestly texts, and (2) the source-critical (Hegelian and Darwinian) reconstructions of Israelite religion.[150] A number of subsequent works

---

144. Following the discussion in Sailhamer, *Introduction*, 36–85.

145. Wright, *God Who Acts*, 13, 107 (and as cited in Sailhamer, *Introduction*, 36).

146. See further, Perdue, *The Collapse*, 1–24. Note also the chapter entitled "The Question of History, History of Tradition, Salvation History, and Story," in Hasel, *Old Testament Theology*, 115–38.

147. For a recent critique of Wellhausen's source criticism (and Gunkel's from criticism), see Kurtz, "Axes of Inquiry," 247–95.

148. See Wellhausen, *Prolegomena*, especially 1–10, 368–92.

149. Indeed, Hasel, *Old Testament Theology*, 23, has argued that 1887 (the year *Prolegomena* was first published) "marks the beginning of the triumph of the 'history-of-religions' (*Religionsgeschichte*) approach over OT theology."

150. Hasel, *Old Testament Theology*, 23. Note further Porteous, "Old Testament Theology," 312.

embraced this dominating historicism by basically dismantling: the unity of OT texts, the nature of their inherent theological message(s), the full-fledged salvation-historical relationship of the OT with the NT, and the connection between divine revelation and biblical text.[151] Scobie, for instance, has defined (with others) this development as a move from "theology" to "religion." He has also challenged the usefulness of such an approach for a *theologically* fruitful study of the canonical Scriptures.[152]

This second major stage in the history of OTT helps brings another ongoing methodological issue to the fore—that of the structure of OT theologies. Should theological reflection on OT (and biblical) texts be represented following a diachronic or a synchronic outline?[153] The labors of the "history-of-religions" school can be considered mainly diachronic in their structure, as can also, for instance, the later work of von Rad.[154] However, other OT biblical theologians have approached their task by more systematically elucidating the OT's teaching on God, on humanity, and on salvation and final hope—such as Jacob, Selling, or Köhler (see below). Hence, a number of biblical scholars have argued for the benefit of synchronically integrating OT materials—although an agreed-upon *means* for such integration can remain elusive or disputed.[155]

---

151. Several of these writers used the term "OTT" in their titles, while the study was following the history-religions format. This is true, for instance, of Stade, *Biblische Theologie*, 1–23 (which follows Wellhausen's "J, E and D" scheme in analyzing early Israelite religion) and Stade and Bertholet, *Biblische Theologie* 3–82, (which further assumes Wellhausen's late apparition of the cultic apparatus in "P," including the "ideal" religion of Chronicles [73–82]). Others engaged in a historical-critical study of Old Testament religion, such as Budde, *Die altisraelitische Religion*, 3–13, 47–52, 121–30, 148–56.

152. Scobie, *The Ways*, 21–22.

153. Also following the discussion in Sailhamer, *Introduction*, 185–94.

154. As Mead, *Biblical Theology*, 34, remarks on the history-of-religions movement, "[f]rom the late nineteenth century and well past the opening decade of the twentieth century, many biblical scholars adopted a perspective and methodology which came to be called the history of religions school. Building on the advances in historical research achieved by the long line of scholars who came before them, the representatives of this school studies the Bible not so much for its theological message as for what it could tell us about Israelite or Christian religion. Ascendancy of this movement was accompanied by a corresponding decrease in scholarly attention to biblical theology in any of its previous manifestations, be they rationalistic, Hegelian, or conservative in expression." See Mead, *Biblical Theology*, 35, goes on to argue that at least three major differences may be noticed between BT and history of religion (HoR) approached by the later nineteenth century: (1) Goal: BT is focused on theological content (rooted in the words of Yahweh and/or Christ) while HoR is focused on the religious beliefs and practices of the peoples of Scripture; (2) Method: HoR is developmental and comparative, in contrast to the final form/canonical approach of BT; (3) Purpose: HoR is essentially descriptive, while BT seeks to be normative.

155. Sailhamer, *Introduction*, 192.

This issue, then, also relates to the possibility of working out an OTT with a firm structural center or a dialectical one.[156]

Furthermore, the rebirth of a genuinely theological perspective represents a *third* major turning point in the field of OTT. Following World War I, a number of factors combined to rejuvenate the discussion regarding revelation in OTT—among them were: (1) a waning confidence in evolutionary naturalism, (2) an equally waning confidence in attaining pure scientific "objectivity," and (3) a resurging confidence in *revelation*, as elaborated in dialectical, neo-orthodox theology especially.[157] From the early 1930s through the 1960s, a number of biblical scholars sought to renew the quest to write a theologically focused OTT (albeit from different perspectives).[158] On the German scene, and beyond, the works of Eichrodt and von Rad came to dominate. Eichrodt wrote an extensive theology based on the organizing principle of "covenant."[159] Von Rad emphasized the basic historical *creeds* of Israel and the way they were then *re-formulated* throughout biblical history—even into NT times.[160] Other scholars also contributed to this (seemingly paradoxical) resurgence of a *theological* sensitivity in OT *theology*.[161]

On the North American side, as noted above, Wright accentuated the activity of God through salvation-historical categories, since he viewed OTT through the lens of history conceived as "event." Wright was an especially prominent scholar in the post-World War II "BT movement" in America, in which the theological character of the Bible was sought, biblical unity was emphasized, revelation was centered in history, static and rational Greek thought was contrasted to verbal and personal biblical thought,

---

156. Note the related discussion of certain biblical theologians below, and see further, "The Center of the OT and OT Theology," in Hasel, *Old Testament Theology*, 139–71; Schmidt, "The Problem of the 'Centre,'" 46–64; Ollenburger, "Discoursing," 617–28.

157. Following Dentan, *Preface*, 61–71. Note, for example, that Jacob begins his section on God's character with a discussion of Barth's concept of divine identity. See Jacob, *Théologie*, 23–24.

158. On this early period, note further the helpful analysis in Jacob, *Théologie*, 18–21.

159. See Eichrodt, *Theologie des Alten Testaments*, 188.

160. See von Rad, *Theology of the Old Testament I*, 3–94, for his basic approach. Note as well, von Rad, *Theology of the Old Testament II*, 319–429.

161. For other significant German OT theologies of this period note Sellin, *Theologie des Alten Testaments*, 1–3 (for the introduction; the work is structured in three parts: God in relationship to the world, Man and Sin, and Law, Salvation, Hope) and Procksch, *Theologie des Alten Testaments*, 1–47, 713–14; and (originally in Dutch), see Vriezen, *An Outline*, 12–38, 118–27, for key methodological statements.

and finally (against the history-of-religions school) the uniqueness of OT thought was strongly upheld.[162] This multifaceted movement was, eventually, criticized especially for its view of divine revelation in history, its de-emphasis of creation and wisdom traditions, its (claimed) overly-confident stance on reconstructing a history of Israel, and finally, its strong emphasis on a particularly *biblical* thought-world and, hence, its strongly perceived contrast between Hebrew and Greek thinking.[163]

This third major stage in the history of OTT highlights a further methodological issue in the practice of OTT: the relationship between biblical criticisms and the biblical canon.[164] First, a number of scholars continue to argue that OTT should be based on the results of the historical-critical study of OT texts: the sources, forms, and ideologies perceived in various literary layers ought to play a decisive role in the final theological construct.[165] However, other writers have focused more firmly on the canonical text: the locus of divine revelation is seen in the text itself or in the events referred to by the text.[166]

In fact, since about the 1970s, the expanding methodological diversity found in OTT represents a *fourth* major turning point. First, a number of writers have approached OTT on the basis of contrasted centering ideas. For instance, McKenzie argued for the centrality of the Israelite cult, Kaiser advanced the paradigm of a promise and fulfillment dialectic, and VanGemeren centered his BT on Jesus Christ, "the revelation of the salvation of God."[167] Terrien worked with the contrasting categories of divine presence

---

162. See Wright, *God Who Acts*, 33–35; Wright, *The Old Testament and Theology*, 55–58. And following Perdue, *The Collapse*, 22 (who is interacting with Childs, *Biblical Theology in Crisis*, 32–50).

163. Following Scobie, *Ways of Our God*, 24–25. Note also Childs, *Biblical Theology*, 11–29; Barr, *The Concept of Biblical Theology*, 1–61. On creation and wisdom in OTT, see for instance, Rendtorff, *Canon and Theology*, 92–113; and further, Perdue, *The Collapse*, 113–50.

164. Following Sailhamer, *Introduction*, 86–113.

165. Such is the view, for example, held in Gerstenberger, *Theologies*, especially 5–18.

166. Gerstenberger, *Theologies*, 113. Vos' method in *Biblical Theology*, 3–18, for example, emphasized the *historical* and *canonical* nature of biblical theology, as it traced the development of divine revelation through the Mosaic and prophetic (OT and NT) periods. Sailhamer emphasized the inherent nature of the canonical *text* as the locus of theological meaning. See Sailhamer, *Introduction to Old Testament Theology*, 36–85.

167. See McKenzie, *A Theology of the Old Testament*, 5–36; Kaiser, *Toward an Old Testament Theology*, 1–40; VanGemeren, *The Progress of Redemption*, 26 (and 17–41 as a whole).

and absence, while Westermann highlighted a different dialectic: that of divine judgment and divine mercy.[168]

Second, other scholars have adopted entirely different methodological structures—often guided by postmodern approaches to knowledge and interpretation.[169] The sociological theories of Gottwald and feminist approaches to biblical interpretation have influenced many of these expressions of OTT.[170] The critique of the BT movement also led to views of OTT that have been strongly dependent on creation theology and/or wisdom literature. And as noted above, still others have continued with more traditional historical-critical methods by pursuing multiple "theologies" within the OT.[171] Perdue has argued that in many of these approaches, traditional views of history (as event or tradition) have "collapsed" to give way to less referential views: where "history" is merely viewed in terms of myth, metaphor, or imagination.[172] A number of these stances may be gathered under Brueggemann's umbrella methodological statement, in which he asserts that OTT's "fresh" work must be "in reading texts always toward contemporary horizons, recognizing that reality is 'linguistic' as well as 'historical.'"[173] These approaches, which focus on the imaginative construct of the writer, stand in some contrast to a critically-realist epistemology.[174]

At the same time, several scholars have argued, at different levels, that the OT *canon* is the most appropriate basis on which to properly conceive of

---

168. Terrien, *The Elusive Presence*, 1–62, 161–226, 470–83; Westermann, *Elements*, 35–84, 118–52.

169. Note the related discussions in Perdue, *Reconstructing*, 1–24, 239–79, 340–52; Brueggemann, "Contemporary Old Testament Theology," 108–16; Martens, "The Shape of an Old Testament Theology," 5–15.

170. On sociological and liberation theory, see for instance Gottwald, "Sociological Method," 154–71; Gottwald, *The Politics of Ancient Israel*, 1–6, 32–112, 158–60, 246–52; Perdue, *Reconstructing*, 76–101; Ceresko, *Introduction to the Old Testament*, 3–28, 341–50. On feminist theology, note for example Trible, "Five Loaves and Two Fishes," 285–95; MacKenzie-Shepherd, *Feminist*, 3–12, 216–34.

171. See, most notably, Gerstenberger, *Theologies*, especially 5–18, 161–206, 283–306.

172. See further Perdue, *The Collapse*, 1–15. In this context, note especially Levenson, *Creation*; Trible, *God and the Rhetoric*, 1–59. In his conceptions of OTT, Brueggemann has adopted the imaginative constructs of "structure legitimation" and the "embrace of pain," and the metaphors of the courtroom drama (with Israel's testimony, counter testimony, unsolicited testimony, and embodied testimony) towards theological interpretation in a pluralistic context. See his *Old Testament Theology*, 117–44, 317–32, 407–12, 567–77, 707–20.

173. Brueggemann, "Editor's Foreword," in Perdue, *The Collapse*, x. Note, in contrast, the critique of this postmodern linguistic turn presented in Evans (above).

174. For instance, see the essay by Chapman, "Imaginative Readings," 409–47.

and construct an OTT. A few even, such as Childs or Scobie, have renewed the practice of a "whole" BT. In his volume on BT, Childs first looks at the main theological witness of the Old Testament, following canonical and salvation-historical lines of development, and then proceeds similarly with NT texts.[175] He then develops a thematic scheme (largely following a God-Humanity principle), where interlocking biblical topics are analyzed.[176] Rendtorff has also strongly argued that the Hebrew canon is the natural basis for developing an OTT.[177] Similarly to Childs (in structure), he first analyzes the flow of the Torah, Prophets, and Writings, before presenting an extensive discussion of relevant OT themes—as witness to Israel's religious "experience."[178] Moreover, with (Christian) canonical approaches to OTT, the question of how one relates the OT with the NT remains particularly acute.[179] As Goldingay argues, in part, in his reflection on the OTT and the canon, "Old Testament Theology considers the insight that emerges from the *form* of the Old Testament canon."[180]

In the end, the plethora of recent and current methods for OTT spans the epistemological spectrum. Postmodern, pluralistic approaches have particularly raised the question of validity in theological meaning—which draws attention to a final, and key, methodological point.[181] Should theological reflection on OT (and biblical) texts merely *describe*—either

---

175. See Childs, *Biblical Theology*, 95–106, 209–18.

176. Childs' earlier OTT first dealt with his canonical approach to OTT, and then discussed the Old Testament's view of the knowledge and revelation of God, the means of the relationship between God and Israel, and the benefits and responsibilities of Israel's covenant life. See Childs, *Old Testament*, 1–27.

177. See Rendtorff, *The Canonical Hebrew Bible*, 1–10. For other recent and canonically-driven (though still varied in the details of their approaches) theologies of the OT, see for example Goldingay, *Old Testament Theology 1*, 15–35, 859–83 (focused on narrative and story); Martens, *God's Design*, 3–36 (focused on the developments of God's promises from Exodus).

178. Note some of the key statements of theological synthesis in Rendtorff, *The Canonical*, 89–93, 157–66, 315–16, 413–14, 415–17, 717–39.

179. See further, for instance, Goldsworthy, "Relationship," 81–89; Baker, *Two Testaments, One Bible*, 19–33, 257–70; Goppelt, *Typos*, 1–22, 198–208; Seitz, *Figured Out*, 3–34, 193–202; Kuntzmann and Beauchamp, *Typologie biblique*; Legarth, "Typology," 143–55; Scobie, *Ways*, 88–91; Hasel, *Old Testament*, 172–93.

180. Goldingay, "Old Testament Theology," 2 (emphasis added). For a recent discussion of the positive interplay of literary approaches and the OT canon as the appropriate foundation for OTT, see Pereira, "An Evaluation," 303–14.

181. For some recent statements on theological method, note the views of Gese, Trible, Levenson, Sailhamer, Wittenberg, Barr, Moberly, and Brett in Ollenburger, *Old Testament Theology*, 377–496. For succinct discussion of the reasons for the explosion of methods in OTT, see Ollenburger, "Contexts," 377–80.

the historical religious situation perceived in the text, or, perhaps, the contemporary religious situation of a particular reading "community"? Or, may the process also *confess*—by affirming certain theological truths raised by a particular text, in relationship to NT and, even, current church contexts?[182] Stendhal strengthened the separation between a descriptive BT and a prescriptive ST by arguing that BT must relate to "what it meant," while only ST should seek out "what it means" (in line with Gabler).[183] BT, then, would only pursue what the text originally meant; it would only be the purview of ST (and not biblical scholars) to elucidate, in contemporary language and categories, what a particular biblical text might mean today for a particular community. However, the implications for biblical interpretation found in Stendahl's (Kantian) distinction between public and private values have been effectively criticized as overly limiting to BT.[184] The question of the final purpose of *biblical* hermeneutics arises, then. Ollenburger, for instance, has contended for a more cooperative role between BT and ST.[185] And Osborne, interestingly, has argued that the proper end of the biblical and theological interpretive task is the "sermon," the exposition and application of the biblical text in the context of the gathered people of God—which represents a distinctly confessional move from exegesis through BT and certain aspects of ST.[186]

182. For a constructive discussion of the elements of description and prescription in BT, note the essay by Reno, "Biblical Theology," 385–408. See also Moberly, "Theological Interpretation," 651–70.

183. Note Sailhammer, *Introduction*, 115–83; Hasel, *Old Testament Theology*, 28–38. And see Stendahl, "Biblical Theology," 418–32.

184. See especially Ollenburger, "What Krister Stendahl," 61–98. Note also Vanhoozer, "Exegesis," 54, who writes, "Stendahl appears to have translated Kant's distinction between public fact and private values into the practice of biblical interpretation, with fateful results. The impact on hermeneutics is no less damaging. Once one distinguishes between 'past facts' from 'present values,' how may one then relate them? Stendahl's distinction between 'what it meant' and 'what it means' opens up a rift in biblical interpretation and hermeneutics alike, for it is not at all clear how one can move from description of the past to present or future application."

185. Ollenburger, "Old Testament Theology," 81–103. For a recent exploration on the tensions between BT and ST, note Callahan, "Must Biblical," 1–26.

186. And also historical theology, see Osborne, *The Hermeneutical Spiral*, 5–16, 353–57. Similarly, note Kaiser, *Toward an Exegetical Theology*, 235–48; Kaiser, "Preaching from Historical Narrative," 439–546.

Biblical Theology in Chronicles: Approaching Levitical Song Theologically

From this broader perspective of the field of OTT/BT, the purpose of chapter five will be to synchronically explore the means by which, from aspects of 1 Chr 16:4-43, and also 1 Chr 25:1-8 and Ps 73 (as a further example of canonical Levitical hymnody), the Levites facilitate the *song* of God's people. To that end, some of the major theological themes in Chronicles will next be pointed out as a backdrop, two key works on Levitical song will be noted, and, finally, a specific method for exploring salient aspects of this theme of Levitical song will be laid out.

Based on the renewed interest in literary structure and theological meaning, scholars have more fully investigated the Chronicler's presentation of such key topics as God, humanity, sin and salvation, worship, and humanity's hope for the future. Some such earlier efforts can be seen, for instance, in essays by Myers, North, Goldingay, Ackroyd, or in fuller works by Brunet, Willi, Japhet, or Petter.[187] Several more recent contributions have further analyzed Chronicles from a number of biblical-theological perspectives.[188] Working on the basis of the canonical text as reliable Scripture, Thompson's theological synthesis of Chronicles is useful, so it will be followed here as a matrix for highlighting eight key theological themes in the book.[189]

First, scholars have noted the Chronicler's emphasis on "all Israel." The people of God include both the southern and northern kingdoms. This can be seen in the twelve-tribe focus of the genealogical introduction or in the effort at showing that all Israel supported David and Solomon (cf. 1 Chr 11:1 or 29:21-26).[190] That is, at least from the point of view of

---

[187]. See Myers, *I Chronicles*, lxiv-lxxxv; Myers, "The Kerygma," 259-73; North, "Theology of the Chronicler," 369-81; Goldingay, "The Chronicler as Theologian," 99-126; Ackroyd, "History and Theology," 51-55. And note Brunet, *La théologie*, 384-97; Willi, *Die Chronik als Auslegung*, 48-189 (on the Chronicler's theological interepretation); Japhet, *The Ideology*, 11-40 (for instance, for a study of the nature of God in Chronicles); and Petter, "A Study of the Theology," 162-254, for a discussion of major themes in the Chronicler's theology.

[188]. Of the large amount of literature produced more recently in this area, see, for example, Bell, "The Theology," 53-60; Kelly, "'Retribution' Revisited," 206-27; Ben Zvi, "The Book of Chronicles," 5-26.

[189]. See the section "8. Important Theological Themes," in Thompson, *1, 2 Chronicles*, 32-42. Similarly, see Pratt, *1 and 2 Chronicles*, 14-54.

[190]. For example, on the inclusive nature of the genealogical introduction in Chronicles, Jonker, *1 & 2 Chronicles*, 30, remarks, "[t]he strong indication of continuity with the past emphasizes Yahweh's faithfulness. It becomes clear from the genealogies that the Chronicler considered the history from Adam to David to be authored

God's promises, the unity of God's people is emphasized and centered on proper worship of Yahweh.[191] Second, the theme of temple and worship is an obvious and pervasive theme for all of Chronicles. On the basis of God's paradoxical presence at the temple in Jerusalem, all of the Davidic kings were to properly maintain the temple cult—this was a key measure of their fidelity to Yahweh.[192]

Third, the concept of kingship is also prevalent in Chronicles. The eternal nature of the covenant with David (1 Chr 17:11-15) shows that failed human kingship (acutely felt in the postexilic period) points toward an eternal and divine kingship—as rooted in the covenant at Sinai. On the basis of such biblical covenants, divine kingship provided hope for God's people.[193] Fourth, the dialectic of retribution and repentance represents another key element in the Chronicler's biblical-theological palette. Earnest seeking of God would be rewarded by God; forsaking the LORD would lead to rejection—though this is far from a mechanical theology overshadowing God's compassion (cf. 1 Chr 28:9; 2 Chr 7:11-22).[194]

Fifth, the *response* of God's people is also significant: they are to adopt the heart-attitudes of openness, willingness, and, especially, joy. The recurrent theological vocabulary in Chronicles is related: spanning the language of unfaithfulness, obedience, and divine response.[195] Sixth, some have adduced eschatological and messianic themes—especially in relationship to the ultimate

---

by Yahweh, the God of Israel. This theological emphasis would have readily found an audience in the changed socioreligious and sociopolitical circumstances of the Persian era. Those living in Yehud would be comforted to hear that Yahweh is steering history."

191. See further, for instance, "A. The Idea of All Israel," in Japhet, *The Ideology*, 267-307; Williamson, "The Concept of Israel in the Books of Chronicles," in Williamson, *Israel in the Books*, 87-140.

192. Note Kalimi, "Jerusalem, The Divine City," 185-205.

193. See further the comments in Thompson, *1, 2 Chronicles*, 36-37.

194. See, for example, Murray, "Retribution and Revival," 77-99; Dillard, "Reward and Punishment," 164-72. And as Boda, *1-2 Chronicles*, 17, argues, "[f]or the Chronicler, those who embrace this renewal experience blessing ... while those who reject it suffer curse. . . . Through this theme, the Chronicler sought to show his community how the power of renewal and faithfulness in the present circumstances but also to warn them of the potential damage for a community that rejects his call."

195. On the language related to God's people, see for instance the uses of: שמח (to rejoice) in 1 Chr 29:9; 2 Chr 7:10; לבב (heart) in 1 Chr 29:17, 19; 2 Chr 15:12; מָעַל (verb: act unfaithfully) in 1 Chr 5:25; 2 Chr 26:16; מַעַל (noun: unfaithful act) in 2 Chr 28:19; 36:14; הלך (to walk) 2 Chr 17:3; 20:32; כנע (to humble oneself) in 2 Chr 7:14; 12:6-7; פלל (to pray) in 1 Chr 17:25; 2 Chr 7:1; בקש (to seek) in 1 Chr 16:10-11; 2 Chr 11:16; שוב (to turn away) 2 Chr 15:4; 36:13. On key terms related to God's response, note the uses of: חסד (loyal love, loving-kindness) in 1 Chr 16:34; 2 Chr 5:13; 7:13; and the combination of שמע (to hear), סלח (to forgive), and רפא (to heal) in 2 Chr 7:14. Note further the uses of סלח in Solomon's prayer: 2 Chr 6:21, 25, 27, 30, 39.

fulfillment of the Davidic hope.[196] Seventh, typological patterning is also an important theological tool for the Chronicler—as a number of characters are related to earlier biblical figures; this is especially seen in the connection made between David and Solomon with Moses and Joshua.[197] This also concerns, finally, the Chronicler's exegesis of former biblical texts and his interpretation of Israel's past in light of a "postexilic present."[198]

This broader spectrum represents the appropriate basis from which to exegetically pursue *theological* aspects of Levitical service, since it stands as a corollary to the larger theme of temple and worship in Chronicles. From distinctly synchronic and biblical-theological angles, two scholars especially (as noted in chapter 1, Kleinig and Leithart) have explored key facets of Levitical *song* in Chronicles.[199] Kleinig's study stands as a broad analysis of the LORD's song (performed by the Levites) throughout the whole of Chronicles. Although Kleinig is not directly addressing historical questions, his work goes a long way in demonstrating how David can appropriately be regarded as the founder of Levitical song both in history *and* the biblical text. That is, Kleinig ably defends the cohesive and interlocking relationship of the following three elements: (1) that 1 and 2 Chronicles are faithful to earlier, "nascent" Pentateuchal principals of musical worship; (2) that David sets up a full Levitical choral ministry for the temple, which becomes the benchmark for such service with later Judean kings; and (3) that this entire liturgical tradition has a decidedly hopeful effect on the Chronicler's postexilic audience, precisely because it represents an *existing* tradition.

Kleinig's monograph, then, provides a helpful basis from which to explore, in more detail, certain canonical and biblical-theological implications related to Levitical song during David's kingship. After dealing with introductory issues, and assuming a canonical stance on the relevant texts for all of Chronicles, the major part of Kleinig's work concerns the *ritual* aspects of the Levitical choral rite: its nature as an institution, its various and sacred components, and its function as the LORD's song.[200] One of the

---

196. Note the views discussed in Kelly, *Retribution*, 135–55; Williamson, "Eschatology," 115–54.

197. See for instance De Vries, "Moses and David," 619–39.

198. Note the conclusion in Japhet, *I and II Chronicles*, 48. See further, Kalimi, *The Reshaping*, 1–17, 404–12.

199. See Kleinig, "Bach, Chronicles," 140–46; Kleinig, "The Divine Institution," 75–83; Kleinig, *The Lord's Song*, 13–27; and Leithart, "Attendants of Yahweh's House," 3–24; Leithart, "Embracing Ritual," 6–20; Leithart, *From Silence to Song*, 11–18.

200. See the conclusions to chapters 2, 3, and 4, in Kleinig, *The Lord's Song*, 62–63, 96–99, 129–32.

key aspects in this regard concerns the place of the musical ritual in the daily sacrificial service of the temple: it was performed before the altar for burnt offering in the inner court of the temple—under priestly supervision and with the principal function of prophetically announcing the presence of the LORD to his people.[201]

A final section of Kleinig's work deals with the theology of sacred song performed by the Levitical singers. The following issues are emphasized: (1) the Levites proclaimed God's name and his works as they praised him; (2) they acted as the LORD's prophets through the choral rite; (3) they evoked the glorious presence of the LORD at the temple and enabled a proper response for all those gathered; (4) they engaged in "supernatural warfare against the LORD's enemies"; and finally (5) "the nations of the world benefited and suffered from Israel's performance of sacred song."[202] Hence, in a theological sense, Kleinig concludes:

> Since the Chronicler holds that sacred song was instituted by the LORD himself to announce his presence with his faithful people and to proclaim his acceptance of them, J. S. Bach may be considered justified in having understood 1 Chron. 25 to be the foundation for all God-pleasing church music and in having used 2 Chron. 5.13 to assert that the ritual function of liturgical music was to proclaim the gracious presence of the LORD with his people in their worship of him.[203]

---

201. Note further the expanded conclusions on the ritual aspects of the Levitical choral rite in Kleinig, *The Lord's Song*, 185–89. For a whole Bible canonical exploration of biblical priestly theology, see Malone, *God's Mediators*, especially 13–124. In one of his conclusions, Malone, *God's Mediators*, 181 (emphasis added), affirms that "[t]he missionary God has always envisaged his name being worshipped in every place and in every language. It is in only one sense that, as God's worshipers grow in number and in variety, the number of vocational priests need to expand to accommodate this worship. Far more prevalent in a biblical theology of priesthood is the inverse observation that, at the key nexus where the new covenant reality extends the races invited to worship and eases their entry into the people of God, *the number of vocational priests necessary to facilitate this is reduced to one*." For some broader studies of the biblical theology of worship, see Block, *For the Glory of God*, especially 1–80; Ross, *Recalling the Hope*, especially 169–220.

202. See chapter 5 in Kleinig, *The Lord's Song*, 133–81, and the theological conclusions in 190–91.

203. Kleinig, *The Lord's Song*, 191. Note further, Kleinig, "Bach, Chronicles," 140–46. For a broader study of Bach and also, the biblical-theological aspects of musical liturgy, see for instance, Stapert, *My Only Comfort*, 7–11; and McGann, *Exploring Music*, 61–79, who, from a Roman Catholic perspective, reflects on various aspects of liturgy and musical worship—she argues that Christian worship music can be engaged as: theological-trinitarian, pneumatological, sacramental, biblical, ecclesiological, and eschatological.

Leithart's work, in turn, focuses on the peculiar liturgical situation present in 1 Chr 15–16, when, at the conclusion of chapter 16, the ark resides in Jerusalem and the Mosaic tabernacle continues to operate just northwest of Jerusalem, in Gibeon (before the sacred tabernacle furniture is reunited with the ark in the Solomonic temple, cf. 1 Kgs 8:1–11; 2 Chr 5:2–14). Leithart's goal is to explore the typological and theological significance of this temporary phase in salvation history—what he calls the "Davidic liturgical revolution."[204]

To these ends, he first demonstrates how the Chronicler's presentation of David in 1 Chr 15–16 shows him to be a faithful innovator of the pattern of Pentateuchal worship—thus moving the theological understanding of worship forward in salvation history.[205] This is seen especially in the Davidic function of priests and Levites—whose roles in the "revolution" both conform to, and build on earlier priestly teachings. Interestingly (from a NT typological perspective), Leithart also argues that the Obed-Edom of 1 Chr 15–16 is the same Obed-Edom the Gittite—a Philisitine—of 1 Chr 13:13–14. If true, he argues, this could stand as one of the OT precursors of Gentile inclusion into God's people and their worship—through the intermediary role of a "Davidic" ruler.[206]

Furthermore, an important point in Leithart's discussion is related to his observation that sacrificial ministry did not cease at the ark (while it continued at the tabernacle in Gibeon), but was *transformed* through the service of the Levites. He writes:

> Though no blood was shed, no altar erected, no smoke ascended, yet sacrifice was still taking place. The ark had ascended to its place; it is the beginning of the end. At such a moment, nothing is more natural than song ... *[T]he Levites begin to offer their bodies as living sacrifices, their voices ascending to Yahweh in a cloud of song.*[207]

Also, Leithart argues that the tent of David, encompassing the ark in Jerusalem during this transitional situation, was significant *theologically* in the development of Israel's worship. He further contends that it plays a key role *typologically* within a larger canonical perspective. Essentially, Leithart posits that the "booth of David" in Amos 9 refers to this temporary Davidic tent housing the ark—a passage that would promise a revival of choral worship related to "David's tent." The use of the Amos 9 prophecy

---

204. See Leithart, *From Silence to Song*, 11–18.
205. Leithart, *From Silence to Song*, 19–30.
206. Leithart, *From Silence to Song*, 31–52.
207. Leithart, *From Silence to Song*, 72, emphasis added, and see 53–72 as a whole.

at the Jerusalem council in Acts 15 would help tie the typological picture together. Leithart provides a tentative suggestion (based on this Christological interpretation of Amos 9:11–12) on the relationship of the Davidic booth and Christ himself: "[w]hen Jesus ascended to take the throne at the Father's right hand, He fulfilled what was pictured in David's enthronement in the ark-shrine. . . . Jesus is both the restored booth, and the one who sits as judge within it."[208]

Finally, based on the Reformed regulative principle of worship, Leithart offers a discussion of liturgical *hermeneutics*. This is related to the Christian application of Scripture to Christian worship and Leithart emphasizes *analogy*: seen in David's expansion of musical temple worship on the basis of an analogy between the Pentateuchal injunction that merely trumpets be used and the monarchical need for a larger musical service.[209]

On a theology of liturgical song, Leithart concludes (often in direct and positive interaction with Kleinig): (1) the fulfillment of the New Covenant in Jesus Christ invites the analogical application of Levitical song to the "New Israel" and her bursting forth in musical praise for Jesus, the "incarnate Yahweh;" (2) as the Levites performed "under the hand" of David (1 Chr 25:2), so should the body of Christ gather for worship and be united in song as Jesus offers praise to the Father (Heb 2:12)—thus, "the Greater David gives praise" *by the hand* of God's New Covenant people; (3) God's people may *seek* Him through song; (4) the song of God's people also memorializes Him; (5) Levitical song in Chronicles further shows how the song of God's people should proclaim the *glory* of the LORD; (6) aspects of the edification and empowerment of Levitical song may also be applied to New Covenant worship; (7) the qualifications of the Levites for their task is significant: they were skilled leaders who had a "good understanding of Yahweh" (2 Chr 30:21–22)—this should have implication for New Covenant worship; (8) liturgical song should, furthermore, *proclaim* the biblical message of mission—in line with the emphasis of Levitical song: the truth of Yahweh is preached and proclaimed; (9) an important aspect of New Covenant worship is, finally, to emphasize how *liturgical* song fulfills the yearnings of *Levitical* song—since New Covenant song ought to respond in thanks and praise to the proclamation found in the *final* Davidic victory of Christ's atonement.[210]

208. Leithart, *From Silence to Song*, 95, and note the broader discussion at 73–100 for the larger implications of this point.

209. Leithart, *From Silence to Song*, 103–5.

210. Leithart, *From Silence to Song*, 110–29, for the full discussion of these biblical-theological conclusions, and see further, Leithart, "Embracing Ritual," 6–20. For perspectives on music and song in the OT (and the Levant of the ANE) more generally,

These themes are all synthesized in Leithart's more recent theological commentary on Chronicles. For instance, on the musical function set up for the Levites by David in 1 Chr 25, Leithart observes both priestly and royal aspects. On the latter, he argues:

> Music is a royal activity. David the *king* organizes the Levitical choir and its orchestra. It is fitting business for David, sweet psalmist of Israel, harpist of Saul's court, inventor of musical instruments, whose hands fight with the sword while his fingers fight with the lyre . . . The link between music and kingship is not accidental. To sing, we have to rule our bodies and breath . . . To say God made Adam to make musicians is to say that God made Adam to produce priestly singers, royal musicians, and Spirit-mad prophetic chanters. God made us to make music and to be made by the music we make.[211]

Applying Biblical Theology to Levitical Song in 1 Chr 16 and 25

The two scholars discussed above have explored the theological implications of Levitical song within its presentation throughout Chronicles. They have also pointed to further canonical connections. In this phase of the study, we will seek to further root such discussion exegetically in 1 Chr 16 and 25—within the primary context of the Davidic narratives of 1 Chronicles—and then also synchronically expand into one example of a Levitical song, Asaphite Ps 73 in the biblical Psalter. The goal is to build on insights provided by the rhetorical and historical sections and further contribute to the type of analysis offered by scholars such as Kleinig and Leithart.

Also, the discussion of biblical theology to this point should enable the concise statement of several guiding principles of the particular approach envisaged for this section. First, the focus of the investigation, at this juncture, will be primarily *textual*. That is, the main data for the investigation will be the pericopes in 1 Chr 16 and 25, along with selectively related texts in the OT

---

see Mitchell, "Music in the Old Testament," 124–43; Tumbarello, "La Musica," 73–79; Dirk, "Cultic Music," 45–52; Braun, "Music and the Bible," 7–19; Braun, *Music in Ancient Israel*; van Dyk, "Music in Old Testament Times," 373–80; Burgh, *Listening to the Artifacts*; Shahar, "Women in the Bible," 97–115; Pilch, "Singing in the Bible," 38–43; Souza Nunes Wöhl Coelho, "Música," 231–38; Seidel, *Musik in Altisrael*; Music, "Musical Instruments," 51–55. More broadly, for brief discussions on OT aesthetics, note Loader, "Making Things," 100–14; Gillingham, "The Arts," 53–74.

211. Leithart, *1 & 2 Chronicles*, 82–83 (emphasis original).

and in the NT—especially Levitical Ps 73, as a further example of such Levitical song. Secondly, thus, the primary means of presentation for this theological examination will be *synchronic*. Particular themes will be discerned from these texts and analyzed in conjunction with one another.

Third, especially when elucidating the primary data from the biblical passages, the approach will be based on the final canonical form, rather than on theoretical reconstructions of compositional layers. Fourth, this study will also ultimately be taken up from a Christian, confessional theological perspective. The assumption is that these OT texts may ultimately contribute to a deeper understanding of new covenant Christian worship. When God's people are gathered, how might this theme of sacred Levitical song contribute to a more detailed understanding of musical worship and service? Kleinig has suggested that further study of the relationship between this OT theme in Chronicles and its implications for the NT is needed. Specifically, in his conclusions, he suggests exploring the way the NT presents Jesus as the replacement of David in becoming the new leader of *praise* in the New Testament. On this, he writes:

> Just as David had given his words to the Levitical singers in 1 Chron. 16.7–36 for them to use in praise, so the word of Jesus is said in Col. 3:16 to provide the content of the songs sung by his disciples in their instruction and encouragement of each other.[212]

Overall, an overarching method similar to that of Scobie's is proposed for this section. This author has produced an extensive biblical theological study based on a canonical view of Scripture and a proclamation/promise and fulfillment/consummation methodological scheme. He structures his study following an overarching outline that moves from God's *order*, to God's

---

212. See Kleinig, *The Lord's Song*, 185. And note similar issues discussed in Leithart, *From Silence to Song*, 121–29. Block, in fact, draws a parallel between the order, glory, and praise of the Levitical worship musical choirs set up by David, and the need for such characteristics in NT Christian worship. See "Music as Worship," in his *For the Glory of God*, 221–45. For a broader and engaging study by a musicologist on the nature of music in human society in general, see Small, *Musicking*. In the introduction to this study, Small argues that "music is not a *thing* at all but an *activity*, something that people *do*. The apparent 'thing' music is a figment, an abstraction of the action, whose reality vanishes as soon as we examine it at all closely" (emphasis added). Small, *Musicking*, 2. He goes on to coin the noun "musicking" and the verbal idea of "to music," which he defines as "[t]o take part, in any capacity, in a musical performance, whether by performing, by listening, by rehearsing or practicing, by providing material for performance . . . or by dancing" (emphasis original). Small, *Musicking*, 9. An interesting question for our purposes might be, "to what extent do the Levites in the OT enable the people of God to engage in 'musicking' and what are the theological implications of that activity?"

servant, to God's *people*, and to God's *way*.²¹³ Scobie develops these main themes with a variety of interlocking sub-themes, by: (1) synthesizing the aspects of proclamation and promise for relevant OT texts, and (2) discussing NT passages related to the sub-theme following the categories of fulfillment and consummation. For instance, with the overarching theme of "God's way," Scobie notes: (1) the OT *proclaims*, in the Torah, Prophets, and Writings the way of Wisdom as the means of achieving blessing in life; however, (2) Israel's repeated disobedience leads to a better understanding of human sin and also, to the *promise* of a new type of life in a new age to come; thus, (3) these latter promises find *fulfillment* in the new way pointed to by Jesus; (4) this new life can be experienced to a certain extent in the present, but only fully in the final *consummation*.²¹⁴ In this way, Scobie's overarching structure of BT is shaped according to the pattern in table 1 below.²¹⁵

Old Testament		New Testament	
Proclamation	Promise	Fulfillment	Consummation
God's Order	A New Order	The New Order	The Final Consummation
God's Servants	A New Servant	The New Servant	The Final Consummation
God's People	A New People	The New People	The Final Consummation
God's Way	A New Way	The New Way	The Final Consummation

Table 1: The Structure of Scobie's BT

In this scheme, public worship falls under the rubric of "God's people." The OT cult is examined, followed by the NT view of worship, and finally, a synthetic discussion of Christian worship is included. This allows Scobie to deal with contemporary "prescriptive" matters (such as the manner of baptism, or of Sabbath observance for Christians in light of *both* OT and NT witnesses).²¹⁶ Thus, he counters the argument that his method might

---

213. Scobie, *Ways*, 93–99.

214. Scobie, *Ways*, 98.

215. Scobie, *Ways*, 99. And note further the study of Scobie's method in Möller, "The Nature," 41–64.

216. Scobie, *Ways*, 567–612.

undervalue the "rich diversity of the biblical witness," by maintaining "that it is precisely a canonical BT that will seek to do justice to the whole sweep of biblical thought."[217]

Old Testament		New Testament	
The *Proclamation* of Sacred Song	The *Promise* of Sacred Song	The *Fulfillment* of Sacred Song	The *Consummation* of Sacred Song

Table 2: Sacred Song and BT

On this basis, the theological section, in chapter five of our study, will be worked out by generally applying Scobie's structural scheme to the topic of sacred Levitical song rooted in chapters 16 and 25 of 1 Chronicles, and also, by exploring one other further Levitical psalm (Ps 73). Accordingly, these two broad following steps are envisaged: (1) an analysis of the psalm in 1 Chr 16, as an example of the "proclaimed" aspects of Levitical song; and (2) an analysis of Ps 73, as an example of a Levitical psalm displaying the features of the "promised" aspects of Levitical song.

217. Scobie, *Ways*, 99.

3

The Rhetorical Aspect of 1 Chronicles 15:1—16:3

The Levites and the Symbol of God's Presence

THIS STUDY'S THESIS STATES that aspects of 1 Chr 15, 16, 23, and 25 contribute cohesively to the rhetorical argumentation, the historiographic method, and the biblical-theological meaning of the canonical books of Chronicles, generally, and the Davidic narratives of 1 Chr 10-29 more specifically (the Davidic kingship narrative—hereafter cited as the DKN), as they emphasize the central role played by proper Levitical worship leadership at the time of David *and* for the challenging situation of the Chronicler's postexilic audience.[1]

Moreover, the previous chapter sought to establish some of the appropriate methodological parameters for fleshing out this thesis. We may, then, move to the first step in the exegetical argumentation proper—that of presenting a rhetorical-critical reading of the biblical text relating the entry of the ark into Jerusalem in 1 Chr 15-16. As detailed earlier, this segment of the exegesis will be structured according to the following sections: (1) detailed textual observations will first be made; (2) a methodical literary and rhetorical critical analysis of 1 Chr 15:1—16:3 will follow (focused on this first section of the ark procession narrative itself—hereafter cited as the APN1);[2] (3) in conclusion, the ensuing rhetorical emphases of the APN1 will

---

1. In this section, 1 Chr 10:1—22:1 will be cited as the "DKN1" (the first major literary segment of the Davidic kingship narrative) and 1 Chr 22:1—29:30 will be cited as the "DKN 2" (the second major literary segment of the Davidic kingship narrative).

2. The Ark Procession Narrative as a whole (chs. 15–16) will be cited as the "APN." The first segment in 15:1—16:3 will be cited as the "APN1," while the second segment in 16:4-43 will be referred to as the "APN2."

be summarized. The argument in this chapter posits that the APN1 displays a coherent rhetorical message in relationship to the DKN1.

1 Chr 15:1—16:3: Translation and Rhetorical Unity

The aim of this first major section is to provide a carefully established textual basis and a proper literary context on which to build a more focused rhetorical analysis. Hence, a translation will first be presented with relevant textual notes. Some remarks on the setting of the APN1 within the DKN1 will follow. Finally, some basic comments on the relationship of this text with 2 Samuel 6 will be given.

Text and Translation

The translation will be provided following five distinct units. The justification for these unit divisions will be explained throughout the ensuing exegetical analysis.

Unit A: 1 Chr 15:1–3

1. When he [David][3] built houses for himself in the city of David, he prepared[4] a place[5] for the ark of the LORD and pitched a tent for it. 2. Thereafter, David said, "No one may carry the ark of God except the Levites, for the LORD chose them to carry the ark of the LORD[6] and to minister to

---

3. MT reads ויעש־לו בתים בעיר דויד, where the noun "David" is not expressed as the subject of ויעש. It is, however, implied in the flow of the argument in chapter 14. The previous sentence in 14:17 includes a statement summarizing the growing fame of David. The grammatical subject of this immediately preceding verse is David: ויצא שם־דויד בכל־הארצות. For further discussion, note Japhet, *I and II Chronicles*, 296–97, who remarks that the subject of the text in 1 Chr 15:1 is clear, although "its phrasing in the MT is not."

4. Following the MT, which reads וַיָּכֶן (from כון), and which is reflected in the LXX reading of ἡτοίμασεν. A number of other Hebrew manuscripts, as well as the Syriac and the Vulgate read or reflect וַיִּבֶן (from בנה), "and he built." Note further Knoppers, *I Chronicles 10–29*, 604–5.

5. Boda, *1-2 Chronicles*, 138, argues that the term "'place' (*maqom*) . . . is a key leitmotif in Chronicles for the location that God showed David for the temple site (21:22, 25) and where Solomon built the sanctuary."

6. A number of Hebrew manuscripts read here "the ark of God" (האלהים, not יהוה)—most likely as an attempt to concur with the earlier mention of the phrase (ארון האלהים) in verse 2. Also, the phrase את־הארון לשאת in the MT (v. 2b, its second

him forever." 3. David then assembled all Israel to Jerusalem to bring up the ark of the LORD to its place, which he had prepared for it.

Unit B: 1 Chr 15:4–17

4. And David gathered the sons of Aaron and[7] the Levites: 5. of the descendants of Kohath, Uriel the officer and 120[8] of his kinsmen[9], 6. of the descendants of Merari, Asaiah the officer and 220[10] of his kinsmen, 7. of the descendants of Gershon[11], Joel the officer and 130[12] of his kinsmen, 8. of the descendants of Elizaphan, Shemaiah the officer and 200[13] of his kinsmen, 9. of the descendants of Hebron, Eliel the officer and 80 of his kinsmen, 10. of the descendants of Uzziel, Amminanab the officer and 112 of his kinsmen. 11. David then called for Zadok and Abiathar, the priests, and for the Levites—Uriel, Asaiah, Joel, Shemaiah, Eliel, and Amminandab—12. and said to them, "You are the heads of the fathers' houses of the Levites. Consecrate yourselves, you and your kinsmen, so that you may carry the ark of the LORD, the God of Israel, to (the place)[14] I have

---

occurrence) is omitted in certain LXX versions, probably due to homoioteleuton between יהוה and יהוה. In other LXX versions, the phrase appears as αἴρειν τὴν κιβωτὸν. See further Knoppers, *I Chronicles 10–29*, 605.

7. LXXB (codex Vaticanus) omits the copula (a similar omission occurs in 1 Chr 13:2), to read "the Levitical sons of Aaron." In this reading, the distinction between the Aaronides Levites and the non-Aaronides Levites is not made.

8. Here, following the MT (מאה ועשרים). LXXBS (Vaticanus and Sinaiticus) read "110."

9. Translating אח as "kinsman." See further Hamilton, "אָח," 343–44.

10. Again, following the MT (מאתים ועשרים). LXX reads "250."

11. The MT reads גרשום ("Gershom"). LXXN (Basiliano Vaticanus) reads Γυρσον and LXXL (Lucianic recension) reads Γνδσον (with a confusion of ד and ר). The NIV, for instance, translates with the more typical "Gershon," (see the common spelling in 1 Chr 5:27; 23:6), while the RSV or the ESV preserve the MT's "Gershom."

12. For the MT's מאה ושלשים ("130"), a few other Hebrew manuscripts read מאתים ושלשים ("220"). LXX reads "150."

13. One Hebrew manuscript reads "80" (שמנים).

14. A number of textual witnesses (a few Hebrew manuscripts, Syriac, Targum, Vulgate, and Arabic) have attempted to clarify the MT's cryptic expression of אל־הכינותי לו (the relative pronoun seems to be missing) by reading אל־מקום אשר הכינותי לו, "to the place I have prepared for it." *BHS* suggests inserting 'ה האהל instead, to read "to the tent I have prepared for it." Some commentators follow this emendation, such as Williamson, *1 and 2 Chronicles*, 124. Most English versions supply "to the place," as in the NIV, ESV, or RSV. Knoppers, *I Chronicles 10–29*, 606, basically follows the versions here, but also notes that in BH, the relative particle can be omitted and the preposition may also precede the verb, as in 1 Chr 29:2 or 2 Chr 1:4.

prepared for it. 13. Because you did not carry it[15] the first time,[16] the LORD our God broke out against us—because we did not seek him according to the legal specifications."[17] 14. So the priests and the Levites consecrated themselves to carry the ark of the LORD, the God is Israel. 15. And the Levites carried the ark of God, as Moses had commanded according to the word of the LORD, by means of[18] poles[19] on their shoulders.

Unit C: 1 Chr 15:16–25

16. David also instructed the chiefs of the Levites to appoint their kinsmen (as) the singers, to loudly play with instruments of music—harps, lyres, and cymbals—by raising a joyful sound.[20] 17. So the Levites appointed: Heman, son of Joel; and from his kinsmen: Asaph son of Berechiah; and

---

15. This note and the following note are related. Here, the MT cryptically reads למבראשונה לא אתם (reflected in LXXB ὅτι οὐκ ἐν τῷ πρότερον ὑμᾶς). A number of scholars have argued that the MT originally read לא אתם נשאתם, where נשאתם has been dropped by haplography (due to the repeated ם). See for instance Klein, *1 Chronicles*, 345. Most recent English versions (such as the NIV, ESV, or RSV) reflect this emendation with a form of "because you did not *carry* the first time." The NKJ, however, supplies a different verb, with "for because you did not *do* it the first time." BHS suggests adding אִתָּנוּ, to read לא אתם אתנו.

16. As seen in note 15 above, the MT's לְמַבָּרִאשׁוֹנָה is something of a vexing construction that seems to conflate למה ("why") with בראשונה ("at the first"). BHS suggests reading, along with a few Hebrew manuscripts, לְמִבָּרִאשׁוֹנָה, which would conflate למן ("since") and בראשונה and read "since at the first time." Japhet suggests the initial למ- prefix represents a textual corruption, so that one should simply read בראשונה, "at the first." See Japhet, *I and II Chronicles*, 301. Knoppers, *I Chronicles 10-29*, 606, notes that LXXB reads ὅτι οὐκ ἐν τῷ πρότερον ὑμᾶς εἶναι ("because you were not at the former occasion"). Most English versions follow a combination of Japhet's type of emendation and the Septuagint's reading, such as the RSV: "because you did not carry it the first time."

17. Following Enns, "מִשְׁפָּט," 137–38. Evans, "Let the Crime," 73, notes that in this verse, "David explains that the failure to have Levites [carry the ark] was the reason that YHWH's anger 'burst out' (פרץ) against them (clearly referencing the death of Uzzah in 1 Chr 13:11)."

18. Reading the preposition in במטות as an instrumental ב.

19. For the MT's בכתפם ("on their shoulders"), LXX reads κατὰ τὴν γραφήν ("according to the Writings/Scriptures"), which BHS suggests reflects the different Hebrew reading of בכתוב. Most commentators and English versions are disinclined to follow this emendation—such as the ESV or Japhet, *I and II Chronicles*, 301-2.

20. For the MT's בקול לשמחה, BHS suggests deleting the preposition ל on שמחה, for reason of dittography with the previous ל. Several earlier commentators followed this emendation, such as Rudolph in his commentary, who was also the BHS editor of Chronicles. See Rudolph, *Chronikbücher*, 116, or more recently Klein, *1 Chronicles*, 345. Knoppers, *I Chronicles 10-29*, 607, notes, however that the ל preposition can denote mode or manner.

from the sons of Merari, their kinsmen: Ethan son Kushaiah²¹ 18. and with them their brother of the second rank: Zechariah,²² Jaaziel,²³ Shemiramoth, Jehiel, Unni, Eliab,²⁴ Benaiah, Masseiah, Mattithiah, Eliphelehu,²⁵ Miqneiah, Obed-Edom, Jeiel,²⁶ and Azaziah—the gatekeepers;²⁷ 19. the singers—Heman, Asaph, Ethan to sound the bronze cymbals; 20. Zechariah, Uzziel, Shemiramoth, Jehiel, Eliab, Maaseiah, Benaiah with harps

21. LXX reads Κισαιου for the MT's קוּשָׁיָהוּ. A similar contrast of readings between the LXX and the MT also exists at 1 Chr 6:29 (MT).

22. Here, MT adds בֶּן with וִיעֲזִיאֵל. This additional word "son" clashes distinctly with the listing of these Merarite Levites (none of the other names in the verse are preceded by בֶּן). Furthermore, a few Hebrew manuscripts do not have this additional בֶּן and neither it is reflected in the LXX. On this basis, most commentators and current versions do not translate this noun, following the suggestion of *BHS*. See, for instance, Klein, *1 Chronicles*, 345; and the RSV, NIV, or ESV.

23. The MT reads יַעֲזִיאֵל ("Jaaziel"), while the LXX versions read Οζιηλ. Some commentators prefer "Uzziel" in English, based on a dittography in Hebrew; a similar contrast occurs of readings in 1 Chr 15:20 between the MT and LXX witnesses. See, for instance, Knoppers, *I Chronicles 10–29*, 607; Klein, *1 Chronicles*, 345. Most current versions, however, keep the MT's reading of this name (such as the ESV, NIV, or NRSV).

24. While in the Hebrew text each of the proper nouns in this verse is preceded by the ו conjunction, the ו is missing in the MT with אליאב (a parallel issue exists in verse 20 of this chapter). Several Hebrew manuscripts, the LXX witnesses, and the Syriac version all reflect the presence of the coordinating conjunction. *BHS* suggests adding it in Hebrew. This is followed by recent studies such as Knoppers, *I Chronicles 10–29*, 608, and Klein, *1 Chronicles*, 345. The implications for the English translation are minor.

25. Following the spelling of the MT (אֱלִיפְלֵהוּ). Certain LXX versions read καὶ Ελιφαλια, which leads *BHS* to posit emending the Hebrew spelling to אֱלִיפָלָה (based on a perceived dittography between the ו of the next clause). Knoppers, *I Chronicles 10–29*, 604, follows the LXX. Most English versions follow the MT (see RSV or ESV).

26. Here, the LXX adds καὶ Οζιας. *BHS* suggests adding here וַעֲזַזְיָהוּ, which is present in verse 21. The English versions do not follow this emendation.

27. *BHS* suggests that the MT's השערים ("the gatekeepers") is a later gloss, which needs to be deleted. English versions do not follow. This issue is related to the overall discussion of the composition of this chapter—especially for those adopting historical and literary critical approaches. Dirksen, for instance, notes that scholars operating in this vein argue, in various ways, that *four* sets of texts are *later* additions to the original version of the Chronicler's account. These texts are: (1) verses 4–10 (the initial roster of Levites gathered by David); (2) verses 16–24 (the roster to the Levitical musicians and their duties); (3) the mention of (Aaronides) priests in verses 4, 11, 14, and 24; (4) the mention of the gatekeepers in verses 18, 23, 24. For a discussion of the relevant views, see further Dirksen, *1 Chronicles*, 206–8. Knoppers, *I Chronicles 10–29*, 604, 608, reads all of verse 18 as referring to gatekeepers in general.

according to *alamoth*;²⁸ 21. Mattithiah, Eliphelehu,²⁹ Miqneiah, Obed-Edom, Jeiel, and Azaziah³⁰ to lead with lyres according to *sheminit*;³¹ 22. Cheneniah,³² officer of the Levites for music, to direct³³ the music,³⁴ for he

28. *BHS* suggests emending the MT's אל־עלמות to עֲלָמִית ("in the Elamite way"). The meaning of the MT is obscure, but the emendation seems unnecessary. Knoppers suggests it could mean "set to the voice of young women," deriving from the Hebrew phrase for "young woman" (עַלְמָה, *BDB* 761, lists 1 Chr 15:20 as an occurrence [which are few in total] and defines the phrase as "to [the voice of] young women, either lit., or of soprano or falsetto boys;" *HALOT-SE* 835–36, lists the principal meanings of this term as "marriageable girl," "a girl who is able to be married," or "a young woman;" 1 Chr 15:20 is also listed with the על preposition of which the clear meaning is uncertain, but "in the style of young girls, soprano" is proposed; *HALOT-SE* also notes that Mowinckel argued the term was related to עלם [to conceal]). Musically, this *could* then be alluding to a higher pitch of playing (in the mid to high range), while the "Sheminith" (שמינית) which can be seen as deriving from the Hebrew for "eight," *could* be referring to a lower range of playing—that is the lyres, in verse 21 would be played at an octave below the harps of verse 20 (*BDB* 1033, lists the basic meaning as "eight" and also lists 1 Chr 15:21 as an example, and further suggests "according to the eight key," or "on the octave" as possible but, in the end, "dubious" meanings). See further *HALOT-SE*, 1562, which lists 5 possible meanings for the phrase על־שמינית: (1) on an instrument of eight strings; (2) the eighth string of an instrument; (3) in contrast to על־עלמות, meaning "lower octave;" (4) Mowinckel, again, suggested the term referred to the eighth and concluding ceremony of an autumnal new year festival; (5) some have also argued the term is gentilic, referring to the Canaanite city of שִׁמְרוֹן. In the context of 1 Chr 15, which is discussing the musical service of certain Levites, options 1, 2, and 3 seem the most plausible. If the term does refer to the lower-octave pitch of playing, this would suggest a careful, harmonious and organized musical performance. For further discussion, see Knoppers, *I Chronicles 10–29*, 608–9; Japhet, *I and II Chronicles*, 303–4. Note also that the terms appear in a few psalm titles: עלמות in Ps 46:1 (a Levitical Korahite psalm); שמינית in Ps 6:1; 12:1 (both Davidic psalms).

29. See note 22 above for an LXX variant.

30. For this name, the MT reads עֲזַזְיָהוּ; two Hebrew manuscripts read עֲזִיָּהוּ, perhaps in parallel to the LXX's καὶ Ὀζίας.

31. See note 28 above.

32. The MT reads וּכְנַנְיָהוּ. The LXX and the Vulgate reflect a Hebrew reading of וְכֹנַנְיָהוּ. A few Hebrew manuscripts read וּבְנָיָהוּ. Also, MT adds במשא after שר־הלוים, possibly because of a dittography on the same clause later in the verse, but the MT still makes sense, if one allows for a bit of repetition. In the Vulgate, this phrase is rendered "Cheneniah had the duty to *chant the melody*" (. . . ad praecinendam melodiam).

33. For the MT's יָסַר ("to discipline"), a few Hebrew manuscripts read יָשַׂר (based on the root שׂרר, "to lead, to have authority") and this is also reflected in the LXX, Targum, and Vulgate.

34. The first במשא is not reflected in the LXX, and the second one is translated as τῶν ᾠδῶν, "of the songs/odes." The Vulgate understands this as a prophetic activity (*prophetiae* [praarat]). Knoppers notes that במשא can be translated in one of three ways: (1) "in the porterage," based on the verb נשא; (2) "with the oracle," following the allusion in the Vulgate; (3) "in music" following the LXX. Although the translation here follows the majority of English versions (such as the NIV, ESV, RSV, or NRSV),

understood it;³⁵ 23. Berechiah and Elkanah—gatekeepers of the ark; 24. Shebaniah, Joshaphat, Nethanel, Amasai, Zechariah, Benaiah, and Eliezer, the priests—sounding³⁶ the trumpets before the ark of God; Obed-Edom and Jehiah—gatekeepers for the ark.

Unit B': 1 Chr 15:25–29

25. So David, together with the elders of Israel and the officers of the thousands, went forth³⁷ to bring up the ark of the covenant of the LORD from the house of Obed-Edom with rejoicing. 26. And as God helped the Levites who were carrying the ark of the covenant of the LORD, they sacrificed seven bulls and seven rams. 27. David was clothed in a robe of fine linen, as were also all the Levites who were carrying the ark, and the

---

Knoppers' point (as he chooses the *first* translation) is well taken. He notes that most opt for the third translation, based on the immediate context of Levitical music, but for him this still "ignores the larger context (15:1–5, 25–28) and presents a false choice of Levitical duties as either singers or porters. Clearly, the situation is both/and, not either/or. The whole purpose of David's appointing the Levites is, among other things, to transport the Ark. In Chronicles the Levitical duties include carrying the Ark, gatekeeping, and music." On this, see Knoppers, *I Chronicles 10–29*, 609; and also Japhet, *I and II Chronicles*, 305–5. This is also seen in BDB 672–3, which lists משא in relationship to the verb נשא. For משא, three basic glosses are given (the first two being the more common for this somewhat rare word in the OT): (1) load, burden, lifting, bearing, tribute; (2) utterance, oracle; (3) lifting up.

35. This verse presents some interesting variations, then, in the versions. The LXX reads, more succinctly: καὶ Χωνενια ἄρχων τῶν Λευιτῶν ἄρχων τῶν ᾠδῶν, ὅτι συνετὸς ἦν ("and Cheneiah *was* the leader of the Levites of the songs/odes, for he possessed understanding [συνετὸς]"). In the Arabic Polyglot, the text can be translated as: "and the elders (literally, 'the big ones') of the Levites were taking turns every day, because they had fixed places" (based on Walton's Latin translation: "Principes Levitarum alternis utebantur fingulis diebus, quoniam loca errant eis parata"). The Arabic Polyglot, then, reflects an expanded translation, which adds the idea of Levitical rotations (present later in 1 Chr 25, for instance) and subtracts the idea of Cheneniah as a single and skilled Levitical musical leader. This modified and expanded reading of verse 22 is also reflected in the Syriac—although the Syriac maintains the emphasis on Cheneniah. Walton's Latin translation of the Syriac is: "Benaia verò principes Levitarum onus quotidie portabat, qui locus erat ei paratus." For the Syriac and Arabic texts of the Polyglot, see Walton, *Biblica Sacra Polyglotta*, 674–75.

36. Following the Kethib for the Piel participle, מְחַצְּצְרִים, ("sounding"). The Qere is מַחְצְרִים. The issue has to do with the spelling of the root "to sound a clarion," either the more difficult חצצר or the more regular three-consonant root of חצר (cf. *BDB* 348).

37. For the MT participle ההלכים ("the ones going"), the LXX reads οἱ πορευόμενοι. Certain LXX miniscule manuscripts, however, lack the plural article οἱ on the participle—possibly because of a haplography on οἱ in the clause οἱ χιλίαρχοι οἱ πορευόμενοι. The Vulgate reads *ierunt* for the MT's participle.

singers and Cheneniah the leader of the music[38] of the singers. And David wore a linen ephod. 28. Thus, all Israel[39] brought up the ark of the covenant of the LORD with shouting, with the blast of the horn, trumpets and cymbals, with cymbals sounding,[40] with harps and lyres. 29. And as the ark of the covenant of the LORD came to[41] the city of David, Michal the daughter of Saul gazed through the window and saw King David, dancing and celebrating, and she despised[42] him in her heart.

Unit A': 1 Chr 16:1–3

1. When they brought up[43] the ark of God, they set it in the midst of the tent that David had pitched for it, and they offered burnt offerings and peace offerings before God. 2. And when David had finished sacrificing the burnt offerings and the peace offerings, he blessed the people in the name of the LORD 4. Also, he distributed to all Israel—both male and female alike—a loaf of bread,[44] a portion of meat, and a cake of raisin.[45]

---

38. At this juncture, the MT reads השר המשה. *BHS* suggests reading השר במשה, in line with verse 22.

39. In the parallel text of 1 Sam 6:15, the MT reads ודויד וכל־ישראל ("and David and all Israel"), while here in 1 Chr 15:28, the MT reads, in a shorter fashion, וכל־ישראל ("and all Israel"). A haplography on the ו is possible.

40. The participle for "sounding," משמעים, has no conjunction in the MT. *BHS* suggests adding one.

41. The MT here reads עד־עיר דויד. In several Hebrew manuscripts, the preposition עד is not present, as in the parallel text of 2 Sam 6:16.

42. *BHS* suggests reading וַתָּבָז (from the root בוז, "to have contempt") for the MT's וַתִּבֶז (from the root בזה, "to despise"). Both roots carry essentially the same nuance.

43. Here in 1 Chr 16:1, the MT reads ויביו את־ארון, "and they brought up the altar," the subject implied being David and the Levites. In 2 Sam 6:17, the parallel text, the MT reads ויעל דויד, "and David went up;" the focus is on David in the Samuel text, whereas in Chronicles the emphasis is both on David and the Levites' participation in the process.

44. The MT reads ככר־לחם (literally, a "round" or "measure" of bread). In the parallel text of 2 Sam 6:19, the phrase reads חלת־לחם (literally, a "cake" of bread).

45. The MT reads ואשישה ("and a raisin cake," see *BDB* 84). The LXX reads καὶ ἀμορίτην (more simply: "and a cake").

The Basic Setting of the APN1 (and the APN2) within the DKN1

In this first step of the argument, the purpose is to demonstrate that the APN1, as a part of the whole APN in 1 Chr 15 and 16, represents the central rhetorical unit for the DKN1 (that is, of 1 Chr 10:1—22:1). Indeed, when observing the APN in the context of the entire DKN1 from a literary and rhetorical perspective, it is possible to observe a thematic and concentric parallelism. In the following, the function of *three* sets of texts within this overall structure of the DKN1 will be noted: the textual center, the outer frame, and the inner units. These broad structural comments build on some basic insights in studies of 1 Chr 10-21 by Dorsey and Eskenazi, while the rhetorical structure for the APN1, proposed later in this chapter, is original to this study and flows from these larger structural observations.[46]

First, then, chapters 15 and 16—the APN—represent the structural center of the DKN1. These two chapters, indeed, are the only sections in this larger narrative that emphasize David's leadership with the priests and the Levites and with the ark and its liturgical celebration in Jerusalem. Stated differently, the APN is structurally central because, in the scope of the entire DKN1, it is the one section that *uniquely* deals with this multifaceted topic of David's relationship to the priests and Levites and their role with the ark in Jerusalem. Furthermore, the outer frame and the inner units of the DKN1 display parallel themes, which reinforce the central position played by the APN as a whole.

The APN1 focuses intently on David's cultic preparations for, and his leadership of, the correctly organized procession of the ark into Jerusalem. The particulars of this thematic development are unique to the APN.[47] Also, 1 Chr 16:4-43 follows as the APN2 by highlighting the Levitical ministry of thanksgiving in song and the establishment of proper cultic ministry both at the tabernacle in Gibeon and at the tent housing the ark in Jerusalem—all made possible by the developments in chapter 15. Consequently, the APN1 moves from David *pitching* a tent for the ark in 15:1 (וַיִּבֶן מקום לארון האלהים

---

46. See Dorsey, *The Literary Structure*, 145-48, and further, Eskenazi, "A Literary Approach," 258-74.

47. The APN2, as a liturgical and joyful *celebration*, is made possible by the *process* set up in the APN1. As Wilcock has argued, the APN1 (among other issues) especially points out the blessing of the LORD on David's careful preparation of the Levites for the ark's transport—as noted specifically in 1 Chr 15:26, האלהים את־הלוים ויהי בעזר. In contrast to the earlier effort at ark-transportation (which had failed), Wilcock indeed writes, "this time 'God helped the Levites' (15:26); the careful attention given both to the principles and to the practice of the ritual relating to the ark meant that now [God's] favour was assured." See Wilcock, *The Message of Chronicles*, 70.

וַיֶּט־לוֹ אֹהֶל) to David leading in worship *at that tent*, once the ark comes to rest within it (16:1–3; cf. v. 1: א הָאֹהֶל בְּתוֹךְ אֹתוֹ וַיַּצִּיגוּ הָאֱלֹהִים אֲרוֹן־אֶת וַיָּבִיאוּ, שֶׁר נָטָה־לוֹ דָּוִיד).[48]

The APN2, also, begins with a call to Asaph and his brothers to lead in music and celebration (1 Chr 16:4–7; cf. verse 4: מִן־ יְהוָה אֲרוֹן לִפְנֵי וַיִּתֵּן בַּיּוֹם הַהוּא, and verse 7: הַלְוִיִּם מְשָׁרְתִים וּלְהַזְכִּיר וּלְהוֹדוֹת וּלְהַלֵּל לַיהוָה אֱלֹהֵי יִשְׂרָאֵל אָז נָתַן דָּוִיד בָּרֹאשׁ לְהֹדוֹת לַיהוָה בְּיַד־אָסָף וְאֶחָיו); this section continues with a psalm of praise and thanksgiving (1 Chr 16:8–36) and ends with a statement on the temporary maintenance of two worship sites: at the ark's tent in Jerusalem (1 Chr 16:37–39, notice verse 37: וַיַּעֲזָב־שָׁם לִפְנֵי אֲרוֹן בְּרִית־יְהוָה לְאָסָף וּלְאֶחָיו לְשָׁרֵת לִפְנֵי הָאָרוֹן תָּמִיד לִדְבַר־יוֹם בְּיוֹמוֹ) and at the tabernacle in Gibeon (1 Chr 16:40–43). Consequently, within the DKN1, the whole of the APN is characterized by a unique focus on the liturgical *preparation for* and ensuing *celebration of* the presence of the "ark of the covenant of the LORD" in Jerusalem (following the wording of 1 Chr 16:37).[49]

A second major factor is the relationship of the *inner* units of the DKN1 to the APN. Indeed, the parallel inner texts of the DKN1 (around the central texts of chs. 15 and 16) further accentuate the key function of the APN (both sections 1 and 2). First, these passages emphasize the military successes of David and his army and reveal God's presence with, and blessing over, David (1 Chr 11:10—12:40 and 18:1—20:8). These inner units also stress the dual paradox between David's expressed desires towards the LORD, on the one hand, and the contrasted responses given by God, on the other hand (cf. 1 Chr 13:1—14:7 and 17:1—27, which are the inner units *closest* to the APN).

In these latter inner sections, indeed, David first desires to bring the ark into Jerusalem—to properly "seek" the LORD, but is prevented by God for not having properly transported it (ch. 13; note David's words in 13:3: וְנָסֵבָּה אֶת־אֲרוֹן אֱלֹהֵינוּ אֵלֵינוּ כִּי־לֹא דְרַשְׁנֻהוּ בִּימֵי שָׁאוּל). Instead, the Chronicler shows how the LORD blessed and expanded David's own house (ch.

---

48. For further discussion of this *inclusio*, see Kalimi, *The Reshaping*, 306–7.

49. McKenzie supports this argument, which relates to the central function of the APN. For chapter 16, he especially highlights the theological contributions made towards the Chronicler's view of the place of worship in the Jerusalem cult and ritual—of which he writes, "it does not simply consist of following a set of prescriptions. Ritual activities alone are not enough to please God. The Chronicler uses this occasion [of the twin-worship sites at the end of 1 Chr 16] to introduce the importance of music into the cult. While sacrifices continue in Gibeon, since the temple is not yet built, the Chronicler has David institute the Levitical orders as musicians as a permanent feature of the worship in Jerusalem. *In Chronicles, true worship is a joyful expression of the human heart, celebrated in community with music.*" See McKenzie, *1–2 Chronicles*, 151–52 (emphasis added).

14; see the conclusion in 14:17: ויצא שם־דויד בכל־הארצות ויהוה נתן את־פחדו על־כל־הגוים). Second, as David becomes firmly secured in his "house" and growing kingdom, he also wishes to build a "house" for the LORD (1 Chr 17:1–2; note David's words in 17:1a: הנה אנכי יושב בבית הארזים וארון ברית־יהוה תחת יריעות). Instead, the LORD prophetically announces that David will be endowed with an eternal house (or line/dynasty) of his own (cf. 1 Chr 17:3–27, especially vv. 11–14, of which notice verse 14—where God emphasizes the eternal nature of the Davidic covenantal promise—drastically important in a postexilic context: והעמתיהו בביתי ובמלכותי עד־העולם וכסאו יהיה נכון עד־עולם).[50]

Also, in the inner units furthest removed from the APN, David's military successes are highlighted—this is the political dimension of David's divinely-provided blessing.[51] In 1 Chr 11:10—12:40, David receives full support from his military representatives. This helps towards the firm establishment of his kingdom (note the lists and notices of the strong military leaders who join David and win victories for him in chapters 11 and 12). It is also a sign of God's blessing over David's leadership (cf. for instance 1 Chr 11:10: ואלה ראשי הגבורים אשר לדויד המתחזקים עמו במלכותו עם־כל־ישראל להמליכו כדבר יהוה על־ישראל). Such military support is also a sign of the fuller support David receives from *all* of the tribes (as seen, for

---

50. As Pratt remarks on this passage, "God promises that David's line would be the permanent dynasty over God's people.... This promise was especially important for the Chronicler's postexilic community. Postexilic Israel hoped for national security against her enemies. It was through David and her seed that God promised such security. *The promises served the Chronicler's purpose of turning attention to the house of David as the permanent hope for Israel.*" See Pratt, *1 and 2 Chronicles*, 154 (emphasis added). Notice also that the phrase "*your* [David's] house and kingdom" (בֵּיתְךָ וּמַמְלַכְתְּךָ) from 2 Sam 7:16 has been modified here to "*my* house and kingdom" (בְּבֵיתִי וּבְמַלְכוּתִי) in 1 Chr 17:14. Pratt, *1 and 2 Chronicles*, 154, makes a further point of connecting this modification to the Chronicler's understanding of God's kingdom— since the Chronicler "drew a close connection between the human throne of Israel and God's throne because the son of David ruled as God's vice-regents . . . *the kingdom did not belong to David but to God*. This aspect of the Chronicler's viewpoint on David's throne provides an essential background for understanding the New Testament teaching on the Kingdom of God (Heaven). *With the re-establishment of the Davidic throne in Christ, the reign (Kingdom) of God was re-established*" (emphasis added). Similarly, see the discussion in Hill, *1 and 2 Chronicles*, 240–45.

51. As Cazelles wrote of the reasoning behind the Chronicler's placement of the military texts in chapters 11–12 before the texts dealing with the ark (which he calls David's "great action" which *sanctifies* Jerusalem), "avant de décrire le grand acte qui va faire de Jérusalem la cité sainte, le transfert de l'arche de la présence de Yahvé, le Chroniste donne un tableau de la puissance de David (11 et 12). Il y a les grands qui l'entourent (le Chroniste les évoque en reproduisant la liste de 2 Sam 23); mais il y a aussi des représentants des tribus non judéennes et des guerriers de toutes les tribus." See Cazelles, *Le livres des Chroniques*, 71.

example, in MT 1 Chr 12:39 [EV 12:38]: כל־אלה אנשי מלחמה עדרי מערכה בלבב שלם באו הברונה להמליך את־דויד על־כל־ישראל וגם כל־שרית ישראל לב אחד להמליך את־דויד).[52]

Further, in the parallel sub-units of 1 Chr 18:1—20:8, David is presented as victorious over his enemies (over the Philistines in 18:1-13 and 20:4-8; for which note 18:13b: ויושע יהוה את־דויד בכל אשר הלך; and over the Ammonites in 19:1-19, 20:1-3). King David is also described as receiving full support from *all of Israel* in response to his effective political leadership (note 18:14, for instance, וימלך דויד על־כל־ישראל ויהי עשה משפט וצדקה לכל־עמו—in the context of the complete statement of broad support in 18:1-17). These texts, in chapters 18-20, make only quick reference to the complicated narrative of David's court intrigue in the latter section of 2 Samuel (following his sin with Bathsheba in 2 Samuel 11). However, the way they have been preserved and shaped in Chronicles remains consistent with the Chronicler's emphasis on David's rise to power to secure the place for the *temple* and to establish its proper *cultic* structures. In this sense, it is perhaps an overstatement to assert, as Michaeli has, that the Chronicler has simply "sanctified" David in 1 Chr 10-21 (since, in comparison with 2 Samuel, some of David's egregious sins are omitted in this section of Chronicles—such as the sin with Bathsheba and all of its repercussions in David's kingship).[53]

In fact, the Chronicler actually *preserves* certain mistakes by David, but they are sins that are consistent with his postexilic literary and theological purposes. In chapter 13, David is at fault in the first attempt at moving the ark, and in chapter 21, David commits sin with his desire for a census.[54] In fact, Allen has noted that for the Chronicler, David's request for a military census demonstrated a particular lack of faith in the LORD, since "Joab's protest [in 1 Chr 21:3] implies that David's sin was an act of presumption

---

52. This is sustained, for instance, in Klein's discussion, when he notes of 1 Chr 12:39, "[a]fter expending so much space in demonstrating military loyalty, from 11:10–12:38 (37), the Chronicler affirms that all the civilian population ('all the rest of Israel') had the same singlemindedness." See Klein, *1 Chronicles*, 325.

53. Michaeli, *Les livres des Chroniques*, 106.

54. Michaeli's comments in *Les livres des Chroniques*, 106-7, are also pertinent in this regard, as he notes of the purposeful shaping of the Chronicler's David narrative: "[c]e qui compte pour [le Chroniqueur] c'est non seulement de souligner l'importance et la gloire de la figure royale de David, mais aussi de mettre en relief tout ce qui concerne Jérusalem et le Temple, ainsi que l'organisation du culte. Les autres considérations pour lui sont secondaires. C'est pourquoi, dans la longue histoire de la cour royale de David, le Chroniqueur ne va retenir que les quelques éléments susceptibles d'éclairer son sujet et d'être utiles à son plan; tout le reste peut être omis comme inutile dans la grande fresque qu'il présente" (emphasis added).

against the LORD as giver of national blessing."[55] Duke also sees chapter 21 as the sole overall negative portrayal of David by the Chronicler, since it is "the only break in the paradigm" that was necessary for the overall purpose of introducing the location of the temple.[56]

Fourth and finally, the framing units (on the outer extremities of the DKN1) both emphasize David's royal leadership and, especially, the location of the future temple. Dorsey has commented on this feature concisely when he writes:

> While David's other accomplishments are also recounted in the unit [the DKN1], David's activities involving the temple are emphasized by being placed at the beginning, in the middle, and at the end. This structural design reflects the author's agenda—to encourage the postexilic community to pay attention to the temple as King David did.[57]

Thus, the central unit and the framing sections of the DKN1 consistently point the reader towards the significance of Jerusalem as the location of God's holy and atoning presence. Indeed, the *place* of Jerusalem is reinforced in chapter 10 and also in chapter 21. First, in 1 Chr 10:1—11:9, the Chronicler contrasts Saul's breach of faith (10:1-14; note the key statement in 10:14 ולא־דרש ביהוה וימיתהו ויסב את־המלוכה לדויד בן־ישי) to God's choice of David as successor. David is then shown as the successful shepherd king unto whom the LORD has turned over the kingdom and to whom all Israel granted support—this, based on a previous prophetic word (11:1-3; note 3b: וימשחו את־דויד למלך על־ישראל כדבר יהוה ביד־שמואל).[58] David also leads his army in taking over Jebus/Jerusalem, to establish the city as the center of his reign—and in the Chronicler's perspective, of God's presence. Thus, based on the analysis of Saul's failure in 1 Chr 10:13-14 and the national defeat by the Philistines, the Chronicler immediately implies in 1 Chr 11:1-9 that David represents God's *paradigmatic choice* for kingship. The conclusion of the pericope detailing David's conquest of Jebus/Jerusalem is, hence, straightforward in 1 Chr 11:9: וילך דויד הלוך וגדול ויהוה צבאות עמו.[59]

---

55. See Allen, "Chronicles," 426.
56. Duke, *The Persuasive Appeal*, 59–60.
57. Dorsey, *The Literary Structure*, 146.
58. Two elements dominate the pericope in 11:1-3: (1) the "word of the LORD" and (2) the "sacramental act of anointing." As Selman notes, these two elements "speak of God's purposes for David: the former emphasizing God's call and promise, the latter demonstrating that God equips those whom he calls." See Selman, *1 Chronicles*, 138.
59. Duke roots his observations on chapter 11 in the larger context of chapters 11–12. He notes an *inclusio* on the "all Israel" theme in 11:1-3 and 12:38-40. The military

Second, in 1 Chr 21:18—22:1, David secures the place for the future temple, Ornan's threshing floor (גרן ארנן היבסי), following the sinful census and the ensuing national plague (21:1-17).[60] In 1 Chr 22:1, God announces to David that in this location: (1) the house of the LORD God will be erected, and (2), the altar for burnt offering will also be built.[61] In highlighting this incident, the Chronicler concludes the DKN1 with a final emphasis on the future location of the temple in Jerusalem, as this unit also represents the last section of the whole DKN1. Also, the Chronicler prepares the reader for the DKN2 (chs. 22-29) by alluding to this temple location—since the DKN2 is chiefly concerned with the various preparations for the leadership, the construction, and the ministry of the future temple—all of which will eventually be overseen by Solomon. That is, the final unit in the frame of the DKN1 also becomes a *hinge unit* leading naturally into the DKN2.[62]

---

men who give allegiance to David shows that the LORD was with him. As Duke writes, "by such structuring of his account, the Chronicler conveys that the king chosen by Yahweh and endorsed by all the people was concerned first of all with establishing the proper worship of Yahweh—despite the fact that David's first attempt to bring up the ark actually met with failure." See Duke, *The Persuasive Appeal*, 57-58.

60. For a recent analysis of the sin of David in this context, see Evans, "Let the Crime Fit the Punishment," 65-80. In essence, Evans argues that the Chronicler has marshalled the law of Exodus 30 by applying casuistic law related to the tabernacle to the temple site. As Evans, "Let the Crime Fit the Punishment," 80, notes, "[t]hus the Chronicler's association of this legislation [in Exodus 30] with David's failed census allowed the Chronicler to make the 'crime fit the punishment' regarding the otherwise baffling sin of the census." For further analysis of 1 Chr 21 in the context of Persian Yehud, see Jonker, "Of Jebus, Jerusalem," 81-102.

61. The LORD commands David to purchase the threshing floor site from Arunah, a Jebusite, and to prepare, there, a place for the temple, the altar, and its sacrificial ministry. On these commands, Allen notes with perspicacity, "the altar David is commanded to build is, for the chronicler, a monument to God's forgiving grace. Hitherto the narrative had witnessed to a David dedicated to the will of God whose only fault was an unwitting ritual ignorance that he gladly resolved. But sooner or later forgiving grace cannot stay out of any divine/human relationship. There is a need for a 'God who is rich mercy,' who redirects misused energies into new and wholesome channels." See Allen, "Chronicles," 426.

62. McConville highlights the theological significance present both in the content of chapter 21 and in its placement at the end of the first section of the Davidic narrative, before the texts that deal specifically with the temple ministry—note that the center of the DKN2 is 1 Chr 24:1-19 which deals with the envisaged atoning sacrificial ministry of the Aaronides priests at the temple. McConville writes, "in David's penitence [in chapter 21] intercession and the purchase of the threshing-floor we have seen the subjective cost, the cost experienced by the person who would be in fellowship with God. The objective cost is symbolized by the Temple and the sacrificial system for which it was intended. That system was not new. It dates to Moses' period (v. 29), and was currently being carried on at the high place (or sanctuary) of Gibeon. But there is a reaffirmation in this chapter that God has provided a way of atonement for

In conclusion, the parallels between the framing units and the inner units reveal a chiastic or concentric patterning within the DKN1.[63] This structure firmly locates chapters 15 and 16 at the rhetorical center. In the DKN1, David is portrayed by the Chronicler as the LORD's choice for the proper king in Israel, who, despite certain national failures, secured the city and the place for the temple—all the while "seeking" the LORD and effectively leading "all Israel" cf. (the frame of 10:1–11:9 and 21:1–22:1). Thus, as Duke has affirmed, "in the narrative which follows the [genealogical] lists, the Chronicler painted a picture in which he portrayed David and Solomon as one who properly sought Yahweh by instituting and upholding the official temple cultus."[64]

Further, with the first set of inner units, the DKN1 also presents David as a successful military leader (in contrast to Saul's deadly defeat in chapter 10) who enjoys the full support of his able military personnel—an army that is itself representative of "all Israel" (see the first inner units of chapters 11:1—12:40 and 18:1—20:8). The second inner units also reveal: (1) that God chooses to bless David with a secured "physical" kingdom, despite David's initially flawed desire to bring the ark into Jerusalem (1 Chr 13 and 14), and (2) that God also chooses to bless David with a secured "eternal" kingdom, despite David's initial desire to build a physical temple for the LORD (1 Chr 17). These parallel sections, then, reinforce the central placement of chapters 15 and 16, where David is ultimately presented as the able, liturgical, priestly and kingly leader in Israel—the leader of the Levites who allows for the proper, joyful, and musically-imbued worship of the LORD in the new location of Jerusalem. Table 3 summarizes the preceding broad-scaled rhetorical discussion of the function of the APN with the DKN1.[65]

---

the sin of his people. The rituals testify to God's decision to deal with sin" (emphasis original). See McConville, *I and II Chronicles*, 75. On the issue of the atonement in Chronicles, see further, Johnstone, "Guilt and Atonement," 113–38, who argues that Chronicles is largely an ideological work responding to the reality of the exile. For him, the exile would be a result of transgressive unfaithfulness (מעל, understood in the technical, cultic sense of Leviticus) for which atonement continues to be needed, since in Johnstone's view, "Chronicles grapples with the mystery that, despite 'The Return,' Israel is still in 'Exile,' still poised on the eve of the definitive 'Return.'" See Johnstone, "Guilt and Atonement," 114.

63. A similar pattern can be observed in the DKN2 with chapter 24 (focused on the ministry of the Aaronides priests at the temple). See further Dorsey, *The Literary Structure*, 147.

64. Duke, *The Persuasive Appeal*, 56.

65. This chart is adapted from Dorsey, *The Literary Structure*, 147.

A. Following the Philistine defeat, David conquers Jebus (Jerusalem) and is anointed king: 1 Chr 10:1–11:9

וילך דויד הלוך וגדול ויהוה צבאות עמו 11:9

B. David receives full support from his military: 1 Chr 11:10—12:40

כל־אלה אנשי מלחמה עדרי מערכה בלבב שלם באו הברונה להמליך את־דויד [38] 12:39

על־כל־ישראל וגם כל־שרית ישראל לב אהד להמליך את־דויד

C. David desires to transport the ark into Jerusalem, but the LORD chooses to bless his house instead: 1 Chr 13:1—14:17

ויחר לדויד כי־פרץ יהוה בעזה ויקרא למקום ההוא פרץ עזא עד היום הזה 13:11

וידע דויד כי־הכינו יהוה למלך על־ישראל כי־נשׂאת למעלה מלכותו בעבור עמו ישראל 14:2

D. Center (APN): David properly leads the Levites in bringing the ark into Jerusalem and in celebrating with all Israel (APN[1 and 2]): 1 Chr 15:1—16:43

ויעשׂ־לו בתים בעיר דויד ויכן מקום לארון האלהים ויט־לו אהל 15:1

ויביאו את־ארון האלהים ויציגו אתו בתוך האהל אשר 16:1

נטה־לו דויד ויקריבו עלות ושלמים לפני האלהים

C'. David desires to build the LORD a house, but the LORD promises David an eternal house instead: 1 Chr 17:1–27

ויהי כאשר ישב דויד בביתו ויאמר דויד אל־נתן הנביא 17:1

הנה אנכי יושב בבית הארזים וארון ברית־יהוה תחת יריעות

B'. David receives full support from his military: 1 Chr 18:1–20

וימלך דויד על־כל־ישראל ויהי עשׂה משפט וצדקה לכל־עמו 18:14

A'. Following the national plague, David secures the temple site in Jebus (Jerusalem): 1 Chr 21:1—22:1

ויאמר דויד אל־ארנן תנה־לי מקום הגרן ואבנה־בו מזבח ליהוה בכסף מלא תנהו לי 21:22

ויאמר דויד זה הוא בית יהוה האלהים וזה־מזבח לעלה לישראל 22:1

Table 3: The Placement of the APN within the DKN1

The Relationship between 1 Chr 15:1—16:3 and 2 Sam 6:1–23: Some Basic Features

Having established some of the key features of the placement of the APN within the DKN1 of 1 Chronicles, the overall argument of this chapter may also be elucidated by some brief consideration of parallel texts. Indeed, the text of 1 Chr 15:1—16:3 (the APN1): (1) assumes background information from 1 Chr 13 and 1 Sam 4–7, generally; (2) incorporates and/or omits source material from 2 Samuel, and provides new material related to the successful entry of the ark into Jerusalem. Scholars continue to debate (and disagree on) how the Chronicler may have used his *Vorlage* in this case. Street strikes a balance when he notes of this issue:

> The lack of scholarly consensus causes one to remain cautious about the historical value of these changes to the text. However, the overall perspective between the text of Chronicles and Samuel along with the fact that a case can be made for this organization occurring during the time of David, at least implicitly by the text of Samuel, suggests that this organization and festival took place at the time that David brought the ark to Jerusalem.[66]

As such, the Chronicler assumes a certain amount of background information, both from his own work and from 1 Samuel. In 1 Chr 13:1–14, David gathers and consults with his leaders and announces to the "assembly of Israel" (v. 2) that all Israelites throughout the land should be gathered together for the ark of God to be brought into Jerusalem from Abinadab's house in Kiriath-Jearim. This first attempt is unsuccessful since David fails to order the proper Levitical leadership to carefully bring in the ark—although Obed-Edom, the Gittite, receives the ark in his home for a period of three months; he also receives God's blessing (see 1 Chr 13:14: וישב ארון האלהים עם־בית עבד אדם בביתו שלשה חדשים ויברך יהוה את־בית עבד־אדם ואת־כל־אשר־לו).[67]

---

66. Street, *The Significance*, 19. Jonker, *1 & 2 Chronicles*, 108, notes how the Chronicler appears to use quotations from 2 Sam 6 "to bracket the whole episode of the actual ark procession in 1 Chr 15:25—16:3 (cf. 2 Sam 6:12–19a) and the conclusion in 16:43 (cf. 2 Sam 6:19b–20a)."

67. On the inclusion of this early ark narrative in chapter 13 (in the context of David's military and political successes), Knoppers, *I Chronicles 10–29*, 592, makes some salient points as he notes, "the Chronicler's coverage of David's early reign deals with a number of matters, such as the Philistine wars, that have little to do with the Ark. Nevertheless, given the many references to the Ark during the reign of David, it is appropriate to enquire as to the nature of the coverage the Chronicler does devote to the sacred artifact. The references both to Israel's ancient palladium and to the Tabernacle, for that matter, are reverential in character." Knoppers, *I Chronicles 10–29*, 592–93, goes

The Chronicler, then, appears to assume that the reader is aware of the events recorded in 1 Sam 4:1—7:1, which led up to the ark being placed in Kiriath-Jearim. In this related historical narrative, the capture of the ark by the Philistines during battle is a sign of judgment on Israel. This also brings divine judgment upon the Philistine Pentapolis. In fact, as Beitzel has noted, altogether "it was inevitable that tensions between [the Israelites and the Philistines] should develop [as seen in the movements of the ark], particularly as they both sought to colonize and exploit [the Shephela]."[68] The ark is eventually returned to Israelite lands where it is brought to the house of Abinadab in Kiriath-Jearim, west of Jerusalem. Eleazar, Abinadab's son, is subsequently consecrated to care for the ark (see the conclusion of this unit in 1 Sam 7:1 ויבאו אנשי קרית יערים ויעלו את־ארון יהוה ויבאו אתו אל־בית אבינדב בגבעה ואת־אלעזר בנו קדשו לשמר את־ ארון יהוה).[69] This represents a transitional period for the ark—following its earlier and careful transport by the Levitical clans in the wilderness, and before it is placed in a tent in Jerusalem by David, in preparation for its eventual placement by Solomon in the physical temple.[70]

Second, the Chronicler's text of the successful procession of the ark into Jerusalem is partly based on the presentation of this event in the

---

on to argue that this aspect of the Chronicler's presentation serves two purposes for a late Persian or early Hellenistic age: (1) the reality of the Second Temple is linked both to the First Temple and to the Sinaitic age, so that "the prestige and importance of the Jerusalem Temple are enhanced by such ties to Israel's distant past;" (2) "the writer can argue (by implication) that the Yahwistic cultus is no longer inherently portable, but tied to one centralized, portable sanctuary . . . The author's account of the early monarchy and of David's attempts to retrieve the Ark ultimately ratify the historical primacy, central status, and continuing privileges of the Jerusalem Temple."

68. Beitzel, *The New Moody Atlas*, 143–44.

69. Arnold has recently pointed out the irony of blessing and judgment with the transitional stage of the ark being in Kiriat-Jearim (following the battle at Beth Shemesh in 1 Samuel 6). He writes, "Israel had been equally guilty of attempting to manipulate Yahweh [as the Philistines were as well]. The use of the ark of the covenant to guarantee military victory came perilously close to imitative magic, or at least pagan religious warfare. And now the losses at Beth Shemesh reveal a propensity to disregard him, failing to glorify him and give thanks to him (Rom 1:21). *Israel had been given the riches of divine self-disclosure. God had revealed his nature to ancient Israel, and this was to make her unique in the ancient world*" (emphasis added). See Arnold, *1 and 2 Samuel*, 124.

70. On the final outcome of the ark, note that Beitzel, *The New Moody Atlas*, 144–45, concludes it is most reasonable to assume that it remained in Jerusalem until it was destroyed by Nebuchadnezzar's invading army in the sixth century BC (note the stark claim by the prophet in Jer 3:16 והיה כי תרבו ופריתם בארץ בימים ההמה נאם־יהוה לא יאמרו עוד ארון ברית־יהוה ולא יעלה על־לב ולא יזכרו־בו ולא יפקדו ולא יעשה עוד)—although apocryphal legends exist, which claim the ark survived that fall of the southern kingdom (such as accounts in 1 Esdras 1; 2 Baruch 6 and 2 Macc 2). See also Sparks, "Ark of the Covenant," 89–92.

narrative of 2 Samuel. In fact, the Chronicler keeps certain materials, modifies others, and also omits yet other sections from this source.[71] The unit dealing with this procession plays a different role in the literary structure of Samuel and, hence, displays different emphases than in Chronicles. 2 Sam 1–8 deals with the rise and consolidation of David's kingdom after the extensive presentation of Saul's failed kingship in 1 Samuel chapters 8–31 (the Chronicler assumes knowledge of this period and simply marks its end with 1 Chr 10). In 2 Sam 1–4, the establishment of David's kinship over Judah is detailed, while in 2 Sam 5–8, David's developing rule over all Israel is recorded. Arguably, the climax of this latter section is found in 2 Sam 7:1–17, with the LORD's promise of an eternal dynasty for David (thus, the climactic section of the parallel unit in Chronicles is *different*). Arnold, for example, has commented on the key function of this text (2 Sam 7) within the whole narrative of David's kingdom in Samuel. He writes:

> The dialogical nature of the chapter reflects the significance of David and his dynasty in salvation history, past and future. David expresses his intentions to build a temple for Yahweh in 7:1–3. . . . David's line will not end; Yawheh will be a father to David's descendants, and they will be Yahweh's sons (2 Sam 7:13–16).[72]

Also, this central section is framed in 2 Sam 6:1–23 and in 2 Sam 7:18–29 with the joyful procession of the ark *into* Jerusalem and David's joyful praise *at* the ark—in thanksgiving for the LORD's covenantal promise. Thus, while in 2 Sam 6, the ark procession narrative anticipates the structurally central *Davidic promise* narrative, in 1 Chronicles, the ark procession *itself* is part of the structural literary center (1 Chr 15 and 16)—which is then followed by

---

71. Many commentators have produced systematic presentations of the textual parallels and divergences between the two sources at this juncture. See for instance, Knoppers, *I Chronicles*, 628–29; Japhet, *I and II Chronicles*, 292–96; Williamson, *1 and 2 Chronicles*, 119–22. A thorough textual analysis of the parallels may be found in several chapters in Rezekto, *Source and Revision*, 86–285. Rezekto concludes, source-critically (essentially), that some amount of "secondary" layers are present in the synoptic passages, as he notes, "I closely examined 2 Sam 6 and the synoptic portions of 1 Chron 13, 15–16. I argued that many details in MT Samuel's story of the ark are secondary, are connected to the language of stories in 1 Samuel, and aim to advance David's kingship and character. I discerned three *interconnected* themes which influenced the revision of the story we eventually inherited in the received Hebrew version: an apology of Davidic kingship, an apology of Davidic and Yahwistic character, and cultic practice" (emphasis original). See Rezekto, *Source and Revision*, 287. Hence, Rezekto is focused on the theoretical addition of "pro-David" and "pro-Yahweh" stances. The rhetorical-critical analysis proposed in the chapter stands in contrast, as is it pursuing the cohesive message of the MT itself.

72. Arnold, "Samuel," 869. Note also the discussion of the literary structure of 2 Samuel in Dorsey, *The Literary Structure*, 133–36.

the Chronicler's presentation of the LORD's covenant-making with David (in 1 Chr 17 and in concentric parallel with 1 Chr 13 and 14).[73]

These general observations on the relationship between 2 Sam 6 and 1 Chr 15 lead to the following four specific observations. (1) *All* of 1 Chr 15:1–24 is unique to the Chronicler. The entire description of David's gathering of the priests and the Levites and of David's institution of Levitical music is given only in Chronicles. Just one verse in 1 Samuel describes the movement between Obed-Edom's house and the tent in Jerusalem. 2 Sam 6:12 should be noted here: ויגד למלך דוד לאמר ברך יהוה את־בית עבד אדם ואת־כל־אשר־לו בעבור ארון האלהים וילך דוד ויעל את־ארון האלהים מבית עבד אדם עיר דוד בשמחה. The events surrounding that one event are given much greater emphasis in Chronicles (all of chapter 15). In fact, the final clause in 2 Sam 6:12 (...וילך) indicates that David oversaw the transportation of the ark from Obed Edom's home to Jerusalem and that this process was done "with rejoicing" (בשמחה). In a sense, this brief statement of "rejoicing" in 2 Sam 6 is developed fully into chapter 15 of the Chronicler's account, with his detailed emphasis on the priests and the Levites. This is a strong clue as to the particular emphasis of Chronicles. As Endres comments at this juncture:

> These chapters [of 1 Chr 15–16] constitute a very important text for the Chronicler, who transforms a brief notice in 2 Samuel 6:12–19a (about David's transfer of the ark of Jerusalem) into a major liturgical festival of transfer and dedication of the ark. It

---

73. In her literary analysis of the movement of the ark in Chronicles, Eskenazi sees chapter 13:1–4 as defining the objective—that is, of bringing the ark into Jerusalem with full consensus. Chapter 15 represents the end of the actualization process—after the complications of the rest of chapters 13 and 14. The objective is reached in chapter 16 so that "the arrival of the ark in Jerusalem is a fulfillment of all that has been promised (16:15–22) and of global, even cosmic significance (16:29–33). *No other event in Chronicles, not even the dedication of the temple, is enshrined in such broad-reaching terms and imagery*" (emphasis added). Eskenazi, "A Literary Approach," 270. Eskenazi's study is also helpful in synthesizing the issues regarding the relationship between Chronicles and Samuel at this point. As such, Eskenazi, "A Literary Approach," 272, argues for three major points: (1) The more expansive treatment in Chronicles highlights the "importance, beauty, and joy of the ark and the cult," which includes David's careful concern for the ark; (2) whereas in Samuel, the emphasis is solely on David's role in the transportation and celebration, in Chronicles, "the wide-ranging participation of the people in the life of the nation and the cult stands out;" (3) the Levites, which are very prominent in Chronicles, simply do not appear in Samuel. The term "the ark of the covenant" doesn't appear either (in Samuel). As Eskenazi notes at this point, "the term 'covenant' is the Chronicler's addition. *These observations help clearly confirm and help refine Chronicles' distinctive focus. The focus itself, however, can be garnered from the text even without comparison with Samuel*" (emphasis added). See Eskenazi, "A Literary Approach," 270.

also includes a lengthy psalm of thanksgiving, which portrays the spiritual climate of the celebration.[74]

(2) In his narrative structure (note the discussion of the DKN1 above), the Chronicler also makes a separation between the initial attempt at moving the ark from Kiriath-Jearim, which only ends up at Obed Edom's home (ch. 13), and the successful attempt three months later (ch. 15). In 2 Samuel, and in the context of the broader literary structure of 2 Samuel, the entire movement from Kiriath-Jearim to Jerusalem is included in the *same* narrative context of 2 Samuel 6 (vv. 1–12). As noted above, the varying placements relate to the function in each narrative context.[75]

(3) 1 Sam 6:13-16 gives an initial description of the ark's entry into Jerusalem. The emphasis in Samuel is on David's actions (vv. 13–15), followed by a brief and initial notice of Michal's scorn of David (v. 16). On the other hand, in Chronicles, this stage is amplified, as the presence of David *and* the elders and military commanders (as well as the priests and Levites, implied by earlier statements in 1 Chr 15) is noted. The Chronicler also includes the notice of Michal's scorn (1 Chr 15:29, as a further example in line with 1 Chr 10 of the faithlessness of, and judgment upon, the house of Saul) but especially emphasizes the joy and celebration present with the large procession surrounding the ark (1 Chr 15:25–29). The Chronicler does *not* include the further detail on Michal, which is included at the conclusion of Samuel's narrative (in 2 Sam 6:20–23, a notice that accentuates the blessing of David's house and lineage vis-à-vis Saul's).

(4) Finally, the introduction to the celebration *in* Jerusalem is very similar in both accounts. The Chronicler makes close use, indeed, of 2 Sam 6:17-19 in the composition of 1 Chr 16:1–3. Both texts similarly highlight David's oversight of a sacrificial service in Jerusalem and of his provision of food for the people of Israel. A minor difference, however, is worth noting. While 2 Sam 6:17 puts the emphasis on *David's* role with the sacrifices (ויעל דוד עלות לפני יהוה ושלמים), 1 Chr 16:1 modifies this text slightly to put the accent on David *and* the various leaders present in the procession (the elders, the military leaders, the priests and the Levites from 1 Chr 15; compare

---

74. Endres, *First and Second Chronicles*, 37.

75. In fact, Kalimi shows how 1 Chr 15:1 to 16:1 (part of the APN1 in this discussion) are tied together with an *inclusio* between the preparations for the arrival of the ark from Obed-Edom's home (1 Chr 15:1–3) and the actual transportation into Jerusalem in 1 Chr 15:25—16:3. He also argues that this section (again, what is defined here as the APN1) is concentrically arranged and framed with this *inclusio*. See further Kalimi, *The Reshaping*, 306-7, and also the fuller discussion below.

1 Chr 16:1b וַיַּקְרִיבוּ עֹלוֹת וּשְׁלָמִים לִפְנֵי הָאֱלֹהִים).[76] Table 4 summarizes the basic relationship between the two parallel passages.[77]

Biblical Event	Samuel	Chronicles
Initial, unsuccessful ark-transfer	2 Sam 6:1–8	1 Chr 13:1–11
Three-month stay of the ark with Obed-Edom	2 Sam 6:9–11	1 Chr 13:12–14
David's desire to move the ark to Jerusalem	2 Sam 6:12	1 Chr 15:1–3
David's institution of Levitical regulations for the procession	--	1 Chr 15:4–24
Joyful procession of the ark into Jerusalem	2 Sam 6:13–15	1 Chr 15:25–28
David's joyful worship leadership in Jerusalem	2 Sam 6:16–18	1 Chr 16:1–3
Michal's despondent reaction to David	2 Sam 6: (16), 20–23	1 Chr 15:29

Table 4: Relationship between 1 Sam 6 and 1 Chr 15

1 Chr 15:1—16:3: Internal Rhetorical Development

The text of the APN1 has been analyzed; its relationship to the immediate context in the DKN1 has been observed; its relationship to key parallel texts in Samuel has been elucidated. It remains, then, to provide a closer literary and rhetorical reading of the APN1 itself. A number of scholars have

---

76. Notice as well that in the clauses quoted from 1 Chr 15:1 and 2 Sam 6:17, the Chronicler demonstrates his aptitude at varying the original text (here the verbal root, the name for God, and the syntactical structure), while still keeping the essential information similar. Kalimi argues that this is one example of the Chronicler's use of "chiasmus between parallel texts by use of alternate words." Kalimi, *The Reshaping*, 247 (and see pages 247–52 for the whole section), notes that on these occasions, "the transcribed text not only displays inverted word order but also substitutes words with the same general meaning. Thus, the Chronicler twice varied the earlier texts without changing their content."

77. For further helpful comment on the relationship between the two texts, see Pratt, *1 Chronicles*, 139–40.

observed some overarching literary patterns in 1 Chr 15 and 16. Pratt, for instance, sees this section as a rhetorical center for the Davidic narratives. He also observes a thematic progression within the unit—the transition between the two being found at 1 Chr 16:3 and 1 Chr 16:4.[78]

In the following, the structure of the *first* major unit (that is, the APN1/1 Chr 15:1—16:3; the rest of chapter 16 will be examined in more detail in chapter five of this study) of this central section will be investigated. We will argue here that this passage (the APN1) displays *five distinct and essentially concentric* parallel units (ABCB'A') that are distinguishable by key grammatical, lexical, and topical points of commonality. This section will lay out the structure of each unit. The focus will be on demonstrating the cohesiveness of the Hebrew text in each unit and, hence, in the Chronicler's message present in that structure. The final section will suggest ways to reflect on the interrelatedness of these units and, thus, more fully identify and appreciate the flow of the rhetorical argument. We will show, most basically, how the overall structure emphasizes David's correct choice of a properly established musical Levitical leadership. The inherent message found in that structure can be seen as addressing some of the key issues in postexilic Judah—such as the call for continued trust in, and worship of, the LORD despite challenging circumstances, or such as learning how to revive the hopes inherent in earlier Scripture in the light of a weakened and oppressed postexilic Israel. The following discussion is based on the detailed rhetorical outline of the Hebrew text of the APN1—found in the appendix to this study.

Unit A (1 Chr 15:1–3): In Jerusalem, David Correctly Chooses the Levites to Carry the Ark

In the flow of the Chronicler's argument, this unit follows David's first unsuccessful attempt at bringing the ark into Jerusalem. This failure of leadership on the part of David in chapter 13 (essentially due to his lack of concern for Torah precedent on the correct transportation of the ark—the preeminent

---

78. See Pratt, *1 and 2 Chronicles*, 126. A number of scholars also approach chapters 13 through 16 as a unit generally concerned with the movement of the ark. See, for instance, Eskenazi, "A Literary Approach," 258–73; Hill, *1 and 2 Chronicles*, 224–45; McKenzie, *1–2 Chronicles*, 131–51. For instance, McKenzie's (*1–2 Chronicles*, 131) literary analysis of this larger section includes three sections: (1) an etiology for the place-name of Perez-uzzah (ch. 13); (2) reports on David's family and military successes; (3) the successful transfer and installation of the ark (chs. 15–16, which he further breaks down; see McKenzie, *1–2 Chronicles*, 131–32). Many recent authors argue for some type of literary unity within chapters 15 and 16, whether connections to chapters 13 and 14 are very strongly drawn or not.

symbol of the LORD's presence among his people) contrasts quite vividly with the statement of David's physical blessing of house, family (1 Chr 14:1-5), and military conquest (1 Chr 14:6-17). Key statements in 14:2, 17, indeed, emphasize the Chronicler's presentation of David as an ideally blessed and successful king: וידע דויד כי־הכינו יהוה למלך על־ישראל כי־נשאת למעלה מלכותו בעבור עמו ישראל, ויצא שם־דויד בכל־הארצות ויהוה נתן את־פחדו על־כל־הגוים. The use of the verb כון in verse 2 is characteristic of the Chronicler's vocabulary—it functions to point out God's firm establishment and blessing of his chosen leaders.[79] In contrast, as seen in verse 17, this establishment of the LORD's chosen leader induces fear in those nations outside of Israel. Such are the immediately preceding concerns leading into 15:1-3.

Also, unit A can be defined as the narrative introduction to the entire APN, generally, and to its first section, specifically (15:1—16:3, the APN1). The argument here posits that this unit is structured around David's short speech in verse 2, which introduces the key concern for the APN1—the responsibility of the Levites in properly transporting the ark, in this case, into Jerusalem. The following comments will highlight this structure (as outlined in table 5 below): (1) the initial narrative statement (v. 1); (2) the central direct discourse (v. 2); (3) the framing narrative notice (v. 3).

Verse 1, Davidic Preparation: General building projects and preparation for the ark

(ויעש ויכן ויט)

Verse 2, Davidic Proclamation: Levitical duty in carrying the ark

(אמר דויד)

Verse 3, Davidic Assembly: "All Israel" involved in carrying the ark

(ויקהל דויד)

Table 5: Structure of Unit A (1 Chr 15:1-3)

The initial statement of unit A reveals a narrative movement encapsulated in a series of three *wayyiqtol* verbs—all of which are actively voiced and describe verbal actions that are grammatically simple: ויעש ויכן ויט.[80]

---

79. The verb כון occurs about fifty times in Chronicles. For other significant uses, see, for instance, 1 Chr 17:11-12, 14, 24; 22:10; 28:7; 29:18; 2 Chr 1:4; 12:1, 14; 17:5; 19:3; 20:33; 27:6; 29:35; 30:19.

80. This is an example of the *waw consecutive* with the imperfect, which indicates, in this case, similar temporal and aspectual connotations (past and completed) than the perfect, but also, with the added nuance of "progression" emphasizing both sequence and the logical relationship of the events.

The first ("and he *made*") relates to David's construction projects within Jerusalem. This is in keeping with the Chronicler's statement of David's physical blessing as he is being established by God in his kingdom (much of the emphasis of chs. 10–14).[81]

The second two verbs ("and he *prepared*," "and he *pitched/stretched out*") highlight the two-step process David oversees, as he focuses on the proper *liturgical* and *cultic* set-up for Jerusalem. First, a physical space is prepared with the city of David—the object of ויכן is מקום, followed by the prepositional phrase לארון האלהם. Second, a physical, though temporary, structure (אהל, the tent), is erected on that physical place for housing the ark of God. The ark has not arrived within the city limits, since this remains the preparatory stage for its coming. Thus, three imperfect verbs modified by a *waw consecutive* have the same subject, David (the 3ms suffix of the first construction, ויעש־לו, refers naturally in the MT to the previously expressed subject of 14:17, David). The three actions on David's part represent two acts of preparation—seen in the series of three objects: (1) houses or buildings within the city; (2a) a place and (2b) a covering structure for the ark.[82]

Verse 2, David's direct statement and the central section in this unit, is introduced by the particle אז followed by a *qatal* + subject construction (אמר דויד).[83] Structurally, it can be divided into two segments: (1) the fundamental assertion; and (2) the reason sustaining that assertion. The basic assertion, communicated with a לא + infinitive construct (לא לשאת), affirms that only the Levites are to carry the ark (in direct contrast to the events alluded to in chapter 13).[84] The reason for this statement is introduced by a כי clause: God *chose* (בהר) the Levites for this task. This divine choice is further characterized through two other ל + infinitive constructs (indicating purpose): (1) to allow proper transport of the ark (לשאת) and (2), to minister (לשרתו) to the LORD forever.

---

81. Also, Knoppers notes that the statement of David's building projects at this juncture is significant for two further reasons: (1) a strong tie between David and the city of Jerusalem is established; (2) construction activity by kings is viewed very positively in Chronicles generally. See Knoppers, *I Chronicles 10–29*, 612.

82. Klein sees the use of מקום in 15:1b as having a "sacred" denotation in contrast to the "secular" aspect of the בתים in 15:1a. See Klein, *1 Chronicles*, 351.

83. The particle אז is a temporal marker, which, in this context, could indicate a time after the ark's three-month stay at Obed-Edom's house (1 Chr 13:42) or a time, more specifically, after the building projects detailed in 1 Chr 15:1. See further Knoppers, *I Chronicles 10–29*, 613.

84. The infinitive emphasizes, here, the aspect of obligation, while the לא negative "absolutizes" the infinitive. See further, GKC §114l; Joüon §160j; and Knoppers, *Chronicles 10–29*, 605.

David's statement in verse 2, reported by the Chronicler, links back to three Pentateuchal passages, which further reinforce David's command. First, the emphasis on God's election (his choosing) of the Levites for sacred service recalls Moses' final blessing of Israel, specifically Deut 33:8–10, where verse 10 emphasizes the Levites' core duties of teaching and religious leadership (ישימו קטורה באפך וכליל על־מזבחך). Second, a direct connection is also made to Deut 10:8, which states that some of the basic duties of the (non-Aaronide) Levites were: to carry the ark (לשאת את־ארון ברית־יהוה) and to minister in front of the LORD (לעמד לפני יהוה לשרתו ולברך בשמו). Two passages in the early chapters of Numbers (detailing the precise preparations for the temporary period of the wilderness travels) also present the general duty of the Levites in caring for the Tabernacle complex, which included the ark (cf. Num 1:50–53; 3:5–9).[85]

Verse 3 resumes the narrative flow with a *wayyiqtol* construction, again with David as the subject (ויקהל דויד). The direct object of this religious gathering is, typically for the Chronicler, "all Israel" (see also 11:1 and 12:39, for instance). Two other prepositional phrases give further definition to the *purpose* of David's call to gather the people of Israel: (1) they are called to Jerusalem itself (אל־ירושלם); and (2), for the purpose of bringing up the ark to its place (להעלות).

Two issues stand out in verse 3. First, verse 2 specifically emphasizes that only the Levites are to carry the ark, while in verse 3, "all Israel" could be seen as the subject of the infinitive construct להעלות ("to bring up"). As McKenzie notes, this has led certain commentators to view verses 3 and 4 (which both emphasize the presence of a large religious assembly) as later additions.[86] That is, some perceive a tension between the sole duty of the Levites in carrying the ark in verse 2 and the apparent participation of the whole congregation in this transport in verse 3. However, the structure proposed for unit A here seems to mitigate against this tension, as David's command for the Levites to *carry* the ark in verse 2 makes it possible (in a proper, cultic sense) for all Israel to participate in the procession around the ark.

Second, four aspects tie verses 1 and 3 together and, thus, further reinforce the central function in this brief unit of David's words in verse 2. (1)

---

85. This is in keeping with the Chronicler's desire to present David as a faithful "second Moses." As Selman, *1 Chronicles*, 161, has noted, "the main aim of chapter 15 is not to describe the Levites' history and organization. The two central themes seem to be David's role vis-à-vis the Levites and the priority of worship in Israel. . . . [The Chronicler seeks] to emphasize [David's] stature as a second Moses, adapting Moses' original instructions . . . to new circumstances. This theme, however, is subsidiary to the primary aim of giving specific encouragement about the activities and personnel of Israel's worship."

86. McKenzie, *1–2 Chronicles*, 142–43.

Broadly, *wayyiqtol* constructions with David as the subject are used in both verses 1 and 3; (2) the theme of properly finding a place for the ark is introduced in verse 2 (defined as the ארון האלהים), while in verse 3 this theme of the ark (here defined as the ארון יהוה) is developed with the statement of David's choice of the Levites (in the context of the whole congregation); (3) two lexemes (and also, the varying expressions defining the ark of God) are used both in verses 1 and 3: the noun מקום, in reference to the sacred place prepared for the ark—the symbol of God's presence, and the verb כון, in reference to David's actions led by God. (4) Verse 1 affirms that David established the place, while verse 3 echoes back to that statement, following David's command concerning the Levites in verse 2.[87]

Unit B: Before the Congregation, David Prepares the Priests and Levites For the Ark-Procession (1 Chr 15:4–15)

The second section of this unit displays a narrower topical focus. The text shifts from the broader interest in David's gathering of "all Israel" (כל ישראל) in verse 3 to his specific gathering of the members of the sacerdotal tribe of Levi (in verse 4). In fact, the Chronicler is careful to point out that David gathers together *both* the Aaronide members (בני אהרן) and the non-Aaronide members of the tribe of the Levi (הלוים) and, as such, arguably highlights the *interdependent* nature of these distinct Levitical clans for the Israelite cult.[88]

Furthermore, this section is also carefully structured around five *wayyiqtol* verbs. The first three are singular and introduce two actions by David, which are related to his calling forth the various Levitical personnel (ויאסף ויקרא ויאמר, vv. 3, 11, 12). The last two forms are plural and point to the subsequent and obedient response of the Levites (ויתקדשו וישאו, vv. 14, 15). Hence, these imperfect forms with the *waw consecutive* are the key structural markers to this unit; the other verbal forms are non-imperfects and describe verbal realities *within* the sub-sections of the overall unit: two imperatives and one perfect in David's discourse of verses 12–13 (התקדשו והעליתם פרץ), one infinitive construct in the grammatical object of verse 14 (להעלות), and one perfect in the grammatical object of verse 15 (צוה).

---

87. Dirksen further notes that the Hiphil form of קהל in verse 3 "marks a special event," and is similarly used in 1 Chr 28:1 (another formal Davidic assembly). See Dirksen, *1 Chronicles*, 209.

88. See further Knoppers, "Hierodules, Priests, or Janitors?" 49–72; Leithart, "Attendants of Yahweh's House," 3–24. Others see various pro-Levitical and pro-priestly redactions in chapter 15. On these views, see especially Hanson, "1 Chronicles 15–16," 69–78.

Also, within this verbal structure, three literary forms have been woven together—in keeping with the style found throughout the whole of the APN1. Narrative comments indeed complete the *wayyiqtol* forms and describe the principal movements found in this section (in vv. 4, 11, 14, 15); in verses 5-7, an extended Levitical genealogical notice reinforces the identity of the Levites that David calls forth; and as with the first unit (vv. 1-3), David's reported direct speech in verses 12 and 14 represents the pivot point in unit B. In this way, a concentric-type outline may also be ascertained at this micro-structural level within the APN1, as table 6 illustrates.[89]

Verses 4-10: <u>Narrative:</u> David gathers (ויאסף) the priests and the Levites

    Verse 11: <u>Narrative:</u> David calls forth (ויקרא) the priests and the Levites

        Verses 12-13: <u>Direct discourse:</u> David's dual orders to the Levites: consecration (התקדשו) and transportation (והעליתם)

    Verses 14-15: <u>Narrative:</u> The priests and the Levites consecrate themselves (ויתקדשו)

Verse 15: <u>Narrative:</u> The Levites transport the ark (וישאו)

Table 6: Structure of Unit B (1 Chr 15:4-15)

The preceding observations demonstrate the overarching cohesiveness of unit B. That is, the MT itself reveals a purposeful structure, focused on David's actions and the immediate response by the Levites. It is a structure that is also centered on David's verbal commands. The first action is found in David's gathering of the tribe of Levi. The general statement in verse 1 is supported in verses 5-10 by more specific genealogical statements. Verse 4 indeed displays the typical syntactical structure of a straightforward statement in Hebrew narrative: (1) verb (ויאסף); (2) subject (דויד); (3) object (a twofold direct object: את־בני אהרן ואת־הלוים). Verse 4, then, represents the foundation upon which the Chronicler provides further identifying detail for the *second* direct object (ואת־הלוים).

---

89. Thus, it is possible to see the genealogical lists in chapter 15 as contributing to the narrative and not distracting from it—the latter position is taken by several commentators (for instance Klein, *1 Chronicles*, 347-51). However, Selman, *1 Chronicles*, 159-60, has noted that the genealogical lists (in vv. 4-10 and 16-24) "have an important function in anticipating the next section of narrative," as the Levites who sanctified themselves in vv. 11-15 "are shown to have had a valid ancestry (vv. 4-10; this was a live issue in postexilic Israel, cf. Ezr. 2:59-63 = Ne. 7:61-65), while the presence and qualifications of the musicians in verses 27-28 is explained by their selection in verses 16-24."

The genealogical expansion is thus directly connected to verse 4. It is also developed following two groups of Levites. First, in verses 5–7, the text reveals that members from each of the main non-Aaronide Levitical clans are properly represented in David's gathering.[90] Indeed, the text systematically shows that leaders and a large group of kinsmen from the Kohathite (Uriel and his kinsmen in v. 5), Merarite (Asaiah and his kinsmen in v. 6), and Gershonite (Joel and his kinsmen in v. 6) non-Aaronide Levitical clans are present. Second, in verses 8–10, the Chronicler further points out that each of the main sub-clans of the *Kohathite* clan are also represented by a key Kohathite leader and his kinsmen. The Kohathite sub-clan of Elizaphan is led by Shemaiah and his kinsmen in verse 8; the sub-clan of Hebron is present through Eliel and his kinsmen in verse 9; the sub-clan of Uzziel is represented by Aminadab and his kinsmen in verse 10.

The larger biblical witness reveals that each of these leaders in verses 8–10 are representative of significant Kohathite Levitical sub-clans. It is known from Num 3:29–30 (משפחת בני־קהת יחנו על ירך המשכן תימנה ונשיא בית־אב למשפחת הקהתי אליצפן בן־עזיאל; and note as well the implication of 2 Chr 29:12–13) that Elizaphan was a central Kohathite leader during the wilderness period, whose genealogical line, then, represented an important Kohahite sub-clan. Specifically, Elizaphan was a great-grandson of Levi through Kohath and Uzziel (see also Exod 16:18). Furthermore, key texts in Exod 6:18 (ובני קהת עמרם ויצהר וחברון ועזיאל), Num 3:19 ובני קהת, 1 Chr 6:2 (MT 5:28 למשפחתם עמרם ויצהר חברן ועזיאל), and 23:12 ובני קהת עמרם ויצהר וחברון ועזיאל, 6:18 (MT 6:3 וחברון ועזיאל) (בני קהת עמרם יצהר חברון ועזיאל ארבעה) all maintain the tradition that Hebron and Uzziel (the Kohathite sub-clans mentioned in 1 Chr 15:9–10) are also known to be one of the four sons of Kohath,[91] who in turn was known as the second son of Levi (cf. Exod 16:16—within the traditional triad of Gershon, Kohath, and Merari).

The inclusion of this expanded notice describing the Kohathite sub-clans makes sense as an *extension* of the Mosaic model, since in the initial Pentateuchal description of the duties of the Kohathites, Merarites, and Gershonites, the *Kohathites* are specifically given guard duty over the central items of the ark, table, lampstand, vessels, and screen of the tabernacle.[92]

---

90. On the slightly different order of the three main Levitical clan names between here and in the genealogies of 1 Chr 5:27–41 and 6:1–66, see Street, *The Significance*, 86–87.

91. The other two sons being Amram and Izhar (עמרם יצהר); Moses and Aaron come from Levi through Kohath and Amram (see Exod 6:16, 18 and 20).

92. See especially Num 3:30, and further, Num 4:17–20, which emphasizes the special position of the Kohathites within the Levitical (and non-Aaronide) clans because

Thus, David's *first* action specifies the *general* nature of the Levitical gathering (priests and Levites) as well as the *specific* nature of the (non-Aaronide) Levites being gathered (Kohathites [including their three specified sub-clans], Merarites, and Gershonites). David's *second* action follows naturally, then, in verse 11 and is introduced by the second *wayyiqtol* form ויקרא. Hence, out of the larger gathering of the Levitical personnel (note the use of the root אסף in verse 4) comes a specific calling (note the use of the root קרא in verse 11) of the Levitical *leadership*. These leaders are specified by means of the object of the verb/subject clause (ויקרא דויד) of verse 11.

Again, the Chronicler is careful to show how David focused *both* on Aaronide and non-Aaronide Levitical leaders. In fact, the narrative comment in verse 11 relates coherently to verses 4, 5-7, and 8-10 and sets the stage for David's dual commands (David's third grammatical *action* in this unit) in verses 12-13 by introducing the first recipients of those commands—the combined Aaronide and Levitical leaders. That is, the grammatical *objects* of David's direct and active verbal action of "calling" in verse 4 are directly related to the Levitical personnel specified in verses 4-10. Zadok and Abiathar (in verse 11: לצדוק ולאביתר הכהנים) represent the leading Aaronide priests who are representative of the "sons of Aaron" first gathered in verse 4 (בני אהרן). Conversely, first, Uriel, Asaiah, and Joel (of verse 11: וללוים לאוריאל עשיה ויואל) are the key leaders in David's time of the Levitical clans of Kohath, Merari, and Gershon—listed genealogically in verses 5-7; second, Shemaiah, Eliel, and Aminadab of verse 11 (שמעיה ואליאל ועמינדב) are the key leaders of the Kohathite sub-clans of Elizaphan, Hebron, and Uzziel—listed genealogically in verses 8-10.

The center section of unit B, in verses 12-13, is characterized by the occurrence of direct discourse, highlighted by the third *wayyiqtol* form of ויאמר. David's third action, then, culminates in this verbal command given to the Levitical leaders. Thus, the three actions by David in verses 4-11 arrive at a literary climax in verses 12-13 with his direct command for the Levites to consecrate themselves and prepare themselves to transport the

---

of their guard duty over the sacred tabernacle vessels, which included the ark. With Pratt, *1 Chronicles*, 137, it should also be noted that this sixfold Levitical division does not have precedent in Mosaic law (which typically emphasizes the basic threefold division of Kohath, Merari, and Gershon.) The added emphasis on the Kohathite sub-clans reveals a particular focus on the Chronicler's part that "may have been in response to controversies among the Levites in his day." See Pratt, *1 Chronicles*, 137. Note also the related comments in McKenzie, *1-2 Chronicles*, 143. Thompson has suggested that the Kohathite lines of Elizaphan, Hebron, and Uzziel "must have attained sufficient numbers or prestige to gain independent status." See Thompson, *1, 2 Chronicles*, 135. Hill, however, suggests, as above, that the Kohathites' role in relationship to the ark in the Pentateuch is most telling. See Hill, *1 and 2 Chronicles*, 234.

ark. The resulting sections of verses 14 and 15 highlight the two actions taken by the priests and Levites in response to this central command in verses 12–13—in parallel to the initial narrative/genealogical statements of verses 4–11.[93]

In verse 13, David's dual command to the Levites is sustained by a concomitant dual warrant—seen with two כי clauses. First, the proper consecration of the Levites and their sole transportation is needed, because at the first attempt (recorded in 1 Chr 13), the *Levites* did not carry the ark, which caused God's judging anger to break out. This dual command is also supported by another allusion to previous legal tradition in the second כי clause: כי־לא דרשנהו כמשפט—that is, Levitical consecration and transportation is needed to properly move the ark into Jerusalem because such is the only way to properly *seek* the LORD according to his *rule*. Thus, the Chronicler emphasizes David's faithfulness in properly *seeking* the ways of the LORD, as the law of God is evoked in a later circumstance.

In verse 14, the fourth *wayyiqtol* of unit B (ויתקדשו) appears in direct relationship to David's *first* imperative in verse 12a, התקדשו. David is again presented as carefully following Pentateuchal precedent as he ensures that the Levites have engaged in the proper cleansing rituals before engaging in the actual transport of the ark.[94] Hence, in verse 15, the fifth *wayyiqtol* of unit B (וישאו) occurs also as a direct response to David's *second* imperative in verse 12b, והעליתם. The second aspect of David's command involves the act *per se* of transporting the ark, which is described fully (ארון יהוה אלהי ישראל). The prepositional phrase in 12b, אל־הכינותי לו, indicating the end location for the transport, connects David's command in this unit back to unit A through the use of the lexeme כון (v. 1, with David as the subject: ויכן מקום לארון האלהם). In Num 7:9, the Mosaic rules give the detail for the ark transportation by the Levites, which is emphasized in 1 Chr 15:15, including bearing the ark with the poles on their shoulders.[95]

---

93. As McKenzie, *1–2 Chronicles*, 143–44, has written, "verses 12–15 follow a pattern of command and completion. David's speech in 12–13 consists of a command to the Levites to bring up the ark (v. 12) followed by the reason for the command in verse 13. Then verse 14, in language nearly identical to verse 12, reports that the Levites sanctified themselves and brought up the ark."

94. Note the relevant background texts in Exod 19:14–15; Lev. 21:1–4, 13–14.

95. However, on some of the discrepancies in terminology with this issue, see Japhet, *I and II Chronicles*, 302, who concludes more generally on verse 15, "the words 'as Moses had commanded' are therefore only of general import. They do not refer the reader to any specific precept or to any given text found in the Pentateuch, but only state that the transfer was carried out with legal precision, in full conformity with the will of God, as expressed in the Mosaic command."

Unit C: David Appoints the Priests and Levites for Musical Ministry (1 Chr 15:16–24)

Unit C, in verses 16–24, represents the center of the APN1, with its core focus on the establishment of Levitical *musical* service. Units A and B, in verses 1–15, focus on David's general preparation for the movement of the ark into Jerusalem and on his specific gathering of the appropriate Levitical clans. These first two units then set up the necessary conditions for the focus on Levitical music in the central unit C: (1) the need of a place for the ark in Jerusalem; (2) the oversight of the king; (3) the gathering of "all Israel," (4) the specific gathering of the priests and Levites.[96] Also, units B' and A', in verses 15:25—16:3, which narrate the actual celebratory transportation of the ark into Jerusalem, are made possible by the turning point effected in unit C—the proper set-up of the procession.

The Chronicler thus emphasizes to his readers the need for celebratory music surrounding the procession of the ark. Yet, as Thompson reminds us, the ark that is at the center of this narrative is actually non-existent for the Chronicler's audience. That is, "the original readers of this book had no more opportunity to worship God before the ark than we do."[97] Why, then, would the Chronicler accentuate the "joy" and the "holiness" associated with the ark? Thompson answers by noting that "for the Chronicler it was not the object itself but what the object *represented* that mattered."[98] In this sense, three aspects stand out: (1) God was with the Israelites and would go with them wherever they went; (2) the ark represented the holiness of God, since it contained the tables of the Ten Commandments—the essence of the Torah; (3) thus, 1 Chr 15 teaches God's compassionate forgiveness in allowing Israel a second chance. As such, "Israel's initial failure was not final and God's judgment was not just positive but instructive."[99] Ahn has

---

96. As Japhet, *I and II Chronicles*, 302, has pointed out for the transition begun in verse 16, "when the arrangements for a proper carrying of the ark are complete, David's attention is turned to another matter: the organization and singing to accompany the ark. The very fact that the bringing of the ark was accompanied by music is also mentioned in II Sam. 6.12–15, but in Chronicles there is much more detail, and the task is entrusted to those who are best qualified for it—the levitical singers."

97. Thompson, *1, 2 Chronicles*, 134, emphasis added.

98. Thompson, *1, 2 Chronicles*, 134.

99. Thompson, *1, 2 Chronicles*, 134–35 (emphasis added). For an overview of the physical features of the ark, see Hill, *1 and 2 Chronicles*, 225. Hill comments further, "the Chronicler's audience has no opportunity to worship before the ark as did David because the sacred chest was lost or destroyed during the Exile. At least there is no record that this piece of furniture was part of the inventory of temple vessels and articles returned to Jerusalem under Persian auspices (cf. Ezra 1:7–11)" (p. 234). For Hill, *1 and 2 Chronicles*, 225, there are three crucial aspects to the symbolism of the ark: (1) God's

also pointed to this feature in the rhetorical setting of David's speech here in 1 Chr 15:12-13—when he writes:

> For the [Chronicler], the focus is on the meaning of the ark which the ark conveys. In effect, the ark is absent from the Judahites' life in the time of the [Chronicler]. Much earlier, with the destruction of Jerusalem, the ark had disappeared and the Israelites had been deported to Babylon. . . . Thus, as the symbol of YHWH's presence, the ark of the covenant of YHWH is significantly linked to the temple. . . . David's speech functions to persuade the assembly of Israel and the Levites to go carry out the task of transferring of the ark according to YHWH's instructions to Moses. . . . [Eventually] David plays the role as a worship leader like the high priest on behalf of the Israelites (1 Chr 15:27). . . . David is portrayed as a worship leader who recognizes YHWH's ordinances.[100]

Thus, the APN1, as it centers on the ark, stresses the divine qualities of presence, holiness, and forgiveness—qualities which are celebrated in the musical ministry of the Levites established in unit C of the APN1. The emphasis is not on the "ark as a sacred object, but what that piece of furniture represents: *the mobile presence of God among his people and his uncompromising holiness.*"[101] This central unit is framed by two *wayyiqtol* clauses. As in unit B, a command of David is followed by direct (and obedient) Levitical response.[102]

This response involves the establishment of the Levitical singers, going beyond the precedent set by the Priestly and Deuteronomic writings (which made provisions for priests, prophets, judges, and kings, but not for musicians and singers)—so that Kaufmann was apt at describing the Priestly sanctuary as a "sanctuary of silence," in comparison to Davidic liturgical practice.[103] At this juncture, many commentators view the Chronicler's emphases on

---

presence in the midst of Israel, based on descriptive texts in Exodus (the ark's lid [Exod 37:6-9] and the place of meeting between God and Israel—above the cover of the ark and between the cherubim [Exod 25:22]); (2) the Mosaic covenant at Sinai (since the law of Moses was contained in the ark—which provides a natural tie-in to the Davidic covenant in 1 Chr 17); (3) the rule of God over Israel and all creation.

100. Ahn, *The Persuasive Portrayal*, 112-13.

101. Hill, *1 and 2 Chronicles*, 234, emphasis added.

102. As Knoppers notes, *I Chronicles 10-29*, 619, while earlier in this chapter David has made direct appointments to prepare for the entry of the ark into Jerusalem, "in this case (15:15-24), he delegates authority to the Levitical officers themselves."

103. As noted by Knoppers, *I Chronicles 10-29*, 619-20. See further Kaufmann, *The Religion of Israel*, 175-211.

Levitical singers and musicians as merely reflecting his own postexilic situation. With Knoppers, we are arguing that this description of David's cultic innovations very likely resonated with and provided a "historical *precedent* for the practice of worship at the Jerusalem Temple in the late Persian or early Hellenistic period."[104] As Knoppers then states, "this is undoubtedly true," and would show the relevance for the use of *preexilic* sources since "the historical situation is surely more complex."[105]

Knoppers points to three areas of evidence in this regard: (1) the existence of musicians and singers as a "constituent feature of temple worship in a variety of ancient Near Eastern societies;"[106] (2) the appearance of male or female singers in other biblical texts (2 Sam 19:36; 1 Kgs 10:12; Ezek 40:44; Qoh 2:8; Ps 68:26; 87:7); (3) the existence of extra-biblical evidence that "indicates that musicians existed in *preexilic* Jerusalem."[107] Based on the text of 1 Chr 15 and on the lines of evidence cited above, Knoppers argues that evidence connecting the Levitical singers and musicians to David's time is strong and that the connection between the origin of this Levitical music service and the Chronicler's own time is often too quickly made. His conclusion is worth repeating at this juncture, before the analysis of the central section of the APN1. Knoppers writes:

> *The complete absence of singers from the Pentateuch and from most of the Deuteronomistic work tells us more about the limitations of these sources than it does about the conditions at the Jerusalem Temple during the monarchy.* Rather than viewing the Chronicler as inventing the tradition of song and music at the temple, it may be the better part of wisdom to say that he took a special interest in Levitical singers (Kleinig 1993) and sought to advance their cause. *His work provides an impeccable precedent for a certain kind of worship at the Jerusalem Temple.* The central role given to the Levitical singers during the reign of David justifies an integral liturgical role for their descendants in the author's own time.[108]

Such broader considerations are reinforced by a close inspection of this central unit C, which displays a carefully established structure that both

---

104. Knoppers, *I Chronicles 10–29*, 620.
105. Knoppers, *I Chronicles 10–29*, 620.
106. Knoppers, *I Chronicles 10–29*, 620. (And note chapter four of this work)
107. Sennacherib's list of tribute from king Hezekiah includes both male and female musicians. See Knoppers, *I Chronicles 10–29*, 620, emphasis added, and 620–21 as a whole.
108. Knoppers, *I Chronicles 10–29*, 621, emphasis added.

relates the development of Levitical music and song to David and, by virtue of its rhetorical shaping and placement, stresses the significance of this tradition for the Chronicler's postexilic audience.

The first *wayyiqtol* clause of unit C, in verse 16, ויאמר דויד, introduces the sub-section of verse 16, which presents David's command for establishing a Levitical musical ministry for the transportation of the ark. The second *wayyiqtol* clause, in verse 17, ויעמידו, introduces the Levitical response resulting from David's command. The lexeme עמד ties verses 16 and 17 together, since it is found both in David's command (v. 16: להעמיד) and in this narrative introduction to the Levitical response (the *wayyiqtol* form). This response entails a carefully stated twofold process: (1) the establishment of the *leaders* for the Levitical musical service in verses 17-18, and (2) the careful organization of the *duties* which the leaders (established in verses 17-18) are to oversee.[109] As Kleinig notes, the Chronicler demonstrates here that David did not go about this organization on his own but carefully selected Levitical leaders to carry out the task (the chief priests and the six Levitical leaders of verse 11). Thus, David "did not usurp their rights in sacral matters, but paid due respect to them."[110]

The leaders, introduced in verses 17-18, are also carefully presented in two phases, both with genealogical notices. The Levitical "heads" (set up in unit B) first call on Heman, Asaph, and Ethan (הימן אסף איתן) in verse 17 to be the primary Levitical *musical* leaders. Verse 18 introduces the second-order Levitical musical leaders: ועמהם אחיהם המשנים. Here, ten Levites are presented as this type of second-order musical leaders (thus, under the primary authority of Heman, Asaph, and Ethan). Also, two other Levites are described as gatekeepers (השערים: Obed-Edom and Jeiel).

This Levitical music leadership structure forms the core basis on which the musical *duties* are established in verses 19-24. In this sub-section of unit C, five non-Aaronide duties are introduced along with one Aaronide Levitical musical duty. The key Levitical leaders introduced in verses 17-18 are responsible for the first three set of duties related to three distinct musical instruments: (1) Heman, Asaph, and Ethan (introduced in v. 17 as the core musical leaders) are defined as singers (משררים) responsible for sounding the

---

109. Thus, the lack of organization and proper preparation in David's first unsuccessful attempt at moving the ark in 1 Chr 13 is set in contrast at this juncture of 1 Chr 15 with the appropriate and elaborate care taken to prepare for the successful procession of the ark. As Johnstone has remarked on the emphasis of 1 Chr 15:17-25, "in contrast to the free exuberance of the abortive first attempt to bring in the ark (1 Chron. 13), [Chronicles] now stipulates that only Levites duly consecrated for the task can appropriately conduct the procession." See Johnstone, *1 and 2 Chronicles*, 1:184.

110. Kleinig, *The Lord's Song*, 47.

cymbals in verse 19 (מצלתים);[111] (2) Zechariah, Aziel, Shemiramoth, Jehiel, Unni, Eliab, Maaseiah, and Benaiah—introduced in verse 18a as the first group of second-order Levitical musical leaders—are responsible in verse 20 for the *harps* (נבלים) according to a specific style (על־עלמות); (3) Mattithiah, Eliphelehu, Mikneiah, Obededom, Jeiel, and Azaziah—introduced in verse 18b as the second group of second-order Levitical musical leaders—are responsible in verse 21 for the *lyres* (כנרות), directing according to a different style (על־השמינית).[112] As Japhet has noted, the point to emphasize here is that the Chronicler is careful to show: (1) the precise organizational set-up for Levitical music at this temporary stage of worship at the ark, and (2) its anticipation of the more permanent temple service.[113]

Thus, for the procession to transport the ark into Jerusalem, the central leaders Heman, Asaph, and Ethan are responsible for the percussive instruments, while the second-order Levites are responsible for the stringed instruments (vv. 19–21). Furthermore, the Chronicler notes three other duties established by the Levitical music leaders for the procession, in verses 22–24: (1) in verse 22, a single musical director is established over the whole procession, Cheneniah—based on his overall skill (כי מבין הוא);[114] (2) two notices of Levitical gatekeepers *for the ark* (vv. 23 [Berekiah and Elkanah] and 24b [Obededom and Jehiah]) frame the list of, (3) the seven priests who were to sound the trumpet before the ark.[115]

Several scholars see the inclusion of the gatekeepers as problematic.[116] But, if one allows for some repetition in the Chronicler's style, the

111. These three singers appear in the major Levitical genealogy of 1 Chr 6:16–32. Ethan is also noted in the superscription of Ps 89. However, in 1 Chr 25:1–31, Jeduthun appears in place of Ethan, along with Asaph and Heman—so there is compositional variation at this juncture. See further the discussions in Knoppers, *I Chronicles 10–29*, 620; Japhet, *I and II Chronicles*, 303.

112. Note the textual discussion of these musical terms in note 25 above. Japhet simply remarks that the terms "Alamoth," "Sheminith," and "lead" (נצח) which "also occur in the Psalms and belong to the realm of Temple musical functions, have not yet been fully clarified . . . the unusual phrases here, combining the names of the musical instruments with the titles of the psalm headings, are evidence that their meaning had already become obscure and their use is archaic." See Japhet, *I and II Chronicles*, 304.

113. Japhet, *I and II Chronicles*, 303–4.

114. מבין also occurs in relationship to the permanent temple rotations of the Levitical (prophetic) singers in 1 Chr 25:6–7.

115. For further discussion of the nature of the liturgical procession, see Kleinig, *The Lord's Song*, 44–51, who concludes, "1 Chron. 15.16–24 thus contains David's command to the leaders of the Levites to arrange a choir for the transport of the ark, as well as the fulfillment of that command" (emphasis added). See Kleinig, *The Lord's Song*, 51.

116. Japhet, for instance, sees the mention of gatekeepers in verse 23 as an interruption in the sequence between verse 22 (Cheneniah the music leader) and verse 24 (the

importance of the gatekeepers is apparent. As Johnstone has written, "the threefold reference to 'gatekeepers' (vv. 18, 23, 24; cf. 1 Chron. 9:17-26) emphasizes the absolute necessity for *preserving* the sanctity of the ark and supervising all the rites associated with it."[117]

Also, Knoppers argues that the gatekeepers play an important role in the various texts of the Chronicler. This was not simply an honorific title, but the role came with important duties since "the main obligation of gatekeepers was to guard the sanctuary from possible encroachment."[118] 1 Chr 9:17-32 shows that gatekeepers had a variety of duties—from military, to administrative and even culinary duties. For Knoppers, one should approach the gatekeepers in 1 Chr 15 on the basis of this *complex* pattern of duties. First Chr 15:18 attests to the general title of the gatekeepers, while verses 23 and 24 refer to more specific duties within the procession.[119] Further, Kleinig notes that the role of gatekeeper in 1 Chr 15 should be seen as *temporary*, and thus distinct from the *earlier* tabernacle gatekeepers in 1 Chr 9:17-26 and the *later* gatekeepers for the temple in 1 Chr 26:1-19. Also, as table 7 below shows, the literary shaping of verses 16-24 points to the significance of the gatekeepers. Verse 22 lists Chemeniah, the overall music leader for the procession, at the center. Three sets of broader duties then frame this central verse: (1) vv. 19-21: the cymbal, harp, and lyre players, and (2) vv. 23-24: the gatekeepers, priestly trumpet players, and additional gatekeepers.

Overall, this reading posits that verses 17-18 (Levitical leaders) and verses 19-24 (Levitical duties) are closely interlinked and are *not* representative of two distinct lists, which would have been later redacted and supplemented into the narrative of 1 Chr 15—as in Braun's view for instance.[120] In fact, the Chronicler first shows that the newly established service of celebratory music surrounding the procession of the ark into Jerusalem is led mainly by non-Aaronide Levites; at the same time, however, he is also careful to demonstrate the participation of Aaronide priests as well, which stands as a further measure of the *interdependent* nature of

---

Aaronides trumpet players). She argues, then, that verse 23 is probably a later gloss. The two names of verse 23 appear in a genealogy in 1 Chr 9:16, but for Japhet, the significance "of the gloss can no longer be ascertained." See Japhet, *I and II Chronicles*, 304. Similarly, note the arguments of Klein, *1 Chronicles*, 354-56, for verses 18, 23, and 24.

117. Johnstone, *1 and 2 Chronicles*, 185 (emphasis added). See also Selman, *1 Chronicles*, 164-65.

118. Knoppers, *I Chronicles 10-29*, 622.

119. Knoppers, *I Chronicles 10-29*, 622. Note, also, that Knoppers reads verse 18 as defining the whole list as gatekeepers. See Knoppers, *I Chronicles 10-29*, 607-8.

120. Braun, *1 Chronicles*, 190-91. Similarly, note also Klein, *1 Chronicles*, 349-51; Dirksen, *1 Chronicles*, 206-15.

these Levitical clans—in contrast to the oft-mentioned perceived rivalries between Aaronide and non-Aaronide clans at this juncture. As Johnstone has judiciously noted:

> It is the prerogative of the *priests* alone to sound the trumpets. ... In shattering sound that is beyond the expression of words, the blaring trumpets announce the theophany (Num. 10.9-10; 31.1-12), the arrival of God the victor in battle, now ritualized by the arrival of his ark in his sanctuary. The *Levites* with their psalms sing the *ordered* verbal response of the community to this self-manifestation of God.[121]

Wilcock has also observed the significance of the institution of Levitical music generally in 1 Chr 15 as it both reflects on the past and anticipates the future. It also promotes both careful organization and exuberant proclamation, since "the principles underlying [the worship] are rooted in the past, but the expression of them is very much in the present."[122] All in all, this unit stands out in the APN1, since it is closely focused on the *musical* duties of the priests and the Levites for the procession; it also *anticipates* the more permanent Levitical musical function at the temple, established formally in 1 Chr 23 and 25. Table 7 summarizes the structure of unit C presented above.

I. David's <u>Command</u> for the Establishment of a Levitical Musical Service: 1 Chr 15:16

II. The Levites' Obedient <u>Response</u>: Institution of Levitical Musical Leaders and Duties: 1 Chr 15:17-24

    A. Levitical Musical Leaders: vv. 17-18 (Three principals and one group of second-order Levitical leaders)

    B. Sixfold Levitical Musical Duties: vv. 19-24

        1. Three Main Instrumental Leaders on *Cymbals*: v. 19

        2. First Set of Second-Order Leaders on *Harps*: v. 20

        3. Second Set of Second-Order Leaders on *Lyres*: v. 21

        4. One Skilled and Principal Musical Leader: v. 22

        5. Two Levitical Gatekeepers: v. 23

        6. Seven Aaronide Levitical Trumpet Players: v. 24a

        7. Two Levitical Gatekeepers: v. 24b

Table 7: Structure of Unit C (1 Chr 15:16-24)

---

121. Johnstone, *1 and 2 Chronicles*, 186, emphasis added.
122. See Wilcock, *The Message of Chronicles*, 69.

Unit B': With the Congregation, David Leads the Priests and the Levites in the Procession (1 Chr 15:25–29)

Following the central unit focused on the institution of the musical service of the Levites, unit B' initiates the narrative description of the ark's movement by means of the joyous procession from the house of Obed-Edom to its prepared place in Jerusalem. As with the other sections of the APN1, unit B' (15:25–29) also presents the reader with an interrelated structure that holds the unit together from = grammatical and thematic point of views. In verses 25, 26, and 29, three *wayyiqtol* temporal forms of היה (ויהי) delineate the description of the ark's procession. The *wayyiqtol* in the middle of verse 26, ויזבחו, falls within the sequence introduced by the second past tense narrative temporal marker (ויהי) at the beginning of verse 26. Unit B', then, entails a two-stage *preparatory* process and the *execution* proper of the procession. Because the central unit in verses 16–24 has established the needed set-up for the proper procession of the ark (namely, the Levitical and priestly organization), the text in B' moves quickly to show how David, the priests and the Levites, and the whole congregation join forces in preparing for and executing the liturgical celebration.

The ויהי clause in verse 25 (וַיְהִי דויד וזקני ישראל ושרי האלפים) leads to the first stage of the preparation for the procession. With this initial step, David and key leaders are described as moving towards the ark, which is still at Obed-Edom's house. The Chronicler emphasizes the participation of the large congregation, in contrast to the emphasis in 2 Sam 6:12–16 on David's personal faith.[123] As Hill remarks, "the divine 'help' afforded David (1 Chron. 15:26; cf. 12:18) is now extended to the Levitical corps as confirmation that this time the plans for the transfer of the ark are truly sanctioned by God."[124] The second ויהי clause, in verse 26 (וַיְהִי בעזר האלהים), shifts the narrative to the second stage in the preparation for the procession—of celebratory sacrifices at the ark, introduced in the second *wayyiqtol* in 26b.

Furthermore, verses 27 and 28, being introduced by a *waw* + non-verbal (ודויד), are set outside the structure of the narrative movement proper. In this descriptive section, the Chronicler emphasizes: (1) the priestly overtones to David's leadership of the Levites and the priests; (2) the execution of the Levitical musical ministry around the ark, properly led by Cheneniah; (3) the participation of "all Israel" in the exuberant proclamation of celebratory instrumental music and song. This unit, then, accentuates the

---

123. Following Selman, *1 Chronicles*, 165.
124. Hill, *1 and 2 Chronicles*, 236.

movement of the ark into Jerusalem and its positive effect on the congregation. As Hill concludes on this section:

> David is reestablishing God's rule over Israel and Israel's loyalty to Yahweh's covenant with his chosen people. The relationship between God and Israel, the relationship of Israelite to Israelite, and the relationship of Israel to the nations are once again restored under the umbrella of the Mosaic covenant.[125]

The ark is thus presented as a key symbol of the LORD's covenantal promise and, hence, of the presence of the LORD God of Israel with his people—here, specifically through properly established means of liturgical leadership. Further, the ark (ארון) is variously described in the APN as the "ark of God," (15:1, 2, 24, 16:1: ארון אלהים), the "ark of the LORD," (15:2, 3, 16:4: ארון יהוה), the "ark of the LORD, the God of Israel," (15:12, 14: ארון יהוה אלהי ישראל), "the ark of the covenant of the LORD," (15:25, 26, 28, 29, 16:37: ארון ברית־יהוה). However, the latter description, which includes the term "covenant," ברית, is included after the establishment of the Levitical procession. This shows the Chronicler's special concern for the Levites. As they have been endowed with this musical ministry, they have also been blessed with the opportunity to announce the covenant promises, as the LORD symbolically enters the holy place of Jerusalem. That is, as Eskenazi has remarked of this feature, "it is inevitable that one recognizes the Levites, not the ark alone, as the vehicle of the covenant."[126] Or, as Johnstone has commented:

> The ark is now designated by [the Chronicler] with the title, "the ark of the covenant of the LORD" (v. 25). While in the preceding chapter in the context of the international recognition of David, and in the previous verses in celebration of God's cosmic victory, it had been the universal term for Deity that had been used. . . . [The Chronicler] is now concerned about the inner-Israel significance of the ark: at this formal moment of the final integration of symbol and reality at the center of the nation's life, it is Israel in relation to the LORD, the name by which the Deity had been made known to Israel alone, as the people of the LORD that stands now in the forefront of interest.[127]

Finally, the third ויהי clause followed by a *qatal* form, in verse 29 (ויהי ארון ברית יהוה בא עד עיר דויד), moves to the execution of the procession as

---

125. Hill, *1 and 2 Chronicles*, 237.
126. See Eskenazi, "A Literary Approach," 270–71.
127. Johnstone, *1 and 2 Chronicles*, 186.

the narrative refers to the physical movement of the ark into Jerusalem. As the ark finally arrives to its new location, the Chronicler is showing how, on the one hand, "all of Israel" (represented by the gathered congregation) is faithfully *supporting* David, while Michal, representing Saul's *failed* royal house unfaithfully rejects God's chosen king. As Selman notes, "the isolation of Saul's daughter was a further demonstration of the unfitness of Saul's house to lead the people of God."[128] Table 8 summarizes the rhetorical development of unit B'.

I. *Preparation* for the Procession—Stage 1: Movement to the Ark: v. 25

II. *Preparation* for the Procession—Stage 2: Celebratory Sacrifices and Music: vv. 26–28

    1. Narrative *Movement*: v. 26

    2. Narrative *Background*: vv. 27–28

III. *Execution* of the Procession: v. 29

    1. Narrative *Movement*: v. 29a

    2. Narrative *Background*: v. 29b

Table 8: Structure of Unit B' (1 Chr 15:25–29)

Unit A': In Jerusalem, David Leads in Worship Around the Ark the Levites Have Correctly Carried (1 Chr 16:1–3)

In the final section of the APN1, the focus moves to the *effect* of the ark on the people gathered for the occasion—now that it has been properly brought into Jerusalem by David and the Levites. Several authors, such as Knoppers or McKenzie, view the pericope in 16:1–3 as concluding the APN1, which is the position taken here.[129] Others approach 16:1–3 with a stronger connection to the APN2 (the rest of chapter 16). Japhet especially connects this text with 1 Chr 16.[130] In fact, 16:1–3 could be seen as a literary

---

128. Johnstone, *1 and 2 Chronicles*, 166.

129. See the textual delimitation in Knoppers, *I Chronicles 10–29*, 604–5 (and similarly Klein, *1 Chronicles*, 345–56). For Knoppers, 16:1–3 represents the final stage of the APN1 and he defines the unit as a "national celebration for the ark." See Knoppers, *I Chronicles 10–29*, 605. McKenzie, *1–2 Chronicles*, 146, notes that 16:1–3 "continue the account [in Chronicles] of the movement of the ark [from chapter 15] in parallel to 2 Sam 6:17–19a."

130. See Japhet, *I and II Chronicles*, 311–13. Selman, *1 Chronicles*, 166, also reads 16:1–3 in parallel with 16:43, connected with the theme of blessing.

"hinge" unit—since it both concludes some of the emphases of the APN1 (the ark being properly moved) and introduces the geographical location and context for the liturgical celebration of the APN2.[131]

Overall, unit A' in 16:1-3 reveals a twofold structure. First, verse 1 focuses broadly on the return of the ark to Jerusalem, at the conclusion of the procession. This narrative sequence is tied together with three *wayyiqtol* forms with a *plural* subject. The plural subject of the *wayyiqtol* forms in this first sub-section at least represents the members of the formal procession (David, the Levites, and other leaders) or, possibly, the congregation as a whole. The Chronicler seems to emphasize the total participation of the LORD's people, in contrast to the emphasis in 2 Samuel 6 (as noted above). As the ark comes to rest in its place in Jerusalem, the initial actions involved not only David but the larger group—perhaps as a sign that the blessing inherent in the symbol of the ark is for the entire congregation. As McKenzie suggests on this point:

> The difference between 1 Chr 16:1-3 and its Samuel predecessor is slight. The only one worthy of note is in verse 1 where Chronicles uses a plural verb without an expressed subject and thus has the people as a whole rather than David alone offer sacrifices to God. The people, therefore, are not merely present but are active participants in the cultic celebrations.[132]

Thus, verse 1 presents the reader with a three-step progression detailing the arrival of the ark in its place. The first *wayyiqtol*, ויביאו, indicates the first movement enacted by the group involved—of formally bringing in the ark at the end of the procession. The second verb in the sequence, ויציגו, shows the cessation of movement as the ark is set in the tent (האהל) pitched for it (נטה) by David. Again, both of these latter lexemes produce a literary echo directly back to unit A, where David initially pitched the tent for the ark. The third verb in the narrative sequence of verse 1, ויקריבו, demonstrates the *result* of the ark having been *moved* and *set* by the congregation. The object of this third *wayyiqtol* clarifies the result: sacrificial celebration (עלות ושלמים) in front of God (whose broader name is used at the end of verse 1 in the phrase לפני האלהים).[133] As Johnstone writes, "the joyous spontaneity of the new order is

---

131. This is similar to Leithart, *1 & 2 Chronicles*, 49, who argues that 1 Chr 16:1-3 "both concludes the ark's ascent and begins the following chapter."

132. McKenzie, *1-2 Chronicles*, 147.

133. As Hill, *1 and 2 Chronicles*, 236, remarks, the burnt offerings indicate dedication for God and sacrifices for sin (Leviticus 1); the fellowship offerings point to the completion of a vow (David vowed to honor the LORD with the ark in 1 Chr 13) and thankfulness to God.

expressed by whole burnt offerings and communion sacrifices (v. 1) offered on the brazen altar as in 1 Chron. 15.26."[134]

Second, verses 2 and 3 conclude this final unit of the APN1 with a narrower focus on David's role in the initial stages of the celebration in Jerusalem. David's role in offering blessing and food to the congregation has been variously defined as the extension of a "supreme mediatorial role as priest," or as a "semi-priestly-role, mediating temporal (v. 3) as well as a spiritual blessing."[135] As Selman notes, only David and Solomon are known to have exercised this particular privilege in Israel, which highlights the spiritual solemnity of the event (one that explodes into liturgical praise in the APN2).[136]

In these last two verses of the APN1 three *wayyiqtol* forms with a *singular* subject (here, expressed clearly as David) encase the narrative sequence highlighting these actions towards the congregation. The first verb, ויכל, indicates the conclusion of David's priestly activity—as he "finishes" (from the root כלה) offering the whole burnt and peace offerings. Thus, the first singular *wayyiqtol* in the sequence expressly denotes David's focused priestly activities, following the celebration at the ark led by the priests and the Levites. David's first priestly activity, then, was properly directed towards the LORD in the offering of sacrifices (the vertical axis). The next two *wayyiqtol* forms in the sequence (vv. 2b and 3) denote two further priestly acts on David's part, which flow from the first one, and which are now focused on the LORD's congregation (the horizontal axis). Indeed, in verse 2b, ויברך, introduces David's act of imparting a blessing on the people—specifically by means of the covenantal name of God (בשם יהוה). This act represents the spiritual aspect of David's ministry to the people—as it proceeds from the celebration at the ark.

In verse 3, the third *wayyiqtol* with a singular subject, ויהלק, denotes David's final act towards the congregation—a physical act of blessing—as he provides the people with three sets of food items. The stated comprehensiveness of the recipients (לכל־איש ישראל מאיש ועד־אשה לאיש), as well as the detail given for these foodstuffs in verse 3 (ככר־לחם ואשפר ואשישה) suggests a great largesse in David's provision.[137] Table 9 summarizes the basic outline of this final unit within the APN1.

---

134. Johnstone, *1 and 2 Chronicles*, 189.

135. The first definition is from Johnstone, *1 and 2 Chronicles*, 189; the second is from Selman, *1 Chronicles*, 166–67.

136. Selman, *1 Chronicles*, 166.

137. This priestly activity of David is a key feature in the typological relationship made by the Chronicler between David and Moses, the initial cult founder. For example, even Klein, who remains skeptical of the compositional integrity of the APN1,

I. The Ark Arrives in Jerusalem: *Broad* Focus (three *wayyiqtols* with plural subject): 16:1
II. Celebration at the Ark in Jerusalem: *Narrower* Focus (three *wayyiqtols* with singular subject): 16:2–3

Table 9: Structure of Unit A' (1 Chr 16:1–3)

Conclusion: Relationship of Units and Inherent Emphases of the APN1

The particular rhetorical reading of the APN1 proposed here relates well with some of Duke's more general observations on the rhetorical shape of Chronicles. For him, the Davidic narratives (and the Solomonic narratives) are texts which have been specifically shaped by the Chronicler for the purpose of promoting the message of properly seeking after the LORD. As Duke writes of the ideal of "seeking after the LORD" (in 1 Chr 10—2 Chr 9 especially):

> The narrative employment [of this paradigmatic ideal] also carries with it an argument about the course of history and the nature of reality. As a result, the audience is implicitly called on to accept an ideology about how to live in this reality. *Inherent to the narrative is an attempt to persuade an audience to evaluate their present situation in light of this paradigm and to take appropriate action. The possibility of following the ideal model offers the audience the hope of blessing.*[138]

In essence, at the end of the APN1, the Chronicler is eager to show: (1) how the participation of both the leaders (David, the priests, the Levites especially) *and* the whole congregation is germane to the celebration of the ark's movement, and (2) how the movement of the ark and the ensuing musical celebration sets the proper stage for David to act as a key liaison between the God of heaven and earth—symbolically and spiritually present at the ark—and God's people—physically present as the gathered congregation. In this manner, the APN1 contributes fully to the overall argument of the Davidic narratives, which acknowledge David as a human and historical

---

observes this phenomenon—if only at the literary level. Klein, *1 Chronicles*, 358, writes on the text of the APN1, "David in this chapter is a second Moses, who also pitched a tent and blessed the people."

138. Duke, *The Persuasive Appeal*, 54 (emphasis added).

embodiment of the spiritual paradigm of properly seeking after the ways of Yahweh. Such is the way of future hope and blessing in the perspective offered in the Chronicler's text.[139]

On this basis, the following concluding comments will: (1) present the basic logic present in the *relationship* of the various rhetorical units analyzed, and (2) suggest certain rhetorical emphases present in the overall shape of the APN1 as analyzed.

Basic Logic

The rhetorical structure proposed in this chapter for the APN1 may be represented by the data in table 10.[140]

Unit A: In Jerusalem, *David* correctly chooses the Levites to carry the *ark* (1 Chr 15:1–3)

> **Unit B:** Before the *congregation*, *David* prepares priests and Levites for the procession (1 Chr 15:4–15)
>
>> **Unit C:** David *appoints* the priests and the Levites for musical ministry (1 Chr 15:16–24)
>
> **Unit B':** With the *congregation*, *David* leads priests and Levites in the procession (1 Chr 15:25–29)

Unit A': In Jerusalem, *David* leads in worship at the *ark* the Levites have correctly carried (1 Chr 16:1–3)

Table 10: Overall Structure of the APN1 (1 Chr 15:1—16:3)

---

139. Alster has commented on the different rhetorical strategies between the ark narratives in 2 Samuel and 1 Chronicles. He writes that "both versions of the David story portray two characteristics of the king at the beginning of his reign. Both show David as founder of the Temple in Jerusalem. But while 2 Samuel depicts David the warrior, the Chronicler chooses instead to show the king as unifier of the Israelite people, while playing down his military role for the time being (until 1 Chron. 28:3). In order to show these double portraits, the two books use different strategies. *Both use the primary effect—Samuel to show David the warrior, and Chronicles to show David the unifier. But David's image as Temple founder is brought up differently: 2 Samuel uses surprise, and Chronicles uses sheer length, to produce their respective recency effects*" (emphasis added). See Alster, "Narrative Surprise," 463–6.

140. For a slightly different chiastic reading of 1 Chr 15:2–16:3, see Leithart, *1 & 2 Chronicles*, 48, who sees 15:2 and 15:25–29 in parallel as A/A' units and 15:3 and 16:1–3 in parallel as B/B' units.

First, the outer units of A and A' both focus on the physical location of Jerusalem as the sacred place of God's symbolic presence in the ark and its tent—in anticipation of the more permanent structure of the physical temple. Thus, the whole unit is framed by an emphasis on the sacred geographical location of Jerusalem. The city, from which God's word and God's law emanate (as stated in Micah 4:2–5), is at the heart of David's concern with the ark and of the Chronicler's appropriation of this key theme. Also, both units focus intently on the dynamic existing between David's choice for the Levites to carry the ark into Jerusalem—and in the *effect* of this choice on the congregation. It is *because* the Levites are properly chosen in unit A that eventually, the blessings of unit A' are *available* for the congregation gathered around the ark in Jerusalem.[141]

Second, the inner units of B and B' both focus on David's relationship with the congregation vis-à-vis the role of the priests and the Levites. Hence, both units define and develop the dynamic of David's relationship to the priests and the Levites before and after the central event of the institution of Levitical music for the procession. In unit B, the congregation is gathered in Jerusalem (15:4), out of which David calls forth the head priests and Levites. In unit B', David and his Levitical leaders join the congregation in moving out of and back to Jerusalem, to the "city of David," (15:29 עד־עיר דויד). Third, then, the distinct parallels between units A/A' and B/B' locate unit C (15:16–24) at the structural center.

Consequently, in the structure of the APN1, Jerusalem and the temple are central. The establishment of the musical ministry of the Levites enables the symbol of God's presence to properly enter the holy city. Much of the narrative action is either in Jerusalem itself or leading back to Jerusalem in relationship to David's leadership at the ark, the response of priests and Levites, and the larger congregation. As Knoppers has noted, "to speak of the position of Jerusalem in the Chronicler's work is to deal with one of the most consistent and beloved subjects addressed by the biblical author.... The city plays a central role in his worldview."[142]

A key factor for the Chronicler's rhetorical emphasis on Jerusalem would have indeed been his desire to address both internal and external challenges to the maintenance of the temple cult in Persian-dominated Jerusalem.

---

141. As for example McConville has noted on the celebration in Jerusalem narrated in unit A', "David presides over the whole affair, evidently directing, or temporarily taking over, the priestly duty of 'blessing the people' (v. 2; cf. Deut. 10:8). The distribution of various foods is no mere royal bounty, but has a symbolic character, re-affirming to the people God's good intention to let theme enjoy the good things of the promised land." See McConville, *I and II Chronicles*, 50.

142. See Knoppers, "'The City Yhwh Has Chosen,'" 307–26.

Internally, even as Judaism had become something of an international movement, in the city of Zion "the heart of the religion was relatively small."[143] Jerusalem was economically challenged and the support of the temple was limited and in need of full support from the fledgling Jewish community. Externally, during the Achaemenid era, the possible religious and economic challenges of other shrines in the postexilic period (such as Lachish or Gerizim), the rise of other Jewish communities (such as at Elephantine), and the economic domination of larger cities in the Levant (such as Samaria) were all factors (at least from a basic historical perspective) that combined in raising the need for a strong defense of the significance of an enduring temple service in Jerusalem.[144] In fact, as Knoppers concludes:

> All of this promotion of Jerusalem makes eminent sense. In the time the Chronicler wrote, Jerusalem was pivotal to the economy, social identity, and religious life of Yehud. . . . The Chronicler situates Jerusalem's position internationally in his own time by recourse to establishing such a status for the city in preexilic history.[145]

> The issue is not whether Yhwh needed this place but how much the people did. *Israel's temple city had proven its great value on numerous occasions in the past. The question in the present is whether the people would have recourse to it.*[146]

Key Rhetorical Emphases

The preceding remarks lead to finally noting *three* major areas of inherent rhetorical emphases particularly raised in the text of the APN1. First, this passage makes it clear that in the Chronicler's perspective, there exists in sacred music and song the ability to express worshipful gratitude for the blessing of God's presence among his people. This is certainly borne out by the central function of the unit dealing with the establishment of Levitical musical leaders and duties. It is further made apparent by the responsibility given to Asaph and his kinsmen to lead in a full-fledged liturgical celebration in the APN2 (as well as the further developments on Levitical duty in the DKN2 in chapters 23, 25, and 26). In this context, Matthews has noted

---

143. Knoppers, "'The City Yhwh Has Chosen,'" 307.

144. Note the fuller discussion on these internal and external challenges to the temple in Jerusalem, in Knoppers, "'The City Yhwh Has Chosen,'" 314–21.

145. Knoppers, "'The City Yhwh Has Chosen,'" 314.

146. Knoppers, "'The City Yhwh Has Chosen,'" 326, emphasis added.

that the role of the Levitical guilds was key in enabling the praise and the lament of Israel before the LORD, with the more formal cultic developments of the ark and temple in Jerusalem. Of these guilds, he states:

> They in essence represent the movement of music into a formal liturgical setting with a set religious calendar of performances. . . . Each guild would have ultimately created and become associated with a particular repertoire of songs—thereby aiding in the transmission and survival of this sacred music.[147]

Ross, among others, has also pointed to the inherent prophetic power of the ministry of the Levitical musical guilds set up by David. In reference to David's role in the prophetic nature of the temple guilds (1 Chr 25), he writes:

> [David] was signifying that their singing, and especially what they were singing, was due to prophetic inspiration. . . . There is [thus] a level of artistic skill in music and poetry that deserves to be called "inspired"; it is truly evidence that the human spirit shares something of the divine work of creating.[148]

Second, part of the intent of the APN1 also appears to be an emphasis on the significance of spiritually mature and musically trained leadership for the production of God-pleasing instrumental and vocal music. As Leithart notes in general of David's role in this context of 1 Chr 15–16, David proves himself to be a good shepherd by constructing a "holy house of musicians, a place for Yahweh's throne filled with the glory of song, a refreshing pasture for the sheep."[149] So, in the context of the internal challenges in Jerusalem during the Chronicler's period (mentioned above), this accent on trained musical leaders would also be relevant to the postexilic audience's need for such type of leadership. There is recognition of genealogical roots to the

---

147. Matthews, "Music," 933. For a historical study of the liturgical chant of psalms, a feature inherent to the musical guilds of ancient Israel, see Randholfer, "From the Present to the Past," 23–62. It is also important to note the earlier discussion of Mowinckel in relationship to the temple guilds. In line with certain source- and from-critical assumptions, he argued that the ascendancy of the temple singers was late in the history of Israel as they attempted to achieve Levitical status. This would be seen specifically in the Chronicler's later treatment of this group. See further Mowinckel, *The Psalms*, 2:79–84, 90–95.

148. Ross, *Recalling the Hope of Glory*, 258. Sendrey argued that the terms related to the prophetic aspect of ancient Israelite music "refer to various forms of a prophetic message (or pronouncement), which weighs like a burden upon the prophet's soul, a burden imposed on him by the LORD's commandment, and which he transmits to the people in a tangible form, akin to a solemn song of the levitical singers." See Sendrey, *Music in Ancient Israel*, 508.

149. Leithart, *1 & 2 Chronicles*, 54.

tribe of Levi and connection to David's involvement in the organization of skilled musical leaders. From a historical perspective, Sendrey points out that by the time of Saul and Samuel, "an organized profession of musicians, music instruction, and skilled craftsmen for building instruments"[150] most likely already existed. This musical organization was then "professionalized" under David. Sendrey writes further:

> This detailed account proves abundantly that the levitical organization must have passed a previous extended stage of development, enabling David to select the most qualified men out of the multitude of trained singers. . . . Thus, the transfer of the ark of the covenant to Jerusalem was at the same time the birth-hour of the organized and permanent Temple music.[151]

Hill has also commented on this aspect of organized leadership and reinforced some of its broader implications. He argues that this emphasis in 1 Chronicles represents a paradigmatic call for the leadership of God's people in worship that is focused on proclaiming the LORD's truth in community by means of liturgical personnel.[152]

Third, another key aspect to the message inherent in the shape of the APN1 is the significance of both respecting biblical (and textual) precedent, while also *extending* this precedent based on God-centered developments. The intent of the biblical precedent remains true and stable, while the new development makes possible a fuller expression of that original emphasis. Thus, it might be argued that as the Chronicler observed such a principle at work with David's establishment of the new musical facet of Levitical service, he also saw the significance of applying that principle to a new development in Israel's history—the postexilic predicament. Satterthwaite, for instance, has defended the historicity of the Davidic literary traditions and their complex presentation of this crucial king. In so doing, this author also highlights the Chronicler's particular interest in David, as he argues:

> David as depicted in the OT Historical Books is seen from many angles: as an Israelite leader zealous for God . . . as a man whose personal failings undermined many of his earlier achievements; and (in Chronicles) as a symbol of hope for the postexilic generations. . . . *The depth, complexity and (at times) ambivalence of these portrayals suggest that they are rooted in historical fact*.[153]

In a sense, then, from the perspective of a musical metaphor, it could be stated that the Chronicler is *modulating* on a theme that itself was already

---

150. Sendrey, *Music in Ancient Israel*, 529.
151. Sendrey, *Music in Ancient Israel*, 529, 531–32.
152. See Hill, *1 and 2 Chronicles*, 335–40.
153. Satterthwaite, "David," 206, emphasis added.

adapted from an earlier theme. In the postexilic period, the Chronicler is applying a principle that had itself been reapplied in the Davidic period *from* the Mosaic period. These aspects further suggest that the rhetorical message of the APN1 is related to a major emphasis in the DKN—that of seeking after the LORD through proper channels—especially as it relates to the *meaning* of David's faithful institution of crucial aspects of worship, liturgy, and temple practices.

Relationship to Broader Methodology

Finally, we may point out that the preceding rhetorical study of the APN brings up key issues that are interrelated with the historical and the biblical-theological discussions of the Levites in 1 Chr 10–29, presented in the following two chapters.

First, from a historical perspective, the APN presents the Levites' role in the formal procession of the ark as a significant historical occurrence during the reign of David, at the period of the United Monarchy. The Chronicler develops his biblical historiography on the presupposition that his readers have knowledge of David's kingdom (with all of the other details presented in Samuel/Kings assumed as broader background information). He then chooses to emphasize this particular aspect of Davidic kingship (the role of the Levites), as well as the formal preparations for the Solomonic temple—among other issues. In this sense, the rhetorical emphases discussed in this chapter are built out from the historical aspects of David's early reign—dealt with in the next chapter.

Second, from a more distinctly theological perspective, the APN clearly emphasizes the meaning of God's presence in Jerusalem, and prefigures its significance (in blessing and in judgment) for the temple complex. As the ark is brought into Jerusalem, the fact of, and the implications stemming from, the divine presence become a key foundation on which the Davidic promises of 1 Chr 17 are built. Also, the theological significance of worshipful instrumental and vocal music is emphasized. The APN as a whole offers a rich Scriptural deposit relating to the ability of God's people to properly express joy and gratitude to God, the creator and sustainer of life. The theological issues, emanating from the Levitical texts of 1 Chr 10–29, are more formally investigated in chapter 5 of this study.

In conclusion, in this chapter we have explored the *symbol* of God's presence, as it is sustained by the ministry of the Levites. It remains to further engage with the *service* the Levites render unto God, in chapter 4, and the *song* the Levites lift up to God, in chapter 5.

4

The Historical Aspect in 1 Chronicles 23

On the Plausibility of David's Establishment of an Expanded
Levitical Duty in the Early First Millennium

As noted in the methodological discussion of chapter two, the second major step of this study involves an examination of the *historical* aspect of David's organization and expansion of the Levitical duty at the temple—i.e., the *service* the Levites render unto God. In the previous chapter, we have sought to point out some of the rhetorical cohesiveness related to the presentation of Levitical duty, especially their music and song in 1 Chr 15, as this theme can be understood as serving an important function in the overall literary shape and theological message of 1 Chr 10–29 (and of chapters 10–21 in particular). Based on these insights, some of the historical questions related to this theme will now be considered.

The Chronicler claims in these narratives that as the king, David was responsible for expanding Levitical service during the united monarchy to include a variety of organized duties (music and worship among them)—especially in preparation for, and in support of, the formal temple complex which would be inaugurated in Jerusalem by Solomon his son.

However, as has been noted at various junctures throughout our study thus far, a number of scholars both past and present argue that this claim by the Chronicler—of the Davidic establishment of the expanded Levitical temple service—is artificial and even anachronistic. That is, a large number of authors would contend that these duties, including the musical ones, are included in Chronicles because of postexilic social realities and *not* based on any preexilic historical precedent. In these views, the complex and organized Levitical service would only represent a reflection of the Chronicler's (and/or later redactors') interest in promoting postexilic Levitical and/or priestly concerns. For instance, in De Vries' reading, the texts of Levitical musicians in 1 Chr 25 are not from the time of the Chronicler, let alone the preexilic period of David. Indeed, for him, there is a "high degree of artificiality" in the lists of singers in this passage, which would reveal a "secondary expansion" *beyond* the time of the Chronicler, even, and from the circles of late postexilic second temple singers and musicians.[1] Thus, it is often taken for granted that David simply could not have instigated nor overseen such a developed cultic and liturgical Levitical corps in Jerusalem at the time of the early first millennium BC.

However, based on the careful methodological discussion presented earlier, the *plausibility* that David was responsible for the establishment of Levitical music will be investigated and defended in this chapter. As noted, the following question then guides this aspect of our overall argument seeking to demonstrate that the theme of Levitical duty contributes cohesively to the Chronicler's text: namely, is it *plausible* that the Chronicler's claim for the Davidic modification and expansion of Levitical duties seen first in 1 Chr 23—which included musical duties—is based on reliable and preexilic traditions/sources that preserved the witness of this early monarchic development?

In this way, the focus will be on the historical plausibility of the duties the Chronicler claims David set up for the Levites in preparation for their temple ministry in the context of 1 Chr 22-29. The method for fleshing out a positive defense of the question stated above will be twofold. *First*, aspects of Levitical duty in 1 Chr 23 will be reviewed in relationship to David's preparations for the temple building in 1 Chr 22-29, to demonstrate the possibility of a cohesive reading of the duties of priests and Levites from a historical perspective. *Second*, based on the claims of the text in Chronicles, some illustrative data from the ANE related to temples, priests and attendants, ritual, and music will be synthesized as appropriate and relevant background historical information that further sustains our plausibility argument.

Focused Biblical Evidence: Levitical Temple Duty under David in 1 Chr 23

The first major step in his chapter, then, entails a discussion of some of the evidence related to Levitical temple duties in 1 Chr 23, as set in the overall

---

1. De Vries, *1 and 2 Chronicles*, 204, 206. De Vries (p. 206) engages with Gese's theoretical stages of the postexilic development of the Levites (cf. Gese, "Zur Geschite," 223-34).

context of 1 Chr 22–29. As such, we begin by suggesting that the historical plausibility of the Chronicler's claim may be defended from the basis of this biblical textual evidence. This claim will be considered in two steps: (1) the Levitical duties in context of chapters 22–29 broadly; (2) particular issues related to chapter 23.

Levitical Duties and 1 Chr 22–29

In discussing the Levitical duties of 1 Chr 23 and 25, it is first helpful to have a grasp of the immediate setting of these texts.[2] As previously noted, the first section of the Davidic narratives in 1 Chronicles focuses especially on David's establishment of his royal rule and the proper establishment of the ark in Jerusalem (1 Chr 10:1—22:1). This first unit concludes with a narrowed interest on David's obedience to the LORD's desire for a temple and a place for atoning sacrifices (the altar of burnt offering) in Jerusalem, as is evident in the last verse of the unit in 1 Chr 22:1: ויאמר דויד זה הוא בית יהוה האלהים וזה־מזבח לעלה לישראל.

The second major section of 1 Chr 10–29 is then concerned with David's preparations for the temple building and its service, his various charges, and the worship celebration he oversees in the process. This section reveals a literary frame in chapters 22 and 28–29, around a core set of texts dealing with the duties of the leaders of Israel, of the priests, and of the Levites in chapters 23–27 (following the initial statement of 1 Chr

---

2. Dorsey has suggested a chiastic outline for this section, where the frame is found in David's assemblies in 22 and 28–29 and the center is found in 24:1–9, focused on the priests and their duties. The inner parallel layers would be found first in 23:1 and 27:1–34, focused on civil leadership (Solomon and other civil leaders), and second in 23:2–32 and 24:20—26:32 (focused on the Levites and their duties). See Dorsey, *The Literary Structure*, 147. That the first section of the first inner parallel unit hangs on one verse alone (23:1) is perhaps problematic, but Dorsey still seems to appropriately highlight the interplay between David's role in the frame and the central function of the texts relating to the priests and Levites. He highlights the literary integrity of 23–27 vis-à-vis 22 and 28–29:

  A David assembles people concerning the temple, 22:1–19

    B Civil ruler: Solomon appointed as king, 23:1

      C Levites: duties in assisting the priests, 23:2–32

        D Center: Aaronides priests and their duties, 24:1–9

      C' Levites: duties as musicians and gatekeepers, 24:20—26:32

    B' Civil rulers: government officials appointed, 27:1–34

  A David assembles people concerning the temple, 29:1—29:30

23:2: (ויאסף את־כל־שׂרי ישׂראל והכהנים והלוים)—that is, leaders directly, or indirectly, connected with the establishment of the temple in Jerusalem.[3] Thus, the description of Levitical duties in chapters 23 and 25 is due to the momentous historical and theological occasion found in this preparation for the physical temple in Jerusalem—especially following the central event in the earlier narratives of the ark coming to rest in the city.

In this regard, it is interesting to note the way in which David characterizes his desire to build a temple for the LORD in Jerusalem. In 1 Chr 28:2, in one of his last recorded public charges, David expresses his desire to construct a "house of rest" since the "ark of the covenant," which is the "footstool" of God" has been properly established in the city of Zion, Jerusalem (v. 2 reads: שמעוני אחי ועמי אני עם־לבבי לבנות בית מנוחה לארון ברית־יהוה ולהדם רגלי אלהינו והכינותי לבנות). At basic contextual and cultural levels this language naturally connects to the general ancient Near Eastern cognitive perception of temples representing a connection point between the human and the divine; the biblical covenantal language used by David in relationship to the ark, however, especially relates this temple-building theme with the specificity and the exclusivity of Yahweh's revelatory claims.[4]

The contention here is that the literary frame for this unit provides the overall context for the various lists and comments on the duties of the personnel in chapters 23–28.[5] The introductory section of the literary frame, in chapter 22, is divided into two main sections. First, the entire unit opens with David's royal orders to physically prepare for the temple-building (22:2–5). David gathers the workforce and materials needed for the construction project. Even as he was barred by God from engaging in the building process himself, the text also accentuates David's commitment to fully preparing his son for it—as seen in 22:5b ויכן דויד לרב לפני מותו.

---

3. McKenzie summarizes the impetus of this overall section when he writes, "basically, these chapters (22–29) describe David's accomplishment of two important tasks: his transfer of the kingdom to Solomon and his preparation for building the temple.... David is clearly the central figure. Like Moses with the tabernacle—and the comparison is all but explicit at points—David is credited with the entire organization of the temple worship. Thus, for all practical purposes, *David replaces Moses as the founder of Israel's worship*. Also, like Moses with Joshua, David transfers succession to Solomon" (emphasis added). See McKenzie, *1–2 Chronicles*, 178. Although McKenzie's statement certainly captures the essence of this section well, his insistence that David *replaced* Moses as the cultic founder is perhaps overstated. It might be fairer to state that David *completed* and *expanded* Moses' role as cult founder.

4. For a helpful discussion of the term "a house of rest" and a contrasting perspective found in Ps 132, see Knoppers, *I Chronicles 10–29*, 926.

5. On this frame, note Braun, "The Significance of 1 Chronicles 22, 28, 29," especially 10–99, 200–224.

Secondly, in verses 6–19, a more specific charge to Solomon is recorded. As Ahn notes, the rhetorical situation of this speech by David may be thought about at two levels: first, the narrative *historical* situation itself, and, second, the rhetorical situation of the *Chronicler* himself in his postexilic setting. As such:

> The [Chronicler] brings the narrative situation of David's preparation of the temple building to his own situation. Through David's speeches, the [Chronicler] attempts to persuade the Yehudite community as his audience. . . . The [Chronicler] recognizes the necessity of the identity formation of the Yehudite community on the basis of the Jerusalem temple as the worship place given by YHWH in the Persian period.[6]

In this way, David provides the rationale for the LORD's choice of Solomon for kingship and temple-building; David also prays for divine guidance in accomplishing the building process. David, as a man of war, has shed much blood and is thus ritually disqualified from building the sacred sanctuary. Vivid language in the charge (in 22:9–10), however, shows how the LORD has promised a son who would be fully qualified for this task: הנה־בן נולד לך הוא יהוה מנוחה והנחותי לו מכל־אויביו מסביב כי שלמה יהיה שמו ושלום ושקט אתן על־ישראל בימיו הוא־יבנה בית לשמי והוא יהיה־לי לבן ואני־לו לאב. David further notes the preparations he has overseen for material and personnel; he then charges Solomon to take up the leadership of the building process (note, for instance, the careful description given of the material in v. 14 and of the workers in vv. 15–16). At the end of this address, the king challenges the leaders of Israel to fully support Solomon in this process.[7]

Consequently, this introductory section sets the stage for the entire unit by emphasizing: (1) the transition of royal leadership between David and Solomon—David will prepare for the building; Solomon will oversee the construction itself; (2) the basic preparations for the construction of the temple; (3) the commitment required by Solomon and the various leaders

---

6. Ahn, *The Persuasive Portrayal*, 180.

7. Selman, for instance, agrees that chapter 22 appears to have "no obvious source in earlier biblical literature." However, he further contends that three separate strands of earlier, more generally parallel OT traditions are "readily identifiable": (1) the Davidic covenant promise of 1 Samuel 7 (in vv. 7–10); (2) Moses' appointment of Joshua (Deuteronomy 31; Joshua 1)—serving as the model for the transition between David and Solomon; (3) the general association with 1 Kings' presentation of Solomon. See Selman, *1 Chronicles*, 211–12. On this issue, Japhet adds, "if this unit [22:2–19] is regarded as nothing more than a compilation of various literary layers or fragments, it loses much of its significance for the understanding of the literary-historiographic methods of the Chronicler and his views of major aspects of the history of Israel." See Japhet, *I and II Chronicles*, 392.

under him for the entire process. In the end, then, it is important to note that the temple, even in its preparatory phases here, is not being celebrated merely as an awe-inspiring physical edifice, but as an important *historical and theological* development in Yahweh's relationship to his covenant people. As Hill points out, for example, in this context of 1 Chronicles, "the temple is a theological statement to the nations (1 Chron. 22:5) about God's faithfulness to his covenant with David and the embodiment of his kingdom in the Israelite monarchy."[8]

The concluding section of this literary frame is found in chapters 28 and 29. Chapter 28 begins with two charges delivered in public, while chapter 29 concludes the Davidic narratives as a whole with the record of a joyful worship celebration in preparation for the temple. After the initial address to Solomon and his leaders in chapter 22 and the ensuing personnel detail given in chapters 23–27, the final section opens with a public address to a large congregation that seems to be representative of the whole nation (notice the detailed description of the assembly gathered by David in 1 Chr 28:1).

In this section, God's choice of having David serve over Israel "forever" is affirmed (v. 4a: ויבחר יהוה אלהי ישראל בי מכל בית־אבי להיות למלך על־ישראל לעולם), as well as God's choice of having Solomon build the temple—not David. The conclusion to this charge, in verse 8, gives the command of *observing* and *seeking* the commandments of the LORD (שמרו ודרשו כל־מצות) so that: (1) the "good land" (הארץ הטובה) of Israel may be possessed, and (2) it may be an *eternal* inheritance (והנחלתם לבניכם אחריכם עד־עולם) for the children of Israel.[9]

After this general charge to the Israelite congregation, David delivers a more specific charge to Solomon, recorded in 1 Chr 28:9–21. This text is framed by direct discourse from David and encompasses rich language encouraging Solomon to be wholeheartedly committed to seeking and serving the LORD (in vv. 9–10 and 20–21; note v. 9a, for example: ואתה שלמה־בני דע את־אלהי אביך ועבדהו בלב שלם ובנפש חפצה כי כל־לבבות דורש יהוה). This section is centered on the narrative comments in vv. 11–19 that highlight David's giving of the plan for the temple complex—the תָּבְנִית (see v. 11a: ויתן דויד לשלמה בנו את־תבנית האולם ואת־בתיו). It seems crucial

---

8. See Hill, *1 and 2 Chronicles*, 297; and similarly, Selman, *1 Chronicles*, 214.

9. Pratt suggests this language is related to Joshua. He writes, "these words alluded to God's commission of Joshua after the death of Moses. The Chronicler pointed to the parallel between Joshua and Solomon earlier (see 22:11–16). Similar allusions to Joshua's commission appear at several points in the material (28:1–10). As Joshua completed Moses' work, so Solomon must complete David's work." See Pratt, *1 and 2 Chronicles*, 192.

to notice here that this plan includes both the layout of the temple facilities with a number of its cultic accoutrements *and* the instructions for the divisions of priests and Levites, with "all of the work of the service in the house of the LORD" (v. 12).[10]

In this way, the Chronicler appears to be presenting David in typological relationship to Moses. Both of these OT leaders received plans via divine revelation for a physical sanctuary of God—Moses, for the tabernacle, and David, for the temple. There is continuity *and* development, as the text includes in the plan the divisions of priests and Levites. On the other hand, the תַּבְנִית Moses received from God did not directly emphasize the duties of the Levites, but focused on the structure itself, its various furnishings, and the priesthood of Aaron. The LORD tells Moses in Exod 25:9: ככל אשר אני מראה אותך את תבנית המשכן ואת תבנית כל־כליו וכן תעשו. As a constituent feature of the frame of chapters 1 Chr 23–27, this inclusion in chapter 28 of Levitical divisions would firmly suggest that the Levitical duties as laid out by David are deeply rooted in the divine plan being given to Solomon.[11]

Finally, the historical and theological significance (both at David's time and for the Chronicler's postexilic audience) of the temple-building preparation is magnified by the celebratory worship service recorded in chapter 29. Verses 1–5 show how David has made great provisions for the building of God's temple and, then, challenges the people of Israel to fully support the temple as well. This support is highlighted by the freewill offerings given by the Israelite leaders in vv. 6–9. David's celebratory prayer and leadership over the sacrificial service in 29:10–22 serves as a fitting capstone to the temple-building narratives, before the concluding notices of Solomon's royal anointing and David's death in 29:22–30. David's prayer, in particular, presents a full-fledged affirmation of the LORD's power and dominion over all creation—a statement that stands in stark contrast to the ancient Near Eastern historical concept of the limited locality and influence of a god in his or her temple. Note the theological effusion, hence, of 1 Chr 29:10–11:
ויברך דויד את־יהוה לעיני כל־הקהל ויאמר דויד ברוך אתה יהוה אלהי ישראל אבינו

---

10. Regarding the plan, Japhet affirms, "God's promise to David that his son will build the Temple is most emphatically confirmed by the communication to David of the actual plans through divine inspiration. The Chronicler, who has described David as the one responsible for making all the preparations for the building of the Temple, here goes one step further: *God himself was a partner to God's preparations.*" See Japhet, *I and II Chronicles*, 493 (emphasis added).

11. This is supported by Knoppers who writes, "[t]he plans David delivers to Solomon pertain to the sanctuary complex, its furnishings, and its sacerdotal organization. *In this respect, the Temple plans resonate with the Tabernacle plans in Exodus.* Yhwh's provisions cover the Tabernacle, its furnishings, the priesthood of Aaron, and its consecration" (emphasis added). See Knoppers, *I Chronicles 10–29*, 932.

מעולם ואד־עולם לך יהוה הגדלה והגבורה והתפארת והנצח וההוד כי־כל בשמים
ובארץ לך יהוה הממלכה והמתנשא לכל לראש.[12]

This literary frame encloses texts dealing with the organization of the temple complex in Jerusalem and certain leadership needs in Israel as a whole. That is, the Chronicler shows: (1) the joyful and exultant nature of the celebration surrounding the temple-building preparations in the literary frame (with the charges emphasizing God's faithfulness and the joy surrounding the worship service), and (2) the careful and well-planned nature of the organization needed for the proper implementation of the temple ritual services in the central duty texts of 23–27. Chapters 23–27 are, indeed, mainly concerned with listing, and commenting on, the temple (and related) duties of the various members of the tribe of Levi (chs. 23–26). The final chapter in this central section broadens the perspective by ensuring the proper establishment of monthly military divisions (27:1–15) and tribal leaders (27:16–32) for the nation, which is now being further established to be centered on Jerusalem and its nascent temple cult.

With regard to the duties of the tribe of Levi, chapter 23 should be seen as the *general* statement on the census, genealogies, and temple-duties of the non–Aaronide Levites. In 24:1–19 (which can be viewed as the chiastic center of 22–29), the Chronicler shows that David is also following Pentateuchal precedent by ensuring that the Aaronide priests were properly organized to continue in their duty as sacred officers. The remaining texts dealing with Levitical personnel focus on four more specific sets of roles for the non-Aaronide Levites, most of which are related to the temple: (1) the group assisting the Aaronide priests (24:20–31); (2) the group performing regular musical duty (25:1–31); (3) the group organized into temple gatekeeping watches (26:1–17); and (4) the group concerned with administrative or support tasks (temple "treasurers," 26:20–28; external "officers and judges," 26:29–32).

---

12. McConville notes the connection between this prayer and the psalm of 1 Chr 16. He writes, "[i]t has been well pointed out that [David's prayer in 1 Chr 29] takes up themes also present in ch. 16, the praises which attended the bringing of the ark to Jerusalem. There, as here, there is an emphasis on the fact that greatness of Israel does not lie within, but rather is granted by God.... The prayers of chs. 16 and 29, therefore, mark two of the great events of David's reign, the bringing of the ark and the commissioning of Solomon to carry out his plans for the Temple." See McConville, *I and II Chronicles*, 104.

Levitical Duties in 1 Chr 23

From the outset, a few remarks ought to be made related to the compositional discussions surrounding 1 Chr 23. Indeed, as alluded to above, one of the key interpretive issues with this whole section concerns the compositional relationship of 23:3—27:34 (all the lists of duties) with the outer frame of 22:2—23:1 and 28:1—29:26 commented on above (various charges, prayers, and narrative comments). Specifically, some scholars have considered the central lists of duties (chs. 23-28) as later additions to the original text composed by the Chronicler (chs. 22, 28-29)—since certain tensions are perceived within the section itself and in relationship to other parts of Chronicles.[13]

Klein has summarized the compositional views related to 1 Chr 23-27 in a helpful manner.[14] He argues that since the beginning of the twentieth century, scholars have taken one of three basic positions on these compositional issues. (1) "All of the lists are secondary."[15] In this view, 28:1 is seen as a repetition of 23:2 (both deal with a Davidic assembly in Jerusalem). Hence, here, *all of* 23:3—27:34 is viewed as an interruption in the narrative. Most scholars who hold this view argue for a number of contradictions in the duty lists section and that the lists were added at different times (the main representative scholars in this tradition are Noth, Welch, and Rudolph).[16]

(2) "Some of the lists are original and the others belong to a secondary level."[17] Williamson is the main advocate for this position. He argues that 28:1 and 23:3 are not exact duplicates, but build on each other. Based on the census list of 23:3-6a, Williamson sees four basic roles for the Levites as originally expounded by the Chronicler in the rest of 23-27: (a) core temple work (23:4a/23:6b-13a, 15-24); (b) officers and judges (23:4b/26:20-32);

---

13. So, *first*, historical critics have often considered chapters 22 and 28-29 as original to the Chronicler and as his *own* creation. Such, for example, was the view sustained by Curtiss and Madsen, who wrote, "[t]his chapter [22] is a free composition by the Chronicler, full of general and exaggerated statements, with a number of short quotations from earlier canonical books woven together." See Curtis and Madsen, *A Critical and Exegetical Commentary*, 255. *Secondly*, chapters 23-27, in these views, are regarded as compositionally *secondary* to this initial, free composition by the Chronicler. Note the concise discussion in Japhet, *I and II Chronicles*, 406-11, and see also, for example, Rudolph, *Chronikbücher*, 152-59; and Noth, *The Chronicler's History*, 31-35—who argued that chapters 22-29 display "a rank growth of literary accretions." See Noth, *The Chronicler's History*, 31.

14. See Klein, *1 Chronicles*, 445-47. And see further Wright, "Narrative Function," 229-42.

15. Klein, *1 Chronicles*, 445.

16. Klein, *1 Chronicles*, 445.

17. Klein, *1 Chronicles*, 445.

(c) gatekeepers (23:5a/26:1-3, 9-11, 19); and (d) singers and musicians (23:5b/25:1-6). These four sets of duties and their texts are original for Williamson (and mainly reflective of postexilic history). A *second* redactional layer is then adduced in 23-27: (a) 23:13b-14, 25-32 (later glosses on the temple duties); (b) 24:1-19 (the twenty four priestly courses would be later additions); (c) 24:20-31 (perceived genealogical tensions); (d) 25:7-31 (this would be a later supplementary list of singers); (e) 26:4-8, 12-18 (the Obed-Edom material would be a later addition); and (f) 27:1-32 (not directly related to priests and Levites).[18]

(3) "All, or almost all, of the lists are original."[19] Japhet is the main proponent discussed for this position. For her, 23:2 to 28:1 build on each other and the tensions apparent in 23:3-27:34 are due to the variety of sources the Chronicler used in shaping this section. For example, in reaction to the literary-critical arguments of the first position delineated by Klein, Japhet indeed notes that two main factors should be considered (among other arguments), namely, that the use of "varying sources in the composition, which could give rise to many discrepancies, and the threshold of tolerance for such incompatibilities of detail, are certainly much broader for the Chronicler than for the modern reader."[20]

In light of the third position discussed by Klein, McKenzie notes, in fact, that a number of recent writers are of the opinion "that if the Chronicler's compositional techniques are *properly understood there is no need to see this section as secondary.*"[21] Still, as noted previously, scholars who argue for compositional *unity* in this section also often contend that its *content* is mostly (or completely) reflective of postexilic history.[22]

---

18. Klein, *1 Chronicles*, 445-47. And note further, Williamson, *1 and 2 Chronicles*, 159-78. For example, Williamson writes, "two major and related problems face the commentator of this section of Chronicles. First, many have observed that there is a close link between 23:2 and 28:1, so that from a narrative point of view 23:3-27:34 seems to be intrusive [and is considered to be secondary]. Second, whatever the attitude adopted to this first point, various literary levels have been detected even within these chapters. The whole of chs 23-27 is found to fall neatly into two, internally self-consistent [redactional] layers.... [Thus,] the account of David's last acts [in 28:1-29:30] leading to Solomon's accession is picked up from 23:2." See Williamson, *1 and 2 Chronicles*, 159-60, 178. One of the main goals of this section of the chapter, in contrast, is to highlight the possibility of a more constructive relationship between the literary frame of this section and its center.

19. Klein, *1 Chronicles*, 447.

20. Japhet, *I and II Chronicles*, 408; see 406-11 for her full argument.

21. McKenzie, *1-2 Chronicles*, 179, emphasis added. Such is the opinion of Japhet, *I and II Chronicles*, 409-10; and of Williamson, *1 and 2 Chronicles*, 157-59.

22. Note the related discussion in Wright, "The Legacy of David in Chronicles," 229-42; Wright, "The Origin and Function of 1 Chronicles 23-27," 248-57. Wright

These matters arise clearly when looking at 1 Chr 23:24–32. On the one hand, as McKenzie remarks, "the duties of the Levites laid out in verses 25–32 are explicitly described as the result of a change in *historical circumstances* [during the Davidic monarchy]."[23] On the other hand, in certain approaches, ideological tensions are perceived within this text: between the claim that David modified the duties of the Levites during the united monarchy and the "ideologies" of later literary strands (such as the sharp division between priest and Levite in "P," or the view of divine rest in "D").[24]

On this basis, some of the issues arising from chapter 23 will be considered in more detail in the following. First Chr 23 is part of the "additions" of the Chronicler's presentation of David's kingdom.[25] From a basic canonical perspective, as the first step in the "duties" section of 23–27, this chapter carefully and broadly delineates Levitical duties for the temple service. This is a key chapter in the *biblical* history of Levitical duty. It follows the initial transformations that have occurred with the procession of the ark into Jerusalem in chapter 15 and the *provisional* liturgical situation noted at the end of chapter 16, where some Levites remained as assistants with the Aaronide priests at the tabernacle in Gibeah and a whole group of other Levites were assigned to a new, temporary liturgical service at the tent housing the ark in Jerusalem. In chapter 23, the Chronicler is communicating to his audience the way in which David prepared the non-Aaronide Levites for their regular liturgical and cultic duties at the temple.

Generally, then, the argument posited here asserts that certain perceived compositional, and thus historical, tensions do not appear to be insurmountable; hence, it seems plausible to contend that in this text, the Chronicler is reflecting on a preexilic tradition related to David's preparations for Levitical leaders at the temple in the united monarchy. Chapter 23 will be broadly analyzed following its principal divisions, which can be read as: (1) 23:1 Solomonic Kingship Heading; (2) 23:2–5 Levitical Census by David;

---

defends the literary integrity of chapters 23–27 within the larger frame of 22 and 28–29. However, he is much more skeptical of the *historical* connection of these passages to the Davidic monarchy, as he notes of 1 Chr 23–27, "this passage can tell us nothing concerning preexilic Israel or even early postexilic Judah." See Wright, "The Origin and Function of 1 Chronicles 23–27," 252.

23. McKenzie, *1–2 Chronicles*, 180, emphasis added.

24. Note, for instance, the discussion in Knoppers, *I Chronicles 10–29*, 817–26.

25. This text is in keeping with the "re-focusing" of David in 1 Chronicles that emphasizes his role in instigating proper worship, so that, as one author aptly notes, "the historian recasts a vision of David's role to present him as the priest of praise, a founder and leader of a pattern the Chronicler believes will bring peace and wholeness to a community that is wrestling with new circumstances and shifting political boundaries." See Hoglund, "The Priest of Praise," 190.

(3) 23:6–23 Levitical Genealogical Organization by David; and (4) 23:24–32: Levitical Temple-Duties Instituted by David. Some of the key compositional and historical issues arising from this text will also be considered.[26]

Solomonic Kingship Heading: 23:1

The initial statement in 23:1 emphasizes David's establishment of Solomon as king—this notice is introduced by a non-verbal clause: ודיד זקן ושבע ימים וימלך את־שלמה בנו על־ישראל. Occurring at this juncture in the context of chapters 22–29, the emphasis on Solomon's accession to the throne after David appears to be more theologically focused. As the Chronicler is beginning his presentation of the various lists of temple duties in 23–27, it is important to show the relationship between the royal Davidic house and the temple ministry. As Selman has noted of this initial statement in 23:1:

> Its primary purpose seems to be to show that the organization of priests and Levites was a consequence of God's covenant promise to David. *The temple and its personnel were not to be regarded as an independent religious establishment, but as a symbol of the two "houses" of chapter 17 and ultimately of the kingdom of God.*[27]

Japhet further argues that this heading serves as a general introduction to all of chapters 23–29, since it focuses the reader on the final days of David, who is "old and full of days," (ודיד זקן ושבע ימים). This means for Japhet that it is unnecessary to posit a two-staged Solomonic coronation process (in dealing with the liturgical gathering introduced in 28:1 and the subsequent statement of the anointing of Solomon in 29:22–25).[28]

The general statement of the transition from David to Solomon is provided in this heading; the details of what this transition entails are given in the remainder of the duties section especially.[29] Japhet also notes

---

26. Jonker is helpful in clarifying issues of the *naming* of temple personnel in 1 Chr 23–27. We first have "generic Levites," those who belong to the tribe of Levi as a whole (so, *both* Aaronide priests and non-Aaronide Levites, such as the thirty-eight thousand total of Levites in 23:3–5); we also find the "Aaronides," that is, the "priests," such as in 1 Chr 24; finally, we find the non-Aaronide Levites, whom Jonker calls the "Generic Levites," such as the Levitical musicians in 1 Chr 25 or the gatekeeping Levites in 1 Chr 26. See the chart in Jonker, *1 & 2 Chronicles*, 149.

27. Selman, *1 Chronicles*, 223, emphasis added.

28. Japhet, *I and II Chronicles*, 411.

29. On the synoptic issues with 1 Kgs 1 (and the possibility of two different ceremonies for Solomon—the one in Chronicles being grander) and the possibility of co-regency between David and Solomon, see the succinct discussion in Merrill, *A Commentary*, 273. Boda, *1–2 Chronicles*, 187, 189, in contrast, does not see the necessity of a co-regency in this context.

that this positively-focused presentation of David's final acts as king in Chronicles stands in sharp contrast to the focus in 2 Kings on David's sin with Bath-Sheba and the subsequent political intrigue. As Japhet writes of 23:1, "in this verse as it stands, and the following chapter in general, the Chronicler depicts in a most sympathetic light David's activities at this stage of his life, clearly contravening the negative picture of his sources in King."[30] Overall, this would suggest that the Chronicler is intent on rooting his presentation of the texts dealing with the duties of the temple (and other) officials (in chs. 23–27 generally and ch. 23 particularly) in the historical transition of royal power from David to Solomon. That is, this final section of Chronicles represents a reflection on, as well as a record of, the last formal acts of David as king related to his preparations for transitions from temporary religious structures to more permanent ones.

Levitical Census by David: 23:2–5

The initial statement affirming the kingship of Solomon is followed by the record of a Levitical census in 23:2–6a. This census may be further divided into two sub-sections—on the basis of David's actions. Each of these sections represents a natural progression in David's preparations.

(1) *Gathering*: Three sets of leaders (leaders of Israel, priests, and Levites) are first gathered by David in 23:2 (ויאסף)—an organizational statement that sets up the structure of all of 23–27 as a whole and, further, alerts the reader to the immediate focus of chapter 23. The act of "gathering" by David is a key concept in the Chronicler's Davidic narratives, which highlights the influence and ideal authority of this king.[31]

A number of commentators argue that 23:2 represents a preliminary and preparatory gathering where David is assigning duties to key leaders, while in 28:1, this gathering focuses on the larger liturgical celebration subsequent to the first, more focused gathering. Others, however, see 23:2 and 28:1 as referring to the *same* assembly, where the lists in 23:2–27:34 summarize the duties of all those David has gathered together to anoint Solomon as king. 28:1–29:25, then, presents what actually happened at the coronation assembly. Given the fact that 23:1 specifically alludes to the transfer of power, and that the tenor of 23:2–27:34 is of setting the proper duties for the new temple and the new kingship of Solomon, the latter position seems more tenable.[32]

---

30. Japhet, *I and II Chronicles*, 411.
31. See, for example, Klein, *1 Chronicles*, 448.
32. See further, for instance, Pratt, *1 and 2 Chronicles*, 181–203.

(2) *Numbering*: David then numbers the Levites of thirty years and older for a total of thirty-eight thousand in vv. 3–5. This total and the subtotals in the following verses all seem to be extremely high and rounded numbers. As such, they are often taken as literary devices to indicate the importance of this census at this period in David's reign (or, alternatively, the word for thousand has also been interpreted as "unit" or "tribe").[33] Klein, for instance, simply calls it an "exaggerated number."[34] Nonetheless, once David has assessed the total number of available members of the tribe of Levi, he proceeds in vv. 4–5 to subdivide them into four categories of service in preparation for the changes brought by the building of a major temple complex: (a) the largest subdivision (twenty-four thousand) of Levites is made responsible for work directly related to the temple—for the "charge of the work in the house of the LORD" (על מלאכת בית־יהוה); (b) the next level of subdivision (six thousand) are assigned the administrative duties of "officers and judges;" (c) the last two subdivisions are equal in number (four thousand): gatekeepers, and (d) Levites who will generally be engaged in a worship ministry of "offering praises to the LORD" (מהללים ליהוה) with musical instruments closely associated with David. Also, each of the basic Levitical functions described here in David's numbering (vv. 3–5) is expanded upon in the rest of the duty lists of 23–27.

---

33. Knoppers provides a helpful survey of the various theories: (1) "thousand" (אלף) should be understood either as a sub–tribal division or military units (a view defended by the likes of Medenhall, Myers, Gottwald, Boling, Milgrom, and Humphreys), so that the total number of Levites would read something like "38 tribal divisions"; (2) "thousand" (אלף) is an imprecise traditional term; the real numbers denoted would be far less (a view defended by de Vaux); (3) אלף should be re-vocalized not to read "thousand" but "chief," so that the thirty-eight Levitical chiefs would be in question (a view defended by Payne and J. Wenham); (4) these very large and round numbers are used as a "literary convention" or "scribal embellishment" (a view defended by Braun, Levine, Fouts, Skolnic, Klein, and Heinzerling). For the full discussion, see Knoppers, *I Chronicles 10–29*, 57–71. Knoppers (p. 71) concludes, "of the four positions, then, some combination of theories 2 and 4 would seem to have the most merit. Large numbers are one means by which the Chronicler configures what is for him a heroic past. In writing about the so-called 'Catalogue of Ships' in the *Illiad* (2.484ff.), [one author] comments that 'big numbers mean big events.' *Incredible quantities of people, troops, bullion, and sacrifices contribute to a highly stylized presentation of Israel's past.*" McKenzie similarly argues that the number of thirty-eight thousand here is much larger than other Levitical totals (such as in Num 4:36; 1 Chr 12:27, or Ezra 2:40–58) and notes that "the inflated number may indicate the greater value placed upon [the Levites] here." See McKenzie, *1–2 Chronicles*, 185.

34. Klein, *1 Chronicles*, 448.

Levitical Genealogical Organization by David: 23:6–23

In this sub-section of the chapter, the Chronicler begins with a general statement that is supported by a larger genealogical warrant.

(a) *General Statement*: To ensure the proper and regular execution of these various duties, David then sets up regular divisions (מחלקת) following the fundamental threefold genealogical clans of Gershon, Kohath, and Merari (v. 6). At this juncture, Japhet supports the basic literary integrity of the passage (though she also assumes that the reality of "divisions" and "courses" is better traced to the Second Temple context). She writes:

> This comprehensive unit [in 23:6–23] presents an organization of the whole tribe of Levi into "divisions," registered according to their "fathers' houses," beginning with the ancestral triad: Gershon, Kohath, and Merari. In spite of some difficulties in the details of the list, it is easily seen that it contains twenty-four such fathers' houses: ten of Gershon, nine of Kohath, and five of Merari. The number twenty-four is integral to the list and is not secondarily imposed on it. This accords well with the heading, "David organized them in divisions."[35]

(b) *Genealogical Warrant*: After this general statement on David's establishment of the Levitical divisions of labor, the Chronicler then provides for his audience short, broadly stated and authority-bearing genealogies related to each of the Levitical clans (Gershonites in vv. 7–11; Kohathites in vv. 12–20; Merarites in vv. 21–22). A key feature of these genealogical notices is found in the structurally central position of the Kohathites in vv. 12–20, emphasizing both the special traditional role of the Kohathite Levites (i.e., their care for the sacred vessels) and the fact that the Aaronides also descend from Levi's son Kohath through one of his sons, Amram.

In fact, in v. 13, the Chronicler specifically points out, in the midst of these generally non-Aaronide Levitical genealogies, that Aaron and his descendants were "set apart" (וַיִּבָּדֵל) for four reasons: to "dedicate the most holy things," (להקדישו קדש קדשים), to "forever make offerings to the LORD," (עד־עולם להקטיר לפני יהוה), to "minister" to the LORD (לשרתו), and to "pronounce blessings" in his name forever (לברך בשמו עד־עלם). Thus, as the Chronicler is supporting the non-Aaronide divisions of labor, he is again highlighting the interdependence of all Levitical clans in the work of the LORD at the temple.

Verses 13 and 14 are often taken as later additions to the text (and similarly, the Levitical list of duties in vv. 28–32), since they appear to be

---

35. Japhet, *1 and 2 Chronicles*, 413.

an interruption in the Levitical genealogy by reflecting on the duties of the Aaronide priests.[36] A number of scholars, however, view this notice of priestly duties as *coherent* with the flow of the passage, despite the change in literary form. In fact, as Knoppers remarks, the fact that the biblical writer "contextualizes Aaron within the larger lineage is significant, because in Chronicles Aaronides are, broadly speaking, Levites."[37] Japhet further views this priestly comment as a homiletic "midrash" on Moses' instruction for the anointing of Aaron and his sons in Exod 30:29–30.[38] And as Knoppers points out further, digression or anecdotes "are a common feature of genealogies in the Near Eastern and classical worlds."[39] The Chronicler, indeed, seems to be pointing out that the Aaronides, while being Levites, are still set apart for the envisaged ministry of the temple, following the priestly precedent of the Pentateuch. That is, we find priests and the non-priestly Levites continuing in their distinct calling from within the tribe of Levi, now adapted for the temple setting. Also, we may note here mutuality and cooperation, not rivalry, competition, or a rigid hierarchy. Boda supports this argument, and roots it clearly in the actions of David, when he writes in this context:

> The Levites were commissioned to work in the Temple to assist the descendants of Aaron. The priests in Aaron's line are envisioned in chapter 23 as supervising the Temple worship. . . . Nevertheless, the other members of the tribe of Levi were to play a role as well. . . . [So] in this section Chronicles grants the non-priestly Levites space in the worship of Israel. They are legitimized through the voice of David himself, who links this transition in their role to the transition from Tabernacle to Temple. . . . Thus, to have the Temple is to afford the Levites these roles in the new worship phase. . . . *The non-priestly Levites,*

---

36. See, for example, Dirksen, *1 Chronicles*, 284, who writes of 23:13–14, "this passage interrupts the genealogy, and must be regarded as an insertion. . . . The tenor of the digression accords entirely with the author's interest in the cult." Similarly, see Williamson, *1–2 Chronicles*, 161, who notes of vv. 13–14, "the explanatory expansion included in these verses is *out of place* in a list of heads of fathers' houses. It exactly reflects, however, the viewpoint of the *priestly reviser* whose hand has been detected elsewhere, and so should probably be attributed to him" (emphasis added).

37. Knoppers, *I Chronicles 10–29*, 807.

38. Japhet, *I and II Chronicles*, 415. She is especially pointing to Exod 30:30–31: ואת־אהרון ואת־בניו תמשח וקדשת אתם לכהן לי ואל־בני ישראל תדבר לאמר שמן משחת־קדש יהיה זה לי לדרתיכם.

39. Knoppers, *I Chronicles 10–29*, 807–8. De Vries, in fact, has defined the genre of 23:6–20, not as a genealogy, *per se*, but as a "table of organization, in which both the census figures and the tallies are schematic and ideal." See De Vries, *1 and 2 Chronicles*, 192.

therefore, were legitimated by the authority of David, as well as by their faithful response to his royal commission.[40]

Additionally, a number of scholars have perceived tensions in the relationship between the listing of the divisions David establishes in vv. 7–23, the Levitical census of vv. 3–5, and the notices in v. 6 and in v. 24. However, it seems unwarranted to assume that (1) the census of vv. 3–5 needs to be the organizational pattern for the remainder of the chapter, and (2) that the genealogical list of vv. 7–23 is misplaced. Also, the Levitical duties listed in 23:28–32 are specifically focused on *temple* duties; they do not cover every Levitical set of responsibility laid out by David in his census.[41] Furthermore, the Levitical divisional organization is broadly genealogical and need not correspond directly to the census. As Knoppers suggests, in fact:

> David's partitioning of the Levites into divisions honors and slightly redraws their genealogical segmentation into a variety of ancestral houses. Yet the partitioning is simply an act of conservation, as it is associated with a revision of the Levitical minimum age (vv. 25–27) and a restructuring of the Levitical work profile (vv. 28–32).[42]

Levitical Temple–Duties Instituted by David: 23:24–32

The third and final section of chapter 23 occurs in vv. 24–32 and is focused more specifically on (a) the *reality* of Levitical work at the temple (v. 24); (b) the *reasons* for modified Levitical service (vv. 25–27); and (c) the *nature* of that duty (vv. 28–32).

THE REALITY OF LEVITICAL WORK AT THE TEMPLE: 23:24

In this sub-section, the basic claims will be discussed along with a key compositional/historical issue.

(1) *Basic Claims.* The reality of this work is noted in v. 24. The Chronicler essentially makes two basic claims in this verse. First, he carefully summarizes and enumerates the various genealogical organizational levels of the Levites who were to work at the temple: they have been counted and listed as "the sons of Levi," (בני־לוי), following their "father's houses," (בית אבתיהם)

---

40. Boda, *1–2 Chronicles*, 188–89, emphasis added.
41. Based on Knoppers, *I Chronicles 10–29*, 818.
42. Knoppers, *I Chronicles 10–29*, 818.

and the "heads of the father's houses" (ראשי האבות). This lends traditional authority and credibility to the new work David is assigning at the temple. Second, the Chronicler also notes that those who are actually employed from the Levitical base, for these new temple responsibilities, are twenty years and older. Thus, only Levites who are carefully organized following the traditional sub-divisions are the ones who are assigned to "do the service of the house of the LORD." (עשה המלאכה לעבדת בית יהוה).[43]

(2) *Compositional/Historical Issue: The Age of Levitical Service.* The data of chapter 23 offers the possibility of a contradiction and a challenge to its historical plausibility.[44] On the one hand, in the census of vv. 2–5, David is noted as numbering the Levites who were *thirty* years and older (מבן שלשים שנה ומעלה). On the other hand, in v. 24 (and v. 27), the text indicates that the Levites who were organized for the temple service were *twenty* years and older (מבן עשרים שנה ומעלה). A discrepancy then exists in the "legal minimum age" of the Levites in these verses.[45]

Scholars have approached this issue from basically one of five different angles.[46] (1) There are two stages in David's numbering of the Levites in chapter 23. First stage: David numbered the Levites from thirty years old following the precedent of Num 4:3; second stage: David then numbered the Levites from twenty years old when they were no longer needed for Tabernacle duty (as with Qimhi or Koester, for instance). (2) The issue is present because the Chronicler based his work on *two traditions* that contained different Levitical age minimums (as in the work of Bertheau or Schniedewind, for example). (3) One of the two readings simply has to be a mistake (as with Keil, for instance). (4) One or both of the readings is/are a later addition to the original text of 1 Chr 23 (see Kittel, Braun, or Rudolph, for instance), or is part of the pro-priestly revision layer perceived in 23 (and 23–27 as a whole, as with Welch, Williamson, or DeVries for instance).[47] (5) The Chronicler has David "introduce a (postexilic)

---

43. As Merrill, *A Commentary*, 275, comments on this issue, "the Chronicler makes note that a task previously reserved to the Levites was the transport of the holy ark, a task now obsolete because the ark would come to rest forever in the temple. The Levites then would share all the other responsibilities that had always been theirs."

44. In the broader historical periods of the OT, there does seem to have been a measure of fluctuation in the minimum age for Levitical service. (1) Twenty years old: here in 1 Chr 23:24, 27; and in 1 Chr 31:17; Ezra 3:8 (2) Twenty-five years old: Num 8:24; (3) Thirty years old: Num 4:3, 23, 30, and here in 1 Chr 23:3.

45. Knoppers, *I Chronicles 10–29*, 818.

46. Following the discussion in Knoppers, *I Chronicles 10–29*, 818–19.

47. Note, for instance, Braun, *1 Chronicles*, 235.

innovation,"[48] making a difference between those Levites who could work at building the temple (v. 3) and those who serve in the temple sanctuary (v. 24, as with Curtis and Madsen for instance).

Knoppers argues for a combination of views 1 and 5, where the Chronicler would have first shown David to be in legal compliance with Numbers 3 (and the age of thirty), and then the Chronicler would also show how David subsequently modified the age of service to twenty years with the transition from the movable Tabernacle to the permanent temple. Knoppers also seems to suggest that this latter point would have been especially made to defend the postexilic innovation of having Levites serve from twenty years and up.[49]

However, even if the practice in the postexilic period was to employ, at least at certain periods, Levites at the younger age (perhaps due to the overall lack of numbers in the restoration), it doesn't necessitate that the Chronicler's assignment of the age modification to David at the initial stages of the first temple period be deemed "legendary," as with Knoppers on this point.[50] The statement of verse 24 suggests that Levites from twenty years and up were gathered specifically to *temple* service. This is given a warrant in verse 25 by a royal proclamation by David—as verse 25 is introduced by a כי clause: כי אמר דויד. The *content* of that proclamation strongly accentuates the historical transition from tabernacle to temple.

Thus, while the general census of vv. 2-6 is both concerned with Pentateuchal precedent (thirty years) and the numbering of Levites for a variety of Levitical duties (including, but not limited to temple duty), the text, beginning in verse 24, concentrates more thoroughly on the transition to temple duty and the changes necessitated therein, including David's recruitment of a larger number of Levites for temple duty. The point is that *practical requirements* at the time of David's preparations for the temple personnel probably required the larger Levitical corps—especially if it is accepted that during the pre-monarchic period, the organization of the Levites had deteriorated after settlement in the land (as suggested, for instance, by the negative portrayal of Levites in Judges 17-19). As Selman contends:

> Nowhere in the Old Testament is it envisaged that the age at which the Levites began their service was determined by other than practical considerations. Temple service will certainly have

---

48. Knoppers, *I Chronicles 10-29*, 818.
49. Knoppers, *I Chronicles 10-29*, 820.
50. Knoppers, *I Chronicles 10-29*, 820.

brought increased work, even though the occasional duty of transporting the ark was now to be abolished.[51]

The Reasons for Modified Service: 23:25–27

Further, the Chronicler is careful to root, for his audience, the *reasons* for David's modification of Levitical duty in the early united monarchy. In v. 25, the theological reason is given and it is twofold. First, the Levitical divisions of temple labor are needed because the LORD has provided "rest" to his people. This is in reference to Deut 12:8–11, where in v. 10, the promise of "land" and "rest" from enemies is affirmed, so that in v. 11, God's "name" may "dwell" in his chosen place so that his people might be able to properly bring offerings and sacrifices.

The second and directly related reason is that the rest of God's people in the land has then allowed for God's "name," his identity (cf. the coming of the ark to Jerusalem in 1 Chr 15 and 16) to make his dwelling place in Jerusalem eternally. In v. 26, a concomitant practical reason is noted. Since God has given his people rest from their enemies (at least temporarily, from the point of view of Israel's later history), and since his holy name now dwells in their midst via the ark and soon-to-be established temple, the earlier duties of the Levites related to the care and the transportation of the movable tabernacle tent and complex have become obsolete (duties detailed especially in the earlier chapters of Numbers). Their function within the tribes of Israel is still directly related to sacred religious duty; however, this sacred duty will now be more formally centered on the physical structure of the temple complex in Jerusalem. This is supported by Jonker, who notes, "[t]he background to David's new dispensation is the planned temple building as well as the promise that Yahweh will grant rest to All-Israel through Solomon."[52]

Verse 27 concludes this sub-section (of 23:24–27) with the reaffirmation that the Levites David designated for temple duty were counted from those who were twenty and older. This section also emphasizes that these decisions come as the "last words of David," indicating that the LORD has enabled David to secure the kingdom and establish the LORD's symbolic

---

51. Selman, *1 Chronicles*, 226. Similarly, Hill suggests either the solution based on need or level of maturity for certain tasks. He writes, "perhaps the Chronicler splices together sources that represent different traditions of Levitical service based on need at the time, or certain tasks performed by the Levites require men with more maturity and experience." See Hill, *1 and 2 Chronicles*, 303.

52. Jonker, *1 & 2 Chronicles*, 151.

presence in Jerusalem, for which the establishment of the needed temple-service to God is crucial.

The Nature of the Modified Service: 23:28–32

The Chronicler concludes chapter 23 with a delineation of the nature of the new duties centered on the ministry at the temple. The claims in this final sub-section (vv. 28–32) can be delineated following these movements: general statement (v. 28a); description of particular duties (vv. 28b–31); and concluding statement (v. 32).

In this section, in verse 28a, the Chronicler provides his readers with a general statement of the *overall* responsibility envisaged by David for the Levites engaged in temple work. This duty can be defined from this text as *ritual assistance* to the sons of Aaron for a complete establishment of the "service of the house of the LORD." Again, the Chronicler is careful to emphasize the interdependent nature of the various segments of the tribe of Levi in ensuring the proper working-out of the temple ministry. Arguably, this represents a rhetorical device in the Chronicler's historiographic method, so as to encourage his postexilic audience, including priests and Levites, to cooperate as well during the restoration period.

Second, the general definition of Levitical temple duty as ritual assistance to the sons of Aaron in the temple house is further explicated in the middle section (of vv. 28b–32), by distinguishing *four* sets of duties. The first *three* ritual duties relate to the sphere of the *sacred space* of the physical temple and the work done by the Levites in its adjoining chambers. The *fourth* duty relates to contributions made by the Levites to the sphere of *sacred time* seen in the regular service of worship and music.

(1) *Caring*: The first duty in v. 28b is a basic responsibility of maintenance—that of caring for the physical space, the courts and chambers, of the areas in the temple complex surrounding the sanctuary within the temple complex. This is a practical duty of ensuring that this physical space is able to appropriately serve as the ritual, sacred space of God's house.

(2) *Cleansing*: The second duty in v. 28c moves from the general nature of caring for the physical space to the more specific responsibility of ensuring the ritual purity of every holy implement used in the service of the temple complex (this is the more *specific* nature of this ritual cleansing). In fact, any ritual work that is performed within the holy space of the temple complex must be done properly and purely—and the Levites ensure this is possible (this is the more *general* nature of their ritual cleaning).

(3) *Assisting*: The third type of duty detailed in v. 29 is one of assistance, or service, entailing the preparation of the materials needed for some of the sacrificial food elements used by the Aaronide priests. As Merrill notes, "[n]othing is left to chance or human creativity at this point because each and every function speaks to some aspect of his being and his purposes. The Levites must understand that their role was subordinate to the priests."[53]

Further, the Levites participate in this sacrificial ministry by preparing at least six different baked items for the ritual service: (a) the showbread, (b) the flour of the grain offering, (c) the wafers of unleavened bread, (d) the baked offerings, (e) oil-laden offerings, (f) all other measures—seemingly related as well to any sacrificial food items. This represents a further measure of the interdependent nature of the work of the Levites vis-à-vis the priest; as the Aaronide priests offer the offerings to Yahweh and enable the spiritual service that accompanies this ritual act, so the Levites make this ministry *practically* possible as they are to prepare the physical elements for this part of the temple service.

(4) *Standing for Worship*: Finally, in vv. 30–32, the Levites are also assigned the duty of "standing" to lead the worship of thanksgiving and praise on a daily basis and during the regular festivals. In this, the Levites become a symbolic connection between the people and God, as the temple represents the symbolic connection between God and his people. The Levites, then, become part of the ritual point of union between a glorious heavenly Yahweh and his people, who need a regular connection to him through the sacred calendar (the emphasis of sacred time).

This last aspect of musical duty should be seen as a confirmation and formalization of the liturgical musical ministry David organized for the procession of the ark into Jerusalem in chapter 15 and the temporary liturgical set-up noted at the end of chapter 16. Leithart, in fact, observes that the *musical* Levites, along with the Aaronide priests are the only cultic leaders who are "set apart" in Chronicles—with the use of the verb בדל (cf. 1 Chr 23:13 for the Aaronide priests and 1 Chr 15:1 for the musical Levites, headed by Asaph, Heman, and Jeduthun). As such, Leithart points out the key aspect of the *service* of Levitical music in the general context of 1 Chr 22–29, and also links them to the creation theme. He writes indeed:

> In Chronicles, only the priests and [Levitical] singers are "set apart," a datum that calls attention to the parallels of priestly and musical ministry, of sacrifice and the sacrifice of praise. More, the division of singers from the rest of the Levites is yet another fresh creation within the new creation that is Israel. Forming a

---

53. Merrill, *A Commentary*, 275.

specialized company of singers and musicians at the heart of the temple repeats the first moments of creation.... Inspired by the Spirit, [the Levites] are seer-singers.[54]

Also, this musical duty should be seen as a focused temple musical responsibility; the Levites charged with offering praises in David's census in 23:5 can then be understood as taking up a more *general* musical responsibility. As Selman notes on this issue, "Chronicles seems to draw a distinction between the Levites in general who led the nation in praise (2 Ch. 8:14-15; 20:19; 30:22; 31:9) and the special group of Levites responsible for providing musical accompaniment [1 Chr 15]."[55]

The Levitical duty text in chapter 25 can then be seen as a further definition of the role of the Levites assigned to the temple and, even more narrowly, to temple music under David. In 25:1, David and the chiefs of service (seemingly Levitical chiefs) assign the Levitical Asaphites, Hemanites, and Jeduthunites as musical prophets, in a sense, who performed this musical duty with the specific instruments of the lyre, harp, and cymbal.[56] Some later texts in Chronicles appear to confirm this focused role of Levitical musicians at the temple of the united monarchy. For instance, in 2 Chr 5, when the ark is brought into the physical structure of the temple, it is the Levitical singers (Asaphites, Hemanites, and Jeduthunites) who lead appropriately with the same three sets of instruments noted in 1 Chr 25 (harps, lyres, and cymbals), in *cooperation* with the priestly trumpeters.[57] At this occasion, Levitical song is raised, accompanied by the Levitical instrumental music, "in praise to the LORD."[58]

Also, there are texts in Ezra and Nehemiah which suggest that in the early postexilic period, the tradition of Levitical service of leading worship and music with song and instrumental music was firmly remembered as rooted in *David's* period. In Ezra 3:10-11, at the rebuilding of the temple, Asaphite Levites lead in praise to the LORD, "with cymbals," and especially "according to the directions of David king of Israel." Similarly, in the list of priests and Levites returning with Zerubbabel, noted in Nehemiah 12, certain Levites are recorded, who stood "to praise and give thanks," also "according to the commandment of David" (Neh 12:24). Further, in

---

54. Leithart, *1 & 2 Chronicles*, 81.
55. Selman, *1 Chronicles*, 226.
56. See 1 Chr 25:1.
57. The three types of musical instruments (stringed, blown, and percussive) are known throughout the ANE and from very early periods, beginning well before the time of David. See the further discussion later in this chapter.
58. See further 2 Chr 5:2-24.

the context of Nehemiah's dedication to the Jerusalem city wall, Asaphites are recruited to lead in worship and praise at this event, "with the musical instruments of David the man of God" (Neh 12:36). Finally, in the context of the worship service at the end of Nehemiah 12, at the second temple, Levites are organized for their temple duties, "according to the command of David and his son Solomon, for long ago in the days of Asaph there were directors of the singers, and there were songs of praise and thanksgiving to God" (Neh 12:45-46).[59]

In summary, the textual data from 1 Chr 23, at it is set in the broader context of 1 Chr 22-29, strongly suggests that David, in preparing for the temple complex in Jerusalem in the early first millennium, *transformed* the service of the Levites to allow for the full practical and liturgical support of the ritual services necessary for the proper operation of the temple. This expansion and transformation of Levitical duty included the emphasis on musical service, began in 1 Chr 15-16 by David, and formalized in 1 Chr 23 and 25. Biblical texts in 1 Chr 5, at the dedication of the Solomonic temple, and in Ezra 3 and Nehemiah 12 (at the re-dedication of the rebuilt temple and wall) all stand as further OT examples, which suggest the central importance of David's *earlier* role in establishing the musical function of the Asaphite Levites, especially (as well as the Hemanites and the Jeduthunites, at least in the preexilic period).

However, it is this type of reading of the canonical data that is often challenged. Even if the pertinent passages in 1 Chr 23 and 25 (in the context of 1 Chr 22-29 as a whole) are deemed cohesive at a literary level, the inherent content *communicated* (for example, the establishment of an Asaphite Levitical musical service) is deemed to be of postexilic origin. Further, the strong connection made in these biblical texts to *David* in relationship to the establishment of Levitical music—both in Chronicles, as well as in Ezra and Nehemiah—is further characterized as idealized or artificial.

Yet, based on a critically-realist historiographic appreciation of these biblical texts, it certainly seems *plausible*, from the texts themselves, that David could have instituted such expanded Levitical service, to include even musical service. In this light, to build the argument further, the next major section of this chapter will now seek to further root our discussion of historical plausibility in some of the contextual data of the broader ANE.

---

59. For some recent studies on the priests and Levites in the postexilic Persian period and later, see Pajunen, "The Saga of Judah's Kings," 565-84; Sanders, *Judaism*, 270-310; Werman, "Levi and Levites," 211-25; Begg, "The Levites in Josephus," 1-22; and more broadly note the section "Textual Judaism," in Grabbe, *An Introduction to Second Temple Judaism*, 40-65.

Broad Background Evidence: The Contextual Method in Relationship to the Themes of Temple, Ritual, and Music in the ANE

With regards to the historical discussions of the Chronicler's claim of the Davidic establishment of a Levitical musical organization at the temple, background data from the ANE *relevant to the Davidic period* is rarely brought to bear directly, although it is sometimes suggested.[60] This section will offer a brief synthesis of such data as it emanates from the major cultures in the ANE.

The Contextual Method in OT Studies: Some Methodological Considerations

The benefit of the historical *contextual* method in Old Testament studies is affirmed at this juncture. On the one hand, the history of comparative studies in academic biblical studies has often demonstrated a disconnect between those seeking to use comparative data *apologetically* and those viewing the biblical texts merely as *late* adaptations of earlier ANE texts. Indeed, as Walton has recently noted of the rise of comparative studies in the twentieth century:

> The result was a growing ideological divide between those who viewed comparative studies from a confessional standpoint seeking to use Assyriology in their apologetics, and those who viewed it from a scientific or secular standpoint viewing the Bible as a latecomer in world literature, filled with what were little more than adaptations from the mythology of the ancient Near East.[61]

A number of scholars (including Walton) have argued for the benefit of carefully evaluating the evidence of the ANE and its ability to enlighten certain aspects of the biblical texts—without downplaying the specific (and inherently exclusivist from a cultic, religious point of view) theological

---

60. In more recent literature, Knoppers represents one of the scholars who has made some specific suggestions related to the relevance of early ANE evidence for the historical plausibility of a *Davidic* Levitical musical service. See Knoppers, *I Chronicles 10–29*, 620–21. This section of the present study is seeking to build on the insights offered by Knoppers.

61. See Walton, *Ancient Near Eastern Thought*, 4, and 3–30, for the larger methodological discussion. Note as well Chavalas, "Assyriology and Biblical Studies," 21–67.

claims of the Old Testament.[62] Hallo's work has been seminal in this regard. As Chavalas has noted:

> Hallo's goal "is not to find the key to every biblical phenomenon in some ancient Near Eastern precedent, but rather *silhouette* the biblical text against its wider literary and cultural environment." Thus we must not succumb to either "parallelomania" or to "parallelophobia."[63]

Hence, many have argued for the benefit of interacting with literature and other evidence from the ANE while studying biblical texts. For these authors, the positive results of the comparative approach may be assessed particularly by means of the concept of "propinquity," which relates to various levels of proximity between biblical and ancient Near Eastern texts especially. Younger, for instance, argues that at least four axes of propinquity should be assessed in relating texts from the ANE with biblical texts. These are: (1) linguistic; (2) geographic; (3) chronological; and (4) cultural.[64] Of these, Younger notes further:

> A parallel that is closer to the biblical material in language, in geographic proximity, in time, and culture, is a stronger parallel than one that is removed from the biblical material along one or more of these lines. That does not mean that a parallel further removed is not relevant evidence. There may be circumstances that strengthen its relevance.... By implementing such a

---

62. Walton makes a difference, in this regard, between background/cultural and comparative studies. He writes, "[u]ltimately the goal of *background* studies is to examine the literature and archaeology of the ancient Near East in order to reconstruct the behavior, beliefs, culture, values, and worldview of the people—that is, to explore the dimensions and nature of the ancient cultural river. These could alternatively be called *cultural* studies. *Comparative* studies constitutes a branch of cultural studies in that it attempts to draw from data from different segments of the broader culture (in time and/or space) into juxtaposition with one another in order to assess what might be learned from one to enhance the understanding of another" (emphasis original). See Walton, *Ancient Near Eastern Thought*, 7.

63. Chavalas, "Assyriology and Biblical Studies," 43 (emphasis added). On Hallo's views and his defense of this contextual method, see further, Hallo, "Biblical History in Its Near Eastern Setting," 1–18; Hallo, "The Limits of Skepticism," 187–99; Hallo, "Ancient Near Eastern Texts," xxiii–xxviii; Hallo, "The Bible and the Monuments," xxi–xxvi; Hallo, "Sumer and the Bible," xlix–liv. More broadly, for a recent introduction to biblical archaeology and its key periods, see Gitin, "Introduction," 39–46, and for a recent essay focused on the united monarchy in the context of the ANE, see Ortiz, "The United Monarchy," 208–15.

64. See Younger, "The 'Contextual Method,'" xxxvii.

four-pronged assessment process, caution signs may appear that slow down the tendency to over-state the evidence.⁶⁵

Sparks represents another scholar who has developed the idea of propinquity for the application of the contextual method. In his study of texts from the ANE and their relationship to the biblical text, he defines his approach as a "generic method," in which eight axes are considered: (1) the content and theme of relevant texts; (2) the linguistic and stylistic features of texts under consideration; (3) the context of a text's use (where *Sitz im Leben* is understood more broadly than with Gunkel—as a generic text could have been used in a variety of life-settings); (4) the broader sociological function of the written texts (as far as it can be determined, especially through form-critical considerations); (5) the form and structure of a text (understood as its structure and format); (6) the material attributes of texts—as sometimes useful indicators of literary genre; (7) the mode of composition and reception; (8) issues of genre criticism related to aspects of textual, redaction, source and redaction criticisms.⁶⁶ On the variegated nature of this contextual approach, Sparks concludes:

> This somewhat eclectic posture is perhaps not theoretically rigorous, but then again, on issues as mysterious as interpretation, provisional and heuristic postures are perhaps preferable to more comprehensive theories. I hope that the theoretical presuppositions outlined here will provide readers with an adequate, if not provisional, basis for considering the generic character of Hebrew and Near Eastern literature.⁶⁷

In these ways, scholars such as Younger and Sparks, and others, have affirmed the benefit of bringing certain aspects of ancient Near Eastern texts to bear towards the elucidation of the form or content of a given biblical text.⁶⁸ In fact, in his recent discussion, Walton argues that the contextual method has enabled certain methodological correctives which "have exposed the dangers inherent in research that ignores either similarities or differences between the Bible and the ancient Near East."⁶⁹

---

65. Younger, "The 'Contextual Method,'" xxxvii.
66. See Sparks, *Ancient Texts*, 12–21.
67. Sparks, *Ancient Texts*, 21.
68. See also the discussion of the contextual method in relationship to temple-building texts from Sumer and from the Old Testament in Averbeck, "Sumer," 88–125. In his study, Averbeck advances four axes to consider in a comparative study: (1) proximity in time and place; (2) the priority of inner biblical parallels; (3) correspondence of social function; (4) the holistic approach to texts and comparisons.
69. See Walton, *Ancient Near Eastern Thought*, 8.

For Walton, then, comparative or contextual study is relevant to biblical study as it helps to clarify or give more precision to a variety of cultural dimensions. He discusses four such dimensions. First, with a properly formulated contextual method, the cultural dimension of *language and literature* may be better understood, since contemporary thinking needs to be adjusted to the communication process between members of an ancient culture. Here, Walton argues for the benefit of pursuing and elucidating the commonalities of the "cognitive environment" present throughout the various cultures of the ANE. He writes indeed:

> We can now introduce the discipline of "cognitive environment criticism" as a branch of critical scholarship. Critical scholarship as a whole represents an attempt to bring scientific rigor and thereby a putative objectivity to an interpretation of a text by recovering the historical, literary, and cultural world behind the text as a means to unravel the layers that have brought it to its current state. "Cognitive environment criticism" specifically focuses on the cultural element. It includes both background/cultural studies and comparative studies.[70]

Second, Walton accentuates (as others have as well) the importance of considering the similarities and/or differences within the cultural dimension of the *literary genres* of ancient Near Eastern and biblical texts.[71] Third, Walton also makes an important point regarding the cultural dimension of *religious practice*. On the one hand, the consistent claim of the biblical text is that Israel's religion ought to be distinctive vis-à-vis its neighbors in the ANE and, hence, monotheistic. On the other hand, "the text does not hide the fact that the distinctions that were articulated in *theory* often did not

---

70. Walton, *Ancient Near Eastern Thought*, 11 (emphasis added). In a more recent essay, "Interactions in the Ancient Cognitive Environment," 333–35, Walton briefly looks at the various ways ancient Israelite writers may have interacted with the broader literary environment of the ANE (by borrowing, by the use of polemics, by the use of counter-texts, by echoes, and/or by diffusion). On this, he concludes, "I have suggested that [the writers of the OT] may make use of the literature [more broadly in the ANE] in any number of ways but that for the most part the similarities we observe can be accounted for by diffusion. Polemical passages exist in the Hebrew Bible, but not every touchpoint with the ancient Near East should be considered polemical, and most can be understood in other ways." See Walton, "Interactions in the Ancient Cognitive Environment," 339. Here, Walton is arguing against those OT scholars who contend that many OT texts demonstrate awareness of a key concept from the literature of the ANE and are then refuting it. Walton defines the "diffusion" model by noting that "what we know as literary traditions circulated around in informal ways and often in oral form." See Walton, "Interactions in the Ancient Cognitive Environment," 335.

71. Walton, *Ancient Near Eastern Thought*, 11–12.

translate into *practice*."[72] Thus, Walton argues that assessing the religious practices found in the "cognitive environment" of the ANE is helpful in understanding more *precisely* the nature and impact of Israelite syncretistic practices. That is, "both similarities and differences must be observed [in relationship to religious practice], documented, and evaluated, not for the sake of critiquing, but for the sake of *understanding*."[73]

Fourth, regarding the cultural dimensions of theology (broadly understood here as the religious concepts found within the literary expressions of a particular culture), Walton similarly contends that texts from the ANE help in providing a clearer appreciation of the distinct focus found in the biblical text. In this sense, "as our interpretation of the text requires us to fill in the gaps, we want to be careful to consider the option of filling those gaps from the cultural context before we leap to fill them with a theological significance coming out of our own experience or understanding."[74]

Following the tenor of the contextual methodological issues outlined above, the presence of a key feature within ancient cultures of the Near East will be discussed in what follows. Some relevant data regarding the main theme of temple and ritual will be presented following three sub-themes: (1) temple-building and temple structures; (2) temple rituals, priests, and attendants; and (3) temple rituals and music. For each of these topics, some basic data from the major cultural contexts of the ANE (when applicable—Mesopotamian, Hittite, Levantine, Egyptian) will be briefly noted—*especially* from the third and second millennia and into the first millennium.

The goal is to provide some support to the following basic claim: that up to the early first millennium (and beyond), a significant and prevalent feature of the "cognitive environment" of ancient Near Eastern cultures was the presence of religious temples, within which organized systems of priests and other attendants performed a variety of religious rituals, which also included rituals of instrumental music and vocal music. Again, we are seeking to defend the historical *plausibility* of David's establishment of (1) a corps of non-priestly/non-Aaronide Levites (i.e., as distinct, though related, to the priestly/Aaronide corps) during the early united monarchy (early Iron Age/early first millennium) which (2) was to play an important role in the support of the cultic ministry of the Jerusalem temple, and (3) whose role included an organized musical system—and which, (4) ultimately played a key role in the rhetorical

---

72. Walton, *Ancient Near Eastern Thought*, 23 (emphasis added). Walton also provides ten concluding principles of comparative study and four goals for cognitive environment criticism in Walton, *Ancient Near Eastern Thought*, 17–18.

73. Walton, *Ancient Near Eastern Thought*, 13, emphasis added.

74. Walton, *Ancient Near Eastern Thought*, 16.

structuring and messaging of the Chroniclers for his postexilic Judean audience related to the need of ongoing faithful worship of Yahweh.

Jerusalem in the Early First Millennium: Minimalist and Maximalist Views

Before looking at this ANE evidence *per se*, some reflections related to more recent understanding of the status of Jerusalem in the tenth century BC are relevant to this discussion. On the one hand, it will be shown below that data do exist that reveal the presence of complex temple systems in urban settlements throughout the geographical area of the ANE, and also from various historical periods. On the other hand, however, the ability of Jerusalem to sustain a complex temple system, as an urban settlement of the early Levant has been challenged by a number of recent scholars. A debate continues with regards to the historicity of the biblical presentation of David's period, especially his developments in Jerusalem at the time of the united monarchy. Mazar, an archaeologist in Israel, notes that, indeed, "severe debates" have been raised on these issues. He has recently remarked that on the one hand, "there are those [like him] who accept the United Monarchy [from the OT/Hebrew Bible] *as a historical reality, though its scope can be questioned*, while others (like Israel Finkelstein) *deny the historicity of the United Monarchy altogether*, claiming that the structures [noted in archaeological discoveries from the early Iron Age period] are later than the tenth century and that the earliest Israelite kingdom was northern Israel. This issue remains unresolved."[75]

As such, with Provan, Long, and Longman, it may first be noted that the historical and archaeological study of Jerusalem has particularly been fraught with a number of challenges. They have argued recently:

> At the heart of the debate over the historical plausibility of a Davidic kingdom as described in the Bible is the archaeology of Jerusalem. If the biblical accounts of the tenth-century kingdom of David (and Solomon) are accurate, so the argument goes, should one not expect to find considerable material remains from the tenth century in Jerusalem? The question, logical enough on the face of it, is often posed by revisionist historians who then proceed to argue that, since by their reckoning few if any tenth-century remains have been discovered in Jerusalem,

---

75. Mazar, "Archaeology of the Iron Age II," 64 (emphasis added).

the biblical accounts must be legendary at best, or simply retrojections from a much later age.[76]

Many of these questions, which have arisen in relationship to Jerusalem, are directly related to the ongoing maximalist vs. minimalist debates in OT historiography and in biblical/Syro-Palestinian archeology (the main elements of which were noted in the earlier methodological chapter of this study).[77] Several scholars have argued that the archaeological data from Jerusalem and other sites, which are more traditionally viewed as evidence for the tenth century emergence of an urban center, need to be down-dated to the ninth century or even later into the first millennium. In these perspectives, the biblical data affirming that early in the united monarchy, David (and Solomon) oversaw a number of building projects in Jerusalem are understood, in the main, to be basically tendentious and unreliable in nature.

As noted by Mazar, a principle advocate here has been Finkelstein, who argues for this type of down-dating, based on interpretive theories related to such issues as the (re)interpretation of Philistine/Mycenaean pottery at Tel Jezreel and other sites.[78] From a biblical/literary outlook, Finkelstein's position on the nature of Jerusalem during the early Iron Age is clear when he states the following:

> Textually, we have little reliable information about Iron I Jerusalem. The story of the conquest of Jebus by David cannot be considered a straightforward historical testimony. *Most probably*, ancient folktales, the core of which are impossible to trace, were *manipulated* by the Deuteronomistic Historian in order to describe the way in which the Davidic dynasty established itself in Jerusalem. The biblical description of Jerusalem in the days of Solomon as an illustrious capital of a glamourous empire should be seen as a picture of an idyllic golden age.

---

76. Provan et al., *A Biblical History*, 300 (emphasis added). For further background study on the archaeology and history of Jerusalem in the early First Millennium/United Monarchy, see for instance Mazar, *Archaeology of the Land of Bible*, 368–402; Mazar, "Archaeology and the Iron Age II," 62–69; Hoerth, *Archaeology and the Old Testament*, 253–76.

77. For a recent survey of the writing of OT/Hebrew Bible history, see Moore and Kelle, *Biblical History*, 1–42. Moore and Kelle also provide a brief discussion of their views of the ongoing maximalist/minimalist debates. Similarly, see Grabbe, *Ancient Israel*, 23–25, for a recent discussion of these broader debates in OT historiography. Grabbe argues that the only recent history of Israel that he would call truly maximalist is the one written by Provan, Long, and Longman.

78. See for example Finkelstein, "The Archaeology of the United Monarchy," 177–87; Finkelstein, "The Rise of Jerusalem," 105–15; Finkelstein, "The 'Large Stone Structure,'" 1–10; Finkelstein and Silberman, *The Bible Unearthed*.

As such, they are wrapped in later theological and ideological goals and thus based on very little original material. At the same time, the fact that David was the founder of a dynasty in Jerusalem cannot be challenged, since the Tel Dan Stela refers to Judah as the "house of David."[79]

This suggests that Finkelstein is willing to agree that a certain "David" existed in the early tenth century (for this, he is willing to trust the evidence of the extra-biblical mention of the "house of David" from the Tel Dan Inscription), but that the *biblical witness* to a powerful Davidic kingdom in that period is not to be trusted. As Cahill has noted, Finkelstein in fact "infers that Israel did not exist as a distinct entity in the Iron I period, that no Israelite state existed before the ninth century B.C.E., and that no Judahite state existed before the late eighth century."[80] Finkelstein-type positions on these matters would imply that a complex temple structure, as well as an organized Levitical priestly and cultic system (which the Chronicler affirms David set up in Jerusalem in preparation for the building of the temple, along with other building projects) would not have been sustainable in the Jerusalem of the very early first millennium. Finkelstein's views are in accord with the work of other archaeological studies, such as those of Steiner and Ussishkin.[81]

Cahill, however, has clearly laid out the implications of these minimalist archeological understandings of Jerusalem at this early period, when she writes: "Finkelstein has rocked the archaeological community by challenging the consensus of scholarly opinion regarding the historicity of the united monarchy."[82] A number of scholars have responded strongly to these challenges, in defense of the historicity of the united monarchy and of David's building programs in Jerusalem at this period.

The basic views of three studies from such maximalist advocates (Cahill, Kitchen, and Provan et al.) will be noted briefly here to show that: (1) it can be reliably assumed that Jerusalem was growing into a larger, urban settlement in early Iron Age Levant (in contrast to the Late Bronze Canaanite settlement of Jebus),[83] (2) such an understanding of the archae-

---

79. Finkelstein, "The Rise of Jerusalem," 88–89 (emphasis added).

80. Cahill, "Jerusalem and the Time," 74.

81. See for example: Steiner, "The Archaeology of Ancient Jerusalem," 143–68; Steiner, "Jerusalem in the Tenth and Seventh Centuries," 280–88; Ussishkin, "Solomon's Jerusalem," 103–16; Ussiskhin, "The Temple Mount in Jerusalem," 473–83.

82. Cahill, "Jerusalem and the Time," 75.

83. On the modest but still growing size of the site of Jerusalem at this period, Mazar, "The Archaeology of the Iron Age II," 64, notes, "Jerusalem was no more than 5 hectares (12.5 acres) in area during the time of David, but could have been 12 hectares (30 acres) in area when the Temple Mount was added."

ological and literary evidence shows that it can also be reliably assumed that a temple complex was prepared/built by David/Solomon at this early period—one that would sustain an organized priestly and Levitical service, and (3) that the basic data from other urban settlements in the ANE are thus germane to a more precise understanding of the *historical* aspect of the Chronicler's presentation of Levitical service (seen in David's temple-preparations).

Cahill, first, has approached this debate from several perspectives. Fundamentally, she has contended that the theories advanced by scholars such as Finkelstein and Ussishkin are based on *negative* evidence and, often, what she defines as "disingenuous appeal" to the archaeological data for Jerusalem in the early Iron Age. As can be seen in the following (lengthy) quote, Cahill has strongly argued against the methodological underpinnings found in these minimalist views of Jerusalem's early archaeological status. She writes:

> *Theories based on negative evidence should never be preferred to theories based on positive evidence.* Stated another way: absence of evidence is not evidence of absence, especially at sites such as Jerusalem that are located in hilly terrain.... [Further,] whether relying primarily on the interpretation or archaeological data or on critical interpretation of the Hebrew Bible, modern writers who have challenged the historical existence of the united monarchy cite archaeological evidence from Jerusalem—or rather the supposed lack thereof—in support of their historical conclusions. In most cases, these citations are either grossly misleading, illogical, disingenuous, or all three.... The most extreme example of these assertions are those made by David Ussishkin, who maintains that following approximately 150 years of intense archaeological excavation, Jerusalem has failed to produce any evidence of an occupation stratum, a fortification wall, or even pottery ascribable to the period of the united monarchy. From these and similar assertions, Ussishkin and others conclude that the archaeological evidence contradicts the biblical descriptions of Jerusalem at the time of the united monarchy. These assertions—and the conclusions drawn from them—are not only grossly misleading because virtually every archaeologist to have excavated in the City of David claims to have found architecture and artifacts dating to these periods, but they are also illogical and disingenuous because they purposefully ignore the limited contexts available for archaeological investigation in Jerusalem, sound principles of stratigraphic interpretation, site formation processes characteristic of all

hill-country sites, and contradictory conclusions reached by archaeologists familiar with not only the published record but with the entire excavated material.[84]

Cahill also points out that archaeological evidence of continued urban development in Jerusalem does in fact exist for early Iron Age Jerusalem, even if distinct remains of David's temple and royal palace remain difficult to ascertain, though more recent excavations in Jerusalem by Eilat Mazar actually suggest the existence of just such types of Davidic (and Solomonic) remains (see further on this below). Cahill also notes that the Tel Dan Stela fragments discovered in the early 1990s by Biran and Naveh have for the most part dispelled "doubts concerning the existence of David and his progeny as truly historic figures."[85] Moreover, synchronisms with the Assyrian eponym king lists and Egyptian records allow David to be dated firmly in the tenth century.

Further, Cahill remarks that earlier excavation work by Shiloh, the main archaeologist working in Jerusalem's city of David in the 1970s and 1980s, demonstrates a consistent occupation of, at least, the eastern area of Iron Age Jerusalem. Cahill writes on this:

> Although fragmentary and largely unpublished, stratigraphic evidence for the uninterrupted occupation of Jerusalem from the Iron Age I to the early Iron Age II (ca. twelfth/eleventh—tenth/ninth centuries B.C.E.) has come to light in almost every area excavated by Shiloh on the City of David's eastern slope but has not been found elsewhere in Jerusalem.[86]

Thus, based on her study of this relevant evidence, Cahill has concluded that in the tenth century Levant, Jerusalem can be confidently defined

---

84. Cahill, "Jerusalem and the Time," 73, 76–77 (emphasis added).

85. Cahill, "Jerusalem and the Time," 55. On the Tel Dan Stela fragments (containing the reference בית דוד, "house [or dynasty] of David," at line 9) see the original articles: Biran and Naveh, "An Aramaic Stele Fragment from Tel Dan," 81–98; Biran and Naveh, "The Tel Dan Inscription," 1–18. Recently, Mazar has noted that the Tel Dan inscription represents the only extrabiblical source affirming the "house of David" (*bytdwd*) as the name of kingdom of Judah during the united monarchy of the OT's witness. However, as Mazar notes, "[t]hough later than David by almost 150 years, *the mere occurrence of the name indicates the historical reality behind this ruler, who was considered even among the neighbors of Israel as the founder of the dynasty and state of Judah*" (emphasis added). See Mazar, "Archaeology and the Iron Age II," 64. For a recent discussion of the Tel Dan inscription and some implications for the divided monarchy, see Younger, "The Tel Dan Inscription," 293–98, as well as the further literature cited there.

86. Cahill, "Jerusalem and the Time," 55–56. And note Shiloh, *Excavations at the City of David I*.

as a developing urban settlement in the Levant.[87] That is, she argues that the archaeological data firmly support the biblical presentation of David's kingdom centered in Jerusalem in the early united monarchy. Her final conclusion is quoted here:

> In sum, the developing archaeological evidence demonstrates that during the time of Israel's united monarchy, Jerusalem was fortified, served by two water-supply systems, and populated by a socially stratified society that constructed at least two new residential quarters—one located inside and the other outside—the city's fortification wall. The administrative and economic strength required both to generate and to support the city evidenced by the archaeological record is best identified with the period of the united monarchy rather than with the subsequent period during which rulers of the rump state of Judah struggled to maintain their autonomy.... Stratum 14 of Shiloh's excavations in the City of David appears to evidence the time during which Jerusalem emerged as capital of Israel's united monarchy in the mid-to-late tenth century B.C.E.[88]

Kitchen has also argued that the presentation of the united monarchy in Scripture can be shown to accord well with known extra-biblical evidence. He first acknowledges that no external explicit mention of biblical kings such as Saul, David, or Solomon occurs until 853 BC, with Shalmaneser III's hostile contacts with Ahab of Israel. And this is because no Assyrian king had contact with local rulers in Palestine before 853. In Egyptian sources, Kitchen similarly notes that between Ramesses III (ca. 1184–1153) and Shoshenq (ca. 954–924), there is equally little mention of rulers from the Levant, be they Canaanite, Philistine, or Israelite. On both of these points, Kitchen argues, however, "this is *not* the fault of the kings in Canaan ... and does *not* prove their nonexistence."[89] Again, we find another example of the absence of evidence *not proving* the evidence of absence.

Further, Kitchen reminds us of the specific challenges of doing archaeological work at the heart of modern-day Jerusalem. He especially contends that three factors "entirely exclude any hope of retrieving significant inscriptions from Jerusalem at any period before Herodian times": (1) the "deplorable state" of pre-Herodian remains in oldest Jerusalem (the Ophel and the eastern ridge), (2) the inaccessibility of much of its terrain, and (3)

---

87. On the detailed summary of the archaeological evidence, see Cahill, "Jerusalem and the Time," 19–70.
88. Cahill, "Jerusalem and the Time," 72.
89. Kitchen, *On the Reliability*, 156 (emphasis original).

the "fact that [old Jerusalem] is 95 percent undug/undiggable (100 percent of the Temple Mount itself, where royal stelae may have been erected)."[90] Despite this situation, Kitchen points out further that extra-biblical "traces" of written evidence for the existence of David in the tenth century have begun to emerge: the "House of David" mention in the Tel Dan inscription and (with virtual certainly) the Moabite Stone, within 150 years of David's death, and the probable mention of the "heights of David" in the list of Shoshenq I (ca. 925), merely fifty years after David's death.[91]

Also, Kitchen argues that broader contextual evidence is germane to the historical reality of a Davidic empire in the tenth century Levant. On this issue, he concludes:

> David's "empire" (inherited by Solomon) belongs to a particular type of "mini-empire," of a *scope and nature only present and feasible within the interval between about 1180 and 870 and at no other time in the first millennium*, being known also from Neo-Hittite and Aramean analogies.[92]

Finally, on the archaeological remains, Kitchen argues that the strata for tenth-century Canaanite sites are "consistent with the formal existence of a unified state on its terrain then."[93] This cannot be fully elucidated in Jerusalem because of the reasons noted above, but the contemporary sites of Hazor, Gezer, and Megiddo (for the most part) do reveal such evidence. With a bit of irony, then, Kitchen concludes on the overall archaeological evidence for Davidic Jerusalem/Israel in the tenth century, by writing:

> The occupation of the rest of the area [of ancient Canaan beyond the sites of Jerusalem, Hazor, Gezer, Hazor, and Megiddo] is also consistent with this; *it was not a land of ghosts*. The clever attempt to down-date the archaeological remains of the twelfth-to-eight century substantially into the eleventh-to-late-eight century will not really work, throws up bizarre anomalies, requires the invention of new Aegean invasions, and is wholly needless. . . . *Thus normal dating should be retained, with its entire network of good correlations with social and political conditions also reflected in the biblical sources.*[94]

---

90. Kitchen, *On the Reliability*, 157.
91. Kitchen, *On the Reliability*, 157.
92. Kitchen, *On the Reliability*, 157 (emphasis added).
93. Kitchen, *On the Reliability*, 157 (emphasis added).
94. Kitchen, *On the Reliability*, 158 (emphasis added).

Finally, in the 2015 edition of their history of Israel, Provan, Long, and Longman have helped synthesize both the broader picture of archaeological study of Jerusalem, and also, some of the more recent advances. First, we note that in the 1960s, Kathleen Kenyon's work represents the first modern excavation in Jerusalem, and that in the 1970s and the 1980s, the second major excavation was led by Yigael Shiloh. Steiner has been assigned the task of preparing the final report on Kenyon's work, while Cahill has been assigned the task for Shiloh.[95] As Provan et al. note, "curiously, the conclusions to which Steiner and Cahill come could not be more different."[96] Essentially, Steiner has argued that Jerusalem's evidence is lacking in such a way that the biblical picture of David, Jerusalem, and the united monarchy cannot be viewed as historical fact in the early Iron Age, nor in the Late Bronze Age, for that matter.[97] On the other hand, Cahill remains startled by Steiner's conclusions and cannot see them as substantiated by Jerusalem's archaeological record.

In fact, as Provan et al. write further, "[o]n the basis of preliminary reports by both Kenyon and Shiloh, Cahill shows that at least four separate areas in the city of David exhibit 'stratified remains containing architecture, pottery, and other artifacts attributable to the Late Bronze Age.'"[98] Na'aman has also countered the minimalist conclusions of Steiner. He notes that neither Kenyon nor Shiloh themselves ever noticed the gap in occupation in Jerusalem of the Early Iron Age—the gap that Steiner was confidently arguing for. In fact, Na'aman further reminds us that in the earlier Amarna Letters (from New Kingdom Egypt of the *fourteenth century BC*, detailing correspondence between Egypt and various Canaanite peoples), we find evidence of Jebus (Jerusalem) already being a significant city.[99]

More recently, the archaeologist Eilat Mazar has made two significant discoveries in Jerusalem. (1) Eilat Mazar has argued that the "large-stone structure" of the Ophel area of Jerusalem's City of David may very well represent part of the royal palace complex of the biblical king David. (2) Also, for Eilat Mazar, the further discovery of a large section of city wall (seventy

---

95. See Steiner, *Excavations by Kathleen M. Kenyon*; Cahill's volume is still in preparation (following Provan et al., *A Biblical History*, 301, note 161), but note Cahill, "Jerusalem in David," 20–31; Shiloh et al., *Excavations at the City of David*.

96. Provan et al., *A Biblical History*, 301.

97. See Steiner, "David's Jerusalem," 26–33. And see further Steiner, "The Archaeology," 143–68; Steiner, "Jerusalem in the Tenth," 280–88.

98. Provan et al., *A Biblical History*, 301.

99. See Na'aman, "David's Jerusalem," 42–44; note as well Na'aman, "Cow Town," 43–47.

meters high and six meters long) may come from the time of king Solomon.[100] Some have challenged Eilat Mazar's connection of the large stone structure to David altogether, such as Finkelstein.[101] Others, like Faust, have suggested that this structure was likely built *before* David, but that he would have used and ameliorated it.[102] More generally, Amihai Mazar notes that "the 'stepped stone structure' and 'large building' [evident from excavations at Jerusalem's City of David] to its west comprise a large monumental structure, *which could be the largest structure in the southern Levant in the tenth century BCE*."[103] All in all, with Provan et al., on this type of evidence for a developing Jerusalem in the early tenth century, led by David, we conclude that, to the ongoing questions of whether or not Jerusalem "was a city of sufficient standing to have served as the capital of David's kingdom," that "the answer, on present evidence, would seem to be yes."[104]

As a conclusion to this first methodological section, we now draw out two aspects, which will especially frame our subsequent review of some of the basic data from the ANE: (1) the benefit of carefully investigating parallels and contrasts in related ANE cultures will be assumed; (2) the maximalist view of Jerusalem in the tenth century will be assumed—one that affirms: (a) the historical reality of a developing urban settlement led by David, in the Levant of the tenth-century early Iron Age, and (b) the resultant ability, at this earlier period, of the city to support a temple and palace system (and its needed personnel) similar to other urban settlements in the Levant and in the ANE more generally.

On these bases, the presence of a key feature within ancient cultures of the ANE may now be discussed in what follows. As noted above, relevant data regarding the main theme of temple and ritual will be presented following three sub-themes: (1) temple-building and temple structures; (2) temple rituals, priests, and attendants; and (3) temple rituals and music. For each of these topics, some basic, illustrative data from the major cultural contexts of the ANE (when applicable—Mesopotamian, Hittite, Levantine, Egyptian) will be noted—especially from the third and second millennia, and then into the first millennium, for the sake of developing the picture of a common cognitive environment related to these themes.

100. See Mazar, *The Palace of King David*; Mazar, *Discovering the Solomonic Wall*.
101. See Finkelstein, "The 'Large Stone Structure,'" 1–10.
102. See Faust, "Did Eilat Mazar," 47–52; Faust, "The Large Stone Structure," 115–30.
103. Mazar, "The Archaeology of Iron Age II," 64. And see further Mazar, "Archaeology and the Biblical Narrative," 29–58.
104. Provan et al., *A Biblical History*, 303. And also note Pioske, "David's Jerusalem," 4–15, for a study of tenth century Davidic Jerusalem, its agrarian context, as well as its broader contrasts and connections to other major sites in the ANE from the period.

Again, the goal is to give some measure of substance to the following claim: that from much earlier and down to the early first millennium, a significant and prevalent feature of the cognitive environment of ancient Near Eastern urban settlements was the presence of religious temples, within which organized systems of priests and other attendants supported a variety of religious rituals, and which further included rituals with instrumental music and vocal music. Since Jerusalem can also be shown to have been a developing urban settlement in the tenth-century Levant, this discussion represents the second step in the overall argument of our study—seeking to defend the historical *plausibility* of David's establishment of (1) a corps of Levites during the early United Monarchy (early Iron age/early first millennium), which (2) was to play an important role in the support of the cultic ministry of the Jerusalem temple, and (3) whose role included an organized musical system (and, of course, all of this *then* served as a key rhetorical device for the Chronicler in encouraging his postexilic audience to continue in the proper worship of Yahweh, which was to include the faithful liturgical and cultic leadership of the priests and Levites).

ANE Data: Temples and Temple-Building

Both in ancient Israel and in the broader ANE, temples were a central feature of life: the divinity resided there, worship provided for the divinity, and sacred space was centered on a given temple complex. In fact, Walton has highlighted this all-encompassing influence of the temple, as he has written:

> The temple [generally in the ANE] was the central and fundamental component of the cosmos, the centerpiece of the function and identity of the community and the interface between humans and the divine. As the god sat enthroned in the temple, the order established through creation was maintained, the forces threatening that order were held at bay, and the viability of the human community was maintained.[105]

For instance, in the earliest Sumerian and later Akkadian contexts of Mesopotamia, texts exist that describe both (1) the building of religious temples, and (2) the inherent physical presence, and cultural and religious influence of these temples.[106] In the context of Mesopotamian city-states,

---

105. Walton, "The Temple in Context," 349 (and note the further literature cited there on temples in the ANE). For Walton, further, Israel's temple shared many general features with those of the broader cultures of the ANE, but also stood in contrast in many ways. See further Walton, "The Temple in Context," 352–54.

106. See further Robertson, "Temples and Sanctuaries," 372–76; Robertson, "The

Robertson has noted that most scholars agree that the temple played a key role in the community's self-understanding of a fruitful and meaningful life. Of this aspect, he writes:

> In the minds of ancient Mesopotamians themselves [from the fourth through the first millennia], the temple's most crucial function was to provide for the city's patron deity a secure, permanent residence of appropriate spaciousness and luxury. . . . In the unstinting performance of the duties [performed by the temple attendants] lay the community's only hope, if not assurance, for its continued safety and prosperity.[107]

In Sumerian and Akkadian views, the "temple" is understood as the "house of a god," (É.DINGIRA in Sumerian; bīt *ilim* in Akkadian).[108] Kraus, for example, has noted that during the Neo-Sumerian period of the third Ur dynasty (late third millennium), the city ruler was seen as the master temple-builder, since he was to promote appropriate contact between the people and their gods. The temple is, then, the perceived locus of that divine-human connection. Once a temple was dedicated to a god, appropriate cultic services were setup following a regular calendar; these temple complexes, such as the Shara Temple at Umma (and the temple for the spouse of Shara, Nin-ara), very likely also played important social and economic roles within the larger community.[109]

Castel and Joannès have further pointed out some of the key features related to Mesopotamian temples.[110] Since temples were conceived and perceived as the earthly dwelling place of the deity for a particular geographical

---

Social and Economic Organization," 443–54. On the broader historical background of the principal Mesopotamian civilizations of the ANE, see, for example, Kuhrt, *The Ancient Near East*, 1:19–73 (third millennium), 1:74–116 (Old Babylonian and Old Assyrian periods), 2:473–546 (Neo–Assyrian period), 2:573–622 (Babylonian period). More generally, note also Hallo and Simpson, *The Ancient Near East*, 1–146 (on the major Mesopotamian historical periods), and 151–82 (on Mesopotamian culture generally). See also the section on Mesopotamian city–states in Van De Mieroop, *A History of the Ancient Near East*, 19–118. Also, for recent, broader surveys of some of the key cultures of the ANE covered in this section of this chapter, see Hays and Machinist, "Assyria and the Assyrians," 31–106; Vanderhooft, "Babylonia and the Babylonians," 107–38; Smith, "Ugarit and the Ugaritians," 139–68; LeMon, "Egypt and the Egyptians," 169–96; Collins, "The Hittites and the Hurrians," 197–228.

107. See Robertson, "Temples and Sanctuaries," 376, and 372–75, on the basic archeological and textual evidence.

108. The single terms for "house" are É in Sumerian and *bîtu* in Akkadian. See further, for instance, Kraus, *The Role of Temples*, 1.

109. See further Kraus, *The Role of Temples*, 5–11.

110. See Castel and Joannès, "Temple," 838–41.

location, divine couples or even larger groups of gods were perceived as having taken residence in these temples once they were built. Only certain personnel, such as the priests, attendants, or the king and certain members of his entourage, could enter the temple complex. It was also the kings' responsibility to oversee the building, maintenance, and/or restoration of a particular temple. Indeed, as these authors note of the close relationship between the king and the required building and maintenance of a particular city's religious temple and cult:

> The sovereigns ensure that the memory of their sacred works would be preserved, with the help of baked bricks marked with their name, or with other deposits or foundation documents. They have a duty, also, to watch over the proper functioning of the cult: taking care of the foundation rites for the cultic buildings, of the service in the sacred spaces, but also of the offerings, libations, processions. To provide for the needs of the gods is thus part of the duties of the king and ensures that he will have a blessed reign. To fail in this essential duty is to threaten the peace and the prosperity of the state.[111]

These physical temple structures are attested from the Ubeid period (fifth to fourth millennia), though it is difficult to ascertain the sacred/religious quality of these earliest remains. From the third and second millennia, however, and especially with the third Ur dynasty, it is possible, at various sites, to distinguish a religious quarter laid out around a temple structure dedicated to the principal deity of the city. More specifically, Robertson has noted that the "earliest substantial evidence of a truly complex temple organization incorporating the temple households" appeared in the Uruk and Jamdad Nasr periods (late fourth to early third millennium, especially with the Eanna complex at Uruk).[112] In such places as the temple to Ištar at Mari or the temple of Šin at Tutub, for example, the central temples represent imposing complexes; smaller "chapels" dedicated to the same deities are also present throughout the cities.[113] The data associated with these types of Mesopotamian cultures are indeed quite rich and varied, as Castel and Joannès have further argued:

> All of the cultic locations present specific building set ups. . . . Furthermore, inventory texts, descriptions in hymns and rituals, as well as objects of art all display gods in their sanctuaries and

---

111. Castel and Joannès, "Temple," 839 (my translation).
112. Robertson, "Social and Economic Organization," 449.
113. Castel and Joannès, "Temple," 840.

give us an idea of the richness and of the variety of the materials and the furniture that was found in the temples.[114]

Thus, this type of evidence suggests that Mesopotamian temples were supported by the larger community, that they were carefully managed and involved the maintenance of large flocks, herds, and other sources of support.[115] That is, to "serve the god properly, the temple was equipped like a household. Essential and omnipresent were the provisions for the god's meal."[116] Hence, the religious nature of the temple and its perceived impact on the stability of the community appears to have played a significant role in the cultures of these early Mesopotamian city-states. This begins to paint the portrait of the common cognitive environment in the ANE related to temples, temple attendants, and the function of these in the communities.

Averbeck, for example, has argued that the texts of the "Cylinders of Gudea" can be properly defined as a Sumerian subgenre of the royal hymn known as "building and dedication hymns."[117] This Sumerian composition was most likely written "to celebrate or perhaps commemorate Gudea's building and dedication of a new Enninu temple for the god Ningirsu, the patron deity of Lagash."[118] Averbeck also suggests the text could be dated to just before the Third Dynasty of Ur (or overlapping with it)—that is, sometime during the late third millennium. The Gudea cylinders present a careful literary structure which, among other aspects, emphasizes the construction of the new Enninu temple, the detailed preparations for this temple complex, and the entry of its god.[119] In the section which Averbeck defines as "Gudea's preparations for the induction of Nigirsu and Baba into the new Eninnu" (Cyl. B i.12-ii.6), Gudea's prayer shows how: (1) the temple is perceived as a point of *liaison* between the divine and human realms, and (2) the temple is understood as the proper dwelling place for the gods Ningirsu and Baba. At various points in this section, the text reads:

> The temple, mooring pole of the land, which grows (high) between heaven and earth; The Enninu, the true brickwork, (for) which Enlil decreed a good destiny ... The temple, being a big mountain, reached up to heaven; Being Utu, it filled heaven's

---

114. Castel and Joannès, "Temple," 840 (my translation).
115. See further Robertson, "Social and Economic Organization," 444–48.
116. See Wiggermann, "Theologies, Priests," 1861.
117. See Averbeck, "The Cylinders of Gudea," 417 (417–33 for the full translation); Averbeck, "Sumer," 113–21 for further comparative discussion related to these texts.
118. Averbeck, "The Cylinders of Gudea," 417.
119. See especially, Averbeck, "The Cylinders of Gudea," 424–28 (preparation for the Enninu), and 429–33 (furnishing of the temple complex).

midst . . . O Nigirsu, I have built a temple for you, (so) may you enter (it) in festive joy. O my Baba, I have set up your bed-chamber(?) for you, (so) settle into it comfortably.[120]

Significantly, Averbeck points out some of the temple-building parallels between ancient Near Eastern texts such as these Gudea Cylinders and biblical texts like 1 Chr 22–29 or 2 Chr 8 (and others). He essentially shows that the strong cultural tradition of temple and temple-building present in the early Sumerian culture was preserved in these Sumerian texts and partially influenced the *shape* of related biblical texts—at least in their *cognizance* of cultural factors related to basic historical realities of temples and temple-building.[121] Averbeck concludes, in fact:

> Sumer and the Sumerian language and literature influenced ancient Near Eastern culture in a *formative* way. This is due in no small part to the fact that they were the originators of many of the cuneiform cultural and scribal traditions that dominated much if not all of the fertile crescent for almost two millennia. The underlying cultural foundations that developed through this influence penetrated into and persisted in many cultures near and far, both geographically and chronologically, from ancient Sumer. Some reflections of this influence are found also in the Hebrew Bible.[122]

Thus, first, Averbeck shows that temples and temple-building (with complex building and maintenance programs) were an essential part of Sumerian/Mesopotamian culture, *well before* Iron Age I. Second, he also argues that this very early temple culture was *transmitted throughout* the ANE—especially via Sumerian and Akkadian literature—making the cultural emphasis on the centrality of a religious temple for a city or a larger territory a known entity since *at least* the time of the early third millennium.

One example of this formative influence of Sumero-Akkadian principles may be found in the Hittite culture of eastern Anatolia.[123] As Archi has

---

120. Averbeck, "The Cylinders of Gudea," 427–28. Note here the distinct "cognitive cultural" parallel with Solomon's prayer of dedication in 1 Kgs 8 and 2 Chr 6. In the English version, 2 Chr 6:1–2 reads: "Then Solomon said, 'The LORD has said that he would dwell in thick darkness. But I have built you an exalted house, a place for you to dwell in forever'" (ESV).

121. Note Averbeck, "Sumer," 119–21.

122. Averbeck, "Sumer," 121, emphasis added.

123. See further Archi, "Hittite and Hurrian Literatures," 2367–77. On broader historical background to the Hittite culture, see for instance Houwink ten Cate, "Hittite History," 219–25; Kuhrt, *The Ancient Near East, Volume*, 1:225–82, 2:547–72; Van De Mieroop, *A History of the Ancient Near East*, 112–15 (Old Hittite Kingdom), 145–55 (Hittite New Kingdom); "Hurrians and Hittites," in Hallo and Simpson, *The Ancient*

noted, the archives from the Temple I site within the ancient Hattic/Hittite capital of Kattusha (Boğazköy) have revealed numerous cuneiform tablets showing dependence on earlier Sumerian and Akkadian texts—including texts related to the temple cult. In this vein, Archi notes:

> In addition to Sumerian-Akkadian word lists (necessary for a correct use of cuneiform), which had to be provided with Hittite equivalences, the scribal school *absorbed* literary models that were curricular because of the prestige of Mesopotamian culture and because Akkadian was the written language in the entire Syrian region. And so it follows that discoveries in the archives of Kattusha . . . turned up rituals, auguries, hymns, wisdom texts, and some parts of the Gilgamesh and Atrakhasis poems, all in Babylonian, in addition to the legends about Sargon and Naram-Sin, the two great kings of the Akkad dynasty, in Hittite translation.[124]

The older Hittite historical periods are generally defined as Old Kingdom (1750–1550), Middle Kingdom (1550–1380) and New Kingdom (1380–1200).[125] The Temple I site is especially connected to the New Kingdom (the late second millennium).[126] This site suggests a very large temple complex, as it comprises a main entrance and large temple courtyard near the center. This central area is flanked by several other rooms and halls—including an "archive" room.[127] Twenty-seven smaller temples have also been identified in excavations of the Upper City at Kattusha.[128] The point to highlight here is that Hittite culture, in cultural and chronological *propinquity* to the early first millennium and David's United Monarchy, also demonstrates the presence of an established physical temple complex. The texts discovered within this site further denote a particular concern for cultic and administrative organization—including records for "cultic equipment, personnel, and traditions for local cults throughout the empire," as well as ritual texts detailing "Hittite festivals, prayers, mythology, and divination."[129] Early Hittite texts describing a ritual for building

---

Near East, 106–11. Note as well the essay by Hoffner, "Hittite–Israelite Cultural Parallels," xxviii–xxxiv.

124. Archi, "Hittite and Hurrian Literature," 2367 (emphasis added).
125. Following the chronology in Sparks, *Ancient Texts*, xxxiii.
126. See, for instance, Houwink ten Cate, "Hittite History," 220.
127. See further McMahon, "Theology," 1983–84.
128. McMahon, "Theology," 1983.
129. McMahon, "Theology," 1983. And see further, for example, on the varied nature of Hittite literature, Archi, "Hittite and Hurrian Literatures," 2368–71.

a temple (CTH *413*) and for establishing a new temple (CTH *481*), for instance, are also extant.[130]

Consequently, this type of example further suggests that the ancient Near Eastern temple culture that originated in Mesopotamian Sumerian and Akkadian contexts was then *transmitted* in different regions of the ANE. Religious temples can further be discerned within the ancient cultures of Syria-Palestine, since temples and other sanctuaries are evident there, especially in Canaanite, Philistine, and Israelite contexts.

Indeed, in the Levant, from the earliest Chalcolithic era (ca. 4500–3400 BC), the examples of two key structures stand out. The Ghassulian site at En-Gedi overlooking the Dead Sea represents, for Dever, the earliest "real" temple in Palestine, "in the sense of being a monumental public structure dedicated exclusively to cult practice."[131] This is a religious complex that includes a central temple building, a courtyard and a circular basin structure, as well as a gatehouse and postern gate. In fact, the cache of copper and ivory cultic artifacts, discovered in the nearby Nahal Mishmar cave, is often believed to have belonged to the En-Gedi temple and, hence, suggests the possibility of a developed cultic ritual even at this early date. Smaller temples, such as at Tuleilat al-Ghassul or Gilat, are also attested.[132]

During the stages of the Bronze Age (ca. 3400 BC–1200 BC), remains from a number of monumental temples also exist. In the Early Bronze Age, several *Breithaus* temples are attested—such as the Meggido XIX temple (a single-room structure), two temples at Ai, or the "Twin Temple" at Arad (unique in its preservation of two *Breithaus* structures side-by-side). The temples from this period are "simple, one-room structures, with no particular orientation, with only occasionally an altar as an item of furnishing."[133]

For the Middle Bronze Age period, a greater number and variety of religious temples are evident. Larger fortress-type temples are present at this level at Meggido, Shechem, and Hazor. These and other temple sites reveal either bipartite or tripartite structures. The original features of these temples, however, are difficult to discern fully as most of them were rebuilt in later periods. The Late Bronze Age, furthermore, bears witness to a "proliferation of earlier style temples" and, also, to the introduction of newer "local and Egyptian style temples."[134] The Late Bronze Age strata at

---

130. On these, see further Sparks, *Ancient Texts*, 156–57.

131. Dever, "Temples and Sanctuaries," 376. For a broad discussion of the major historical periods of the ancient Levant, see for example Kuhrt, *The Ancient Near East*, 1:283–331, 2:385–472.

132. Dever, "Temples and Sanctuaries," 377.

133. Dever, "Temples and Sanctuaries," 378.

134. Dever, "Temples and Sanctuaries," 378.

Meggido and Shechem, for instance, reveal a rebuilt *migdal* temple, while a number of temples at Beth-Shan appear to have a more Egyptian style. In the end, for this period, although a large number of architectural temple-styles exist, Dever notes that:

> There is apparently a homogeneity of cult practice reflected. This is no doubt typical of fully developed Canaanite religion, as is best documented by the Ugaritic texts. There is a multiplicity of male and female deities, most of them connected with the fertility cults of greater Canaan.[135]

Early Iron Age temple remains continue to bear witness to Canaanite-style structures, but also to (1) smaller Israelite shrines early on (and fuller temple structures by the tenth century) and (2) Philistine structures revealing Aegean and Cypriot influences (which highlights this culture's connection with the Sea Peoples movement.)[136]

Finally, in the context of ancient Egypt, "the history of the [temple] is extremely long."[137] Ward has pointedly commented on the prevalence of temples in ancient Egypt by noting:

> Egypt can truly be called a land of temples. From the great sprawling complex of the Amon temple at Karnak to the tiny shrines found along village streets, temples and sanctuaries devoted to the cults of the gods were a dominant feature in every city and town.[138]

The best evidence for highlighting Egyptian temple complexes seems to be related to the New Kingdom of the Late Bronze Age (ca. 1500–1000 BC). On this period, O'Connor remarks first that a complex "socioeconomic matrix" is discernable around the major temple structures of the Nile Valley (in general propinquity to the Davidic United Kingdom in Israel). Some of the principal urban centers from this period include Memphis and Thebes. Also, the state had a dominating control over matters social, economic, and religious. Similarly to Mesopotamian patterns, the religious cult was then

---

135. Dever, "Temples and Sanctuaries," 379.

136. Dever, "Temples and Sanctuaries," 379. For a discussion of the impact of the Sea Peoples' movements at the end of the Bronze Age, see Mumford, "The Late Bronze Age Collapse," 260–72.

137. See O'Connor, "The Social and Economic Organization," 319.

138. Ward, "Temples and Sanctuaries," 369. For fuller discussion of the principal periods of ancient Egyptian history, see further Kuhrt, *The Ancient Near East, Volume*, 1:118–84 (Dynasties 1–7), 1:185–224 (New Kingdom period); note also Hallo and Simpson, *The Ancient Near East*, 185–295. Note as well, on comparative issues between Egyptology and biblical studies, Hoffmeier, "Understanding Hebrew," xxi–xxvii.

supported by governmental leadership to promote "cosmic stability" for which a "steady and growing revenue stream" was needed.[139] The administrative district had the responsibility of maintaining local temples, and securing revenue. As Ward has then noted, "the cult temple was first and foremost the home of a deity and thus the point of contact between that deity and the mundane world of man."[140] Egyptian culture also had temple-foundation rituals, and as early as the third millennium. One of the primary functions of the temple was thus to provide a location for the complex worship ritual, the main goal of which was to call the deity to action on behalf of the community. Here the temple-foundation ritual—in which the king and priests participated—was central to properly setting up a temple and allowing for the establishment of a god in its "house."[141]

A distinction is also made in Egyptology between these "cult temples," which housed a variety of deities from the pantheon, and "funerary temples," whose primary function was to maintain the existence of a human soul into eternity. These funerary temples range from the large pyramid complexes devoted to the Pharaohs to much smaller shrines for lower classes of society. The cult temples were perceived as allowing for human contact with the divine, while the funerary temples allowed for contact between the "soul of the deceased and the living."[142]

Religious temple structures of varying size and complexity were present. The central building of the temple complex was known as the "god's temple." The supporting temple establishment, which included the priesthood and attendants, ancillary structures (various residences, workshops and storehouses), lands and other property, was known as the god's "house," (the *pr*).[143] The three royal capital cities of Thebes, Memphis, and Pi-Ramses and Heliopolis, the city of Re (the cosmic ruling deity), contained the wealthiest temple structures. The temple of Amun-Re in the Karnak complex (in Thebes) was spread over seven acres and was the largest Egyptian temple. The temple devoted to Ptah in Memphis, and the temple of Re in Heliopolis are further example of such major temples.

Thus, overall, this brief discussion of some of the basic features of ancient religious temples in the ANE suggests that they can be defined as a pervasive, complex, and dominating feature within the "cognitive worldview" of the major ancient Near Eastern cultures. Vis-à-vis the biblical presentation

---

139. O'Connor, "The Social and Economic Organization," 320.
140. Ward, "Temples," 369.
141. Ward, "Temples," 371.
142. Ward, "Temples," 370.
143. Ward, "Temples," 321.

of the temple theme and the ANE in general, Walton has further affirmed a certain amount of cultural connection and a specific contrast, which is worth noting here. He writes:

> The actual ritual practices [connected to temples] show some degree of commonality across the ancient world, including Israel. Likewise, the role of ritual as undergirding the smooth operation of the cosmos and securing the favor and presence of the deity is everywhere evident. *The main difference seen in the cognitive worldview of Israel concerned the extent to which Yahweh had needs that were met by rituals, or the way in which the giving of gifts influenced deity.*[144]

ANE Data: Temple Priests, Attendants, and Ritual

In this section, the general nature and function of temple priests and other attendants throughout different contexts in the ANE will be examined. The chronologically earlier evidence in this area has not often been brought to bear to support the *Davidic* expansion of Levitical duty in Chronicles. For example, Ko, in a recent study, has examined the concept of the "scholar-singer" in Mesopotamian scribal musical culture, but he only does so from the *later* Neo-Babylonian period, to explore its influence on the Chronicler himself and the socio-ideological setting of the postexilic citizen-temple community.[145]

Overall, the ubiquity of ancient temple structures is matched by recurring patterns of priestly organization and ritual duties within these temples. In fact, as Sparks has noted recently, "[p]riests and other religious specialists were part of an elite in ancient Near Eastern cultures whose services were to secure the well-being of king, people, and land by representing them before the deity.... Priests functioned as mediators between the human and divine spheres and were generally considered attendants of the deity."[146]

Following Grimes, Sparks has further proposed a helpful definition of the concept of ritual, which he suggests is a "symbolic religious act" that is: (1) repeated, (2) sacred (in relationship to the divine), (3) formalized (through set patterns), (4) traditional (perceived as ancient), and (5) intentional (not unconscious). The exercise of religious ritual further entails the twin concepts of sacred space ("the physical domain that is in contact with the divine") and

---

144. Walton, *Ancient Near Eastern Thought*, 95–96 (emphasis added).
145. See Ko, *The Levite Singers*, especially 29–61.
146. Klingbeil, "Priests in the Ancient Near East," 355, 360.

sacred time ("the period within which the divine connection is intact").[147] Modern scholars disagree on the *implications* of such ancient rituals—namely, whether they point to an actual spiritual world or merely to a human construct.[148] In what follows, however, the goal is, more basically, to summarize some of the data related to the early existence, in the ANE, of organized ritual leaders in temple contexts.

In Mesopotamia, the relevant information shows that the temple clergy was set up according to various functions within the worship rituals and ancillary services. First, there is evidence revealing the existence of carefully structured priestly and attending roles. The temple complex in Mesopotamian city-states required both religious and administrative personnel—although, even from the earliest Sumerian period in the third millennium, the king still had final authority.[149] Charpin, for instance, has noted that Mesopotamian temple attendants can be understood following three types of responsibilities: administrative, cultic, and domestic.[150]

First, the *šangû* was at the head of administrative personnel; another key administrator just below the *šangû* was the *šatamu*, whose role became even more important in the later Babylonian periods of the first millennium.[151] Charpin also suggests that the *šangû* should not be viewed as a type of high-priest; nonetheless he remarks, of the *šangû*, "this was indeed the most important functionary in the temple in terms of hierarchy, but, above all, he directed the temple cult from a material point of view."[152] These principal leaders seemed to have exercised oversight with other administrative leaders and their personnel: such as, for instance, the head beer-maker (*šâpir sirašê*), the head bread-maker (*šâpir nuhatimmi*), those responsible for herds in general (*rab buli*), those responsible for the fattening of the herds (*re'û sattukki*), those responsible for farming (*rab ikkari*), or the administrator of the religious personnel (*rab širki*). A head treasurer (*zamartappu*) also supported the work of the *šangû*.[153]

The principal religious or ritual leaders were the high "priest" (EN) or high "priestess" (*entu*). Under these, different types of "purifiers" (especially well-documented for the service to Nanna/Sîn in Ur during the

---

147. Sparks, *Ancient Texts*, 144.

148. Sparks, *Ancient Texts*, 144. Note also the discussion of various theories related to the understanding of ritual in the ANE in Klingbeil, *A Comparative Study*, 18–60.

149. Joannès, "Administration des Temples," 9.

150. See Charpin, "Prêtres, Prêtresses," 681.

151. Joannès, "Administration," 9.

152. Charpin, "Prêtres," 681 (my translation).

153. Charpin, "Prêtres," 681.

Old Babylonian period) maintained the sanctity of the temple, while, often, lamenting singers (*kalû*) also participated in the temple rituals. For example, during the Old Babylonian period of the second millennium, a type of religious cloister is evident in Sippar, where religious women called *nadîtu* lived under the supervision of administrative leaders.[154] The detail and organization of these duties, even at this early period in the ANE, is to be noted for our argument.

In the Old Babylonian period of the early second millennium, cuneiform texts from Ur provide a good example of personnel working at a temple sanctuary—in this case the Erkišgunal for the moon-god Nanna or Sîn. From these texts, Charpin points out the existence of a well-structured system of temple attendants.[155] He notes that the temple priests lived near the sanctuary and were ready to serve at all times. He writes, "if the clergy resided in proximity of the Erkišgunal, it was because of the needs of the cult: the priests, we shall see, were devoted to the service of the gods, both night and day."[156]

Charpin also discusses the organization of these cultic agents, based on a list of rations for the various cultic leaders and workers at the Erkišgunal.[157] The list reveals a number of roles: such as the gal-zu-ukkin-na (the wise man of the gathering), the zabar-dab$_5$ (a type of treasurer), the nar-gal (the chief musician), the nar-sa (a stringed-instrument specialist), the gala-mah (the chief singer), and others as well.[158]

If evidence exists related to the organization of Mesopotamian temple clergy, a number of texts are also extant, which give further insight into the *nature* of the rituals and various liturgical services led by these temple workers. Prayers, hymns, laments, and other liturgical texts indeed survive from the early Sumerian and Akkadian periods and thus further illustrate the *content* of the religious ritual performed by the temple clergy.[159]

For instance, an Akkadian text from Emar, "The Installation of the Storm God's High Priestess," provides some insight into the cultic rites related to a clergy member.[160] This text provides a carefully structured set of

154. Joannès, "Administration," 9.

155. See Charpin, *Le Clergé d'Ur*, especially 233–302 (on the "agents" of the cult at Ur).

156. Charpin, *Le Clergé d'Ur*, 232 (my translation).

157. Charpin, *Le Clergé d'Ur*, 234–35.

158. Charpin, *Le Clergé d'Ur*, 235–50.

159. Note the following overview essays related to this topic: Michalowski, "Sumerian Literature," 2279–91; Bottéro, "Akkadian Literature," 2293–303; Wiggermann, "Theologies, Priests and Worship," 1857–1870.

160. See Fleming "The Installation," 427–31. And note further, Fleming, *The Installation*, especially 80–105 for the human participants in the rite.

instructions surrounding the installation of the priestess. On the first day, "the daughter of any son of Emar" is selected for the rite. On the second day, a number of servants perform a shaving rite with the high priestess, who is formally installed on the third day. A seven-day celebratory feast follows (on days 3–9), before the conclusion of the celebration on the last day. This final day includes involvement from a number of temple attendants: men performing sacrifices, a diviner, and singers. Celebrations of the deity are also part of the Mesopotamian canon, such as the Sumerian hymn in honor of Enki. Hallo suggests that this hymn could have been used for worship, when it was perceived that Enki was visiting the temple (his dwelling place) at Eridu.[161]

Careful organization of a temple clergy is also attested in the Hittite context. In fact, as McMahon has noted, some key Hittite administrative documents have been preserved, and thus:

> The Hittites' concern with organization manifested itself in a variety of administrative documents. Among these are the instruction texts detailing the duties of various state officials. The *Instructions for Border Guards* contain explicit directions for maintaining local cults in the outlying provinces. The *Instructions for Temple Officials* are a rich source for understanding the administration of the temple and throw light on Hittite conceptions of human-divine relations.[162]

This last text, the "Instructions to Priests and Temple Officials" is particularly pertinent to the present discussion since it reveals the existence of temple personnel with different responsibilities in the cult.[163] McMahon notes that the extant copies of this text date to the later Empire period, "but the text itself seems to go back to the pre-New Hittite period, before the reign of Šuppiliuma I" (or around the mid-second millennium).[164] This lengthy text provides detailed instructions for a number of temple priests and other workers. These include: the *bakers* (§2), with their important duty of propitiating "the spirit and body of the gods;" the *temple officials* (§9), in general, who are further subdivided (as "priests," "anointing priests," and "*šiwanzanni*-priestesses"); the *kitchen attendants of all the gods* (§14); the *farmers of the god* (§15); those who *have the plow oxen of the threshing floor* (§17); those who are *cowherds and shepherds of the gods* (§18); those who

---

161. See Hallo "The Blessing of Nisaba," 531–32.

162. Note McMahon, "Theology," 1982.

163. See McMahon "Instructions to Priests," 217–21; this translation is organized following 19 numbered paragraphs (§1–19) and a colophon.

164. McMahon "Instructions to Priests," 217.

cut out a selection of animals and *drive them to the gods* (§19). The nature of the duties for the different temple officials are particularly well delineated according to their situation in the temple (§10):

> Whoever is a temple official—all [high] priests, lesser priests, anointing priests—whoever regularly crosses the threshold of the gods: let each not neglect to sleep up in the temple. Further, let sentries be posted at night, and let them continue to make rounds all night. Outside, let the guards keep their watch. But inside the temples let the temple official make the rounds all night. Let there be no sleep for them. Each night one high priest is to be in charge of the sentries. . . . Guard the temples very carefully, and let there be no sleep for you. Further, let the watch be divided among you.[165]

This text concludes with a colophon that affirms the end of the "rules" given to four specific sets of temple workers: (1) "all the temple officials," (2) "the kitchen attendants of the gods," (3) "the farmers of the gods," (4) "the cowherds of the god and shepherds of the god."[166]

If the Hittite literary corpus evinces such detail on the roles of temple personnel, it also presents several texts relating the content of the actual performance of the sacred rituals. For example, the "Ritual and Prayer to Ishtar of Ninevah" contains: (1) a prayerful exultation to the goddess Ishtar (§3–10; which concludes: "O Ištar of Ninevah, Lady, do you know not know how the land of Ḫatti is damaged by this deadly plague?"), and (2) some instructions on the ritual surrounding this prayer to Ishtar (§11–16).[167] It is further interesting to note, for our larger purposes here, that when the ritual for Ishtar is concluded, vocal and instrumental music plays a key part in the final stage (§16). Through their musical procession, the singers are indeed to "bring the god back into the temple."[168] In so doing, they are to both play

---

165. McMahon "Instructions to Priests," 219. As Sturtevant and Bechtel noted of this text from the royal library at Hattusas, it "included regulations for various classes of officials and public servants. Those for temple officials happen to have been well preserved." See Sturtevant and Bechtel, *A Hittite Chrestomathy*, 168.

166. Sturtevant and Bechtel, *A Hittite Chrestomathy*, 219. Jensen, "לִין‎," 722, following earlier research by Milgrom, draws a comparison between the Hittite guards in this "Temple Officials" text, who "guard the inside of the temple" and "another class, comparable to the Levite guards [who guard] the outside. Foreigners who approach must be killed, and if the guards fail to prevent such a sin, they themselves are to be put to death."

167. See Collins, "Ritual and Prayer to Ishtar," 164–65.

168. Collins, "Ritual and Prayer to Ishtar," 165.

instruments (the INANNA-instrument and the cymbals) and sing at the end of this prayer and ritual.[169]

Furthermore, in the Levantine context, a number of texts are preserved, which record the cultic rituals related to various sites in Syria/Palestine. For instance, within the Ugaritic corpus (in the chronological context of the Bronze Age), Xella has argued that ritual texts can be subdivided into seven categories: (1) monthly liturgies and lists of cultic offerings; (2) divination texts and oracles; (3) prayers; (4) incantations; (5) atonement sacrifices; (6) liturgies for the king; and (7) votive texts.[170] The clergy within this cultic system were particularly close to the king, who was viewed in these contexts as a religious officiant. The priest (*khnm*) and high priest (*rb khnm*) were part of the temple personnel.[171] The Ugaritic ritual texts also mention a few other cultic participants—such as a cantor (*šr*), a purifier (*qdš*), and a type of exorcist (*mḥllm*)—and all of these functionaries seemed to have been "dependants of the royal house (*bnš mlk*)."[172] The cultic role of the *inš ilm, nqdm, tnnm, mlsm, šib mqdšt*, and the *'bd mlk*, have also been discussed.[173] Xella and Merlo have further commented on the distinct levels of cultic personnel found in a variety of Ugaritic texts, all in close geographical, cultural, and linguistic propinquity to the OT's united monarchy. They note:

> The rare mention of personnel with religious functions in the cultic texts is partly completed by references which can be derived from the administrative and economic texts . . . [with several references: such as those to "priests", "a community of priests," a "chief priest"] . . . There are also the "consecrated ones," *qdšm*, for whom a divinatory function has also been proposed, hypothetically, and then the "singers," *šrm*, personnel connected in various ways with music in the cult . . . and lastly the "water

---

169. Collins, "Ritual and Prayer to Ishtar," 165.
170. See Xella and Merlo, "The Ugaritic Cultic Texts," 291.
171. On the Ugaritic and Pheonician *khnm*, see further Cody, *A History*, 18–22.

172. Xella and Merlo, "The Ugaritic Ritual Texts," 300. For further discussion of the liturgy of Ugarit, see Del Olmo Lete, *Canaanite Religion*, especially 87–138 ("Sacrifical Rituals"), 139–65 ("Non-Sacrifical Liturgies"), and 292–323 ("The Royal Liturgy of the Word"); Tarragon, *Le Culte à Ugarit*, 55–130.

173. See further Tarragon, *Le Culte à Ugarit*, 131–44. Similarly to Xella and Merlo, Tarragon also notes the difficulty in clearly deciphering the particular identities of various cult members at Ugarit. He writes indeed, "l'étude du personnel du culte à Ugarit nous conduit aux mêmes précautions qu'à propos du vocabulaire cultuel: bien des termes semblent proches d'un parallèle connu, surtout hébreu, mais les contextes ou la pauvreté des attestations forcent à rester en deçà de ces parallélismes." See Tarragon, *Le Culte à Ugarit*, 131.

carriers of the sanctuary," *sīb mqdšt*, a function which has parallels in the Hebrew world, in Hellenistic-Syria, and elsewhere.[174]

Of the many such liturgical Ugaritic texts, one can perhaps point to RS 1.0009 (*KTU* 1.46) as an example, which is a tablet of 18 lines preserving instructions for the cultic functionaries to undertake sacrificial rituals for various Canaanite gods. This involved offering two rams and a bull for *'Anatu* or one ram for *Ba'lu*, *Yammu*, or *Dagan*.[175] The fragmented text also contains a few chronological notices (such as: "the king shall wash on the fourteenth of the month" [line 9], and "on the day of the full moon, two bulls will be sacrificed for *Yariḫu*" [line 10]), which leads Pardee to conclude that the full text probably contained similar rituals for a month-long period.[176]

Lastly, ancient Egyptian culture also reveals an emphasis, within the temple contexts, on the prescription of careful duties for a variety of cultic personnel—with a specific emphasis on the priests' representative role vis-à-vis the king/pharaoh.[177] Sauneron has defined the core duty of the Egyptian priest as follows:

> Of the two royal functions, the religious and the legislative, only the former was delegated to the priests. This immediately indicates the limited and specialized role of their activities: it would be their duty to ensure the cults of the gods and the goddesses along with the various external manifestations in the temples that these services entailed. . . . As substitutes for the king, who was the sole titular officiant, *the priests of Egypt had a very specific role to play: to maintain the integrity of divine presence on earth, in the sanctuaries of the temples where this presence had consented to dwell.*[178]

Te Velde concurs, then, when he notes that especially in the third and second millennia, the king and the priests were very closely aligned. In theory, the pharaoh was the only being who was able to approach the gods—since he was both a human being and a god or the son of a god, and, hence, he became "the intermediary between the world of humanity and the world of the gods."[179]

174. Xella and Merlo, "The Ugaritic Ritual Texts," 301.

175. See Pardee, *Les Textes Rituels*, 265–87.

176. Pardee, *Les Textes Rituels*, 286.

177. For a detailed discussion of various dimensions of the temple cult, its rituals and attendants, see for example Assman, *The Search for God*, 15–52.

178. Sauneron, *The Priests*, 34, (emphasis added)—and note further, 28–50 ("The Priestly Office"), 51–74 ("The World of the Temples").

179. Te Velde, "Theology," 1731.

However, as representatives of the king, Egyptian priests, in turn, engaged in carefully planned daily rituals designed to symbolically care for the god in its "house." All of the ritual activities had the effect of making the deity "disposed to do what was needed in order to maintain order and justice (*ma'at*) in the cosmos."[180] For Te Velde, a typical ritual would include the following elements: (1) pre-dawn offerings and vessel preparation; (2) a ceremonial purification; (3) a solemn procession of a group of priests; (4) the intonation of the morning hymn by the principal singer (to awaken the god) with antiphonal answers by the choir (the hymn-singing at the Edfu temple, for example, was very long); (5) the uncovering of the god's face following the hymn and further worship; (6) offerings given to the god, such as incense, myrrh, and a golden image of Ma'at, the goddess "symbolizing order and justice," with further spells and hymns;[181] (7) a maintenance ritual involving the cleansing and dressing of the god, accompanied by solemn texts; (8) food offerings given to the god; (9) a closing ceremony involving the covering of the god, purification rites, and closing of the shrine.[182] Tarragon summarizes the implications of these Egyptian priestly rituals well, when he writes:

> From sunrise to sunset, [the temple-gods] were bathed [by the temple priests], clothed, perfumed, fed, distracted by song and music, and put in good humor, so that they might perform their divine task, which was to ensure the smooth functioning of the universe. The priests functioned as the domestic servants of these superior beings.[183]

In the end, we would note that this type of data from a broad swath of ancient Near Eastern cultures show that Israel, from its inception, was set in a context replete with religious temple culture, polytheistic theologies, and a number of priests and other attendants responsible for all types of cultic rituals. This was the nature of their cognitive environment. On the one hand, awareness of such background helps clarify some of the basic notions related to biblical conceptions of the temple. However, on the

---

180. Te Velde, "Theology," 1741.

181. Te Velde, "Theology," 1742.

182. Te Velde, "Theology," 1741–42 as a whole. And see further for greater detail on these priestly ritual services, Sauneron, *The Priests of Ancient Egypt*, 75–109 ("The Sacred Services").

183. Tarragon, *The Priests of Ancient Egypt*, 75. For a helpful example of a text detailing this type of temple ritual, see Ritner, "Daily Ritual," 55–57. Ritner calls this text "one of the best sources for the standardized morning liturgy used for divine and royal cults throughout Egypt from the New Kingdom until Roman times." See Ritner, "Daily Ritual," 55.

other hand, *biblical* temple life and priestly rituals, beginning with David's time, were also distinct from the broader ritual culture of the ANE—especially in the detail of the conception of divine nature and human interaction with the divine.

In fact, Sparks suggests three concrete avenues of contrast: (1) Israelite Yawhistic religion was aniconic—i.e. no cultic images of the LORD were allowed; (2) the national temple cult, which began to be centralized under David, also did not tolerate polytheistic practices that were prevalent throughout the larger ANE; (3) the history of Israelite religion also demonstrated a growing desire to quell the use of various magical rites (cf., for instance, Deut 18:10–11).[184] Thus, while Israelite religious culture reflected certain basic aspects present throughout ancient contexts (such as the presence of a sanctuary, of priests, of ritual practices, of sacrifices, of hierarchical attendants, of music rituals and so on), the fundamental distinction found in the core message of biblical monotheism shows that it was also interpreted as a continuing polemic against neighboring religions. Tensions, furthermore, exist in the biblical text between the *ideal* religious dispositions required of God's people and the concurrent witness of the repeated *failures* of the Israelites to remain faithful—most notably revealed in recurrent habits of syncretistic religious practices. As Sparks remarks, the nature of this polemical strain against the religions of the ANE inherent in the biblical text "and archaeological evidence . . . suggests that many ancient Israelites practiced the very rituals and incantations that the biblical polemic demonized."[185] All in all, it appears quite plausible to affirm that David, in the early tenth century lived and led in a time in the ANE that was firmly rooted in the knowledge of, and experience with, temples and organized, hierarchical temple attendants.

ANE Data: Temple Ritual and Music

The final step of this study of ANE contextual evidence entails a brief analysis of one specific aspect of temple ritual—that of music.[186] Instrumental and

---

184. Sparks, *Ancient Texts*, 211.

185. Sparks, *Ancient Texts*, 212.

186. Note the large ancient Near Eastern musicological bibliographies in Sparks, *Ancient Texts*, 122–26. And as general background for music in ancient Israel, note the section "Music, Song, and Dance," in King and Stager, *Life in Biblical Israel*, 285–99. They (p. 290) write that "musical instruments, all apparently dating from early times (harps, lyres, and lutes to the third millennium B.C.E.), are divided into three basic categories—string, wind, and percussion, although some cannot be satisfactorily identified."

vocal music is indeed present throughout these ancient religious cultures, and beginning in early millennia. In earliest Mesopotamian settings, music represents a distinct component of religious temple ritual.[187] When it comes to the musical instruments in general, Caubet has noted that their names, "listed in literary sources vary . . . with the different cultures. Their identification with 'real' instruments poses any number of problems. The precise definition of the *balag*, the *kinnaru*, or the *alû*, for instance, is still open to speculation, one reason being that ancient Near Eastern people did not classify musical instruments along the same criteria that we use nowadays, such as cordophones, membranophones, and so forth."[188] What is not problematic is that ancient Near Eastern literary sources point to a variety of musical activities, especially in the sacred context, in all of the major cultures before the time of David, and in parallel with his kingship.

The interest in musical activities is evident not only in temple contexts, but also in royal and more mundane settings. Furthermore, in Sumerian mythology, music is considered to be a part of the ME, which the goddess Innana/Ištar gave to Uruk.[189]

The patron deity of music was Enki/Ea. Singing or instrumental playing was conveyed through the verb *zamarû* (NAR in Sumerian). The subject of this verb is the *nâru* (male) or the *nartu* (female)—indicating a singer or an instrumental player. Furthermore, ancient Mesopotamian musical instruments are known through Sumero-Akkadian lexical lists, although the precise nature of many of the instruments listed remain obscure.[190]

The stringed instruments (chordophones) especially include forms of the lyre (ZÀ.MÍ/*sammû*), harp (BALAG/*balaggu*; also *sabbatu*), lute (GÙ.DI/*inu*), and zither (GUDI). Wind instruments are also attested (the aerophones), of various materials (such as reed, wood, bone, or metal) and shapes. The vocabulary for these instruments is smaller than the chordophones and includes more commonly the reed pipe (GI.GÍD/*embūbu*—the long reed), the flute (GI.DA.DA/*malīlu*—the sounding reed), and the horn (SI/*qarnu*). The percussion instruments (membraphones) include a

---

187. Note, for instance, Kilmer, "Music and Dance," 2601–13; Michel, "Musique," 545–46.

188. Caubet, "Music and Dance," 470. And see also Caubet, "Musical Practices and Instruments," 172–84.

189. See, for instance, Lafont, "ME," 514–15. The concept of ME is notoriously difficult to define very precisely, however, Lafont suggests generally that "le concept sumérien de ME se rattache à l'idée que les Sumériens se faisaient de l'univers, du monde des dieux, du monde des hommes, et de la façon dont s'articulait l'ensemble." A key text in this regard is Faber, "Inanna and Enki," 522–26.

190. See further Michel, "Musique," 545.

variety of small frame drums (ÙB/uppu), a number of larger drums (like the cultic kettle drum, the LILIZ/lilissu), metal drums (MEZE/manzû; SEM/ ḫalḫallatu), and wooden drums (Á.LÁ/alû).[191]

The religious cults of the city-states also included full temple orchestras and choral performances directed by professional cult musicians (such as the GALA/kalû and NAR/nâru). Various texts bear witness to the fact that these temple-music directors oversaw a host of instrumentalists and vocalists. Sumerian and Akkadian texts further preserve a rich musical vocabulary in general, as well as a technical record of modal theory (in the "Sumerian" system), Akkadian music theory for stringed instruments (for the SA/pintu, the "string"), and extended modal scales (seven tunings which correspond to the later Greek modes—such as the išartu, the normal [Dorian] mode or the qablītu, the middle [Mixolydian] mode). A large number of precise musical performance notations are also extant in these types of texts.[192] From the Mari archive, for instance, there is a record of female choristers, who were under the authority of the queen or of a music master.[193]

Likewise, some Hittite texts and iconographic materials from the late third through the early first millennium also suggest the existence of a developed system of musical instruments and of vocal and instrumental musical performers in this ancient eastern Anatolian setting. As in the Mesopotamian milieu, the lyre (often represented by the Sumerogram GIŠ^{d}INANNA, and corresponding to the Hattic term zina/ir) is the most attested instrument, usually occurring in the context of ritual song. These lyres were also of different sizes and materials, and two verbs are related to it—one denoting "plucking" or "picking" (ḫazziya-/ḫazzik(k)-), the other meaning "striking" or "beating" (walḫ-). The playing of the lute is also recorded in Hittite literature, as well as a larger number of membraphones—such as a basic wooden drum (^{GIŠ}arkam(m)i-), a cymbal (ḫuḫupal), castanets (galgalturi-), a type of tambourine (^{GIŠ}BALAG.DI), and a sistrum (^{GIŠ}mukar). A few aerophones are also attested, such as the horn (^{SI}šawatar/šawitra) or the flute (GI.ÍD).[194]

191. See further Kilmer, "Music and Dance," 2601–4.

192. Kilmer, "Music and Dance," 2605–13. And further, for a detailed analysis of Sumero-Akkadian musical theory texts, see Vitale, "La Musique Suméro–Accadienne," 260–72. Interestingly, Vitale discusses a tablet (H.6) pertaining to music theory; he also suggests a transcription in modern musical notation of the musical content, which is in the Dorian mode (in this text called the nid qibli mode). He concludes that the recorded piece is most likely a religious poem, which he suggests ought to be played in a very slow rhythm. Note as well the essay by Bathja, "The Mesopotamian Theory of Music," 15–91.

193. See Ziegler, Les musiciens, 23–26 (and as cited by Caubet, "Music and Dance," 469).

194. See further the discussion in de Martino, "Music," 2661–69.

These instruments were played in the Hittite temples by a number of professional musicians and singers—who are defined in the texts with Sumerograms and Hittite words, although it is difficult to assess precise definitions for many of these (such as $^{LÚ}ḫalli(ya)ri$-, or $^{MUNUS}SÌR$). These texts also reveal some specificity related to the ability of musicians to play particular instruments. These skills were also defined according to particular language specialties—either Hattic, Luwian, or Hurrian. Overall, this carefully defined system of music was a key part of Hittite religious ceremonies in the historical periods leading up to the first millennium. De Martino thus highlights the well-structured nature of this music ritual in the Hittite contexts, as he writes:

> Musicians and singers were part of the personnel in temples and palaces. Probably every palatial or temple institution, whether in the capital of Kattusha or elsewhere, had a group of musicians at its disposal. It is possible to recover a hierarchical system among such personnel on the basis of titles such as "the master of singers" or "the superintendent of performers."[195]

Furthermore, it is important to highlight evidence related to religious music ritual found in the Levant. As in other areas of the ANE, this type of religious ritual was present in a variety of Levantine cultures, including the Canaanite religions. A number of musical instruments are in fact evident.[196] More specifically, Burgh has argued that three principle sources exist for the study of the "archaeomusicology" of Israel/Palestine: (1) artifacts; (2) texts; and (3) ethnographic data. Artifacts include the elements found in various examples of iconography (drawings of figures and/or musical instruments) and various figurines.[197] Texts may describe musical instruments, activity, and/or musicians. Burgh notes that ethnographic data emanates "from various cultures and their musical practices over time and space [and] are

---

195. de Martino, "Music," 2664.

196. For example, Koitabashi has studied how two Ugaritic texts (*KTU* 1.108 and *KTU* 1.3) use the terms *mṣltm* in the context of Baal cultic worship with song and musicians. This author compares and contrasts this with the use of cymbals in 1 Chr 15:19. See Koitabashi, "Significance of Ugaritic *mṣltm*," 5–6.

197. See also Jones, "Music and Musical Instruments," 934–39, who analyzes ancient Israelite instruments following the principal categories alluded to above of idiophones, membranophones, aerophones, and chordophones. He notes overall (p. 939), "the evidence concerning musical instruments in the Bible includes scriptural references and archaeological discoveries, the latter provide a context for the scriptural references in the musical usage of the ANE and in the range and character of musical instruments known there."

employed to conduct cross-cultural studies of the past and present."[198] An example of such ethnographic research can be found in an older paper by Spector, who studied ancient Samaritan chant based, in part, on interviews with small twentieth-century groups of Samaritans in modern Israel and their traditional methods of liturgical chant.[199]

Braun, further, has produced a recent study of the musical ritual culture of ancient Israel/Palestine. As with Burgh above, Braun also emphasizes the need to consider a broad variety of sources in assessing the musical culture of the ancient Levant—which presents continuities and contrasts in comparison with the rest of the ANE. Braun also shows how the majority of musical instruments mentioned in the Bible can be traced at least to *Bronze Age* Israel/Palestine (that is, earlier than David's early Iron Age setting).[200]

The point to emphasize here is that Braun provides a careful discussion of musical instruments and their function related to each of the major historical periods of ancient Israel/Palestine. The main musical instruments discussed by Braun from the Bronze and Iron ages will be noted here.[201]

For the Bronze Age (ca. 3200–1200 BC), Braun emphasizes the prominence of seven aspects of the musical culture: (1) various lyres and drums were used in dance; (2) the lute was also a prominent feature of musical rituals; (3) Canaanite religious music rituals were highly developed and also give evidence of interrelationships with Egyptian culture; (4) several engravings suggest a developed musical culture in the upper echelons of Canaanite society (5); clay rattles were another significant feature of Levantine ritual music; (6) priestly bronze cymbals are equally attested; and (7) flutes played a significant role.[202]

For the Iron Age (1200–587 BC), Braun highlights developments found in the following five aspects of the ancient Israelite/Palestinian musical culture: (1) clay figurines depicting female drummers appear more prominently in this archeological stratum; (2) male and female aerophone (reed pipe) players are also attested; (3) other evidence also depicts organized lyre performances, both in solo and in ensemble contexts; (4) the Philistine and Phoenician cultures of the Levantine coastal areas also reveal

---

198. Burgh, "Ancient Music in Israel/Palestine," 2–3. See also Dever, "Some Observations," 9–21.

199. See Spector, "Samaritan Chant," 66–69. On this type of study, note, more recently, Randholfer, "From the Present to the Past," 23–62.

200. See Braun, *Music in Ancient Israel/Palestine*, 1–46.

201. Braun also looks at the earliest period (Stone Age) and the later period (Hellenistic–Roman Period) in his *Music in Ancient Israel/Palestine*, 47–66, 189–320.

202. For further discussion of each of these issues, note Braun, *Music in Ancient Israel/Palestine*, 71–112.

a developed musical culture using a variety of instrument-types; and (5) a number of trumpet-types are also attested for this period. Overall, Braun concludes that the evidence for the musical culture of the Bronze and Iron Ages in Israel/Palestine is well developed.[203]

Finally, in the long and varied history of Egyptian culture, we note that music equally played an important role within the religious context of temple ritual. Also, as a form of entertainment, music was an important feature within the higher echelons of the social classes. In this latter more secular context, dancing and singing was highly prized. Song was usually performed by choirs and a lead harpist.[204] Performed hymns and poems were an inherent part of the religious rituals led by the priestly classes at the temples. The term *dw'w* (a "praising") encompasses the overall genre of "hymn," under which the supplication (*snmhw*) and adoration (*snsw*) forms can be subsumed. Especially during the First Intermediate Period and the Middle Kingdom, laments (*nhwt*) were a prominent feature of musical performance, as "long dirge-like declamations deploring the social and economic conditions in the land."[205] This lament form could also be infused with an element of perceived predictive prophecy—as signified by the use of the verb *sr* ("predict," "prophesy"), which generally finds contextual connection to the prophetic aspect of Levitical music, established by David in 1 Chr 25:1.[206]

Anderson has also argued that in Egyptian literature and the culture it memorialized, the power and influence of music is indeed attested and recognized.[207] Although no specific texts dealing with musical theory or choreography remain, four areas of evidence sustain the claim that complex and developing music culture existed from the Old Kingdom on, in ancient Egypt: (1) references to music in Egyptian literature and in classical literature about Egypt; (2) preserved musical instruments; (3) religious music scenes depicted on temple walls; (4) detailed representations of musical chamber groups in tomb scenes.[208] Certain gods were especially connected to music, like Hathor, Isis, or Osiris. The temple rituals related to these gods were infused with the musical elements of song, dance, and

---

203. Braun, *Music in Ancient Israel/Palestine*, 113–88. Braun also argues that the archeological gap in the record for the musical culture of ancient Israel/Palestine during the Babylonian/Persian period (587–333 BC) makes it more difficult to assess the musical culture of the biblical exilic and postexilic books.

204. Redford, "Ancient Egyptian Literature," 2225.

205. Redford, "Ancient Egyptian Literature," 2225.

206. Redford, "Ancient Egyptian Literature," 2225.

207. See Anderson, "Music and Dance," 2555–68.

208. Anderson, "Music and Dance," 2555.

instruments.[209] The four main types of musical instruments were regularly used by the priestly class in the performance of the sacred temple rituals in ancient Egypt: idiophones (percussion), membraphones (drums), aerophones (wind), and chordophones (strings).[210]

Percussive clappers are among the earliest attested musical instruments, dating back to the beginning of the Dynastic period (third millennium). The sistrum (a type of drum) was especially prominent from the Middle Kingdom (late second millennium) forward and was used both in military and religious contexts. Within the temple cult, the *naos* sistrum "had mainly religious significance in attracting the attention of a god or warding off evil."[211] The careful use of various other wind instruments (flutes and horns/trumpets especially) and stringed instruments (harps and lyres especially) are also attested from the earliest dynasties on through the later ones, especially in religious contexts. For example, Anderson has commented on the early and prevalent use of the harp, as he writes:

> The harp was the mainstay and only indigenous instrument among the chordophones, or strings. It took many shapes during its long history. . . . The harp was both an ensemble and a solo instrument. In the tomb of Mereruka at Saqqara, it is shown in the hands of a royal princess, the daughter of King Teti of the Sixth Dynasty [in the late third millennium]; alone and seated on a divan or bed, she plays to the high official, her husband. In Old Kingdom chamber groups, the harpists are usually male; seven are shown playing together in a tomb at Dayr al-Gebrawi.[212]

Furthermore, in the context of the temple rituals, the priests sung, chanted, or intoned poetic compositions—texts which display meter based on the stich of two cola. These sacred chants were accompanied by wind instruments (such as the reed pipe or lyre), string instruments (such as the lyre), and strong rhythmic percussion (with clapping and/or castanets).[213] This complex pattern of poetic literary artistry and musical accompaniment was indeed a key factor in the temple rituals in ancient Egypt during the second and first millennia. As Redford has noted of this hymnic literature:

---

209. Anderson, "Music and Dance," 2555-6.
210. Anderson, "Music and Dance," 2557.
211. Anderson, "Music and Dance," 2558.
212. Anderson, "Music and Dance," 2561.
213. Redford, "Ancient Egyptian Literature," 2237.

Hymns abound, finding their context in the cult. Temples employed choirs of male and female singers to intone morning and evening hymns. Some hymns achieve a sublimity of concept that raises them to a prominent place in the ranks of world hymnology: one may cite the hymns to and lamentations over Osiris, the prayers of Isis for her baby, the hymns of Amun-Re and Re, the sun hymn to Akhenaten, and the great didactic paean to Ptah.[214]

The Harper's Songs, for example, are specifically defined as musically-focused compositions; they indicate the musical function of the performer (a singer) and the instrument used (a harp). Thus, the "Song from the Tomb of King Intef"[215] opens with the introductory statement, "song which is in the tomb of King Intef, the justified, in front of the singer with the harp."[216] Similarly, the opening of the "Song from the Tomb of Neferhotep," identifies the musical function of the performer and the type of accompaniment: "says the singer-with-harp of the divine father of Amun, Neferhotep, justified."[217]

In conclusion, this discussion of contextual evidence from the ANE points to the prevalence of at least three aspects of the cognitive environment of temples and temple attendants. First, complex physical temple structures along with temple-building and temple-installation texts are common features in the ancient record. Second, organized, hierarchical temple priests and various attendants working within these temple complexes and performing a variety of religious rituals represent a further prevalent feature of ancient Near Eastern religious culture. Third, the evidence also shows that temple attendants or priests who focused on the religious ritual of music stands as another important feature of this aspect of ancient Near Eastern culture. In fact, the prevalence of vocal and instrumental music in the religious culture of these ancient societies is sustained by a significant amount of textual, iconographic, and material evidence from the ANE.

Moreover, this evidence is spread over all of the principal geographical areas of the ANE (Mesopotamia, Eastern Anatolia, Syria/Palestine, Egypt). Additionally, from a chronological perspective, this evidence occurs in early archaeological contexts, especially in the third and second millennia and

---

214. Redford, "Ancient Egyptian Literature," 237. For hymns of praise, see for example, Lichtenheim "The Great Hymn to Osiris," 41–43; Lichtenheim, "The Great Hymn to the Aten," 44–46. For an individual prayer of supplication, see Fox "Prayers to Re–Harakhti," 47–48. Note as well the comments and bibliography under "Egyptian Hymns, Prayers, and Laments," in Sparks, *Ancient Texts*, 104–12.

215. See Lichtenheim, "Song from the Tomb of King Intef," 48–49.

216. Lichtenheim, "Song from the Tomb of King Intef," 48.

217. See Lichtenheim, "Song from the Tomb of Neferhotep." 49–50.

continues into the first millennium. Furthermore, the data related to temple culture generally, and to temple rituals and temple music more specifically, reveal measures of conceptual continuity among the various cultures, while also presenting regionally distinctive traits.

Hence, from the perspective of this broad contextual data, the Chronicler's claim under investigation appears historically possible. That is, the comparative evidence presented seems to sustain the historical plausibility of David's careful preparations for (1) building a temple in a developing urban center of the early Iron Age Levant, and for (2) preparing clergy to oversee the proper maintenance of the temple cult—which included Levitical attendants supporting the work of the priests and also leading in ritual vocal and instrumental music.

Conclusion

Fundamentally, in this chapter we have sought to defend the historical plausibility of David's institution of Levitical duty during the early united monarchy, in preparation for the First Temple in Jerusalem. From the perspective of 1 Chr 23 and in the broader context of 1 Chr 22–29, the historical *plausibility* of the Chronicler's claim has been suggested, both in relationship to the presentation of David's modification of Levitical duty and in relationship to the purposes of the Chronicler's work.

Furthermore, both from the perspective of a maximalist view of the archaeology of early tenth-century Jerusalem and of contextual evidence in the ANE, we have pointed out that various ancient Near Eastern cultures reveal a consistent emphasis on temples and temple-building, on temple priests and attendants engaged in hiearchical ritual activities, and on temple attendants particularly engaged in ritual *musical* activities.

Thus, one the one hand, it seems *possible* that the Chronicler's presentation of David's organization of the Levitical attendants (to include focused responsibilities in the temple with significant music and worship duties) may be coherently read from the biblical text in compositional and historical perspectives. Also, the cultural, cognitive environment of the ANE further reveals the presence and influence of the themes of temple, temple attendants, and temple music as early as the third and second millennia. Both of these aspects would suggest and, indeed, reinforce the historical plausibility of David's organization and modification of Levitical duty in the early United Monarchy, in preparation for the ongoing services of the preexilic Solomonic temple.

Finally, we note that this focus on the *historical* aspect of the Levites' ministry under David further reinforces the emphases of the other methodological aspects of our entire study, which is seeking to provide a multidimensional and constructive reading of key passages concerning the Levites in 1 Chr 10–29. First, the historical significance of David's institution of Levitical leadership for the temple is mirrored by the rhetorical significance of the placement of chapters 23–27 within chapters 22–29 as a whole. As noted earlier in this chapter, the center of chapters 22–29 is found in chapters 23–27 and is focused on the duties of the Aaronide priests and Levites. Thus, the rhetorical emphases of chapters 15–16, the Ark Procession Narrative as a whole (equally centered on priests and Levites), are further developed in chapters 23–27 of 1 Chronicles. In this sense, the historical issues related to David's expansion of Levitical duty for the temple are intermingled with the Chronicler's continued rhetorical-critical argument that emphasizes to his postexilic audience the importance of proper worship procedure and personnel—as was noted in the rhetorical study of chapter three of this work.

Second, the historical significance of David's institution of a complex Levitical corps for first temple duty is also closely related to the theological implications of the texts concerning the Levites in 1 Chr 10–29 as a whole. Just as the Ark Procession Narrative of chapters 15 and 16 particularly emphasizes the importance of God's presence symbolically residing with his people and joyfully leading his people to praise, so the Levitical duty texts of chapters 23–27 further develop the significance of divine presence, especially in relationship to temple-preparation. The overall biblical-theological implications of Levitical duty in 1 Chr 10–29 are then closely connected to the historical development of the Levites under David. Particularly in chapters 22–29, the Chronicler is indeed developing the significance of a proper space for corporate worship, as well as the importance of properly established worship and ministry personnel. These twin themes, of worship space and worship personnel, work together to further expand the theological significance of Levitical song, especially as it relates to the aspects of divine proclamation and divine promise, which is the overarching focus of our next chapter, dealing specifically with the theological implication of the *song* of the Levites in the Chronicler's perspective.

5

A Biblical-Theological Reflection on Levitical Song

Proclamation about God in 1 Chronicles 16
and Promise from God in Psalm 73

FIRST CHRONICLES 25 LISTS David's establishment of the Levitical choristers for the Israelite temple. In the margin of his Bible, Johann Sebastian Bach (1685–1750) wrote that "this chapter is the true foundation for all God-pleasing music." In so doing, Bach reminds us of the theological significance of biblical texts dealing with Levitical song. By his comment and in his body of work, Bach in fact posited the continuing relevance of this OT theme for the NT Christian.[1]

This example from Western music history highlights some of the theological implications of the OT witness to sacred Levitical song and leads to the emphasis of this final chapter. After having analyzed the theme of Levitical duty in 1 Chr 10–29 from rhetorical and historical perspectives,

---

1. See Stapert, *My Only Comfort*, 11. Bach understood the intertwined nature of music and theology. As such, we might argue that he stands in the tradition of Levitical singers, whose song communicated key aspects of God's person and work to the Israelite community, both in preexilic and postexilic contexts. For further analysis of the theologically communicative aspect of Bach's musical corpus, see, for instance, Leaver, *Music as Preaching*, especially 3–5, 12–34. French notes the strong influence of Chronicles on Bach as he writes, "some fellow German Lutherans of [Bach's] day rejected playing musical instruments in worship. *Bach's reading of Chronicles, however, affirmed their rightful place in the sanctuary as well as the sacredness of his own calling. His notations to various Chronicles verses indicate that he understood himself to occupy in some vital sense the same office as the Temple musicians*" (emphasis added). See French, *Chronicles through the Centuries*, 89.

we will now proceed to consider some of the *theological* aspects of OT Levitical song.

In fact, this biblical-theological study of Levitical duty will focus on the *content* of Levitical song. The musical duty of the Levites is here understood as one prominent aspect of the Levites recorded in Chronicles, and beyond (especially in the Psalms). Specifically, as noted in the methodological chapter above, it is assumed from the outset that the approach of biblical theology will be helpful in elucidating some of the particular theological contributions made by OT texts either defined as a Levitical song or hymn, or set in a literary context that is centered on Levitical song and worship.

To these ends, Scobie's biblical-theological method will be applied when considering this theme. As also noted earlier, Scobie argues that biblical-theological reflection can be a productive interpretive method for arriving at a thicker and richer analysis of individual texts or sets of texts. In practice, Scobie applies the analytical scheme of "promise" and "proclamation" in looking at OT texts, while NT texts are approached through the grid of "fulfillment" and "consummation." This approach is not the only one possible, nor is it authoritative, in the end.[2] It should, however, provide a helpful exegetical tool, among others available, for analyzing this topic.[3]

We will thus proceed on the basis of a "proclamation" and "promise" dialectic in relationship to the theme of Levitical song. Methodologically, our enquiry will first focus on the notion of OT "proclamation." Scobie defines this concept as follows:

> In relation to all the major themes of Scripture, the OT proclaims what God has done, both in nature and his history. It proclaims God as the One on whom all living things depend, and whose order can be discerned. And it proclaims God as the One who chose Israel and entered into special relationship with her.[4]

Secondly, Scobie defines the aspect of "promise" in this way:

> But if the OT proclaims what God has done, within every major theme there is also a strong element of promise. The God of the OT is "the God who makes promises." . . . Amid the chaos and

---

2. For other constructive, and contrasted, approaches to biblical theology and for their methodological statements, see for instance: Schreiner, *The King in His Beauty*, xii–xvi; VanGemeren, *The Progress of Redemption*, 17–41; Vos, *Biblical Theology*, 3–18; Childs, *Biblical Theology*, 70–94. More broadly, on method and history in the field of Biblical Theology, see Klink and Lockett, *Understanding Biblical Theology*, 134–28; Meade, *Biblical Theology*, 13–60.

3. For his fundamental methodological statement, see Scobie, *The Ways*, 91–104.

4. Scobie, *The Ways*, 92 (emphasis original).

darkness caused by Israel's rebellion and disobedience, and the rebellion and disobedience of all humankind, again and again the OT sees the only hope as lying in some future action of God on behalf of his people and of his world.[5]

This two-pronged approach will be worked out from the basis of two examples of biblical hymns or songs set in the context of Levitical praise and worship. First, in canonical perspective, issues related to the psalm in 1 Chr 16:4-38 will be investigated, focusing on how this Levitical hymn contributes to "proclamation about God." In 1 Chr 16, the Chronicler has edited sections from three psalms now in the canonical Psalter (Ps 105:1-15 // 1 Chr 16:8-22; Ps 96:1b, 2b-10b, 11a-13a // 1 Chr 16:23-33; Ps 106:1, 47-48 // 1 Chr 16:34-36).[6] This "new psalm" was placed in the immediate narrative context of Levitical worship, once the ark was properly set in Jerusalem (1 Chr 15-16). For the Chronicler, the theological message of this psalm is clearly reflective of Levitical praise and worship, as begun at the ark in Jerusalem under David and as especially taken up by Asaph and his brothers. On this, note especially the statement preceding the psalm in 1 Chr 16:7: ב־יום ההוא אז נתן דויד בראש להדות ליהוה ביד־אסף ואחיו, and the notice following the psalm in 1 Chr 16:37 (and the ensuing pericope in vv. 37-43): ויעזב־שם לפני ארון ברית־יהוה לאסף ולאחיו לשרת לפני הארון תמיד לדבר־יום ביומו. In fact, in his study of Levitical choral music in Chronicles, Kleinig concludes that the psalm of 1 Chr 16 represents a key example of sacred Levitical song *proclaiming* crucial divine attributes to God's gathered people. In his conclusion on 1 Chr 16:8-36, Kleinig writes in part:

> According to the evidence from 1 Chron. 16:4-42, choral music was instituted to proclaim the LORD's name and announce his presence to the congregation and the whole world at Jerusalem. While this was basically the task of the singers, they performed it for David and the people . . . Motivated by the LORD's promises and manifest goodness to his people as expressed in their praise, they petitioned him for their deliverance. Thus, with the transferal of the ark to Jerusalem and the appointment of the singers, provision was made for the public proclamation of the LORD's name there together with the presentation of the petitions for Israel.[7]

---

5. Scobie, *The Ways*, 92 (emphasis original).

6. For a general study of the re-use of earlier biblical tradition in the prayers of 1 Chronicles, including the psalm of 1 Chr 16, see Nowell, "Teach Us How to Pray," 208-13.

7. Kleinig, *The Lord's Song*, 148 (emphasis added).

First Chronicles 25 continues to associate Asaph, and the Asaphites generally, with prophetic musical worship at the temple established by David (along with the Hemanites and Jeduthunites). Kleinig has also aptly defended the significance of the *prophetic* overtones of Levitical song, as he concludes on 1 Chr 25:

> In 1 Chron. 25:1-6, the Chronicler explains the significance of the choral service by treating it as a species of prophecy. All the singers exercised a prophetic role in their singing at the temple. Even though the singers did not usually act as prophets by communicating divine oracles to the people, their regular musical performance was regarded by the Chronicler as a "kind of ritualized prophecy in which God spoke to his people." . . . It announced gracious acceptance of their burnt offering and his favourable disposition to them.[8]

This strong tradition of Asaphite psalmody and Levitical song, instituted by David, continues to be recognized in the postexilic period (see for instance Ezra 3 and Nehemiah 12) and in the canonical shape of the biblical Psalter.[9] On this basis, the angle of "promise" in Levitical song will be rooted in a study of the text of Ps 73—a Levitical psalm in the Asaphite tradition that introduces Book III of the Psalter. The statement of 1 Chr 25:1a (ויבדל דויד ושׂרי הצבא לעבדה לבני אסף והימן וידותון הנביאים בכנרות בנבלים ובמצלתים), related to the prophetic nature of Levitical song, provides a sychronic canonical hinge between the "proclamation" of 1 Chr 16 and the "promise" of Ps 73, especially as each of the texts (1 Chr 16, 25 and Ps 73) are united by the theme of Asaphite psalmody.[10]

Hence, the claim of this chapter is that biblical-theological reflection on Levitical song, as it is rooted in 1 Chr 16, formalized in 1 Chr 25, and canonically recognized in the final form of the Psalter, further demonstrates that aspects of 1 Chr 15, 16, and 23 contribute cohesively to the rhetorical argumentation, the historiographic method, and the biblical-theological meaning of the canonical books of Chronicles generally and the Davidic narratives of 1 Chr 10–29 more specifically, as they emphasize the central role played by proper Levitical worship leadership at the time of David *and* for the challenging situation of the Chronicler's postexilic audience.

---

8. Kleinig, *The Lord's Song*, 156–57, and 148–57 for his analysis of 1 Chr 25 overall.

9. It has been argued that the Chronicler had available to him the final form of the canonical Psalter, which included, hence, Pss 96, 105, and 106. On this argument, see for instance, Koch, "Der Psalter," 243–77.

10. The prophetic or "divine forth telling" nature of the content of Levitical song, both in Chronicles and in the Psalter, has been defended in Ross, *Recalling the Hope*, especially 209–16, 254–61. See also Leithart, *1 & 2 Chronicles*, 82–83.

A parallel twofold method will be presented in discussing this "proclamation about God" in 1 Chr 16 and "the promise from God" in Ps 73. First, a foundation will be laid by interacting with some of the key scholarly discussions related to each text. Second, exegetical reflections will be presented on the basis of these texts.

Proclamation about God in the Levitical Song of 1 Chr 16

The study of the psalm in 1 Chr 16 will proceed by first interacting with select scholarship focused on this section of the Chronicler's work. The investigation will then present some pertinent exegetical reflections rooted in the text of 1 Chr 16:8–36 itself.

Scholarly Foundations: The Proclamation about God in 1 Chr 16:8–36 in the History of Scholarship

A number of studies have focused on the psalm of 1 Chr 16:8–36. A focused sampling of this scholarly history will be considered in what follows, to bring out the key literary and theological issues inherent in this text. Specifically, more recent analyses by Butler, Hill, Kleinig, Gosse, Auffret, Nielsen, Throntveit, Doan and Giles, and Ahn will be discussed in chronological order.

Butler, "Theological Cohesiveness"

In a 1978 essay, Butler was one of the first, in recent generations, to challenge a prevailing notion regarding the study of the psalm of 1 Chr 16:8–36.[11] For the most part, from his perspective at least, this text in the Chronicler's work had suffered from acute scholarly neglect, as "commentaries refer to the relevant Psalm commentaries [and] monographs ignore it."[12] If scholars were interested in this passage, it was mainly from a textual perspective to explain the forty-five differences between the source passages in Pss 105, 96, and 106 and the resulting psalm in 1 Chr 16.[13]

---

11. See Butler, "A Forgotten Passage," 142–50.
12. Butler, "A Forgotten Passage," 142.
13. See Butler, "A Forgotten Passage," 142–43, for a concise discussion of these textual differences. For further analysis, see especially Knoppers, *I Chronicles 10–29*, 644–61. Knoppers recognizes the emergence of scholarly work that affirms that "the poetry of vv. 8-36 is not a collage of disconnected pieces, but a skillful and artfully

Butler suggested that studies merely focused on textual differences were, in the end, of little value in deciphering the theological significance of the passage. His main question in the essay was then to ask if the psalm of 1 Chr 16 fit with the other known theological emphases in the rest of the Chronicler's work. He first commented on some of the specific changes that occur when the sections from the Psalter are tailored into their new contexts. For example, he notes that the emphasis in Ps 105 on patriarchal salvation history is transformed in 1 Chr 16 to address the politics of the postexilic period—namely, to encourage the postexilic "wanderers."[14] Thus, Butler essentially suggested that the re-shaping of the passages in the Psalter were meant to encourage the postexilic community, in line with the overall purposes of the Chronicler's work.

On this basis, Butler further showed that the emphases of the "new" psalm in 1 Chr 16 fits well with major themes in the rest of Chronicles. That is, "the basic themes [of 1 Chr 16:8–36] are those of the Chronicler."[15] For Butler, the themes connecting the psalm in 1 Chr 16 and the rest of Chronicles are the following: (1) the covenant of the "God of the fathers;" (2) kingship of man and of God; (3) prophetic themes (though to a lesser extent); (4) the motif of God's sovereignty; and (5) the call for judgment upon the nations.[16] Hence, "theological motifs within 1 Chr. xvi. 8–36 thus prove to be leading motifs for the Chronicler's history as a whole."[17]

Butler's analysis was seminal in encouraging subsequent scholars to consider the unique literary qualities and the theological contributions of 1 Chr 16:8–36 more fully—especially as he supported his claims with the key observation of major themes connecting the psalm and the rest of Chronicles. Butler, however, did not offer any precise exegetical study of the text in these regards; his observations were also limited by his acceptance of the theory that the Chronicler was responsible for all of Chronicles and

---

arranged composition." See Knoppers, *I Chronicles 10–29*, 644. For a study focused on a particular textual aspect of 1 Chr 16, see Seiler, "Theologische Konzepte," 197–225 (Seiler looks at four concepts emphasized in the LXX translation of 1 Chr 16: the confession of the "kyrios" before the nations, the attitude towards the foreign gods, the epiphany of the "kyrios," and the cult). For further recent commentaries arguing for the constructive contributions made by the psalm in 1 Chr 16 to the Chronicler's overall message, see especially Boda, *1–2 Chronicles*, 146–51; Jonker, *1 & 2 Chronicles*, 111–22; Merrill, *A Commentary*, 198–215; Leithart, *1 & 2 Chronicles*, 54–58; Konkel, *1 & 2 Chronicles*, 172–74.

14. Butler, "A Forgotten Passage," 144.
15. Butler, "A Forgotten Passage," 147.
16. Butler, "A Forgotten Passage," 147–49, for the basic discussion of these themes.
17. Butler, "A Forgotten Passage," 147.

Ezra-Nehemiah—in more recent Chronicles scholarship, distinct authors for Chronicles and Ezra-Nehemiah are usually posited.[18]

Hill, "Connective Structure"

In a subsequent essay in 1983, Hill built on Butler's work by offering more precise exegetical insights into the text of 1 Chr 16:8–36.[19] His comments further support the cohesive nature of the "new" psalm existing in the Chronicler's context. Hill agrees that "Butler is correct in arguing that the hymn of 1 Chr. xvi is the result of the theological intentions underlying the Chronicler's reinterpretation of the early monarchical period."[20] However, Hill notes further that Butler did not discuss this theological interpretation by the Chronicler within "the internal poetic structure of the composite psalm."[21] Neither, for Hill, did Butler investigate the possible relationship of the poetic structure of the composite psalm in correlation "with the dominant theological theme of the psalm of praise within the context of the events described in 1 Chr. xv–xvii."[22]

Therein lies Hill's principal contribution, since he suggests, beyond Butler, that the writer of the composite psalm in 1 Chr 16 was: (1) "led by the theological motifs of the immediate context in the selection of Psalms," but also, (2) his combination of the source-passages from the Psalter "was consciously governed by Hebrew poetic device and structure."[23]

Thus, Hill suggests that it is important to consider the thematic flow of the composite psalm of 1 Chr 16 in the context of the ark narratives in 1 Chr 15 and 16 especially. For Hill, the fact that the statement of the Davidic covenant (ch. 17) and David's victories over Israel's enemies (chs. 18–20) follow the proper establishment of the ark in Jerusalem is significant. Hence, "plainly, this cohesive historical and theological scenario penned by the Chronicler can ultimately be ascribed to the covenantal interests symbolically embodied in the sacred box [of 1 Chr 15–16]."[24]

---

18. See Butler, "A Forgotten Passage," 148, for Butler's views on Chronicles and Ezra-Nehemiah. On the issue of composition and authorship, see further Klein, *1 Chronicles*, 1–18.

19. Hill, "Patchwork Poetry or Reasoned Verse?" 91–101. And see further the section on 1 Chr 16 in his commentary, Hill, *1 and 2 Chronicles*, 237–40.

20. Hill, "Patchwork Poetry or Reasoned Verse?" 98.

21. Hill, "Patchwork Poetry or Reasoned Verse?" 98.

22. Hill, "Patchwork Poetry or Reasoned Verse?" 98.

23. Hill, "Patchwork Poetry or Reasoned Verse?" 98.

24. Hill, "Patchwork Poetry or Reasoned Verse?" 99.

More specifically, Hill suggests that a broad connective structure is evident in the composite psalm. He argues that the composer selected sections from the Psalter that each began with an imperative followed by the "divine name introduced by the preposition *le*."[25] This broad connective structure is further reinforced, for Hill, by a "network of lesser connectors that serve to further the consolidation of the three Psalms into a poetic unity."[26] The broad connective structure mirrors הודו and שירו and is defined as follows: 16:8 הודו ליהוה (= Ps 105:1); 16:9 שירו לו (= Ps 105:2); 16:23 שירו ליהוה (= Ps 96:1); 16:34 הודו ליהוה (= Ps 106:1).

By emphasizing the inherent connective structure of the psalm in 1 Chr 16 and by accentuating the significance of this psalm in the historical and theological movements inherent to 1 Chr 10–22 as a whole (and chs. 14–17 especially), Hill's work built on Butler's claim that the psalm was rhetorically cohesive, as its main themes connected well with the rest of the Chronicler's work.[27] Thus, Hill advanced the discussion related to the poetic structure of the Chronicler's psalm, although without commenting fully on the biblical-theological significance or implications of that structure.

Kleinig, "Israel's Praise, International Praise, and Cosmic Praise,"

Kleinig's overall work on the function and meaning of Levitical choral music in Chronicles also contributed to the study of the Chronicler's psalm, since his analysis included a significant discussion of the psalm in 1 Chr 16:8–36.[28] As noted above, Kleinig specifically sees this text as a *proclamation* about God—eventually directed towards the world at large. His structural analysis of the psalm is also sensitive to the issues of lexematic connectivity suggested by Hill.

Broadly, Kleinig reads first a "psalm of thanksgiving": in vv. 8–34, and second, a "summary petition" in vv. 35–36a. He further subdivides the psalm of thanksgiving following the main imperative calls (which, for the most part, mirror the original passages in the Psalter). They read as follows: 1. General call to Thanksgiving (v. 8); 2. Israel's praise (vv. 9–22); 3. International praise (vv. 23–30); 4. Cosmic praise (vv. 31–33).

---

25. Hill, "Patchwork Poetry or Reasoned Verse?" 99.

26. Hill, "Patchwork Poetry or Reasoned Verse?" 99. The "lesser" connectors include, for instance, the divine name יהוה in vv. 10, 11, 14, 25, 26, 31, 33, 36.

27. This connective structure also serves as the basis for his analysis of the psalm in his commentary on Chronicles. See Hill, *1 and 2 Chronicles*, 238.

28. For this discussion, see Kleinig, *The Lord's Song*, 133–48.

Consequently, Kleinig is sensitive to the literary development of the psalm as it stands in Chronicles. He also points to the inherent theological message by noting the progressive call to praise that is rooted in the structure of the text and that escalates from a call to praise for Israel, for all nations, and, finally, for all creation.[29] Kleinig's work on the theological themes of divine proclamation is especially suggestive. His analysis of the poetic structure of the psalm, however, has been refined by subsequent studies.[30]

Auffret, "Remember His Marvelous Works!"

Using his particular structural method for analyzing psalms, Auffret, in 1995, also offered a study of the psalm under consideration.[31] Essentially, in his analysis, Auffret further defends the literary integrity of the Chronicler's psalm, and as such, builds on the scholarly trajectory begun in part by Butler, and developed by Hill and Kleinig, among others.

Auffret begins with the obvious point that 1 Chr 16:3-36 utilizes three canonical psalms or fragments thereof. He then poses the following question in relationship to the psalm, "would one then conclude that this is not an original work, but just a pure and simple compilation, juxtaposition, and that one would need, to study it, to simply consult each of the three [psalms] that [the Chronicler] pieces together?"[32] While some scholars would give a positive answer here, Auffret is not satisfied and argues that careful consideration of the structure of the text as it stands in 1 Chr 16:8-36 is needed. His work, then, gives a positive answer to the further questions posed:

> Aren't we encountering here a new text, which has its own structure, one that displays an interplay of new relationships vis-à-vis the source texts, thus creating a new literary unity? Do we need to speak of a compiler or an author? Because he has used portions of text already structured, must one conclude that he himself has not created a literary work?[33]

Auffret then presents the results of his own analysis in a threefold manner. First, he shows how the literary structure of vv. 8-9, 23-24 and 34-36

---

29. Kleinig, *The Lord's Song*, 143-44, for this thematic outline.

30. See especially the essay by Throntveit, "Songs in A New Key," discussed below.

31. See Auffret, "Merveilles à nos yeux," 289-307.

32. Auffret, "Merveilles à nos yeux," 280 (my translation). Auffret is asking this question based on the views expressed in the French commentary by Michaeli, *Les livres des Chroniques*, 84-97.

33. Auffret, "Merveilles à nos yeux," 280 (my translation).

are coherently displayed in the text, and also, how they are parallel to each other. These small pericopes relate to the original source-texts found in the Psalter. For example, both vv. 8–9 and vv. 23–24 are shaped with verbal imperatives, which first invite the worshiper to praise the LORD and, then, give the reason supporting this invitation. Auffret further argues that parallels exist between vv. 8–9 and vv. 23–24 and between vv. 23–24 and vv. 34–36—a structure that, for him, ties the whole psalm together.[34]

Second, Auffret goes on to show that in vv. 10–22 and 25–33, the alternating structure found at a smaller scale in vv. 8–9 and in vv. 23–24 (the dialectic between God's person and the nature of his work) is more fully developed with lexematic links and parallels in vv. 10–22 and in vv. 25–33. Of vv. 25–33, for example, Auffret accentuates the strong movement between the power of God's person and his work in creation. He notes of this section, "we here make a distinction between that which is connected to the power (P) of Yahweh . . . and that which is connected to [Yahweh's] work (C) in creation in [vv.] 26b and 30b, this creation is invited to rejoice in [vv.] 31aba and 32–33ba."[35]

Third, and finally, by way of highlighting the cohesiveness of the overall structure of the psalm, Auffret demonstrates, with close attention to detailed thematic and lexematic links in the Hebrew text, that vv. 10–22 and 25–33, as they are introduced by vv. 8–9 and vv. 22–24, stand at the broadest level of organizing structure. In all of this, Auffret is arguing that with this composite psalm in 1 Chr 16, the Chronicler has adroitly redacted his source passages. The detail of Auffret's analysis supports, then, the tenor of his conclusion, in which he states firmly, "even if the author has used three psalms or sections of psalms to compose his work, he has clearly produced an original work with regards to his 'sources.' We truly find here an author's work, structured in a way that is his own, thus creating a new text, which can't be simply reduced back to the original sources."[36]

In his study, Auffret has gone deeper into the detailed analysis of literary structure. In so doing, he solidifies the claim made by earlier writers supporting the unique literary features of the psalm in 1 Chr 16. However, Auffret makes no contribution with regards to the possible meaning and implication (and granted, this is not part of his stated objective) of such a carefully established literary structure. That is, the discussion is advanced in relationship to a more precise understanding of the language and

---

34. See Auffret, "Merveilles à nos yeux," 290–95, for the full analysis.
35. Auffret, "Merveilles à nos yeux," 299 (my translation).
36. Auffret, "Merveilles à nos yeux," 307 (my translation).

arrangement of the text, but not necessarily in relationship to its contextual and larger biblical-theological implications.

Gosse, "Theological and Historical Re-readings"

In 1998 and 1999, Gosse produced two studies focused on specific aspects of the use of earlier Scripture in 1 Chr 16.[37] In these, he reflects more thoroughly on some key theological topics raised in the Chronicler's psalm.

In the first study, Gosse comments on the progression of reflections on the Abrahamic covenant in four sets of OT texts: (1) the postexilic Levitical song of praise recorded in Neh 9, which provides a long rehearsal of God's past faithfulness to Israel; (2) Pss 105 and 106, which also reflect extensively on God's past faithful acts with Israel; (3) Pss 135 and 136, which are exultant songs of praise, and which both include reflection on God's actions in Israel's history; and finally, (4) 1 Chronicles 16, the psalm of the Chronicler, which preserves in its proclamation a reflection of God's faithfulness to Abraham particularly.[38]

From a historical perspective, Gosse assumes that each text, in order, emanates as a final canonical passage from earlier to later postexilic periods. Essentially, Gosse notes that with each of these passages, the history of Israel is read and re-read with a growing focus on the patriarchal period, especially on the promise of land inherent in the Abrahamic covenant first proclaimed in Gen 12—which would have been particularly pertinent in the developing biblical message of the postexilic period. Gosse notes, indeed:

> These different passages are characterized by re-readings of the history of Israel [and they] are united by the evermore fundamental role given to the covenant with Abraham, and then, in a more general way, to all of the patriarchs. This covenant is characterized by the gift of the land of Canaan, a problem still at the forefront [when the Jews] return from exile. Thus, this postexilic community could self-identify with the patriarchs, and this identification was strengthened by a shared sense of weakness.[39]

---

37. See Gosse, "Deux Usages," 266–78; Gosse, "L'alliance avec Abraham," 123–35. And note further Gosse, "Le texte 1 Chr 16," 145–58, where Gosse argues for Davidic reinterpretation of the servant motif in 1 Chr 16, and where he also links this to Isa 41 and 42.

38. See Gosse, "L'alliance avec Abraham," 134–35, for his discussion of 1 Chr 16 "au terme de l'évolution de Ne 9 et du psautier."

39. Gosse, "L'alliance avec Abraham," 123 (my translation).

This growing emphasis on the land-promise of the Abrahamic covenant stands in parallel, for Gosse, to the de-emphasis, in the progression of these texts, of the traditions related to God's acts of saving Israel from Egypt and providing the law at Sinai. For instance, the giving of the law at Sinai is alluded to in Neh 9, but this reference disappears altogether in the psalm of 1 Chr 16. Gosse in fact notes further:

> In contrast, in [successive re-readings of these texts], the role of the liberation from Egypt in this history of Israel is diminished. In any case, the covenant at Sinai is now only mentioned as a "covenant," without any further detail, in contrast to the covenant with the patriarchs, even if the gift of the Law at Sinai is still recalled in Neh 9. In 1 Chr 16, all allusion to the covenant at Sinai would disappear, the "forever" covenant with the "patriarchs" no longer needing any other covenant.[40]

Similarly, Gosse has also commented on the use of the theme of salvation in Ps 96 in Isa 56–59 and in 1 Chr 16. He essentially argues that in Ps 96 (and the Psalter in general), divine salvation is understood in the broadest context of God's intervention with Israel and with creation at large. He writes:

> It is clear that in the Psalter, the presentation of the coming of salvation comes to fruition in the context of the coming of salvation and in the context of references to grand, divine interventions [such as] the Exodus, the return from exile, and finally, the ultimate intervention of Yahweh.[41]

On this basis, Gosse further contends that this broad theme of salvation, as presented in the Psalter, is *transformed* both in the Isaiah and in the Chronicles passages. In 1 Chr 16, the realities of the postexilic period, he claims, lead to a modulation of the understanding of divine salvation, to be focused more narrowly on the Patriarchal period and the cult of the Second Temple (as seen in certain modifications, for example, in the quotes in 1 Chr 16 from Pss 105 and 106). Thus, for 1 Chr 16, Gosse concludes:

> In 1 Chr 16, the citation of Pss 105–106 demonstrate that salvation is conceived as participation in the covenant with Abraham, through the cult of the Second Temple, cf. the role of the messiah-priests and the prophet-Levites. Transitional events, between the age of the patriarchs and the Second Temple cult no longer play a role in the coming of salvation. . . . As it is quoted in 1 Chr 16, Ps 96 participates in the celebration of

---

40. Gosse, "L'alliance avec Abraham," 127 (my translation), and see further, 127–33.
41. Gosse, "Deux usages," 273 (my translation).

salvation brought to the Second Temple faithful, by means of the covenant with Abraham.[42]

In these two studies, Gosse has perhaps overemphasized the Chronicler's *reduction* of the themes of Exodus and Sinai (and the inherent tradition of the giving of the Law). For example, in 1 Chr 15, the (re-)organization of the Levites for the musical procession is accomplished by David in keeping at least with the *spirit* of Mosaic law, as the Chronicler writes in 1 Chr 15:15b, that the process proceeded "as Moses had commanded according to the word of the LORD" (כאשר צוה משה כדבר יהוה). Or, more broadly in 1 Chronicles, the presentation of David's organization of the priests and Levites for their duties at the temple remains in accord with priestly and legal prerogatives requiring the separation of duties between Aaronides and non-Aaronides Levites, while allowing for the developments required for the maintenance of a large temple complex (compare, for instance, 1 Chr 23 and 24).

However, Gosse still makes helpful contributions to our understanding of the theological message of 1 Chr 16, by noting the repositioning and refocusing that the realities of the postexilic period most likely wrought on the struggling Israelite community. Overall, Gosse's reflections on some of the key themes of the psalm, as it is rooted in the patriarchal age to address the postexilic audience directly, seem to advance the theological aspect of the discussion generally. As Knoppers has noted on this issue, "in both Ps 105 and in Chronicles, the Ancestral age is formative to Israel's constitution."[43]

Nielsen, "Whose Song Praise?"

In a 1999 essay, Nielsen focused on the question of the *purpose* of the psalm in 1 Chr 16.[44] Nielsen's brief study raises this question in relationship to the text: "whose song of praise?" Is it being attributed to David, to the Levites, to all the nations? Nielsen notes, for example, how Myers did not think the Chronicler's uses of the Psalms passages changes the meaning or purpose of the resulting composite psalm.[45] The point Nielsen makes is that, at least with older commentators, the purpose *in Chronicles* of the composite psalm was not perceived as a significant issue (similar to Butler's earlier comments).

Also, building on insights from Watts, Nielsen argues that it ought to be more productive to focus, in fact, on the psalm as a coherent piece

---

42. Gosse, "Deux usages," 277–78 (my translation).
43. Knoppers, *I Chronicles 10–29*, 646.
44. See Nielsen, "Whose Song of Praise," 327–36.
45. In reference to Myers, *I Chronicles*, 121.

of poetic literature—produced by the Chronicler himself, and for a definite purpose.⁴⁶ She further notes the striking feature, that in the context of Chronicles, the psalm is set in a Levitical/Asaphite context, while the source-texts in the Psalter are neither Levitical, nor expressly Davidic.⁴⁷ Thus, why would the Chronicler insert this particular composite psalm at this particular juncture? On this, Nielsen insightfully suggests:

> One possible reason for the insertion of poetic material is that the citation of the psalm is proof that the levites did what David appointed them to do. Whereas the narrative itself may legitimate the role of the levites in the temple cult, the psalm may illustrate how carefully the levites pursued their duties. Hardly had they been ordered to sing for the LORD, when they begin to sing a specific song of praise. That this must have been an important motif for Chr. was demonstrated by Watts in his profound analysis of the language of the psalm and its narrative setting. The narrative explaining what the levites were ordered to do contains precisely the vocabulary used in the psalm.⁴⁸

In the end, Nielsen creatively notes that as it operates as sacred Scripture, the composite psalm does not end up merely being a psalm sung in the tradition of David and the Levites, since:

> It is every reader's song of praise. . . . The psalm is rooted in the book of Psalms; it is composed and inserted in Chr's narrative as an example of the song of praise of the levites; but through its poetic style it also becomes the reader's song of praise, which makes the reader part of the everlasting song of praise.⁴⁹

As such, Nielsen's main contribution to this discussion is found in her reflection on the varying interpretive contexts of the composite psalm. Although we would not argue for the reader's perspective to be the *initial or primary* interpretive stance, it seems to be, in the end, a proper extension for the meaning of a composite psalm whose parts were originally rooted in the Psalter, to then be combined in the postexilic period to reflect, arguably, on the significance of an earlier preexilic event for the postexilic community. That is, an extended interpretive progression is already noticeable in the Chronicler's placement of the text at this juncture of his work.

---

46. Nielsen is appealing here to Watts, *Psalm and Story*, 155–64.
47. Nielsen, "Whose Song of Praise," 330.
48. Nielsen, "Whose Song of Praise," 332. Nielsen is referring to Watt's observation that the vocabulary of David's order to "bring remembrance, to give thanks, and to praise" in 16:4 (להזכיר ולהודות ולהלל) is used multiple times throughout the composite psalm. See Watts, *Psalm and Story*, 158.
49. Nielsen, "Whose Song of Praise," 335.

Throntveit, "A Psalm in a New Key"

Throntveit's 2003 essay on the literary structure of the psalm is especially deemed helpful here and will serve as the basis for further exegetical reflections on the biblical-theological theme of the "proclamation about God" in the subsequent section of this chapter.[50]

As other scholars mentioned in this discussion, Throntveit begins by noting that generally "matters of unity and authorship have dominated scholarly interest until fairly recently," and this "neglects the importance of context and falsely suggest that these psalms mean the same thing in both canonical settings."[51] He then notes the contributions of more recent essays, including some of those mentioned above, which have re-directed attention to matters of literary structure and theological meaning. However, he still observes that in more recent commentaries on this passage, for instance, a plethora of structural analyses exist, ranging from two to eight perceived principal divisions. On these bases, Throntveit further argues that "identification of structure [should lead] to clearer perception of function and message."[52] He then applies this stance to 1 Chr 16:8–36; the following three steps shape his analysis.

(1) He provides his own annotated translation.[53] (2) He interacts with the structural analyses of three scholars—namely, those of Shipp, Kleinig, and Watts.[54] Shipp proposes that the triad of "causing remembrance of, giving thanks to, and praising" Yahweh found in David's order to the Levites in 16:4b are then reflected in the psalm with an introductory section (vv. 8–14), a "remember" section (vv. 15–22), a "praise section" (vv. 23–33), and finally, a "giving-thanks" section (vv. 34–36). Throntveit finds the structure appealing, but the actual divisions in the psalm problematic.[55] For Kleinig's basic outline, which was noted above (and which moves from Israel's praise, to the praise of the nations, and finally to cosmic praise), Throntveit suggests that it is "an elegant approach to the structure of the hymn based upon the placements of [the key] imperatives [and that it] invites acceptance."[56] However, three main questions mitigate against full acceptance of Kleinig's outline: (a) the possible structural isolation of vv. 9–11; (b) the early unknown identity of the addressees in the imperatives

---

50. Throntveit, "Songs in A New Key," 153–70.
51. Throntveit, "Songs in A New Key," 154.
52. Throntveit, "Songs in A New Key," 155.
53. Throntveit, "Songs in a New Key," 156–59.
54. On these, see specifically Shipp, "'Remember His Covenant Forever,'" 34–37; Kleinig, *The Lord's Song*, 141–44; Watts, *Psalm and Story*, 155.
55. See Throntveit, "Songs in a New Key," 160–62 for his analysis of Shipp's views.
56. Throntveit, "Songs in A New Key," 164.

until v. 13; (c) the strong weight given to the switch in the MT from "He (God) remembers" (Ps 105:8) to "You (Israel) remember" (1 Chr 16:15); though not all of the textual witnesses support this.[57]

Watts' proposal, descriptively, moves from "invocation" (vv. 8–13), to "covenant-exhortations" (vv. 14–22), to a call to recognize the LORD among the nations (vv. 2–29), to nature's reverence of the LORD (vv. 30–33), to a final exhortation, communal plea, and blessing/congregational response (v. 36). One of the main differences with Watts (and his view is similar to the commentaries of Williamson, Johnstone, or Thompson, for instance) is his willingness to *not* be tied necessarily to the underlying source-texts from the Psalter. Throntveit agrees with the basic thematic development found in Watts. But his proposal moves further in seeking to relate the constituent parts together more precisely. Throntveit's structural outline is presented here in table 11:[58]

I Thanksgiving Hymn (vv. 8–34)

A Introductory Calls to Thanksgiving (vv. 8–13) (הודו ליהוה)

B For Past "Judgments" (vv. 14–22) (כל־הארץ)

C *For Present Sovereignty* (vv. 23–29) (שירו ליהוה כל הארץ)

B' For Future "Rule" (vv. 30–33) (כל־הארץ)

A' Concluding Call to Thanksgiving (v. 34) (הודו ליהוה)

II Concluding Liturgy (vv. 35–36a)

A Liturgical Summons (v. 35a) (ואמרו)

B Petition (v. 35b)

B' Benediction (v. 36a)

A' Congregational Response (v. 36b) (ויאמרו)

Table 11: Throntveit's Structure for 1 Chr 16:8–36

On this structure, he notes that "the Chronicler's hymn is a rhetorically sophisticated example of the classic hymn of praise: a call to praise the

---

57. Throntveit, "Songs in A New Key," 164–65.
58. Throntveit, "Songs in A New Key," 168.

LORD followed by a motive clause giving the reasons for praise."[59] As such, vv. 8–13 represent the introductory calls to worship and conclude with the main addressees (Israel his servant, sons of Jacob, his chosen ones). Verses 14–22 provide the "initial motivation for praise" in reciting God's mighty acts in history. Verses 23–29 focus on praise for God's present sovereignty (especially with the double כי statements at the heart of the hymn in vv. 24–25), while vv. 30–33 build on the reflection on "past judgements" of vv. 14–22 to focus on an appeal to praise God for his "future rule." The hymn proper is then concluded with a final call for thanksgiving in v. 34. The final liturgy calls for reaction from the congregation, on the basis of the preceding proclamation about God. As Throntveit concludes:

> At the heart of the Chronicler's sixteenth chapter, as David completes the important task of centralizing the ark, the symbol of the LORD's presence, in Jerusalem, the narrator pauses to remind his readers of the centrality of worship. The Chronicler's hymn, these songs in a new key, provide a model for worship in which proclamation leads to prayer and culminates in praise.[60]

Doan and Giles, "Performance Criticism"

Doan and Giles have produced an engaging essay that both builds on some of the previous studies mentioned here, but also adds a new element to the discussion—that of "performance criticism," which they define as "the examination of conventions, content, structure, and style of presentation, generally oral, that may be transferred to a written medium and leave characteristic marks on resultant literature."[61] For these authors, 1 Chr 16:8–36 represents an ideal candidate for performance-critical analysis, as they argue the Chronicler's editorial changes from the original psalms are intended for a "desired effect," namely, "audience formation."[62] After reviewing some key issues in the field of performance criticism (drawing from theater), they note that "twice-used songs" in the OT, such as 1 Chr 16:8–36,

> composed earlier, sung and performed as pieces in their own right, have been appropriated by narrative writers and inserted in strategic places within narrative compositions. When so used by a narrator, more than a lyric is appropriated. The social place

---

59. Throntveit, "Songs in A New Key," 169.
60. Throntveit, "Songs in A New Key," 170.
61. Doan and Giles, "The Song of Asaph," 29.
62. Doan and Giles, "The Song of Asaph," 29.

and influence, that is, the performative power of the song, are also appropriated by the narrator to influence the power of the composition. Narrators borrow these songs in order to add persuasive power to their own narrative compositions.[63]

These authors also build on Throntveit's chiastic analysis noted above, and then argue that the Chronicler's edits of the original psalms "seem to have been intended to help shape a social identity by moving the spectator into the role of character."[64] In contrast to Butler's essay, Doan and Giles argue that the specific edits by the Chronicler were intended to help his postexilic audience to still consider themselves as full participants in "Israel" and in Yahweh's ongoing work with his people—the edits are to encourage audience participation. In a helpful way, the authors highlight 7 key edits: (1) from "Abraham" in Ps 105:6 to "Israel" in 1 Chr 16:13; (2) from "he remembers" in Ps 105:8 to "you remember" (plural imperative) in 1 Chr 16:15; (3) from "they were few in number" to "you were few in number" (plural imperative) in 1 Chr 16:19; (4) from "let all the people say" in Ps 106:48 to "they said" in 1 Chr 16:36; (5) from "in his sanctuary" in Ps 96:6 to "in his place" in 1 Chr 16:27; (6) from "come into his courts" in Ps 96:8 to "come before him" in 1 Chr 16:27; and (7) from the idea that neighboring countries declare that Yahweh reigns in Ps 96:10 to the idea that heaven and earth declare that Yahweh reigns in 1 Chr 16:30–31.

Ultimately, based on their analysis of these edits, and also based on their method of performance criticism that explores the specific ways an author is seeking to engage an audience, Doan and Giles conclude:

> In the context of the narrative dialectic, the Chronicler presents, in song, an iconic interlude, one that allows the spectators to embrace identity and a history. Their participation in the song allows the Chronicler's audience to claim the identity of past heroes as their own identity.[65]

Ahn, "Rhetorical Situation and Effectiveness"

Finally, we make note of Ahn's rhetorical treatment of 1 Chr 16:8–36, from his broader study of the rhetorical effectiveness of the speeches and prayers found in the Chronicler's Davidic and Solomonic narratives.[66]

---

63. Doan and Giles, "The Song of Asaph," 31.
64. Doan and Giles, "The Song of Asaph," 36.
65. Doan and Giles, "The Song of Asaph," 43.
66. Ahn, *The Persuasive Portrayal*, 113–24.

First, Ahn briefly notes some of the previous scholarship on this text, including the studies by Butler, Hill, and Kleining. Ahn provides his own textual analysis of the MT and then proceeds to further reflect on the rhetorical situation and effectiveness of this new psalm. For Ahn, the rhetorical situation is rooted in the initial narrative situation, broadly set in David's ascension to throne (1 Chr 11–12) and, especially, the initial attempts at transferring the ark (1 Chr 13–14). That is, Ahn argues that at the narrative level, the psalm in 1 Chr 16 is enabling the narrative audience (from David's time) to celebrate the successful transfer of the ark to Jerusalem.

However, as Ahn notes further, "the rhetorical situation of the [Chronicler] is more embedded in the Persian period. . . . [As] [i]n this new psalm, the [Chronicler] emphasizes that the Yehudite community should praise YHWH, reminding them of YHWH's presence. . . . The Chronicler underscores that God made an everlasting covenant with Israel, which is strongly reinforced by his appealing to God's covenant with the patriarchs."[67] Finally, Ahn argues that the Chronicler is *effective* in his rhetorical goals for both the narrative audience, as well as the Chronicler's own, postexilic audience. As Ahn concludes, "in a time when the worship of YHWH appears to have been the only way to confirm their identity as God's people under the Persian leader,"[68] the Chronicler has sought, through this psalm in 1 Chr 16, to persuade his postexilic audience of the necessity to continue to worship Yahweh in faithfulness.

Other studies could be examined, where many of the same conclusions are reached. For instance, Jonker has argued that the Chronicler's psalm in 1 Chr 16 definitely reflects the needs of a post-exilic, Persian-dominated audience, where the Chronicler is encouraging a certain amount of loyalty to the Persian empire, but also, where Yahweh-worship remains central.[69] Also, Grol has noted that in the psalm of 1 Chr 16, the Chronicler is not simply quoting from the earlier psalms; the Chronicler's psalm is also functioning fully in its own literary setting and displays the theological purpose of instilling hope into a vulnerable postexilic community—that eventually God will gather his people fully.[70] Jendrek, in turn, argues that 1 Chr 16:8–36 stands as a key prayer text for the Chronicler, as it bridges Israel's past and an ideal present for the Chronicler. In this case, the Davidic past is seen as "utopian" in comparison to the Chronicler's postexilic present.[71] Weber, in his synchronic study, examines details on how the use of Ps 18 in 1 Sam 22 focuses on David as a *military* leader,

---

67. Ahn, *The Persuasive Portrayal*, 121.
68. Ahn, *The Persuasive Portrayal*, 124.
69. See Jonker, "The Chronicler Singing Psalms," 115–31.
70. See Grol, "1 Chronicles 16," 97–121.
71. See Jendrek, "Taking the Reader," 171–82.

while the Chronicler's uses of Pss 96, 105, and 106 in 1 Chr 16 emphasizes the notion of David as a *cultic* leader, which is in keeping with the Chronicler's purposes.[72] Gillingham, furthermore, has explored the liturgical aspect of the Chronicler's psalm, with an emphasis on the concept of teaching through historical recollection; she has also looked at the reception history of the psalm.[73]

All in all, the preceding discussion of select scholarly analyses of the psalm of 1 Chr 16 leads to the following observations related to a theological analysis of this text. First, recent scholarship has emphasized the significance and fruitfulness of approaching this psalm of 1 Chr 16 on its own literary terms—that is, a purposeful theological message is being developed by the Chronicler for his audience. Second, the importance of the literary modulations inherent in the final form of this composite psalm have also been studied to greater interpretive benefit—that is, we may find distinctive theological points in the particular literary shape the Chronicler has given to this Asaphite Levitical song. Finally, the theological significance of various literary and historical contexts has been suggested. On the one hand, in the flow of the Chronicler's narrative, the text stands as a celebratory proclamation of the faithfulness of God on the occasion of the establishment of his symbolic presence in Jerusalem. At this basic narrative level, the connection to David and the Levites is strong. In turn, this text also becomes a source of encouragement for the struggling postexilic community. At the rhetorical level of addressing his implied audience, the Chronicler is claiming that celebration and hope for the postexilic people of God is still possible, and necessary, since the LORD has returned them to the ancient land promised to Abraham, and since faithful worship of Yahweh is still required for the Yehudite community yet under the human control of the Persian empire.

Exegetical Reflections: Outlining the Nature of the Proclamation about God in 1 Chr 16:8–36

Based on the previous interaction with scholarly discussions of 1 Chr 16:8–36, the biblical-theological perspective of *proclamation* about God will now be further explored. As Nielsen has suggested, the "proclamation" features of this text are meant to define the works of God both in relationship to the *origin* of Levitical song under David in Jerusalem, but also in connection to the *extension* of the worship-principles of Levitical song for the Chronicler's audience, and eventually, to a contemporary reader. As

---

72. See Weber, "Die doppelte Verknoting," 14–27.
73. See Gillingham, "Psalms 105 and 106," 450–75.

such, the claim of this exegetical reflection is that, in 1 Chr 16:8–36, the content of Levitical song proclaims: (1) the necessity of, and benefit for, God's people to express thanksgiving to Him, (2) the necessity of, and benefit for, God's people to reflect on His acts of salvation—past, present, and future, and (3) the necessity of, and benefit for, God's people to respond to His acts of salvation. This theological outline is building on the concentric structure proposed by Throntveit, introduced above.

Proclamation about God and Thanksgiving from God's People, 1 Chr 16:8–13, 35–36

The psalm of proclamation, set in the context of Levitical song in 1 Chr 15 and 16, invites the reader-worshiper to reflect on the responsibility of expressing thanksgiving to God. That is, a call to thanksgiving frames the hymn proper. The initial call in vv. 8–13 is lengthy and replete with imperatival injunctions, while the closing call in v. 34 is much shorter.

Basic Data and Scholarly Interaction

Structurally, two issues stand out in vv. 8–13. First, the hymn of proclamation opens with a series of ten imperatival clauses and one jussive form. The imperative forms are as follows: הודו קראו הודיעו שירו זמרו שיחו התהללו דרשו בקשו זכרו. The jussive ישמח introduces the second segment of verse 10 (which is introduced with התהללו). The general act of thanksgiving (introduced in v. 8 with הודו) should be understood as a liturgical call of proclaiming the divine attributes through at least four progressive steps: (1) acknowledging God (v. 8, which implies turning away the other gods of the nations); (2) expressing joyful praise to God (vv. 9–10); (3) pursuing the person and presence of God alone (v. 11); (4) recalling the faithful acts past of God (v. 12).

Second, the final poetic line in this opening call to thanksgiving, in v. 13, is set off from the imperatival sequence, since it begins with a non-verbal form: זרע ישראל, in parallel to בני יעקב. Hence, this final statement in the opening stanza defines the primary addressees of the hymn—namely, the people of Israel.

Finally, in the final call to praise in v. 34, the *inclusio* with v. 8 is made with the identical imperatival introduction of הודו. While the initial call to praise is more fully developed with its definition of the various stages of thankful proclamation, v. 34 ties the hymn together with its single imperative followed by two supporting כי clauses.

It is interesting, then, to note that in his commentary, Williamson did not deal with vv. 8–13 in any detail. At least in this earlier commentary, Williamson was one those scholars who referred the reader to the Psalm commentaries. He writes, "it is generally agreed that the Chronicler is here dependent on the Psalter, not *vice versa*, so that the reader must be referred to the commentaries on the book of Psalms for questions of general exegesis."[74] Thus, Williamson does not deal with vv. 8–13 at all in the context of 1 Chr 16, nor does he look at the final call of thanksgiving in v. 34.

Japhet, on the other hand, presents a more involved discussion of the literary structure as a whole. Generally, she sees the psalm as the rhetorical center of chapter 16, framed by three levels of material: connecting links (vv. 7, 37), notices of permanent liturgical arrangements (vv. 4–6, 38–42), and, finally, references to the basic source text of 2 Sam 6:17–20a (vv. 1–3, 43).[75] Further, Japhet would also support Throntveit's structural outline, in general at least, as she reads the psalm first as a hymn of thanksgiving in vv. 8–33, followed by a concluding thanksgiving and supplication in vv. 34–36. By means of a "sophisticated literary technique" of layered textual rings, Japhet sees vv. 8–36 as the centrally inserted psalm, with v. 7 and v. 37 as the connecting links, then with vv. 4–6 and vv. 38–42 as describing a permanent arrangement, and finally with vv. 1–3 and v. 43 as the Chronicler's use of the basic source (2 Sam 6:17–20a).[76]

However, since v. 35 begins with the only imperative prefixed with a *waw* (ואמרו), it seems that the הודו clauses in vv. 8 and 34 function more precisely as the enclosing literary frame for the hymn proper in vv. 8–34 as a whole. As such, and as Throntveit points out, vv. 35–36 stand out as the concluding liturgy (not vv. 34–36, as with Japhet). This seems further supported by the fact that the summons introduced by the *weqatal* ואמרו in v. 35 is parallel to the response of v. 36 introduced by the *wayyiqtol* ויאמרו. This reveals some literary creativity on the part of the Chronicler, as he uses Ps 106:1 to *conclude* the central section of his psalm, from v. 14 to v. 34, and then he places the conclusion of Ps 106 (vv. 47–48 from that psalm) to close out his psalm in 1 Chr 16, at vv. 35–36 (again, set off by ואמרו).

Observations

First, the hymn begins with a long call to thanksgiving in vv. 8–13 (quoted from the historical Ps 105). This section is full of imperatives moving the attention of the worshiper to proclaiming the varied facets of God's nature and

---

74. Williamson, *1 and 2 Chronicles*, 128.
75. See further, Japhet, *I and II Chronicles*, 312.
76. Japhet, *I and II Chronicles*, 312.

work. This opening section does not, however, included any formal *reasons* for the call. The reasons for such proclamation of thanksgiving represent the heart of the composite psalm in vv. 14–33. Verse 34, then, stands as a natural resumption of *both* the initial call to praise, which is briefly reiterated (הודו ליהוה), and the *reasons* for the proclamation expounded in the body of the psalm, which it also briefly reiterates with two short כי clauses (כי טוב כי לעולם חסדו), which the initial call to thanksgiving did not contain.

Second, the initial thanksgiving section selected and shaped by the Chronicler (vv. 8–13) connects directly with the narrative introduction in 16:4–7 by demonstrating the relevance of Levitical song and its musical expression of praise to the LORD. Once the ark was established in Jerusalem, David instructed in v. 4 the Asaphite Levites, in particular, "to invoke, to thank, and to praise" (להזכיר ולהודות ולהלל) before the ark of the LORD. In the opening call of thanksgiving proper, then, the Chronicler is apt to show how the praise to the LORD should include these various liturgical actions— as the imperatives early in the hymn repeat the language of David's exactly: "remember" (v. 12 זכרו); "give thanks" (v. 8 הודו); and "praise" (v. 10 התהללו) and also sustain the notion of outright musical praise (v. 9 שירו לו זמרו־לו). In fact, Knoppers has noted that this emphasis on music at the ark in 1 Chr 16, and the fact that the sacrificial service was maintained at Gibeah, shows that at least for this temporary stage, the celebratory aspect of musical worship is being emphasized in the context of the city of Jerusalem.[77]

Further, a significant editorial update made by the Chronicler should be noted. First, in 16:13a, we read that it is the offspring (זרע) of *Israel* (ישראל) who are called out as the servant of Yahweh, while the original text, in Ps 105:6, reads the offspring (זרע) of Abraham (אברהם). This is the first significant nuance introduced by the Chronicler. As Doan and Giles have noted, "[t]he Chronicler's use of the seed of 'Israel' drew the attention into the performance of the song as they—those now reading or listening to the Chronicler's work and considering themselves 'Israel'—suddenly found the song was about them!"[78] Ps 105 as a whole is focused on God's goodness to Israel in the past, rooted in the covenant with Abraham. The Chronicler quotes the first praise section from Ps 105, and modulates the mention of Abraham, so as to encourage his audience to remember that God would remain faithful to his proclaimed promises, including those promises made to Abraham. As Boda remarks, "[t]his part of the drama resonates with the vulnerable remnant living in the Chronicler's time with the land still ruled by other nations even as they longed for the reconquest of the land."[79]

---

77. See Knoppers, *I Chronicles 10–29*, 659–61.
78. Doan and Giles, "The Song of Asaph," 36.
79. Boda, *1–2 Chronicles*, 149.

Finally, we note that the Chronicler's psalm concludes in 1 Chr 16:35-36 with a quote from the conclusion of Ps 106, found at vv. 47-48 of that psalm. In the Psalter, Ps 106 concludes book IV. In canonical analyses of the potential historical-theological progression of the Psalms, some scholars relate Book IV to Israel's experience of the exile, and its desire to be gathered from the nations (Ps 106:47). Book V is then introduced with Ps 107, and some scholars then relate this psalm (and book V as a whole) to Israel's postexilic experience, as they are gathered back by Yahweh from the lands (Ps 107:1-3).[80] All in all, it seems the Chronicler is speaking directly to his postexilic audience with this conclusion. As Merrill notes of 1 Chr 16:36, "the Chronicler has the exilic community of his own time in mind. He promises on their behalf that the people will give thanks to the name of Yahweh (cf v. 29) and offer him glorious praise."[81]

As such, the Chronicler's psalm concludes with a liturgy that encourages the full involvement of the congregation with the proclamation made about God in the hymn proper. Throntveit's structuring of this final liturgy is insightful and adapted in table 12 below.[82] Note that Throntveit reads 1 Chr 16:34 (// Ps 106:1) as the conclusion to the central section (vv. 14-34):

ואמרו	A Liturgical summons (v. 35a)
הושיענו אלהי ישענו וקבצו והצילנו מן־הגוים להדות לשם קדשך להשתבח בתהלתך	B Petition (v. 35b)
ברוך יהוה אלהי ישראל מן־העולם ועד העלם	B' Benediction (v. 36a)
ויאמרו כל־העם אמן והלל ליהוה	A' Congregation Response (v. 36b)

Table 12: Throntveit's Structure for 1 Chr 16:35-36

The frame is evident in 35a and 36b with the contrasting uses of אמר, while the enclosed center is divided into a call for salvation in 35b (הושיענו) and liturgical benediction (ברוך). If this concentric structure is accepted, then the Chronicler, in concluding the hymn of proclamation, emphasizes (1) the petition for salvation and gathering from among the nations for the purpose of declaring thanksgiving and praise to the LORD (v. 35b), and (2) the benediction of v. 36a which highlights both the special relationship of God with Israel and his eternal nature.

Unlike Japhet, as noted earlier, but following scholars like Throntveit, Klein has argued that the conclusion of the hymn is found in vv. 35-6 and

---

80. See for instance deClaissé-Walford et al., *The Book of Psalms*, 35-38.
81. Merrill, *A Commentary*, 215.
82. See Throntveit, "Songs in a New Key," 168.

the final call of thanksgiving in v. 34 serves as an appropriate *inclusio* with v. 8.[83] Klein does not focus on a concentric outline for vv. 35 and 36 but simply reads these two verses as a final summary petition. He does note however, that the addition of "and they [the people] said" (ויאמרו) in v. 35 (in comparison to the source text in Ps 106) is significant in showing that "the Chronicler emphasizes that his audience is to utter the following prayer."[84]

In the end, the Chronicler is reminding his audience that just as Israel celebrated in joy and unity at David's leadership with the ark, after the divisive period of Saul's monarchy, so the postexilic audience could be encouraged because, as Jonker notes, "the fulfillment of the prayer to gather the nation and save them had begun to be fulfilled."[85]

Proclamation about God and God's Actions Past, Present, and Future, 1 Chr 16:14–33

The heart of the proclamation involves the *reasons* supporting the call to proclaim thanksgiving to God and frames the central hymn found in vv. 8–34. Building on the structure proposed by Throntveit, the data of the three main sections will be briefly discussed in the following, before making some key observations on the whole of the passage.[86]

Basic Data and Scholarly Interaction

The chiastic structure of vv. 14–33 places vv. 23–29 at the center and provides the key reason for proclaiming thanksgiving to God: his *present* rule. This central section is framed on the one hand by vv. 14–22 and its emphasis on God's past actions, and on the other hand by vv. 30–33 and its accentuation of the future acts of God. The phrase "all the earth" (כל־הארץ) also sets off each section as it is found in the introductory verse of each (vv. 14, 23, and 30). The thanksgiving frame, then, in vv. 8–13 and in v. 34 connects the hymn proper into a coherent whole.

Indeed, in the first unit (vv. 14–22) of this central section, in vv. 14–15, the text first affirms the nature of God and of his universal rule (see 14b בכל־הארץ משפטיו) and then turns the worshiper's attention in v. 15 to God's *past* covenantal promises through an imperative phrase of

---

83. See Klein, *1 Chronicles*, 367.
84. See Klein, *1 Chronicles*, 367.
85. Jonker, *1 & 2 Chronicles*, 174.
86. See Throntveit, "Songs in a New Key," 168.

remembrance: זכרו לעולם בריתו דבר צוה לאלף דור. Following the call to past remembrance, the text highlights God's covenantal promise to Abraham, confirmed to Isaac and Jacob (vv. 16–17); it particularly reflects on God's past promise of *land* for the Israelites and the protection he offered them when they were of little account vis-à-vis neighboring nations. This past truth of God's proclaimed goodness would be especially relevant to the Chronicler's postexilic audience.

Furthermore, in comparison to the original text in Ps 105, the Chronicler has made two editorial changes of note in this unit of vv. 14–22. First, for "he remembers" (זכר) in Ps 105:8, we now have "*you* remember (זכרוּ)," a second plural imperative, in 1 Chr 16:15. Similarly, for "they were few in number" (בהיותם מתי מספר) in Ps 105:12, we now read "*you* were few in number," (בהיותכם מתי מספר) another second plural form, in 1 Chr 16:19.[87] So we see that the Chronicler wishes to engage his audience more directly, by making the proclamation about God's past faithfulness directly applicable. As such, "[t]he story in the psalm of generations gone by becomes the audience's story in Chronicles."[88]

Then, in vv. 23–29, the focus of the proclamation turns to God's present rule on the earth as a whole. The phrase in v. 23 sets up this shift: שירו ליהוה כל־הארץ and is further developed with two other initial imperatival phrases introduced by בשרו (v. 23b) and ספרו (v. 24). In vv. 25 and 26, two parallel כי clauses follow, which can be understood as the center of this core unit and of the psalm as a whole. The reasons for the overall call to thanksgiving are spelled out in vv. 25–26—namely that (1) God is the one and true LORD of *all creation* and that (2) *all other gods* claimed by man are worthless human creations.

This is a crucial statement in relationship to the ark being in the city of Jerusalem. That is, as noted earlier in our study, a prevalent notion in the ancient Near Eastern context was that a god was perceived to dwell in his temple and have dominion over his particular city. The Chronicler, however, is reminding his hearers that a central feature in a faithful proclamation about God (and joyfully here communicated in the context of Levitical song) is the affirmation of God's exclusivity in creation—hence the need for thanksgiving as a whole (vv. 8–34) and for a response from God's people (vv. 35–36).

As Throntveit has remarked, this fundamental statement is communicated in the MT by a smaller chiastic structure in vv. 25 and 26 around the

---

87. As noted by Doan and Giles, "The Song of Asaph," 38.
88. Doan and Giles, "The Song of Asaph," 37.

contrasted themes of God's sovereignty and the idols' futility.[89] This can be expressed as follows in table 13:

כי גדול יהוה ומהלל מאד	A	For great is Yahweh, and greatly to be praised (25a)
ונורא הוא על־כל־אלהים	B	Indeed, revered is he above all gods (25b)
כי־כל־אלהי העמים אלילים	B'	For all the gods of the people are nothing (26a)
ויהוה שמים עשה	A'	But Yawheh the heavens has made (26b)

Table 13: Chiastic Outline of 1 Chr 16:25–26

This section concludes with further imperatives reinforcing the present orientation of the proclamation: הבו (three times, in v. 28a–b and in v. 29a), שאו and ובאו (v. 29b), and השתחוו (v. 29).

Also, two small modifications made by the Chronicler further show that his message was ultimately intended, rhetorically speaking, for his postexilic audience. First, for "in his sanctuary" in Ps 96:6 (במקדשו), we read "in his place" (במקמו) in 1 Chr 16:27. Also, for "come into his courts" in Ps 96:8 (ובאו לחצרותיו), we read "come before him" (ובאו לפניו) in 1 Chr 16:29. At the postexilic period of the Second Temple, the First Temple complex devised by David and built by Solomon was no longer in existence, so "the alteration of references to the sanctuary and those courts was a necessary condition if the Chronicler's audience was to feel part of the song and to have the ability to 'enter' the song as participants."[90]

The final section of the core of the hymn, in vv. 30–33, is also introduced by a direct imperative paired with the "all of the earth" phrase in v. 30: הילו מלפניו כל־הארץ. However, unlike the previous section in vv. 24–29, these imperatives (focused on the present situation of the Chronicler's original audience) are replaced by a series of imperfect verbal forms that can be read, grammatically, as pointing to the future work of God in all of creation. These verbal forms are (vv. 30–33): תכון תמוט ישמחו ותגל ויאמרו ירעם יעלץ ירננו. At this future time, the rule of God will fully extend to the whole heavens, to the whole earth, and to all nations (v. 31). All of creation will rejoice in this future establishment of God's rule (vv. 32–33). The faithfulness of God's past acts will be confirmed, then (vv. 15–22), as will be the utter futility of the nations' gods (vv. 23–27). In this sense, the biblical-theological aspect of "proclamation" in this hymn is also infused

---

89. Throntveit, "Songs in a New Key," 170. The table is based on Throntveit's discussion at this point in his essay.

90. Doan and Giles, "The Song of Asaph," 37.

with an aspect of "promise" in this final section, by pointing the worshiper towards the fulfillment of God's future rule.[91]

McKenzie supports the notion that the Chronicler's psalm in chapter 16 contributes fully to the narrative structure and theological implications of the surrounding texts.[92] For instance, in the second section of vv. 14–22, he notes that the switch from the perfect form "he has remembered" in Ps 105:8, to the plural imperative "remember" in 1 Chr 16:15 is a significant modification brought in by the biblical writer. As McKenzie notes in this case:

> God's faithfulness is beyond question; what is needed is for the Israelites to recognize that they are God's covenant people and to learn to trust in his faithfulness. The Chronicler thus adapts the psalm to address the audience of his day, encouraging them to bolster their faith. The psalm's function in this context, then, is both liturgical and theological. It encourages the people to greater faith while illustrating the significance of music in Israel's worship.[93]

Observations

The key observation related to the central sections of vv. 13–34 is that they provide the rich *content* of the proclamation about God, while also serving as examples of proper and joyful worship. The LORD is celebrated in multiple dimensions in this text and this full picture is intended to become a source of encouragement for the Chronicler's readers. The core proclamation (especially at the center in vv. 25–26) affirms the absolute distinction between Yahweh and any other humanly conceived deity. This is the heart of the "present" proclamation. God's power and faithfulness was demonstrated to the Israelites in his promises to the Patriarchs especially and the concomitant promise of land and protection; this historical example of God's continued sovereignty over the nations will explode into every aspect of creation when his future rule will be completely and firmly established.

Thus, in affirming and encouraging the proclamation by God's people of the theological truths of God's sovereignty, the Chronicler is encouraging

---

91. This point relates to the both/and eschatology that can be discerned in Chronicles. For a thorough study of the history of scholarship focused on eschatology in Chronicles (often polarized between views sustaining a literal fulfillment in the Davidide line and a broader fulfillment in the community of God's people), see Boda, "Gazing Through the Cloud of Incense," 215–45. Boda argues for a both/and approach.

92. See McKenzie, *1–2 Chronicles*, 147–50.

93. McKenzie, *1–2 Chronicles*, 148, emphasis added.

his readers to a musically rooted worship that leads to divinely-centered joy. As McKenzie has noted further on 1 Chr 16:

> Ritual activities alone are not enough to please God. The Chronicler uses this occasion to introduce the importance of music into the cult. . . . [T]rue worship is a joyful expression of the human heart, celebrated in community with music. . . . Thus, worship in Chronicles is reverent and joyful—reverent but not somber, joyful but not frivolous. Another factor motivating the people to joy is their perception of the fruition of God's plan and the fulfillment of his promises in their day. The narrative thus emphasizes the faithfulness of God.[94]

This overall study of the Chronicler's hymn in 1 Chronicles, set in the context of Levitical song instituted in Jerusalem by David under the direction of Asaph and his kindred, suggests: (1) the rich biblical-theological perspectives related to divine *proclamation* present in the song, and (2) the useful contributions made by the psalm in the flow of the Chronicler's Davidic narrative. It remains to present a further study of the aspects of divine *promise* inherent in the text of another Levitical song in the Asaphite tradition, that of Ps 73, and the potential for finding in it the affirmation of a divinely-established personal eschatological hope.

Promise from God in the Levitical Song of Ps 73

To recapitulate, the aim of this chapter is to present an exegetically-rooted biblical-theological reading of the *content* of Levitical song as it is presented in 1 Chronicles and as it relates further to the "temple hymnbook" of ancient Israel, the biblical Psalter. Furthermore, the interpretive matrix adopted is that of Scobie's "proclamation and promise" method for looking at a particular theme. In the previous section, we suggested that the psalm in 1 Chr 16 stands as an example of Levitical psalmody that particularly emphasizes the need for a "present" proclamation of God's actions on behalf of his people and throughout his creation. We also pointed out that an element of future hope and promise exists in the text (especially in 1 Chr 16:31–33) related to the consummation of God's rule.

Further, we have argued in this study, overall, that the theme of Levitical service plays a central role in the rhetorical structure of 1 Chr 10–29. And from a historical perspective, we have sought to defend the idea that the Chronicler's witness of *David's* expansion or re-focusing of the duties

---

94. McKenzie, *1–2 Chronicles*, 152, emphasis added.

of the Levites—though clearly shaped by his postexilic concerns—is at least *plausible* and may be trusted as a reliable witness to tenth-century developments in Israel.

An important feature of this modified Levitical service is its *musical* component, especially at the temple complex in Jerusalem. If these types of arguments are persuasive in any way, then a theological understanding of Levitical song may be fruitfully examined from at least two perspectives. First, the discussion of Levitical service in Chronicles provides the historical framework for the establishment and development of the Levitical musical guilds in the sacred services of the Jerusalem temple. A biblical-theological understanding of Levitical song may then be appropriately rooted in this historical setting of Chronicles. Some examples of the *content* of Levitical psalmody are preserved in the context of this historical framework, namely, the psalm of 1 Chr 16 just analyzed. Second, the Levitical psalms preserved in the Psalter present further data from which to investigate the theological emphases of Levitical song. As they are set in the context of poetic texts, the Levitical psalms represent another important source for ascertaining the larger theological contributions of Levitical song, at least from the perspective of a synchronic theological reading.

Scholarly Foundations: Ps 73 and the Levitical Tradition of Psalmody

A number of psalms in the biblical Psalter are connected through their titles to the Korahite and Asaphite Levitical musical guilds—the Levitical musical groups described in such historical narrative contexts as 1 Chr 6, 15, 16, 25. Since in Chronicles the Levites are especially connected to the temple and the magnified experience of divine presence the temple brings forth, so the Korahite and Asaphite psalms in the Psalter share some theological emphases that naturally link them back to the historical narrative setting in Chronicles. Two major connecting themes (and other points of commonality exist) of the Levitical psalms will be briefly analyzed here, as foundational data for further examination of Ps 73.[95]

---

95. In the scope of this study, I cannot fully engage the broader examination of the function of the Levitical collections in the canonical shape of the Psalter; my purpose is to simply engage the theological *content* of one such psalm (Ps 73) as an example of Levitical song, while maintaining broader awareness of the canonical setting of Ps 73 in the Psalter. For some helpful essays related to the canonical approach for the Psalter and the implications of the editorial shaping of the five books of the Psalter, see deClaissé-Walford, "The Canonical Approach," 1–12; Nasuti, "The Editing of the Psalter," 13–20. For some recent discussions of the function of the Levitical psalm collections within

First, the Levitical psalms often reflect a particularly acute awareness of the power of God's reign and of his sovereignty—especially as it symbolically emanates from God's habitation/temple in Zion. This Levitical perception of divine sovereignty is often expressed in relationship to the blessings it brings to the righteous and to the judgment it gives to the wicked. Since the Levitical musical guilds were regularly involved in the temple services and were leading Israel in praise, and thus in spiritual connection to Yahweh, it would make sense that the literary deposit of their psalmody would evince a particular interest in the connected themes of God's presence in Jerusalem/Zion and of God's utter sovereignty in creation.[96] As general support for the preceding claim, a few examples in each of the Korahite and Asaphite psalm collections will be noted here. Six passages that particularly highlight this theme of Yahweh's sovereignty from Zion may be pointed out in the Korahite collection.

(1) In Ps 44, God's sovereignty is remembered from historical precedent (vv. 1–8). The further perception of God's distance leads to an intense lament and call for God to make his power known anew to the psalmist (vv. 9–26). If God is known to have been so powerful and sovereign in past dealings with Israel, then the experience of divine separation is all the more intense, as seen in the psalmist's desire for the LORD to renew the expression of his love and power—as in v. 26 (MT v. 27): קומה עזרתה לנו ופדנו למען חסדך.[97] (2) Ps 45 also contains intense expressions directed towards Yahweh that evoke the eternal nature of God's royal dominion, his sovereign and heavenly kingdom—such as in v. 6 (MT v. 7): כסאך אלהים עולם ועד שבט מישר שבט מלכותך.

(3) In Psalm 47, the people of God are joyfully invited to join in songs of praise and exultation *because* God's sovereign, kingly power is complete—this represents the grounds for the call to praise, beginning in vv. 2–3 (MT vv. 3–4): כי יהוה עליון נורא מלך גדל על־כל־הארץ ידבר עמים תחתינו ולאמים תחת רגלינו. We also note the strong musical language of praise in vv. 1, 5, 6, and 7. In a sense, this poem stands as a reminder that as Yahweh is fully revealed as king on his heavenly throne, his presence throughout creation cannot be

---

the Psalter, see Gillingham, "The Levites," 201–13; Jones, "The Message," 71–86. Gerald Wilson's work on the purposeful editing of the Psalms was significant for recent generations. See Wilson, *The Editing*, especially 139–230.

96. For a discussion of Psalms scholarship exploring the relationship between the biblical psalms and the OT cult, see Creach, "The Psalms and the Cult," 119–38.

97. As Limburg, *Psalms*, 148, notes of Ps 44, "the people have not sinned but have remained faithful. So why should these innocent people suffer? The psalm does not answer the 'why' question.... The best the psalmist can do is affirm continued trust and hope in the Lord's 'steadfast love' (v. 26)."

missed by anyone, Israel or the nations.⁹⁸ (4) The language of Zion is strong in Ps 48, where the LORD is particularly related to the sacred geography of the "city of our God," of "his holy mountain," of "mount Zion," and the sovereign power of God in his "fortress," as in vv. 1-2 (MT vv. 2-3): גדול יהוה ומהלל מאד בעיר אלהינו הר קדשו יפה נוף משוש כל־הארץ הר ציון ירכתי צפון קרית מלך רב. The architecture of Zion also becomes the symbolic basis from which the witness of God's eternal guidance can go forth (vv. 12-14).⁹⁹

(5) In Psalm 49, the folly of being distant from God's sovereign power is claimed as human folly. Those who trust in themselves will be judged and condemned in death (v. 14), but the Korahite psalmist remains faithful in God's ability to overcome the power of death itself: אך־אלהים יפדה נפשי מיד־שאול כי יקחני (v. 15; MT v. 16). Being near the sovereign God of creation is the only means of being "received" by him beyond death—unlike the fate of the ungodly in v. 19 (MT v. 20): תבוא עד־דור אבותיו עד־נצח לא יראו־אור. (6) In the short Korahite Ps 87, the theme of Zion is presented and directly connected to God's power. For example, in vv. 1-2, the LORD is shown to have founded the "holy mount" and to have a particular love for the "gates of Zion" (v. 1b-2a): יסודתו בהררי־קדש אהב יהוה שערי ציון. It is also interesting to note the allusion to music and dance in Levitical worship in v. 7: ושרים כחללים כל־מעיני בך. In Ps 87, in particular, the glorious presence of Yahweh in Zion extends to the nations as well.¹⁰⁰

Further, six passages from the Asaphite psalms may also be highlighted, as further evidence that these collections emphasize God's power and sovereignty in creation symbolically emanating from Zion. (1) Ps 50 opens with a dual statement highlighting: (a) the sovereign and judging power of Yahweh, and (b) the fact that Zion is viewed as the symbolic center from which his presence radiates—note vv. 1-2: אל אלהים יהוה דבר ויקרא־ארץ ממזרח־שמש עד־מבאו מציון מכלל־יפי אלהים הופיע.¹⁰¹ From the foundation

---

98. As Wilson, *Psalms Volume 1*, 727, notes of Ps 47, "[t]his 'Most High' and 'fear-producing' God, Yahweh, is here proclaimed to be more than the national God of Israel, taking his place among the panoply of national deities worshiped in the ancient Near East.... Therefore, all people ought to acknowledge his authority."

99. Mays, *Psalms*, 188, argues that as a song of Zion, Ps 48 is centered on a theological conception where "[t]he LORD is the great king who is sovereign over the world and all the nations in it; Zion, the city and the hill on which it stands, is the great king's capital and site of his temple-palace."

100. Broyles, *Psalms*, 351, for instance, argues that Ps 87 "makes the most positive, explicit statement about the nations" as a psalm of Zion.

101. VanGemeren, "Psalms," 373, notes the theological nuance between divine presence at Sinai and then Zion when he comments "[t]he God who at one time revealed himself at Mount Sinai 'shines forth' from Jerusalem, where he made his name to dwell. The 'light' of God's presence was evident in the glory-cloud in the desert."

of this dual theme of divine power and divine "perfection" in Zion, the psalm also addresses the flourishing of the godly and the floundering of the wicked. The godly, who are called upon to offer genuine "sacrifices and thanksgiving" will indeed experience God's deliverance and glory—in v. 15: וקראני ביום צרה אחלצך ותכבדני. But the wicked (vv. 16–23) stand in judgment before the LORD on the basis of their distance from him—as in v. 21b, where God addresses them directly: אוכיחך ואערכה לעיניך. (2) In Ps 73, it is the renewed *perception* of God's sovereignty (occasioned in v. 17 by the experience of the Asaphite psalmist in the holy space of the temple complex) that enables a change in perspective. This renewed focus on God's eternal sovereignty in fact enables the psalmist to understand the final blessing of the godly and the final judgment of the wicked.

(3) Divine judgment, as a crucial aspect of God's sovereign power, is emphasized in Asaphite Ps 75. For example, God is the *origin* of judgment in v. 7 (MT v. 8): כי־אלהים שפט זה ישפיל וזה ירים. The conclusion of this psalm again emphasizes the fairness of God's sovereign judgment, with the drastic distinction made between the fate of the wicked and the fate of the righteous (v. 10, MT v. 11): וכל־קרני רשעים אגדע תרוממנה קרנות צדיק.

(4) Ps 76 also opens with the dual themes of divine power and Zion. In v. 2 (MT v. 3), for instance, parallel phrases accentuate the theme of divine presence in Jerusalem: ויהי בשלם סכו ומעונתו בציון, while v. 3 (MT v. 4) illustrates, with warfare imagery, the intensity of the divine power that emanates from the LORD's abode in Zion/Jerusalem: שמה שבר רשפי־קשת מגן וחרב ומלחמה. (5) In Ps 82, the Asaphite psalmist generally appeals to the LORD to rescue the weak and the oppressed (cf. vv. 4–5). The basis on which this appeal is made is the sovereign power of God, who holds his divine court of judgment in v. 1: אלהים נצב בעדת־אל בקרב אלהים ישפט, and who is called upon to exercise his power to judge the earth in v. 8: קומה אלהים שפטה הארץ כי־אתה תנחל בכל־הגוים. (6) Finally, in Ps 83, an intense appeal is made to the LORD for him to fully exercise his sovereign power to judge the enemies of God. The framing verses of this psalm are telling in this regard. In vv. 1–2 (MT vv. 2–3), the appeal for God to judge the wicked is made: אליהם אל־דמי־ לך אל־תחרש ואל־תשקט אל כי־הנה אויביך יהמיון ומשנאיך נשאו ראש, and in vv. 17–18 (MT vv. 18–19), the psalmist urges the LORD, in his power, to shame the enemy for the purpose of proclaiming the exclusive reign of God: יבשו ויבהלו עדי־עד ויחפרו ויאבדו וידעו כי־אתה שמך יהוה לבדך עליון על־כל־הארץ.[102]

Furthermore, a second major connecting theme in the Levitical psalms is evident. These texts indeed accentuate the fundamental blessing

---

102. As Tate, *Psalms 1–50*, 349, remarks, "[l]et all kings and tyrants, all oppressors whatever their role and status, take notice. Let the people of God whenever they are ringed about with threatening foes lift up their hearts."

of being in God's *presence*—which ties into the Levitical experience of serving in the context of the temple itself. In fact, this theme of the blessing of God's presence is communicated through at least two basic and interlocking themes. (1) The Levitical psalms often express sentiments of worship that *directly* yearn for God himself—without intermediary. (2) These texts also bear witness to the symbol of the *temple* as a significant foundation for experience the blessing of God's presence.

Seven passages in the Korahite psalms may be highlighted, as strong examples of this overall theme in this collection. (1) With Ps 42, the entire tone of the poem emphasizes the desire to be close to God and to be renewed in his presence—as in v. 2 (MT v. 3): צמאה נפשי לאלהים לאל חי מתי אבוא ואראה פני אלהים. The language of hope that comes from being *near* to God is especially accentuated in this first Korahite psalm—as seen for example in the refrain of vv. 5b and 11b (MT vv. 6b and 12b): הוחילי לאלהים כי־עוד אודנו ישועות פניו. (2) In Ps 43 (which is often understood as closely connected to Ps 42, since Ps 43 does not have a title and we find the same refrain in Ps 42:5, 11 and in Ps 43:5), the themes of finding refuge and hope (vv. 2, 5) in God's presence are further developed and correlated with the benefit of being in God's presence, and here, in the context of the sacred service of the temple. This is evident in the central call of vv. 3-4: שלח־אורך ואמתך המה ינחוני יביאוני אל־הר־קדשך ואל־משכנותיך ואבואה אל־מזבח אלהים אל־אל שמחת גילי ואודך בכנור אלהים אלהי (and note also the emphasis on instrumental praise in v. 4).[103] (3) In Ps 46, the theme of finding refuge in the presence of God is amplified—as in v. 1 (MT v. 2): אלהים לנו מחסה ועז עזרה בצרות נמצא מאד. The joy of God's presence is also poetically related to the themes of Jerusalem and the temple in v. 4 (MT v. 5): נהר פלגיו ישמחו עיר־אלהים קדש משכני עליון.

(4) In Korahite Ps 48, in praise to Zion, the temple is also viewed as a means of experiencing God's love. It is the center from which God's name and praise fan out through creation—as in vv. 9-10a (MT vv. 10-11a): דמינו אלהים חסדך בקרב היכלך כשמך אלהים כן תהלתך על־קצוי־ארץ צדק מלאה ימינך. (5) In Korahite Ps 84, the theme of finding blessing in God's presence through the intermediary of God's house, of his temple, is found throughout the poem. Language directly related to the temple and the joy of worship therein is present in vv. 1, 2, 3, 4 and 10. For example, the psalmist strongly yearns for the

---

103. Craigie, *Psalms 1-50*, 328, has noted the emphasis in the psalm to the blessing of God's presence at the temple: "[l]ight would bring the psalmist out of darkness and into the divine presence in the temple, here symbolized by the 'holy mountain' and divine 'dwelling place'. . . . God's temple had been merely the object of nostalgic remembrance; now it comes closer to the reality of experience in the prayer addressed to the living God."

temple courts, where connection can be made to the "living God" in v. 2 (MT v. 3): נכספה וגם־כלתה נפשי לחצרות יהוה לבי ובשרי ירננו אל אל־חי.

(6) Ps 85 demonstrates that nearness to God's presence is viewed as a source of restoration—as in v. 4 (MT v. 5): שובנו אלהי ישענו והפר כעסך עמנו. This yearning for divine restoration is communicated in terms of unmediated worship—in the sense that the psalmist expresses his desire to directly enjoy the blessings of the LORD *himself*. (7) In the prayer of Ps 88, the yearning for God's presence and for his response is expressed with depth and with spiritual anguish—as in vv. 1-2 (MT vv. 2-3): יהוה אלהי ישועתי יום־צעקתי בלילה נגדך תבוא לפניך תפלתי הטה־אזנך לרנתי.[104]

Additionally, the Asaphite collection of psalms also reveals connected emphases on this yearning for God's presence, with and without the theme of the temple being expressed outright. Eight passages may be noted in this regard. (1) In Ps 50, the temple cult is alluded to, as the LORD is quoted as desiring more than mechanically-offered sacrifices (vv. 7-11), but for a "sacrifice of thanksgiving" (v. 14) to experience deliverance from God. This Asaphite psalm, then, modulates on the meaning of the historical temple sacrifices, by showing that internal thanksgiving for God's power and presence is ultimately the type of sacrifice that will glorify the LORD and demonstrate his salvation—as seen in the conclusion of v. 23: זבח תודה יכבדנני ושם דרך אראנו בישע אלהים.

(2) And again, in Ps 73, it is the experience of God's presence (and hence, the renewed perception of his sovereignty as well) in the temple complex that enables the shift from despair over the wicked to a renewed confidence in God's ultimate justice. (3) In Ps 74, the physical destruction of the temple leads to mourning and the sense of distance from God—as in vv. 2-3: זכר עדתך קנית קדם גאלת שבט נחלתך הר־ציון זה־שכנת בו הרימה פעמיך למשאות נצח כל הרע אויב בקדש. This sense of separation from the LORD leads the psalmist to forcefully call on the LORD to respond to the apparent strength of the wicked (cf. vv. 22-23).[105] Even as the psalmist laments the sense of desperation from God's judgment and perceived distance (74:1-11), we find a complete reversal of tone in the middle section (74:12-17), which emphasizes God's control and power over all of creation, before a

---

104. Terrien, *The Psalms*, 626, 627, argues that at the opening of this psalm of lament of a "man mortally sick," the psalmist is first challenging the sense of God's "remoteness."

105. With its clear language of a destroyed temple (such as v. 4), Kidner, *Psalms 73-150*, 264, has argued that Ps 74 bears "the marks of the national disaster that produced Psalms 79 and 137 and the book of Lamentations: i.e., the Babylonian destruction of Jerusalem and Temple in 587 BC."

final appeal is made for Yahweh to remember his people, and be near to them, in the midst of a severe trial (74:18-23).

(4) Ps 77 emphasizes the *need* to pursue the presence of God in time of trouble. Asaph's lament first describes the nature of his disorientation and of his desire to be close to God (vv. 1-9); the poem then moves to reflect on the faithfulness of God's past acts in Israel's history (vv. 10-20), which shows that presence with God in lament and in worship leads to a renewal of perspective. (5) Ps 78, on a larger scale, also reflects on God's past actions in Israel's history. Despite the sin of the Israelites, God remained present with them and eventually chose to reveal his presence more fully at Zion, through David and through the temple (cf. vv. 67-72)—as seen in vv. 68-70: ויבחר את־שבט יהודה את־הר ציון אשר אהב ויבן כמו־רמים מקדשו כארץ יסדה לעולם ויבחר בדוד עבדו ויקחהו ממכלאת צאן. (6) Ps 79 connects back to Ps 74 in the sense of being a song of lament over the destruction of the temple (v. 1); one also finds a *renewed* confidence in God for the care he provides for his people—as in v. 13: ואנחנו עמך וצאן מרעיתך נודה לך לעולם לדר ודר נספר תהלתך.

(7) Ps 80 stands as a Levitical worship song that expresses the desire for restoration from God—since the renewed presence of God is sought. This is noted in the repetition of a call for divine restoration in vv. 3, 7, and 10—v. 19 (MT v. 20), for instance, highlights the relationship between God's presence (his "shining" face) and the renewal and restoration of his salvation: יהוה אלהים צבאות השיבנו האר פניך ונושעה. (8) Ps 81, finally, reads as a reflection on the blessing of God's presence in the context of Israel as a whole.[106] As God is present with his people, he will also provide for them (as in vv. 10 or 16). The opening call to praise in vv. 1-3 is particularly replete with musical terms and allusions to the sacred calendar, as in vv. 2-3 (MT vv. 3-4) especially: שאו־זמרה ותנו־תף כנור נעים עם־נבל תקעו בחדש שופר בכסה ליום חגנו. These musical and cultic terms link to the duties of the Levites at temple—laid out in 1 Chr 23 and 25.

This brief survey of some of the data in the Levitical psalms shows that these texts often reflect the experience of the Levitical musical guilds at the temple worship services. They also reflect the experience of a heightened awareness of the sovereign power of God in creation. Based on this broader textual data, we will now proceed to the analysis of a particular aspect of God's promise presented in the example of Ps 73, a Levitical song of Asaph at the beginning of Book III of the canonical Psalter.

---

106. Kraus, *Psalms 60-150*, 152, notes the strong focus on divine presence in Ps 81, as he writes: "The community is let in for an encounter with the God who is present in his word. אנכי יהוה—in the fully authoritative message of him who is inspired … Yahweh with his majestic *I* appears on the scene. Idolatry and disobedience suddenly come under the spotlight of the *deus praesens*" (emphasis original).

Again, the connection between 1 Chr 16 and Ps 73 (and to the Levitical psalms in general) is made here on the basis of a *synchronic and canonical* stance. Specifically, the following three sets of observations further suggest that looking at these two psalms can strengthen a theological appreciation of Levitical *song*, as it is rooted in Chronicles and further expanded in the Levitical psalms of the biblical book of Psalms.

First, as the basic OT data on the Levites shows (see chapter 1), there is much connection between the Levitical singers identified in 1 Chr 6, 15 and 25 (especially) and the Levitical psalms of the Psalter (as briefly discussed above). In his historiography, the Chronicler appears, then, to have recorded the function of the Levitical singers established by David, and also appears to have provided an example of their song; to a greater extent, the Psalter, in its final canonical arrangement, has preserved significant *content* of Levitical song.

Second, the compositional placement of Ps 73 in the book of Psalms is also relevant. Psalm 73 is an Asaphite text that (a) follows immediately after the colophon of Ps 72, which indicates to the reader-worshiper that "the prayers of David, the son of Jesse, are ended" (כלו תפלות דוד בן־ישׁי), and that (b) introduces Book III of the Psalter, which extends from Ps 73 to Ps 89, and which preserves a high concentration of Levitical psalms. Indeed, in Book III, Pss 73–83 are Asaphite; Pss 84–85 and 87–88 are Korahite and they also frame the sole Davidic psalm of Book III (Ps 86); the final Ps 89 is also Levitical, since it is canonically assigned to Ethan the Ezrahite. Thus, although Davidic psalms occur after the colophon at Ps 72:11 (even in Book III, then, at Ps 86), the fact that ten Asaphite psalms (73–83) follow this colophon suggests at least the following general points: (a) the Asaphite lineage of Levitical singers became well-established and recognized in the religious life of ancient Israel; (b) the relationship between Davidic psalmody and Levitical Asaphite psalmody was viewed as closely related; (c) Ps 73 was viewed as a significant example of Asaphite psalmody for the purposes of the transition between Books II and III, and, hence, for the final structure of the Psalter as a whole. Many Psalms scholars further argue that the Levitical voice takes center stage in Book III of the Psalter, as a counterpoint to the Davidic voice (of especially Book I, and in part Book II) and as an expression of the disorientation that occurred with Israel's divided kingdom, and ultimately with the divine judgment of the destroyed Jerusalem temple and the Babylonian exile.[107]

---

107. On this line of thinking, see further the section, "IV. The Canonical Shape of the Psalter," in deClaissé-Walford et al., *The Book of Psalms*, 21–38.

Third, both Chronicles and the Psalter, then, emphasize the significance of Asaphite Levitical song, especially as it was rooted in the religious life of temple worship services. In particular, the psalm in 1 Chr 16 is set *after* David's command to Asaph and his brothers to worship the LORD as the ark has come to rest in Jerusalem, in anticipation for the temple (1 Chr 16:7). First Chr 25, in turn, shows how the Asaphite Levitical genealogical line played a crucial role in the formalized choral ministry of the established temple services. It is then interesting to note that the Asaphite Levitical Ps 73 begins with a type of despairing lament over the apparent success of the ungodly (Ps 73:2–15), but then transforms into a firm statement of God's future blessing of the godly and judgment of the wicked (Ps 73:16–28) only *after* the spiritually reorienting experience Asaph goes through in the *temple*, the sanctuary of God (the מקדשי־אל of Ps 73:17).

Many interpreters maintain that this spiritual movement in Ps 73 is merely reflective of the biblical wisdom tradition, since the Asaphite psalmist transitions from despair and jealousy over acutely evil and unrighteous persons, to a renewed sense of confidence in the goodness and fairness of God's overarching plans for the righteous.[108] However, Gowan, for instance, has noted that the Zion theme, particularly as it relates to the temple and God's presence, can be seen as the center of OT *eschatology*, the "[fundamental] concern [of which] is the future existence of a holy people enjoying the presence of God in their midst."[109] I would argue, then, that the central role of holy space in this psalm naturally raises the issue of eschatology and, hence, of the biblical-theological dimension of "promise" in this OT text.

Thus, a question arises in the interpretation of Ps 73 concerning the correlation of the way of wisdom, the experience in God's holy place and the possibility of an existing eschatological dimension that is rooted in God's promise for both the godly and the wicked. Could the renewed personal hope of this psalm, as it is achieved at least partly through a wisdom frame, possess any element of a personal *eschatological* hope, of a *promise* from God about the eventual situation of the godly and the ungodly? That is, could this Levitical psalm be offering insight into "the direction and goal of God's covenant faithfulness in and for his created order," by reflecting on "the way God's good purposes in history correspond to *ultimate reality*?"[110] Or, is the text merely exemplifying a mostly horizontal move-

---

108. For analyses of Ps 73 particularly focused on the wisdom axis, see for example Luyten, "Psalm 73 and Wisdom," 49–81. Note as well: Ross, "Psalms 73," 161–75; Crenshaw, *A Whirlpool of Torment*, 93–108; Spangenberg, "Psalm 73," 151–75; Cheung, *Wisdom Intoned*; Jacobson and Jacobson, *Invitation to the Psalms*, 72–75.

109. Gowan, *Eschatology in the Old Testament*, 13, emphasis added.

110. Brower, "Eschatology," 459 (emphasis added).

ment *from* the folly of human observation *to* the wisdom of living one's earthly existence rightly, according to the blessing and confidence gained through the divine presence?

Specifically, the argument presented in this section of the chapter posits that an element of personal eschatological hope does in fact exist in Ps 73 and that it is mediated by the experience in the מקדשי־אל. On these bases, this central "promise from God," inherent in the meaning of the temple for Asaph, will be further elucidated as a fruitful biblical-theological counterpoint to the central "proclamation about God" in the Levitical song of 1 Chr 16. As with the earlier analysis of the psalm in 1 Chr 16, some focused interaction with certain scholarly discussions will precede further exegetical reflections on a few key aspects of Ps 73. First, then, the discussion will deal with two salient issues: (1) the relationship between the themes of wisdom and eschatology, and (2) the genre and structure of Ps 73.[111]

Ascertaining Eschatology vis-à-vis Wisdom

On the one hand, if the fundamental aspect of wisdom is defined as "the capacity of judging rightly in matters relating to life and conduct [and] as the ability to cope [with life],"[112] then such a dimension certainly exists in this psalm and bears a very "present" focus. Indeed, the psalmist is seeking to cope with the experience of the apparent blessing of the wicked. Yet, if an eschatological dimension exists, how might it be defined? Marshall notes

---

111. This second major unit of this chapter is adapted from a section in Clayton, "An Examination of Holy Space in Psalm 73," 117–42.

112. Such is the introductory definition given by Schnabel in his article, "Wisdom," 843. Schnabel argues for five emphases of biblical wisdom: (1) Wisdom is a divine gift, never intended as an independent human enterprise. (2) Wisdom acknowledges the inscrutability of God's ways, which can defy rational explanation. (3) Genuine wisdom manifests itself in proper behavior that pleases God. (4) Wisdom emphasizes teaching: "proper behavior has to be learnt and must be passed on from one generation to the next" (Schnabel, "Wisdom," 847). (5) A particular NT accent is that Jesus Christ climactically embodies God's wisdom. Schnabel's second emphasis seems especially pertinent to the realities expressed in Ps 73. Crenshaw, *Old Testament* Wisdom, 3, defines the biblical concept of wisdom as a "reasoned search for specific ways to ensure personal well-being in everyday life, [of an attempt] to make sense of extreme adversity and vexing anomalies?" Such an aspect is certainly present, at least on one level of reading, in Ps 73. See also, Wilson, "חכם," 134. Wilson points out that the Qal form of חָכַם usually denotes "the possibility of acquiring wisdom," (as in Deut 32:39 or Prov 6:6, for example), while the factitive aspect of the Piel form implies that "as it is possible to increase and enhance one's innate wisdom through appropriate study and experience, others can influence and direct this process of learning through appropriate instruction and encouragement (as in Job 35:11 or Ps 119:98)."

that the term "eschatology" is both useful and dangerous, but when properly defined and used with care, the word rightfully points to "a forward look and the consciousness that the promises of God regarding the future are already being fulfilled in the present."[113] Could both a forward aspect and a present consciousness be present?

Some scholars, indeed, hint at possible eschatological overtones in this text. Kraus, for example, has argued that a definite prophetic component is present as "there is information and direction concerning the righteous rule of God on the basis of a new dimension." He notes that in most psalms, God's power is celebrated in the midst of life, "but Psalm 73 prophetically proclaims on the basis of the [אחרית in verse 17] a final certainty no longer visible."[114] Mitchell even argues for an overarching eschatological programme in the Psalter, with a prophetic role played by the Asaphite collection.[115] More generally, Reisenauer has argued that Ps 73, as it is focused on the goodness of God, ultimately points the reader to the notion that union with God enables an *eternal* experience of God's goodness.[116]

Such views call for further exploration of the particular nature of any eschatological overtones in Ps 73. Gowan centers OT eschatology on the theological (and paradoxical) notion of God's presence in the temple on

---

113. Marshall, "Slippery Words," 268. In his synopsis of biblical eschatology, Todd, "Biblical Eschatology," 3–16, perhaps overemphasizes the claim that OT eschatology borrowed extensively from ANE mythical motifs. He also places the emphasis of OT eschatology on "the evidence for a strong futuristic hope . . . from the very beginning of Israel's history, whether this history be traced from Abraham, Jacob, or Moses." See Todd, "Biblical Eschatology," 5.

114. Kraus, *Psalms 60–150*, 20. Broyles' conclusion on Ps 73 may also point to a broader eschatological context as he writes, "Psalm 73 is extraordinary among the psalms in that a resolution is won, but it does not consist in a deliverance from troubling circumstances but a new understanding of God's ultimate design." Broyles, *Psalms*, 303. Furthermore, Westermann notes that with the strength of renewed certainty (found in the text after v. 17), the wisdom motif takes on a deeper theological aspect that emphasizes the possibility of a never-ending fellowship with God. See Westermann, *The Living Psalms*, 141.

115. Mitchell, *An Eschatological Programme*; see especially pp. 82–89 for the main thesis. Mitchell discusses the Asaphite collection in the third chapter, noting that "this group of psalms can be read as representing as eschatological ingathering of Israel, culminating in battle." See Mitchell, *An Eschatological Programme*, 107. Note however that Vincent questions the validity of such a compositional program for a liturgical collection of Psalms. See Vincent, "The Shape of the Psalter," 61–82. For further discussion on the Asaphite collection, see Buss, "The Psalms of Asaph and Korah," 382–92; Illman, *Thema und Tradition*, 63–64; Nasuti, *Tradition History*; Weber, "Der Asaph-Psalter," 141. Goulder argues that the Asaphite psalms represent some of the earliest written traditions in Israel that would bear witness to an eighth century and largely oral E source for the Pentateuch. See his *The Psalms of Asaph and the Pentateuch*, 328–41.

116. Reisenauer, "The Goodness of God," 11–28.

Mount Zion. Gowan indeed remarks that this "important biblical theme—the presence of God—takes on an eschatological form with the promise of God's immediate and continuing presence with his people on Mt. Zion."[117] This would suggest that an important facet of the OT's eschatological conception is more closely linked with a state of *being*, rather than merely with a sharp focus on end-time chronology. Such a view appears fruitful when reflecting on the language of Ps 73.

In fact, in his analysis of OT eschatological hope, Thomas relates God's holiness to the requisite holiness of God's people. His conclusions are pertinent, as he writes, "eschatology in the OT has more to do with the ultimate, than with last things. The ultimate hope is not linked to any particular time.... The fulfillment of the eschatological hope can be expressed then in precisely this way: it is of a holy God dwelling in the midst of a holy people in a holy land."[118]

In this way, the ultimate reality of eschatological hope is not only relegated to a future reality, but it is also part of a present yearning and expectation, especially as it relates God's holiness and God's subsequent desire for the holiness of his people.[119] It might be stated, generally, that this aspect of OT divine promise was rooted in the religious life of ancient Israel and focused on the implications of God's transcendent nature. Hence, does the transformation evidenced in Ps 73 bear out *this* type of hope—a personal hope that is eschatologically oriented, with a focus on the ultimate nature of God's holiness? The following discussion on the centrality of the holy space experience and the twofold dimension of the psalmist's hope should provide a positive answer to this question. However, some comments should first be made in relationship to the overall structure of Ps 73.[120]

---

117. Gowan, *Eschatology in the Old Testament*, 15.

118. He notes further, "[a] holy God among a holy people in a holy place—the enduring eschatological hope of the Scriptures, [that is] God's ultimate purpose for his world, not just in the far-off future but here and now and always." See Thomas, "A Holy God," 62, 63, 69. Thomas discusses such passages as Ezekiel 36:22–35; 37:25–28 and others.

119. In Thomas' words, "ultimate reality is not just what will transpire at the end of time, but that which has always existed in the heavenlies and which God apparently has always sought to make a present reality, according to the Law and Prophets." See Thomas, "A Holy God," 55. Or, as Terrien puts it in relationship to prophetic ministry, "prophets are usually mistaken for predictors. The prophets of Israel unveiled not the future but the absolute." See Terrien, *The Elusive Presence*, 227, and as quoted by Thomas, "A Holy God," 55.

120. For a recent and detailed analysis of the carefully wrought ring structure of Ps 73, see Wong, "Psalm 73," 16–40.

Underscoring the Genre and Structure of Ps 73

The contention here is that issues of genre and structure support our argument on at least two grounds. The first reason is broad and relates to the overarching composition of the text. Commentators agree concerning the central function of the מקדשי־אל theme in v. 17. Brueggemann, for instance, argues that in a sense, the whole Psalter turns on this verse.[121] Tanner notes that while the transformation encountered in v. 17 is clear, "the 'how' and the 'why' of the change are as enigmatic as the earlier dilemma."[122] Nonetheless, in the first section (vv. 1–12), the prosperity of the wicked stands in tension with the expectation of God's fairness. This dissonant perception is transformed through the encounter in the holy space. This moves Asaph to a reversal in perception, since he grasps the eventual floundering of the wicked and the flourishing of the godly.

Yet from a form-critical perspective, scholars continue to debate the setting and genre of Ps 73.[123] Broyles, for instance, notes particular echoes with Pss 24 and 26 and he argues extensively for a "temple entrance liturgy" setting.[124] McCann remarks that although opinions vary as to original setting, v. 17 leads most writers to posit some type of *cultic* setting. It is likely impossible to know what transpired specifically in the temple to change the opinion of the psalmist, but "what is much clearer is that the structure of Ps 73 reinforces the conclusion that the psalmist underwent a remarkable transformation of perspective."[125] In this sense, Tate's typological approach to this issue is helpful.[126] He notes that Ps 73 is certainly rooted historically in a temple worship experience; however, by

---

121. Brueggemann, *The Psalms and the Life*, 207, and as cited by Tanner in deClaissé-Walford et al., *The Book of Psalms*, 591.

122. deClaissé-Walford et al., *The Book of Psalms*, 591

123. Tate notes that a number of different cultic or non-cultic genres have been offered: Ps 73 is understood either as a song of wisdom, of thanksgiving, of confidence, or of lament. The critical pursuit of a particular *Sitz im Leben* is in disarray as well, from non-cultic wisdom settings, to individual or corporate cultic settings. See Tate, *Psalms 51–100*, 36–37.

124. Broyles writes, "Psalm 73 probably functioned as a testimony that reflects on the liturgy of entering Yahweh's temple." See his *Psalms*, 301.

125. McCann, "The Book of Psalms," 968. McCann suggests that the psalmist could have experienced "a priestly oracle of salvation, some sort of festal presentation, a Levitical sermon, or some kind of mystical experience," but certainty on the precise nature of the experience is not possible.

126. He writes in relationship to Ps 73, as biblical literature "the psalms are not locked into any one particular setting in history, but their openness in language and universality of concerns invite the sincere participation of twentieth century Americans with fifth century BCE Israelites." See Tate, *Psalms 51–100*, 233.

divine intent, it is now also rooted in a literary canonical "experience" that emphasizes the need for a "Godward" orientation.[127]

The possibility of a cultic setting and the overall structural movement in the text open the way for a reading that reflects movement beyond a merely "present-time" focus—one that is not limited to the human sphere of reflection and life-engagement. Broader issues related to the place of Ps 73 in the Psalter and its potential as a theological microcosm further strengthen the aspect of an eschatologically oriented hope, in context of the overarching theological move from lament to praise.[128]

Secondly, some more specific issues related to structure should be noted.[129] Indeed, Ps 73 is bound up with a literary *inclusio* that determines its limits: the particle טוב ("good") occurs in v. 1 and again, in v. 28. From

---

127. Brueggemann emphasizes the reorientation that is centered on the literary function of verse 17. He writes of the experience that this was "a decisive time, a turn in perspective. A new orientation was wrought. A refocusing of reality happened in the 'sanctuary of God.' The holy place offered another look and freed the speaker from the mesmerizing evidence at hand." See Brueggemann, *Message of the Psalms*, 118.

128. As noted above, space precludes full discussion of these significant issues, but note that the interpretive move from the historical-critical method to a literary and compositional method, adopted by many in Psalms studies, has been fruitful in emphasizing the function of Ps 73 in the Psalter. Besides the recent essays noted above, see also Mays, "Past, Present and Prospect," 147–56; Howard, "The Psalms and Current Study," 23–40; Howard, "Recent Trends," 329–68. Both Brueggemann and McCann, for example, propose that Ps 73, at it opens Book III, occupies a crucial role in the whole Psalter. McCann sees Ps 73 as a microcosm of OT theology, as it holds "in tension the legitimation of [social] structures and the embrace of pain." See McCann, "Psalms 73," 253. Brueggemann argues that the Psalter thematically moves from obedience to praise, via the embrace of suffering and hope. In his view, Ps 73 is then central, as it summarizes the thesis in Ps 1 of God's reliable faithfulness, develops it into doubt, but ends up with an "ultimate embrace of [this thesis] in trust and confidence." See Brueggemann, "Bounded by Obedience," 80–88. Brueggemann and Miller extend this further by noting the possibility that Ps 73 represents the voice of the king in juxtaposition to Torah and piety. See Brueggemann and Miller, "Psalm 73 as a Canonical Marker," 45–56. They argue along two lines: (1) that the language in Ps 73 recalls Pss 15–24, kinship Torah piety psalms; and (2) that the canonical placement after Ps 72 represents a redefinition of the Solomonic ideal.

McCann, for instance, supports this notion when he sees Ps 73 as "a sort of summary of what the reader of the Psalter would have learned after beginning with Psalms 1 and 2 and moving through the prayer of Psalms 3–72." See McCann, *A Theological Introduction*, 143. Overall, it seems clear that Ps 73 resumes and develops the twofold conclusions of Pss 1 and 2—namely, that the wicked will certainly perish and the righteous seeking refuge in God will certainly find blessing—which fits well into the concept of a personal eschatological hope.

129. For a text-linguistic analysis of Ps 73 that includes interaction with speech-act theory, see Wendland, "Introit," 128–53. See also Wendland, "Aspects of the Structure," 135–49.

the point of view of the psalmist, the more *external* language in the heading of verse 1, אַךְ טוֹב לְיִשְׂרָאֵל אֱלֹהִים לְבָרֵי לֵבָב, turns into a more *internal* conclusion in verse 28, וַאֲנִי קִרֲבַת אֱלֹהִים לִי־טוֹב, a conclusion that follows the consideration of severe evil in vv. 2–13, the experience of the מִקְדְּשֵׁי־אֵל in vv. 13–17 and the reflection on the consequences of God's reorienting presence in vv. 18–27.[130] In his rhetorical study of Ps 73, McCann surveys thirty-two different proposals for understanding the internal structure of this unit.[131] He argues, however, that the threefold repetition of the adverbial particle אַךְ ("truly") in vv. 1, 13 and 18, serves to delineate the primary structure of the text.

Additionally, the repetition of the כִּי / וַאֲנִי ("but I"/"for") sequence in vv. 2–3 and its reversed form וַאֲנִי / כִּי ("for"/"but I") in vv. 27–28 provides a secondary underlying structure that introduces the main *problem*—i.e. the dissonance of the *tradition* of God's goodness to those who are upright with the actual *experience* of the temporal blessing of the wicked—and concludes with its core *solution*—i.e. the distance in judgment of the wicked and the proximity in blessing of the godly.

In sum, the rhetorical structure of the Psalm places the מִקְדְּשֵׁי־אֵל experience squarely at the center of the text.[132] The essential language and structure of this psalm moves from anthropocentric doubt to theocentric certainty, via the momentous experience of the godly individual in God's holy presence. As such, a textual structure with a progressive threefold metaphor is possible: "Anthropocentric Dissonance (vv. 1-12)," "Towards Re-establishing Consonance (vv. 13-17)" and "Theocentric Consonance (vv. 18-28)."[133] The claim here is that, as it is tied to the poetic arrangement of the psalm, such a thematic progression at least makes an eschatologically oriented reading

---

130. For a thorough study of the לֵבָב theme in Ps 73, see Bubei, "The Heart Determines: Psalm 73," 109–18. Also, the superscription in 73:1, מִזְמוֹר לְאָסָף, and the superscription in 74:1, מִזְמוֹר לְאָסָף, further delimit the text as a literary unit in the MT. On this issue of the superscriptions, I agree with the conclusion of Dillard and Longman in their OT handbook, where they argue, "the best solution is to regard the titles as early reliable tradition concerning the authorship and setting of the psalms. The titles, however, should not be taken as original or canonical ... [as] the psalms are always relevant to the needs of the nations as well as to individual Israelites." See Dillard and Longman, *An Introduction to the Old Testament*, 215–216.

131. See McCann, "Psalm 73," 49–63. See also the discussion in Allen, "Psalm 73," 93–107. He notes that although agreement exists as to the core subject matter of this Psalm, "general agreement [regarding structure] proves to be an elusive quarry." See Allen, "Psalm 73," 94.

132. Wong, "Psalm 73," 40, sees vv. 16–17 as the turning point in the tight ring structure of Ps 73.

133. See also for example, Terrien, *The Psalms*, 531, who presents a tripartite strophic structure to the Psalm: Part 1: vv. 1–12; Part 2: vv. 13–22 and Part 3: vv. 23–28.

focused on the ultimate nature of God *possible*—on the basis that Asaph has encountered and recorded a momentous reorienting spiritual experience, based on the renewal in perspective of the divine promise of ultimate blessing for the godly and judgment of the wicked.

Exegetical Reflection: Promise from God and Eschatological Insight with the Holy Space of Ps 73

Some further exegetical reflections will now be offered regarding two specific aspects of the poem: (1) the nature of the "sanctuaries of the God" in v. 17, and (2) the thematic development of vv. 21–28.

Promise from God and "The Sanctuaries of God"

How should one understand מקדשי־אל in v. 17 of Ps 73? Since מקדש ("sanctuary, sacred place") occurs in the plural, some wonder how to understand these "*sanctuaries* of God." Ross identified this question as a major issue in the history of the study of the psalm and discusses four major traditions related to the definition of this expression.

The first area of interpretive tradition is quite imaginative. For example, Gunkel simply emended the MT to read, "the snares of God," whereby God would have somehow trapped the wicked. Birkeland suggested that illegitimate sanctuaries are being referenced, following the establishment of centralized worship in Jerusalem.[134] Schmidt thought the author of Ps 73 "saw one of the wicked struck by a heart-attack on the stones of the temple court."[135]

A second group of scholars argues for more spiritualized meanings of the expression.[136] In these readings, the מקדשי־אל are not places, rather, they represent ideas or concepts. Following Hitzig's supposed parallel in the Wisdom of Solomon, some have seen in this expression the idea of "secret purposes" or "hidden plan." Kittel thought the expression referred to a kind of mystical retraction to God. Oesterly similarly argued that the idiom not only referred to God's physical holy places, but also, to "that inner shrine of the

---

134. See Birkeland, "The Chief Problems of Ps 73 17ff," 100.

135. Ross, "Psalm 73," 165.

136. An example of this view may be found in Schaefer's commentary, *Psalms*, 179. Although he notes v. 17 most likely refers to some type of religious experience, he remains unwilling to decide between the "pagan shrines" view, or the view that supports merely a "contemplative experience."

spirit where God and man may more surely meet." Eichrodt concluded that a type of esoteric knowledge of God's holiness is at hand in verse 17.[137]

The third area of interpretation contends for more literal renderings of the expression and argues for various cultic associations to the earthly temple complex.[138] In the fourth interpretive tradition, some think that the reorientation of the psalmist is such "that the author, although really in the temple, took part in deliberations of the wisdom schools, where discussions of problems of theodicy took place." This is the interpretive strategy Ross opts for—that is, the psalmist would have arrived at his transformation, not by means of religious faith, but through a scholarly wisdom discussion.[139]

However, as some views of the third area of interpretation reveal, this stress on the wisdom tradition may be at odds with the use of מקדש and its broad reference to OT cultic faith and practice. For instance, in her succinct study of the biblical concept of sacred space, Japhet emphasizes the reality of cultic holiness related to מקדש and its derivatives (such as the verb קָדֵשׁ or the noun קֹדֶשׁ) as these terms both refer "to the deity and to the entire spectrum of phenomena and objects that are associated with him: sacred space, sacred persons, sacred objects and so on."[140] Haran also examines the wide referential range of מקדש. He observes that the basic nominal form doesn't "necessarily refer to a house of God," in priestly language it can also indicate "any article or object possessing sanctity."[141]

Why then does מקדשי־אל occur in the plural in Ps 73:17? The LXX and Syriac emend the expression to a singular, but this seems unnecessary, as מקדש can occur in the plural in the OT and refers then to "the multiple holy precincts within the tabernacle or temple complex."[142] Besides the reference

---

137. See Schaefer, *Psalms*, 166.

138. Schaefer, *Psalms*, 166–67. For example, Mowinckel argued that Ps 73 should be seen as a thanksgiving psalm. The psalmist was ill, went to the sanctuary for ritual purification and, as Nielsen, "Psalm 73," 276, notes of Mowinckel's view, "[f]rom the [psalmist's] experiences at the sanctuary [Mowinckel] draws the conclusion that the rich and unjust persons who afflicted him with illness by means of sorcery will be punished by God." Although Mowinckel's view is theoretically plausible, the textual evidence suggests it remains a historically tendentious reconstruction of the *Sitz im Leben* of Ps 73.

139. Ross, "Psalm 73," 167.

140. Japhet, "Some Biblical Concepts of Sacred Place," 56–57. Japhet further notes that "holiness obligates people to observe certain rules of behavior, prohibitions and obligations of various degrees, and their very observance attests to the fact that the place is 'sacred.'" See Japhet, "Some Biblical Concepts of Sacred Place," 57.

141. Haran, *Temples and Temple-Service*, 14–15.

142. See Averbeck, "מִקְדָּשׁ," 1079. Also, note that during the transitional liturgical and cultic stage noted at the end of 1 Chronicles (with the ark in Jerusalem and the remainder of the tabernacle complex still in Gibeon), the Asaphite psalmist could have

in Ps 73, this can also be seen in Lev 21:23 or Jer 51:51. Indeed, for Haran, the form of Ps 73:17 represents a case when it "is applied to the temple in the plural, [and thereby points to] the temple's various structures and appurtenances, all of which were considered holy."[143]

Consequently, it appears warranted to affirm that the מקדשי־אל theme refers to an experience of the Asaphite psalmist in the *temple complex*, with *primarily* religious and cultic overtones. Whether or not the temple complex includes "wisdom schools" is uncertain,[144] since the textual evidence bears out the fact that "the answer to the psalmist's heart-rending problem comes from religious faith and personal experience at *worship, not from discussing with sages in the vicinity of the temple.*"[145] This issue is significant as it helps establish the religious overtones of the theme and a theological connection to the eschatological trajectory of the dwelling place of God—which, thus, provides further support to the idea that the wisdom element in Ps 73 is infused by an eschatologically-oriented hope, a "promise" from God in Levitical song.

Promise from God and Thematic Development in Ps 73:13–17

Some discussion of the developments in vv. 13–17 may give further substance to the centrality of holy space. Indeed, this section forms a literary unit that presents the paradoxical interplay of *limiting* human perspective with the *broadening* force of an "in-breaking" divine perspective. God's

---

had worship experiences in multiple sacred places. However, the fact that 1 Chr 16 emphasizes how Asaph and his brothers were instructed by David to remain at the ark in Jerusalem to minister at the ark (16:37) suggests that the Asaphite musical service was centered in Jerusalem from the beginning (while Heman and Jeduthun were assigned to Gibeon with the priests during the temporary stage). Still, in the end, it remains a historical possibility that Asaph *could* have experienced Yahweh's renewal in Jerusalem and in Gibeon.

143. Haran, *Temples and Temple-Service*, 15. Even-Shoshan lists two major glosses for מִקְדָּשׁ: "a holy place for the service of God," and "the house of God for the holy service of sacrifices in Jerusalem," and he lists 73:17 as referring to the "house of God." See Even-Shoshan, *A New Concordance*, 702–3. For references of the cultic usage of מִקְדָּשׁ, see for example: Lev 12:4; 19:30; 20:3; 21:12; Num 18:1; 19:20; Lam 2:7; 1 Chr 22:10; 2 Chr 28:10; 30:8; 36:17; Neh 10:39.

144. As Ross argues in his essay, "Psalm 73," 167–69.

145. Crenshaw, *A Whirlpool of Torment*, 108 (emphasis added), who is reacting directly to Ross' view. Note also Allen's conclusion on this issue, as he writes "the wisdom elements in [Psalm 73] present no obstacle to cultic usage since wisdom and cult need not be regarded as mutually exclusive entities." See Allen, "Psalm 73," 93–118.

presence is being affirmed in the experience of the psalmist. The particular contribution of this section to the larger pattern of the divine presence motif has to do with the *effect* of God's presence, as God lifts the godly out of despair over evil.¹⁴⁶

Structurally, vv. 13–17 open with the second occurrence of the אך adverbial particle in v. 13 and close with the עד־אבוא ("until I went") prepositional phrase in v. 17, which provides some clues regarding the transformations taking place. As alluded to above, whereas the first אך clause in v. 1 follows a quasi-recitation of what the psalmist knows *should* be true, namely that טוב לישראל אלהים לברי לבב, the disjunctive ואני ("and I") of v. 2 introduces an existential dissonance to this initially objective statement. In v. 13, the text reveals a speaker whose perspective flows from a consciousness centered on self and on evil, that is, a limited consciousness lacking any perspective on God's person and plan.

In this way, vv. 13–16 present the reader with the consequences of a *limiting* human perspective; the perspective in which the divine presence motif needs to operate. The connection with לבב ("heart") is revealing. Whereas the proverbial statement of v. 1 of אך טוב לישראל אלהים לברי לבב stands in direct contrast to the wicked in v. 7, whose hearts are expanding in their pride, עברו משכיות לבב, the speaker now doubts the integrity of his own heart in v. 13 (אך־ריק זכיתי לבבי). In the perspective of Ps 15, for example, integrity of heart and sound ethical actions (cf. Ps 15:2, הולך תמים ופעל צדק ודבר אמת בלבבו) are representative of the godly person who is able to enter into God's presence—into the tabernacle, on the holy hill (cf. Ps 15:1). He who walks in truth and in righteousness is *supposed* to enjoy deep fellowship with God—yet, the reality of prospering wickedness causes doubt concerning the validity of ritual purity. The psalmist remains distracted in his experience with God, because of the overwhelming presence of wickedness.

This despairing perspective is amplified in Ps 73:14 with existentially percussive words, such as נגוע and ותוכחתי. This language highlights the all-encompassing nature of the troubling perspective. It seems inescapably present "all the day, every morning." At the same time, in vv. 15 and 16, the text indicates movement towards the radical transformation that in

---

146. As Broyles remarks of the reorienting function of this text, "[n]ow Ps 73 shows us that God personally is the reward of faith and relationship with him is its chief value. While God, in fact, *may* give evidence of his goodness in material terms, the only guarantee we have as believers is that he will evidence that goodness in personal terms. *Ps 73 is extraordinary among the psalms in that a resolution is won, but it does not consist in a deliverance from troubling circumstances but a new understanding of God's ultimate design*" (emphasis added). See Broyles, *Psalms*, 303.

fact occurs in v. 17. Introduced by the אם ("if") conjunction, the speaker indicates that while in this state of despair—one of limited perspective—at least an *intellectual* dilemma is occurring, denoted by verbs of expression, reflection, and rumination: אספרה, אמרתי, and אחשבה.[147]

If on the one hand, the speaker is tempted to give in to this perspective of wickedness, he also *intellectually* recognizes the unfaithfulness of such a move. The conclusion of v. 16 reveals the limits of the disoriented perspective, one that lacks the recognition of God's presence with the godly. This is highlighted by the linguistic connection between vv. 11 and 16. In v. 11, the wicked assert one cannot ידע־אל ("know God"), so when the psalmist attempts to find דעת ("knowledge") in v. 16, it comes to nothing, to עמל ("trouble, toil"). Thus, vv. 13–16 present the reader with the effects of *self-centeredness*: it remains limited; it causes pain and doubt, as it leads to a withering perspective on life. This middle section then *prepares* for the divine blessing, by highlighting the personal despair experienced without the perspective gained in the midst of God's presence.

The larger perspective begins to take shape only as the psalmist is actively engaged in the מקדשי־אל in v. 17. One aspect of the perspective can be seen as personal and eschatologically oriented, as it will return the focus of the psalmist on God's ultimate plan both for the wicked and the godly. What then does the experience in the מקדשי־אל provide? It leads the speaker to assert his comprehension of *their end*, לאחריתם the *ultimate* destination for the proud and arrogant wicked. The מקדשי־אל brings about the transformation from despair to renewed perception. Kraus comments on this new dimension, by noting that "what in this world can no longer be demonstrated empirically is cleared up prophetically."[148]

If the LORD's holiness is encountered in the holy space, clarification on the ultimate judgment of the profanity of evil is natural. Keel, in fact, argues that the very *nature* of God is inherent in the notion of sanctuary. In Hebrew, the difference between "sanctuary" and "holiness" can be ambiguous. For Keel, the crucial element is that "in the Israelite view, holiness is not inherent in any created thing. It receives the quality of holiness through *relation* to Yahweh."[149] The religious experience in the sanctuary enables communication with the LORD, which moves the psalmist's perspective from the profanity of outright evil to the sacredness of God's holy presence. In sum, the מקדשי־אל theme represents a multi-faceted literary motif of theological

---

147. Verses 15–16: "If *I had said* 'I will talk' on in this way I would have been untrue to the circle of your children. But *when I thought* how to understand this, it seemed to me a wearisome task."

148. Kraus, *Psalms 5–150*, 89 (emphasis added).

149. Keel, *The Symbolism*, 174 (emphasis added).

reorientation for the psalmist, by means of an intricate mediation between God and his people.[150] This is an eschatologically oriented hope that begins with a renewal of perspective—a perspective rooted in God's own immanent, yet transcendent, presence.[151] Despite the reality of wickedness, sin, and evil, this text demonstrates that God's presence leads not only to an earthly perspective of wisdom but also, to the *reinforcement* of the hopeful certainty of evil's demise. The text has not yet presented what that destiny *actually is*; what the text *does* point out at this juncture is the expanding perspective gained by the immediate presence of God. On this basis, a brief analysis of two dimensions of personal hope (the distance of the wicked and the proximity of the godly) *produced* by the central experience of holy space will further establish the argument presented here.

Promise from God and the Wicked Ones' Judgment in Distance

The third אך particle of the psalm introduces the final section in v. 18 and is concluded by the reversed ואני / כי sequence in vv. 27 and 28 (in contrast to the sequence of vv. 2 and 3). Verse 18 presents some linguistic reversals. Whereas the first אך clause eventually led to the slippery state of the speaker in v. 2—seen in the נטוי and שפכו verbs ("stumbled," "slipped"), the "post-holy space-encounter" אך clause in v. 18 reveals that God has set the *evil ones* on the slippery places—בהלקות.

---

150. Averbeck provides a helpful exegetical synthesis of the overall use of the מִקְדָּשׁ theme in Old Testament traditions. He argues that first, the temple was the focal point of the world of ancient Israel—all existing space was oriented around it. Secondly, he notes that the temple is understood as a place of contact between the LORD and his people. Thirdly, the temple served as a microcosm of the heavenly realm and mirrors the heavenly realm on earth, by means of its concepts of purity and holiness. (See for instance, 1 Kgs 8:30, where Solomon's prayer at the dedication of the Temple illustrates this concept, "Hear the plea of your servant and of your people Israel when they pray toward this place; O hear in heaven your dwelling place; heed and forgive" [NIV]) Finally, "the temple was a place of immanent and transcendent presence in which the LORD was present, even though he was also transcendent and could not be contained there." See Averbeck, "מִקְדָּשׁ," 1081.

151. Terrien is helpful in elucidating the paradoxical nature of this spiritual experience, though he may be overemphasizing the notion of a mystical union, not present in the text—the psalmist remains aware of his creaturely existence vis-à-vis his Creator—as he writes, "the line of demarcation is blurred. The I-Thou dialogue in prayer reaches almost the level of identification. The psalmist may not have intended to produce such an impression. Nevertheless, the communion is so intense and so continuous that, although he does not speak of my God in the sense of proprietorship, he knows that he possesses none in heaven, no saint, no angel, no member of the heavenly council, besides the Lord." See Terrien, *Psalms*, 533.

Furthermore, textual irony exists in the reversed use of the שׁית ("set") root. In v. 9, the wicked ones *set* (שׁתו) their tongues in the heavens, most likely an image of their utter contempt and pride. However, the reversed perspective reminds the psalmist that God will set the evil ones towards their final destination in v. 18—תשׁית. This is the language of finality, the אהרית of the wicked ones in v. 17 is made evident in v. 18. The use of the hiphil form—הִפַּלְתָּם ("you make them fall") further emphasizes the central role that God plays in the final judgment of the oppressors. Hence, the text reminds the reader of the divine promise—namely, that God is the cause and origin of such judgment; therein lies the eschatological hope of the godly, as it connects to the pattern of God's certain judgment of evil. No matter how prideful and arrogant the wicked may appear to be, this text demonstrates that an ultimate transformation *will* take place for the wicked and it will be certain.

Still, Kraus strikes a note of caution when he writes, "it must become clear that *aharot* in Ps 73 has to do with personal activity of God, with Yhwh's final intervention and operation. The term 'eschatology' would, however, go too far—unless we should explain precisely how this term is to be understood."[152] However, it should be possible to argue for an eschatological overtone at work in the imagery of the psalm, by noting that the text is pushing the consciousness of the psalmist forward, to a more certain realization of the *ultimate end* of evil.

The certainty of God's judgment of the wicked, in v. 18, is strengthened by the developments in vv. 19 and 20 that highlight the *finality* of this judgment. Verse 19 contains a rapid-fire succession of verbal clauses that draw attention to the irrevocability of the fate of the wicked: היו ספו תמו. Three prepositional phrases serve to objectify the actions of these verbs: לשׁמה כרגע מן־בלהות. Verse 20 presents some text critical problems. Literally, the MT reads, "like a dream awakening LORD, in the city their image you despise." The suggested emendation made by *BHS* is probably valid, whereby the clause "like a dream, when one awakes, LORD, upon awakening, you despise their image" can be read (also reflected in the NIV for example).

As VanGemeren notes, this is the most likely sense of the verse, which highlights the notion that "when God rouses himself to action the wicked are nothing but an image in relation to God. Though they have set themselves up as 'gods,' they are not real and will be dealt with quickly."[153] Both vv. 19 and 20 thus emphasize the finality of God's dealings with the wicked. Complemented with the certainty of God's judgment of the impious in v. 18,

---

152. Kraus, *Psalms 60–150*, 91.
153. VanGemeren, "Psalms," 481.

this portion of text substantiates the suggestion that an aspect of personal eschatological is present, whereby the wicked move from present haughtiness to the certainty of a future devastation and distance from God.

In sum, the first dimension of a renewed personal eschatological hope may be found in the motif of divine judgment, as it is communicated by the image of the final distance of the wicked from God. This is a spiritual distance in God because of his judgment.

Promise from God and the Godly Ones' Blessing of Proximity

Verses 21 to 26 represent the middle segment of this second half of the psalm. The כי clause introduces this section, which is dominated by the repetition of both לבבי and עמך.[154] The reorientation of the psalmist is taking hold in his own consciousness. The text is now moving from the external, more objective pronouncement of v. 1 to an internal, more subjective affirmation of the blessed relationship of the godly to the Creator. This movement reflects the pattern of transformative godliness. Because of the reorienting experience of v. 17, not only is the psalmist able to regain his outlook on the true end of the wicked, but also, he is able to renew the perception of his own relationship to God.

This begins in vv. 21 and 22 with a re-visitation of past disorientation. In v. 21, the text presents a reflection that emanates from the innermost parts of the psalmist: לבבי וכליותי. As the psalmist had envied the elusive blessing of the wicked, he experienced the testing of depression and anguish, seen in these strong verbs: חָמֵץ in the hithpael (a *hapax* in this stem: a "soured, leavened heart") and שָׁנֵן in the hithpolel (another *hapax*: "pierced through"). The agony and distress of v. 21 caused the speaker to behave brutishly before God.

However, the disjunctive ואני at v. 23 reaffirms the consonance of the psalmist's new theocentric perspective. Whereas the לבבי/עמך pair was repeated once in the flashback section of vv. 21 and 22, the same pair of terms is repeated twice in this section, emphasizing the centeredness the psalmist has found in and through God's presence in the holy space. In v. 23, the psalmist experiences protection from God, seen in the use of ימין. This leads him both to a renewal in the way of wisdom in v. 24a and to the affirmation of the eternal nature of God's relationship with the godly in v. 24b, ואחר כבוד תקחני.[155] Some scholars argue for a definite postmortem resurrection in this clause. Because Terrien posits the possibility of a later Persian period for this psalm,

---

154. On the repeated use of עִמָּךְ, see Mannati, "Sur le quadruple *avec toi*," 59–67.

155. NIV: "and afterward you will take me into glory." And note the NRS: "and afterward you will receive me with honor."

and thus, heightened Jewish eschatological expectations, he views this clause as a clear reference to the resurrection.[156]

Other interpreters only see a reference in v. 24b to a glorified present life, as Tate does, "it does not refer to postmortem existence in a heavenly realm. Thus, the meaning in verse 24 is most probably that of a life guided by the counsel of God and coming to its end with a 'glory' which testifies of its worth and fulfillment."[157] Other scholars present a more nuanced outlook. For example, Westermann notes that this verse expands on a traditional theological "confidence." The certainty of the psalmist has reached such a point that a new development is added, but the reference to a future life remains ambiguous. He writes, "[a]ll that is said is that the psalmist's fellowship with God cannot be destroyed even by death. Such certainty does not need any particular concept of a life beyond."[158]

It seems, however, warranted to argue with others yet, who note that the language of this text supports the notion of definite *continuation* of the relationship between God and the godly, while not giving any *precision* as to the nature of that continuation (we may allow for the rest of the canonical voice to do so). Both the language of "taking into glory," as well as the adverbial particle אחד, a close cognate to the אחרית particle in v. 18, reinforce the eschatological connotation of this verse.[159] Verse 25 bolsters the psalmist's expression of God's nearness, which leads him to a theocentric confession of faith. In all of creation, proximity to God is paramount. This segment concludes with a poetic line that sets human frailty in contrast to divine consistency. And in v. 26, the psalmist perceives God as his צור and his חלק—for what duration of time? לעולם. Just as the Levites received the LORD himself as their inheritance (Num 18:20), so this poetic modulation leads the psalmist to affirm his total reliance on God *himself*.

A final transformational motif is implied throughout the psalm, made evident in the conclusion of vv. 27 and 28 and is introduced by the final כי־הנה clause. On the one hand, through his experience in the holy space of the sanctuary, the psalmist is secure in the notion that the wicked will not prevail in their pride and contempt—the use of the אבד and צמת roots, which denote God's final actions in relation to the wicked, make this certain. Proximity to God is now secured in the experience of the psalmist.[160] Not only do

---

156. Terrien, *Psalms*, 533.

157. Tate, *Psalms 50–100*, 236.

158. Westermann, *The Living Psalms*, 141.

159. For further discussion on this issue, see Witte, "Auf dem Weg," 15–30; Alexander, "The Psalms and the Afterlife," 2–17; Jellicow, "The Interpretation of Psalm lxxxiii. 24," 209–10; Tournay, "Le psaume LXXIII," 187–99; Johnston, "Psalm 49," 73–84.

160. As Terrien remarks, "the nearness of God becomes the supreme good. It is

the concluding lines to the text present a *secured* proximity to God, but they also display an *intimate* proximity to God. The final disjunctive clause of the psalm, ואני, introduces a personalized experience of God's presence.[161]

The *inclusio* on the adjective טוב is now complete. Whereas the psalmist could argue that God is good to the *community* of Israel in v. 1, having now gone through his reorienting experience, he is able to confidently affirm the goodness of God to *himself*: קרבת אלהים לי־טוב.[162] The celebration of his renewed perspective concludes with another contrasting use of the שית root. While he had observed that the evil ones *set* their "mouths to the heavens" in verse 9, the godly individual is now able to firmly *set* his refuge in the LORD God for the purpose of declaring the wondrous works of God.[163]

Conclusion: Basic Claims and Relationship to Larger Methodology

Primarily, in this chapter we have sought to argue that the *content* of Levitical song, as it is rooted in the Chronicler's work and further presented in the Levitical psalms of the Psalter, can be fruitfully analyzed along biblical-theological trajectories. These lines of investigation reveal how the theme of Levitical worship duty plays a coherent role in the overall method and message of 1 Chr 10–29.

Among other possible theological emphases, two in particular have been pointed out. First, the psalm in 1 Chr 16, as it is set in the narrative context of Asaphite worship at the ark under David's supervision,

---

both a desire and a gift.... Theology is born out of the quest for truth and its doubts. It matures into creedal statements after the sublimity of divine possession." See Terrien, *Psalms*, 534–35.

161. As Brueggemann notes of this final statement in verse 23, "the symmetry of 'But I' in verse 2 and 'But I' in verse 23 traces the dynamic of this life with God. And this is preceded by a parallel 'surely' in verse 1, 18 which provide the intellectual, religious, and moral point of discontinuity with what had been assumed until this point. Thus the psalm narrates two break points." See Brueggemann, *The Message of the Psalms*, 119.

162. "But for me it is good to be near God." On the issue of nearness to God, see further Asension, "Una faceta bíblica del acercamiento," 5–19, who deals with the קרב lexeme.

163. Creach argues that the theme of the godly finding refuge in God is a crucial development throughout the Psalter. See Creach, *Yahweh as Refuge*. Note also the emphasis given by Beaucamp, *Le Psautier: Ps 73–150*, 5, on the blessing of proximity to God in the conclusion to Ps 73, who writes "[i]l ne s'agit pas de résoudre un problème, en l'occurrence celui de la réussite des méchants; il s'agit de décider si l'on continuera à s'engager à la suite de Yahvé, vu le peu de profit qu'apparemment on en retire. La question est moins de savoir si Yahvé est avec nous, que de vouloir, envers et contre tout, demeurer avec lui; l'expression revient trois fois (v. 22, 23, 25)."

especially demonstrates for God's people the significance of proclaiming, in a worship context, the *present* dominion of the LORD in creation—even if human circumstances might point to the contrary. This theme of Levitical worship would have certainly been of significant value to the original audience of Chronicles—namely, the struggling restoration community of postexilic Judah.

Second, Ps 73, an Asaphite psalm at the head of Book III of the Psalter (which is primarily Levitical), further points to the emphasis in Levitical song on an important *promise* from God. Despite the human reality of wickedness (seemingly) prevailing, God's ultimate rule and justice will certainly prevail, per the conclusion of this psalm. In the end, the promise of the proximity of God is understood as the highest blessing (cf. Ps 73:28a ואני קרבת אלהים לי־טוב), since Yahweh himself is experienced as a safe refuge (cf. Ps 73:28b שתי באדני יהוה מחסי—a clause that alludes back to a fundamental statement in the conclusion of Ps 2: (אשרי כל־הוסי בו), from which, ultimately, further proclamation about God is able to radiate (cf. Ps 73:28c לספר כל־מלאכותיך). This promise of the blessing of the godly and the judgment of the wicked appears rooted, for the Asaphite psalmist, in the tradition of Levitical worship and music at the sacred Jerusalem temple complex.

Finally, we may briefly note how these biblical-theological implications regarding Levitical song interact with the larger methodological approach of our study. From a historical point of view, the initial establishment of the ark in Jerusalem (1 Chr 15–16) and the subsequent preparations for the permanent temple complex in the city of Zion (1 Chr 22–29) both provide important foundations on which the theology of Levitical song may actually develop—which is related to the historical discussion from earlier in this work. That is, we are seeking to develop the argument that it is *because* Yahweh has chosen to paradoxically *dwell* in Jerusalem, and it is *because* he has chosen David and certain Levites to lead in musical praise, that the tradition of Levitical psalmody is, indeed, able to find roots in, and flourish from, the period of the early monarchy. Hence, a theological reflection on the implications of Levitical song in 1 Chr 10–29 can be fruitfully connected to the historical development of the Levitical choristers—from their foundations at the time of David, to their influential role throughout the religious life of Israel beyond the time of David, on through the postexilic period, and as especially preserved, ultimately, in the Levitical collections of the Psalter.

In the end, the theological implications of Levitical song, discussed from the point of view of two discreet Levitical psalms in this chapter, should also be considered in relationship to the rhetorical emphases of the Chronicler—another major methodological aspect of our study. The significant theological issues of divine proclamation and divine promise are key to the rhetorical impetus of 1 Chr 10–29, since they occur within centrally located literary units—i.e., chapters 15–16 and chapters 22–27. When these various elements are kept in balance, a more vivid rhetorical, historical, and theological prism begins to emerge and helps enlighten the meaning and significance of the texts concerning the Levites in 1 Chr 10–29.

6

Conclusion

Summary, Contributions,
and Final Reflections

The main goal of our study has been to propose a multidimensional reading of select texts related to the Levites in 1 Chr 10–29, the section of the Chronicler's biblical history focused on the kingship of David in the early united monarchy of ancient Israel. In the modern critical study of this topic, the historicity of the Chronicler's presentation of the Levites has often been challenged. A related scholarly trajectory in the critical study of these texts also contends that they are not, in the main, original to the Chronicler's work *per se*. In fact, at least in academic studies of the Chronicler's history, these types of approaches continue to be influential and have often led, arguably, to readings of the passages under consideration here, which have remained focused on matters of historical reconstruction, and related theories of redactional layers. In these discussions, the possibility of arriving at a fuller appreciation of the function and contribution of the literary units in the Chronicler's corpus seems often to have been downplayed.

In contrast, some of the more recent literary-critical and canonical-based studies have offered something of an alternative approach—in the sense of viewing the Chronicler's text as a more coherent literary and theological whole. It is on the basis of the latter scholarly developments that we have sought to provide a reading of texts related to the expanded cultic service of the Levites under David in 1 Chronicles. Reflections on the function of these passages from the perspective of the Chronicler's postexilic setting have also been a significant element of our study.

To these ends, our work began in chapter one by providing a summary of the basic biblical data related to the Levites in the OT. The rationale was to highlight the key biblical texts, before noting some of the related scholarly theories. Thus, first, the principle aspects of texts related to the identity, function, and purpose of the non-Aaronide Levites in passages outside of Chronicles were highlighted, to provide a larger backdrop to the ensuing discussion. This section summarized the presentation of the Levites' establishment in their sacred roles during the tabernacle wilderness period and up to the preparations for entry into the land. Texts related to the pre-monarchic period were also noted, as well as the passages pertaining to the Levites in the biblical historiography of Samuel-Kings. The data present in the biblical books of Ezra and Nehemiah was also highlighted, as were some key texts related to the Levites in other OT books, such as the Levitical psalms.

This first (biblical data-driven) section was followed by a discussion of two major streams of scholarly theories related to the Levitical texts of the OT as a whole. On the one hand, we sought to demonstrate that historical-critical approaches have emphasized both source-critical and redaction-critical theories. In these views, the final form of the text is carefully analyzed to decipher the possibility of various redactional layers and, hence, of various developmental, historical stages for the Levites' roles. In such approaches, these stages are often deemed to be contradictory, or as providing evidence for ideologically-driven rivalries between various Levitical factions. On the other hand, we also sought to highlight the way canonical-based readings of the Levites more directly support the ability to relate the final canonical form of relevant passages to principal historical stages of ancient Israel—at least on a maximalist reading of that history.

Furthermore, this first major introductory step of the study attempted to summarize some of the basic biblical data related to the Levites in 1–2 Chronicles. This summary was developed following the largest literary divisions of the Chronicler's text: the genealogical introduction of 1 Chr 1–9, the Davidic narratives of 1 Chr 10–29, the Solomonic narratives of 2 Chr 1–9, and the lengthy presentation of the divided kingdom (focused on the southern kingdom) in 2 Chr 10–36.

On the basis of textual data, three principle scholarly research trajectories in relationship to the Levites in Chronicles were discussed. First, historical-critical approaches have contended for the composite and ideological nature of these texts related to the Levites. In these views, the reality of a developed Levitical service is usually seen as a historical possibility only in the postexilic period. On the other hand, newer literary-critical discussions of this topic have accentuated more of the textual integrity in the Chronicler's work, while still exploring the various (postexilic) ideological factors that could have given rise to the Chronicler's strong emphasis on a complex Levitical temple cult. That is, while literary approaches demonstrate an emphasis on the coherence of the Chronicler's text, often, it is also assumed that much of the "historical" description of the Levitical cult at the time of David is more reflective of the Chronicler's own postexilic time and/or of even later postexilic redactors. Finally, we also attempted to show that a number of more recent canonical-based theories have recognized that the passages dealing with the Levites in the Chronicler's work can be seen as: (1) being rooted in reliable preexilic traditions, even as they have been purposefully shaped by the demands of a postexilic audience, and (2) as properly functioning as theologically-focused historical narratives.

Hence, chapter one concluded with the thesis statement driving the whole study—one that has been built on the basis of the canonical-based scholarly theories related to the Levites in the OT generally, and in Chronicles specifically. In our thesis statement, we have contended that aspects of 1 Chr 15, 16, and 23—key texts for the Chronicler concerning the function of the Levites under David—contribute significantly to the rhetorical argumentation, the historiographic method, and the biblical-theological implications of the Davidic narratives of 1 Chr 10–29, as they emphasize the central role played by proper Levitical worship leadership at the time of David *and* during the challenging situation of the Chronicler's postexilic audience.

Hence, the second major step of our study involved the definition of a distinct multidimensional methodological approach—one that would enable fleshing out the three-pronged statement found in the operating thesis. The purpose of chapter two, then, was to provide a succinct discussion of some of the key aspects of three distinct exegetical methodologies, and their application to three control texts in 1 Chr 10–29.

First, the method of OT rhetorical criticism was considered and a specific approach to the study of 1 Chr 15:1—16:3 (a passage dealing with David's preparation of the Levites for the processional entry of the ark into Jerusalem) was laid out. The approach adopted emphasized the need to carefully consider the literary structure of the Chronicler's canonical text and the potential impact of its inherent message on a postexilic audience. Second, the method of OT historiography was briefly analyzed. An approach to the historical study of 1 Chr 23 (a passage dealing with David's expansion of Levitical duty at the temple for the temple service in Jerusalem) was given. In the basic approach proposed, we noted the benefit of a critically-realist epistemological stance, which would enable the defense of the historical plausibility of an expanded Levitical service in David's united monarchy (i.e., the early first millennium). Finally, the method of biblical theology was also discussed, and an exegetical approach that focused on the theological ramifications of 1 Chr 16 was laid out.

Specifically, the matrix of "proclamation" and "promise" was proposed as a helpful tool in elucidating some of the theological implications of Levitical song, as rooted in the historical setting of 1 Chr 16 (a text that is set in the context of a leading Levite, Asaph, who was instructed by David to lead in music and praise at the installation of the ark in Jerusalem) and as also related to the Levitical literature of the book of Psalms (Ps 73, a Levitical psalm of Asaph, was proposed as a specific example).

This synthesis of the biblical data on the Levites, as well as the discussion of various scholarly theories related to the function of the Levites in the OT, and the underlying threefold methodological approach, could all be seen as basic contributions of this study to the ongoing, broader analysis of the Levites in the OT, and especially in Chronicles. However, the more substantive contributions of this work are to be found in the subsequent exegetically-focused chapters. As such, and as a final concluding synthesis, the following points will be noted in relationship to chapters three, four, and five of this work: (1) a basic summary; (2) a statement related to the most significant contribution; and (3) some suggested implications for ongoing research.

The Rhetorical Aspect: Summary, Contribution, and Implications

In chapter three, we began with a translation of the MT of 1 Chr 15:1—16:3. This is the first full-fledged narrative unit focused on the Levites in the Chronicler's work (save for the sections in the genealogies devoted to the Levites). In this pericope, David is preparing for the successful procession of the ark of Yahweh into Jerusalem. In so doing, he assigns the Levites to a carefully established musical ministry of praise and worship. The basic setting of this unit within 1 Chr 10:1—22:1 (the first major unit of the Chronicler's Davidic texts) was discussed, to demonstrate its central rhetorical function at this broader literary level. Further, some of the key features of the relationship between 1 Chr 15:1—16:3 and 2 Sam 6:1-3, the parallel text in the Samuel-Kings narrative, were noted. The Chronicler obviously made use of this (and some other OT texts), though he also carefully included unique material, namely, the passages emphasizing Levitical leadership for the ark procession.

Most notably, a concentric rhetorical structure of the Hebrew text was suggested for 1 Chr 15:1—16:3 as a unit. This proposed structure, and its related discussion, may be viewed as the principle contribution of this section of our study. This rhetorical structure reveals the way in which the emphasis on the Levitical ministry in the passage plays a key role in the overall flow of the unit, and hence, in the larger rhetorical development of 1 Chr 10:1—22:1. While it was noted that this structure is not the only possible literary/structural reading possible for this unit, we argued that Chr 15:1—16:3 *could* be read, from the basis of the Hebrew text, as comprising five concentric sub-sections. Sections A (15:1-3, David's actions in Jerusalem) and B (15:4-15, David's preparations of the Levitical leaders for the procession), were suggested to be in parallel with sections B' (15:25-29, David's execution of the procession with the Levitical leaders) and A' (16:1-3, David's actions in Jerusalem). These external and parallel units were then shown to focus the reader's attention on the central section C, in 15:16-24, the rhetorically unique sub-unit concerned with the establishment of the Levitical musical ministry for the procession of the ark.

Finally, based on the rhetorical structure proposed, some suggestions were made in relationship to the impact of the unit on the Chronicler's postexilic audience, especially with its emphasis on the coming of the ark into Jerusalem and the liturgical support provided by the joyful ministry of the Levites. A key observation in this regard was that a historical consciousness of earlier preexilic traditions of the Levites and their ministry at the ark seems to have played an especially significant role in this text—since the Chronicler was seeking to *encourage* a struggling postexilic audience towards a renewed identity as a Yahweh-centered worshipping community, based on God's past faithfulness to, and paradigm-shifting work with, David. Thus, we have suggested that the emphasis on a developed and complex Levitical corps serves a full-fledge rhetorical purpose within the flow of the Chronicler's Davidic narratives.

Based on these rhetorical observations, a few implications for further research may be noted. First, for example, the Levitical duty rosters in 1 Chr 23-27 occupy a basically central position in the second major unit of the Davidic narratives (chs. 22-29). A more precise understanding of the relationship between these core units (chs. 23-27) and the outer framing units (chs. 22 and chs. 28-29) could be further investigated. Also, there are a number of other places in the Chronicler's work (that is, in 2 Chronicles) where similar studies could be fruitful, to further reinforce the central role of pericopes focused on the ministry of the Levites at the temple, and the ensuing significance of proper, joyful worship envisaged by the Chronicler for his postexilic audience. We may note, for example, the text narrating the coming of the ark in the Solomonic temple proper, which includes a clear emphasis on the cultic support of Aaronides and non-Aaronide Levites (1 Chr 5:2-14). That is, the rhetorical structure of this unit could be further investigated, along with its relationship to the Solomonic narratives of 2 Chr

1–9. Also, the latter unit focused on the reign of Hezekiah (2 Chr 29–31) could also be investigated along these rhetorical methodological lines. Each of the chapters in this unit in 2 Chronicles emphasize, in different ways, the roles of the priests and Levites: at the restoration of temple worship (ch. 29), at the ensuing Passover celebration (ch. 30), and at the organization of the service of the priests and the Levites (ch. 31)

The Historical Aspect: Summary, Contribution, and Implications

The second major step of this work, in chapter four, entailed a focus on the historical aspect of the Chronicler's presentation of the Levites—at the time of David in the early first millennium. The control text for this section was 1 Chr 23, the first chapter in the formal duty rosters of 1 Chr 23–27. Chapter 23 focuses on the nature of the Levites' role in preparation for the establishment of the physical temple complex in Jerusalem. A number of scholars have argued that either all, or certain sections, of the duties laid out in this text should be seen as reflections of various (theoretically established) postexilic historical stages of Levitical ministry at the *second* temple.

However, in this work, we have sought to defend the historical *plausibility* of David's establishment of a more complex and carefully organized corps of Levites for temple service in the early first millennium. It was deemed possible, and indeed plausible, that the Chronicler could have based his narrative on trustworthy preexilic traditions related to David's expansion of Levitical duties at the *first* temple. This would further reinforce the salvation-historical impact of the Chronicler's work. Namely, from the Chronicler's perspective, as God was faithful to David in the preexilic past (in allowing him to fully organize and set up the crucial ministry for the Solomonic temple), so Yahweh would enable the postexilic generations to similarly organize their needed temple cult, and, most significantly, to renew their life as a worshiping community.

This historical argument was presented in two phases. First, the possibility of a cohesive reading of chapter 23, in the context of chapters 23—27 and of the literary frame of chapters 22 and 28–29, was proposed. That is, we argued that chapter 23 presents a historically understandable expansion of Levitical duty based on: (1) the obsolescence of the Levites' earlier tabernacle transportation duty, and (2) the requirements of the soon-to-be established Solomonic temple complex in Jerusalem. From a canonical perspective, and at least in chapter 23, the possibility of reading the data in this manner was suggested.

CONCLUSION

Second, the historical angle proposed for the reading of chapter 23 was further reinforced by (1) a contextual appeal to some of the relevant data in the ANE and (2) from the basis of a *maximalist* understanding of some of the basic archaeological data related to Jerusalem in the early first millennium. In this section, an approach to the contextual method in OT studies was first sketched out. The method adopted particularly emphasized the benefit of reflecting on the "common cognitive environment" (as seen in Walton's work) of the cultures of the ANE. On this basis, three aspects of the data from the ANE related to temples and clergy were synthesized, to further reinforce the historical plausibility of David's early first millennium establishment of a complex Levitical temple corps: (1) temples and temple structures, (2) temple rituals, priests and attendants, and (3) temple rituals and music, more specifically. Some data from each of the principle cultures from the ANE, from the third and second millennia as well, were considered for each of these categories.

On these bases, the following historically-focused conclusion was given: (1) it seems possible that the Chronicler's presentation of David's organization of the Levitical attendants—to include focused responsibilities at the temple (with significant music and worship duties) can be coherently read from the biblical text, in compositional and historical perspectives, and (2) the cognitive environment of the ANE further reveals the presence and influence of the historical realities of temple, temple attendants, and temple music, as early as the third and second millennia. Both of the aspects tend to reinforce the historical plausibility of the Chronicler's inherent claims regarding David's organization, and modification, of Levitical duty in the early united monarchy (of the early first millennium) in preparation for the ongoing worship ministries of the preexilic Solomonic temple.

The principle contribution of this phase of the study should then be viewed as twofold. First, unlike many studies related to 1 Chr 23–28, priority in the analysis was not given to theoretical suggestions related to postexilic Levitical developments. When 1 Chr 23, at least, is considered first from the basis of the data of the MT text as it stands, it seems possible to make some historical sense of it—both as it relates to the period of David, and as it functions rhetorically in the Chronicler's postexilic setting. The benefit of a canonical, textual approach to this passage was then suggested. Second, and also unlike many studies related to the complex nature of the Levitical ministry presented in 1 Chr 23 and other chapters in this context (such as chapters 24, 25, and 26), our study was further intent on interacting with some of the earlier contextual data related to ancient temple cults and their complex organizations, including musicians and other ritual attendants.

A major voice in ongoing Chronicles scholarship (especially when it comes to the Levites in Chronicles) is focused on historical-critical reconstructions of the postexilic period. An alternative approach is pointed to here. It relates to further investigating the relationship between the Chronicler's presentation of a developed Levitical ministry and much earlier and parallel contextual evidence. This suggests that, in fact, it is very well possible that in chapter 23, the Chronicler was reflecting on God's past involvement with David and the Levites at a high point in Israel's religious history, to further encourage his postexilic audience and to motivate his original audience towards a proper continuation of the central temple services in postexilic Jerusalem.

From these historical perspectives, two areas of further research might be suggested. This could serve to further strengthen this notion of the historical plausibility of David's expansion of the Levites' role at the first temple. First, building on some of the canonically-based theories of Levitical history discussed in chapter one, further work could be done towards elucidating the salvation-historical stages of the history of the non-Aaronide Levites and their relationship to the Aaronide priests. Second, further studies could also be done to better understand, from these perspectives, the relationship between the presentation of the Levites in the postexilic work of Ezra-Nehemiah and in the Chronicler's postexilic work. At different junctures in Ezra-Nehemiah, for example, we appear to have a strong historical consciousness of the founding role of David vis-à-vis certain groups of Levites, and of Asaph in particular for the musical Levites (such as in Ezra 3:10–11, or in Neh 12:26–46). The heritage of both David and Asaph play important roles in the reestablishment of worship in the postexilic period.

The Theological Aspect: Summary, Contribution, and Implications

The final stage of our study's overall argument included a reflection on the theological aspects of Levitical ministry in 1 Chronicles. The focus was especially on the theological nature of Levitical *song*. The intent here was to show how the inherent theological message of the psalm in 1 Chr 16 contributes effectively to certain theological trajectories in 1 Chr 10–29. The purpose was also to suggest how the theological emphases of the psalm of 1 Chr 16 intersects with the Levitical psalms of the Psalter. Hence, Ps 73, an Asaphite Levitical psalm, was chosen as a specific example for further exploration of the theology of Levitical song.

As noted above, the methodological matrix of "proclamation" and "promise" was used to flesh out the theological section of the study. The psalm of 1 Chr 16 was first investigated. A selection of studies on the structural and theological development of this text were discussed, as they have pointed out fruitful insights on its meaning and message. Subsequently, the exegetical structure of this psalm (both in relationship to its use of several canonical psalms from the Psalter and with respect to its final shape in Chronicles) was examined further to demonstrate that a high point in the text may be found in the *present-focused proclamation* of God's supreme rule over all peoples and all gods. This was seen as a key feature of the theological message of Levitical song: (1) in the primary context of the celebration of the ark coming to Jerusalem, when David ordered Asaph and his brethren to lead in celebration for the symbolic presence of Yahweh in Jerusalem, (2) in the larger context of the Chronicler's message to this postexilic audience of highlighting the truth of God's sovereignty, even in difficult circumstances, and (3) in the "extended" context of the present biblical reader, who is able to interact with both of these primary contexts, to appropriate the theological message of God's continuing rule in creation.

Second, by means of the hinge-text in 1 Chr 25, we shifted our discussion to the theological message of Ps 73. Specifically, we argued that his psalm, as one further example of (Asaphite) Levitical temple song, reveals an emphasis on divine "promise," with its accentuation, arguably, of a personal eschatological hope (even in the midst of the consciousness of the temporal prosperity of the wicked). In these ways, it was suggested from these two example texts that the *content* of Levitical song preserves a rich theological tradition, focused on the proclamation of divine rule and the promise of divine blessing. This reflection on the nature of Levitical song could then be seen as a main contribution to this aspect of the present study—especially as it develops the potential relationship between the psalm in 1 Chr 16 and the example of Ps 73.

In fact, further studies could be taken up in the area of the theological meaning of Levitical song specifically, and of the Levitical music ministry in Chronicles more generally. First, it could be helpful to further investigate in this manner the theological meaning of other short examples of Levitical song, such as 2 Chr 5:2–14 (the ministry of the priests and Levites at the dedication of the Solomonic temple), both in relationship to the message of Chronicles, and to further theological connections with the broader Levitical psalms in the Psalter.

Second, certain theological trajectories could also be pursued from the basis of Levitical service as it is presented in Chronicles, and as it then relates to other postexilic OT texts. For example, the role of the Levitical high priest

Joshua (יְהוֹשֻׁעַ) in Zechariah (chapter 3, for example), or the commentary on the faithfulness of the Levitical priests in Malachi (in sections of chapters 1 and 2, for example), could be further examined in this manner.

Third, theological connections between the meaning of Levitical ministry in Chronicles and certain NT texts could also be investigated. For instance, the theme of joyful song and/or proclamation being expressed at a key salvation-historical juncture could be typologically examined. That is, in 1 Chr 15 and 16, the Levites help God's people proclaim songs of joy and worship when the name of Yahweh comes to symbolically reside in Jerusalem. And significantly, the formal Levitical choir rotations, set up in 1 Chr 23 and 25, enable the *regular* proclamation of God's people at the temple complex.

Since Chronicles also emphasizes Davidic theology, it could be worthwhile to reflect further on the potential connection to the theological proclamation and *song* at the announcement of the coming of Jesus Christ, the Davidic king and Messiah, in the NT. For instance, in Luke 1, both Mary and Zechariah's songs poetically and prophetically proclaim the announcement of the birth of Jesus (see Luke 1:67, for example: καὶ Ζαχαρίας ὁ πατὴρ αὐτοῦ ἐπλήσθη πνεύματος ἁγίου καὶ ἐπροφήτευσεν λέγων). Further in Luke 2, the angels also proclaim praise and worship, along with the shepherds near Bethlehem, as does Simeon at the temple (the temple location in itself seems to be significant), who blesses the Lord for the coming of his salvation for Jews and Gentiles alike (see Luke 2:43, for instance, at the end of Simeon's words to the Lord: φῶς εἰς ἀποκάλυψιν ἐθνῶν καὶ δόξαν λαοῦ σου Ἰσραήλ). The potential fruitful relationship between the messianic overtones of the temple services in the OT texts of Chronicles and the fulfillment of these aspects by Jesus himself is suggested here.

Finally, and from a more practical perspective, it seems that the theology and practice of church worship could be further strengthened with a greater appreciation for, and a proper appropriation of, the meaning and function of Levitical temple-service as the Chronicler presents it. From an OT perspective, the Chronicler shows that as God's people gathered in the special setting of the temple complex, the Levites were carefully organized religious leaders who enabled *exuberant* and *joyful* worship of the gathered community, but also within a *carefully* and *respectfully* understood sense of sacred space and sacred time.

In this way, the presentation of OT Levitical song could provide further theological and practical bases for the gathering of God's NT people in the context of the worshipping church community. That is, the song of God's people could be viewed as a rich "whole-Bible" theme that calls for continued theological reflection and application within the life of the church. The contribution of song to the worship of God's people, which is presented as an eternal activity of the church in the NT, could then be more valued and carefully understood. As Nicholls wrote, "[w]orship is the supreme and only indispensable activity of the church. It alone will endure . . . into heaven when all other activities will have passed away."[1]

For example, Asaphite Ps 81 encourages the worshiper to strongly raise a song to Yahweh (MT 81:2 הרנינו לאלהים עוזנו הריעו לאלהי יעקב) and, more generally, in Isa 51, the "voice of song" (v. 3, קול זמרה) is seen as one component of God's comfort to his people. In the NT, Paul makes it clear that song ought to play an important part for the life of God's people in the church—along with the ministry of the Word (note especially Col 3:16: Ὁ λόγος τοῦ Χριστοῦ ἐνοικείτω ἐν ὑμῖν πλουσίως, ἐν πάσῃ σοφίᾳ διδάσκοντες καὶ νουθετοῦντες ἑαυτούς, ψαλμοῖς ὕμνοις ᾠδαῖς πνευματικαῖς ἐν τῇ χάριτι ᾄδοντες ἐν ταῖς καρδίαις ὑμῶν τῷ θεῷ). Furthermore, we remember that in the new heaven and the new earth, song, indeed, represents an integral part of the praise of God's people. In the end, a "new song" will be proclaimed in the new creation (Rev 5:9a: καὶ ᾄδουσιν ᾠδὴν καινὴν λέγοντες· ἄξιος εἶ λαβεῖν τὸ βιβλίον), as there will also be intense proclamation of joy and gratitude on the part of God's saints (Rev 19:1: μετὰ ταῦτα ἤκουσα ὡς φωνὴν μεγάλην ὄχλου πολλοῦ ἐν τῷ οὐρανῷ λεγόντων· ἁλληλουϊά·ἡ σωτηρία καὶ ἡ δόξα καὶ ἡ δύναμις τοῦ θεοῦ ἡμῶν). Ultimately, this final song of God's people may be understood as one key theological fulfillment of the proclamation and promise of OT Levitical song.

---

1. Nicholls, *Jacob's Ladder*, 9, as cited in Engle, *Baker's Worship Handbook*, 15.

Appendix

A Rhetorical-Critical Outline of 1 Chronicles 15:1—16:3

SECTION A: 1 Chr 15:1–3
David's Preparations
<u>Narrative</u>
three wayyiqtol forms with David as subject, v. 1

ויעש לו בתים בעיר דויד
ויכן מקום לארון האלהים
ויט לו אהל

David's Proclamation
<u>Direct Discourse</u>
v. 2

אז אמר דויד
Core assertion
לא לשאת את ארון האלהים כי אם הלוים
Warrant
כי בם בחר יהוה לשאת את ארון יהוה ולשרתו עד עולם

David's Gathering
<u>Narrative</u>
wayyiqtol with David as subject
v. 3

ויקהל דויד
Nature and location of gathering
את כל ישראל
אל ירושלם
Purpose of gathering:
להעלות את ארון יהוה
אל מקומו
אשר הכין לו

SECTION B: 1 Chr 15:4–15
David's <u>first</u> action: Gathering the tribe of Levi
<u>Narrative</u>
wayyiqtol with David as subject
v. 4

ויאסף דויד
General object: Aaronites and (non-Aaronite) Levites
את בני אהרן
ואת הלוים

Genealogical list
Vv. 5–7: Three major non-Aaronite clans of the tribe of Levi and their leaders
First level of genealogical specification

לבני קהת
אוריאל השר ואחיו מאה ועשרים
לבני מררי
עשיה השר ואחיו מאתים ועשוׄיׄם
לבני גרשום
יואל השר ואחיו מאה ושלשים

Vv. 8–10: Three major sub-clans of Kohath and their leaders
Second level of genealogical specification

לבני אליצפן
שמעיה השר ואחיו מאתים
לבני חברון
אליאל השר ואחיו שמונים
לבני עזיאל
עמינדב השר ואחיו מאה ושנים עשר

APPENDIX: A RHETORICAL-CRITICAL OUTLINE OF 1 CHR 15:1—16:3

David's <u>second</u> action: Calling forth the Levitical leaders
Narrative
wayyiqtol with David as subject
V. 11

ויקרא דויד
לצדוק ולאביתר הכהנים
וללוים לאוריאל עשיה ויואל שמעיה ואליאל ועמינדב

David's <u>third</u> action: Commanding the Levitical leaders
<u>Direct discourse</u>
V. 12

ויאמר להם
Supporting assertion
אתם ראשי האבות ללוים
Dual command
התקדשו אתם ואחיכם
והעליתם את ארון יהוה אלהי ישראל אל הכינותי לו

Dual warrant
V. 13

כי למבראשונה לא אתם
פרץ יהוה אלהינו בנו
כי לא דרשנהו כמשפט

Levitical response—stage 1: Consecration
<u>Narrative</u>
V. 14

ויתקדשו הכהנים והלוים
Purpose of consecration
להעלות את ארון יהוה אלהי ישראל

Levitical response—stage 2: Transportation
V. 15

וישאו בני הלוים
Object of transportation
את ארון האלהים
Dual warrant for transportation
כאשר צוה משה
כדבר יהוה בכתפם במטות עליהם

SECTION C: 1 Chr 15–24
David's <u>command</u> for the Levitical musical service
Narrative
v. 16

ויאמר דויד
Object of command
לשרי הלוים
Purpose of command
להעמיד את אחיהם המשררים
Nature of the appointment
General means
בכלי שיר
Specific means
נבלים וכנרות ומצלתים
Purpose
משמיעים להרים בקול לשמחה

Levitical <u>response</u>: Institution of leaders and duties
Leaders
3 principle musical leaders
<u>Narrative comment</u> (*wayyiqtol*)
v. 17

יעמידו הלוים
את הימן בן יואל
ומן אחיו אסף בן ברכיהו ס
ומן בני מררי אחיהם איתן בן קושיהו

Second order leaders: Levitical brothers
v. 18

ועמהם אחיהם המשנים
זכריהו בן ויעזיאל
ושמירמות
ויחיאל
וענִי אליאב
ובניהו
ומעשיהו
ומתתיהו
ואליפלהו
ומקניהו
ועבד אדם
ויעיאל השערים

Six-fold duties (five non-Aaronite Levitical duties; one Aaronite duty)
1. Three principal leaders on *cymbals* (following names in v. 17)
V. 19

והמשררים
הימן אסף ואיתן במצלתים נחשת להשמיע

---

2. First set of Levitical brothers on *harps* (following names in v. 18a)
V. 20

וזכריה ועזיאל ושמירמות ויחיאל וענִי ואליאב ומעשיהו ובניהו
בנבלים על עלמות

---

3. Second set of Levitical brothers on *lyres* (following names in v. 18b + Azaziah)
V. 21

ומתתיהו ואליפלהו ומקניהו ועבד אדם ויעיאל ועזיהו
בכנרות
על השמינית לנצח

---

4. One skilled and principal Levitical musical director
V. 22

וכנניהו שר הלוים במשא יסרבמשא
כי מבין הוא

5. Two Levitical ark gatekeepers
v. 23

וברכיה ואלקנה
שערים לארון

6. Seven Aaronite ark trumpet players
vv. 24a

ושבניהו ויושפט ונתנאל ועמשי וזכריהו ובניהו ואליעזר הכהנים מחצצרים
בחצצרות לפני ארון האלהים

5'. Two further ark gatekeepers
v. 24b

ועבד אדם ויחיה שערים לארון

SECTION B': 1 Chr 15:25–29
Framed by three *wayyiqtol forms of* היה

1. Preparations for the procession—stage 1: movement to the ark (to Obed-Edom)
<u>Narrative movement</u>
v. 25

ויהי דויד וזקני ישראל ושרי האלפים
ההלכים להעלות
את ארון ברית יהוה
מן בית עבד אדם בשמחה

2. Preparations for the procession—stage 2: celebratory sacrifices and music
<u>Narrative movement</u>
v. 26

ויהי בעזר האלהים
את הלוים נשאי ארון ברית יהוה
ויזבחו שבעה פרים ושבעה אילים

<u>Narrative background description</u> (*waw* + <u>non-verbal</u>)
v. 27

ודויד מכרבל במעיל בוץ
וכל הלוים
הנשאים את הארון
והמשררים
וכניה השר המשא המשררים
ועל דויד אפוד בד

v. 28

וכל ישראל
מעלים
את ארון ברית יהוה
בתרועה ובקול שופר ובחצצרות ובמצלתים משמעים בנבלים וכנרות

3. Execution of the procession
<u>Narrative movement</u>
v. 29

ויהי ארון ברית יהוה
בא
עיר דויד עד

Narrative background description (*waw* + non-verbal):

ומיכל בת שאול
נשקפה בעד החלון

<u>Narrative movement:</u>

ותרא את המלך דויד מרקד ומשחק
ותבז לו בלבה

SECTION A': 1 Chr 16:1–3
The ark arrives in Jerusalem: Broad focus
<u>Narrative movement: three *wayyiqtol* forms with plural subject</u>
16:1

ויביאו
את ארון האלהים
ויציגו
אתו
בתוך האהל אשר נטה לו דויד
ויקריבו
עלות ושלמים
לפני האלהים

Celebration at the ark in Jerusalem: Narrower focus
Narrative movement: three *wayyiqtol* forms with singular subject
vv. 2–3

ויכל דויד
מהעלות העלה והשלמים
ויברך
את העם
בשם יהוה
ויחלק
לכל איש ישראל
מאיש ועד אשה לאיש ככר לחם ואשפר ואשישה

Bibliography

Abadie, Philippe. "David, innocent ou coupable? Nouveau regard sur 1 Chronique 21." *Foi et vie* 96 (1997) 73-83.

———. "From the Impious Manasseh (2 Kings 21) to the Convert Manasseh (2 Chronicles 33): Theological Rewriting by the Chronicler." In *CaT* 89-104.

———. "La figure de David dans le livre des Chroniques." In *Figures de David à travers la Bible*, edited by L. Desrousseaux and J. Vermeylen, 156-86. Paris: Cerf, 1999.

Abba, R. "Priests and Levites." In *IDB* 2:876-91.

———. "Priests and Levites in Deuteronomy." *VT* 27 (1977) 257-67.

———. "Priests and Levites in Ezekiel." *VT* 28 (1978) 1-9.

Abraham, William J. *Divine Revelation and the Limits of Historical Criticism*. Oxford: Oxford University Press, 1982.

Abrams, M. H. *The Mirror and the Lamp: Romantic Theory and the Critical Tradition*. Oxford: Oxford University Press, 1953.

Ackroyd, Peter R. *I & II Chronicles, Ezra, Nehemiah*. London: SCM, 1973.

———. *The Chronicler in His Age*. JSOTSup 101. Sheffield: JSOT Press, 1991.

———. *Exile and Restoration: A Study of the Sixth Century B.C*. OTL. Philadelphia: Westminster, 1968.

———. "Faith and Its Reformulation in The Post-Exilic Period: II. Prophetic Material." *Theology Digest* 27 (1979) 335-46.

———. "History and Theology in the Writings of the Chronicler." *CTM* 38 (1967) 501-15.

Adam, A. K. M. *Reading Scripture with the Church: Toward a Hermeneutic for Theological Interpretation*. Grand Rapids: Baker, 2006.

Adam, P. J. H. "Preaching and Biblical Theology." In *NDBT* 104-12.

Adler, Joshua J. "David's Last Sin: Was It the Census?" *Jewish Bible Quarterly* 23 (1995) 91-95.

Ahlström, Gösta W. *Ancient Palestine: A Historical Introduction*. Facets. Minneapolis: Fortress, 2002.

———. *Aspects of Syncretism in Israelite Religion*. Horae Soederblomianae 5. Lund: Gleerup, 1963.

———. *The History of Ancient Palestine*. 2nd ed. Minneapolis: Fortress, 1994.

———. *Royal Administration and National Religion in Ancient Palestine*. Studies in the History of the Ancient Near East 1. Leiden: Brill, 1982.

———. *Who Were the Israelites?* Winona Lake: Eisenbrauns, 1986.
Ahn, Suk-il. *The Persuasive Appeal of David and Solomon in Chronicles: A Rhetorical Analysis of the Speeches and Prayers in the David-Solomon Narrative*. McMaster Biblical Studies Series 3. Eugene: Pickwick, 2018.
Albertz, Rainer. *A History of Israelite Religion in the Old Testament Period. Volume I: From the Beginnings to the End of the Monarchy*. Translated by John Bowden. OTL. Louisville: Westminster John Knox, 1994.
Alexander, T. Desmond. *From Paradise to the Promise Land: An Introduction to the Pentateuch*. 3rd ed. Grand Rapids: Baker, 2012.
———. "The Psalms and the Afterlife." *Irish Biblical Studies* 9 (1987) 2–17.
Allan, M. W. T. "The Priesthood in Ancient Israel with Special Reference to the Status and Function of the Levites." PhD diss., University of Glasgow, 1971.
Allen, Leslie C. *1, 2 Chronicles*. Nashville: Nelson, 1987.
———. "The First and Second Books of Chronicles: Introduction, Commentary, and Reflections." In *NIB* 3:299–659.
———. *The Greek Chronicles: The Relation of the Septuagint of I and II Chronicles to the Massoretic Text*. VTSup 25. Leiden: Brill, 1974.
———. "Kerygmatic Units in 1 & 2 Chronicles." *JSOT* 41 (1988) 21–36.
———. "Psalm 73: An Analysis." *TynBul* 33 (1982) 93–107.
———. "The Structuring of Ezekiel's Revisionist History Lesson (Ezekiel 20:3–31)." *CBQ* 54 (1992) 448–63.
Allen, Lindsay. *The Persian Empire*. Chicago: University of Chicago Press, 2005.
Alster, Baruch. "Narrative Surprise in Biblical Parallels." *BibInt* 14 (2006) 456–85.
Alter, Robert. *The Art of Biblical Narrative*. New York: Basic, 1981.
———. *The Art of Biblical Poetry*. New York: Basic, 1985.
Amador, J. D. H. "Where Could Rhetorical Criticism (Still) Take Us?" *Currents in Research: Biblical Studies* 7 (1999) 195–222.
Ameriks, Karl. "The Critique of Metaphysics: The Structure and Fate of Kant's Dialectic." In *The Cambridge Companion to Kant and Modern Philosophy*, edited by Paul Guyer, 269–302. Cambridge: Cambridge University Press, 2006.
Anbar, Moshé. "'Joab fils de Cerouya monta le premier' (1Ch 11:6) à la lumière des archives royales de Mari." *Ugarit-Forschungen* 32 (2000) 23–26.
Anderson, Bernard W. "Introduction: The New Frontier of Rhetorical Criticism: A Tribute to James Muilenburg." In *Rhetorical Criticism: Essays in Honor of James Muilenburg*, edited by Jared J. Jackson and Martin Kessler, ix–xvii. Pittsburgh: Pickwick, 1974.
Anderson, Robert D. "Music and Dance in Pharaonic Egypt." In *CANE* 4:2555–68.
Anderson, Bernhard W. *Contours of Old Testament Theology*. Minneapolis: Fortress, 1999.
Anderson, Gary A. "The Praise of God as Cultic Event." In *Priesthood and Cult in Ancient Israel*, edited by Gary A. Anderson and Saul M. Solyan, 15–33. JSOTSup 125. Sheffield: Sheffield Academic, 1991.
Anderson, Gary A., and Saul M. Olyan. *Priesthood and Cult in Ancient Israel*. JSOTSup 125. Sheffield: JSOT Press, 1991.
Anderson, Hugh. *Historians of Israel: 1 and 2 Chronicles, Ezra, Nehemiah*. Bible Studies 6. New York: Abingdon, 1962.
Ankersmit, F. R. "Historiography and Postmodernism." *History and Theory* 28 (1989) 137–53.

Archi, Alfonson. "Hittite and Hurrian Literatures: An Overview." In *CANE* 4:2367–77.
Aristotle. *The "Art" of Rhetoric*. Edited by Jeffrey Henderson. Translated by J. Henry Freese. Loeb Classical Library 193. Cambridge: Harvard University Press, 1926.
Arnold, Bill T. "Pentateuchal Criticism, History of." In *DOTP* 622–31.
———. "Religion in Ancient Israel." In *FAOTS* 391–420.
Arnold, Bill T., and Richard S. Hess, eds. *Ancient Israel's History: An Introduction to Issues and Sources*. Grand Rapids: Baker, 2014.
Assman, Jan. *The Search for God in Ancient Egypt*. Translated by David Orton. Ithaca: Cornell University Press, 2001.
Aron, Raymond. *Introduction à la philosophie de l'histoire: Essai sur les limites de l'objectivité historique*. Bibliothèque des idées. 4th ed. Paris: Gallimard, 1938.
Asension, Félix. "Una faceta bíblica del acercamiento humano-divino en el A. Testamento." *Estudios Biblicos* 36 (1977) 5–19.
Ash, Paul S. *David, Solomon and Egypt: A Reassessment*. JSOTSup 297. Sheffield: Sheffield Academic, 1999.
Auffret, Pierre. "Merveilles à nos yeux: Étude structurelle de vingt psaumes dont celui de 1 Ch 16, 8–36." BZAW 235. Berlin: de Gruyter, 1995.
Aufrecht, Walter E. "Genealogy and History in Ancient Israel." In *Ascribe to the Lord: Biblical and Other Studies in Memory of Peter C. Craigie*, edited by Lyle M. Eslinger and J. Glen Taylor, 205–35. JSOTSup 67. Sheffield: JSOT Press, 1988.
Augustine, Saint. *On Christian Doctrine*. Edited by D. W. Robertson Jr. Library of Liberal Arts. Upper Saddle River: Prentice Hall, 1997.
Auld, A. Graeme. *Kings Without Privilege: David and Moses in the Story of the Bible's Kings*. Edinburgh: T&T Clark, 1994.
———. "Prophets Shared—But Recycled." In *The Future of the Deuteronomistic History*, edited by Thomas Römer, 19–28. Bibliotheca Ephemeridum Theologicarum Lovaniensium 147. Leuven: Peeters, 2000.
———. "Salomo und die Deuteronomisten—eine Zukunftsvision." *Theologische Zeitschrift* 48 (1992) 343–55.
———. "What was the Main Source of the Books of Chronicles?" In *ChrA* 91–99.
Austel, Hermann. "The United Monarchy: Archaeological and Literary Issues." In *GtS* 160–78.
Averbeck, Richard E. "Ancient Near Eastern Mythography as It Relates to Historiography in the Hebrew Bible: Genesis 3 and the Cosmic Battle." In *The Future of Biblical Archaeology: Reassessing Methodologies and Assumptions*, edited by James K. Hoffmeier and A. R. Millard, 328–56. Grand Rapids: Eerdmans, 2004.
———. "The Cylinders of Gudea." In *COS* 2:417–33.
———. "Factors in Reading the Patriarchal Narratives: Literary, Historical, and Theological Dimensions." In *GtS* 115–37.
———. "Leviticus: Theology of." In *NIDOTTE* 4:907–23.
———. "מִקְדָּשׁ." In *NIDOTTE* 2:1071–79.
———. "Sacrifices and Offerings." In *DOTP* 706–33.
———. "Sumer, the Bible, and Comparative Method: Historiography and Temple Building." In *Mesopotamia and the Bible: Comparative Explorations*, edited by Mark W. Chavalas and K. Lawson Younger Jr., 88–125. Grand Rapids: Baker, 2002.
———. "The Sumerian Historiographic Tradition and Its Implications for Genesis 1–11." In *FTH* 79–102.
———. "Tabernacle." In *DTOP* 807–27.

Bae, Hee-Sook. *Vereinte Suche nach JHWH: Die Hiskianische und Josianische Reform in der Chronik.* BZAW 355. Berlin: de Gruyter, 2005.
Bailey, Moses. "The Reliability of the Chronicler as a Jewish Historian for the Persian Period." PhD diss., Boston University, 1926.
Bailey, Noel. "David and God in 1 Chronicles 21: Edged with Mist." In *ChrA* 337–59.
———. "David's Innocence: A Response to J. Wright." *JSOT* 64 (1994) 83–90.
Baker, D. L. *Two Testaments, One Bible: A Study of the Theological Relationship Between the Old & New Testaments.* Revised ed. Downers Grove: InterVarsity Press, 1991.
Baker, David W. "Source Criticism." In *DOTP* 798–805.
Ball, Ivan Jay. "Additions to a Bibliography of James Muilenburg's Writings." In *Rhetorical Criticism: Essays in Honor of James Muilenburg*, edited by Jared J. Jackson and Martin Kessler, 285–87. Pittsburgh: Pickwick, 1974.
Balla, P. "Challenges to Biblical Theology." In *NDBT* 20–27.
Balzaretti, Claudio. *I Libre delle Cronache.* Guide Spirituali All'Antico Testamento. Rome: Città Nuova, 2001.
Bar-Efrat, Shimon. *Narrative Art in the Bible.* Sheffield: Sheffield Academic, 1989.
———. "Some Observations on the Analysis of Structure in Biblical Narrative." *VT* 30 (1980) 154–73.
Barilli, Renato. *Rhetoric.* Theory and History of Literature 63. Minneapolis: University of Minnesota Press, 1989.
Barker, David G. "The Theology of the Chronicler: A Synoptic Investigation of 1 Chronicles 13, 15–17 and 2 Samuel 6–7." ThD diss., Grace Theological Seminary, 1984.
Barnes, William Emery. *The Books of Chronicles, with Maps, Notes, and Introduction.* The Cambridge Bible for Schools and Colleges. Cambridge: Cambridge University Press, 1899.
Barnes, William Hamilton. "Non-Synoptic Chronological References in the Books of Chronicles." In *CaH* 106–31.
Barr, James. *The Concept of Biblical Theology: An Old Testament Perspective.* Minneapolis: Fortress, 1999.
———. *History and Ideology in the Old Testament: Biblical Studies at the End of a Millennium.* Oxford: Oxford University Press, 2000.
———. *The Semantics of Biblical Language.* Oxford: Oxford University Press, 1961.
———. "The Theological Case Against Biblical Theology." In *Canon, Theology, and Old Testament Interpretation: Essays in Honor of Brevard S. Childs*, edited by Gene M. Tucker et al., 3–19. Philadelphia: Fortress, 1988.
Barrois, Georges. "The Notion of Historicity and the Critical Study of the Old Testament." *Greek Orthodox Theological Review* 19 (1974) 7–22.
Barstad, Hans M. "History and the Hebrew Bible." In *Can a 'History of Israel' Be Written?*, edited by Lester L. Grabbe, 37–64. European Seminar in Historical Methodology 1. Sheffield: Sheffield Academic, 1997.
Barthélemy, Dominique. *Critique textuelle de l'Ancien Testament. 1. Josué, Juges, Ruth, Samuel, Rois, Chroniques, Esdras, Néhémie, Esther.* Orbis Biblicus et Orientalis 50/1. Göttingen: Vandenhoeck & Ruprecht, 1982.
Barthes, Roland. *Image, Music, Text.* Translated by Stephen Heath. New York: Hill & Wang, 1977.
Bartholomew, Craig G. "Biblical Theology." In *DTIB* 84–90.

Bartlet, Andrew H. *The Book Around Immanuel: Style and Structure in Isaiah 2-12*. Biblical and Judaic Studies 4. Winona Lake: Eisenbrauns, 1996.

Barton, John. *Reading the Old Testament: Method in Biblical Study*. Louisville: Westminster John Knox, 1996.

Bathja, Bayer. "The Mesopotamian Theory of Music and the Ugarit Notation: A Reexamination." In *Music in Antiquity: The Near East and the Mediterranean*, edited by Joan Goodnick et al., 15-91. Berlin: de Gruyter, 2014.

Baudissin, Wolf. W. W. *Die Geschichte des altestamentlichen Priesterhums*. Leipzig: S. Hirzel, 1889.

Bauer, Georg Lorenz. *Theologie des Alten Testaments, oder, Abriss der religiösen Begriffe der alten Hebräer*. Leipzig: Weygand, 1796.

———. *The Theology of the Old Testament, or, A Biblical Sketch of the Religious Opinions of the Ancient Hebrews*. London: Fox, 1838.

Beale, G. K., ed. *The Right Doctrine from the Wrong Texts? Essays on the Use of the Old Testament in the New*. Grand Rapids: Baker, 1994.

Beaucamp, Évode. *Le Psautier 2: Ps. 73-150*. Sources Bibliques. Paris: Gabalda, 1979.

Becker, Joachim. *2 Chronik*. Die Neue Echter Bibel 20. Würzburg: Echter, 1988.

———. "'Söhne' oder 'Bauleute' der Atalja in 2 Chr 24,7?" *BN* 111 (2002) 5-11.

Becking, Bob. "Continuity and Discontinuity After the Exile: Some Introductory Remarks." In *Crisis of Israelite Religion: Transformation of Religious Tradition in Exilic and Post-Exilic Times*, edited by Bob Becking and Marjo C. A. Korpel, 1-8. Leiden: Brill, 1999.

Beckwith, R. T. "The Canon of Scripture." In *DTIB* 27-34.

Beentjes, Pancratius C. "Jerusalem in the Book of Chronicles." In *Centrality of Jerusalem: Historical Perspectives*, edited by Marcel Poorthuis and Safrai Chana, 15-28. Kampen: Kok Pharos, 1996.

———. "Prophets in the Book of Chronicles." In *The Elusive Prophet: The Prophet as a Historical Person, Literary Character and Anonymous Artist*, edited by Johannes Cornelis de Moor, 45-53. Oudtestamentische Studiën 45. Leiden: Brill, 2001.

———. "Tradition and Transformation: Aspects of Innerbiblical Interpretation in 2 Chronicles 20." *Bib* 74 (1993) 258-68.

———. "Transformations of Space and Time: Nathan's Oracle and David's Prayer in 1 Chronicles 17." In *Sanctity of Time and Space in Tradition and Modernity*, edited by Alberdina Houtman et al., 27-44. Jewish and Christian Perspectives Series 1. Leiden: Brill, 1998.

Begg, Christopher, and Flavius Josephus. *Josephus' Account of the Early Divided Monarchy*. Bibliotheca Ephemeridum Theologicarum Lovaniensium 108. Leuven: Leuven University Press, 1993.

———. *Josephus' Story of the Later Monarchy*. Bibliotheca Ephemeridum Theologicarum Lovaniensium 145. Leuven: Leuven University Press, 2000.

Begg, Christopher T. "David's Capture of Jebus and Its Sequels According to Josephus: Ant 7, 60b-70." *Ephemerides theologicae Lovanienses* 74 (1998) 93-108.

———. "David's Initial Philistine Victories According to Josephus." *Skrif en kerk* 20 (1999) 1-14.

———. "The Levites in Josephus." *Hebrew Union College Annual* 75 (2004) 1-22.

Beitzel, Barry J. *The New Moody Atlas of the Bible*. Chicago: Moody, 2009.

Bell, Robert D. "The Theology of the Book of Chronicles." *Biblical Viewpoint* 38 (2004) 53-60.

Ben Zvi, Ehud. "A Gateway to the Chronicler's Teaching: The Account of the Reign of Ahaz in 2 Chr 28,1–27." *Scandinavian Journal of the Old Testament* 7 (1993) 216–49.

———. *History, Literature, and Theology in the Book of Chronicles*. London: Oakville, 2006.

———. "Shifting the Gaze: Historiographic Constraints in Chronicles and Their Implications." In *The Land that I Will Show You: Essays on the History and Archaeology of the Ancient Near East in Honor of J. Maxwell Miller*, edited by J. Andrew Dearman and M. Patrick Graham, 38–60. JSOTSup 343. Sheffield: Sheffield Academic, 2001.

Bennett, W. H. *An Exposition of the Books of Chronicles*. London: Armstrong, 1908. Reprint, Minneapolis: Klock & Klock, 1983.

Benzinger, I. *Die Bücher der Chronik*. Kurzer Hand-Commentar zum Alten Testament 20. Tübingen: Mohr, 1901.

Berger, Yitzhak. "Chiasm and Meaning in 1 Chronicles." *The Journal of Hebrew Scriptures* 14 (2014) 1–28.

Berquist, Jon L. "The Social Context of Postexilic Judaism." In *Passion, Vitality, and Foment: The Dynamics of Second Temple Judaism*, edited by Lamontte M. Luker, 20–54. Harrisburg: Trinity, 2001.

Berry, George R. "Priests and Levites." *JBL* 42 (1923) 227–38.

Bertheau, Ernst. *Die Bücher der Chronik*. Kurzgefasstes exegetisches Handbuch zum Alten Testament 15. 2nd ed. Leipzig: Hirzel, 1873.

Bertholet, Alfred, and W. Robertson Smith. "Levites." In *Encyclopædia Biblica: A Critical Dictionary of the Literary Political and Religious History, the Archeology, Geography, and Natural History of the Bible*, edited by T. K. Cheyne and J. Sutherland Black, 3:2770–76. 10 vols. New York: MacMillan, 1902.

Biberfeld, Heinrich. *Der Übergang des levitischen Dienstgehaltes auf die Priester, eine historich-kritische Untersuchung*. Berlin: Itzkowski, 1888.

Biran, Avraham, and Joseph Naveh. "An Aramaic Stele Fragment from Tel Dan." *Israel Exploration Journal* 45 (1993) 81–98.

———. "The Tel Dan Inscription: A New Fragment." *Israel Exploration Journal* 45 (1995) 1–18.

Birkeland, Harris. "Chief Problems of Ps 73:17ff." *ZAW* 67 (1955) 99–103.

Bizell, Patricia, and Bruce Herzberg. "General Introduction." In *The Rhetorical Tradition: Readings from Classical Times to the Present*, edited by Patricia Bizell and Bruce Herzberg, 1–15. Boston: St. Martin's, 1990.

Blenkinsopp, Joseph. *Ezekiel*. Interpretation: A Bible Commentary for Teaching and Preaching. Louisville: John Knox, 1990.

———. *Sage, Priest, Prophet: Religious and Intellectual Leadership in Ancient Israel*. Louisville: Westminster John Knox, 1995.

———. "Wisdom in the Chronicler's Work." In *In Search of Wisdom: Essays in Memory of John G. Gammie*, edited by John G. Gammie et al., 19–30. Louisville: Westminster John Knox, 1993.

Block, Daniel I. *The Book of Ezekiel: Chapters 25–48*. NICOT. Grand Rapids: Eerdmans, 1998.

———. *For the Glory of God: Recovering a Biblical Theology of Worship*. Grand Rapids: Baker, 2014.

———. "Tell Me the Old, Old Story: Preaching the Message of Old Testament Narrative." In *GtS* 409–38. Grand Rapids: Kregel, 2003.
Blomberg, C. L. "The Unity and Diversity of the Old Testament." In *DTIB* 364–72.
Bloomquist, L. Gregory. "A Possible Direction for Providing Programmatic Correlations of Textures in Socio-Rhetorical Analysis." In *Rhetorical Criticism and the Bible*, edited by Stanley E. Porter and Dennis L. Stamps, 61–96. JSNTSup 195. London: Sheffield Academic, 2002.
Boda, Mark J. *1–2 Chronicles*. Cornerstone Biblical Commentary 5a. Carol Stream: Tyndale, 2010.
———. *The Heartbeat of Old Testament Theology: Three Creedal Expressions*. Acadia Studies in Bible and Theology. Grand Rapids: Baker, 2017.
———. "Gazing Through the Cloud of Incense: Davidic Dynasty and Temple Community in the Chronicler's Perspective." In *CtC* 215–45.
———. "Reenvisioning the Relationship: Covenant in Chronicles." In *Covenant in the Persian Period: From Genesis to Chronicles*, edited by Richard J. Bautch and Gary N. Knoppers, 391–406. Winona Lake: Eisenbrauns, 2015.
Bodner, Keith. "Reading the Lists: Several Recent Studies of the Chronicler's Genealogies." In *CtC* 29–42.
Boer, Roland T. "Utopian Politics in 2 Chronicles 10–13." In *ChrA* 360–94.
Böhler, Dieter. "Das Gottesvolk als Altargemeinschaft. Die Bedeutung des Tempels für die Konstituierung kollektiver Identität nach Esra-Nehemia." In *Gottesstadt und Gottesgarten: Zu Geschichte und Theologie des Jerusalemer Tempel*, edited by Othmaar Keel and Erich Zenger, 207–30. Quaestiones Disputatae 191. Freiburg: Herder, 2002.
Bolin, Thomas M. "History, Historiography, and the Use of the Past in the Hebrew Bible." In *The Limits of Historiography: Genre and Narrative in Ancient Historical Texts*, edited by Christina Shuttleworth Kraus, 113–40. Mnemosyne, bibliotheca classica Batava: Supplementum 191. Leiden: Brill, 1999.
Bonneau, Normand. "Socio-Rhetorical Interpretations' 'Narrational Texture' in Dialogue with Narratology." *Theoforum* 46 (2015) 3–52.
Bottéro, Jean. "Akkadian Literature: An Overview." In *CANE* 4:2293–303.
Bowman, Craig D. "An Analysis of the Chronicler's Use of Sources: Methodological Concerns and Criteria." PhD diss., Princeton Theological Seminary, 1997.
Brandes, Heinr. *Die Königsreihen von Juda und Israel nach den biblischen Berichten und den Keilinschriften*. Leipzig: Edelmann, 1873.
Bratcher, Robert G. "Where Was David? A Note on 2 Samuel 7.18 and 1 Chronicles 17.16." *Bible Translator* 52 (2001) 440–41.
Bräumer, Hansjörg. *Das zweite Buch der Chronik*. Wuppertal: Brockhaus, 2000.
Braun, Joachim. "Music and the Bible." *Analecta Bruxellensia* 12 (2007) 7–19.
———. *Music in Ancient Israel/Palestine: Archeological, Written, and Comparative Sources*. The Bible in Its World. Grand Rapids: Eerdmans, 2002.
Braun, Roddy. *1 Chronicles*. WBC 14. Waco: Word, 1986.
———. "1 Chronicles 1–9 and the Reconstruction of the History of Israel: Thoughts on the Use of Genealogical Data in Chronicles in the Reconstruction of the History of Israel." In *CaH* 92–105.
———. "Chronicles, Ezra, and Nehemiah: Theology and Literary History." In *Studies in the Historical Books of the Old Testament*, edited by J. A. Emerton, 53–64. VTSup 30. Leiden: Brill, 1979.

———. "Cyrus in Second and Third Isaiah, Chronicles, Ezra and Nehemiah." In *CaT* 146–64.

———. "The Message of Chronicles: Rally 'Round the Temple." *CTM* 42 (1971) 502–14.

———. "The Significance of 1 Chronicles 22, 28, 29 for the Structure and Theology of the Work of the Chronicler." ThD diss., Concordia Seminary, 1971.

———. *Understanding the Basic Themes of 1, 2 Chronicles*. Dallas: Word, 1991.

Braw, J. D. "Vision as Revision: Ranke and the Beginning of Modern History." *History and Theory* 46 (2007) 45–60.

Brett, Marc G. "The Future of Old Testament Theology." 469–88 in *Congress Volume: Oslo 1998*, edited by A. Lemaire and M. Sæbø. VTSup. Leiden: Brill, 2000.

Brett, Mark G. *Biblical Criticism in Crisis? The Impact of the Canonical Approach on Old Testament Studies*. Cambridge: Cambridge University Press, 1991.

Brettler, Marc Zvi. *The Creation of History in Ancient Israel*. New York: Routledge, 1995.

———. "From the Deuteronomist(s) to the Chronicler: Continuities and Innovations." In *Proceedings of the Eleventh World Congress of Jewish Studies, Div. A: The Bible and the World*, edited by David Assaf, 83–90. Jerusalem: World Union of Jewish Studies, 1994.

Briant, Pierre. *Alexander the Great: Man of Action, Man of Spirit*. Translated by Jeremy Leggatt. Discoveries. New York: Abrams, 1996.

———. *Alexandre le Grand, vérité et légende: Un tyran visionnaire: Terreur impérialiste et séduction culturelle. La création d'un monde nouveau*. Document Archéologia 5. Dijon: Archéologia, 1974.

———. "Bulletin d'histoire achéménide." In *Recherches récentes sur l'Empire achéménide*, edited by Jean Andreau et al., 5–127. Topoi: Orient-Occident: Supplement 1. Paris: De Boccard, 1997.

———. *Darius dans l'ombre d'Alexandre*. Paris: Fayard, 2003.

———. *Darius, les Perses et l'Empire*. Découvertes Gallimard: Histoire 159. Paris: Gallimard, 1992.

———. *From Cyrus to Alexander: A History of the Persian Empire*. Winona Lake: Eisenbrauns, 2002.

———. *Histoire de l'Empire Perse: De Cyrus à Alexandre*. Paris: Fayard, 1996.

Broyles, Craig C. *Psalms*. New International Biblical Commentary: Old Testament Series. Peabody: Hendrickson, 1999.

Brower, K. E. "Eschatology." In *NDBT* 459.

Bruce, F. F. "The Theology and Interpretation of the Old Testament." In *Tradition and Interpretation: Essays by Members of the Society for Old Testament Study*, edited by G. W. Anderson, 385–416. Oxford: Clarendon, 1979.

Brueggemann, Walter. "Bounded by Obedience and Praise: The Psalms as Canon." *JSOT* 50 (1991) 63–92.

———. *The Book that Breathes New Life: Scriptural Authority and Biblical Theology*. Minneapolis: Fortress, 2004.

———. "Futures in Old Testament Theology: Dialogic Engagement." *Horizons in Biblical Theology* 32 (2015) 32–49.

———. *Interpretation and Obedience: From Faithful Reading to Faithful Living*. Minneapolis: Fortress, 1991.

———. *The Message of the Psalms: A Theological Commentary*. Minneapolis: Augsburg, 1984.

———. *The Psalms and the Life of Faith*. Minneapolis: Fortress, 1995.
———. *Reverberations of Faith: A Theological Handbook of Old Testament Themes*. Louisville: Westminster John Knox, 2002.
———. *Texts Under Negotiation: The Bible and Postmodern Imagination*. Minneapolis: Fortress, 1993.
———. *Theology of the Old Testament: Testimony, Dispute, Advocacy*. Minneapolis: Fortress, 1997.
———. "Theology of the Old Testament: Testimony, Dispute, Advocacy Revisited." *CBQ* 74 (2012) 28–38.
Brueggemann, Walter, and Patrick D. Miller, eds. *Old Testament Theology: Essays on Structure, Theme, and Text*. Minneapolis: Fortress, 1992.
Brueggemann, Walter, and Patrick D. Miller. "Psalm 73 as a Canonical Marker." *JSOT* 72 (1996) 45–56.
Brunet, Adrien M. "Le Chroniste et ses sources." *RB* 60 (1953) 481–508.
———. "Le Chroniste et ses sources." *RB* 61 (1954) 349–86.
———. *Théologie du Chroniste: Théocratie et messianisme*. Gembloux: Duculot, 1959.
Bryant, Donald C., ed. *The Rhetorical Idiom: Essays in Rhetoric, Oratory, Language, and Drama Presented to Herbert Augustus Wichelns*. New York: Russell & Russell, 1966.
Buber, Martin. "The Heart Determines: Psalm 73." In *Theodicy in the Old Testament*, edited by J. L. Crenshaw, 109–18. Philadelphia: Fortress, 1983.
Bückers, Hermann. *Die Bücher der Chronik; oder, Paralipomenon*. Die Heilige Schrift für das Leben erklärt IV/1. Freiburg: Herder, 1952.
Buechner, Frederick. "The Bible as Literature." In *CLGB* 40–48.
Bullinger, E. W. *Figures of Speech Used in the Bible*. London: Eyre & Spottiswoode, 1898.
Bullock, C. Hassel. "History and Theology: The Tale of Two Histories." In *GtS* 97–114.
Burgh, Theodore W. "Ancient Music in Israel/Palestine: What are the Sources?" In *Sources of Music in Ancient Israel/Palestine*, edited by Regina Randholfer, 1–7. Orientwissenschatliches Hefe. Halle: Orientwissenschatliches Hefe Zentrum der Martin Luther Universität, 2003.
———. *Listening to the Artifacts: Music Culture in Ancient Palestine*. New York: T&T Clark, 2006.
Burke, Peter. "Overture: The New History, Its Past and Its Future." In *New Perspective on History*, edited by Peter Burke, 1–23. University Park: Pennsylvania State University Press, 1991.
———. "Ranke the Reactionary." In *Leopold von Ranke and the Shaping of the Historical Discipline*, edited by Georg G. Iggers and James M. Powell, 36–44. Syracuse: Syracuse University Press, 1990.
Buss, Martin. "The Psalms of Asaph and Korah." *JBL* 82 (1963) 382–92.
Cabrera, Miguel A. "Linguistic Approach or the Return to Subjectivism? In Search of An Alternative to Social History." In *Historiography: Critical Concepts in Historical Studies: Volume II: Society*, edited by Robert M. Burns, 68–88. Critical Concepts in Historical Studies. London: Routledge, 2006.
Cahill, Jane. "Jerusalem at the Time of the United Monarchy: The Archaeological Evidence." In *Jerusalem in Bible and Archaeology: The First Temple Period*, edited by Andrew G. Vaughn and Ann E. Killebrew, 13–80. Atlanta: SBL, 2003.
———. "It is There: The Archeological Evidence Proves It." *BAR* 24 (1998) 34–41.
———. "Jerusalem in David and Solomon's Time." *BAR* 30 (2004) 20–31.

Callaham, Scott N. "Must Biblical and Systematic Theology Remain Apart? Reflection on Paul van Imschoot." *Journal for the Evangelical Study of the Old Testament* 5 (2016) 1–26.
Campbell, Antony F. *Joshua to Chronicles: An Introduction*. Louisville: Westminster John Knox, 2004.
Cardellini, Innocenzo. *I Leviti, l'esilio e il Tempio: Nuovi elementi per una rielaborazione storica. Lezione inaugurale*. Cathedra: Facoltà di teologia. Rome: Lateran University Press, 2002.
Castel, Corinne, and Francis Joannès. "Temple." In *DCM* 838–41.
Carr, Gordon Lloyd. "The Claims of the Chronicler for the Origin of the Israelite Priesthood." PhD diss., Boston University, 1972.
Carson, D. A. "Systematic Theology and Biblical Theology." In *NDBT* 89–104.
Carter, Charles E. *The Emergence of Yehud in the Persian Period*. JSOTSup 294. Sheffield: Sheffield Academic, 1999.
Caubet, Annie F. "Music and Dance in the World of the Bible." In *BSOT* 468–81.
———. "Musical Practices and Instruments in Late Bronze Age Ugarit (Syria)." In *Music in Antiquity: The Near East and the Mediterranean*, edited by Joan Goodnick et al., 172–84. Berlin: de Gruyter, 2014.
Cavedo, Romeo. *1–2 Cronache Esdra e Neemia*. Leggere oggi la Bibbia 9/10. Brescia: Queriniana, 1991.
Cazelles, H. *Le livres des Chroniques*. La Sainte Bible traduite en Français. Paris: Cerf, 1961.
Ceresko, A. R. "Chiastic Word Patterns in Hebrew." *CBQ* 38 (1976) 303–11.
———. "The Function of Chiasmus in Hebrew Poetry." *CBQ* 40 (1975) 1–10.
Charpin, Dominique. "Prêtres, Prêtresses." In *DCM* 681.
———. *Le Clergé d'Ur au siècle d'Hammurabi*. Hautes Études Orientales 22. Genève: Droz, 1986.
Chavalas, Mark W. "Assyriology and Biblical Studies: A Century of Tension." In *Mesopotamia and the Bible: Comparative Explorations*, edited by Mark W. Chavalas and K. Lawson Younger Jr., 21–67. Grand Rapids: Baker, 2002.
Cheung, Simon Chi-Chung. *Wisdom Intoned: A Reappraisal of the Genre "Wisdom Psalms."* LHBOTS 613. London: Bloomsbury T&T Clark, 2015.
Childs, Brevard S. *Biblical Theology in Crisis*. Philadelphia: Westminster, 1970.
———. *Biblical Theology of the Old and New Testaments: Theological Reflections on the Christian Bible*. Minneapolis: Fortress, 1992.
———. *The Book of Exodus: A Critical, Theological Commentary*. OTL. Philadelphia: Westminster, 1974.
———. *Introduction to the Old Testament as Scripture*. Philadelphia: Fortress, 1979.
———. *Old Testament Theology in a Canonical Context*. Philadelphia: Fortress, 1985.
Chisolm, Robert B., Jr. "History or Story? The Literary Dimension in Narrative Texts." In *GtS* 54–73.
Cicero. *On Oratory and Orators*. Edited by J. S. Watson. Landmarks in Rhetoric and Public Address. Carbondale: Southern Illinois University Press, 1970.
Clark, Gordon Haddon, and John W. Robbins. *Historiography: Secular and Religious*. 2nd ed. Jefferson: Trinity Foundation, 1994.
Clayton, J. Nathan. "An Examination of Holy Space in Psalm 73: Is Wisdom's Path Infused with an Eschatologically Oriented Hope?" *Trinity Journal* 27 (2006) 117–42.

Classen, Carl Joachim. *Rhetorical Criticism and the New Testament*. Wissenschaftliche Untersuchungen zum Neuen Testament 128. Tübingen: Mohr Siebeck, 2000.
Clements, R. E. *Old Testament Theology: A Fresh Approach*. New Foundations Theological Library. Atlanta: John Knox, 1979.
———. "Wellhausen, Julius." In *Historical Handbook of Major Biblical Interpreters*, edited by Donald McKim, 380–85. Downers Grove: InterVarsity Press, 1998.
Cody, Aelred. *Ezekiel, with an Excursus on Old Testament Priesthood*. Old Testament Message 11. Wilmington: Glazier, 1984.
———. *A History of the Old Testament Priesthood*. AnBib 35. Rome: Pontifical Biblical Institute, 1969.
Coggins, R. J. "1 and 2 Chronicles." In *Eerdmans Commentary on the Bible*, edited by James D. G. Dunn and John W. Rogerson, 282–312. Grand Rapids: Eerdmans, 2003.
———. *The First and Second Books of the Chronicles: Commentary*. Cambridge Bible Commentary. Cambridge: Cambridge University Press, 1976.
Cohen, G. A. "Functional Explanation: In Marxism." In *Readings in the Philosophy of Social Science*, edited by Michael Martin and Lee C. McIntyre, 391–402. Cambridge: MIT Press, 1994.
Cohen, John S. "The Achievements of Economic History: The Marxist School." In *Historiography: Critical Concepts in Historical Studies: Volume I: Foundations*, edited by Robert M. Burns, 301–28. Critical Concepts in Historical Studies. London: Routledge, 2006.
Cole, R. Dennis. *Numbers*. NAC 3B. Nashville: Broadman & Holman, 2000.
Collier, Andrew. "Critical Realism." In *The Politics of Method in the Human Sciences: Positivism and Its Epistemological Others*, edited by George Steinmetz, 327–44. Politics, History, and Culture. Durham: Duke University Press, 2005.
———. "Realism, Relativism, and Reason in Religious Belief." In *Transcendence: Critical Realism and God*, edited by Margaret S. Archer et al., 41–48. Routledge Studies in Critical Realism. London: Routledge, 2004.
Collingwood, R. G. *The Idea of History*. Oxford: Clarendon, 1946.
Collins, Billie Jean. "The Hittites and the Hurrians." In *WOT* 197–228.
———. "Ritual and Prayer to Ishtar of Ninevah." In *COS* 1:164–65.
Collins, John J. *The Bible After Babel: Historical Criticism in a Postmodern Age*. Grand Rapids: Eerdmans, 2005.
———. "Is a Critical Biblical Theology Possible?" In *The Hebrew Bible and its Interpreters*, edited by William Henry Propp et al., 1–17. Biblical Judaic Studies 1. Winona Lake: Eisenbrauns, 1990.
———. "Israel." In *Religions of the Ancient World: A Guide*, edited by Sarah Iles Johnston, 181–88. Cambridge: Belknap, 2004.
Compier, Don H. *What is Rhetorical Theology? Textual Practice and Public Discourse*. Harrisburg: Trinity, 1999.
Condit, Celeste M. "Contemporary Rhetorical Criticism: Diverse Bodies Learning New Languages." *Rhetoric Review* 25 (2006) 368–72.
Connors, Robert J., et al. "The Revival of Rhetoric in America." In *Essays on Classical Rhetoric and Modern Discourse*, edited by Robert J. Connors, 1–15. Carbondale: Southern Illinois University Press, 1984.
Cook, Stephen L. "Innerbiblical Interpretation in Ezekiel 44 and the History of Israel's Priesthood." *JBL* 114 (1995) 193–208.

Cooper, Derek, and Martin J. Lohrman. *1–2 Samuel, 1–2 Kings, 1–2 Chronicles*. Reformation Commentary on Scripture V. Downers Grove: InterVarsity Press, 2016.
Coote, Robert B. *Early Israel: A New Horizon*. Minneapolis: Fortress, 1990.
———. *In Defense of Revolution: The Elohist History*. Minneapolis: Fortress, 1991.
Coote, Robert B., and Mary P. Coote. *Power, Politics, and the Making of the Bible: An Introduction*. Minneapolis: Fortress, 1990.
Coote, Robert B., and David Robert Ord. *The Bible's First History*. Philadelphia: Fortress, 1989.
———. *In the Beginning: Creation and the Priestly History*. Minneapolis: Fortress, 1991.
———. *Is the Bible True? Understanding the Bible Today*. Maryknoll: Orbis, 1994.
Coote, Robert B., and Keith W. Whitelam. *The Emergence of Early Israel in Historical Perspective*. Sheffield: Sheffield Phoenix, 2010.
Cook, Ryan. "Prayers That Form Us: Rhetoric and Psalms Interpretation." *JSOT* 39 (2015) 451–67.
Corduan, Winfried, and Max E. Anders. *I & II Chronicles*. Holman Old Testament Commentary 8. Nashville: Broadman & Holman, 2004.
Cotterell, Peter. "Linguistics, Meaning, Semantics, and Discourse Analysis." In *A Guide to Old Testament Theology and Exegesis*, edited by Willem A. VanGemeren, 131–57. Grand Rapids: Zondervan, 1997.
Cotterell, Peter, and Max Turner. *Linguistics and Biblical Interpretation*. Downers Grove: InterVarsity, 1989.
Craigie, Peter C. *Psalms 1–50*. WBC 19. Waco: Word, 1983.
Creach, Jerome F. D. "The Psalms and the Cult." In *Interpreting the Psalms: Issues and Approaches*, edited by David First and Philip S. Johnstone, 119–38. Downers Grove: InterVarsity Press, 2005.
———. *Yahweh As Refuge and the Editing of the Hebrew Psalter*. JSOTSup 217. Sheffield, Sheffield Academic, 1996.
Crenshaw, James L. *Old Testament Wisdom: An Introduction*. Louisville: Westminster John Knox, 1998.
———. *A Whirlpool of Torment: Israelite Traditions of God as Oppressive Presence*. Philadelphia: Fortress, 1984.
Croce, Benedetto. *History: Its Theory and Practice*. New York: Russell & Russell, 1960.
Cross, F. M. *Canaanite Myth and Hebrew Epic: Essays in the History of the Religion of Israel*. Cambridge: Harvard University Press, 1973.
Crossley, Sanford Lyle. "The Levite as a Royal Servant During the Israelite Monarchy." PhD diss., Southwestern Baptist Theological Seminary, 1989.
Cummins, S. A. "The Theological Interpretation of Scripture: Recent Contributions by Stephen E. Fowl, Christopher R. Seitz and Francis Watson." *Currents in Biblical Research* 2 (2004) 179–96.
Curtis, Edward Lewis, and Albert Alonzo Madsen. *A Critical and Exegetical Commentary on the Books of Chronicles*. International Critical Commentary. Edinburgh: T&T Clark, 1910.
Curtiss, Samuel Ives. *The Levitical Priests: A Contribution to the Criticism of the Pentateuch*. Edinburgh: T&T Clark, 1877.
Dahm, Ulrike. *Opferkult und Priestertum in Alt-Israel: Ein kultur-und religionswissenschaftlicher Beitrag*. BZAW 327. Berlin: de Gruyter, 2003.
Dahmen, Ulrich. *Leviten und Priester im Deuteronomium: Literarkritische und redactionsgeschichtliche Studien*. Bonner Biblische Beiträge 110. Bodenheim: Philo, 1996.

Davaney, Sheila Greeve. *Historicism: The Once and Future Challenge for Theology.* Guides to Theological Inquiry. Minneapolis: Fortress, 2006.

Davidson, Richard M. "The Legacy of Gerhard Hasel's Old Testament Theology: Basic Issues in the Current Debate Revealed in Old Testament Scholarship of the Last Four Decades." *Journal of the Adventist Theological Society* 26 (2015) 3–25.

Davies, Philip R. *The History of Ancient Israel: A Guide for the Perplexed.* Bloomsbury Guides for the Perplexed. London: Bloomsbury T&T Clark, 2015.

———. *In Search of 'Ancient Israel'.* 2nd ed. Sheffield: Sheffield Academic, 2003.

———. *Scribes and Schools: The Canonization of the Hebrew Scriptures.* Library of Ancient Israel. Louisville: Westminster John Knox, 1998.

———. *Whose Bible is it Anyway?* JSOTSup 204. Sheffield: Sheffield Academic, 1995.

———. "Whose Israel? Whose Bible? Biblical Histories, Ancient and Modern." In *Can a 'History of Israel' Be Written?* Edited by Lester L. Grabbe, 104–22. European Seminar in Historical Methodology 1. Sheffield: Sheffield Academic, 1997.

Davis, Casey Wayne. *Oral Biblical Criticism: The Influence of the Principle of Orality on the Literary Structure of Paul's Epistle to the Philippians.* JSNTSup 172. Sheffield: Sheffield Academic, 1999.

deClaissé-Walford, Nancy, et al. *The Book of Psalms.* NICOT. Grand Rapids: Eerdmans, 2014.

———. "The Canonical Approach to Scripture and *The Editing of the Hebrew Psalter.*" In *The Shape and Shaping of the Book of Psalms: The Current State of Scholarship*, edited by Nancy DeClaissé-Walford, 1–12. Ancient Israel and Its Literature 20. Atlanta: SBL, 2014.

Deboys, David G. "History and Theology in the Chronicler's Portrayal of Abijah." *Bib* 71 (1990) 48–62.

Del Olmo Lete, Gregorio. *Canaanite Religion According to the Liturgical Texts of Ugarit.* Translated by W. G. E. Watson. Bethesda: CDL, 1999.

de Martino, Stefano. "Music, Dance, and Processions in Hittite Anatolia." In *CANE* 4:2661–69.

de Tarragon, Jean-Michel de. *Le Culte à Ugarit d'après les textes de la pratique en cunéiformes alphabétiques.* Cahiers de la Revue Biblique 19. Paris: Gabalda, 1980.

de Vaux, Roland. *Les institutions de l'Ancien Testament. Volume II: Institutions militaires, institutions religieuses.* Paris: Cerf, 1960.

Dennerlein, Norbert. *Die Bedeutung Jerusalems in den Chronikbüchern.* BEATAJ 46. Frankfurt: Lang, 1999.

Dentan, Robert C. *The First and Second Books of the Kings. The First and Second Books of the Chronicles.* The Layman's Bible Commentary 7. Richmond: John Knox, 1964.

———. *Preface to Old Testament Theology.* Rev. ed. New York: Seabury, 1963.

Dever, William G. *Beyond the Texts: An Archaeological Portrait of Ancient Israel and Judah.* Atlanta: SBL, 2017.

———. "Histories and Non-Histories of Ancient Israel: The Question of the United Monarchy." In *SPreIs* 65–94.

———. "Some Observations on Comparative Method and Ancient Music in Near Eastern Archaeology." In *Sources of Music in Ancient Israel/Palestine*, edited by Regina Randhofer, 9–21. Halle: Orientwissenschatliches Zentrum der Martin Luther Universität, 2003.

———. "Temples and Sanctuaries: Syria-Palestine." In *ABD* 6:370–85.

———. *What Did the Biblical Writers Know and When Did They Know It?* Grand Rapids: Eerdmans, 2001.

———. *Who Were the Early Israelites and Where Did They Come From?* Grand Rapids: Eerdmans, 2003.
de Vries, P. "Hegel. Georg Wilhelm Friedrich (1770–1831)." In *EDT* 55.
De Vries, Simon J. *1 and 2 Chronicles*. FOTL 11. Grand Rapids: Eerdmans, 1989.
———. "Festival Ideology in Chronicles." In *Problems in Biblical Theology: Essays in Honor of Rolf Knierim*, edited by Henry T. C. Sun et al., 104–24. Grand Rapids: Eerdmans, 1997.
———. *The Forms of Prophetic Address in Chronicles*. Columbus: Ohio State University Press, 1986.
———. "The Schema of Dynastic Endangerment in Chronicles." *Eastern Great Lakes Biblical Society Proceedings* 7 (1987) 59–77.
De Wette, W. M. L. *Beiträge zur Einleitung in das Alte Testament*. Halle: Schimmelpfennig, 1823.
———. *A Critical and Historical Introduction to the Canonical Scriptures of the Old Testament*. Translated by Theodore Parker. 2 vols. 3rd ed. Boston: Leighton, 1859.
———. *Kritischer Versuch über die Glaubwürdigkeit der Bücher der Chronik mit Hinsicht auf die Geschichte der Mosaischen Bücher und Gesetzgebung: Ein Nachtrag zu den Vaterschen Untersuchungen über den Pentateuch*. Halle: Schimmelpfennig, 1806.
———. *Lehrbuch der christlichen Dogmatik: in ihrer historischen Entwickelung dargestellt*. 2 vols. 3rd ed. Berlin: Reimer, 1831.
———. *Lehrbuch der historisch-kritischen Einleitung in die kanonischen und apokryphischen Bücher des Alten Testamentes*. Berlin: Reimer, 1845.
Dillard, Raymond B. *2 Chronicles*. WBC 15. Waco: Word, 1987.
———. "The Reign of Asa (2 Chronicles 14–16): An Example of the Chronicler's Theological Method." *JETS* 23 (1980) 207–18.
———. "Reward and Punishment in Chronicles: The Theology of Immediate Retribution." *WTJ* 46 (1984) 164–72.
Dillard, Raymond B., and Tremper Longman III. *An Introduction to the Old Testament*. Grand Rapids: Baker, 1994.
Diller, Carmen. "Der Kompositpsalm 1 Chr 16, 8–36 als theologisches Kompendium." In *"Wer darf hinaufsteigen zum Berg JHWHs?" Beiträge zu Prophetie und Poesie des Alten Testaments: Festschrift für Sigurður Örn Steingrímsson zum 70. Geburtstag*, edited by Hubert Irsigler, 173–203. Arbeiten zu Text und Sprache im Alten Testament 72. Ottilien: EOS, 2002.
Dillmann, August, and Rudolf Kittel. *Handbuch der alttestamentlichen Theologie*. Leipzig: Hirzel, 1895.
Dirksen, Peter B. "1 Chron 22:12: The Chronicler in Actu Scribendi." *Journal of Northwest Semitic Languages* 26 (2000) 135–41.
———. *1 Chronicles*. Historical Commentary on the Old Testament. Leuven: Peeters, 2005.
———. "1 Chronicles 5:1–2." *Journal of Northwest Semitic Languages* 25 (1999) 17–23.
———. "1 Chronicles 9, 26–33: Its Position in Chapter 9." *Bib* 79 (1998) 91–96.
———. "1 Chronicles xxviii 11–18: Its Textual Development." *VT* 46 (1996) 429–38.
———. "Chronistic Tendency in 1 Chr 18, 10–11." *Bib* 80 (1999) 269–71.
———. "The Future in the Book of Chronicles." In *New Heaven and New Earth: Prophecy and the Millennium: Essays in Honour of Anthony Gelston*, edited by P. J. Harland and C. T. R. Hayward, 37–51. Leiden: Brill, 1999.

———. "Kronieken in de recente literatuur: Een overzicht van recente publikaties betreffende Kronieken." *Nederlands Theologisch Tijdschrift* 47 (1993) 6–20.

———. "What Are the Mehabberôt in 1 Chron 22:3?" *BN* 80 (1995) 23–24.

———. "Why Was David Disqualified as Temple Builder? The Meaning of 1 Chronicles 22.8." *JSOT* 70 (1996) 51–56.

Dörrfuss, E. M. *Mose in den Chronikbüchern: Garant theokratischer Zukunftserwartung.* BZAW 219. Berlin: de Gruyter, 1994.

Dorsey, David A. *The Literary Structure of the Old Testament.* Grand Rapids: Baker, 1999.

Dosse, F. *New History in France: The Triumph of the Annales.* Translated by Peter V. Conroy Jr. Urbana: University of Illinois Press, 1994.

Douglas, George C. M. "Levite." In *The Imperial Bible-Dictionary: Historical, Biographical, Geographical, and Doctrinal*, 6 vols., edited by Patrick Fairbairn, 4:85–92. London: Blackie, 1887.

Dozeman, Thomas B. "The Priestly Vocation." *Int* 59 (2005) 117–28.

Dray, W. H. "Narrative vs. Analysis in History." In *Historiography: Critical Concepts in Historical Studies: Volume IV: Culture*, edited by Robert M. Burns, 340–59. Critical Concepts in Historical Studies. London: Routledge, 2006.

Duke, Rodney K. "Chronicles, Books of." In *DOTHB* 161–80.

———. "The Ethical Appeal of the Chronicler." In *Rhetoric, Ethic, and Moral Persuasion in Biblical Discourse: Essays from the 2002 Heidelberg Conference*, edited by Thomas H. Olbricht and Anders Eriksson, 33–51. London: T&T Clark, 2005.

———. *The Persuasive Appeal of the Chronicler: A Rhetorical Analysis.* JSOTSup 88. Sheffield: Almond, 1990.

———. "The Portion of the Levite: Another Reading of Deuteronomy 18:6–8." *JBL* 106 (1987) 193–201.

———. "Priests, Priesthood." In *DOTP* 646–55.

———. "Punishment or Restoration? Another Look at the Levites of Ezekiel 44.6–16." *JSOT* 40 (1988) 61–81.

———. "A Rhetorical Approach to Appreciating the Books of Chronicles?" In *ChrA* 100–35.

———. "The Strategic Use of Enthymeme and Example in the Argumentation of the Books of Chronicles." In *Rhetorical Argumentation in Biblical Texts: Essays from the Lund 2000 Conference*, edited by Anders Eriksson et al., 127–40. Emory Studies in Early Christianity 8. Harrisburg: Trinity, 2002.

Dumbrell, William J. "The Purpose of the Books of Chronicles." *JETS* 27 (1984) 257–66.

Durham, John I. *Exodus.* WBC 3. Nashville: Nelson, 1987.

Dyck, Jonathan E. "Dating Chronicles and the Purpose of Chronicles." *Didaskalia* 8 (1997) 16–29.

———. "The Ideology of Identity in Chronicles." In *Ethnicity and the Bible*, edited by Marc G. Brett, 89–116. Biblical Interpretation Series. Leiden: Brill, 1996.

———. *The Theocratic Ideology of the Chronicler.* Biblical Interpretation Series 33. Leiden: Boston, 1998.

Earl, Douglas S. "'Minimalism' and Old Testament Theological Hermeneutics: The 'David Saga' as a Test Case." *Journal of Theological Interpretation* 4 (2010) 207–28.

Edart, Jean-Baptiste. *L'Épître aux Phillipiens, rhétorique et composition stylistique.* Études Bibliques 45. Paris: Gabalda, 2002.

Edelman, Diana. "Clio's Dilemma: The Changing Face of History-Writing." In *CVO* 247–55.

———. "The Deuteronomist's David and the Chronicler's David: Competing or Contrasting Ideologies?" In *The Future of the Deuteronomistic History*, edited by Thomas Römer, 67–83. Bibliotheca Ephemeridum Theologicarum Lovaniensium 147. Leuven: Peeters, 2000.

———. "Doing History in Biblical Studies." In *The Fabric of History: Text, Artifact, and Israel's Past*, edited by Diana Edelman, 13–25. JSOTSup 127. Sheffield: JSOT Press, 1991.

Eichrodt, Walther. "Does Old Testament Theology Sill Have Independent Significance within Old Testament Scholarship?" In *OTTFF* 21–29.

———. "Hat die Altestamentliche Theologie noch selbständige Bedeutung innerhalb der Altestamentliche Wissenschaft?" *ZAW* 47 (1929) 83–91.

———. *Religionsgeschichte Israels*. Dalp Taschenbücher 394. Bern: Francke, 1969.

———. *Theologie des Alten Testaments: Teil I: Gott und Volk*. 8th ed. Göttingen: Vandenhoeck & Ruprecht, 1968.

———. *Theologie des Alten Testaments: Teil II: Gott und Welt; Teil III: Gott und Mensch*. 4th ed. Göttingen: Vandenhoeck & Ruprecht, 1935.

———. *Theology of the Old Testament*. 2 vols. Translated by J. A. Baker. OTL. Philadelphia: Westminster, 1961.

Eisemann, Moshe. *1 Chronicles: A New Translation With a Commentary Anthologized from Talmudic, Midrashic, and Rabbinic Sources*. Brooklyn: Masorah, 1969.

Eissfeldt, Otto. "The History of Israelite-Jewish Religion and Old Testament Theology." In *OTTFF* 3–11.

———. "Israelitisch-jüdische Religionsgeschischichte und Altestamentliche Theologie." *ZAW* 44 (1926) 1–12.

———. *The Old Testament: An Introduction, Including the Apocrypha and Pseudepigrapha, and Also the Works of Similar Type from Qumran: The History of the Formation of the Old Testament*. Translated by Peter R. Ackroyd. New York: Harper and Row, 1965.

———. *Religionsgeschichte des Alten Orients: Lieferung 1*. Leiden: Brill, 1964.

Elder, Crawford. *Appropriating Hegel*. Scots Philosophical Monographs 65. Aberdeen: Aberdeen University Press, 1981.

Elmslie, W. A. L. *The Books of Chronicles, with Maps, Notes and Introduction*. The Cambridge Bible for Schools and Colleges. Cambridge: Cambridge University Press, 1916.

Emerton, J. A. "Priests and Levites in Deuteronomy: An Examination of Dr. G. E. Wright's Theory." *VT* 12 (1962) 129–38.

Endres, John C. *First and Second Chronicles*. New Collegeville Biblical Commentary. Collegeville: Liturgical, 2012.

———. "Joyful Worship in Second Temple Judaism." In *Passion, Vitality, and Foment: The Dynamics of Second Temple Judaism*, edited by Lamontte M. Luker, 155–88. Harrisburg: Trinity, 2001.

———. "A New Parallel Version of Samuel, Kings, Chronicles." *Forum* 8 (1992) 31–43.

———. *Temple, Monarchy and Word of God*. Message of Biblical Spirituality 2. Wilmington: Glazier, 1988.

Endres, John C., et al. *Chronicles and Its Synoptic Parallels in Samuel, Kings, and Related Biblical Texts*. Collegeville: Liturgical, 1998.

Enns, Peter. "מִשְׁפָּט." In *NIDOTTE* 2:137–38.
Enos, Richard Leo. "Classical Rhetoric and Rhetorical Criticism." *Rhetoric Review* 25 (2006) 361–65.
Eskenazi, Tamara Cohn. "A Literary Approach to Chronicles' Ark Narrative in 1 Chronicles 13–16." In *Fortunate the Eyes That See: Essays in Honor of David Noel Freedman in Celebration of his Seventieth Birthday*, edited by Astrid B. Beck et al., 258–74. Grand Rapids: Eerdmans, 1995.

———. "The Missions of Ezra and Nehemiah." In *Judah and the Judeans in the Persian Period*, edited by Oded Lipschits and Manfred Oeming, 509–29. Winona Lake: Eisenbrauns, 2006.

Estes, Daniel J. "Metaphorical Sojourning in 1 Chronicles 29:15." *CBQ* 53 (1991) 45–49.
Evans, Craig A. "Aspects of Exile and Restoration in the Proclamation of Jesus and the Gospels." In *Exile: Old Testament, Jewish, and Christian Conceptions*, edited by James M. Scott, 299–328. Supplements to the Journal for the Study of Judaism 56. Leiden: Brill, 1997.

———. "New Testament Use of the Old Testament." In *NDBT* 72–80.
Evans, Paul S. "Divine Intermediaries in 1 Chronicles 21: An Overlooked Aspect of the Chronicler's Theology." *Bib* 85 (2004) 545–58.

———. "Let the Crime Fit the Punishment: The Chronicler's Explication of David's 'Sin' in 1 Chronicles 21." In *CthC* 65–80.

Evans, Richard J. *In Defense of History*. New York: Norton, 1999.
Even-Shoshan, ed. *A New Concordance to the Old Testament*. 2nd ed. Jerusalem: Kiryat, 1997.
Ewald, Heinrich. *Die lehre der Bibel von Gott, oder, Theologie des alten und neuen bundes*. 4 vols. Leipzig: Vogel, 1871–76.

———. *Revelation, Its Nature and Record*. Clark's Foreign Theological Library XIX. Edinburgh: T&T Clark, 1884.

Exum, Cheryl J., and David J. A. Clines. "The New Literary Criticism." In *The New Literary Criticism and the Hebrew Bible*, edited by Cheryl J. Exum and David J. A. Clines, 11–25. JSOTSup 143. Sheffield: JSOT Press, 1993.
Faber, Gertrude. "Inanna and Enki." In *COS* 1:522–26.
Farrenkopf, John. "Spengler's Historical Pessimism and The Tragedy of Our Age." *Theory & Society* 22 (1993) 391–41.
Faust, A. "Did Eilat Mazar Find David's Palace?" *BAR* 38 (2012) 47–52.

———. "The Large Stone Structure in the City of David: A Reexamination." *Zeitschrift des Deutschen Palästina-Vereins* 126 (2011) 116–30.

Fernández Marcos, Natalio. "On Double Readings, Pseudo-Variants and Ghost-Names in the Historical Books." In *Emanuel: Studies in Hebrew Bible, Septuagint, and Dead Sea Scrolls in Honor of Emanuel Tov*, edited by Shalom M. Paul et al., 591–604. VTSup 94. Leiden: Brill, 2003.
Finkelstein, Israel. "The Archaeology of the United Monarchy: An Alternative View." *Levant* 28 (1998) 177–87.

———. "The 'Large Stone Structure' in Jerusalem: Reality versus Yearning." *Zeitschrift des Deutschen Palästina-Vereins* 127 (2012) 1–10.

———. "The Rise of Jerusalem and Judah: The Missing Link." *Levant* 33 (2001) 105–15.

Finkelstein, Israel, and Neil Asher Silberman. *The Bible Unearthed: Archaeology's New Vision of Ancient Israel and the Origin of Its Sacred Texts*. New York: Simon & Schuster, 2002.

Finn, Daniel K. "What Is Critical Realism?" In *Moral Agency within Social Structures and Culture: A Primer on Critical Realism for Christian Ethics*, edited by Daniel K. Finn et al., 19–28. Washington, DC: Georgetown University Press, 2020.

Fiore, Benjamin. "Rhetoric and Rhetorical Criticism." In *ABD* 710–19.

Fischer, David Hackett. *Historians' Fallacies: Toward a Logic of Historical Thought*. New York: Harper & Row, 1970.

Fischer, Georg. *Theologien des Alten Testaments*. Stuttgart: Katholisches Bibelwerk, 2012.

Fishbane, Michael. *Biblical Interpretation in Ancient Israel*. Oxford: Clarendon, 1988.

———. "Types of Biblical Intertextuality." In *Congress Volume: Oslo 1998*, edited by A. Lemaire and M. Sæbø, 39–44. VTSup 80. Leiden: Brill, 2000.

Fitzsimons, M. A. "Ranke: History as Worship." *The Review of Politics* 42 (1980) 533–55.

Fleming, Daniel E. *The Installation of Baal's High Priestess at Emar*. Harvard Semitic Studies. Atlanta: Scholars, 1992.

———. "The Installation of the Storm God's High Priestess." In *COS* 1:427–31.

Fohrer, Georg. *History of Israelite Religion*. Translated by David E. Green. Nashville: Abingdon, 1972.

Fouts, David M. "Who Really Killed Goliath? 2 Samuel 21:19 versus 1 Chronicles 20:5." *Journal of Translation and Textlinguistics* 13 (2000) 14–24.

Fox, Michael V. "Prayers to Re-Harakhti." In *COS* 1:47–48.

Freedman, D. N., and David Miano. "Is the Shorter Reading Better? Haplography in the First Book of Chronicles." In *Emanuel: Studies in Hebrew Bible, Septuagint, and Dead Sea Scrolls in Honor of Emanuel Tov*, edited by Shalom M. Paul et al., 685–98. VTSup 94. Leiden: Brill, 2003.

French, Blaire A. *Chronicles through the Centuries*. Wiley Blackwell Bible Commentaries. Chichester: Wiley, 2017.

Fried, Lisbeth. *The Priest and the Great King: Temple-Palace Relations in the Persian Empire*. Biblical and Judaic Studies. Winona Lake: Eisenbrauns, 2004.

Fritz, Volkmar. *An Introduction to Biblical Archaeology*. JSOTSup 172. Sheffield: Sheffield Academic Press, 2001.

Fritz, Volkmar, and Philip R. Davies. *The Origins of the Ancient Israelite States*. JSOTSup 228. Sheffield: Sheffield Academic Press, 1996.

Frisch, Amos. "Jeroboam and the Division of the Kingdom: Mapping Contrasting Biblical Accounts." *JANES* 27 (2000) 15–29.

Gabel, John B., et al. *The Bible as Literature: An Introduction*. 5th ed. Oxford: Oxford University Press, 2006.

Gabler, J. P., et al. "J. P. Gabler and the Distinction Between Biblical and Dogmatic Theology: Translation, Commentary, and Discussion of His Originality." *Scottish Journal of Theology* 33 (1980) 133–58.

Gabriel, Ingeborg. *Friede über Israel: Eine Untersuchung zur Friedenstheologie in Chronik I 10–II 36*. Österreichische Biblische Studien 10. Klosterneuburg: Österreichisches Katholisches Bibelwerk, 1990.

Galling, Kurt. *Die Bücher der Chronik, Esra, Nehemia*. Alte Testament Deutsch 12. Berlin: Evangelische, 1958.

Garbini, Giovanni. *History and Ideology in Ancient Israel*. Translated by John Bowden. New York: Crossroad, 1988.

———. *Myth and History in the Bible*. JSOTSup 362. London: Sheffield Academic, 2003.

Gard, Daniel L. "Warfare in Chronicles." PhD diss., University of Notre Dame, 1991.
Garfinkel, Yosef. "The Birth & Death of Biblical Minimalism." *Biblical Archaeology Review* 37 (2011) 46–78.
Garrett, D. A. "Levi, Levites." In *DOTP* 519–22.
Garsiel, Moshe. "David's Warfare Against the Philistines in the Vicinity of Jerusalem (2 Sam 5, 17–25; 1 Chron 14,8–16)." In *Studies in Historical Geography and Biblical Historiography: Presented to Zecharia Kallai*, edited by Gershon Galil and Moshe Weinfeld, 150–64. VTSup 81. Leiden: Brill, 2000.
Geivett, R. D. "Idealism." In *EDT* 588–89.
Gericke, Jaco W. "Rethinking the 'Dual Causality Principle' in Old Testament Research: A Philosophical Perspective." *OTE* 28 (2015) 86–112.
Gerstenberger, Erhard. *Theologies in the Old Testament*. Translated by John Bowden. Minneapolis: Fortress, 2002.
Gertner, M. "The Masorah and the Levites: An Essay in the History of a Concept." *VT* 10 (1960) 241–72.
Gericke, Jaco W. "When Historical Minimalism Becomes Philosophical Maximalism." *Old Testament Essays* 27 (2014) 412–27.
Gese, H. "Zur Geschichte des Kultsänger am zweiten Tempel." In *Abraham Unser Vater; Otto Michel*, edited by O. Betz, 223–34. Leiden: Brill, 1963.
Gilbert, Felix. "Historiography: What Ranke Meant." *The American Scholar* 56 (1987) 393–97.
Giles, Terry, and William Doan. "The Song of Asaph: A Performance-Critical Analysis of 1 Chronicles 16:8-36." *CBQ* 70 (2008) 29–43.
Gillingham, Susan. "The Arts: Architecture, Music, Poetry, Psalmody." In *The Biblical World*, edited by John Barton, 2 vols., 1:53–74. London: Routledge, 2002.
———. "The Levites and the Editorial Composition of the Psalms." In *The Oxford Handbook of the Psalms*, edited by William P. Brown, 201–13. Oxford: Oxford University Press, 2014.
———. "Psalms 105 and 106 and Participation in History through Liturgy." *Hebrew Bible and Ancient Israel* 4 (2015) 450–75.
Gitay, Yehoshua. *Prophecy and Persuasion: A Study of Isaiah 40-48*. Forum Theologiae Linguisticae 14. Bonn: Linguistica Biblical, 1981.
———. "Rhetorical Criticism and the Prophetic Discourse." In *Persuasive Artistry: Studies in New Testament Rhetoric in Honor of George A. Kennedy*, edited by Duane F. Watson, 13–24. JSNTSup. Sheffield: Sheffield Academic, 1991.
Gittlen, Barry M. *Sacred Time, Sacred Place: Archaeology and the Religion of Israel*. Winona Lake: Eisenbrauns, 2002.
Gitin, Seymour. "Introduction to Biblical Archaeology." In *BSOT* 39–46.
Glatt-Gilad, David A. "The Root *knʻ* and Historiographic Periodization in Chronicles." *CBQ* 64 (2002) 248–57.
Glessmer, Uwe. *Die ideale Kultordnung: 24 Priesterordnungen in den Chronikbüchern, kalendarischen Qumrantexten und in synagogalen Inschriften*. Studies on the Texts of the Desert of Judah 25. Leiden: Brill, 1998.
———. "Leviten in spät-nachexilischer Zeit, Darstellungensinteressen in den Chronikbüchern und bei Josephus." 127–51 in *Gottes Ehre erzählen, Festschrift für Hans Seidel zum 65. Geburtstag*, edited by M. Albani and T. Arndt. Leipzig: Thomas, 1994.

Goettsberger, Johann. *Die Bucher der Chronik oder Paralipomenon.* Bonn: Hanstein, 1939.
Goldingay, John. *Approaches to Old Testament Interpretation.* Issues in Contemporary Theology. Downers Grove: InterVarsity, 1981.
———. "The Chronicler as Theologian." *Biblical Theology Bulletin* 5 (1975) 99–126.
———. "Old Testament Theology and the Canon." *TynBul* 59 (2008) 1–26.
———. *Old Testament Theology. Volume 1: Israel's Gospel.* Downers Grove: InterVarsity Press, 2003.
———. *Theological Diversity and the Authority of the Old Testament.* Grand Rapids: Eerdmans, 1987.
Goldsworthy, G. "Relationship of Old and New Testament." In *NDBT* 81–89.
Goppelt, Leonhard. *Typos: The Typological Interpretation of the Old Testament in the New.* Translated by Donald H. Madvig. Grand Rapids: Eerdmans, 1982.
Gosse, B. "L'Alliance avec Abraham et les relectures de l'histoire d'Israël en Ne 9, Pss 105–106, 135–136 et 1 Ch 16." *Transeu* 15 (1998) 123–35.
———. "Deux usages du Psaume 96." *OTE* 12 (1999) 266–78.
———. "La disparition de la dynastie davidique." *Transeu* 39 (2010) 97–112.
———. "L'insertion des psaumes des chantres–lévites dans l'ensemble rédactionnel livre d'Isaïe–psautier et les revendications des lévites." *Transeu* 19 (2000) 145–58.
———. "Le texte 1 Chr 16 comme réinterprétation davidique de Ps 105, 1–15, la réponse des serviteurs et élus de Ps 105,16–46 et la continuité du livre d'Isaïe." *ZAW* 128 (2016) 221–32.
Gottwald, Norman K. *The Bible and Liberation: Political and Social Hermeneutics.* Maryknoll: Orbis, 1983.
———. *The Hebrew Bible in its Social World and in Ours.* Semeia Studies. Atlanta: Scholars, 1993.
———. *The Hebrew Bible: A Socio-Literary Introduction.* Philadelphia: Fortress, 1985.
———. *The Politics of Ancient Israel.* Louisville: Westminster John Knox, 2001.
———. *The Tribes of Yahweh: A Sociology of the Religion of Liberated Israel, 1250–1050 B.C.E.* Maryknoll: Orbis, 1979. Reprint, Sheffield: Sheffield Academic, 1999.
Gottwald, Norman K., and Richard A. Horsley. *The Bible and Liberation: Political and Social Hermeneutics.* The Bible & Liberation Series. Revised ed. Maryknoll: Orbis, 1993.
Goulder, M. *The Psalms of Asaph and the Pentateuch: Studies in the Psalter, III.* JSOTSup 233. Sheffield: Sheffield Academic, 1996.
Gowan, Donald E. *Eschatology in the Old Testament.* Edinburgh: T&T Clark, 2000.
Grabbe, Lester L. *Ancient Israel: What Do We Know and How Do We Know It?* Revised ed. New York: Bloomsbury, 2017.
———. *An Introduction to Second Temple Judaism: History and Religion of the Jews in the Time of Nehemiah, the Maccabees, Hillel and Jesus.* New York: T&T Clark, 2010.
———. "Israel's Historical Reality After the Exile." In *Crisis of Israelite Religion: Transformation of Religious Tradition in Exilic and Post-Exilic Times*, edited by Bob Becking and Marjo C. A. Korpel, 9–32. Leiden: Brill, 1999.
———. "A Priest Without Honor in His Own Prophet: Priests and Other Religious Specialists in the Latter Prophets." In *The Priests in the Prophets: The Portrayal of Priests and Other Religious Specialists in the Latter Prophets*, edited by Lester L. Grabbe and Alice Ogden Bellis, 79–97. New York: T&T Clark, 2004.

———. *Priests, Prophets, Diviners, Sages: A Socio-Historical Study of Religious Specialists in Ancient Israel.* Valley Forge: Trinity, 1995.

———. "Were the Pre-Maccabean High Priests 'Zadokites'?" In *Reading From Right to Left: Essays on the Hebrew Bible in Honor of David J. A. Clines*, edited by Cheryl J. Exum and H. G. M. Williamson, 205–15. JSOTSup 373. New York: Sheffield Academic, 2003.

———. "Writing Israel's History at the End of the Twentieth Century." In *CVO* 203–18.

Graham, M. Patrick. "Aspects of the Structure and Rhetoric of 2 Chronicles 25." In *History and Interpretation: Essays in Honour of John H. Hayes*, edited by M. Patrick Graham, 78–89. JSOTSup 173. Sheffield: JSOT Press, 1993.

———. "The 'Chronicler's History': Ezra, Nehemiah, 1–2 Chronicles." In *Hebrew Bible Today: An Introduction to Critical Issues*, edited by Steven L. McKenzie and M. Patrick Graham, 201–15. Louisville: Westminster John Knox, 1998.

———. "Setting the Heart to Seek God: Worship in 2 Chronicles 30:1–31:1." In *Worship and the Hebrew Bible: Essays in Honour of John T. Willis*, edited by M. Patrick Graham et al., 124–41. JSOTSup 284. Sheffield: Sheffield Academic, 1999.

———. *The Utilization of 1 and 2 Chronicles in the Reconstruction of Israelite History in the Nineteenth Century.* SBLDS 116. Atlanta: Scholars, 1990.

Gramberg, Carl Peter Wilhelm. *Die Chronik nach ihrem geschichtlichen Charakter und ihrer Glaubwürdigkeit.* Halle: Anton, 1823.

Green, J. B. "Modernity, History and the Theological Interpretation of the Bible." *Scottish Journal of Theology* 54 (2001) 308–29.

Greenberg, Moshe. "The Design and Themes of Ezekiel's Program of Restoration." *Int* 38 (1984) 181–204.

Greenwood, David. "Rhetorical Criticism and Formgeschichte: Some Methodological Considerations." *JBL* 89 (1970) 418–26.

Groff, Ruth. *Critical Realism, Post-Positivism and the Possibility of Knowledge.* Routledge Studies in Critical Realism. New York: Routledge, 2004.

Grol, Harm van. "1 Chronicles 16: The Chronicler's Psalm and Its View of History." In *Rewriting Biblical History: Essays on Chronicles and Ben Sira in Honor of Pancratius C. Beentjes*, edited by Harm van Grol and Jeremy Corley, 97–121. Deuterocanonical and Cognate Literature Studies 7. Berlin: de Gruyter, 2011.

Grosos, Philippe. "Lire Hegel: Avec ou sans la cohérence du système?" *Revue Philosophique de Louvain* 112 (2014) 655–72.

Gunn, David M. "Entertainment, Ideology, and the Reception of 'History': 'David's Jerusalem' as a Question of Space." In *"A Wise and Discerning Mind": Essays in Honor of Burke O. Long*, edited by Burke O. Long et al., 153–61. Brown Judaic Studies 325. Providence: Brown University, 2000.

Gunneweg, A. H. J. *Leviten und Priester. Hauptlinen der Traditionsbildung und Geschichte des israelitisch-jüdischen Kultpersonals.* Forschungen zur Religion und Literatur des Alten und Neuen Testaments 89. Göttingen: Vandenhoeck & Ruprecht, 1965.

Habib, Irfan. "Problems of Marxist Historiography." *Social Scientist* 16 (1988) 3–13.

Hallo, William W. "Biblical History in Its Near Eastern Setting: The Contextual Approach." In *Scripture in Context: Essays on the Comparative Method*, edited by C. D. Evans, 1–18. Pittsburgh: Pickwick, 1980.

———. "The Bible and the Monuments." In *COS* 2:xxi–xxvi.

———. "The Birth of Rhetoric." In *Rhetoric Before and Beyond the Greeks*, edited by Carol S. Lipson and Roberta A. Binkley, 25–46. Albany: State University of New York Press, 2004.

———. "The Blessing of Nisaba by Enki." In *COS* 1:531–32.

———. "Introduction: Ancient Near Eastern Texts and Their Relevance for Biblical Exegesis." In *COS* 1:xxiii–xxviii.

———. "The Limits of Skepticism." *JAOS* 110 (1990) 187–99.

———. "Sumer and the Bible." In *COS* 3:xlix–liv.

Hallo, William W., and William Kelly Simpson. *The Ancient Near East: A History*. Fort Worth: Harcourt Brace, 1998.

Halpern, Baruch. *The First Historians: The Hebrew Bible and History*. University Park: Pennsylvania State University Press, 1988.

———. "Levitic Participation in the Reform Cult of Jeroboam I." *JBL* 95 (1976) 31–42.

Hamilton, Mark W. "The Problem of History in Old Testament Theology: A Review Essay." *Restoration Quarterly* 50 (2008) 197–211.

Hamilton, Victor. "אָח." In *NIDOTTE* 1:343–44.

Hanson, P. D. "1 Chronicles 15–16 and the Chronicler's Views on the Levites." In *ShaTal* 69–78.

Hanspach, Alexander. *Inspirierte Interpreten: Das Prophetenverständnis der Chronikbücher und sein Ort in der Religion und Literatur zur Zeit des Zweiten Tempels*. Arbeiten zu Text und Sprache im Alten Testament 64. St. Ottilien: EOS, 2000.

Haran, Menahem. "Priests and Priesthood." In *EncJud* 13:1070–86.

———. "Studies in the Account of the Levitical Cities. I. Preliminary Considerations." *JBL* 80 (1961) 45–54.

———. *Temples and Temple-Service in Ancient Israel*. Oxford: Clarendon, 1978. Reprint, Winona Lake: Eisenbrauns, 1985.

Harper, William R. *The Work of the Old Testament Priests: A Study of the Development of Ideas Concerning Worship*. Edited by William R. Harper and Ernest D. Burton. Constructive Bible Studies. Chicago: University of Chicago Press, 1908.

Harris, R. Laird. "Chronicles and the Canon in New Testament Times." *JETS* 33 (1990) 75–84.

Harrison, R. K. *Introduction to the Old Testament*. Grand Rapids: Eerdmans, 1969. Reprint, Peabody: Hendrickson, 2004.

Harsgor, Michael. "Total History: The Annales School." *Journal of Contemporary History* 13 (1978) 1–13.

Hartley, John E. *Leviticus*. WBC 4. Dallas: Word, 1992.

Harvey-Jellie, W. *Chronicles: Introduction, Revised Version with Notes, Index and Map*. The New-Century Bible. Oxford: Oxford University Press, 1906.

Hasel, Gerhard F. "The Nature of Biblical Theology: Recent Trends and Issues." *Andrews University Seminary Studies* 32 (1994) 203–15.

———. *Old Testament Theology: Basic Issues in the Current Debate. Revised, Updated & Enlarged*. 4th ed. Grand Rapids: Eerdmans, 1991.

———. "The Problem of History in OT Theology." *Andrews University Seminary Studies* 8 (1970) 23–50.

Hauer, Chris. "David and the Levites." *JSOT* 23 (1982) 33–54.

Hayes, John H. "The History of the Study of Israelite and Judean History: From the Renaissance to the Present." In *Israelite and Judean History*, edited by John H. Hayes and J. Maxwell Miller, 33–69. Philadelphia: Westminster, 1977.

Hays, Christopher, with Peter Machinist. "Assyria and the Assyrians." In *WOT* 31–106.
Hegel, Georg Wilhelm Friedrich. *The Philosophy of History*. Translated by J. Sibree. Mineola: Dover, 1956.
Hegel, Georg Wilhelm Friedrich, and Peter Crafts Hodgson. *Lectures on the Philosophy of Religion*. 3 vols. Berkeley: University of California Press, 1984–1987.
Held, Klaus. "Wonder, Time, and Idealization: On the Greek Beginning of Philosophy." *Epoche: A Journal for the History of Philosophy* 9 (2005) 185–96.
Hempel, Carl G. "The Function of General Laws in History." In *Readings in the Philosophy of Social Science*, edited by Michael Martin and Lee C. McIntyre. Cambridge: MIT Press, 1994 [1942].
Hengstenberg, Ernst Wilhelm. *Christologie des Alten Testamentes und Commentar über die messianischen Weissagungen*. Berlin: Oehmigke, 1854.
———. *Christology of the Old Testament and a Commentary on the Messianic Predictions*. Kregel Reprint Library. Grand Rapids: Kregel, 1970.
———. *Geschichte des Reiches Gottes unter dem alten Bunde*. Berlin: Schlawitz, 1869.
———. *History of the Kingdom of God under the Old Testament*. Edinburgh: T&T Clark, 1871.
Hens-Piazza, Gina. *Of Methods, Monarchs, and Meanings: A Sociorhetorical Approach to Exegesis*. Studies in Old Testament Interpretation 3. Macon: Mercer University Press, 1996.
Herder, Johann Gottfried. *Ideen zur Philosophie der Geschichte der Menschheit*. Darmstadt: Melzer, 1966 [1784–91].
Hess, Richard S. "An Archeological Synthesis of Israel's History." *BBR* 30 (2020) 261–76.
———. "History of Israel." In *DTIB* 299–302.
———. *The Old Testament: A Historical, Theological, and Critical Introduction*. Grand Rapids: Baker. 2016.
Hicks, John Mark. *1 & 2 Chronicles*. The College Press NIV Commentary. Joplin: College, 2003.
Hicks, R. Lansing. "A Bibliography of James Muilenburg's Writings." In *Israel's Prophetic Heritage: Essays in Honor of James Muilenburg*, edited by Bernard W. Anderson and Walter Harrelson, 233–42. New York: Harper, 1962.
Hill, Andrew E. *1 and 2 Chronicles*. NIVAC. Grand Rapids: Zondervan, 2003.
———. "Levitical Cities." In *NIDOTTE* 5:905–7.
———. "Patchwork Poetry or Reasoned Verse? Connective Structure in 1 Chronicles XVI." *VT* 45 (1995) 82–106.
Ho, Craig Y. S. "Conjectures and Refutations: Is 1 Samuel xxxi 1–13 Really the Source of 1 Chronicles x 1–12?" *VT* 45 (1995) 82–106.
Hoerth, Alfred J. *Archaeology and the Old Testament*. Grand Rapids: Baker, 2009.
Hoffmeier, James K. *Ancient Israel in Sinai: The Evidence for the Authenticity of the Wilderness Tradition*. Oxford: Oxford University Press, 2005.
———. *Israel in Egypt: The Evidence for the Authenticity of the Exodus Tradition*. Oxford: Oxford University Press, 1997.
———. "Understanding Hebrew and Egyptian Military Texts: A Contextual Approach." In *COS* 3:xxi–xxvii.
Hoffner, Harry A. "Hittite-Israelite Cultural Parallels." In *COS* 3:xxviii–xxxiv.
Hoglund, Kenneth G. "The Chronicler as Historian: A Comparativist Perspective." In *CaH* 18–29.

———. "The Priest of Praise: The Chronicler's David." *Review & Expositor* 99 (2002) 185–91.
Holdridge, Donald Wesley. "An Argument for a Late Sixth Century Date for the Book of Chronicles." ThD diss., Dallas Theological Seminary, 1992.
Hooker, Paul K. *First and Second Chronicles*. Westminster Bible Companion. Louisville: Westminster John Knox, 2001.
House, Paul R. 2009. "God's Design and Postmodernism: Recent Approaches to Old Testament Theology." In *The Old Testament in the Life of God's People: Essays in Honor of Elmer A. Martens*, edited by Jon Isaak, 29–54. Winona Lake: Eisenbrauns, 2009.
———. *Old Testament Theology*. Downers Grove: InterVarsity, 1998.
———. "The Rise and Current Status of Literary Criticism of the Old Testament." In *Beyond Form Criticism: Essays in Old Testament Literary Criticism*, edited by Paul R. House, 3–23. Winona Lake: Eisenbrauns, 1992.
Houwink ten Cate, Philo H. J. "Hittite History." In *ABD* 3:219–25.
Howard, David M., Jr. "History as History: The Search for Meaning." In *GtS* 25–53. Grand Rapids: Kregel, 2003.
———. *An Introduction to the Old Testament Historical Books*. Chicago: Moody, 1993.
———. "The Psalms and Current Study." In *Interpreting the Psalms: Issues and Approaches*, edited by David Firth and Philip S. Johnston, 23–40. Downers Grove: InterVarsity Press, 2005.
———. "Recent Trends in Psalms Study." In *The Face of Old Testament Studies: A Survey of Contemporary Approaches*, edited by David W. Baker and Bill T. Arnold. Grand Rapids: Baker, 1999.
———. "Rhetorical Criticism in Old Testament Studies." *BBR* 4 (1994) 87–104.
Howard, Thomas A. *Religion and the Rise of Historicism: W. M. L. de Wette, Jacob Burckhardt, and the Theological Origins of Nineteenth-Century Historical Consciousness*. Cambridge: Cambridge University Press, 2000.
Huizinga, Johan. "A Definition of the Concept of History." In *Philosophy and History: Essays Presented to Ernst Cassirer*, edited by R. Klibansky and H. J. Paton, 1–10. New York: Harper & Row, 1963.
Human, Dirk. "Cultic Music in the Ancient Orient and in Ancient Israel/Palestine." *Verkündigung Und Forschung* 56 (2011) 45–52.
Hunt, Alice Wells. "The Zadokites: Finding Their Place in the Hebrew Bible." PhD diss., Vanderbilt University, 2003.
Hunt, Lynn. "French History in the Last Twenty Years: The Rise and Fall of the Annales Paradigm." *Journal of Contemporary History* 21 (1986) 209–24.
Hurvitz, Avi. "Terms and Epithets Relating to the Jerusalem Temple Compound in the Book of Chronicles: The Linguistic Aspect." In *Pomegranates and Golden Bells: Studies in Biblical, Jewish, and Near Eastern Ritual, Law, and Literature in Honor of Jacob Milgrom*, edited by David P. Wright et al., 165–83. Winona Lake: Eisenbrauns, 1995.
Hynson, Leon O. "Toynbee's Approach to the History of Religions." *Journal of Religious Thought* 34 (1877) 40–49.
Iggers, Georg G. *The German Conception of History: The National Tradition of Historical Thought from Herder to the Present*. Middletown: Wesleyan University Press, 1968.
———. *Historiography in the Twentieth Century*. Hanover: University Press of New England, 1997.

Illman, Karl-Johan. *Thema und Tradition in den Asaf-Psalmen*. Åbo: Åbo Akademi, 1976.
Im, Tae-Soo. "Das Davidbild in den Chronikbüchern." PhD diss., Rheinische Friedrich-Wilhelms-Universität, 1985.
Ingeborg, Gabriel. *Friede über Israel: Eine Untersuchung zur Friedenstheologie in Chronik I 10–II 36*. Österreichische Biblische Studien. Klosterneuburg: Österreichisches Katholisches Bibelwerk, 1990.
Jacob, Edmond. *Théologie de l'Ancien Testament*. Manuels et précis de théologie. Neuchâtel: Delachaux & Niestlé, 1955.
Jacobson, Rolf A., and Karl N. Jacobson. *Invitation to the Psalms: A Reader's Guide for Discovery and Engagement*. Grand Rapids: Baker Academic, 2013.
James, E. O. *The Nature and Function of Priesthood: A Comparative and Anthropological Study*. New York: Vanguard, 1955.
Jameson, Fredric. "Marxism and Historicism." *New Literary History* 11 (1979) 41–73.
Janowski, Bernd. "Die heilige Wohnung des Höchsten. Kosmologische Implikationen der Jerusalemer Tempeltheologie." In *Gottesstadt und Gottesgarten: Zu Geschichte und Theologie des Jerusalemer Tempels*, edited by Othmaar Keel and Erich Zenger, 24–68. Quaestiones Disputatae 191. Freiburg: Herder, 2002.
Janzen, David. *Chronicles and the Politics of Davidic Restoration: A Quiet Revolution*. LHBOTS 655. London: T&T Clark, 2017.
Japhet, Sara. "Conquest and Settlement in Chronicles." *JBL* 98 (1979) 205–18.
———. "The Distribution of the Priestly Gifts According to a Document of the Second Temple Period." In *Texts, Temples, and Traditions: A Tribute to Menahem Haran*, edited by Michael V. Fox et al., 3–20. Winona Lake: Eisenbrauns, 1996.
———. "Exile and Restoration in the Book of Chronicles." In *Crisis of Israelite Religion: Transformation of Religious Tradition in Exilic and Post-Exilic Times*, edited by Bob Becking and Marjo C. A. Korpel, 33–44. Oudtestamentische Studiën 42. Leiden: Brill, 1999.
———. *From the Rivers of Babylon to the Highlands of Judah: Collected Studies on the Restoration Period*. Winona Lake: Eisenbrauns, 2006.
———. "The Historical Reliability of Chronicles: The History of the Problem and Its Place in Biblical Research." *JSOT* 33 (1985) 83–107.
———. *I and II Chronicles*. OTL. Louisville: Westminster John Knox, 1993.
———. *The Ideology of the Book of Chronicles and Its Place in Biblical Thought*. BEATAJ 9. Frankfurt: Lang, 1989.
———. "The Israelite Legal and Social Reality as Reflected in Chronicles: A Case Study." In *ShaTal* 79–91.
———. "L'historiographie post-éxilique: Comment et pourquoi?" In *Israël construit son histoire: l'historiographie deutéronomiste à la lumière des recherches récentes*, edited by Rainer Albertz et al., 123–52. Le monde de la Bible 34. Geneva: Labor & Fides, 1996.
———. "Periodization: Between History and Ideology: The Neo-Babylonian Period in Biblical Historiography." In *Judah and the Judeans in the Neo-Babylonian Period*, edited by Oded Lipschitz and Joseph Blenkinsopp, 75–89. Winona Lake: Eisenbrauns, 2003.
———. "Periodization Between History and Ideology II: Chronology and Ideology in Ezra/Nehemiah." In *Judah and the Judeans in the Persian Period*, edited by Oded Lipschitz and Manfred Oeming, 491–508. Winona Lake: Eisenbrauns, 2006.

———. "The Prohibition of the Habitation of Women: The Temple Scroll's Attitude Toward Sexual Impurity and Its Biblical Precedents." *JANES* 22 (1993) 69–87.

———. "The Relationship Between Chronicles and Ezra-Nehemiah." In *Congress Volume: Leuven 1989*, edited by J. A. Emerton, 298–313. VTSup 43. Leiden: Brill, 1991.

———. "Some Biblical Concepts of Sacred Place." In *Sacred Space: Shrine, City, Land*, edited by Benjamin Z. Kedar and R. J. Zwi Werblowsky, 55–72. New York: New York University Press, 1998.

———. "The Supposed Common Authorship of Chronicles and Ezra-Nehemiah Investigated Anew." *VT* 18 (1968) 330–98.

———. "The Temple in the Restoration Period: Reality and Ideology." *Union Seminary Quarterly Review* 44 (1991) 195–251.

———. "The Writings: 1 and 2 Chronicles." In *Hebrew Bible: History of Interpretation*, edited by John H. Hayes, 115–26. Nashville: Abingdon, 2004.

Jarick, John. *1 Chronicles*. Readings: A New Biblical Commentary. London: Sheffield Academic, 2002.

Jeanrond, Werner G. *Text and Interpretation as Categories of Theological Thinking*. Translated by T. J. Wilson. New York: Crossroad, 1988.

———. *Text und Interpretation als Kategorien theologischen Denkens*. Hermeneutische Untersuchungen zur Theologie 23. Tübingen: Mohr, 1986.

———. "Text, Textuality." In *DTIB* 782–84.

———. *Theological Hermeneutics: Development and Significance*. New York: Crossroad, 1991.

Jellicow, S. "The Interpretation of Psalm lxxxiii. 24." *Expository Times* 67 (1956) 209–10.

Jendrek, Matthias. "Taking the Reader into Utopia." In *Worlds That Could Not Be: Utopia in Chronicles, Ezra, and Nehemiah*, edited by Steven J. Schweitzer and Frauke Uhlenbruch, 171–82. LHBOTS 620. London: T&T Clark, 2016.

Jensen, P. *Graded Holiness: A Key to the Priestly Conception of the World*. JSOTSup 106. Sheffield: Sheffield Academic, 1992.

———. "Priest and Levites." In *NIDOTTE* 4:1066–67.

———. "לוי." In *NIDOTTE* 2:772–78.

Jepsen, Alfred. "Mose und die Leviten: Ein Beitrag zur Frügeschichte Israels und zur Sammlung des altestamentlichen Schrifttums." *VT* 31 (1981) 318–23.

Jeremias, Jorg. *Theologie des Alten Testaments*. Grundrisse zum Alten Testament 6. Göttingen: Vandenhoeck & Ruprecht, 2015.

Joannès, Francis. "Administration des Temples." In *DCM* 9–15.

Johnson, Marshall D. *The Purpose of the Biblical Genealogies, with Special Reference to the Setting of the Genealogies of Jesus*. Society for New Testament Studies: Monograph Series 8. Cambridge: Cambridge University Press, 1969.

Johnston, Philip S. "Psalm 49: A Personal Eschatology." In *Eschatology in Bible & Theology: Evangelical Essays at the Dawn of a New Millennium*, edited by Kent E. Brower and Mark W. Elliot, 73–84. Downers Grove: InterVarsity, 1997.

Johnstone, William. *1 and 2 Chronicles*. 2 vols. JSOTSup 253–54. Sheffield: Sheffield Academic, 1997.

———. *Chronicles and Exodus: An Analogy and Its Application*. JSOTSup 275. Sheffield: Sheffield Academic, 1998.

———. "Guilt and Atonement: The Theme of 1 and 2 Chronicles." In *A Word in Season: Essays in Honor of William McKane*, edited by J. D. Martin and Philip R. Davies, 113–38. JSOTSup 42. Sheffield: JSOT Press, 1986.
———. "Solomon's Prayer: Is Intentionalism Such a Fallacy?" *Studia theologica* 47 (1993) 119–33.
———. "The Use of Leviticus in Chronicles." In *Reading Leviticus: A Conversation with Mary Douglas*, edited by John F. A. Sawyer, 243–55. JSOTSup. Sheffield: Sheffield, 1996.
Jones, Christine Brown. "The Message of the Asaphite Collection and Its Role in the Psalter." In *The Shape and Shaping of the Book of Psalms: The Current State of Scholarship*, edited by Nancy DeClaissé-Walford, 71–86. Ancient Israel and Its Literature 20. Atlanta: SBL, 2014.
Jones, Gwilym H. *1 & 2 Chronicles*. Sheffield, England: JSOT Press, 1993.
Jones, Ivor H. "Music and Musical Instruments." In *ABD* 4:934–39.
Jonker, Louis C. *1 & 2 Chronicles*. Understanding the Bible Commentary Series. Grand Rapids: Baker, 2013.
———. "The Chronicler Singing Psalms: Revisiting the Chronicler's Psalm in 1 Chronicles 16." In *"My Spirit at Rest in the North Country" (Zechariah 6.8): Collected Communications to the XXth Congress of the International Organization for the Study of the Old Testament, Helsinki 2010*, edited by Hermann Michael Niemann and Matthias Augustin, 115–31. BEATAJ 57. Frankfurt: Lang, 2011.
———. "Of Jebus, Jerusalem, and Benjamin: The Chronicler's *Sondergut* in 1 Chronicles 21 against the Background of the Late Persian Era in Yehud." In *CtheC* 81–102.
Julius, Christiane-Barbara. *Die ausgeführten Schrifttypologien bei Paulus*. Europäische Hochschulschriften. Reihe XXIII, Theologie 668. Frankfurt: Lang 1999.
Kaiser, Gottlieb Philipp Christian. *Die biblische Theologie*. Erlangen: Palm, 1813.
Kaiser, Walter C. *The Old Testament Documents: Are They Reliable & Relevant?* Downers Grove: InterVarsity Press, 2001.
———. "Preaching from Historical Narrative Texts of the Old Testament." *GtS* 439–546.
———. *Toward an Old Testament Theology*. Grand Rapids: Zondervan, 1978.
Kalimi, Isaac. *An Ancient Israelite Historian: Studies in the Chronicler, His Time, Place and Writing*. Studia Semitica Neerlandica 46. Assen: VanGorcum, 2005.
———. *The Books of Chronicles in Jewish Tradition and Exegesis: Interpretation, Reception and Impact-History from the Earliest Times to the Beginning of Modern Biblical Scholarship*. JSOTSup 415. London: T&T Clark, 2005.
———. "The Capture of Jerusalem in the Chronistic History." *VT* 52 (2002) 66–79.
———. *Das Chronikbuch und seine Chronik: Zur Entstehung und Rezeption eines Biblisches Buches*. Fuldaer Studien 17. Freiburg: Herder, 2013.
———. "The Date of the Book of Chronicles." In *God's Word for Our World: Biblical Studies in Honor of Simon John De Vries*, edited by J. Harold Ellens et al., 347–71. JSOTSup 38. New York: T&T Clark, 2004.
———. "Die Abfassungskeit der Chronik, Forschungstand und Perskpektiven." *ZAW* 105 (1993) 223–33.
———. "Jerusalem, The Divine City: The Representation of Jerusalem in Chronicles Compared with Earlier and Later Jewish Compositions." In *CaT* 189–205.
———. "Könnte die aramäische Grabinschrift aus Ägypten als Indikation für die Datierung der Chronikbücher fungieren." *ZAW* 110 (1998) 79–81.

———. "Models for Jewish Bible Theologies: Tasks and Challenges." *Horizons in Biblical Theology* 39 (2017) 107–33.

———. *The Reshaping of Ancient Israelite History in Chronicles*. Winona Lake: Eisenbrauns, 2005.

———. "The View of Jerusalem in the Ethnographical Introduction of Chronicles (1 Chr 1–9)." *Bib* 83 (2002) 556–62.

———. "Was the Chronicler a Historian?" In *CaH* 73–91.

Kallai, Zekharyah. "Organizational and Administrative Frameworks in the Kingdom of David and Solomon." In *Biblical Historiography and Historical Geography: Collection of Studies*, 130–64. BEATAJ 44. Frankfurt: Lang, 1998.

Kansteiner, Wolf. "Hayden White's Critique of the Writing of History." In *Historiography: Critical Concepts in Historical Studies: Volume IV: Culture*, edited by Robert M. Burns, 379–467. Critical Concepts in Historical Studies. London: Routledge, 2006.

Kant, Immanuel. *Critique of Pure Reason*. Translated by Norman Kemp Smith. New York: St. Martin's, 1965.

———. *Kritik der reinen Vernunft*. Philosophische bibliothek 37a. Hamburg: Meiner, 1956.

Karsenti, Bruno. *Politique de l'esprit: Auguste Comte et la naissance de la science sociale*. Collection Savoir. Paris: Hermann, 2006.

Katz, Ben Zion. "Kimchi and Tanhum ben Joseph Hayerushalmi on Chronicles." *Jewish Bible Quarterly* 26 (1998) 45–51.

Kaufmann, Yehezkel. *The Religion of Israel: From Its Beginnings to the Babylonian Exile*. Translated by Moshe Greenberg. Chicago: University of Chicago Press, 1960.

Kautzsch, E. *Biblische theologie des Alten Testaments*. Tübingen: Mohr & Siebeck, 1911.

Keel, Othmaar. "Der salomonische Tempelweispruch. Beobachtungen zum religionsgeschitlichen Kontext des Ersten Jerusalemer Tempels." In *Gottesstadt und Gottesgarten: Zu Geschichte und Theologie des Jerusalemer Tempel*, edited by Othmaar Keel and Erich Zenger, 9–23. Quaestiones Disputatae 191. Freiburg: Herder, 2002.

———. *The Symbolism of the Biblical World: Ancient Near Eastern Iconography and the Book of Psalms*. London: SPCK, 1978.

Kegler, Jürgen. "Das Zurücktreten der Exodustradition in den Chronikbüchern." In *Schöpfung und Befreiung: Für Claus Westermann zum 80 Geburtstag*, edited by Rainer Albertz et al., 54–66. Stuttgart: Calwer, 1989.

———. "Prophetengestalten im Deuteronomistischen Geschischtswerk und in den Chronikbüchern. Ein Beitrag zur Kompositions und Redaktiongeschichte der Chronikbücher." *ZAW* 105 (1993) 481–97.

Kegler, Jürgen, and Matthias Augustin. *Synopse zum Chronistischen Geschichtswerk*. BEATAJ 1. Frankfurt: Lang, 1984.

Keil, C. F. *Apologetischer Versuch über die Bücher der Chronik, und über die Integrität des Buches Esra*. Berlin: Oehmigke, 1833.

———. *Biblischer Commentar über die Bücher Moses*. Keil, C. F. und F. Delitzsch, Biblischer Commentar über das Alten Testament 1. 3rd ed. Leipzig: Dörffling und Frankke, 1878.

———. *The Pentateuch*. Keil, C. F. and F. Delitzsch: Biblical Commentary on the Old Testament 1. Edinburgh: T&T Clark, 1866.

Kellerman, D. "לֵוִים לֵוִי." In *TDOT* 7:483–503.

Kellerman, Ulrich. "Amerkungen zum Verständnis der Tora in den chronistischen Schriften." *BN* 42 (1988) 49–92.
Kelley, Donald R. "Mythistory in the Age of Ranke." In *Leopold von Ranke and the Shaping of the Historical Discipline*, edited by Georg G. Iggers and James M. Powell, 3–22. Syracuse: Syracuse University Press, 1990.
Kelly, Brad E. *Hosea 2: Metaphor and Rhetoric in Historical Perspective*. Society of Biblical Literature Academia Biblica 20. Atlanta: SBL, 2005.
Kelly, Brian E. *Retribution and Eschatology in Chronicles*. JSOTSup 211. Sheffield: Sheffield Academic, 1996.
———. "Retribution Revisited: Covenant, Grace, and Restoration." In *CaT* 206–27.
Kempshall, Matthew. *Rhetoric and the Writing of History, 400–1500*. Manchester: Manchester University Press, 2011.
Kennedy, George A. *Classical Rhetoric & Its Christian & Secular Tradition from Ancient to Modern Times*. 2nd ed. Revised and enlarged. Chapel Hill: University of North Carolina Press, 1999.
———. *New Testament Interpretation Through Rhetorical Criticism*. Studies in Religion. Chapel Hill: University of North Carolina Press, 1984.
Kerry, Paul E. *Enlightenment Thought in the Writings of Goethe: A Contribution to the History of Ideas*. Studies in German Literature, Linguistics, and Culture. Rochester: Camden, 2001.
Kessler, Martin. "An Introduction to Rhetorical Criticism of the Bible: Prolegomena." *Semitics* 7 (1980) 1–27.
———. "A Methodological Setting for Rhetorical Criticism." *Semitics* 4 (1974) 22–36.
Keulen, P. S. F. van. "A Touch of Chronicles: The Provenance of 3 Reigns 10:26–26a." In *X Congress of the International Organization for Septuagint and Cognate Studies, Oslo, 1998*, edited by Bernard A. Taylor, 441–61. Society of Biblical Literature Septuagint and Cognate Studies Series 51. Atlanta: SBL, 2001.
Kidner, Derek. *Psalms 73–150*. TOTC 14b. Downers Grove: InterVarsity Press, 1973.
Kikawada, Isaac M. "Some Proposals for the Definition of Rhetorical Criticism." *Semitics* 5 (1977) 67–91.
Kilmer, Anne Draffkorn. "Music and Dance in Ancient Western Asia." In *CANE* 4:2601–13.
Kim, Yeong Seon. *The Temple Administration and the Levites in Chronicles*. Catholic Biblical Quarterly Monograph Series 51. Washington, DC: Catholic Biblical Association of America, 2014.
King, Andrew. "The State of Rhetorical Criticism." *Rhetoric Review* 25 (2006) 365–88.
King, Philip J. "The Musical Tradition of Ancient Israel." In *Realia Dei: Essays in Archaeology and Biblical Interpretation in Honor of Edward F. Campbell, Jr. at His Retirement*, edited by Prescott H. Williams Jr. and Theodore Hiebert, 84–99. Atlanta: Scholars, 1999.
King, Philip J., and Lawrence E. Stager. *Life in Biblical Israel*. Library of Ancient Israel. Louisville: Westminster John Knox, 2001.
Kitchen, K. A. *Ancient Orient and Old Testament*. Chicago: InterVarsity, 1966.
———. *The Bible in Its World: The Bible and Archaeology Today*. Downers Grove: InterVarsity, 1977.
———. "The Controlling Role of External Evidence in Assessing the Historical Status of the Israelite United Monarchy." In *Windows into Old Testament History: Evidence, Argument, and the Crisis of "Biblical Israel"*, edited by Philips V. Long, 103–10. Grand Rapids: Eerdmans, 2002.

———. *On the Reliability of the Old Testament*. Grand Rapids: Eerdmans, 2003.

Kittel, Rudolf. *Die Bücher der Chronik*. Handkommentar zum Alten Testament. I. Abteilung, Die historischen Bücher 1. Göttingen: Vandenhoeck & Ruprecht, 1902.

Klawans, Jonathan. *Purity, Sacrifice, and the Temple: Symbolism and Supersessionism in the Study of Ancient Judaism*. Oxford: Oxford University Press, 2006.

Klein, Ralph W. *1 Chronicles: A Commentary*. Hermeneia: A Critical and Historical Commentary on the Bible. Minneapolis: Fortress, 2006.

———. "Chronicles, Book of 1–2." In *ABD* 1:992–1002

———. "How Many in a Thousand." In *CaH* 270–82.

———. "The Ironic End of Joash in Chronicles." In *For a Later Generation: The Transformation of Tradition in Israel, Early Judaism, and Early Christianity*, edited by Randal A. Argall et al., 116–27. Harrisburg: Trinity, 2000.

———. *Israel in Exile: A Theological Interpretation*. Overtures in Biblical Theology. Philadelphia: Fortress, 1978.

———. "The Last Words of David." *Currents in Theology and Mission* 31 (2004) 15–23.

———. "Reflections on Historiography in the Account of Jehoshaphat." In *Pomegranates and Golden Bells: Studies in Biblical, Jewish, and Near Eastern Ritual, Law, and Literature in Honor of Jacob Milgrom*, edited by David P. Wright et al., 643–57. Winona Lake: Eisenbrauns, 1995.

Kleinig, John W. "Bach, Chronicles, and Church Music." *Lutheran Theological Journal* 34 (2000) 140–46.

———. "The Divine Institution of the Lord's Song in Chronicles." *JSOT* 55 (1992) 75–83.

———. *The Lord's Song: The Basis, Function, and Significance of Choral Music in Chronicles*. JSOTSup 156. Sheffield: JSOT Press, 1993.

———. "Recent Research in Chronicles." *Currents in Research: Biblical Studies* 2 (1994) 43–76.

Klingbeil, Gerald A. *A Comparative Study of the Ritual of Ordination as Found in Leviticus 8 and Emar 369*. Lewiston: Mellen, 1998.

———. "Historical Criticism." In *DOTHB* 401–20.

———. "Priests and Levites." In *DOTHB* 811–19.

———. "Priests in the Ancient Near East." In *BSOT* 355–60.

Klink, Edward W., III, and Darian R. Lockett. *Understanding Biblical Theology: A Comparison of Theory and Practice*. Grand Rapids: Zondervan, 2012.

Knierim, Rolf P. "Cosmos and History in Israel's Theology." In *Werden und Wirken des Alten Testaments: Festschrift für Claus Westermann*, edited by Claus Westermann and Rainer Albertz, 59–123. Göttingen: Vandenhoeck & Ruprecht, 1980.

———. "On the Task of Old Testament Theology." In *Reading the Hebrew Bible for a New Millennium: Form, Concept and Theological Perspective. Volume 1: Theological and Hermeneutical Studies*, edited by Wonil Kim, 21–32. Harrisburg: Trinity, 2000.

———. *The Task of Old Testament Theology: Substance, Method, and Cases: Essays*. Grand Rapids: Eerdmans, 1995.

Knierim, Rolf P., and George W. Coats. *Numbers*. FOTL 4. Grand Rapids: Eerdmans, 2005.

Knohl, Israël. *The Sanctuary of Silence: The Priestly Torah and the Holiness School*. Winona Lake: Eisenbrauns, 2007.

———. "Between Voice and Silence: The Relationship Between Prayer and Temple Cult." *JBL* 115 (1996) 17–30.

Knoppers, Gary N. "An Achaemenid Imperial Authorization of Torah in Yehud?" In *Persia and Torah: The Theory of Imperial Authorization of the Pentateuch*, edited by James W. Watts, 115–34. Society of Biblical Literature Symposium Series 17. Atlanta: SBL, 2001.

———. *I Chronicles 1–9*. Anchor Bible 12A. New York: Doubleday, 2004.

———. *I Chronicles 10–29*. Anchor Bible 12B. New York: Doubleday, 2004.

———. "'The City Yhwh Has Chosen': The Chronicler's Promotion of Jerusalem in Light of Recent Archaeology." In *Jerusalem in Bible and Archaeology: The First Temple Period*, edited by Andrew G. Vaughn and Ann E. Killebrew, 307–26. Atlanta: SBL, 2003.

———. "Greek Historiography and the Chronicler's History: A Reexamination." *JBL* 122 (2003) 627–50.

———. "Hierodules, Priests, or Janitors? The Levites in Chronicles and the History of the Israelite Priesthood." *JBL* 118 (1999) 49–72.

———. "The Historical Study of the Monarchy: Developments and Detours." In *FAOTS* 207–35.

———. "History and Historiography: The Royal Reforms." In *Cah* 178–203.

———. "In Search of Post-Exilic Israel: Samaria After the Fall of the Northern Kingdom." In *SPreIs* 150–79.

———. "Jerusalem at War in Chronicles." In *Zion, City of our God*, edited by Richard S. Hess and Gordon J. Wenham, 57–76. Grand Rapids: Eerdmans, 1999.

———. "The Relationship of the Priestly Genealogies to the History of the High Priesthood in Jerusalem." In *Judah and the Judeans in the Neo-Babylonian Period*, edited by Oded Lipschitz and Joseph Blenkinsopp, 109–33. Winona Lake: Eisenbrauns, 2003.

———. "Shem, Ham and Japheth: The Universal and The Particular in the Genealogy of Nations." In *CaT* 13–31.

———. "'To Him You Must Listen': The Prophetic Legislation in Deuteronomy and the Reformation of Classical Tradition in Chronicles." In *CtheC* 161–94.

———. "Treasures Won and Lost: Royal (Mis)appropriations in Kings and Chronicles." In *ChrA* 181–208.

———. "'Yhwh Is Not with Israel': Alliances as a Topos in Chronicles." *CBQ* 58 (1996) 601–26.

Knoppers, Gary N., and Paul B. Harvey. "Omitted and Remaining Matters: On the Names Given to the Book of Chronicles in Antiquity." *JBL* 121 (2002) 227–43.

Ko, Ming Him. *The Levite Singers in Chronicles and Their Stabilising Role*. LHBOTS 657. New York: T&T Clark, 2017.

Koch, Klaus. "Der Psalter und seine Redaktionsgeschichte." In *Neue Wege der Psalmenforschung: für Walter Beyerlin*, edited by Klaus Seybold and Erich Freiburg, 243–77. Herders Biblische Studien 1. Freibrug: Herder, 1994.

———. "Ezra and Mehemoth: Remarks on the History of High Priesthood." In *ShaTal* 105–10.

Kofoed, Jens Bruun. "Epistemology, Historiographical Method, and the 'Copenhagen School.'" In *Windows into Old Testament History: Evidence, Argument, and the Crisis of "Biblical Israel"*, edited by Philips V. Long et al., 23–43. Grand Rapids: Eerdmans, 2002.

———. *Text and History: Historiography and the Study of the Biblical Text*. Winona Lake: Eisenbrauns, 2005.

Köhler, Ludwig. *Old Testament Theology*. Translated by A. S. Todd. Philadelphia: Westminster, 1957.

———. *Theologie des Alten Testaments*. Tübingen: Mohr, 1936.

Köhler, Ludwig, and Walter Baumgartner, eds. *The Hebrew and Aramaic Lexicon of the Old Testament: Study Edition*. Translated by M. E. J. Richardson. 2 vols. Leiden: Brill, 2001.

Koitabashi, Matahisa. "Significance of Ugaritic *msltm* 'Cymbals' in the Anat Text." In *Cult and Ritual in the Ancient Near East*, edited by Mikasa no Miya Takahito, 1–6. Bulletin of the Middle Eastern Culture Center in Japan 6. Wiesbaden: Otto Harrassowitz, 1992

Kraus, F. R. *The Role of Temples from the Third Dynasty of Ur to First Dynasty of Babylon*. Translated by B. Foster. Monographs of the Ancient Near East 2. Malibu: Undena, 1990.

Kremer-Marietti, Angèle, and Auguste Comte. *Auguste Comte et la théorie sociale du positivisme: Présentation, choix de textes, bio-bibliographie*. Philosophes de tous les temps 65. Paris: Seghers, 1970.

Kropat, Arno. *Die syntax des Autors der Chronik verglichen mit der seiner Quellen: Ein Beitrag zur historischen Syntax des Hebräischen*. BZAW 16. Giessen: Töpelmann, 1909.

Krüger, Thomas. "Recent Developments in the History of Ancient Israel and Their Consequences for a Theology of the Hebrew Bible." *BN* 144 (2010) 5–13.

Kuhrt, Amélie. *The Ancient Near East C. 3000-330 BC*. 2 vols. London: Routledge, 1995.

———. "Israelite and Near Eastern Historiography." In *CVO* 257–79.

———. "Some Thoughts on P. Briant, *Histoire de l'Empire perse*." In *Recherches récentes sur l'Empire achéménide*, edited by Jean Andreau et al., 299–304. Topoi: Orient-Occident Supplément 1. Paris: De Boccard, 1997.

Kuntzmann, Raymond. "David, constructeur du temple?" 139–56 in *Figures de David à travers la Bible*, edited by L. Desrousseaux and J. Vermeylen. Paris: Cerf, 1999.

———. "Dieu vient vers son lieu de repos (2 Ch 6,41)." In *Ce Dieu qui vient: Études sur l'Ancien et le Nouveau Testament offertes au Professeur Bernard Renaud à l'occasion de son soixante-cinquième anniversaire*, edited by Raymond Kuntzmann, 205–13. Lectio divina 159. Paris: Cerf, 1995.

Kuntzmann, Raymond, and Paul Beauchamp, eds. *Typologie biblique: De quelques figures vives*. Lectio divina. Paris: Cerf, 2002.

Kurtz, J. H. *Das mosaische Opfer: Ein Beitrag zur Symbolik des Mosaischen Cultus*. Mitau: Lucas, 1842.

———. *Geschichte des alten Bundes*. Berlin: Wohlgemuth, 1858–1864.

Kurtz, Paul Michael. "Axes of Inquiry: The Problem of Form and Time in Wellhausen and Gunkel." *Scandinavian Journal of the Old Testament* 29 (2015) 247–95.

Laato, Antti. "The Levitical Genealogies in 1 Chronicles 5–6 and the Formation of Levitical Ideology in Post-Exilic Judah." *JSOT* 62 (1994) 77–99.

Laberge, L. "Ministères et esprit dans les communautés postexiliques." *Église et théologie* 9 (1978) 379–412.

LaCapra, Dominick. *Rethinking Intellectual History: Texts, Contexts, Language*. Ithaca: Cornell University Press, 1983.

Laffey, Alice L. *First Chronicles, Second Chronicles*. Collegeville Bible Commentary: Old Testament 10. Collegeville: Liturgical, 1985.

Lafont, Bertrand. "ME." In *DCM* 514–15.

Laubach, Fritz. *Das erste Buch der Chronik*. Wuppertal: Brockhaus, 2000.
Leaver, Robin A. *J. S. Bach As Preacher: His Passions and Music in Worship*. St. Louis: Concordia, 1984.
———. *Music as Preaching: Bach, Passions and Music in Worship*. Latimer Studies 13. Oxford: Latimer, 1982.
Lefèvre, A. "Lévitique (Organisation)." In vol. 5 of *Dictionnaire de la Bible Supplément*, edited by Louis Pirot et al., 205–13. 7 vols. Paris: Letouzé & Ané, 1957.
Legarth, Peter V. "Typology and Its Theological Basis." *European Journal of Theology* 5 (1996) 143–55.
Leithart, Peter J. "Attendants of Yahweh's House: Priesthood in the Old Testament." *JSOT* 85 (1999) 3–24.
———. "Embracing Ritual: Sacraments as Rites." *Calvin Theological Journal* 40 (2005) 6–20.
———. *From Silence to Song: The Davidic Liturgical Revolution*. Moscow: Canon, 2003.
———. *1 & 2 Chronicles*. Brazos Theological Commentary on the Bible. Grand Rapids: Brazos, 2019.
Leloir, Louis. "Valeurs permanentes du sacerdoce lévitique." *Nouvelle Revue Théologique* 92 (1970) 246–66.
Lemche, Niels Peter. *Ancient Israel: A New History of Israelite Society*. The Biblical Seminar. Sheffield: JSOT Press, 1988.
———. *The Canaanites and Their Land: The Tradition of the Canaanites*. JSOTSup 110. Sheffield: JSOT Press, 1991.
———. *Early Israel: Anthropological and Historical Studies on the Israelite Society Before the Monarchy*. VTSup 37. Leiden: Brill, 1985.
———. *The Israelites in History and Tradition*. Library of Ancient Israel. London: SPCK, 1998.
———. "Jerusalem and King Solomon: How Writers Create the Past." In *Recenti tendenze nella ricostruzione della storia antica d'Israele: Convegno internazionale: Roma, 6-7 marzo 2003*, 73–86. Contributi del Centro linceo interdisciplinare "Beniamino Segre" 110. Rome: Accademia nazionale dei Lincei, 2005.
———. *Prelude to Israel's Past: Background and Beginnings of Israelite History and Identity*. Peabody: Hendrickson, 1998.
Lemke, Werner E. "Is Old Testament Theology an Essentially Christian Theological Discipline?" *Horizons in Biblical Theology* 11 (1989) 59–69.
———. "The Synoptic Problem in the Chronicler's History." *Harvard Theological Review* 58 (1965) 349–63.
———. "Synoptic Studies in the Chronicler's History." ThD diss., Harvard University, 1963.
———. "Theology (OT)." In *ABD* 6:448–73.
LeMon, Joel M. "Egypt and the Egyptians." In *WOT* 169–96.
Lengendre, A. "Lévi (Tribu de)." In *Dictionnaire de la Bible, contenant tous les noms mentionnés dans les Saintes Écritures, les questions théologiques, archéologiques, scientifiques, critiques relatives à l'Ancien et au Nouveau Testament et des notices sur les commentateurs anciens et modernes*, edited by F. Vigoroux, 4:200–13. 5 vols. Paris: Letouzé & Ané, 1912.
Levin, Yigal. "Who Was the Chronicler's Audience? A Hint from His Genealogies." *JBL* 122 (2003) 229–45.

Levenson, Jon D. *Creation and the Persistence of Evil: The Jewish Drama of Divine Omnipotence*. San Francisco: Harper & Row, 1988.
———. *The Hebrew Bible, the Old Testament, and Historical Criticism: Jews and Christians in Biblical Studies*. Louisville: Westminster John Knox, 1993.
———. *Sinai and Zion: An Entry into the Jewish Bible*. Minneapolis: Winston, 1985.
Lichtenheim, Miriam. "The Great Hymn to the Aten." In *COS* 1:44–46.
———. "The Great Hymn to Osiris." In *COS* 1:41–43.
———. "Song from the Tomb of Neferhotep." In *COS* 1:49–50.
———. "Song from the Tomb of King Intef." In *COS* 1:48–49.
Limburg, James. *Psalms*. Westminster Bible Companion. Louisville: Westminster John Knox, 2000.
Lipking, Lawrence I. "The Genie in the Lamp: M. H. Abrams and the Motives of Literary History." In *High Romantic Argument: Essays for M. H. Abrams*, edited by M. H. Abrams et al., 128–48 Ithaca: Cornell University Press, 1981.
Lipschitz, Oded. "Achaemenid Imperial Policy, Settlement Processes in Palestine, and the Status of Jerusalem in the Middle of the Fifth Century B.C.E." In *Judah and the Judeans in the Persian Period*, edited by Oded Lipschitz and Manfred Oeming, 19–52. Winona Lake: Eisenbrauns, 2006.
———. *The Fall and Rise of Jerusalem: Judah under Babylonian Rule*. Winona Lake: Eisenbrauns, 2005.
Lipson, Carol S. "Ancient Egyptian Rhetoric: It All Comes Down to Maat." In *Rhetoric Before and Beyond the Greeks*, edited by Carol S. Lipson and Roberta A. Binkle, 79–88. Albany: State University of New York Press, 2004.
Liss, Hanna. "The Imaginary Sanctuary: The Priestly Code as an Example of Fictional Literature in the Hebrew Bible." In *Judah and the Judeans in the Persian Period*, edited by Oded Lipschitz and Manfred Oeming, 663-90. Winona Lake: Eisenbrauns, 2006.
Liver, Jacob. *Chapters in the History of the Priests and Levites: Studies in the Lists of Chronicles and Ezra and Nehemiah*. Jerusalem: Magnes, 1968.
Lo, Hing Choi. "The Removal of the Ark of God as Was Recorded in 1 Chronicles: A Study on 1 Chr 13:1–14." *China Graduate School of Theology Journal* 24 (1998) 41–52.
Loader, James Alfred. "Making Things from the Heart: On Works of Beauty in the Old Testament." *OTE* 25 (2012) 100–14.
Long, Frederick J. *Ancient Rhetoric and Paul's Apology: The Compositional Unity of 2 Corinthians*. Society for New Testament Studies Monograph Series 131. Cambridge: Cambridge University Press, 2004.
Long, Philips V. *The Art of Biblical History*. Foundations of Contemporary Interpretation 5. Grand Rapids: Zondervan, 1994.
———. "Historical Interpretation of the OT: Three Basic Relationships." In *NIDOTTE* 1:86–102.
———. "Historiography of the Old Testament." In *FAOTS* 145–75.
———. "In Search of David: The David Tradition in Recent Study." In *FTH* 271–84.
———. "Introduction: Minimalism, Maximalism, and the Crisis in Old Testament Studies." In *Windows into Old Testament History: Evidence, Argument, and the Crisis of "Biblical Israel"*, edited by Philips V. Long, 1–22. Grand Rapids: Eerdmans, 2002.

Longman, Tremper, III. "Literary Approaches and Interpretation." In *NIDOTTE* 1:103–24.

———. "Literary Approaches to Old Testament Study." In *FAOTS* 97–115.

———. "The Literature of the Old Testament." In *CLGB* 95–107.

Longman, Tremper, III, and Leland Ryken. "Introduction." In *CLGB* 15–39.

Luyten, J. "Psalm 73 and Wisdom." In *La sagesse de l'Ancien Testament*, edited by Maurice Gilbert, 49–81. Bibliotheca Ephemeridum Theologicarum Lovaniensium 51. Leuven: Leuven University Press, 1990.

Lorenz, Chris. "Comparative Historiography: Problems and Perspectives." *History and Theory* 38 (1999) 25–39.

———. "Historical Knowledge and Historical Reality: A Plea for 'Internal Realism.'" In *Historiography: Critical Concepts in Historical Studies: Volume IV: Culture*, edited by Robert M. Burns, 434–67. Critical Concepts in Historical Studies. London: Routledge, 2006.

Lowery, R. H. *The Reforming Kings: Cult and Society in First Temple Judah*. JSOTSup 120. Sheffield: JSOT Press, 1991.

Lowth, Robert. *Lectures on the Sacred Poetry of the Hebrews*. New York: Leavitt, 1829 [1787].

Löwisch, Ingeborg. *Trauma Begets Genealogy: Gender and Memory in Chronicles*. Sheffield: Sheffield Phoenix, 2015.

Lund, Nils W. *Chiasmus in the New Testament: A Study in Formgeschichte*. Chapel Hill: University of North Carolina Press, 1942.

Lundbom, Jack R. *Biblical Rhetoric and Rhetorical Criticism*. Hebrew Bible Monographs 45. Sheffield: Sheffield Phoenix, 2013.

Lunsford, Andrea A., and Lisa E. Ede. "On Distinctions Between Classical and Modern Rhetoric." In *Essays on Classical Rhetoric and Modern Discourse*, edited by Robert J. Connors, 37–49. Carbondale: Southern Illinois University Press, 1984.

Lynch, Matthew. *Monotheism and Institutions in the Book of Chronicles: Temple, Priesthood, and Kingship in Post-Exilic Perspective*. Studies of the Sofja Kovalevskaja Research Group on Early Jewish Monotheism 1. Tübingen: Mohr Siebeck, 2014.

Lyons, Martin. "The End of Annales? Some Thoughts on the So-Called Death of the French Historical School." *The European Legacy* 1 (1996) 8–13.

Malamat, Abraham. "Weapons Deposited in a Sanctuary by Zimri-Lim of Mari and David and Saul of Israel." In *Ex Mesopotamia et Syria Lux: Festschrift für Manfried Dietrich zu seinem 65. Geburtstag*, edited by Oswald Loretz et al., 325–27. Alter Orient und Altes Testament 281. Münster: Ugarit, 2002.

Malone, Andrew S. *God's Mediators: A Biblical Theology of Priesthood*. New Studies in Biblical Theology. Downers Grove: InterVarsity, 2017.

Mandelbaum, Maurice. *History, Man, & Reason: A Study in Nineteenth-Century Thought*. Baltimore: Johns Hopkins Press, 1971.

Mangan, Céline. *1–2 Chronicles, Ezra, Nehemiah*. Old Testament Message 13. Wilmington: Glazier, 1982.

Mannati, M. "Sur Le Quadruple 'Avec Toi' de Ps 73:21-26." *VT* 21 (1971) 59–67.

Marshall, I. Howard. *Beyond the Bible: Moving from Scripture to Theology*. Acadia Studies in Bible and Theology. Grand Rapids: Baker, 2004.

———. *The Books of Kings and Chronicles*. Scripture Union Bible Study Books. Grand Rapids: Eerdmans, 1968.

———. "Slippery Words I. Eschatology." *Expository Times* 89 (1978) 264–69.

Martens, Elmer A. "Canon, Literature, Interpretation, and Biblical Theology." In *NIDOTTE* 1:172–205.

———. *God's Design: A Focus on Old Testament Theology*. 2nd ed. Grand Rapids: Baker, 1994.

———. "Moving from Scripture to Doctrine." *BBR* 15 (2005) 77–103.

———. "The Oscillating Fortunes of 'History' within Old Testament Theology." In *FTH*, 313–40.

———. "Tackling Old Testament Theology." *JETS* 20 (1977) 123–32.

Martin-Achard, Robert. "Théologies de l'Ancient Testament et confessions de foi." *Revue de théologie et de philosophie* 117 (1985) 81–91.

Marx, Karl, and Friedrich Engels. *Basic Writings on Politics and Philosophy*. Edited by Lewis S. Feuer. Garden City: Doubleday, 1959.

Mason, Rex. *Preaching the Tradition: Homily and Hermeneutics After the Exile*. Cambridge: Cambridge University Press, 1990.

Mathys, Hans-Peter. "Chronikbücher und hellenistischer Zeitgeist." In *Vom anfang und vom Ende: Fünf alttestamentliche Studien*, 41–155. BEATAJ 47. Berlin: Lang, 2000.

———. "Prophetie, Psalmengesang und Kultmusik in der Chronik." In *Prophetie und Psalmen: Festschrift für Klaus Seybold zum 65. Geburtstag*, edited by Beat Huwyler et al., 281–96. Alter Orient und Altes Testament 280. Münster: Ugarit, 2001.

Matthews, Kenneth A. *Genesis 11:27–50:26*. NAC 1B. Nashville: Broadman & Holman, 2013.

Matthews, Victor H. *Studying the Ancient Israelites: A Guide to Source and Methods*. Grand Rapids: Baker, 2007.

———. "Music and Musical Instruments." In *ABD* 4:933.

Mayes, A. D. H. "The Place of the Old Testament in Understanding Israelite History and Religion." In *Understanding Poets and Prophets: Essays in Honor of George Wishart Anderson*, edited by A. Graeme Auld, 242–57. JSOTSup 152. Sheffield: JSOT Press, 1993.

Mazar, Amihai. "Archaeology and the Biblical Narrative: The Case of the United Monarchy." In *One God—One Cult—One Nation*, edited by R. Kratz and H. Spieckermann, 29–58. BZAW 405. Berlin: de Gruyter, 2010.

———. *Archaeology of the Land of the Bible, 10,000-586 B.C.E.* New Haven: Yale University Press, 2009.

———. "Archaeology and the Iron Age II." In *BSOT* 62–69.

———. "Jerusalem in the 10th Century BCE: The Glass Half Full." In *Essays on Ancient Israel in its Near Eastern Context: A Tribute to Nadav Na'aman*, edited by Y. Amit et al., 255–72. Winona Lake: Eisenbrauns, 2006.

Mazar, Eilat. *Discovering the Solomonic Wall in Jerusalem: A Remarkable Archaeological Adventure*. Jerusalem: Shoham, 2011.

———. *The Palace of King David: Excavations at the Summit of the City of David: Preliminary Report of Seasons 2005-2007*. Jerusalem: Shoham, 2009.

McCann, J. Clinton, Jr. *A Theological Introduction to the Book of Psalms*. Nashville: Abingdon, 1993.

———. "The Book of Psalms: Introduction, Commentary and Reflections." In *NIB* 4:960.

———. "Psalm 73: A Microcosm of Old Testament Theology." In *The Listening Heart: Essays in Wisdom and the Psalms in Honor of Roland E. Murphy, O. Carm.*, edited by K. G. Hoglund et al., 247–57. JSOTSup 58. Sheffield: Sheffield Academic.

McConville, J. G. *I and II Chronicles*. Old Testament Guides. Philadelphia: Westminster, 1984.
———. "Priests and Levites in Ezekiel: A Crux in the Interpretation of Israel's History." *TynBul* 34 (1982) 1–35.
McCready, W. O. "Priest and Levites." In vol. 3 of *The International Standard Bible Encyclopedia, Revised*, 4 vols., edited by Geoffrey W. Bromiley, 965–70. Grand Rapids: Eerdmans, 1986.
McEntire, Mark Harold. *The Function of Sacrifice in Chronicles, Ezra, and Nehemiah*. Lewiston: Mellen, 1993.
McGann, Mary E. *Exploring Music as Worship and Theology: An Interdisciplinary Method for Studying Liturgical Practice*. American Essays in Liturgy. Collegeville: Liturgical, 2002.
McGlasson, Paul. *Invitation to Dogmatic Theology: A Canonical Approach*. Grand Rapids: Brazos, 2006.
McGrath, Alister E. *The Science of God: An Introduction to Scientific Theology*. Grand Rapids: Eerdmans, 2004.
———. *A Scientific Theology. Volume 2: Reality*. Grand Rapids: Eerdmans, 2002.
McKenzie, John L. *A Theology of the Old Testament*. Garden City: Doubleday, 1974.
McKenzie, Steven L. *1–2 Chronicles*. Nashville: Abingdon, 2004.
———. "The Chronicler as Redactor." In *ChrA* 70–90.
———. *The Chronicler's Use of the Deuteronomic History*. HSMS 33. Atlanta: Scholars, 1985.
———. "Why Didn't David Build the Temple: The History of a Biblical Tradition." In *Worship and the Hebrew Bible*, 204–24. Sheffield: Sheffield Academic, 1999.
McKenzie, Steven L., and Stephen R. Haynes, eds. *To Each Its Own Meaning: An Introduction to Biblical Criticisms and Their Application, Revised and Expanded*. Louisville: Westminster John Knox, 1999.
McMahon, Gregory. "Instructions to Priests and Temple Officials." In *COS* 1:217–21.
———. "Theology, Priests, and Worship in Hittite Anatolia." In *CANE* 3:1982.
Mays, James L. "Past, Present and Prospect in Psalm Study." In *Old Testament Interpretation: Past, Present and Future—Essays in Honor of Gene M. Tucker*, edited by Gene M. Tucker et al., 147–65. Nashville: Abingdon, 1995.
———. *Psalms*. Interpretation: A Bible Commentary for Teaching and Preaching. Louisville: John Knox, 1994.
Mead, James K. *Biblical Theology: Issues, Methods, and Themes*. Louisville: Westminster John Knox, 2007.
Meinecke, Friedrich. *Historism: The Rise of a New Historical Outlook*. Translated by J. E. Anderson. London: Routledge & Paul, 1972 [1936].
Merrill, Eugene H. *1, 2 Chronicles*. Bible Study Commentary. Grand Rapids: Zondervan, 1988.
———. "Archaeology and OT Theology: Their Interface and Reciprocal Usefulness." *JETS* 58 (2015) 667–78.
———. *A Commentary on 1 & 2 Chronicles*. Kregel Exegetical Library. Grand Rapids: Kregel, 2015.
———. "Old Testament History: A Theological Perspective." *NIDOTTE* 1:68–87.
Merritt, Melissa McBay. "Science and the Synthetic Method of the Critique of Pure Reason." *Review of Metaphysics* 59 (2006) 517–39.

Meyer, Ivo. *Gedeutete Vergangenheit: Die Bücher der Könige, die Bücher der Chronik.* Stuttgarter kleiner Kommentar: Altes Testament 7. Stuttgart: Katholisches Bibelwerk, 1976.

Meynet, Roland. *Initiation à la rhétorique biblique: "Qui donc est le plus grand?"* 2 vols. Initiations. Paris: Cerf, 1982.

———. *L'analyse rhétorique: une nouvelle méthode pour comprendre la Bible.* Paris: Cerf, 1989.

———. *L'évangile selon Saint Luc: Analyse Rhétorique.* Paris: Cerf, 1988.

———. *Rhetorical Analysis: An Introduction to Biblical Rhetoric.* JSOTSup 256. Sheffield: Sheffield Academic, 1998.

Michaeli, Frank. *Les livres des Chroniques, d'Esdras et de Néhémie.* CAT 16. Neuchâtel: Delachaux & Niestlé, 1967.

Michalowski, Piotr. "Sumerian Literature: An Overview." In *CANE* 4:2279-91.

Michel, Cécile. "Musique." In *DCM* 545-46.

Micheel, Rosemarie. *Die Seher- und Prophetenüberlieferungen in der Chronik.* Beiträge zur biblischen Exegese und Theologie 18. Frankfurt: Lang, 1983.

Milgrom, Jacob. *The Encroacher and the Levite: The Term 'Aboda.* Near Eastern Studies 14. Berkeley: University of California Press, 1970.

———. "The Levitic Town: An Exercise in Realistic Planning." *Journal of Jewish Studies* 33 (1982) 185-88.

———. *Leviticus 23-27: A New Translation with Introduction and Commentary.* AB 3B. New York: Doubleday, 2004.

———. *Studies in Cultic Theology and Terminology.* Studies in Judaism in Late Antiquity 36. Leiden: Brill, 1983.

Mill, John Stuart. *Auguste Comte and Positivism.* Ann Arbor: University of Michigan Press, 1961.

Millar, William R. *Priesthood in Ancient Israel.* St. Louis: Chalice, 2001.

Millard, A. R. *1 Kings-2 Chronicles.* Bible Study Commentary. London: Scripture Union, 1985.

———. "Methods of Studying the Patriarchal Narratives in Ancient Texts." In *Essays on the Patriarchal Narratives*, edited by D. J. Wiseman and A. R. Millard, 35-52. Winona Lake: Eisenbrauns, 1983.

———. "Story, History, and Theology." In *FTH* 37-64.

Miller, J. Maxwell. "Is It Possible to Write a History of Israel Without Relying on the Hebrew Bible?" In *The Fabric of History: Text, Artifact, and Israel's Past*, edited by Diana Edelman, 93-102. JSOTSup 127. Sheffield: Sheffield Academic, 1991.

———. "Separating the Solomon of History from the Solomon of Legend." In *The Age of Solomon: Scholarship at the Turn of the Millennium*, edited by Lowell K. Handy, 1-24. Studies in the History and Culture of the Ancient Near East 11. Leiden: Brill, 1997.

Miller, J. Maxwell, and John H. Hayes. *A History of Ancient Israel and Judah.* Philadelphia: Westminster John Knox, 1986.

Miller, Patrick D. *The Religion of Ancient Israel.* Louisville: Westminster John Knox, 2000.

Miller, Richard H. "An Investigation of the Perspective of the Deuteronomistic Historian Toward the Zadokite Priesthood." PhD diss., New Orleans Baptist Theological Seminary, 2002.

Milton, Spenser Terry. *Chronicles and the Mosaic Legislation*. Essays on Pentateuchal Criticism 7. New York: Funk & Wagnalls, 1887.

Min, Kyung-Jin. *The Levitical Authorship of Ezra-Nehemiah*. JSOTSup 409. New York: T&T Clark, 2004.

Mitchell, Christine. "The Dialogism of Chronicles." In *ChrA* 311–26.

———. "Transformations in Meaning: Solomon's Accession in Chronicles." *Journal of Hebrew Scriptures* 4 (2002) Article 3.

Mitchell, David C. *The Message of the Psalter: An Eschatological Programme in the Book of Psalms*. JSOTSup 252. Sheffield: Sheffield Academic, 1997.

Mitchell, T. C. "The Music in the Old Testament Reconsidered." *Palestine Exploration Quarterly* 124 (1992) 124–43.

Moberly, Roger W. L. *The Bible, Theology, and Faith: A Study of Abraham and Jesus*. Cambridge Studies in Christian Doctrine. Cambridge: Cambridge University Press, 2000.

———. "Theological Interpretation, Second Naiveté, and the Rediscovery of the Old Testament." *Anglican Theological Review* 99 (2017) 651–70.

———. "Theology of the Old Testament." In *FAOTS* 452–78.

Möller, Karl. "The Nature and Genre of Biblical Theology: Some Reflections in the Light of Charles H. H. Scobie's 'Prolegomena to a Biblical Theology.'" In *Out of Egypt: Biblical Theology and Biblical Interpretation*, edited by Craig Barholomew et al., 41–64. Scripture and Hermeneutics Series 5. Grand Rapids: Zondervan, 2011.

———. "Rhetorical Criticism." In *DTIB* 689–92.

Moore, Megan Bishop, and Brad E. Kelle. *Biblical History and Israel's Past: The Changing Study of the Bible and History*. Grand Rapids: Eerdmans, 2011.

Mosis, Rudolf. *Untersuchungen zur Theologie des chronistischen Geschichtswerkes*. Freiburger Theologische Studien 92. Freiburg: Herder, 1973.

Moulton, Richard Green. *The Literary Study of the Bible*. Boston: Heath, 1899.

Movers, Franz Karl. *Kritische Untersuchungen über die biblische Chronik: Ein Beitrag zur Einleitung in das Alte Testament*. Bonn: Habicht, 1834.

Mowinckel, Sigmund. *The Psalms in Israel's Worship*. Translated by D. R. Ap-Thomas. 2 vols. Oxford: Blackwell, 1962.

Muilenburg, James. "Form Criticism and Beyond." *JBL* 88 (1969) 1–18.

Mulder, M. J., and Harry Sysling, eds. *Mikra: Text, Translation, Reading, and Interpretation of the Hebrew Bible in Ancient Judaism and Early Christianity*. Literature of the Jewish people in the period of the Second Temple and the Talmud 1. Assen: Van Gorcum, 1990.

Mumford, Gregory D. "The Late Bronze Age Collapse and the Sea People's Migrations." In *BSOT* 260–72.

Murray, Donald F. "Dynasty, People, and the Future: The Message of Chronicles." *JSOT* 58 (1993) 71–92.

———. "Retribution and Revival: Theological Theory, Religious Praxis, and the Future in Chronicles." *JSOT* 88 (2000) 77–99.

———. "Under YHWH's Veto: David as Shedder of Blood in Chronicles." *Bib* 82 (2001) 457–76.

Music, David W. "Musical Instruments of the Seventh Century B.C." *Biblical Illustrator* 12 (1986) 51–55.

Myers, Jacob M. *I Chronicles*. AB 12. Garden City: Doubleday, 1965.

———. *II Chronicles*. AB 13. Garden City: Doubleday, 1965.

———. "The Kerygma of the Chronicler: History and Theology in the Service of Religion." *Int* 20 (1966) 259–73.

Mykytiuk, Lawrence J. "Strengthening Biblical Historicity vis-à-vis Minimalism, 1992–2008 and Beyond, Part 2.2: The Literature of Perspective, Critique, and Methodology, Second Half." *Journal of Religious & Theological Information* 12 (2013) 114–55.

Na'aman, Nadav. *Ancient Israel's History and Historiography: The First Temple Period. Collected Essays, Volume 3*. Winona Lake: Eisenbrauns, 2006.

———. "Cow Town or Royal Capital? Evidence for Iron Age Jerusalem." *BAR* 34 (1997) 43–47.

———. "David's Jerusalem, It Is There: Ancient Texts Prove It." *BAR* 24 (1998) 42–44.

Nasuti, Harry Peter. "The Editing of the Psalter and the Ongoing Use of the Psalms: Gerald Wilson and the Question of Canon." In *The Shape and Shaping of the Book of Psalms: The Current State of Scholarship*, edited by Nancy DeClaissé-Walford, 13–20. Ancient Israel and Its Literature 20. Atlanta: SBL, 2014.

———. *Tradition History and the Psalms of Asaph*. Dissertation Series. SBLDS 96. Atlanta: Scholars, 1988.

Nel, Henrietta W. "Theopolitics in the Davidic Monarchical System: A Pilot Study." *In die Skriflig* 31 (1997) 421–34.

———. "The Davidic Covenant in 1 and 2 Chronicles: A New Theme for an Old Song." *In die Skriflig* 28 (1994) 429–44.

Nelson, Richard D. *Raising Up a Faithful Priest: Community and Priesthood in Biblical Theology*. Louisville: Westminster John Knox, 1993.

Newsome, James D. "The Chronicler's View of Prophecy." PhD diss., Vanderbilt University, 1981.

———. "Towards a New Understanding of the Chronicle and His Purposes." *JBL* 94 (1975) 201–17.

Nicholls, William. *Jacob's Ladder: The Meaning of Worship*. Ecumenical Studies in Worship. Richmond: John Knox, 1966.

Nicholson, Ernest. "Current 'Revisionism' and the Literature of the Old Testament." In *SpreIs* 1–22.

Nielsen, Kirsten. "Intertextuality and the Hebrew Bible." In *Congress Volume: Oslo 1998*, edited by A. Lemaire and M. Sæbø, 17–31. VTSup 80. Leiden: Brill, 2000.

———. "Whose Song of Praise: Reflections on the Purpose of the Psalm in 1 Chronicles 16." In *ChrA* 327 36.

Nielsen, Eduard. "Psalm 73: Scandinavian Contributions." In *Understanding Poets and Prophets: Essays in Honour of George Wishart Anderson*, edited by Graeme A. Auld, 273–83. Sheffield: JSOT Press, 1993.

Nissinen, Martti. "Reflections on the 'Historical-Critical' Method: Historical Criticism and Critical Historicism." In *Method Matters: Essays on the Interpretation of the Hebrew Bible in Honor of David L. Petersen*, edited by Joel M. Lemon and Kent Harold Richards, 479–504. Atlanta: SBL, 2009.

Noblesse-Rocher, Annie. "Die rezeptionen des Werkes von Paul Ricœur in der französischen Historiographie." *Evangelische Theologie* 73 (2013) 273–82.

North, Robert. "Theology of the Chronicler." *JBL* 82 (1963) 369–81.

Noth, M. "The Background of Judges 17–18." In *Israel's Prophetic Heritage: Essays in Honor of James Muilenburg*, edited by Bernhard W. Anderson and Walter J. Harrelson, 68–85. New York: Harper, 1962.

———. *The Chronicler's History*, edited by H. G. M. Williamson. JSOTSup 50. Sheffield: JSOT Press, 1987.

———. *The Deuteronomistic History*, edited by D. P. Thomas. JSOTSup 15. Sheffield: JSOT Press, 1981.

Nowell, Irene. "Teach Us How to Pray." *The Bible Today* 36 (1998) 208–213.

Nurmela, Risto. *The Levites: Their Emergence as a Second-Class Priesthood*. South Florida Studies in the History of Judaism 193. Atlanta: Scholars, 1998.

O'Connell, Robert. *The Rhetoric of the Book of Judges*. VTSup 63. Leiden: Brill, 1996.

O'Conner, David. "The Social and Economic Organization of Ancient Egyptian Temples." In *CANE* 1:319.

Oehler, Gustav F. *Prolegomena zur Theologie des Alten Testaments*. Stuttgart: Liesching, 1845.

———. *Theologie des Alten Testaments*. Tübingen: Heckenhauer, 1873.

Oeming, Manfred. *Das wahre Israel: die "genealogische Vorhalle" 1 Chronik 1–9*. BWA(N)T 7. Stuttgart: Kohlhammer, 1990.

———. "Die Eroberung Jerusalems durch David in deuteronomistischer und chronistischer Darstellung (II Sam 5,6–9 und 1 Chr 11,4–8) Ein Beitrag zur narrativen Theologie der beiden Geschichtswerke." *ZAW* 106 (1994) 404–20.

Oiry, Béatrice. "L'histoire comme récit: Enjeux d'une lecture narrative de l'historiographie biblique." *Revue Théologique de Louvain* 50 (2019) 329–61.

Olbricht, Thomas H. "Classical Rhetorical Criticism and Historical Reconstructions: A Critique." In *The Rhetorical Interpretation of Scripture: Essays from the 1996 Malibu Conference*, edited by Stanley E. Porter and Dennis L. Stamps, 108–24. JSNTSup 180. Sheffield: Sheffield Academic, 1999.

———. "The Flowering of Rhetorical Criticism in America." In *The Rhetorical Analysis of Scripture: Essays from the 1995 London Conference*, edited by Stanley E. Porter and Thomas H. Olbricht, 94–99. Sheffield: Sheffield Academic, 1997.

Ollenburger, Ben C. "Discoursing Old Testament Theology." *Biblical Interpretation* 11 (2003) 617–28.

———. "Old Testament Theology: A Discourse on Method." In *Biblical Theology: Problems and Perspectives: In Honor of J. Christiaan Beker*, edited by Johan Christiaan Beker et al., 81–103. Nashville: Abington, 1995.

———. "Old Testament Theology Before 1933." In *OTTFF* 3–11.

———. "Old Testament Theology's Renaissance: Walther Eichrodt through Gerhard von Rad: Introduction." In *OTTFF* 33–40.

———. "Review Essay: The History of Israel Contested and Revised." *Modern Theology* 16 (2000) 529–40.

———. "What Krister Stendahl 'Meant'—A Normative Critique of 'Descriptive Biblical Theology.'" *Horizons in Biblical Theology* 8 (1986) 61–98.

Ord, David Robert, and Robert B. Coote. *Is the Bible True? Understanding the Bible Today*. Maryknoll: Orbis, 1994.

Ortiz, Steven M. "The United Monarchy." In *BSOT* 208–15.

Osborne, Grant R. *The Hermeneutical Spiral: A Comprehensive Introduction to Biblical Interpretation*. Downers Grove: InterVarsity, 2010.

———. "Historical Narrative and Truth in the Bible." *JETS* 48 (2005) 673–88.

———. "Type, Typology." In *EDT* 1222–23.

Pagès, Claire. "De Hegel à Herder: Le principe d'historicité: Réflexions sur les relations entre les philosophies Herdérienne et Hégélienne de l'histoire." *Revue Philosophique de Louvain* 111 (2013) 631–60.
Pajunen, Mika S. "The Saga of Judah's Kings Continues: The Reception of Chronicles in the Late Second Temple Period." *JBL* 136 (2017) 565–84.
Pardee, Dennis. *Les textes rituels*. Ras Shamra-Ougarit 12. Paris: Recherche sur les Civilisations, 2000.
Partain, Jack G. "Numbers." In *Mercer Commentary on the Bible*, edited by Watson E. Mills et al., 175–79. Macon: Mercer University Press, 1995.
Patai, Raphael. *Man and Temple in Ancient Jewish Myth and Ritual*. New York: Ktav, 1967.
Patrick, Dale, and Allen Scult. *Rhetoric and Biblical Interpretation*. Bible and Literature Series 26. Sheffield: Sheffield Academic, 1990.
———. "Rhetoric and Ideology: A Debate Within Biblical Scholarship Over the Import of Persuasion." In *The Rhetorical Interpretation of Scripture: Essays from the 1996 Malibu Conference*, edited by Stanley E. Porter and Dennis L. Stamps, 63–83. JSNTSup 180. Sheffield: Sheffield Academic, 1999.
Payne, J. Barton. "1 Chronicles." In *1 Kings–Job*, vol. 4 of *The Expositor's Bible Commentary*, edited by Frank E. Gaebelein, 303–564. Grand Rapids: Zondervan, 1988.
Pearson, Lori. *Beyond Essence: Ernst Troeltsch as Historian and Theorist of Christianity*. Harvard Theological Studies 56. Cambridge: Harvard University Press, 2006.
Peltonen, Kai. "Function, Explanation and Literary Phenomena: Aspects of Source Criticism as Theory and Method in the History of Chronicles Research." In *ChrA* 18–69.
———. *History Debated: The Historical Reliability of Chronicles in Pre-Critical and Critical Research*. 2 vols. Publications of the Finnish Exegetical Soceity 64. Helsinki: Finnish Exegetical Society, 1996.
———. "A Jigsaw Without a Model? The Date of Chronicles." In *Did Moses Speak Attic? Jewish Historiography and Scripture in the Hellenistic Period*, edited by Lester L. Grabbe. Sheffield: Sheffield Academic, 2001.
Perdue, Leo G. *The Collapse of History: Reconstructing Old Testament Theology*. OBT. Minneapolis: Fortress, 1994.
———. *Reconstructing Old Testament Theology: After the Collapse of History*. OBT. Minneapolis: Fortress, 2005.
Perelman, Chaim. *L'empire rhétorique: rhétorique et argumentation*. Bibliothèque des textes philosophiques. Paris: Vrin, 1997.
Perelman, Chaim, and L. Olbrechts-Tyteca. *Traité de l'argumentation*. Logos: Introduction aux études philosophiques. Paris: Presses universitaires de France, 1958.
Pereira, G. C. "An Evaluation of the Canonical Approach: Is It Adequate for the Task of Old Testament Theology in Christian Hermeneutical Endeavour?" *Scriptura* 114 (2015) 303–14.
Petersen, David L. *Late Israelite Prophecy: Studies in Deutero-Prophetic Literature and in Chronicles*. Society of Biblical Literature Monograph Series 23. Missoula: Scholars, 1976.
Petter, Gerald J. "A Study of the Theology of the Book of Chronicles." PhD diss., Vanderbilt University, 1985.

Pickering, Mary. *Auguste Comte: An Intellectual Biography. Volume 1: Auguste Comte and Positivism, 1798–1842*. Cambridge: Cambridge University Press, 1993.
Pierard, R. V. "Troeltsch, Ernst." In *EDT* 1218–19.
Pilch, John J. "Singing in the Bible." *Bible Today* 34 (1996) 38–43.
Pioske, Daniel D. "David's Jerusalem: A Sense of Place." *Near Eastern Archaeology* 76 (2013) 4–15.
Pohlmann, Karl F. "Zur Frage von Korrespondenzen und Divergenzen zwischen den Chronikbüchern und dem Esra/Nehemia-Buch." In *Congress Volume: Leuven, 1989*, edited by J. A. Emerton, 314–30. Leiden: Brill, 1991.
Pola, Thomas. *Das Priestertum bei Sacharja: Historische und traditionsgeschichtliche Untersuchungen zur frühnachexilischen Herrschererwartung*. FAT 35. Tübingen: Mohr Siebeck, 2003.
Polk, T. "The Levites in the Davidic-Solomonic Empire." *Studia Biblica* 9 (1979) 3–22.
Polzin, Robert. *Late Biblical Hebrew: Toward an Historical Typology of Biblical Hebrew Prose*. HSMS 12. Missoula: Scholars, 1976.
Poorthuis, Marcel. "Introduction and Overview: The Centrality of Jerusalem." In *The Centrality of Jerusalem: Historical Perspectives*, edited by Marcel Poorthuis and Chana Safrai, 1–6. Kampen: Kok Pharos, 1996.
Popper, Karl R. *The Poverty of Historicism*. Boston: Beacon, 1957.
Porteous, N. W. "Old Testament Theology." In *The Old Testament and Modern Study: A Generation of Discovery and Research: Essays by Members of the Society for Old Testament Study*, edited by H. H. Rowley, 311–45. Oxford: Clarendon, 1951.
Porter, Carolyn. "History and Literature: 'After the New Historicism.'" In *History and Histories Within the Human Sciences*, edited by Ralph Cohen and Michael S. Roth, 23–43. Charlottesville: University Press of Virginia, 1995.
Post, G. E. "Levi." In vol. 3 of *A Dictionary of the Bible Dealing with Its Language, Literature, and Contents, Including the Biblical Theology*, 5 vols., edited by James Hastings, 99–102. Edinburgh: T&T Clark, 1900.
Pratt, Richard L. *1 and 2 Chronicles*. Fearn: Mentor, 1998.
———. "First and Second Chronicles." In *CLGB* 193–205.
———. "Royal Prayer and the Chronicler's Program." ThD diss., Harvard Divinity School, 1987.
Preston, Ronald H. *Religion and the Ambiguities of Capitalism*. Cleveland: Pilgrim, 1993.
Preuss, Horst Dietrich. *Old Testament Theology*. OTL. Louisville: Westminster John Knox, 1995.
Provan, Iain W. "The End of (Israel's) History? K. W. Whitelam's The Invention of Ancient Israel: A Review Article." *Journal of Semitic Studies* 42 (1997) 283–300.
———. "In the Stable with the Dwarves: Testimony, Interpretation, Faith and the History of Israel." In *CVO* 280–320.
———. "Knowing and Believing." In *"Behind" the Text: History and Biblical Interpretation*, edited by Craig Bartholomew et al., 229–66. Scripture and Hermeneutics Series. Grand Rapids: Zondervan, 2003.
Provan, Iain W., et al. *A Biblical History of Israel*. 2nd ed. Louisville: Westminster John Knox, 2015.
Prussner, Frederick C., and John H. Hayes. *Old Testament Theology: Its History and Development*. Atlanta: John Knox, 1985.

Quintilian. *On The Teaching of Speaking and Writing: Translations from Books One, Two, and Ten of the Institutio Oratoria*. Edited by James J. Murphy. Landmarks in Rhetoric and Public Address. Carbondale: Southern Illinois University Press, 1987.

Rabinowitz, Chaim Dov. *Commentary to the Book of Divrey Hayamim*. Translated by Y. Starett. Da'ath Soferim: Torah, Prophets, Sacred Writings. New York: Vagshal, 2002.

Radday, Yehuda. "Chiasm in Torah." *Linguistica Biblica* 19 (1972) 12–23.

———. "Chiasmus in Hebrew Biblical Narrative." In *Chiasmus in Antiquity: Structure, Analyses, Exegesis*, edited by J. W. Welch, 50–117. Hildesheim: Gerstenberg, 1981.

Rainey, Anson F. "The Chronicler and his Sources: Historical and Geographical." In *CaH* 30–72.

Räisänen, Heikki. *Beyond New Testament Theology: A Story and a Programme*. 2nd ed. London: SCM, 2000.

Raison, Stephen J. "From Theocracy to Kingdom: Royalist Hope in Chronicles." PhD diss., Westminster Theological Seminary, 1992.

Randholfer Regina, "From the Present to the Past: A New Approach to Music in Jewish and Christian Ritual." In *Sources of Music in Ancient Israel/Palestine*, edited by Regina Randholfer, 23–62. Halle: Orientwissentschatliches Zentrum der Martin Luther Universität, 2003.

Raney, Donald C., II. *History as Narrative in the Deuteronomistic History and Chronicles*. Series in the Bible and Early Christianity 56. Lewiston: Mellen, 2003.

Ranke, Leopold von. *The Secret of World History: Selected Writings on the Art and Science of History*. Translated by Roger Wines. New York: Fordham University Press, 1981.

———. *The Theory and Practice of History*. Edited by Georg G. Iggers and Konrad von Moltke. European Historiography Series. Indianapolis: Bobbs-Merrill, 1973.

Ravasi, Gianfranco. *I libri delle Cronache: Ciclo di conferenze tenute al Centro culturale S. Fedele di Milano*. Conversazioni bibliche. Bologna: EDB, 1996.

Reardon, Bernard M. G. *Religion in the Age of Romanticism: Studies in Early Nineteenth Century Thought*. Cambridge: Cambridge University Press, 1985.

Redford, Donald D. "Ancient Egyptian Literature: An Overview." In *CANE* 4:2225.

Rehm, M. D. *Die Bücher der Chronik*. Echter-Bibel: Das Alte Testament. Würzburg: Echter, 1949.

Rehm, Merlin D. "Levites and Priests." In *ABD* 4:297 310.

Reinhold, Then. *Gibt es denn keinen mehr unter den Propheten? Zum Fortgang der alttestamentlichen Prophetie in frühjüdischer Zeit*. BEATAJ 22. Frankfurt: Lang, 1990.

Reisenauer, Augustine Marie. "The Goodness of God in Psalm 73." *Antonianum* 86 (2011) 11–28.

Rendtorff, Rolf. *Canon and Theology: Overtures to an Old Testament Theology*. Translated by Margaret Kohl. OBT. Minneapolis: Fortress, 1993.

———. *The Canonical Hebrew Bible: A Theology of the Old Testament*. Translated by David E. Orton. Tools for Biblical Study 7. Leiden: Deo, 2005.

———. "Chronicles and the Priestly Torah." In *Texts, Temples, and Traditions: A Tribute to Menahem Haran*, edited by Michael V. Fox et al., 259–66. Winona Lake: Eisenbrauns, 1996.

———. "The Image of Postexilic Israel in German Bible Scholarship from Wellhausen to Von Rad." In *ShaTal* 165–73.

———. "The Paradigm is Changing: Hopes—And Fears." *Biblical Interpretation* 1 (1993) 34–53.

———. "Recent German Old Testament Theologies." *Journal of Religion* 76 (1996) 328–37.

Reuss, Eduard. *Die Kirchenchronik von Jerusalem: Chronik, Esra, Nehemia.* Braunschweig: Schwetschke, 1893.

Reventlow, Henning Graf. *Bibelautorität und Geist der Moderne*. Forschungen zur Kirchen und Dogmengeschichte 30. Göttingen: Vandenhoeck & Ruprecht, 1980.

———. *Hauptprobleme der alttestamentlichen Theologie im 20. Jahrhundert*. Erträge der Forschung 173. Darmstadt: Wissenschaftliche Buchgesellschaft, 1982.

———. "Theology (Biblical), History of." In *ABD* 6:483–505.

Reventlow, Henning Graf, and William Reuben Farmer. *Biblical Studies and the Shifting of Paradigms, 1850–1914.* JSOTSup 192. Sheffield: Sheffield Academic, 1995.

Rezetko, Robert. "Dating Biblical Hebrew: Evidence from Samuel–Kings and Chronicles." In *Biblical Hebrew: Studies in Chronology and Typology*, edited by Ian Young, 215–50. JSOTSup 369. New York: T&T Clark, 2003.

———. *Source and Revision in the Narratives of David's Transfer of the Ark: Text, Language, and Story in 2 Samuel 6 and 1 Chronicles 13, 15—16.* LHBOTS 470. New York: T&T Clark, 2007.

Richards, Kent Harold. "Reshaping Chronicles and Ezra–Nehemiah Interpretation." In *Old Testament Interpretation: Past, Present, and Future; Essays in Honor of Gene M. Tucker*, edited by James Luther Mays et al., 211–23. Nashville: Abingdon, 1995.

Ricœur, Paul. *Temps et Récit: Tome I. L'ordre philosophique.* Paris: Seuil, 1983.

Riley, William. *King and Cultus in Chronicles: Worship and the Reinterpretation of History.* JSOTSup 160. Sheffield: JSOT Press, 1993.

Ritchie, John. *Feast of Jehovah: Bright Foreshadowings of Grace and Glory.* Kilmarnock: Office of the Believer's Magazine, 1895. Reprint, Grand Rapids: Kregel, 1982.

———. *The Lord's Work and Workers: An Address on the Levites and Their Service.* Kilmarnock: The Young Watchman, n.d.

Ritner, Robert K. "Daily Ritual of the Temple of Amun-re at Karnak." In *COS* 1:55–57.

Ritter, Harry. *Dictionary of Concepts in History. Reference Sources for the Social Sciences and Humanities* 3. New York: Greenwood, 1986.

Robbins, Vernon K. "From Heidelberg to Heidelberg: Rhetorical Interpretation of the Bible at the Seven 'Pepperdine' Conferences from 1992 to 2002." In *Rhetoric, Ethic, and Moral Persuasion in Biblical Discourse: Essays from the 2002 Heidelberg Conference*, edited by Thomas H. Olbricht and Anders Eriksson, 335–78. London: T&T Clark, 2005.

———. "The Present and Future of Rhetorical Analysis." In *The Rhetorical Analysis of Scripture: Essays from the 1995 London Conference*, edited by Stanley E. Porter and Thomas H. Olbricht, 24–52. JSNTSup 146. Sheffield: Sheffield Academic, 1997.

———. "The Rhetorical Full-Turn in Biblical Interpretation: Reconfiguring Rhetorical-Political Analysis." In *Rhetorical Criticism and the Bible*, edited by Stanley E. Porter and Dennis L. Stamps, 48–60. JSNTSup 195. London: Sheffield Academic, 2002.

Roberts, David D. *Benedetto Croce and the Uses of Historicism*. Berkeley: University of California Press, 1987.

Robertson, John F. "Temples and Sanctuaries: Mesopotamia." In *ABD* 6:372–76.

———. "The Social and Economic Organization of Ancient Mesopotamian Temples." In *CANE* 3:443–54.

Rockmore, Tom. *Kant and Idealism*. New Haven: Yale University Press, 2007.
Rogerson, John W. *W. M. L. De Wette, Founder of Modern Biblical Criticism: An Intellectual Biography*. JSOTSup 126. Sheffield: JSOT Press, 1992.
Rom-Shiloni, Dalit. "Hebrew Bible Theology: A Jewish Descriptive Approach." *Journal of Religion* 96 (2016) 165–84.
Rooke, Deborah W. *Zadok's Heirs: The Role and Development of the High Priesthood in Ancient Israel*. Oxford: Oxford University Press, 2000.
Rosenberg, A. J. *1 Chronicles: A New English Translation*. New York: Judaica, 1992.
Rosner, Brian S. "Biblical Theology." In *NDBT* 3–11.
Ross, Allen P. *Recalling the Hope of Glory: Biblical Worship from the Garden to the New Creation*. Grand Rapids: Kregel, 2006.
Ross, James P. "Psalm 73." In *Israelite Wisdom: Theological and Literary Essays in Honor of Samuel Terrien*, edited by Samuel L. Terrien and John G. Gammie, 161–75. New York: Scholars, 1978.
Rothstein, J. Wilhelm, and Johannes Hänel. *Das erste Buch der Chronik: Überstezt und erklärt*. Kommentar zum Alten Testament 18/1. Leipzig: Deichertsche, 1927.
Rubanowice, Robert J. *Crisis in Consciousness: The Thought of Ernst Troeltsch*. Tallahassee: University Presses of Florida, 1982.
Rudolph, Wilhelm. *Chronikbücher*. Handbuch zum Alten Testament 21. Tübingen: Mohr, 1955.
Ruffing, Andreas. *Jahwekrieg als Weltmetapher: Studien zu Jahwekriegstexten des chronistischen Sondergutes*. Stuttgarter biblische Beiträge 24. Stuttgart: Katholisches Bibelwerk, 1992.
Runnalls, Donna. "The (parwar) A Place of Ritual Separation?" *VT* 41 (1991) 324–31.
Ryken, Leland. "The Bible as Literature: A Brief History." In *CLGB* 49–68.
———. "Literary Criticism." In *DTIB* 457–60.
Ryken, Leland, and Tremper Longman III. "Introduction." In *CLGB* 15–39.
Sabourin, Leopold. *Priesthood: A Comparative Study*. Studies in the History of Religions (Supplements to *Numen*) 25. Leiden: Brill, 1973.
Sacchi, Paolo. *The History of the Second Temple Period*. JSOTSup 285. Sheffield: Sheffield Academic, 2000.
Sailhamer, John. "1 Chronicles 21:1—A Study in Inter-Biblical Interpretation." *Trinity Journal* 10 (1989) 33–48.
———. *First and Second Chronicles*. Chicago: Moody, 1983.
———. *Introduction to Old Testament Theology: A Canonical Approach*. Grand Rapids: Zondervan, 1995.
———. *The Meaning of the Pentateuch: Revelation, Composition and Interpretation*. Downers Grove: InterVarsity, 2009.
Samuel, Harald. *Von Priestern zum Patriarchen: Levi und die Leviten im Alten Testament*. BZAW 448. Berlin: de Gruyter, 2014.
Sanders, E. P. *Judaism: Practice and Belief, 63 BCE–66 CE*. Minneapolis: Fortress, 2016.
Sanders, James A. *Canon and Community: A Guide to Canonical Criticism*. Guides to Biblical Scholarship. Philadelphia: Fortress, 1984.
———. *From Sacred Story to Sacred Text: Canon as Paradigm*. Philadelphia: Fortress, 1987.
Sands, P. C. *The Literary Genius of the Old Testament*. Oxford: Clarendon, 1924.
Satterthwaite, P. E. "Biblical History." In *NDBT* 42–51.

Sauder, Christopher. "L'Ενεργεια selon Hegel: La mise en valeur de l'idéalisme Aristotélicien." *Science et Esprit* 72 (2020) 213–22.
Sauneron, Serge. *The Priests of Ancient Egypt*. Translated by David Lorton. Ithaca: Cornell University Press, 2000.
Saw, Insaw. *Paul's Rhetoric in 1 Corinthians 15: An Analysis Utilizing the Theories of Classical Rhetoric*. Lewiston: Mellen Biblical, 1995.
Scalise, Charles J. *From Scripture to Theology: A Canonical Journey into Hermeneutics*. Downers Grove: InterVarsity Press, 1996.
Schaefer, Glenn Edward. "The Significance of Seeking God in the Purpose of the Chronicler." ThD diss., Southern Baptist Theological Seminary, 1972.
Schaefer, Konrad. *Psalms*. Berit Olam. Collegeville: Liturgical, 2001.
Schams, Christine. *Jewish Scribes in the Second-Temple Period*. JSOTSup 291. Sheffield: Sheffield Academic, 1998.
Schaper, Joachim. *Priester und Leviten im achmäenidischen Juda*. FAT 31. Tübingen: Mohr Siebeck, 2000.
———. "Priestly Purity and Social Organization in Persian Period Judah." *BN* 118 (2003) 51–57.
Schenk, Ferninand S. *The Oratory and Poetry of the Bible*. New York: Hodder & Stoughton, 1915.
Schenker, Adrian. *Une Bible archétype? Les parallèles de Samuel-Rois et des Chroniques*. L'écriture de la Bible 3. Paris: Cerf, 2013.
Schiffman, Lawrtence H. *Texts and Traditions: A Source Reader for the Study of Second Temple and Rabbinic Judaism*. Hoboken: KTAV, 1998.
Schmid, Johannes H. *Biblische Theologie in der Sicht heutiger Alttestamentler: Hartmut Gese, Claus Westermann, Walther Zimmerli, Antonius Gunneweg*. Monographien und Studienbücher 326. Giessen: Brunnen, 1986.
Schmidt, Werner H. "Ansätze zum Verstehen des Alten Testaments." *Evangelische Theologie* 47 (1987) 436–59.
———. "Die Frage nach einer 'Mitte' des alten Testaments." *Evangelische Theologie* 68 (2008) 168–78.
———. "The Problem of the 'Centre' of the Old Testament in the Perspective of the Relationship Between History of Religion and Theology." *OTE* 4 (1986) 46–64.
Schnabel, E. J. "Scripture." In *NDBT* 34–42.
Schniedewind, William M. "The Chronicler as Interpreter of Scripture." In *ChrA* 158–80.
———. "History or Homily: Toward Understanding the Chronicler's Purpose." In *Proceedings of the Eleventh World Congress of Jewish Studies: Jerusalem, June 22–29, 1993*, edited by David Assaf, 91–97. Jerusalem: World Union of Jewish Studies, 1994.
———. "King and Priest in the Book of Chronicles and the Duality of Qumran Messianism." *Journal of Jewish Studies* 45 (1994) 71–78.
———. "Prophets and Prophecy in the Books of Chronicles." In *CaH* 204–24.
———. *The Word of God in Transition: From Prophet to Exegete in the Second Temple Period*. JSOTSup 197. Sheffield: Sheffield Academic, 1995.
Scholder, Klaus. *The Birth of Modern Critical Theology: Origins and Problems of Biblical Criticism in the Seventeenth Century*. Translated by John Bowden. Philadelphia: Trinity, 1990.

Scholer, John M. *Proleptic Priests: Priesthood in the Epistle to the Hebrews.* JSNTSup 49. Sheffield: JSOT Press, 1991.

Scholtz, Gunter. "The Notion of Historicism and 19th Century Theology." In *Biblical Studies and the Shifting of Paradigms, 1850–1914*, edited by Henning Graf Reventlow and William Reuben Farmer. JSOTSup 192. Sheffield: Sheffield Academic, 1995.

Schreiner, Thomas R. *The King in His Beauty: A Biblical Theology of the Old and New Testaments.* Grand Rapids: Baker, 2013.

Schuele, Andreas. "Theology as Witness: Gerhard von Rad's Contribution to the Study of Old Testament Theology." *Int* 62 (2008) 256–67.

Schulz, Hermann. *Leviten im vorstaatlichlen Israel und im mittleren Osten.* Munich: Kaiser, 1987.

Schulz, Richard. "Integrating Old Testament and Exegesis: Literary, Thematic, and Canonical Issues." In *NIDOTTE* 1:185–205.

Schweitzer, Steven. "The Genealogies of 1 Chronicles 1–9: Purposes, Forms, and the Utopian Identity of Israel." In *CtC* 9–28.

———. "The High Priest in Chronicles: An Anomaly in a Detailed Description of the Temple Cult." *Bib* 84 (2003) 388–402.

Scobie, Charles H. H. "The Challenge of Biblical Theology." *TynBul* 42 (1991) 31–61.

———. "History of Biblical Theology." In *NDBT* 11–20.

———. *The Ways of Our God: An Approach to Biblical Theology.* Grand Rapids: Eerdmans, 2003.

Seidel, Hans. *Musik in Altisrael: Untersuchungen zur Musikgeschichte und Musikpraxis Altisraels Anhand biblischer und ausserbiblischer Texte.* BEATAJ 12. Frankfurt: Lang, 1989.

Seitz, Christopher R. "Canon, Narrative, and the Old Testament's Literal Sense: A Response to John Goldingay, 'Canon and Old Testament Theology.'" *TynBul* 59 (2008) 27–34.

———. *Figured Out: Typology and Providence in Christian Scripture.* Louisville: Westminster John Knox, 2001.

———. *Word Without End: The Old Testament as Abiding Theological Witness.* Grand Rapids: Eerdmans, 1998.

Selman, Martin J. *1 Chronicles: An Introduction and Commentary.* TOTC 10a. Downers Grove: InterVarsity, 1994.

———. *2 Chronicles: An Introduction and Commentary.* TOTC 10b. Downers Grove: InterVarsity, 1994.

———. "Chronicler's History." In *DOTHB* 157–61.

———. "Jerusalem in Chronicles." In *Zion: City of Our God*, edited by Gordon J. Wenham and Richard S. Hess, 43–56. Grand Rapids: Eerdmans, 1999.

Sendrey, Alfred. *Music in Ancient Israel.* London: Vision, 1969.

Shalev, Meir. *Rewriting History in the Bible: The Book of Ruth vs. the Book of Chronicles.* Max and Cecelia Leavitt Memorial Lecture 1987. Cambridge: Harvard University Library, 1988.

Shahar, Ntan. "Women in the Bible and in Hebrew Song." *Beit Mikra* 49 (2004) 97–115.

Shaver, Judson Rayford. *Torah and the Chronicler's History Work: An Inquiry into the Chronicler's References to Laws, Festivals, and Cultic Institutions in Relationship to Pentateuchal Legislation.* Brown Judaic Studies 195. Atlanta: Scholars, 1989.

Sheperd, Lorrain M. *Feminist Theologies for a Postmodern Church: Diversity, Community, and Scripture.* New York: Lang, 2002.
Sherwood, Stephen K. *Leviticus, Numbers, Deuteronomy.* Berit Olam. Collegeville: Liturgical, 2002.
Shiloh, Yigal. *Excavations at the City of David I, 1978-1982: Interim Report of the First Five Seasons.* Qedem 19. Jerusalem: Hebrew University of Jerusalem, 1984.
Shiloh, Yigal, et al. *Excavations at the City of David. 6, 1978-1985: Inscriptions.* Jerusalem: Institute of Archaeology Hebrew University of Jerusalem, 2000.
Shipp, R. Mark. "'Remember His Covenant Forever': A Study of the Chronicler's Use of the Psalms." *Restoration Quarterly* 35 (1993) 29–39.
Siedlecki, Armin. "Foreigners, Warfare, and Judahite Identity in Chronicles." In *ChrA* 229–66.
———. "The Literature of Ancient Israel by Hermann Gunkel." In *Relating the Text: Interdisciplinary and Form-Critical Insights on the Bible*, edited by Timothy J. Sandoval and Carleen Mandolfo, 26–83. New York: T&T Clark, 2003.
Simpson, David, ed. *German Aesthetic and Literary Criticism: Kant, Fichte, Schelling, Schopenhauer, Hegel.* Cambridge: Cambridge University Press, 1984.
Sklba, Richard J. *The Teaching Function of the Pre-Exilic Israelite Priesthood.* Pontifica Studiorum Universitas. Rome: University of St. Thomas Press, 1965.
Slomovic, Elieser. "Toward an Understanding of the Formation of Historical Titles in the Book of Psalms." *ZAW* 91 (1979) 350–80.
Slotki, I. W. *Chronicles.* Soncino Books of the Bible 13. London, 1985.
Small, Christopher. *Musicking: The Meanings of Performing and Listening.* Music/Culture. Middletown: Wesleyan University Press, 1998.
Smend, Rudolf. *Die Mitte des Alten Testaments: Exegetische Aufsätze.* Tübingen: Mohr Siebeck, 2002.
Smith-Christopher, Daniel L. *A Biblical Theology of Exile.* Overtures in Biblical Theology. Minneapolis: Fortress, 2002.
———. "Reassessing the Historical and Sociological Impact of the Babylonian Exile (597/587–539 BCE)." In *Exile: Old Testament, Jewish, and Christian Conceptions*, edited by James M. Scott, 7–36. Supplements to the Journal for the Study of Judaism 56. Leiden: Brill, 1997.
Smith, Mark S. *The Memoirs of God: History, Memory, and the Experience of the Divine in Ancient Israel.* Minneapolis: Fortress, 2004.
———. "Ugarit and the Ugaritians." In *WOT* 139–68.
Snyman, Fanie. "Mapping Recent Developments in Old Testament Theology." *HTS Teologiese Studies/Theological Studies* 75 (2019) 1–8.
Snyman, Gerrie. "Who is Responsible for Uzzah's Death: Rhetoric in 1 Chronicles 13." In *Rhetoric, Scripture and Theology: Essays from the 1994 Pretoria Conference*, edited by Stanley E. Porter and Thomas H. Olbricht, 203–17. JSNTSup 121. Sheffield: Sheffield Academic, 1996.
Soggin, J. Alberto. *Israel in the Biblical Period: Institutions, Festivals, Ceremonies, Rituals.* Edinburgh: T&T Clark, 2001.
———. "King David." In *Recenti tendenze nella ricostruzione della storia antica d'Israele: Convegno internazionale: Roma, 6-7 marzo 2003*, 65–73. Contributi del Centro linceo interdisciplinare "Beniamino Segre" 110. Rome: Accademia nazionale dei Lincei, 2005.

Souza Nunes Wöhl Coelho, Helena de. "Música para Textos Bíblicos." *Estudos Teológicos* 31 (1991) 231–38.
Spangenberg, Izak J. J. "Psalm 73 and the Book of Qoheleth." *OTE* 29 (2016) 151–75.
Sparks, Kenton L. *Ancient Texts for the Study of the Hebrew Bible: A Guide to the Background Literature*. Peabody: Hendrickson, 2005.
Spector, Johanna. "Samaritan Chant." *Journal of the International Folk Music Council* 16 (1964) 66–69.
Spencer, John R. "The Tasks of the Levites: šmr and ṣbʾ." *ZAW* 96 (1984) 267–71.
Spengler, Oswald. *The Decline of the West: Volume 1: Form and Actuality*. Translated by C. F. Atkinson. New York: Knopf, 1926.
———. *The Decline of the West: Volume 2: Perspectives of World History*. New York: Knopf, 1928.
Stade, Bernhard, and Alfred Bertholet. *Biblische theologie des Alten Testaments*. Tübingen: Mohr, 1905.
Stapert, Calvin. *My Only Comfort: Death, Deliverance, and Discipleship in the Music of Bach*. Grand Rapids: Eerdmans, 2000.
Steiner, Margreet L. "The Archaeology of Ancient Jerusalem." *Currents in Research: Biblical Studies* 6 (1998) 143–68.
———. "David's Jerusalem, It's Not There: Archaeology Proves a Negative." *BAR* 24 (1998) 26–33.
———. *Excavations by Kathleen Kenyon in Jerusalem, 1961–1967, vol. 3: The Settlement in the Bronze and Iron Ages*. Copenhagen International Series 9. Sheffield: Sheffield Academic, 2001.
———. "Jerusalem in the Tenth and Seventh Centuries BCE: From Administrative Town to Commercial City." In *Studies in the Archaeology of the Iron Age in Israel and Jordan*, edited by Amihai Mazar, 280–88. JSOTSup 331. Sheffield: Sheffield Academic, 2001.
Steiner, Vernon J. "Literary Structure of the Pentateuch." In *DOTP* 544–66.
Steinmetz, George. *The Politics of Method in the Human Sciences: Positivism and its Epistemological Others*. Politics, History and Culture. Durham: Duke University Press, 2005.
———. "Positivism and Its Others in the Social Sciences." In *The Politics of Method in the Human Sciences: Positivism and Its Epistemological Others*, edited by George Steinmetz, 1–58. Politics, History, and Culture. Durham: Duke University Press, 2005.
Steins, Georg. "1 Chr 1–10 als Set Up der Chronikbücher." In *Textarbeit: Studien zu Texten und ihrer Rezeption aus dem Alten Testament und der Umwelt Israels: Festschrift für Peter Weimar zur Vollendung seines 60. Lebensjahres mit Beiträgen von Freunden, Schülern und Kollegen*, edited by Klaus Kiesow and Thomas Meurer, 483–504. Alter Orient und Altes Testament 294. Münster: Ugarit, 2003.
———. *Die Chronik als kanonisches Abschlussphänomen: Studien zur Entstehung und Theologie von 1/2 Chronik*. Bonner biblische Beiträge 93. Weinheim: Beltz Athenäum, 1995.
———. "Zur Datierung der Chronik: Ein neuer methodischer Ansatz." *ZAW* 109 (1997) 84–92.
Stendahl, K. "Biblical Theology, Contemporary." In vol. 1 of *The Interpreter's Dictionary of the Bible*, 4 vols., edited by G. A. Buttrick, 418–32. New York: Abingdon, 1962.

Sternberg, Meir. *The Poetics of Biblical Narrative: Ideological Literature and the Drama of Reading.* Bloomington: Indiana University Press, 1985.
Strauss, Daniël F. M. 2015. "Between Postmodernism, Positivism and (New) Atheism." *Koers* 80 (2015) 1–10.
Strauss, Han. *Untersuchungen zu den Uberlieferungen der vorexilischen Leviten.* Bonn: Rheinische Friedrich Wilhelms Universität, 1960.
Strawn, Brent A. "What Would (or Should) Old Testament Theology Look Like If Recent Reconstructions of Israelite Religion Were True?" In *Between Israelite Religion and Old Testament Theology: Essays on Archaeology, History, and Hermeneutics,* edited by Robert D. Miller, 129–66. Contributions to Biblical Exegesis and Theology 80. Leuven: Peeters, 2016.
Street, James M. *The Significance of the Ark Narrative: Literary Formation and Artistry in the Book of Chronicles.* Studies in Biblical Literature 129. New York: Lang, 2009.
Stuart, Douglas K. *Exodus.* NAC 2. Nashville: Broadman & Holman, 2006.
Stulac, Daniel J. "Charting New Paths in Modern-Critical Exegesis: An Agrarian-Rhetorical Analysis of Isaiah 5." *BibInt* 27 (2019) 390–412.
Sturtevant, Edgar H., and George Bechtel. *A Hittite Chrestomathy.* Philadelphia: University of Pennsylvania, 1935.
Sweeney, Marvin A. "Jewish Biblical Theology and Christian Old Testament Theology." *Theologische Literaturzeitung* 134 (2009) 397–410.
Talshir, David. "A Reinvestigation of the Linguistic Relationship Between Chronicles and Ezra-Nehemiah." *VT* 38 (1988) 165–93.
Talshir, Zipora. "Several Canon-Related Concepts Originating in Chronicles." *ZAW* 113 (2001) 386–403.
Tate, Marvin E. *Psalms 51–100.* WBC 20. Dallas: Word, 1990.
Telfer, Charles K. "The Turbulent Fortunes of Narrativity in Twentieth-Century Historiography." *Mid-America Journal of Theology* 21 (2010) 7–19.
Terrien, Samuel L. *The Bible and the Church: An Approach to Scripture.* Philadelphia: Westminster, 1962.
———. *The Elusive Presence: Toward a New Biblical Theology.* Religious Perspectives 26. San Francisco: Harper & Row, 1978.
———. *The Psalms.* Eerdmans Critical Commentary. Grand Rapids: Eerdmans, 2003.
Tertel, Hans Jürgen. *Text and Transmission: An Empirical Model for the Literary Development of Old Testament Narratives.* BZAW 221. Berlin: de Gruyter, 1994.
Te Velde, Hermann. "Theology, Priests, and Worship in Ancient Egypt." In *CANE* 3:1731.
Thiselton, Anthony C. *New Horizons in Hermeneutics: The Theory and Practice of Transforming Biblical Reading.* Grand Rapids: Zondervan, 1992.
Thomas, Gordon J. "A Holy God among a Holy People in a Holy Place: The Enduring Eschatological Hope." In *Eschatology in Bible & Theology: Evangelical Essays at the Dawn of a New Millennium,* edited by Kent E. Brower and Mark W. Elliot, 53–69. Downers Grove: InterVarsity, 1997.
Thompson, J. A. *1, 2 Chronicles.* New American Commentary 9. Nashville: Broadman & Holman, 1994.
Thompson, Thomas L. *The Bible in History: How Writers Create a Past.* London: Cape, 1999.
———. *Early History of the Israelite People: From the Written and Archaeological Sources.* Studies in the History of the Ancient Near East 4. Leiden: Brill, 1992.

———. *The Historicity of the Patriarchal Narratives: The Quest for the Historical Abraham*. BZAW 133. Berlin: de Gruyter, 1974.
———. *Jerusalem in Ancient History and Tradition*. JSOTSup 381. T&T Clark, 2003.
———. *The Mythic Past: Biblical Archaeology and the Myth of Israel*. New York: Basic, 1999.
Thorsten, Moritz. "Critical Realism." In *DTIB* 147–50.
Throntveit, Mark A. "The Chronicler's Speeches and Historical Reconstruction." In *CaH* 225–45.
———. "Chronicles, Books of." In *DTIB* 109–12.
———. "Songs in A New Key: The Psalmic Structure of the Chronicler's Hymn (1 Chr 16:8–36)." In *A God So Near: Essays on Old Testament Theology in Honor of Patrick D. Miller*, edited by Brent A. Strawn and Nancy R. Bowen, 153–70. Winona Lake: Eisenbrauns, 2003.
———. *When Kings Speak: Royal Speech and Royal Prayer in Chronicles*. Society of Biblical Literature Dissertation Series 93. Atlanta: Scholars, 1987.
Thurén, Lauri. "Is There Biblical Argumentation?" In *Rhetorical Argumentation in Biblical Texts: Essays from the Lund 2000 Conference*, edited by Anders Eriksson et al., 77–94. Emory Studies in Early Christianity 8. Harrisburg: Trinity, 2002.
Todd, Virgil H. "Biblical Eschatology: An Overview." *The Cumberland Seminarian* 22 (1984) 3–16.
Tournay, Raymond Jacques. "Le psaume LXXIII: relectures et interprétation." *RB* 92 (1985) 187–99.
———. *Voir et entendre Dieu avec les Psaumes ou la liturgie prophétique du Second Temple à Jérusalem*. Cahiers de la Revue Biblique 24. Paris: Gabalda, 1988.
Townsend, Jeffrey L. "The Purpose of the 1 and 2 Chronicles." *Bibliotheca Sacra* 144 (1987) 277–92.
Toynbee, A. J. *Christianity Among the Religions of the World*. New York: Scribner's, 1957.
———. *Christianity and Civilisation*. Wallingford: Pendle Hill, 1947.
———. *An Historian's Approach to Religion*. 2nd ed. New York: Oxford University Press, 1979.
Toynbee, A. J., and D. C. Somervell, eds. *A Study of History*. 2 vols. New York: Oxford University Press, 1947.
Trebolle, Julio. "Samuel, Kings and Chronicles: Book Division and Text Composition." In *Studies in the Hebrew Bible, Qumran, and the Septuagint Presented to Eugene Ulrich*, edited by Eugene Ulrich et al., 96–108. VTSup 101. Leiden: Brill, 2006.
Trible, Phyllis. *God and the Rhetoric of Sexuality*. OBT 2. Philadelphia: Fortress, 1978.
———. *Rhetorical Criticism: Context, Method, and the Book of Jonah*. Minneapolis: Fortress, 1994.
———. *Texts of Terror: Literary-Feminist Readings of Biblical Narratives*. OBT. Philadelphia: Fortress, 1984.
Troeltsch, Ernst. *Historicism and Its Problems. Volume 1: The Logical Problem of the Philosophy of History*. Translated by Gerda Hartman. Tübingen, 1922.
Tucker, Aviezer. "The Future of the Philosophy of Historiography." *History and Theory* 40 (2001) 37–56.
Tuell, Steven Shawn. *First and Second Chronicles*. Interpretation: A Bible Commentary for Teaching and Preaching. Louisville: John Knox, 2001.

Tull, Patricia K. "Rhetorical Criticism and Intertextuality." In *To Each Its Own Meaning*, edited by Steven L. McKenzie and Stephen R. Hayes, 156–82. Louisville: Westminster John Knox, 1999.

Tumbarello, Giacomo. "La Musica e Gli Strumenti Musicali Nella Bibbia." *Bibbia e Oriente* 32 (1990) 73–79.

Twersky, Geula. "Genesis 49: The Foundation of Israelite Monarchy and Priesthood." *JSOT* 43 (2019) 317–33.

Ussishkin, David. "Solomon's Jerusalem: The Text and the Facts on the Ground." In *The First Temple Period*, edited by Andrew G. Vaughn and Ann E. Killebrew, 1–10. Society of Biblical Literature Symposium Series 18. Atlanta: SBL, 2003.

———. "The Temple Mount in Jerusalem during the First Temple Period: An Archaeologist's View." In *Exploring the Longue Durée: Essays in Honor of Lawrence E. Stager*, edited by D. Schloen, 473–83. Winona Lake: Eisenbrauns, 2009.

Vanderhooft, David S. "Babylonia and the Babylonians." In *WOT* 107–38.

Van De Mieroop, Marc. *A History of the Ancient Near East, Ca. 3000-323 BC*. Chichester: Wiley-Blackwell, 2016.

van der Lugt, Pieter. *Rhetorical Criticism and the Poetry of the Book of Job*. Oudtestamentische Studiën 32. Leiden: Brill, 1995.

van Dyk, P. J. "Music in Old Testament Times." *OTE* 4 (1991) 373–80.

van Eemeren, Frans H. "Argumentation Theory: An Overview of Approaches and Research Themes." In *Rhetorical Argumentation in Biblical Texts: Essays from the Lund 2000 Conference*, edited by Anders Eriksson et al., 9–26. Emory Studies in Early Christianity 8. Harrisburg: Trinity, 2002.

Van Hoonacker, A. "Les prêtres et les lévites dans le livre d'Ézéchiel." *Revue Biblique* 8 (1899) 177–205.

———. *Sacerdoce lévitique dans la loi et dans l'histoire*. Leuven: Istas, 1899.

Van Rooy, Harry V. "Prophet and Society in the Persian Period according to Chronicles." In *Second Temple Studies, 2: Temple and Community in the Persian Period*, edited by Tamara Cohn Eskenazi and Kent Harold Richards, 163–79. JSOTSup 175. Sheffield: JSOT Press, 1994.

Van Seters, John. *Abraham in History and Tradition*. New Haven: Yale University Press, 1975.

———. "The Chronicler's Account of Solomon's Temple-Building: A Continuity Theme." In *CaH* 283–300.

———. "Creative Imitation in the Hebrew Bible." *Studies in Religion* 29 (2000) 395–409.

———. *In Search of History: Historiography in the Ancient World and the Origins of Biblical History*. New Haven: Yale University Press, 1983. Reprint, Winona Lake: Eisenbrauns, 1997.

———. *A Law Book for the Diaspora: Revision in the Study of the Covenant Code*. Oxford: Oxford University Press, 2003.

———. *Prologue to History: The Yahwist as Historian in Genesis*. Louisville: Westminster John Knox, 1992.

VanderKam, James C. "Ezra-Nehemiah or Ezra and Nehemiah?" In *Priests, Prophets, and Scribes: Essays on the Formation and Heritage of Second Temple Judaism in Honour of Joseph Blenkinsopp*, edited by Eugene Ulrich, 55–75. JSOTSup 149. Sheffield: JSOT Press, 1992.

———. "Jewish High Priests of the Persian Period: Is the List Complete?" In *Priesthood and Cult in Ancient Israel*, edited by Gary A. Anderson and Saul M. Olyan, 67-91. JSOTSup 125. Sheffield: JSOT Press, 1991.

VanGemeren, Willem A. *The Progress of Redemption: The Story of Salvation from Creation to the New Jerusalem*. Grand Rapids: Baker, 1988.

———. "Psalms." In *The Expositor's Bible Commentary, Volume 5*, edited by Frank E. Gæbelein, 1-880. Grand Rapids: Zondervan, 1991.

Vanhoozer, Kevin J. *The Drama of Doctrine: A Canonical Linguistic Approach to Christian Theology*. Louisville: Westminster John Knox, 2005.

———. "Exegesis and Hermeneutics." In *NDBT* 52-64.

———. "Introduction: What is Theological Interpretation of the Bible?" In *DTIB* 19-25.

———. *Is There a Meaning in This Text? The Bible, the Reader, and the Morality of Literary Knowledge*. Grand Rapids: Zondervan, 1998.

Vanhoye, Albert. *La lettre aux Hébreux: Jésus-Christ, médiateur d'une nouvelle alliance*. Collection "Jésus et Jésus-Christ" 84. Paris: Desclée, 2002.

———. *Old Testament Priests and the New Priest: According to the New Testament*. Translated by J. Bernard Orchard. Studies in Scripture. Petersham: St. Bede's, 1986.

Vannutelli, Primo. *Libri Synoptici Veteris Testamenti, seu, librorum Regum et Chronicorum loci paralleli*. 2 vols. Scripta Pontificii Instituti Biblici. Rome: Pontifical Biblical Institute, 1931-1934.

Vasholz, Robert I. *The Old Testament Canon in the Old Testament Church: The Internal Rationale for Old Testament Canonicity*. Ancient Near Eastern Texts and Studies 7. Lewiston: Mellen, 1990.

Vatke, Wilhelm. *Die biblische Theologie*. Berlin: Bethge, 1835.

———. *Die Religion des Alten Testamentes nach den kanonischen Büchern entwickelt*. Berlin: Bethge, 1835.

Vaughn, Andrew G. "Jerusalem in Bible and Archaeology: Dialogues and Discussions." In *Jerusalem in the Bible and Archaeology: The First Temple Period*, edited by Andrew G. Vaughn and Ann E. Killebrew, 1-10. Society of Biblical Literature Symposium Series 18. Atlanta: SBL, 2003.

Vitale, Raoul. "La Musique Suméro-Accadienne: Gamme et notation musicale." *Ugarit-Forschungen* 14 (1982) 260-72.

Vieillard-Baron, Jean-Louis. *Platon et l'idéalisme allemand (1770-1830)*. Bibliothèque des archives de philosophie: Nouvelle série 28. Paris: Beauchesne, 1979.

Vogelstein, H. *Der Kampf zwischen Priestern und Leviten Seit den Tagen Ezechiels*. Stettin: F. Nagel, 1889.

Vincent, M. A. "The Shape of the Psalter: An Eschatological Dimension?" In *New Heaven and New Earth Prophecy and the Millennium*, edited by P. J. Harland and C. T. R. Hayward, 61-82. Leiden: Brill, 1999.

von Götz, Schmitt. "Der Ursprung des Levitentums." *ZAW* 94 (1982) 575-99.

von Hofmann, J. C. K. *Weissagung und Erfüllung im Alten und im Neuen Testamente*. Nördlingen: Beck, 1841.

von Rad, Gerhard. *Das Geschichtsbild des Chronistischen Werkes*. BWA(N)T 4. Stuttgart: Kohlhammer, 1930.

———. "Die Levitische Predigt in den Büchern der Chronik." In *Festschrift Otto Procksch zum sechzigsten Geburtstag*, edited by Albrecht Alt, 113-24. Leipzig: Deichert, 1934.

---. "The Levitical Sermon in 1 and 2 Chronicles." In *From Genesis to Chronicles: Explorations in Old Testament Theology*, edited by K. C. Hanson, 232–42. Minneapolis: Fortress, 2005.
---. *Theologie des alten Testaments. Band 1: Die theologie der geschichtlichen überlieferungen Israels*. München: Kaiser, 1957.
---. *Theology of the Old Testament, Volume I: The Theology of Israel's Traditions*. Translated by D. M. G. Stalker. Edinburgh: Oliver & Boyd, 1962.
Vos, Geerhardus. *Biblical Theology: Old and New Testaments*. Grand Rapids: Eerdmans, 1948.
Wahl, Otto. *Die Sacra-Parallela-Zitate aus den Büchern Josua, Richter, 1/2 Samuel, 3/4 Könige sowie 1/2 Chronik*. Abhandlungen der Akademie der Wissenschaften zu Göttingen 255. Göttingen: Vandenhoeck & Ruprecht, 2004.
Walton, Brian, et al., eds. *Biblia Sacra Polyglotta*. London: Roycroft & Thomas, 1657.
Walton, John H. *Ancient Near Eastern Thought and the Old Testament: Introducing the Conceptual World of the Hebrew Bible*. 2nd ed. Grand Rapids: Baker, 2018.
---. "Interactions in the Ancient Cognitive Environment." In *BSOT* 333–39.
---. "The Temple in Context." In *BSOT* 349–54.
Ward, William A. "Temples and Sanctuaries: Egypt." In *ABD* 6:369.
Warner, Martin. "Introduction: Rhetorical Criticism of the Bible." In *The Bible as Rhetoric: Studies in Biblical Persuasion and Credibility*, edited by Martin Warner. Warwick Studies in Philosophy and Literature. London: Routledge, 1990.
Watson, Duane F. "Paul's Speech to the Ephesian Elders (Acts 20.17–38): Epideictic Rhetoric of Farewell." In *Persuasive Artistry: Studies in New Testament Rhetoric in Honor of George A. Kennedy*, edited by Duane F. Watson, 184–208. JSNTSup 50. Sheffield: Sheffield Academic, 1991.
Watson, W. G. E. "Chiastic Patterns in Biblical Hebrew Poetry." In *Chiasmus in Antiquity: Structure, Analyses, Exegesis*, edited by J. W. Welch, 118–68. Hildesheim: Gerstenberg, 1981.
Weber, Beat. "Der Asaph-Psalter—Eine Skizze." In *Prophetie Und Psalmen: Festschrift Für Klaus Seybold Zum 65. Geburtstag*, edited by Beat Huwyler et al., 117–41. Alter Orient und Altes Testament 280. Münster: Ugarit, 2001.
---. "Die doppelte Verknoting des Psalters. Kanonhermeneutische Erwägungen zu den 'Schnittstellen' Psalm 18//2 Samuel 22 und Psalm 96; 105; 106//1 Chronik 16." *Biblische Zeitschrift* 60 (2016) 14–27.
Weinberg, Joel. *Citizen-Temple Community*. Translated by Daniel L. Smith-Christopher. JSOTSup 151. Sheffield, England: JSOT Press, 1992.
---. *Der Chronist in seiner Mitwelt*. BZAW 239. Berlin: de Gruyter, 1996.
Welch, Adam Cleghorn. *The Work of the Chronicler: Its Purpose and Its Date*. The Schweich Lectures of the British Academy 1938. London: Oxford University Press, 1939.
Welch, J. W. "Introduction." In *Chiasmus in Antiquity: Structure, Analyses, Exegesis*, edited by J. W. Welch, 9–16. Hildesheim: Gerstenberg, 1981.
Wellhausen, Julius. *Prolegomena to the History of Ancient Israel*. Translated by J. S. Black and A. Menzies. Edinburgh: Black, 1885. Reprinted, New York: Meridian, 1957.
---. *Prolegomena zur Geschichte Israels*. Berlin: Reimer, 1883.
Welten, Peter. *Geschichte und Geschichtsdarstellung in den Chronikbüchern*. Wissenschaftlich Monographien zum Alten und Neuen Testament 42. Neukirchen-Vluyn: Neukirchener, 1973.

———. "Lade-Tempel-Jerusalem. Zur Theologie der Chronikbücher." In *Textgemäß: Aufsätze und Beiträge zur Hermeneutik des Alten Testaments. Festschrift für Ernst Würthwein zum 70. Geburstag*, edited by A. H. J. Gunneweg and Otto Kaiser, 168–83. Göttingen: Vandenhoeck & Ruprecht, 1979.

Wendland, Ernst R. "Aspects of the Structure, Style, and Transmission of Psalm 73." *The Bible Translator* 50 (1999) 135–49.

———. "Introit 'Into the Sanctuary of God' (Psalm 73:17): Entering the Theological 'Heart' of the Psalm at the Centre of the Psalter." *OTE* 11 (1998) 128–53.

Wenham, Gordon J. *Genesis 16–50*. WBC 2. Nashville: Nelson, 1994.

———. *Numbers: An Introduction & Commentary*. TOTC. Downers Grove: InterVarsity, 1981.

———. *Story as Torah: Reading Old Narrative Ethically*. Grand Rapids: Baker, 2000.

Werman, Cana. "Levi and Levites in the Second Temple Period." *Dead Sea Discoveries* 4 (1997) 211–25.

Westermann, Claus. *Elements of Old Testament Theology*. Atlanta: John Knox, 1982.

———. *The Living Psalms*. Translated by J. R. Porter. Grand Rapids: Eerdmans, 1984.

———. *What Does the Old Testament Say about God?* Atlanta: John Knox, 1979.

Whitcomb, John Clement. *Solomon to the Exile: Studies in Kings and Chronicles*. Old Testament Studies. Winona Lake: BMH, 1971.

White, Hayden. *The Content of the Form: Narrative Discourse and Historical Representation*. Baltimore: Johns Hopkins University Press, 1987.

———. *Metahistory: The Historical Imagination in Nineteenth-Century Europe*. Baltimore: Johns Hopkins University Press, 1973.

———. *Tropics of Discourse: Essays in Cultural Criticism*. Baltimore: Johns Hopkins University Press, 1978.

White, Marsha. "The Elohistic Depiction of Aaron: A Study of the Levite/Zadokite Controversy." *VTSup* 41 (1990) 149–60.

Whitelam, Keith W. *The Invention of Israel: The Silencing of Palestinian History*. London: Routledge, 1996.

———. *Rhythms of Time: Reconnecting Palestine's Past*. Sheffield: Black, 2013.

Whybray, R. N. "What Do We Know about Ancient Israel?" *Expository Times* 108 (1996) 71–74.

Wiener, Harold M. "Priests and Levites." In vol. 4 of *The International Standard Bible Encyclopedia*, edited by James Orr, 2446–52. Chicago: Severance, 1915.

Wiggermann, F. A. M. "Theologies, Priests and Worship in Ancient Mesopotamia." In *CANE* 3:1859–61.

Wilcock, Michael. "1 and 2 Chronicles." In *New Bible Commentary: 21st Century Edition*, edited by D. A. Carson et al., 388–419. Downers Grove: InterVarsity, 1994.

———. *The Message of Chronicles: One Church, One Faith, One Lord*. Downers Grove: InterVarsity, 1987.

Willi-Plein, Ina. "Warum musste der Zweite Tempel gebaut worden?" In *Gemeinde ohne Tempel: zur Substituierung und Transformation des Jerusalemer Tempels und seines Kults im Alten Testament, antiken Judentum und frühen Christentum*, edited by Beate Ego et al., 57–74. Wissenschaftliche Untersuchungen zum Neuen Testament 118. Tübingen: Mohr Siebeck, 1999.

Willi, Thomas. *Chronik*. Biblischer Kommentar: Altes Testament 24. Neukirchen-Vluyn: Neukirchener, 1991.

———. "Der Weltreichsgedanke im Früjudentum: Israel, Menschheit und Weltherrschaft in den biblischen Chronikbüchern." In *Exegese vor Ort: Festschrift für Peter Welten zum 65. Geburtstag*, edited by Peter Welten and Christl Maier, 389–409. Leipzig: Evangelische Verlagsanstalt, 2001.

———. *Die Chronik als Auslegung; Untersuchungen zur literarischen Gestaltung der historischen Überlieferung Israels*. Forschungen zur Religion und Literatur des Alten und Neuen Testaments 106. Göttingen: Vandenhoeck & Ruprecht, 1972.

———. *Juda, Jehud, Israel: Studien zum Selbstverständnis des Judentums in persischer Zeit*. FAT 12. Tübingen: Mohr, 1995.

———. "Late Persian Judaism and Its Conception of an Integral Israel According to Chronicles." In *Second Temple Studies, vol. 2: Temple Community in the Persian Period*, edited by Tamara Cohn Eskenazi and Kent Harold Richards, 146–62. JSOTSup 175. Sheffield: JSOT Press, 1994.

———. "Leviten, Priester und Kult in vorhellenisticher Zeit." In *Gemeinde ohne Tempel*, edited by Beate Ego et al., 75–98. Tübingen: Mohr Siebeck, 1999.

Williams, Stephen. "The Theological Task and Theological Method: Penitence, Parasitism, and Prophecy." In *Evangelical Futures: A Conversation on Theological Method*, edited by John G. Stackhouse Jr., 159–80. Grand Rapids: Baker, 2000.

Williamson, H. G. M. *1 and 2 Chronicles*. New Century Bible Commentary. Grand Rapids: Eerdmans, 1982.

———. *Confirmation or Contradiction? Archaeology and Biblical History*. The St George's Cathedral Lecture 12. Perth: St. George's Cathedral, 2004.

———. "Eschatology in Chronicles." *TynBul* 28 (1977) 115–54.

———. "Exile and After: Historical Study." In *FAOTS* 236–65.

———. *Ezra, Nehemiah*. WBC 16. Waco: Word, 1985.

———. "Introduction." In *The Chronicler's History*, by Martin Noth. JSOTSup 50. Sheffield: JSOT Press, 1987.

———. *Israel in the Books of Chronicles*. Cambridge: Cambridge University Press, 1977.

———. "The Origins of the Twenty-Four Priestly Courses: A Study of 1 Chronicles xxiii–xxvii." In *Studies in the Historical Books of the Old Testament*, edited by J. A. Emerton, 251–68. VTSup 30. Leiden: Brill, 1979.

———. *Studies in Persian Period History and Historiography*. FAT 38. Tübingen: Mohr Siebeck, 2004.

———. "The Temple in the Book of Chronicles." In *Templum Amicitiae: Essays on the Second Temple Presented to Ernst Bammel*, edited by William Horbury, 15–31. JSNTSup 48. Sheffield: Sheffield Academic, 1991.

Wilson, Gerald. *The Editing of the Hebrew Psalter*. SBLDS 76. Chico: Scholars, 1985.

———. *Psalms Volume 1*. NIVAC. Grand Rapids: Zondervan, 2002.

———. "חכם." In *NIDOTTE* 2:130–34.

Wilson, Robert R. *Genealogy and History in the Biblical World*. Yale Near Eastern Researches 7. New Haven: Yale University Press, 1977.

Winterwowd, W. Ross. *Rhetoric: A Synthesis*. New York: Holt, Rinehart & Winston, 1968.

Witte, Markus. "Auf Dem Weg in Ein Leben nach Dem Tod: Beobachtungen Zur Traditions- und Redaktionsgeschichte von Psalm 73, 24-26." *Theologische Zeitschrift* 58 (2002) 15–30.

Wong, Gregory T. K. "Psalm 73 as Ring Composition." *Bib* 97 (2016) 16–40.

Wood, Richard Alan. "Event and Record: Old Testament Historiography in the Light of Analytical Philosophy of History." PhD diss., Southern Baptist Theological Seminary, 1989.
Wright, Andrew. *Religion, Education, and Post-Modernity*. New York: RoutledgeFalmer, 2004.
Wright, George Ernest. *The Challenge of Israel's Faith*. Chicago: University of Chicago Press, 1944.
———. *God Who Acts: Biblical Theology as Recital*. Studies in Biblical Theology 8. London: SCM, 1952.
———. "The Levites in Deuteronomy." *VT* 4 (1954) 325–30.
———. *The Old Testament Against Its Environment*. Studies in Biblical Theology 1. London: SCM, 1950.
———. *The Old Testament and Theology*. New York: Harper & Row, 1969.
———. *The Rule of God: Essays in Biblical Theology*. Garden City: Doubleday, 1960.
Wright, John W. "Beyond Transcendence and Immanence: The Characterization of the Presence and Activity of God in the Book of Chronicles." In *CaT* 240–67.
———. "The Fight for Peace: Narrative and History in the Battle Accounts in Chronicles." In *CaH* 150–77.
———. "The Founding Father: The Structure of the Chronicler's David Narrative." *JBL* 117 (1998) 45–59.
———. "From Center to Periphery: 1 Chronicles 23–27 and the Interpretation of Chronicles in the Nineteenth Century." In *Priests, Prophets, and Scribes: Essays on the Formation and Heritage of Second Temple Judaism in Honour of Joseph Blenkinsopp*, edited by Eugene Ulrich et al. JSOTSup 149. Sheffield: Sheffield Academic, 1992.
———. "Guarding the Gates: 1 Chronicles 26:1–19 and the Roles of Gatekeepers in Chronicles." *JSOT* 48 (1990) 69–81.
———. "The Innocence of David in 1 Chronicles 21." *JSOT* 60 (1993) 87–105.
———. "The Legacy of David in Chronicles: The Narrative Function of 1 Chronicles 23–27." *JBL* 110 (1991) 229–42.
———. "The Origin and Function of 1 Chronicles 23–27." PhD diss., University of Notre Dame, 1989.
Wright, N. T. *The New Testament and the People of God*. Christian Origins and The Question of God 1. Minneapolis: Fortress, 1992.
Wuellner, Wilhelm. "Reconceiving a Rhetoric of Religion: A Rhetorics of Power and the Power of the Sublime." In *Rhetorics and Hermeneutics: Wilhelm Wuellner and His Influence*, edited by James D. Hester and J. David Hester, 23–77. Emory Studies in Early Christianity. New York: T&T Clark, 2004.
———. "Where is Rhetorical Criticism Taking Us?" *CBQ* 49 (1987) 448–63.
Xella, Paolo, and Paolo Merlo. "The Ugaritic Cultic Texts: The Rituals." In *Handbook of Ugaritic Studies*, edited by Wilfred G. E. Watson and Nicolas Wyatt, 287–304. Handbook of Oriental Studies 1. Leiden: Brill, 1999.
Yamauchi, Edwin M. "The Current State of Old Testament Historiography." In *FTH* 1–36.
———. "The Exilic and Postexilic Periods: Current Developments." In *GtS* 201–16.
Younger, K. Lawson, Jr. *Ancient Conquest Accounts: A Study in Ancient Near Eastern and Biblical History Writing*. JSOTSup 98. Sheffield: Sheffield Academic, 1990.

———. "The 'Contextual Method': Some West Semitic Reflections." In *COS* 3:xxxv–xlii.

———. "Early Israel in Recent Biblical Scholarship." In *FAOTS* 176–206.

———. "The Tel Dan Inscription and the Deaths of Joram of Israel and Ahaziah of Judah." In *BSOT* 293–98.

Zaremba, Michael. *Johann Gottfried Herder: Prediger der Humanität: Eine Biografie*. Köln: Böhlau, 2002.

Ziegler, N. *Les musiciens et la musique d'après les archives de Mari*. Florilgelium marianum 9. Mémoires to NABU 10. Paris: SEPOA, 2007.

Zimmerli, Walther. *Old Testament Theology in Outline*. Atlanta: John Knox, 1978.

Zipor, Moshe A. "On the Presentation of the Synoptic Accounts of the Monarchies (Samuel, Kings, and Chronicles)." *Abr-Nahrain* 28 (1990) 127–35.

Zunz, Leopold. *Die Gottesdienstlichen Vorträge der Juden*. Berlin: Asher, 1832.

Index of Ancient Sources

Old Testament

Genesis

12	215
25:19–35	5
29:31—30:24	5
29:34	6
34	6
34:30–31	6
35:16–18	5
35:23–26	6
46:8–27	6
46:11	6, 19
49:7	6

Exodus

1:1–7	6
2:1	6
6	6, 9
6:13–27	6
6:14–25	6
6:16	118
6:16–19	8
6:18	118
6:20	118
6:23	19
16:16	118
16:18	118
19	5
19–24	6
19–40	5
19:1	5
19:14–15	120
25—27	6
25:9	146
25:22	122
28–29	19
28–30	6
30	103
30:29–30	155
30:30–31	155
32	7, 8, 18
37:6–9	122

Leviticus

1	131
8–10	7
8:2	7
10:11	10
12:4	251
17–27	7
19:30	251
20:3	251
21:1–4	120
21:12	251
21:13–14	120
21:23	251
25:32–34	7, 9, 10

Numbers

1–2	7
1:1–46	7
1:1—10:10	5, 7
1:47	7
1:47–54	7
1:50–53	115
2:17	7
3	7, 158
3–4	7
3:1–13	7
3:2	19
3:5–9	115
3:14–20	7
3:19	118
3:21–39	8
3:29–30	118
3:30	118
3:40–51	8
4	8
4:1–3	8
4:1–17	8
4:3	157
4:17–20	118
4:21–28	8
4:23	157
4:29–33	8
4:30	157
4:34–49	8
4:36	153
7:9	120
8:5–26	8
8:12	8
8:12–26	8
8:19	8
8:24	157
10:1–10	24
10:9–10	127
10:10	5
16	8
16—18	18
16:46–50	8
18	8
18:1	251
18:1–7	8
18:8–24	8
18:20	257
18:25–32	9
19:20	251
25:10–13	19
26	9
26:5–59	9
31:1–12	127
35:1–4	9, 10

Deuteronomy

4:44—11:32	9
10:6–9	9
10:8	115, 135
10:9	6
12–26	9
12:8–11	159
12:10	159
12:11	159
12:11–12	9
12:12	9
14:27	9
16:11–12	9
17:9	9
18	9, 14, 15
18:1	9
18:6–7	9
18:10–11	195
21:5	9
24:8	9
26:12–15	9
27–30	10
27:8	9
27:14	10
27:15–26	10
31	64, 144
31–34	10
31:9	9
31:24	10
32:39	243
33	10
33:8–10	115
33:8–11	10
33:10	115

Joshua

1	64, 144
3:3	10
8:33	10
13:14	10
13:32	10

14:2	10	6:17	97, 110, 111
18:7	10	6:17–19	110
21	21	6:17–19a	130
21:2	10	6:17–20a	226
		6:19	97
		6:19b–20a	106
		6:20–23	110, 111

Judges

		7	64, 108
17–18	10	7:1–3	108
17–19	158	7:1–17	108
18:3–31	10	7:7–10	64
19–20	10	7:13–16	108
19:25–30	10	7:16	100
21:25	10	7:18–29	108
		11	101
		15:24–29	10

1 Samuel

		19:36	123
2:27–36	20	20:25	19
4–7	106	23	100
4:1—7:1	107		
6	107		

1 Kings

6:13–15	110		
6:13–16	110	1	151
6:15	10, 97	1:7	20
6:16	110	1:28–53	12
7	144	2:26–27	20
7:1	107	2:35	20
7:7–10	144	4:1–4	20
8–31	108	8	182
22	223	8:1–11	84
		8:4	10
		8:30	254

2 Samuel

		10:12	123
1–4	108	12:29	10
1–8	108	12:31	18
5–8	108		
6	4, 91, 106, 108, 109, 110, 111, 131		

1 Chronicles

6:1–3	264		
6:1–8	111	1	22
6:1–12	110	1–9	21, 22, 36, 37, 51, 262
6:1–23	106, 108		
6:9–11	111	1:35	12
6:12	109, 111	2:6	13
6:12–15	121	3:17–24	48
6:12–16	128	5	163
6:12–19a	109	5:2–14	265
6:13–15	111	5:25	81
6:16	97, 111	5:27	92
6:16–18	111	5:27–41	21, 118

1 Chronicles (continued)

Reference	Pages
5:28	118
6	19, 21, 234, 241
6:1	21
6:1–2	182
6:1–3	21
6:1–15	21
6:1–48	21
6:1–66	118
6:2	21, 118
6:3	19, 21, 118
6:4	19
6:4–15	21
6:7	12
6:12	19
6:16	21
6:16–17	21
6:16–30	21
6:16–32	125
6:17–19	21
6:18	118
6:20–22	21
6:20–30	21
6:22	12
6:22–24	21
6:24	13
6:25–27	21
6:28	21
6:29	94
6:29–30	21
6:31–48	21
6:33	13, 21
6:33–39	21
6:34	21
6:39–43	21
6:44–47	21
6:48	19
6:49	21
6:49–53	21
6:50–53	21
6:54–70	21
6:71–76	21
6:77–81	21
9	22
9:1–18	28
9:2–17	22, 48
9:10–13	22
9:14–16	22
9:15	13
9:16	126
9:17–26	126
9:17–32	22, 126
9:19	12
9:21	22
9:33–34	22
10	102, 104, 108, 110
10–14	114
10–21	98, 101, 140
10–22	212
10–29	4, 5, 22, 27, 30, 31, 33, 37, 38, 39, 42, 64, 90, 139, 140, 142, 204, 205, 208, 233, 258, 259, 260, 261, 262, 263, 268
10:1–14	102
10:1—11:9	102, 104, 105
10:1—22:1	39, 42, 52, 90, 98, 142, 264, 265
10:13–14	102
10:14	102
11	102
11–12	36, 100, 102, 223
11:1	80, 115
11:1–3	102
11:1–9	102
11:1—12:40	104
11:3b	102
11:9	102, 105
11:10—12:37	101
11:10—12:38	101
11:10—12:40	99, 100, 105
12:18	128
12:26–28	22
12:27	153
12:38	101, 105
12:38–40	102
12:39	101, 105, 115
13	99, 101, 106, 108, 110, 112, 114, 120, 124, 131
13–14	104, 109, 112, 223
13–16	112
13:1–4	22, 109

13:1–11	111		111, 112, 113,
13:1–14	106		134, 263, 264, 265
13:1—14:7	99	15:1—16:43	105
13:1—14:17	105	15:1a	114
13:2	92, 106	15:1b	114
13:3	99	15:2	91, 113, 114, 115,
13:11	93, 105		116, 129, 134, 135
13:12–14	111	15:2–3	132
13:13–14	84	15:2—16:3	134
13:14	106	15:2b	91, 132
13:42	114	15:2b-3	132
14	91, 100	15:3	113, 115, 116,
14–17	212		129, 132, 134
14:1–5	113	15:3–4	115
14:2	105, 113	15:4	94, 116, 117, 118,
14:6–17	113		119, 135
14:17	91, 100, 113, 114	15:4–10	94, 117, 119
15	38, 90, 109, 110,	15:4–11	119, 120
	111, 115, 116,	15:4–15	116, 117, 134, 265
	117, 121, 123,	15:4–17	92, 93
	124, 126, 127,	15:4–24	111
	130, 140, 150,	15:5	118
	161, 162, 208,	15:5–7	117, 118, 119
	211, 217, 234,	15:5–10	117
	241, 263	15:6	118
15–16	3, 4, 22, 27, 28, 34,	15:8	118
	35, 46, 50, 84, 90,	15:8–10	118, 119
	98, 99, 104, 108,	15:9	118
	109, 112, 137,	15:9–10	118
	159, 163, 204,	15:10	118
	207, 225, 259,	15:11	19, 94, 116, 117,
	260, 270		119, 124
15–17	211	15:11–15	117
15:1	91, 98, 105, 111,	15:12	116, 117, 120, 129
	113, 114, 116,	15:12–13	116, 117, 119,
	117, 120, 129,		120, 122
	132, 161	15:12–15	120
15:1–3	91, 92, 110, 111,	15:12a	120
	112, 113, 117,	15:12b	120
	134, 265	15:13	120
15:1–5	96	15:14	94, 116, 117, 120,
15:1–15	121		129
15:1–16	22	15:14–15	117, 120
15:1–24	109	15:15	116, 117, 120
15:1—16:1	110	15:15–24	122
15:1—16:3	39, 40, 42, 46, 50,	15:15b	217
	51, 90, 91, 106,	15:16	121, 124, 127
		15:16–17	124

1 Chronicles (continued)

15:16–24	94, 117, 121, 125, 126, 127, 134, 135, 265
15:16–25	93, 94, 95, 96
15:16–29	22
15:16—16:3	50
15:17	13, 124
15:17–18	124, 126, 127
15:17–24	127
15:17–25	124
15:18	94, 126
15:18a	125
15:18b	125
15:19	13, 22, 125, 127, 198
15:19–21	125, 126
15:19–24	124, 126, 127
15:20	94, 95, 125, 127
15:21	95, 125, 127
15:22	96, 125, 126, 127
15:22–24	125
15:23	94, 125, 126, 127
15:23–24	126
15:24	94, 125, 126, 129
15:24a	127
15:24b	125, 127
15:25	128, 129, 130
15:25–28	96, 111
15:25–29	96, 97, 110, 128, 130, 134, 265
15:25—16:3	106, 110, 121
15:26	98, 128, 129, 130, 132, 159
15:26–28	130
15:26b	128
15:27	122
15:27–28	117, 128, 130
15:28	97, 129
15:29	110, 111, 128, 129, 130, 135, 231
15:29a	130
15:29b	130
16	38, 69, 84, 86, 89, 90, 99, 109, 112, 130, 147, 150, 161, 207, 208, 209, 210, 211, 212, 214, 215, 216, 217, 223, 226, 227, 232, 233, 234, 241, 242, 243, 251, 258, 263, 264, 268, 269
16:1	97, 99, 105, 110, 129, 131, 133
16:1–3	97, 99, 110, 111, 130, 131, 133, 134, 226, 265
16:1–7	23
16:1b	111
16:2–3	133
16:2–29	220
16:3	112
16:3–36	213
16:4	99, 112, 129, 218, 227
16:4–6	226
16:4–7	13, 28, 99, 227
16:4–38	207
16:4–42	207
16:4–43	69, 80, 90, 98
16:4b	219
16:5	13
16:7	13, 23, 99, 207, 226, 242
16:7–36	87
16:8	212, 225, 226, 227, 229
16:8–9	213, 214
16:8–13	220, 221, 225, 226, 227, 229
16:8–14	219
16:8–22	207
16:8–33	226
16:8–34	212, 220, 226, 229, 230
16:8–36	23, 99, 207, 209, 210, 211, 212, 213, 219, 220, 221, 222, 223, 224, 225, 226
16:9	212, 227
16:9–10	225

INDEX OF ANCIENT SOURCES

16:9–11	219	16:30–31	222
16:9–22	212	16:30–33	220, 221, 229, 231
16:10	212, 225, 227	16:30b	214
16:10–11	81	16:31	212, 231
16:10–22	214	16:31–33	212, 233
16:11	212, 225	16:31aba	214
16:12	225, 227	16:32–33	231
16:13	220, 222, 225	16:32–33ba	214
16:13–34	232	16:33	212
16:13a	227	16:34	81, 212, 220, 221, 225, 226, 227, 228, 229
16:14	212, 229		
16:14–15	229		
16:14–22	220, 221, 229, 230, 232	16:34–36	207, 213, 214, 219, 226
16:14–33	227, 229	16:35	226, 229
16:14–34	226, 228	16:35–36	225, 226, 228, 230
16:14b	229	16:35–36a	212, 220
16:15	220, 222, 229, 230, 232	16:35a	220, 228
		16:35b	220, 228
16:15–22	109, 219, 231	16:36	212, 220, 222, 226, 228, 229
16:16–17	230		
16:19	222, 230	16:36a	220, 228
16:22–24	214	16:36b	220, 228
16:23	212, 229, 230	16:37	13, 99, 129, 207, 226, 251
16:23–24	213, 214		
16:23–27	231	16:37–38	23
16:23–29	220, 221, 229, 230	16:37–39	99
16:23–30	212	16:37–43	23, 207
16:23–33	207, 219	16:38–42	226
16:23b	230	16:40–43	99
16:24	230	16:41	23
16:24–25	221	16:42	23
16:24–29	231	16:43	106, 130, 226
16:25	212, 230	17	104, 109, 122, 139, 151, 211
16:25–26	230, 231, 232		
16:25–33	214	17:1	105
16:25a	231	17:1–2	100
16:25b	231	17:1–27	99, 105
16:26	212, 230	17:1a	100
16:26a	231	17:3–27	100
16:26b	214, 231	17:11–12	113
16:27	222, 231	17:11–14	100
16:28a-b	231	17:11–15	81
16:29	228, 231	17:14	100, 113
16:29–33	109	17:24	113
16:29a	231	17:25	81
16:29b	231	18–20	101, 211
16:30	229, 231	18:1–13	101

1 Chronicles (continued)

18:1–17	101
18:1–20	105
18:1—20:8	99, 101, 104
18:13b	101
18:14	101, 105
18:16	19
19:1–19	101
20:1–3	101
20:4–8	101
21	63, 101, 102, 103
21:1–17	103
21:1—22:1	104, 105
21:3	101
21:18—22:1	103
21:22	91, 105
21:29	103
22	64, 65, 142, 143, 144, 145, 148, 150, 265, 266
22–27	260
22–29	2, 4, 27, 65, 67, 103, 141, 142, 143, 147, 148, 151, 161, 163, 182, 203, 204, 259, 265
22:1	103, 105, 142
22:1–19	142
22:1—29:30	90
22:2–5	23, 64, 143
22:2–19	144
22:2—23:1	65, 148
22:2—23:2	23
22:2—29:26	23
22:2—29:30	39, 64
22:5	145
22:5b	143
22:6–19	23, 144
22:9	64
22:9–10	144
22:10	113, 251
22:11–16	145
22:14	144
22:15–16	144
22:17–19	64
23	38, 64, 65, 67, 69, 90, 127, 136, 141, 142, 143, 147, 148, 150, 152, 155, 157, 160, 163, 203, 208, 217, 240, 263, 266, 267, 268, 270
23–26	64, 147
23–27	23, 24, 28, 35, 36, 65, 142, 145, 146, 147, 148, 149, 150, 151, 152, 153, 157, 204, 265, 266
23–28	65, 143, 148, 267
23–29	52, 151
23:1	142, 150, 151, 152
23:1–6	65
23:2	23, 142, 143, 148, 149, 152
23:2–5	150, 152, 157
23:2–6	158
23:2–6a	152
23:2–32	142
23:2—27:34	152
23:2—28:1	149
23:3	23, 157, 158
23:3–5	23, 151, 153, 156
23:3–6a	148
23:3—27:34	23, 65, 148, 149
23:4–5	153
23:4–32	23
23:4a	23, 148
23:4b	23, 148
23:5	162
23:5a	23, 149
23:5b	23, 149
23:6	92, 154, 156
23:6–20	155
23:6–23	23, 151, 154
23:6b-13a	148
23:7–11	154
23:7–23	65, 156
23:12	118
23:12–20	154
23:13	154, 161
23:13–14	23, 154, 155

INDEX OF ANCIENT SOURCES 351

23:13b-14	149	25:1—26:32	23
23:15-24	148	25:1a	208
23:21-22	154	25:2	85
23:24	156, 157, 158	25:6	13
23:24-27	23, 159	25:6-7	125
23:24-32	23, 52, 62, 64, 65, 67, 150, 151, 156	25:7-31	149
		25:9	13
23:25	158, 159	26	136, 151, 267
23:25-27	156, 159	26:1-3	149
23:25-32	149, 150	26:1-12	24
23:27	157	26:1-17	147
23:28	23	26:1-19	126
23:28-32	154, 156, 160	26:4-8	149
23:28a	160	26:9	25
23:28b	160	26:9-11	149
23:28b-31	160	26:12-18	149
23:28b-32	160	26:20-28	147
23:28c	160	26:20-32	24, 148
23:29	23, 161	26:29-32	25, 147
23:30	68	27	64
23:30-31	68	27:1-15	147
23:30-32	23, 161	27:1-32	149
23:32	160	27:1-34	142
24	104, 151, 217, 267	27:16-32	147
24-27	27	28	145, 146
24:1-6	23	28-29	23, 64, 65, 142, 145, 148, 150, 265, 266
24:1-9	142		
24:1-19	103, 147, 149		
24:1-31	23	28:1	116, 145, 148, 149, 151, 152
24:6	19		
24:7-31	23	28:1-10	145
24:11	20	28:1—29:25	152
24:20-31	147, 149	28:1—29:26	65, 148
24:20—26:32	142	28:1—29:30	149
25	4, 24, 31, 36, 37, 69, 83, 86, 89, 90, 91, 96, 127, 136, 137, 141, 142, 143, 151, 162, 163, 205, 208, 234, 240, 241, 242, 267, 269, 270	28:2	143
		28:3	134
		28:4a	145
		28:7	113
		28:8	145
		28:9	81
		28:9-10	145
		28:9-21	145
25:1	68, 162, 200	28:9a	145
25:1-2	13	28:11	24
25:1-5	13	28:11-19	145
25:1-6	149, 208	28:11-21	24
25:1-8	69, 80	28:11a	145
25:1-31	125, 147	28:12	24, 146

1 Chronicles (continued)

28:13	24
28:20–21	145
29	145, 146, 147
29:1–5	146
29:1–30	142
29:2	20, 92
29:6–9	146
29:7	48
29:9	81
29:10–11	146
29:10–22	146
29:17	81
29:18	113
29:19	81
29:21–26	80
29:22–25	151
29:22–30	146

2 Chronicles

1–9	24, 37, 262, 265, 266
1:4	92, 113
5	162
5:2–14	24, 84, 269
5:2–24	162
5:3–6	24
5:7	24
5:11–14	24
5:12	13, 28
5:13	81, 83
6	182
6:21	81
6:25	81
6:27	81
6:30	81
6:39	81
7:1	81
7:1–8	24
7:6a	24
7:6b	24
7:10	81
7:11–22	81
7:13	81
7:14	81
8	182
8:3–4	48
8:14–15	24, 162
10–12	25
10–36	24, 26, 51, 262
11:11–18	25
11:13–17	25
11:14	25
11:16	25, 81
12:1	113
12:6–7	81
12:14	113
13	25
13:8–9	25
13:10–12	25
13:10b	25
13:12	25
15:4	81
15:12	81
16:9	48
17–20	25
17:3	81
17:5	113
17:6	25
17:7–9	25
17:10–19	25
19:3	113
19:8	25
19:8–11	25
20	26, 36
20:13–14	26
20:14	13
20:15–17	26
20:18–19	26
20:19	36, 162
20:32	81
20:33	113
23–24	26
23:2–11	26
23:16–21	26
23:24–32	65
23:25–32	65
24:1–19	26
26:16	81
27:6	113
28:10	251
28:19	81
29	26, 266
29–31	266

29–32	26
29:12–13	118
29:13	13
29:30	13
29:35	113
30	26, 266
30:8	251
30:13–17	26
30:19	113
30:21–22	85
30:22	162
31	26, 266
31:9	162
31:15	20
34–36	26
34:8–20	26
35	26
35:2–6	26
35:15	13
36	31
36:13	81
36:14	81
36:17	251
36:22–23	47, 48

Ezra

1	31
1:7–11	121
2:10	11
2:36–39	11
2:40–42	11
2:40–58	153
2:43–58	11
2:59–63	117
3	163, 208
3:8	157
3:10–11	162, 268
6	11
6:19–22	11
7:10	11
8:15–20	11
8:17	11
9:1–2	11
10:1–4	11
10:23–24	11

Nehemiah

3:17	11
7:43–60	11
7:61–65	117
8:1–12	11
8:13–18	11
9	215, 216
9:1–5	11
9:6–38	11
9:39—10:27	11
10:28–39	11
10:39	251
11:3–19	22, 28
11:10–24	11
12	162, 163, 208
12:1–26	11
12:24	162
12:26–46	268
12:27–47	11
12:36	163
12:45–46	163
13:4–10	11
13:10–14	11
13:22	11
13:30	11

Job

35:11	243

Psalms

1	247
2	247, 259
6:1	95
12:1	95
15	252
15–24	247
15:1	252
15:2	252
18	223
24	246
26	246
42	12, 238
42:1	12
42:2	238
42:3	238

Psalms (continued)

42:5	238
42:5b	238
42:6b	238
42:11	238
42:11b	238
42:12b	238
43	238
43:2	238
43:3–4	238
43:4	238
43:5	238
44	235
44—49	12
44:1	12
44:1–8	235
44:9–26	235
44:26	235
44:27	235
45	235
45:1	12
45:6	235
45:7	235
46	238
46:1	12, 95, 238
46:2	238
46:4	238
46:5	238
47	235
47:1	12, 235
47:2–3	235
47:3–4	235
47:5	235
47:6	235
47:7	235
48	12, 236, 238
48:1	12
48:1–2	236
48:2–3	12, 236
48:9–10a	238
48:10–11a	238
48:12–14	236
49	236
49:1	12
49:14	236
49:15	236
49:16	236
49:19	236
49:20	236
50	12, 13, 236, 239
50:1	13
50:1–2	12, 236
50:7–11	239
50:14	239
50:15	237
50:16–23	237
50:21b	237
50:23	239
68:26	123
72	241, 247
72:11	241
73	80, 86, 87, 89, 208, 209, 233, 234, 237, 239, 240, 241, 242, 243, 244, 245, 246, 247, 248, 249, 250, 251, 252, 255, 258, 259, 264, 268, 269
73–83	13, 241
73–89	241
73:1	13, 247, 248, 252, 256, 258
73:1–12	246, 248
73:2	252, 254, 258
73:2–3	248, 254
73:2–13	248
73:2–15	242
73:7	252
73:9	255, 258
73:11	253
73:13	248, 252
73:13–16	252, 253
73:13–17	248, 251, 252
73:13–22	248
73:14	252
73:15	252
73:15–16	253
73:16	252, 253
73:16–17	248
73:16–17a	12
73:16–28	242
73:17	237, 242, 244, 246, 247, 249,

	250, 251, 252,	78:1	13
	253, 255, 256	78:67–72	240
73:18	248, 254, 255,	78:68–70	240
	257, 258	79	239, 240
73:18–27	248	79:1	13, 240
73:18–28	248	79:13	240
73:19	255	80	240
73:20	255	80:1	13
73:21	256	80:3	240
73:21–26	256	80:7	240
73:21–28	249	80:10–19	240
73:22	256, 258	80:20	240
73:23	256, 258	81	240, 271
73:23–28	248	81:1	13
73:24	257	81:1–3	240
73:24a	256	81:2	271
73:24b	256, 257	81:2–3	240
73:25	257, 258	81:3–4	240
73:26	257	81:10	240
73:27	254	81:16	240
73:27–28	248, 257	82	237
73:28	247, 248, 254	82:1	13, 237
73:28a	259	82:4–5	237
73:28b	259	82:8	237
73:28c	259	83	237
74	239, 240	83:1	13
74:1	13, 248	83:1–2	237
74:1–11	239	83:2–3	237
74:2–3	12, 239	83:17–18	237
74:12–17	239	83:18–19	237
74:18–23	240	84	238
74:22–23	239	84–85	12, 241
75	237	84:1	12, 238
75:1	13	84:2	238, 239
75:7	237	84:3	238, 239
75:8	237	84:4	238
75:10	237	84:10	238
75:11	237	85	239
76	237	85:1	12
76:1	13	85:4	239
76:2	237	85:5	239
76:3	237	86	241
76:4	237	87	236
77	240	87–88	12, 241
77:1	13	87:1	12
77:1–9	240	87:1–2	236
77:10–20	240	87:1b-2a	236
78	240	87:7	123, 236

Psalms (continued)

88	12, 239
88:1	12
88:1–2	239
88:2–3	239
89	12, 125, 241
89:1	12
89:1–37	13
89:38–52	13
96	23, 208, 209, 216, 224
96:1	212
96:1b	207
96:2b–10b	207
96:6	222, 231
96:8	222, 231
96:10	222
96:11a–13a	207
105	23, 208, 209, 210, 215, 216, 217, 224, 226, 227, 230
105–106	216
105:1	212
105:1–15	207
105:2	212
105:6	222, 227
105:8	220, 222, 230, 232
105:12	230
106	23, 208, 209, 215, 216, 224, 226, 228, 229
106:1	207, 212, 226, 228
106:47	228
106:47–48	207, 226, 228
106:48	222
107	228
107:1–3	228
119:98	243
132	143
135	215
135:19–21	11
136	215
137	239

Proverbs

6:6	243

Ecclesiastes

2:8	123

Isaiah

41	215
42	215
51	271
51:3	271
56–59	216
66:14–21	11

Jeremiah

3:16	107
33:17–18	11
51:51	251

Lamentations

2:7	251

Ezekiel

36:22–35	245
37:25–28	245
40–48	11
40:1–4	11
40:44	123
40:44–46	12
40:46	20
43:18–21	12
43:19	20
44	11, 14, 16, 18
44:1–15	20
44:4–31	11
44:6–9	11
44:10–14	11
44:15–28	12
45:1–5	12
48:9–14	12

Amos

9	84
9:11–12	85

Micah

4:2–5	135

Zechariah

3	270
3–4	20
4:10	48
12:1–14	11

Malachi

1	270
2	270
2:1–9	11
3:1–7	11

New Testament

Luke

1	270
1:67	270
2	270
2:43	270

Acts

15	85

Romans

1:21	107

Colossians

3:16	87, 271

Hebrews

2:12	85

Revelation

5:9a	271
19:1	271

Apocrypha

1 Esdras

1	107

2 Baruch

6	107

2 Maccabees

2	107

www.ingramcontent.com/pod-product-compliance
Lightning Source LLC
Chambersburg PA
CBHW071147300426
44113CB00009B/1120